MW00564879

The Construction of Testimony

The Construction of Testimony

Claude
Lanzmann's
Shoah and
Its Outtakes

Edited by
Erin McGlothlin,
Brad Prager, and
Markus Zisselsberger

WAYNE STATE UNIVERSITY PRESS
DETROIT

Contemporary Approaches to Film and Media Series

A complete listing of the books in this series can
be found online at wsupress.wayne.edu.

General Editor

Barry Keith Grant
Brock University
Southern Illinois University

© 2020 by Wayne State University Press, Detroit, Michigan 48201. All rights
reserved. No part of this book may be reproduced without formal permission.

ISBN 978-0-8143-4734-8 (paperback); ISBN 978-0-8143-4733-1 (hardback);
ISBN 978-0-8143-4735-5 (ebook)

Library of Congress Control Number: 2019956854

Wayne State University Press
Leonard N. Simons Building
4809 Woodward Avenue
Detroit, Michigan 48201-1309

Visit us online at wsupress.wayne.edu

Contents

Acknowledgments

Most of the contributions in this volume originated as papers presented at a workshop on Claude Lanzmann's *Shoah* outtakes, which was held at the University of Missouri in November 2015. The editors are grateful to the Research Council of the University of Missouri and the Washington University Center for the Humanities for providing the financial support that made that workshop possible. At the University of Missouri, Robert Greene and Stacey Woelfel helped secure additional funding. We would like to thank Rémy Besson, Sven Kramer, and Michael Renov for their participation in and feedback at the workshop. Further, we are grateful to Heidi Grek of Washington University in St. Louis for assistance in assembling this volume's bibliography.

From the very first stages of this project, we have been able to count on Lindsay Zarwell and Leslie Swift at the United States Holocaust Memorial Museum's Spielberg Film and Video Archive. Without their expert guidance, this project would never have come to fruition.

Finally, Wayne State University Press has been extremely supportive throughout the many stages of publication. We are grateful to Daniel Magilow and an anonymous reviewer, who provided extremely helpful feedback. We are also particularly indebted to our acquisitions editor, Marie Sweetman, to the series editor, Barry Keith Grant, as well as to Kristin Harpster and Emily Shelton, all of whom kept everything moving forward.

Introduction

Inventing According to the Truth: The Long Arc of Lanzmann's *Shoah*

Erin McGlothlin and
Brad Prager

In 2016 Lindsay Zarwell, one of the lead archivists at the United States Holocaust Memorial Museum's Steven Spielberg Film and Video Archive, which is associated with the USHMM's project to restore and digitize the many hours of outtakes from Claude Lanzmann's epic Holocaust documentary *Shoah* (1985), drew our attention to a historically compelling and visually unorthodox interview that Lanzmann chose not to edit for inclusion in the final theatrical release of his film. The "Ziering Oppenheimer" interview is a nearly two-hour discussion with Herman Kempinsky (who later changed his name to Hermann Ziering) and Lore Oppenheimer.[1] At the time of their meeting with Lanzmann, the two were copresidents of the Society of the Survivors of the Riga Ghetto.

In many ways, Lanzmann's joint interview with Kempinsky and Oppenheimer, which was filmed in New York and conducted mostly in English, is consistent with the approach he typically took in the interviews he filmed for *Shoah*. Lore Oppenheimer in particular conforms to the conventional expectations of the interview subject. Extraordinarily self-possessed, she has no trouble gazing directly into the camera as she recounts painful events, including the story of her family's arrival in the Riga Ghetto, where they moved into an apartment that still contained the belongings of Jews who had been torn from their homes in the middle of meals before being deported and murdered. Lanzmann periodically challenges her to supplement her narrative with facts, asking whether it was really true that there were dozens of Jewish suicides in a single day among the residents of the so-called *Judenhäuser* (Jewish houses) in Hannover, where her story began. She directs him to look at the gravestones in the Jewish cemetery, groups of which now display the same date of death.

In terms of its thematic content, Kempinsky's testimony also appears to follow a conventional format. Reading the transcript, one would not notice that anything was unusual about this particular interview. Like many of the other survivors in *Shoah*, Kempinsky, who was born in Kassel in 1926 to Polish Jewish parents and was thus a teenager during the war, recounts stories that must be difficult for him to tell. At the beginning of the war but prior to his deportation from Germany, he was required, as a Polish citizen and therefore an "enemy of the Reich," to appear daily at the local police station on his way to school. The sergeant on duty forced him to say his name aloud, adding to his given name the obligatory "Israel," the middle name that in 1938 was made mandatory by German law for all male Jews. Moreover, because Kempinsky's first name was ostentatiously Germanic—and because he shared it with the Reich Marshal Hermann Göring—the sergeant insisted that he repeat his name with prefatory dehumanizing epithets such as "Saujude" or "Schweinehund." In the interview, Lanzmann asks Kempinsky more than once to repeat these appellations in German, just as he was made to do at the time, and Kempinsky indulges Lanzmann's desire for what must be a painful reenactment.

Lanzmann's interview with Kempinsky is highly significant for both its historical content and the ways in which it conforms to Lanzmann's method of provoking traumatic reenactment. But Zarwell directed us to look at the interview for an additional reason—namely, its unconventional cinematic framing. Astonishingly, Kempinsky keeps his back to the camera as he speaks. Most of the time, we see a close-up of the back of his head in single-quarter profile, wherein the broad back of his shoulder dominates one part of the frame and his yarmulke another. This type of shot composition is hardly ideal for an interview, in that viewers can see little

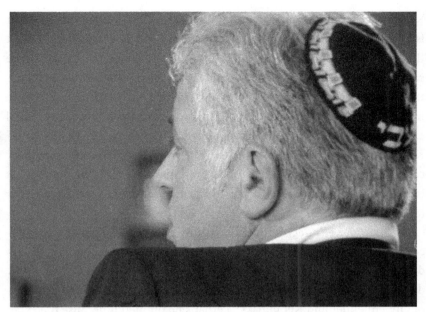

The back of Herman Kempinsky's head. From Claude Lanzmann's interview with Lore Oppenheimer and Hermann Ziering. (Used by permission of the United States Holocaust Memorial Museum and Yad Vashem, the Holocaust Martyrs and Heroes' Remembrance Authority, Jerusalem.)

of Kempinsky's face; indeed, it is difficult to imagine that someone who professionally documented survivor testimony would choose to conduct an interview in this way. The camera position offers viewers few conventional physiognomic signals, and for this reason we are compelled to focus on Kempinsky's words and vocal inflections rather than on his movements and facial expressions. On a couple of occasions, the camera seems to pan around, searching for another angle, but it never finds a shot more comprehensive than this single-quarter profile.

The fascinating framing of this particular outtake intrigued us: What does it mean that Kempinsky had kept his back turned away from the camera, and is this the reason that Lanzmann left this particular footage out of his film? As part of the long restoration and digitization process, Zarwell had first heard the interview's audio track and read the transcript prepared by Lanzmann's team without having seen the image track; only in a later phase of the archiving process did she note the outtake's visual anomalies. Lanzmann, she discovered, waits until the very end of the interview to ask

Kempinsky about his unusual wish to conceal his face. Kempinsky's answer is both philosophical and elliptical: "God, it's really not important. I don't think a face is important. I think the thing that is important is here, if we can give the world a message, what has happened, we shall never forget, that people can do the most cruel things in life, which nobody can believe in his wildest dreams. I . . . I don't think I . . . I could give you the . . . a real explanation how . . . I . . . I feel really. It's . . . it's very hard. It's very hard." Kempinsky implies here his belief that the "message" he wishes to convey can—and should—be effectively delivered apart from its medium—that is, the individual expressive organ constituted by the face of the survivor telling his story.

The interviewee's decision to conceal his face and Lanzmann's acquiescence to that request raise a number of questions concerning Lanzmann's decision to omit the interview from the finished film. To begin with, why did Lanzmann choose not to include the historically compelling testimony of Oppenheimer and Kempinsky? Perhaps he omitted it because the experiences it relates do not fit the narrative that dominates *Shoah*'s theatrical release: the story of mass executions of Jews at killing centers in Poland and, in particular, of the mechanics of gassing deportees and the disposal of their bodies. The Ziering Oppenheimer interview concentrates more on Jewish life in Germany at the beginning of the war and on the deportations of German Jews to Latvia. Topics such as these are fascinating and historically significant, but they do not ultimately correspond with the central theme Lanzmann settled on for the film. Had *Shoah* taken a different thematic focus, how much might he have included of their enlightening discussion of the role of German-Jewish communal leadership in their respective communities? Moreover, assuming Lanzmann had chosen to include parts of this interview, how would he have negotiated the formal challenges posed by the camera's occlusion of the survivor's face? And what does this particular visual anomaly tell us about the status and the nature of the *Shoah* outtakes, whether we conceive of them as raw, "not-yet-edited" footage or as "never-to-be-edited" paratextual remainders?

Even the mise-en-scène of the Ziering Oppenheimer outtakes poses major challenges to any clear distinctions between "not-yet-edited" and "never-to-be-edited" footage. In a moment following one of Lanzmann's cameraman's many changes of reels, when a new shot begins and a clapperboard marked "248" appears, we see something no potential future viewer was ever meant to see: the top of Kempinsky's face, facing forward, toward the camera, but at the same time partially obscured by the clapperboard, possibly in accordance with Kempinsky's wishes. Are we to assume that this odd framing is the creative result of Lanzmann's agreement not to turn the camera on Kempinsky's face, even in the material that, by virtue of its technical nature and formal character, would never have become part of the edited film? Wasn't it Lanzmann's plan to later edit the extraneous footage out, in accord with conventional filmic practice? If no one was ever meant to see this image of the clapperboard falling, then what would it matter whether it captured Kempinsky's face? Did Kempinsky's arrangement with Lanzmann imply on his part a sort of absolute *Bilderverbot*, one that resembles the traditional Judaic ban on visually representing the human face? Or is it possible that Lanzmann knew already at that point that these outtakes would one day be preserved for posterity—that they would

Herman Kempinsky's face, partially obscured by a clapperboard. From Claude Lanzmann's interview with Lore Oppenheimer and Hermann Ziering. (Used by permission of the United States Holocaust Memorial Museum and Yad Vashem, the Holocaust Martyrs and Heroes' Remembrance Authority, Jerusalem.)

be viewed independently of the finished film and eventually constitute an archive of their own?

The *Shoah* Archive: The "Not-Yet-Edited" and the "Never-to-be-Edited"

In 1990, a few years after *Shoah*'s 1985 release, and before it was generally known that over 220 hours of outtakes from the film existed, Lanzmann was asked what he had done with the footage that was not included in the final cut. Lanzmann responded, "You want to know my deep wish? My wish would be to destroy it. I have not done it. I will probably not do it. But if I followed my inclination I would destroy it. This, at least, would prove that *Shoah* is not a documentary."[2] This statement is shocking in its implications. Given the inordinate amount of time that Lanzmann devoted to the *Shoah* project and the extraordinary lengths to which he went to procure the valuable testimony of survivors and perpetrators, it is stunning that he would have contemplated destroying this collection of material. Coming from a man who was a pioneer in the acquisition of survivor testimony and who clearly placed a high value on it as discursive proof of the crimes of the Holocaust as well as the perpetrators' attempts to erase them, the idea that he would suggest destroying the evidence is, to say the least, counterintuitive.

One possible explanation for Lanzmann's position with regard to the unreleased and unedited footage—and one that is suggested by his statement, which is refracted through the lens of the impact that the material's potential destruction would have had on him and his authorship—is that Lanzmann wished to retain absolute control over the filmed material's afterlife, even if this meant essentially suppressing and even destroying survivor testimony. But would an act such as this, because it would contribute to silencing the voices of the interviewed survivors, threaten to reproduce the concealment of the violent crimes that *Shoah* diligently works to undo?

Apart from the troubling implications of Lanzmann's threat to destroy the additional footage, an intriguing dimension of his statement concerns its indication that the possible destruction of the material would "prove that *Shoah* is not a documentary." Lanzmann's rejection of the referential designation "documentary" reveals his own understanding of his film as an artful creation constructed in accord with his vision as an auteur rather than as an assemblage of valuable historical documentation. Lanzmann had a longstanding investment in this distinction. In 2016, when he was asked about the relationship between *Shoah* and the 2015 narrative film *Son of Saul*, Lanzmann once again asserted his vexing claim: "*Shoah* is a fiction film too. Usually in a documentary film you're filming something that exists or existed before—for *Shoah*, nothing existed. I had to make a pure creation and invent according to the truth."[3] The assertion that "nothing existed" before Lanzmann turned his camera on his witnesses is heretical in its implications. He did not in fact create something from nothing, in so far as many of the witnesses who appear in his film had already testified publicly, many of them in courtrooms; for this reason, the facts of their testimonies can hardly be called "a pure creation." Lanzmann's boasts ascribe an outsized if not grandiose role to the documentarian. At the same time, Lanzmann's rejection of the term "documentary" reveals a profound discomfort with the straightforward way in which that term is—at least in his view—conventionally understood. He was reluctant to accept that designation for *Shoah* out of concern that it would belie his authorship.

Despite Lanzmann's histrionic threat to destroy invaluable witness testimony and his insistence that his film is not a documentary by virtue of the fact that he alone bore progenitive responsibility for it, the persistence of the archive of outtakes—alongside Lanzmann's willingness, however reluctant, to authorize its preservation—points to the fact that Lanzmann's *Shoah* project constitutes simultaneously an inventive creation and the creation of an archive. In other words, the archive not only guarantees the indexical and referential status of the film—that is, that the people who can be heard and seen in *Shoah* are not fictional creations, but that they and their experiences exist outside of it—it also underscores Lanzmann's role as the active creator of *Shoah*. Only he was able to bring his film to fruition: "For *Shoah*, nothing existed. I had to make a pure creation and invent according to the truth." Yet the fears behind Lanzmann's threat—specifically, that the existence of the outtakes might undercut the perception that the film is artfully created—were misguided; their existence does exactly the opposite. In fact, the footage highlights Lanzmann's deliberate shaping of the narrative that unfolds in *Shoah*—a point articulated with particular clarity in Jennifer Cazenave's contribution to this volume, which argues that the testimonies Lanzmann filmed can be interpreted as containing a finite number of variables that can be combined in an infinite number of ways. In her chapter, Cazenave draws on the concept of the *incompossible*, a term that Lanzmann employs in his autobiography, *The Patagonian Hare*, to denote the impossibility of the coexistence of two mutually exclusive ideas.[4] The idea of incompossibility here conditions the very act of editing, in that to make an editorial selection means to commit oneself to a particular narrative pathway, one that inherently rules out other narrative possibilities. When Lanzmann was asked directly about how he dealt with the enormous amount of footage he generated, he claimed that he had moved forward "timidly" among what he described as a "superhuman mass of image and sound."[5] He then asserted that there was only one single way through the material, adding, "Several times I felt completely blocked and didn't know how to continue. Just like a mountain climber on an unknown path who might come upon a crevasse or a sudden enormous cliff. You have to find your way. There is one, and only one way."[6] Lanzmann thus vehemently insisted there was only one possible narrative design for *Shoah* and that it happened to be the trajectory he took. The archive of outtakes, however, suggests a nearly infinite number of ways in which the film could have otherwise been constructed. The theatrical release is certainly the only version of *Shoah*, yet the persistence of this "mass of image and sound," particularly now that it has been properly archived, demonstrates that there were countless other paths Lanzmann might have taken through the film's construction and editing, but in fact did not.

Cazenave's conception of the relationship between *Shoah* and its outtakes in terms of its myriad forking pathways reveals a tension between the finished film and the body of the interviews on which it draws. The existence of the archive underlines the three overlapping reference sets that must be accounted for: first, there is the theatrically released film *Shoah*; second, there are the outtakes, i.e., the filmed material and audio recordings that Lanzmann abandoned on the cutting-room floor (the footage not included in *Shoah*); and, third, there is the entire video and audio record of the interviews, which exists only as an abstract, virtual ideal because, owing to the legal conditions stipulated by Lanzmann, the outtakes preserved in the museums' archives may only contain the material that was not included in the film. The first two concrete, available objects of study (the theatrically released film and its ostensibly independent archive) are established by the cleavage of the third set (the original reels of interviews and location footage) into the seen and unseen, into the edited and the not-yet- or never-to-be-edited. While the ideally complete, preedited visual record of the interviews is not the entire historical document of the interviews, since the process of selection in filmmaking is not just one of editing but is operative at all levels and in every moment of filmmaking, it constitutes a common referential point indexed by the theatrical release of *Shoah* and the vast remainder of its outtakes.

The discourse of forking paths reveals that there were certain narratives with which Lanzmann was, at the time of *Shoah*'s production, less comfortable. His fascination with the *Sonderkommandos* of Auschwitz, the *Arbeitsjuden* of Treblinka and other Aktion Reinhard camps, and others who participated—or, more precisely, were compelled to participate—in operating the Nazi death machinery dates back to ongoing discussions in France in the 1960s, when Jean-François Steiner and others asserted that such men were collaborators and should be viewed with suspicion. For Lanzmann, these individuals were faced with little choice, and the issue their testimony raises was the very real one of survival, over and above comparatively abstract ethical principles. With *Shoah*, Lanzmann made an effort to correct the record by emphasizing the extreme situations in which the men were forcibly placed, particularly the circumstances of compelled complicity that Primo Levi termed the "gray zone" and the desperate atmosphere of moral and ethical dilemmas and decision-making that Lawrence Langer called "choiceless choices."[7] In the outtakes, however, we find a number of interviews centered on other "gray zones," including discussions of the Jewish Councils (*Judenräte*). Lanzmann's attention to the very same sensitive theme that emerged in debates surrounding Hannah Arendt's *Eichmann in Jerusalem*—that those Jews who worked in ghetto administration and were thus tasked with enacting the directives of the Nazis were complicit and must be judged—is a running thread throughout the outtakes. As Cazenave points out, one finds among the footage, for example, an extensive interview with Leib Garfunkel, the very first interview that Lanzmann conducted for the *Shoah* project. Lanzmann asks Garfunkel, a survivor and former official of the Jewish Council in the Kovno Ghetto, difficult questions about whether the Jewish Council should have refused to comply with stipulated roundups and deportations. Lanzmann later revisited another such interview with a former Jewish leader in order to make *The Last of the Unjust*, which centers on the Theresienstadt Jewish Council Elder Benjamin Murmelstein. This 2013 film, which makes extensive use of that earlier footage, opens the door to a difficult subject Lanzmann had originally avoided. Similarly, the 2001 film *Sobibór, October 14, 1943, 4 p.m.*, which is largely composed of interviews Lanzmann had conducted with Yehuda Lerner, an instigator of the uprising at Sobibór, deals with the subject of Jewish resistance in the camps, a theme that appears only in the margins of *Shoah*'s theatrical release. These later projects—the results of Lanzmann's edits, embellishments, and releases of material drawn from the archive he had created—invite us to imagine other directions among the forking paths that the theatrical release of *Shoah* might have taken.

As comprehensive and elaborate as Lanzmann's original intentions were, he may not have realized at the time the extent of the intricate archive he was creating. Scholars of the film are now faced with the daunting task of examining the unedited material and taking stock of the competing voices one finds there. Looking solely at the finished film, one might conclude that Lanzmann prioritizes his own agenda above the interests of the survivors and bystanders with whom he speaks. The many decisions he made about testimonies, which included telling witnesses where to stand and even proposing or insisting that they speak in one or another language, align with the practices of a director who is asserting total control over his film. Watching and listening to the footage in the archive, however, one sees and hears numerous perspectives asserting themselves, even though they did not fit into any of *Shoah*'s overarching narratives. By necessity, a documentarian shapes and reshapes witnesses' voices, their ways of expression, and the stories they tell. The footage found in the archive reveals elements of a decision-making process both deliberate and inadvertent. The act of stopping to change the film in the camera, for example, is already one among many processes of shaping; it has the effect of interrupting testimonial speech and of occasionally resetting figures in the frame. The cinematographer also makes editorial choices at each moment with regard to camera distance, depth of field, and the direction—whether toward the interviewer or the interviewee—in which he or she points the camera.

Lanzmann once said that "the structure of a film must itself determine its own intelligibility," but the outtakes have the potential to explode the finished film's structure and call into question its narrative architecture as well as the premises that inform its construction.[8] One's immediate inclination may be to judge the outtakes by the standards of the film and locate within them familiar motifs, yet we might do better to take the opposite approach: to reevaluate the film through the practices revealed in and by the outtakes. The film's theatrical release may thus no longer appear as authoritative as it once did. *Shoah* is, of course, the only version of *Shoah*—what else could it be? But now it stands as one version rather than the sole, authoritative text of the interviews. We believed we knew what led up to the film's interviews and what transpired in them, but we are now beginning to learn how much we did not know.

In the present volume, many aspects of *Shoah* are drawn into contestation, and other aspects, including the very language we use to speak of the film, have to be reconceptualized. To refer to the material under discussion as "outtakes," for example, is to borrow a term from the world of fictional feature film, which risks diminishing the material's character as historical testimony and shortchanging it as both human experience and historical document. On this subject, Sue Vice's chapter has much to say. For her, the existence of the *Shoah* outtakes (along with Lanzmann's post-*Shoah* films that are comprised of some of those outtakes) challenges the conventional frameworks within film studies that distinguish between the theatrically released version of a film and the archive of filmic material that remains after its final editing. She sees the *Shoah* outtakes as constituting not only a "repository" but also a "conceptual field" and argues that their existence reveals the *Shoah* project's status as a syntagmatic continuum in perpetual dialectical tension rather than a paradigmatic hierarchy that would posit the (superior) finished film in opposition to the (inferior) leftover footage. Her chapter responds to the demand for a more descriptive terminology within the study of documentary film, one that can account for the relationship between a finished film and the larger archive of referential material from which it is composed. It lays the groundwork for future analysis in suggesting that, with the outtakes of *Shoah*, we are presented with an opportunity to contribute to a more robust conceptualization of the types of archives that documentary films in general create.

The *Shoah* Scholarship

The study of the outtakes will surely have an impact on the scholarly understanding of *Shoah*. Lanzmann's film has been continuously analyzed and revisited since its 1985 release, and, as this volume's bibliography shows, a vast scholarship has emerged on the topic. In English-language Holocaust studies, the reception to date occurred in two waves. Now, with the availability of the archive of outtakes and the influx of new information about the film's production, we are entering a third phase of study.

In the spirit of the film's public reception, which was by and large positive, the initial critical response to *Shoah* frequently treated it as a masterpiece. Roger Ebert's affirmative reception was akin to that of many American film critics; he described it as "a 550-minute howl of pain and anger in the face of genocide," and he added that *Shoah* was "one of the noblest films ever made."[9] Simone de Beauvoir's 1985 assessment that "there is a magic in this film that defies explanation" was typical of many intellectuals, especially in France.[10] Academic scholarship tended to follow this approbative trend, and the most influential scholarly contributions involved an adoption of Lanzmann's own framework. In this regard, Shoshana Felman's 1991 essay "In an Era of Testimony: Claude Lanzmann's *Shoah*," which discusses how *Shoah* provides a visceral reenactment of trauma in the present, set the stage.[11] Felman's essay has been taken as what Dominick LaCapra calls the "authorized" reading of *Shoah*. Her study of the film is particularly invested in the presence of testimony, which she conceives of in terms of "the finding of the testimony—of its singular significance and functioning as the story of an irreplaceable historical performance, a narrative performance which no statement (no report and no description) can replace and whose unique enactment by the living witness is itself part of a process of realization of historic truth."[12] Felman's emphasis on trauma and on what cannot be shown—the so-called *Bilderverbot*—may have been derived in part from a now-famous workshop she helped to convene at Yale University in 1990.[13] In the protocol of that discussion, Lanzmann unabashedly dictates how his film should be received, delimits the kinds of visual representation that would be, in his opinion, obscene, and highlights the ethical questions that trailed his engagement with his subjects. He implies that not all interviewees are the same, thus providing his rationale for treating Polish witnesses and others differently, and he argues that the imperative to rescue from obscurity and effacement the memories they narrate necessitates an alternate filmmaking ethics.

In Felman's view, Lanzmann captured the secret truth of the Judeocide on film; his work—as she characterizes it, at least—is not inventive cinematic construction, but rather a trove of authentic encounters with traumatized subjects and other firsthand witnesses. Although her essay was ground-breaking when it appeared, from a contemporary perspective it seems to have given relatively little attention to the conditions of the interviews or to the director's powers of invention. In his essay "Lanzmann's *Shoah*: 'Here There Is No Why,'" written in 1997, six years after Felman's article, LaCapra attempted to see in the film numerous perspectives, not only Lanzmann's. He criticized and contextualized Felman's approach, arguing that "a temp-tation in discussing Lanzmann's remarkable film is to transfer to it the ten-dency to sacralize and surround with a taboo the Shoah itself."[14] LaCapra was also among the first to take note of the film's highly produced quality, writing that "*Shoah* is not strictly a documentary film in that scenes in it are carefully constructed. The role of mise-en-scène in the film is indeed crucial."[15] For Felman, the film is a reflection of the real, a perfect reflection of the archive. LaCapra, however, speculates about what didn't appear in the film. He is also interested in the extent to which the scholarship mirrors Lanzmann's own understanding, emphasizing Lanzmann's channeling of the witnesses' experiences with the process of killing and his reification of the perpetrators as an incontrovertibly evil Other. Some scholars, such as Ora Gelley, argue that LaCapra is too concerned with reconstructing Lanzmann's psychology and too little invested in the film as a film.[16] How-ever, LaCapra's efforts to put the director's process and aims under the lens of critical scrutiny was an important step forward.

Included among the responses in this early phase is the essay "Gendered Translations: Claude Lanzmann's *Shoah*," written by Marianne Hirsch and Leo Spitzer, who make a number of critical points that continue to inform our approach to the expanded *Shoah* archive.[17] Hirsch and Spitzer note that *Shoah* focuses on the inner workings of the Nazi killing machine, especially the gas vans and gas chambers; in particular, it closely examines the methods employed at the Aktion Reinhard camps Sobibór, Bełżec, and Treblinka, about which relatively little was known at the time. However, as is much discussed today, over a million people were murdered in mass shootings in the occupied areas of the Soviet Union in what Patrick Desbois has called the "Holocaust by bullets"—an aspect of the Holocaust that plays at best a marginal role in *Shoah*.[18] Lanzmann was more interested in the technologies and processes of genocide as they operated in Auschwitz and in the Aktion Reinhard killing centers, and he was specifically intrigued by the former prisoners and guards who, as a result of their respective tasks, were closest to the death process. Lanzmann did not want to explore the stories of survival of those (mostly male) prisoners; rather, he focused in detail on their proximity, both spatial and temporal, to the deaths of those deported to the killing centers.[19] Female survivors, Hirsch and Spitzer note, are almost completely absent in *Shoah*. The camera avoids their faces, they appear in brief vignettes and sound bites, and they are not featured in the film to the same degree or with the same narrative force as the men. Lanzmann was uncomfortable, they assert, with diverse responses to the machinery of destruction, and his consequent "uneasiness concerning discussions of distinctions—his resolute unwillingness to contemplate and explore differences among the victims in *Shoah*—is most vehement when it comes to gender."[20] Hirsch and Spitzer's analysis of the film's dominant narrative and their suspicions about the narratives Lanzmann suppresses in the film invite us to investigate the outtakes with this paradigm of presence and absence in mind.

By 2001, the reception had entered a second phase: a volume edited by Stuart Liebman, *Claude Lanzmann's* Shoah: *Key Essays*, anthologized the articles by Hirsch and Spitzer and LaCapra, seeking to combine Lanzmann-authorized approaches with critical analyses. The volume signaled a shift in attention from Lanzmann's famous avoidance of archival footage to the images that Lanzmann *did* include.[21] Although some of the contributions in Liebman's anthology, such as Fred Camper's, continued to investigate the problem of incomprehensibility, other essays began to critically examine the director's compositions and his use of mise-en-scène.[22] In those essays Lanzmann appears as an artful creator of images rather than the recorder of a traumatic absolute. While Lanzmann's own approach to the differences between past and present—the notion that images from the archives give the impression that the past is remote and done with—dominated the earliest thinking about the film, scholars now began to historicize the "present" of his moment of filmmaking and indeed Lanzmann himself.

When Lanzmann's autobiography *The Patagonian Hare* was finally published (first in French in 2009 and then in English in 2012), Lanzmann may have seemed less like a contemporary director than a historical figure, a French filmmaker speaking from the perspective of an earlier generation. *The Patagonian Hare* is, of course, in part an extension of its author's own myth-making, as all autobiographies are to some extent, but this too is more complicated: one should not view the book solely in terms of its contribution to Lanzmann's self-stylization. The memoir also provides valuable information about—perhaps even historical context for—the making of *Shoah* in that it allows us to see the historical conditions of its production. Knowing, for example, that Lanzmann was physically assaulted in 1979 by the family of the former Nazi adjutant Heinz Schubert when they discovered that Lanzmann was secretly filming them, or that he paid Franz Suchomel in exchange for his interview, allows us to better understand what was going on behind the camera, even if Lanzmann himself did not realize that with his autobiography he was also contributing to undercutting the very aura of a film that he had carefully worked to construct.[23]

Along similar lines, the publication of the outtakes has altered our thinking about *Shoah* and in the process has punctured many myths. This is not to say that the older scholarship has been superseded—rather, we have embarked on a new phase in our understanding of the film. As we have described above, the object of study now appears new and reframed; we see *Shoah* in a more dialogical mode as an interaction with another, larger archive. The epic film is now revealed to be a fragment of an imagined whole, and yet, on a more concrete level, the archive of additional material challenges, confirms, and deepens the extant scholarship. Further, it answers a number of questions that were previously answered speculatively: it confirms suspicions and corrects long-held assumptions.

One example of the ways in which the *Shoah* archive challenges us to rethink what we once thought was a settled matter is the reconsideration of the problems of gender and voice in the film—the blind spot diagnosed by Hirsch and Spitzer. Several contributions to the present volume engage in reassessment along those lines. The additional material made available in the outtakes contains, for example, the testimony of Auschwitz survivor Ruth Elias, who appears in the finished film, but only for a moment; in the outtakes she provides a much more complex and nuanced view of her experience. Pregnant when she arrived at Auschwitz, she was allowed to give birth but was prevented by the infamous Auschwitz doctor Josef Mengele from breast-feeding and told to watch the child die. Elias chose to give the infant a fatal dose of morphine rather than abide its suffering; she was thus compelled to commit infanticide. Elias differs from the male survivors in the finished film, not least because she refuses to perform the role of permanently traumatized witness or index for those who were murdered at Auschwitz. For instance, she rejects the suggestion that her role as a survivor was to bear witness to the murder of others, saying to Lanzmann, "I didn't want to live to tell people, I wanted to live because I wanted to live." In her story, as well as in that of other survivors such as Ada Lichtman, one sees that Hirsch and Spitzer were absolutely correct in their observations about the representation of gender in *Shoah*. With his attention to the operations of mass murder in Auschwitz and the Aktion Reinhard camps, Lanzmann was interested in bringing some complexity to—and even challenging—then-dominant master narratives of the Holocaust. However, by focusing on the Jewish witnesses who were most involved with the killing and who were inevitably male (because the *Sonderkommandos* at Auschwitz and the *Arbeitsjuden* at the Reinhard camps were always men), he elided certain types of narratives and accounts of survival, as well as those experiences that didn't conform to his preferred narrative of the shock and disbelief Jewish deportees experienced during their arrival at the killing centers and at the entrances to the gas chambers.

Essays by two of the contributors to this volume, Debarati Sanyal and Markus Zisselsberger, examine the outtakes of Lanzmann's interview with Ruth Elias in order to illuminate Lanzmann's aesthetics of testimony in *Shoah* and connect it to a politics of gender. As Sanyal argues, with his determination to complicate popular narratives about the Holocaust, Lanzmann inscribes his own paradigm of Holocaust witnessing, which relies on what she calls "a masculinized model of psychic destruction" in its pursuit of an "antiredemptive ethics and aesthetics." Sanyal writes about the ways in which the outtakes of Ruth Elias's interview challenge dominant assumptions about the gendered character of the outtakes: "Elias's outtakes summon viewers to develop a 'testimonial literacy' that moves beyond the paradigm of witnessing founded by *Shoah*, one that privileges an immersive relationship to past trauma and posits the emergence of 'truth' in the (masculine) witness's breakdown." Through the outtakes, Sanyal is able to identify in the finished film what she calls "'traumatic complicity' in cinematic modes of witnessing." In his essay, Zisselsberger locates what he sees as *Shoah's* emblematic instance of testimony in its protracted scenes featuring Lanzmann's interview with the former Auschwitz *Sonderkommando* Filip Müller. In Zisselberger's view, the Müller we encounter in *Shoah* is Lanzmann's "ideal witness," who survived in order to function as a passive conduit for bearing witness to the people he saw murdered in the gas chambers. He argues that the outtakes of Lanzmann's interview with Müller, which reveal tensions resulting from the role that Lanzmann assigns him, complicate this "paradigm of survival by witnessing." However, in the outtakes of the Elias interview Zisselsberger sees the most forceful challenge to this paradigm, which he argues is predicated on the suppression of female experience and agency (outside of male testimony). Elias rejects the role of passive conduit that Lanzmann attempts to assign her, insisting repeatedly that she can only speak for herself, not for others. Her intransigence in the face of Lanzmann's questioning also suggests a resistance to, if not refusal of, the kind of self-effacement Lanzmann expects from the ideal witness. This resistance to self-erasure is inseparable from—and indeed is constitutive of—the affirmation of life that permeates her testimony; in this way, it offers a counterpoint to the privilege given in *Shoah* to the presence and proximity of death in the male interviewees' testimonies.

In her essay, Leah Wolfson detects a counterpart to the dominant aesthetics of testimony that Sanyal and Zisselsberger identify in *Shoah* in the film's deployment of songs, which Lanzmann shapes into "a tome of witnesses whose voices emanate from inside the machinery of death." However, the multiform acts of singing in the outtakes constitute a set of more diverse and nuanced narratives that, in ways similar to Elias's testimony, contest the dominant narrative Lanzmann establishes in the finished film. In her investigation of the role of vocal performance in the outtakes (especially songs performed by women), Wolfson argues that "Lanzmann's specific framing of these complex musical performances and narratives in the final film excise the complexity of what are multi-layered identities of victimhood and survival." The songs captured on film become something very different from the echoes from the gas chambers that they embody in *Shoah*; they serve as pointed reminders of the complexities of and contradictions within survivor narratives and experiences.

Finally, the archive of outtakes can also prompt a reevaluation of the scholarship on major witnesses or "characters," addressing, for example, the massive lacuna in the languages and national identities through which we understand *Shoah*.[24] At the time of the film's release Anson Rabinbach observed, "The Poles [in *Shoah*] are traditional anti-Semites, unable to conceal their resentments and prejudices, while the Germans are calculating and unrepentant figures hiding behind rational and bureaucratic masks."[25] Even today, Lanzmann's sometimes two-dimensional characterizations along national lines remain controversial. Timothy Snyder wrote in 2010 that the film's dichotomies made it difficult for viewers to see themselves in the bystanders, adding that, "bystanding is what people generally do at times of moral need, and is thus the moral risk that we have confronted ever since the Holocaust." He adds, "Lanzmann makes such an alternative experience of the film impossible: this is its demagogic appeal and substantive weakness."[26] Dorota Glowacka's chapter examines precisely this problem—the depiction of the Polish witnesses and bystanders—and the reception of the film in Poland in light of the surfeit of new information provided by the outtakes. Glowacka notes that Lanzmann repeatedly stated that his intention in the film was to create a chorus of voices, but his interviewing style, his discomfort with Polish witnesses, and his contempt for the Polish language all conspire to suppress the plurality of Polish voices. The extermination of Polish Jews has been assimilated into the narrative of Polish victimhood; Glowacka, in her examination of the outtakes, disentangles the threads that are currently entangled in the "black hole of Lanzmann's (mis)translations." The process of recovery, which the outtakes now make possible, allows us to restructure the testimonial force field in the film and to open up a space for interaction between Polish and Jewish acts of witnessing, a phenomenon that the director and many of the film's commentators had inadvertently foreclosed.

Gary Weissman's essay also addresses the ways in which the practice of translation is inevitably one of distortion and the extent to which every translation is inherently a mistranslation. Weissman analyzes in particular

Lanzmann's 2001 film *Sobibór, October 14, 1943, 4 p.m.* (*Sobibór, 14 octobre 1943, 16 heures*), a documentary that features the testimony of Yehuda Lerner, filmed in October 1979 for the *Shoah* project and then reedited—together with a small amount of additional, newly filmed footage—for theatrical release. Lerner presents his account of his experiences in the Sobibór uprising in Hebrew, which is rendered during the course of the interview into French by Francine Kaufmann, who worked as an interpreter for many of the *Shoah* interviews. Despite Lanzmann's claim to attend carefully to the survivor's "living words," his film's imperative to create a single French narrative out of a Hebrew one relocates Lerner's testimony, pushing it into the background, thereby marginalizing the survivor's story and creating an alternate narrative, with different emphases and effects than the one spoken by Lerner.

The Problem of Authorship

Apart from perspectives of the editors and sound engineers with whom Lanzmann worked and who play integral roles in the production of *Shoah*, the film is also distinguished by the voices of its participants, which include not only Lanzmann himself and his interview subjects, but also the interpreters on whom he relied for transmission of the testimony of interviewees with whom he could not communicate directly. Bill Nichols describes documentaries in which the subjects help shape the film as "participatory," while some British documentarians have taken to calling their subjects "contributors."[27] As we have discussed above, *Shoah* and its outtakes are, in the sense of these terms, replete with participating or contributing witnesses whose presence enable Lanzmann's acts of co-witnessing.[28] Yet the notion that Lanzmann's films are collaborative projects goes against an image he himself carefully cultivated: his self-stylization as an auteur who defined the shape of his films and who had the right to dictate the terms of their reception. In this respect, from the seminar at Yale University in 1990 up through the interviews that constitute the 2015 profile documentary *Spectres of the Shoah*, Lanzmann fashioned himself in ways that resembled the personae of a number of well-known auteur directors. He was in fact part of a generation of French filmmakers who inspired the concept of cinematic authorship. Born in 1925, Lanzmann was a few years younger than Jean Rouch, Chris Marker, and Alain Resnais (director of the groundbreaking 1956 Holocaust documentary *Night and Fog*), and only a few years older than François Truffaut, Agnès Varda, and Jean-Luc Godard, the best-known auteurs of the French New Wave. He was also close in age to Marcel Ophüls, who made the influential documentary film *The Sorrow and the Pity* (1969), which examined the collaborative relationship between the Vichy government and the Nazi regime. All these filmmakers helped to define our understanding of cinematic authorship by audaciously stylizing their films. Lanzmann is squarely in the tradition of those other auteurs and can hardly be considered an outlier.

By the time Lanzmann had begun working on *Shoah*, which was to be his second major film, Resnais and Ophüls had already linked their own authorship to Holocaust documentaries.[29] Lanzmann's connection to them is thus not only formal—that is, it is not only tied to their particular self-stylization as directors of documentaries, a performative mode that continues to shape our contemporary acknowledgement and understanding of the French role in the Holocaust—but it also involves the particular set of questions these filmmakers were asking. The French writer and filmmaker Arnaud Desplechin summarizes a characteristic that defines this group, asserting that "to make a film is to bear witness" and that "the French cinema [bore witness] so poorly in relation to historical events in the beginning of the forties in particular, that it is only logical that people like Resnais, Bazin, Truffaut, Marker, Godard or Rivette stepped up to say: This cannot be, we can't see it; we need to see and it is a moral catastrophe not to see it."[30] No one better epitomized this tendency in French filmmaking than Lanzmann.

In terms of his authorial performance, Lanzmann's practices were difficult to distinguish from those of his countrymen. Authorship is, of course, by no means an exclusively French concept, and the idea that a director would shape a film and mark it identifiably with his or her own overt signatory style was already well established by the time Lanzmann began production on *Shoah*. For this reason he had no cause to be reserved about his aspirations as an auteur. Lanzmann did not try to blend in with the background; he never attempted to vanish like a fly on the wall. Filmmakers such as Rouch, Marker, Resnais and Ophüls have each taken varied approaches, creating in some cases poetic documentaries or essay films in which it is apparent that the filmmaker is constructing the image composition, striving to make a point, and editing the material in accordance with a position or argument. This is particularly true of *Night and Fog*, which Resnais coauthored with the survivor Jean Cayrol, and which linked the crimes of the Third Reich to tendencies that inhere in modern Western societies more generally. (In other words, Resnais and Cayrol wanted to argue that it *can* happen "here.") It is also true of Rouch and Edgar Morin's *Chronicle of a Summer* (1961), one of the first feature-length films to include Holocaust survivor testimony. There is no rule that states that documentarians should not behave like auteurs, that they should not embed their own signatures into the frames of their films. Lanzmann, particularly in light of Resnais's and Rouch's films, saw no reason to be beholden to standards of objectivity or the pretense of invisibility.

Lanzmann was an intellectual, but he was also a remarkably capable and adaptable interviewer.[31] As David Denby observes, "Lanzmann, like [Marcel] Ophüls, is a gently persistent but finally implacable interviewer who manages to coax astounding revelations from his subjects. . . . Lanzmann wants us to grasp the details *physically*; he's like someone going over a mugging or an accident, trying to make it real for himself."[32] Lanzmann proved this already in the interviews that appear throughout *Pourquoi Israël* (1973), a film that significantly defined his filmmaking practice and that can be linked stylistically to his subsequent work. It is thus not surprising to see him on-screen throughout *Shoah*. An example of a scene that is almost entirely shaped by Lanzmann's physical and aural presence is the sequence in which he attempts to interview Josef Oberhauser, the former German SS commander who was convicted of being an accessory to the murder of 300,000 people at Bełżec and who was, at the time of *Shoah*'s filming, serving beer at a pub in Munich. Lanzmann calculatingly makes Oberhauser feel persecuted and pursued, eventually yelling—not at all "gently"— questions at the unresponsive former perpetrator in order to compensate for a lack of public accountability (or in order to provide accountability where there is none). At times, Lanzmann makes himself the star of *Shoah*, particularly when he is at his most cantankerous, difficult, and occasionally misogynistic. He has been criticized for engaging in overly aggressive lines of questioning, even when he interacts with survivors, as when he drives Abraham Bomba, a Treblinka survivor, to tears. Bomba tries to bring the interview with Lanzmann, and his difficult journey into memory, to a halt with the platitudinous rhetorical question, "What could you tell them?" Yet Lanzmann insists on carrying on with the interview, pushing Bomba past his limit for the sake of the film.[33]

Lanzmann performed the role of a detective, pressing his witnesses in pursuit of answers. Some of the essays in this book analyze that pursuit in light of the outtakes, which provide new insights into how Lanzmann shaped his interview scenarios and, in particular, into his use of mise-en-scène. Noah Shenker, for example, takes note of how Lanzmann co-witnessed alongside the historian Raul Hilberg. The particularities of the staging of that interview are uniquely tied to the latter's inimitable persona and his particular historiographical approach. In Shenker's view, the Hilberg outtakes reveal how Lanzmann mitigated and even effaced what he took to be the tensions that mark the intersection between a historian's investigation and the subjective, experiential aspects of testimony. These outtakes provide us with the invaluable opportunity to excavate what Shenker terms the "presence of commentary," whether Lanzmann was working with a firsthand witness or with a scholar such as Hilberg; Lanzmann's changing relationship to the historiography of the Holocaust becomes an instrument for gauging his development as a filmmaker. While he was already quite knowledgeable about the Holocaust when he began to conceive the project that would become *Shoah*, his attendance at a historians' conference on the Holocaust in 1975 energized him. There, for the first time he met Hilberg, whom he found fascinating. As highlighted here by Shenker and by Cazenave, that historians' conference has become more and more important in light of the outtakes, which show how Lanzmann worked with increasing seriousness to emulate great historians while simultaneously pushing for the answers that they, hindered by the limits of the standard historiographical methodologies, had found difficult—if not impossible—to answer.

But it cannot be forgotten that documentary film and cinematic authorship are complicated partners insofar as the documentarian needs his or her contributors. Documentary films are not purely creative or director-authored productions, since they involve real people telling their own stories. One could, therefore, consider whether *Shoah* and the testimonies contained therein even really "belonged" to Lanzmann. Many people think of *Don't Look Back* (1967), for example, as a "Bob Dylan" film, because it is about Bob Dylan, even though most scholars and cinephiles would consider it a D. A. Pennebaker film. The same is true of Lanzmann's work (although in reverse): Lanzmann gave the footage shape. Moreover, these interviews would not have taken place were it not for his perseverance, obduracy, and acts of will. However, the testimonies in the film, whether they come from perpetrators, survivors, or bystanders, may also be described as "property" of those interviewees themselves; the film and footage are also "theirs."

One example of the centrality of the witnesses themselves to Lanzmann's filmic practice is his 2010 documentary about Jan Karksi, *The Karski Report*, which is based on footage Lanzmann filmed in 1978 for *Shoah* and was developed, in part, as a response to what he believed was a misguided novel that had recently been published about Karski.[34] As Regina Longo discusses in the coda to this volume, Sławomir Grünberg used some of the Lanzmann interviews for his film *Karski and the Lords of Humanity* (2015), which aggrieved Lanzmann on account of the fact that someone had the audacity to use "his" footage. But Longo raises an important question: Did Lanzmann possess the claim to total control over those interviews? Other filmmakers, finding themselves in similar situations, might have protested as well. But, from another perspective, one must acknowledge that Karski's testimony also belonged to Karski, the resistance fighter and survivor. Naturally, Lanzmann would have liked to assert control over the footage and the testimony it recorded, but this is slippery ethical terrain when one considers the real persons involved. Should Karksi not also have had the right to claim his testimony?

After ceding ownership and control of the outtakes in the 1990s, Lanzmann maintained all of the rights to the footage that was included in the nine-and-a-half-hour finished film: everything that appears in that original film belonged to him. Everything else (meaning the outtakes to *Shoah*) has been owned jointly by the US Holocaust Memorial Museum and by Israel's Yad Vashem. At this point, anyone who wishes to can access the outtakes; filmmakers are even allowed to use them in their own cinematic productions. Based on her personal encounter with Lanzmann, Longo argues that his position on Grünberg's film amounted to the assertion that Lanzmann was the only one who understood Karski and that others should not have dared to interpret the transcripts and the outtakes of *Shoah*. Longo writes that Lanzmann insisted, implicitly and explicitly, on his exclusive authorship of the material. But Lanzmann's attempt to control Karski's testimony—his struggle to regulate the reception of the outtakes—reveals how the material's structure and, to some extent, its very existence, makes it ungovernable. The fact that real testimony from existing witnesses continues to exist in an unedited, in either a not-yet or never-to-be edited form, pushes against the boundaries of any director's control.

Direction and Misdirection

It is perhaps counterintuitive that a nine-and-a-half-hour film would be acclaimed as having been remarkably well edited, but the theatrical release of *Shoah* has long been admired for having an extraordinary editorial architecture. Without relying on voice-over commentary, the film weaves together details about the stages of the extermination process, particularly a range of stories orbiting around the Chełmno, Treblinka, Sobibór, and Auschwitz-Birkenau killing centers. Although Lanzmann provides occasional rolling intertitles—scrolls of white text against black background—to provide viewers with historical, geographical, and sometimes philosophical orientation, the film at times feels as though it is unfolding organically—that it was birthed whole as a reflection of its copious testimonies. Praising the film's editing, Stuart Liebman writes, "Lanzmann stitches together a number of smaller, local narratives whose overlapping accounts and echoing resonances constitute a temporality unique to the film."[35] Fred Camper finds in *Shoah* a similar subtlety: "*Shoah*'s slow, almost languorous rhythms, rhythms based on this steady accretion of detail, form a monumental jeremiad."[36]

Liebman's and Camper's assessments are both accurate, but one may do well to avoid the trap of imagining (as many scholars—particularly following Felman—have done) that the film's remarkable architecture makes it an unmediated representation of the catastrophe. Leon Wieseltier's response to the film is indicative of this point of view, one that ascribes near-total transparency to *Shoah*. He writes,

> In some sense Lanzmann has literally reassembled the catastrophe. We are shown the sodden woods of Chełmno, the rocky hill of Treblinka, the greening ruins of Auschwitz, as we are told by those who were there what happened there.

The juxtaposition of these words and these images adds up to, or at least approximates, the lived experience of the dead.[37]

Readings along these lines are perhaps encouraged by the film's title, which may underline its claim to mirror the catastrophe itself. Such analyses, however, neglect the necessary awareness that documentaries are always the deliberate constructions of documentarians. Even wholly observational filmmaking does not hold to the pretense of transparency; Jean Rouch, for example, the most famous of vérité filmmakers, boasted of his films' artful constructions. Documentary films should never be mistaken for the things themselves; rather, they are edited in the service of a particular vision or argument.

Shoah's narrative architecture, for which it has been rightly praised, is not equivalent to its editing, and access to the outtakes of the film now allows us to ascertain how much the film was shaped in ways that are not transparent to viewers who only see the final cut, many of whom would willfully or involuntarily interpret Lanzmann's film as an unmediated series of whole, technically unmanipulated testimonies. To look through the archive is to perceive the process of shaping on the conceptual, formal, and technical levels. *Shoah* is edited to reflect Lanzmann's set of interests and organized in accord with his vision. The outtakes reveal more than the fact that the garden was filled with forking paths—that the complex amalgam of narratives and voices we see in *Shoah* was the result of Lanzmann's careful process of selection, juxtaposition and composition. They often also disclose the extent to which individual testimonies were, sometimes at the level of the sentence, edited to convey certain arguments and obscure others. The outtakes teach us about the practice of editing insofar as they remind us that when a documentarian leads us in a particular direction, this is also frequently an act of misleading; every editorial direction, each and every cut, is potentially a misdirection or a sleight of hand.

This volume draws two examples from among the most well-known interviews. Brad Prager's chapter analyzes the outtakes from Lanzmann's encounters with Abraham Bomba, drawing wider conclusions about what was included and what was excluded from Lanzmann's version. In particular, Prager looks at the history of Lanzmann's meetings with Bomba and reveals how the waters of Lanzmann's strategy of co-witnessing were first being tested off-screen from the moment they met. He then analyzes parts of the interview that ended up on the cutting-room floor. Bomba, it turns out, had been pressed to tell his story several times, and Lanzmann was thus aware of his witness's limits prior to the sequence in the barbershop. Perhaps more revealing are the parts of the story that Lanzmann chose to exclude, especially the redemptive aspects of Bomba's testimony. The barbershop interview is generally taken as the most authentic moment of the film—a scene that best embodies what Lanzmann himself termed the "incarnation of truth" and that is carefully structured to give the impression that reality is pouring through the screen in the form of Bomba's tears.[38] However, this impression can also be seen as the product of a succession of painstaking editorial choices.

These editorial constructions are also the subject of Erin McGlothlin's essay, which examines the outtakes of one of the most fascinating (and most troubling) interviews in *Shoah*: Lanzmann's dialogue with the former Treblinka guard Franz Suchomel. By carefully comparing the outtakes of the Suchomel interview with the five sequences in which he appears in *Shoah*, McGlothlin is able to reconstruct in minute detail how Lanzmann shaped—sometimes on the level of the sentence or individual words—the testimony of the apparently unrepentant and even gleeful former perpetrator that we encounter in the finished film. In particular, her analysis of how Lanzmann constructed the scene in which Suchomel sings the so-called Treblinkalied reminds us that moments in *Shoah* that we have come to consider iconic (or, in Felman's words, "a literal residue of the real") should be regarded as neither evidence of the true, essential nature of the witness nor as the unmediated, transcendental reincarnation of the Holocaust past.[39] Rather, they are best understood as the result of a careful, extended, and laborious process of editorial manipulation, one that guides the viewer toward a particular viewpoint vis-à-vis the subject of the interview. McGlothlin's conclusions prod us to re-view other interviews in *Shoah* with eyes more alert to the possibility of similar heavily edited moments, particularly those scenes in which the subject's testimony is deployed as voice-over to location footage rather than synchronized with visual footage of the subject speaking.

The release of subsequent films based on the *Shoah* outtakes also casts Lanzmann's constructions in a different light, particularly because they give us cause to reflect on the film's many temporal layers. Examining *The Last of the Unjust*, Tobias Ebbrecht-Hartmann explores the differences produced when Lanzmann recomposed testimony that had been recorded in 1975 (about the period from 1938 to 1945) in 2011 and 2012. The fact that Lanzmann once again returned to his own archive—that he reworked his own outtakes, sometimes insistently editing his own image into the film such that the present can be seen intervening in the past—significantly structures the temporality and composition of the more recent film. The juxtapositions produce what Ebbrecht-Hartmann terms a "temporality of delay," which not only corresponds to the types of footage presented, but also reveals insights into Lanzmann's deeper perception of the process of remembering.

As the essays in this volume collectively demonstrate, the newly digitized and publicly available archive of *Shoah* outtakes generates the conditions under which a new wave of scholarship on Lanzmann's masterpiece and subsequent films, his practice as a filmmaker, and his enduring legacy as a pioneer in the testimonial retrieval and construction of Holocaust memory can emerge. While the contributors to this collection provide answers to vexing questions that have existed since *Shoah*'s release and further identify and analyze some of the more intriguing aspects of the outtakes, we see this volume as just the tip of the iceberg in what we hope will be a larger, more sustained revival in attention to what is indisputably one of the most seminal cultural texts of the last half century. To take up Cazenave's metaphor of the forking paths once more: in its sheer size and temporal parameters, its remarkable diversity of masterfully filmed interviews with witnesses and location footage, its recovery of invaluable knowledge about the history and legacy of the Holocaust, and its propensity for raising, without unequivocally answering, complex and ambivalent questions about this troubled past, *Shoah* and its outtakes offer a virtually unlimited network of arteries for scholars from a variety of disciplines to traverse. Each of these paths has the potential to take us both backward, into territory we thought we knew—that is, into *Shoah* itself—in a quest to identify previously unexplored areas, as well as forward, into the unknown but vital terrain of the unseen outtakes. This bidirectional journey has the potential to provide insight not only into Lanzmann's film-making practice and the strategies he developed for and employed in *Shoah*, but also into how dominant narratives of the Holocaust, which *Shoah* played such an influential role in shaping, continue to determine our understanding of the events and their aftermaths.

Postscript

On July 5, 2018, while we were editing the last sentences of this introduction, Claude Lanzmann passed away at the age of ninety-two. His final film, *The Four Sisters* (*Les quatre Soeurs*), which included footage from interviews in the *Shoah* outtakes with the survivors Ruth Elias, Hanna Marton, Ada Lichtman and Paula Biren, had premiered the day before.

Notes

1. Claude Lanzmann *Shoah* Collection, interview with Lore Oppenheimer and Hermann Ziering (RG-60.5051), US Holocaust Memorial Museum and Yad Vashem and State of Israel.
2. Claude Lanzmann, "Seminar with Claude Lanzmann 11 April 1990," *Yale French Studies* 79 (1991): 82–99; here, 96.
3. "*Shoah* Filmmaker Claude Lanzmann Talks Spielberg, *Son of Saul*," interview with Jordan Cronk, *Hollywood Reporter*, May 2, 2016, https://www.hollywoodreporter.com/news/shoah-filmmaker-claude-lanzmann-talks-869931 (accessed August 27, 2019).
4. See Claude Lanzmann, *The Patagonian Hare: A Memoir*, trans. Frank Wynne (New York: Farrar, Straus & Giroux, [2009] 2012), 75.
5. Jean-Michel Frodon, "The Work of the Filmmaker: An Interview with Claude Lanzmann," in *Cinema and the Shoah: An Art Confronts the Tragedy of the Twentieth Century*, ed. Jean-Michel Frodon (Albany: State University of New York Press, 2010), 101.
6. Frodon, "The Work of the Filmmaker," 101.
7. Primo Levi, "The Gray Zone," in *The Drowned and the Saved*, trans. Raymond Rosenthal (New York: Summit Books, 1986), 36–69; Lawrence Langer, *Versions of Survival: The Holocaust and the Human Spirit* (Albany: State University of New York Press, 1982), 97.

8. See Marc Chevrie and Hervé Le Roux, "Site and Speech: An Interview with Claude Lanzmann about *Shoah*," in *Claude Lanzmann's* Shoah: *Key Essays*, ed. Stuart Liebman (Oxford: Oxford University Press, 2007), 37–49; here, 40. The original sentence is: "Il faut que la construction du film détermine à elle-seule sa propre intelligibilité," in "Le lieu et la parole," *Cahiers du Cinema* 374 (July–August 1985): 18–23; here, 20.

9. Roger Ebert, "*Shoah* (1985)," *Chicago Sun-Times*, November 24, 1985, https://www.rogerebert.com/reviews/shoah-1985 (accessed August 27, 2019). The film was not without its American detractors. For a critical perspective from a prominent critic, see Pauline Kael, "The Current Cinema: Sacred Monsters," *New Yorker*, December 30, 1985, 70–72.

10. See de Beauvoir's preface to Claude Lanzmann, *Shoah: An Oral History of the Holocaust: The Complete Text of the Film* (New York: Pantheon, 1985), iii. Elements of the film's French reception are more broadly described in Frodon's *Cinema and the Shoah*. Many of the essays in that volume were published in 2007 in French. Frodon has a great deal of enthusiasm for the film. He describes milestones in "the parallel paths of the history of the Shoah and the modernization of the cinema," and adds, "these two paths, that of the construction of the particular place of the extermination of the Jews by the Nazis and that of the modern adventures of the observation of the world by the cinema, would take a long time, forty years to be exact, to reach their exact point of convergence. This point of convergence is the film entitled *Shoah*" (10). Of course, *Shoah* had critics in France, and Georges Didi-Huberman, Gérard Wajcman, and Jean-Luc Godard are among those who more recently came to dispute several of Lanzmann's points of view. See Frodon, 14 note 9.

11. Shoshana Felman, "In an Era of Testimony: Claude Lanzmann's *Shoah*," *Yale French Studies* 79 (1991): 39–81.

12. Felman, "In an Era of Testimony," 58.

13. See Claude Lanzmann, "Seminar with Claude Lanzmann."

14. Dominick LaCapra, "Lanzmann's *Shoah*: 'Here There Is No Why,'" *Critical Inquiry* 23, no. 2 (1997): 231–69; here, 231.

15. LaCapra, "Lanzmann's *Shoah*," 232. Scholars who have taken a particularly film-formal standpoint on the film's inventive constructions include Olaf Berg ("Claude Lanzmann's Approach to the Shoah: Constructing History in Dialectical Time-Images," *Cultural Studies Review* 14, no. 1 [2008]: 124–36), and Michael D'Arcy ("Claude Lanzmann's *Shoah* and the Intentionality of the

Image," in *Visualizing the Holocaust: Documents, Aesthetics, Memory*, ed. David Bathrick, Brad Prager, and Michael D. Richardson [Rochester, NY: Camden House, 2008], 138–61).

16. See Ora Gelley, "A Response to Dominick LaCapra's 'Lanzmann's *Shoah*,'" *Critical Inquiry* 24, no. 3 (1998): 830–32.

17. Marianne Hirsch and Leo Spitzer, "Gendered Translations: Claude Lanzmann's *Shoah*" (1993), reprinted in Liebman, *Claude Lanzmann's* Shoah, 175–90.

18. See Father Patrick Desbois, *The Holocaust by Bullets: A Priest's Journey to Uncover the Truth Behind the Murder of 1.5 Million Jews* (New York: St. Martin's, 2008).

19. According to LaCapra, "On the side of the victims, Lanzmann's predilection is for absolute innocence in closest proximity to death." "Lanzmann's *Shoah*," 260. See also Daniel Listoe, "Seeing Nothing: Allegory and the Holocaust's Absent Dead," *SubStance: A Review of Theory And Literary Criticism* 35, no. 2 (2006): 51–70.

20. Hirsch and Spitzer, "Gendered Translations," 182.

21. Gertrud Koch was among those who wrote eloquently about Lanzmann and the *Bilderverbot*. See "The Angel of Forgetfulness and the Black Box of Facticity: Trauma and Memory in Claude Lanzmann's Film *Shoah*," *History and Memory* 3, no. 1 (1991): 119–34. Translated by Ora Wiskind.

22. See Fred Camper, "*Shoah*'s Absence," in *Claude Lanzmann's* Shoah, 103–11.

23. On the physical assault on Lanzmann and on Lanzmann's payment to Suchomel, see Lanzmann, *The Patagonian Hare*, 457–64 and 446. Although some of the details of the incident offered in Lanzmann's autobiography are new ones, this is not a revelation. As early as the time of *Shoah*'s release Lanzmann told the *Boston Globe*, "Every Nazi in the film was a miracle. . . . I negotiated with Suchomel for a year. Finally, I agreed to pay him. I have film showing him getting paid. I succeeded by telling him, 'Listen, I am not a prosecutor. I am not a judge. I am not a Nazi-hunter.'" See Jay Carr, "A Monument Against Forgetting the Holocaust," *Boston Globe*, November 3, 1985. This source is also cited by Felman in "The Return of the Voice: Claude Lanzmann's *Shoah*," in *Testimony: Crises of Witnessing in Literature, Psychoanalysis, and History*, ed. Shoshana Felman and Dori Laub (New York: Routledge), 204–83; here, 251n29.

24. Prior work on the language question includes Felman, "In an Era of Testimony"; Nelly Furman, "The Languages of Pain in *Shoah*," in *Auschwitz and After: Race, Culture, and "the Jewish Question" in France*, ed. Lawrence Kritzman (New York: Routledge, 1995), 299–312; and Erin McGlothlin, "Listening

to the Perpetrators in Claude Lanzmann's *Shoah*," *Colloquia Germanica* 43, no. 3 (2010): 235–71.

25. Anson Rabinbach, "Films: *Shoah*," *Nation*, March 15, 1986, 313–17; here, 315.

26. Timothy Snyder, "The Holocaust We Don't See: Lanzmann's *Shoah* Revisited," *New York Review of Books*, December 15, 2010, http://www.nybooks.com/daily/2010/ 12/15/holocaust-we-dont-see-lanzmanns-shoah-revisited/ (accessed August 27, 2019). For more on *Shoah*, Lanzmann, and Poland, see Sue Vice, *Shoah* (Basingstoke: Palgrave Macmillan, 2011), especially 73–79. Vice's book-length study of the film also analyzes Lanzmann's explicit role in shaping the testimonies, particularly through his use of mise-en-scène, his method of "reincarnating" the past, and his strategy as an interviewer. A more recent history of Lanzmann's *Shoah* project in light of the outtakes and Lanzmann's autobiography can be found in Jennifer Cazenave's 2019 book *An Archive of the Catastrophe: The Unused Footage of Claude Lanzmann's* Shoah (Albany: State University of New York Press).

27. Bill Nichols specifically cites *Shoah* as an example of "participatory" documentary, one that "emphasizes the interaction between filmmaker and subject." See Nichols, *Introduction to Documentary* (Bloomington: Indiana University Press, 2001), 34.

28. The term "co-witnessing" is borrowed from Irene Kacandes, who notes that victims often find it painful to return to excruciating memories, so "a revisiting of their traumatic experiences seems to require the presence of a sympathetic, committed listener or enabler. The story of the trauma thus comes to be 'co-narrated' or 'co-witnessed.'" See "From 'Never Forgetting' to 'Post-Remembering' and 'Co-witnessing': Memory Work for the Twenty-First Century," in *Being Contemporary: French Literature, Culture, and Politics Today*, ed. Lia Brozgal and Sara Kippur (Liverpool: Liverpool University Press, 2016), 193–210; here, 202.

29. For a comparative reading of *Night and Fog, Shoah*, and Ophüls's *Hotel Terminus: The Life and Times of Klaus Barbie* (1988), see Jay Cantor, "Death and the Image," in *Beyond Document: Essays on Nonfiction Film*, ed. Charles Warren (Hanover, NH: University Press of New England, 1996), 23–49.

30. See the transcript "Conversations at the Mill," in *Cinema and the Shoah: An Art Confronts the Tragedy of the Twentieth Century*, ed. Jean-Michel Frodon, 107–45 (Albany: State University of New York Press, 2010); here, 142.

31. See Vice, *Shoah*, 64–73, and McGlothlin, 245–48.

32. David Denby, "Out of Darkness," reprinted in Liebman, 73–76; here, 74 and 75. Originally in *New York Magazine*, 1985; italics in original.

33. On the style Lanzmann adopts in that interview, see Michael Renov, *The Subject of Documentary* (Minneapolis: University of Minnesota Press, 2004), 127.

34. For Lanzmann's view of the novel, see Claude Lanzmann "Jan Karski de Yannick Haenel: un faux roman," Marianne.net, January 23, 2010, https://www.marianne.net/societe/jan-karski-de-yannick-haenel-un-faux-roman (accessed August 27, 2019). For additional perspective on the relationship between the novel and the film, see Sue Vice, "Supplementing *Shoah*: Claude Lanzmann's *The Karski Report* and *The Last of the Unjust*," in *Holocaust Cinema in the Twenty-First Century: Memory, Images, and the Ethics of Representation*, ed. Gerd Bayer and Oleksandr Kobrynskyy (New York: Columbia University Press, 2015), 38–55.

35. Liebman, "Introduction," in *Claude Lanzmann's Shoah*, 16.

36. Camper, "*Shoah*'s Absence," 104.

37. Wieseltier, "*Shoah*," 91.

38. In Chevrie and Le Roux, "Site and Speech," 41. Lanzmann's original phrase is "l'incarnation en vérité." See "Le lieu et la parole," 20.

39. Felman, "In an Era of Testimony," 75.

1

Inside the Outtakes

A History of the Claude Lanzmann *Shoah* Collection at the United States Holocaust Memorial Museum

Lindsay Zarwell and
Leslie Swift

BERGSON: I said "What are you going to do about it? . . . Surely
you don't say that the government of the United States is going
to do nothing? I am one individual here, a foreigner, and I know
that I am going to do something. What good it will do, I don't
know, but I know I am going to do it." . . . And, I went out and I
called all our active people—our little group of Palestinians, and
all the Americans, Jews and non-Jews—. . . . And I made a speech
that evening which in essence said that from now on, we are
going to get up in the morning and go through the day and go to
bed at night trying to do something to save the Jews of Europe.
Unfortunately we did not succeed. We discovered to our horror
that life went on without much change.

LANZMANN: This was in 1942?

BERGSON: This was November 1942.

—Peter Bergson (aka Hillel Kook)

Nearly thirty-six years after Peter Bergson's interaction with Assistant Secretary of State Adolf Berle, Claude Lanzmann filmed an interview with Bergson for *Shoah* in an effort to document American responses to the Holocaust. Bergson was an activist who organized the "We Shall Never Die" pageant and made bold publicity moves aimed at influencing American policy in desperate hope of saving the Jews of Europe. His passionate testimony, however, did not fit within the scope of *Shoah* as a completed film and remained uncut and unused. Lanzmann's interest in American responses was one of the unknown subjects discovered in the contents of the hundreds of reels of Shoah outtakes now archived at the United States Holocaust Memorial Museum (USHMM).

The Claude Lanzmann *Shoah* Collection at the USHMM is one of the richest audiovisual sources of Holocaust history. This archive of rushes consists of the extraordinary testimony and location footage that was *not* incorporated into the monumental nine-and-a-half-hour film *Shoah*, which weaves together dozens of testimonies to describe in meticulous and devastating detail the step-by-step machinery of the destruction of European Jewry. Almost immediately after the release of *Shoah* in 1985, critics hailed it as "a sheer masterpiece,"[1] "an act of witness,"[2] and a "monument against forgetting."[3] Today, it is still widely regarded as "the most ambitious work ever made examining the Nazi genocide."[4]

Claude Lanzmann and his trusted research team spent nearly twelve years searching for Holocaust survivors, perpetrators, eyewitnesses, and Holocaust scholars, and captured over 220 hours of film footage.[5] The filmed interview subjects are younger—their memories twenty years closer to the events of the Holocaust—than the witnesses in the major oral history video projects that started in earnest in the 1990s. Few other documentarians took the risk to record, for example, members of *Einsatzgruppen* units recounting their experiences of killing thousands of Jews,[6] or the morally complicated stories of *Judenrat* survivors.[7] Lanzmann as an interviewer was sharply focused, intense, confrontational, and emotionally charged, and so are the outtakes. The length and depth of his interviewing approach resulted in powerful responses from Holocaust witnesses.

The USHMM acquired the collection of outtakes, which is co-owned with Yad Vashem, in late 1996. Michael Berenbaum, then-director of the USHMM Research Institute, and Raye Farr, former director of the

USHMM Permanent Exhibition and now-retired director of the USHMM Film Archive, negotiated the acquisition with Lanzmann at the suggestion of Raul Hilberg. Hilberg, an eminent Holocaust historian, had remained close to Lanzmann after being interviewed by him for *Shoah* in January 1979. Following a review screening of the *Shoah* outtake reels in Paris in 1996, Berenbaum and Farr emphasized the high quality of the testimonies, describing them as interviews with "persons of vital historical significance, uniquely placed eyewitnesses to major events."[8] Their written report was crucial in making the case to USHMM stakeholders to support the purchase of such a large and complex collection comprised of various types of media, stored in France under unsuitable conditions. The summary written by Berenbaum and Farr in 1996 remains accurate today:

> We know of nothing available on the subject at this time that equals their scope in probing the difficult issues of human behavior and personal choices during the Holocaust. . . . Lanzmann's deliberate attempt to pull each witness into a re-living of the events—as opposed to a re-telling—has created a series of voyages into the place and the time and the pain and the paradox of Holocaust events, of Holocaust remembering. . . . On some levels they are priceless.[9]

The negotiations that resulted in the acquisition were not without complications, but, in the end, the USHMM received thousands of original films with corresponding sound tapes, negative logs, interview summaries, and transcripts.

It is important to reiterate that the Claude Lanzmann *Shoah* Collection consists *only* of outtakes—that is, the scenes that were shot in the course of making *Shoah* but were not used in the final version. Most of the film material consists of Lanzmann's penetrating interviews with witnesses, but there are also dozens of reels of so-called location footage—illustrative scenes of the forest in Poland, for example, or of the railroad tracks leading up to the gate at Auschwitz—shot by some of France's most skilled camera operators, recruited by Lanzmann to work on the project.[10]

The sheer size and scope of the *Shoah* outtakes collection made it a daunting archival project from the very beginning, and it has been challenging to manage the analog materials and obtain the funds necessary to keep preservation work on track. However, the USHMM staff strongly committed to safeguarding the archive of Lanzmann's signature cinematic achievement and undertook the extensive, complicated, and expensive work (over a million dollars to date) over the course of twenty years to reassemble the film materials. Now, nearly all of the *Shoah* interview and location outtakes fully available for research and freely accessible for viewing on the internet, accompanied by original and/or translated transcripts.[11]

Scope of Materials

Three large shipping containers, containing two tons of film materials, arrived at the USHMM collections storage facility on January 21, 1997. The delivery contained such diverse materials as film negatives, sound tapes, and rushes, the corresponding summaries and transcripts of the major interviews, and handwritten logs of the negative rolls. Our first priority was to unpack, inventory, and arrange the elements, which included several types of original materials: (a) picture content on 16mm silent color negatives; (b) field recordings on quarter-inch sound tapes; (c) 16mm film prints with accompanying magnetic soundtracks created for production and editing purposes, (d) negative trims; and (f) paper items such as transcripts and logs. By the summer of 1997, the collection had been accessioned, checked for damage, compared against content lists and organized numerically on new shelving specially constructed at the offsite facility. A new film archivist staff position was created to provide the expertise needed to evaluate, preserve, and catalog the *Shoah* outtakes, and to supervise the technical requirements for lab work.

It became apparent relatively quickly that we would need to overcome many obstacles in order to archive the materials. We had no way to view the picture content in order to make preservation decisions without jeopardizing the original camera negatives. No names of witnesses were included in the film logs or on the canisters of negatives; instead, the labels included the film manufacturer's edge code number. Most critically, we did not have access to a master log of the *Shoah* outtakes that would allow us to correlate a name, place, and date with corresponding edge code information. Given the tremendous volume of items, we found ourselves confronted by an enormous puzzle.

We attempted to gain some insight into the organization of the analog materials by tracing the methodology of film production employed by Lanzmann in the late 1970s. The film crew in each country where filming for *Shoah* took place (Germany, Poland, Israel, and the United States) consisted of a cinematographer equipped with a camera and 16mm color film, a sound technician with recording equipment and tape, and an interpreter, which was required in cases where Lanzmann did not speak the interviewee's language (for whatever reason, Lanzmann employed only women for this work).[12] Each member of the crew contributed a different and vital component to make up the whole.

The method for clandestine recording was markedly different and yet still required the skills of several crew members. In order to record reluctant interviewees (usually perpetrators or others complicit in Nazi crimes) without their knowledge, Lanzmann concealed a video camera and sound wiring under his clothing to capture a conversation. The distinctive

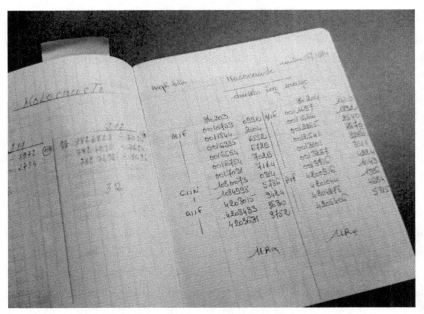

Handwritten log showing one canister with original camera negative identified only by edge codes. (Used by permission of the United States Holocaust Memorial Museum.)

appearance of these clandestine interviews will be familiar to anyone who has seen *Shoah*.[13] Camera equipment was stowed in a purse or bag, usually carried by the interpreter, while the technicians received and recorded the video signal from the back of a Volkswagen van parked on a street outside the house where the dialogue was taking place. This black and white video transmission was later copied onto 16mm film and magnetic soundtrack.

Whether hidden or openly shot, the cameramen employed a range of camera angles; a frame could show the interviewee or Lanzmann, or sometimes both, or sometimes just a place. Clapperboards at the beginning of each picture reel were used to synchronize sound and provide information such as the working title of the film ("Holocauste"), roll numbers, and the names of the cinematographer and the interviewee. Despite our hopes that the method of production might help us unlock the key to the organizing principle behind the materials, the sheer length of the production schedule and number of people involved resulted in little consistency in the administrative systems used to organize the project and therefore hindered our efforts to identify a pattern. Another wrinkle came from the fact that quarter-inch sound tapes run slightly longer than the film rolls, meaning that the otherwise parallel interview contents are actually *not* equivalent in roll numbering. Moreover, the sound technician and camera operator each recorded different information on the respective canisters. For example, only the word "Chelmno" appears on a sound carton containing the interview with Simon Srebnik, while the film cans are labeled with Srebnik's name.[14]

Once shot, the camera negatives and audiotapes captured in the field were immediately processed at Lanzmann's direction and transferred to rough film and soundtrack copies, called rushes or work print. This was done in order to protect the original negatives and sound tapes from damage caused by handling or viewing, enabling them to remain safely untouched until the assembly of the finished version of *Shoah*. Each film work print was stored together with its complementary magnetic track work print in a metal can labeled with the interviewee name and camera roll numbers on color-coded tape that specified geographical area. For example, films shot in Poland were labeled with red tape. Work print copies were often immediately screened by Lanzmann and his assistants during the editing phase of the production. This review process allowed the team to note the contents of an interview and to make a first pass at selecting sequences in the cutting room.

Clapperboards from the beginnings of reels. From the filming of *Shoah*. (Used by permission of the United States Holocaust Memorial Museum.)

Stack of metal film canisters. (Used by permission of the United States
Holocaust Memorial Museum.)

By the end of the making of *Shoah*, the constant process of negative-
cutting during successive editing sessions resulted in a collection of cans
containing unused and unrelated negative rolls—some cut, some complete, and some much smaller "trims"—all identified *only* by edge code
numbers—a series of numbers and letters that is etched into the film
between the sprocket holes every twenty frames.[15] Luckily, edge code information is transferred from the negative to the positive print, so the rush
copies (picture) contain a discernible print-through of edge code numbers.
By winding through the rushes (which Lanzmann and his team had the
foresight to store in cans *with* interviewee names), we were able to identify
the dozens of separate negative rolls that could then be pieced together to
reconstruct an interview. But we could not begin our preservation process
with original negatives, because these elements were stored by Lanzmann
in tin cans *without* interview names.

An understanding of Lanzmann and his crews' varying organizational
schema was a critical step for USHMM staff to begin to establish order over
the 155 boxes of rushes, negatives, quarter-inch tapes, negative trims, and
paper documents. While the diversity and type of formats within the collection is not unusual for a professional film production, the volume of items

Film storage in a climate controlled vault. (Used by permission of the United States Holocaust Memorial Museum.)

and variation in labeling are just one factor that has made the preservation of the *Shoah* outtakes collection a unique challenge. Finding technical staff with deep experience with analog filmmaking and film editing in a digital era was equally difficult. The first motion picture vendor the USHMM hired to work on the *Shoah* collection filed for bankruptcy after five years of collaboration. Our current expert negative cutter at Colorlab retired in March 2015, but became so immersed in the project that he now volunteers his time to continue to reassemble the *Shoah* negatives and synchronize the picture to the audio.[16] Even after two decades, the USHMM's film archivist still regularly handles and analyzes the original films, assesses the physical materials, updates the database, requests and supervises technical laboratory work, and develops new preservation schedules or workflows.

Film Preservation Process

The *Shoah* outtakes acquisition in 1996 was the first major film collection acquired by the USHMM. Today, the USHMM holds a large collection of historically important, unique, and previously unused or unseen archival film documents, both professional and amateur. We rescue, steward, preserve (using state-of-the-art techniques), and make these rich resources accessible to the public. We take all necessary measures to protect our original films from unnecessary handling and slow physical decay by storing the films in climate-controlled vaults. Whenever resources allow, we follow the highest-level film preservation strategy, which requires making copies of original film assets on new motion picture film stock. Many preservationists consider film fully safeguarded only when it is viewable in a form that faithfully replicates its visual and aural content. With regard to *Shoah*, each original camera negative is duplicated onto new polyester film stock, a material that guarantees stability and longevity. This preservation master (called a film interpositive) is then used to create access copies, such as video or digital media, which can be researched and viewed onsite at the USHMM or online.

Film editors work with raw footage, selecting shots and combining them into sequences to create a finished motion picture. For most of the history of filmmaking, analog film was physically cut and then spliced together by hand in order to make a print that could be duplicated and shown in theaters. This was the method used for *Shoah* as well. For example, the film famously opens with Simon Srebnik beside the Narew River in Poland, and

A can of unassembled negatives. (Used by permission of the United States Holocaust Memorial Museum.)

then the scene switches to Mordechai Podchlebnik talking to Lanzmann in Israel. This juxtaposition was carefully constructed by Lanzmann's editor, Ziva Postec, who selected film frames of the interview with Srebnik (filmed in 1978) and spliced them together with similarly edited shots from the Podchlebnik interview (filmed in 1979) to create the opening sequence.[17] The *Shoah* outtakes have been cut to pieces, to greater or lesser degree, depending on how much of a given interview was used in the final film. Our first goal in the preservation process became locating the negatives to re-create an interview as it was originally shot, minus those pieces of footage used by Lanzmann in the 1985 film (to which the USHMM has no copyright permission or access).[18]

The sound was also cut for the finished film, so viewers can hear the voice of a witness play over shots of locations. Thus, in the preserved outtake, when sound is missing and picture remains, one will see the interviewee speaking but not be able to hear corresponding sound.[19] Conversely, when the image has been removed but the sound remains, one will see a blank piece of film leader instead of the interviewee as the voice continues. In practical terms, this means that Abraham Bomba's interview, which was heavily used in the final film, required more extensive and deliberate "conforming," or piecing back together, than did the interview with Ruth Elias, of whom there is merely a glimpse in *Shoah*.[20] Simply put, the more the interviewee appears in the final film, the more work it takes to reconstruct the puzzle, and the more lacunae, in both sound and image, appear in the preserved outtake interview. As one can imagine, the more hand reassembly required by a given set of reels, the more expensive the job at the lab, and the more time it takes to preserve the interview on film.

After staff select an interview subject or location outtake on which to begin work, the disparate film elements are collected from offsite storage and delivered to Colorlab, our outside motion picture preservation facility, where photochemical solutions and cutting-edge technology keep motion picture film stable and viable. Expert technicians carefully inspect, splice, treat, and clean vintage film in order to create the best possible analog and digital copies. The severity of film decay varies widely across the *Shoah* outtakes collection. Original color film of this era is prone to fading, and film can sometimes never be fully repaired. The 16mm image rushes (acetate positive) contain multiple brittle tape splices that often fall apart. The

16mm sound rushes (full-coat magnetic track) shed and are sticky, and they emit an unpleasant vinegar odor, signifying deterioration. Even though the rushes are not the focus of our preservation efforts, they nonetheless serve a critical role as a guide to the reconstruction of the negatives. Therefore, it is also important to apply preservation techniques to stabilize the rushes.

At Colorlab, the negative cutter begins the laborious process of matching the small negative film rolls together in order to reconstruct the picture in relation to the order as it appears in the rushes. If the magnetic sound rushes are severely compromised by decay or exhibit signs of vinegar syndrome or rust deterioration, it is necessary for the lab to go back to the original field recordings to create new soundtracks on a stable polyester film base that must then be resynchronized with the negatives. Not surprisingly, several quarter-inch sound reels required rescuing with special audio conservation treatments, particularly to deal with black mold caused by damp storage conditions in Paris. When conforming tasks are finished, Colorlab creates new film interpositives, thus completing the film duplication phase of the preservation process.

Next, the lab utilizes state-of-the-art film scanning stations that produce high-resolution digital files, such as 2K.[21] Making surrogate versions of an artifact, whether by creating an image, video, or audio file, provides user access to the material without subjecting the original to additional wear and tear. The high-quality digital transfers of the outtakes meet or exceed the industry standard for audiovisual preservation and film production. Digital files are stored in the USHMM digital collections repository where they are maintained, upgraded when necessary, and regularly checked for quality or loss. Prior to 2010, when creative technology applications revolutionized the film industry and the digital age took off, the USHMM's practice was to order videotape viewing copies using telecine, a popular method of transferring film to video.

Once the original reels, new films, and digital surrogates are back at the USHMM, the archivist organizes, rehouses, labels, and shelves the original films and new film copies, video, and digital elements under appropriate archival conditions to facilitate long-term care and use. Staff must maintain control over all of these physical generations and digital files as they, too, are now part of the Claude Lanzmann *Shoah* Collection. With screening copies in hand, staff begin to gain intellectual control over the contents of the interviews or location footage. We view, listen to, and summarize each interview or location outtake and write reel summaries using time codes to identify meaningful segments. This helps researchers locate specific parts of the narrative within a reel, which is especially helpful when the interviews are quite long. Staff also highlight particular clips we think might be of interest to specialists, based on our ever-evolving understanding of the ways in which digital users query the USHMM historical film and oral history collections, as well as our knowledge of developments in Holocaust historiography and changing areas of interest within the field. Given the number and length of the interviews, we often enlist subject specialists, interns, and volunteers to research, translate, transcribe, describe, and otherwise enhance the catalog records. The contents of our descriptive catalog are thus an organic and ever-changing set of data to which many individuals contribute.

Once the catalog record meets the standards for public display, staff enable researcher access by publishing a detailed summary along with streaming video files on the public Collections Search catalog. Lanzmann's working transcripts in their original language (German, Hebrew, English, Polish, or French) as well as English translations are linked to the online catalog. Staff-curated selections or noteworthy highlights are identified and featured as well. The catalog records—which include historical and biographical information—are available online to anyone with access to the internet, greatly expanding the possibilities for discovery, learning, and general use of Lanzmann's important testimonies. Researchers no longer need to travel to Washington, DC, to access large parts of the *Shoah* outtakes archive, which we consider an enormous contribution to Holocaust and film scholarship.

Film preservation is not a onetime operation but an ongoing process, especially in the digital age. Digitization projects may be renewed or workflows reappraised as techniques, equipment, and standards improve. For example, several years ago, thanks to a generous grant, we shifted from our standard practice of working on the complicated reassembly of image elements with sound to focusing only on sound by migrating quarter-inch audio tapes to high-quality digital audio. We chose to do this to provide audio access points to interviews that we had considered less important (often for lack of available information) and therefore had not prioritized for full preservation. Digitizing only the audio was much more cost effective and allowed us to provide faster access to these interviews for researchers, make efficient use of our limited budget, and provide us with information that would help us to determine which interviews were the best candidates for full preservation.

To date, nearly 90 percent of the *Shoah* outtakes collection has been completely preserved on film, transferred to digital format, cataloged, and made available on the internet. That includes all sixty-eight interview outtakes (167 hours) and twenty location films (or 49 hours). The USHMM provides research and reference assistance on the Claude Lanzmann *Shoah* Collection to a growing body of scholars, researchers, students, and film producers. New preservation efforts are currently underway as funding allows, and the collection is on track to be fully preserved and available online by January 2020.

Selection of Interviewees

As film scholar Stuart Liebman aptly observes, "No filmmaker before Lanzmann had devoted so much time to reflecting not only on *what* to represent in a film about the Holocaust, but also on *how* to do so. . . . No director had ever demanded so much dedication and forbearance from his audience in order to confront what many Jews and non-Jews alike, though for different reasons, did not wish to think about."[22] Lanzmann was equally demanding, as the outtakes illustrate, with his interviewees, not only with his persistent questioning, but also in the length of time he spent with them. Consider the unusual length of the Benjamin Murmelstein interview, which runs eleven hours, or Jan Karski's, which runs over four hours.[23] Lanzmann himself classified the film material into three categories:

1) 35 main protagonists of *Shoah* (this means that I actually shot much more than I edited);
2) characters who don't appear in the film (this means that I shot with them but that for length and architectural reasons I decided not to edit them in the film as such); and
3) countless shots of locations, landscapes, countrysides, etc. during the campaigns of filming.[24]

He estimated that he shot 350 hours of film.[25]

We began work on the preservation of the archive in 1998, starting with the interviews of Filip Müller, Leib Garfunkel, Gertrude Schneider, Karl Kretschmer, Ruth Elias, and Paula Biren.[26] We prioritized these witnesses because they were among those that Lanzmann considered the strongest, according to the brief descriptive notes he compiled as part of the acquisition negotiations. In addition, all of these individuals appear, to greatly varying degrees, in the final film. We reasoned that preserving them first could provide a good representation of the types of technical and organizational challenges we would face in dealing with cut negatives and sound tapes. The interview with Andre Steiner was also given priority at the request of the producer of the 1999 documentary, *Andre's Lives*.

All along, we considered a host of factors, both intellectual and practical, as we prioritized the order in which to preserve the *Shoah* outtakes, such as identifying compelling subject matter in anticipation of USHMM exhibition priorities, the amount of work (and therefore expense) necessary to conform the negatives, and the condition of the film or magnetic material. If an interviewee appears frequently in the final film, we would sometimes assume that Lanzmann had incorporated the "best" conversational material from the interview. However, we also knew that Lanzmann's film was famously concerned—primarily, if not exclusively—with the killing process, and therefore other experiences outside this scope would not have "made the cut." For example, he filmed several interviews relating to the story of Rabbi Dov Weissmandel, a Hungarian Jew who, together with other members of the resistance organization known as the Working Group (*Pracovná Skupina*), managed to delay the deportation of Slovakian Jews. He interviewed Hansi Brand, whose work with Rudolf Kasztner resulted in the controversial rescue by train of more than 1,100 Jews from Hungary.[27] Over the course of a week, Lanzmann spoke with Benjamin Murmelstein, the self-anointed "Last of the Unjust" who served as the last chairman of the Jewish council in Theresienstadt and was widely reviled and accused of collaboration with the Nazis.[28] And Lanzmann interviewed Peter Bergson, aka Hillel Kook, a Palestinian Jew living in New York who was relentless in his efforts to alert the American public and politicians as high up as President Roosevelt to the ongoing destruction of the European Jews.[29] None of these individuals appear in the final film, because the subjects that they cover diverge radically from the theme that would eventually prevail as the subject of the film *Shoah* in its final form. And yet these interviews, and many more in the collection, are of immeasurable value, both to scholars of Lanzmann's work, students of testimony in general, and more traditional Holocaust historians. In short, they are wide-ranging, incredibly compelling, and delve deep into many topics that are of interest to Holocaust scholars today.

The language in which the interview was conducted was another significant factor in deciding which interviews to preserve, given our primary audience and location in the United States. Lanzmann conducted interviews directly in the languages he spoke—French, English, and German—or through a French interpreter in Polish and Hebrew. Our staff had language abilities in English, French, and German, so we could read and evaluate those transcripts for historical value. Moreover, since we had no budget to subtitle the interviews, which meant they would stream online in their original languages, it often made sense to us, as representatives of an American institution, to prioritize interviews conducted in English. However, cataloging English-language interviews brought its own set of challenges. For example, English is not the first language of most interviewees, and many use German words that were part of the everyday vocabulary of the concentration and death camps. The transcripts produced during filming contain typographical or historical errors, or incomplete phrases. They also cover the entire interview, even those parts cut by Lanzmann for use in the final film, which can be confusing for researchers who compare a transcript with the video.[30] Original transcripts are available for research in the USHMM's online catalog both as PDF attachments along with English translations produced by volunteers, and as individually-scanned pages (over 7,300 in the collection).[31]

Some of the most powerful interviews Lanzmann conducted were those filmed with perpetrators and collaborators, notable partly because of Lanzmann's provocative style and also because of his innovative use of hidden cameras. According to Lanzmann, "I had to learn to deceive the deceivers, it was my bounden duty."[32] For obvious reasons, interviews with perpetrators were hard to obtain, and so Lanzmann developed a system to record them surreptitiously, using a newly developed hidden camera called a *paluche*.[33] This method of clandestine filming was not always successful—Heinz Schubert, SS officer and adjutant to the staff of

Einsatzgruppe D, discovered that he was being taped and his sons ended up roughing up Lanzmann badly enough to put him in the hospital; one can hear (but not see) the beginning of a violent altercation taking place at the end of the Schubert interview.[34] The first camera rolls of the interview with former *Obersturmführer* with *Einsatzgruppe* 4a (Babi Yar) Karl Kretschmer provides unexpected insight into Lanzmann's process. The viewer is treated to the sight of a shirtless Lanzmann being fitted with the wiring that provided the sound recording for the *paluche*.[35] In such cases, the *Shoah* outtakes provide heretofore-unseen visual evidence of Lanzmann's determined and unique method of clandestine recording. In addition to interviews with perpetrators, Lanzmann also interviewed people who witnessed the Holocaust while it was being carried out, including Jan Piwonksi, a Polish worker who talks about the construction of Sobibór and the killing process in that camp.[36]

Lanzmann's treatment of women and their lack of inclusion in the final film has been and will no doubt continue to be a topic of intense study.[37] Because of this, and because three of the four archive staff making preservation decisions were women, we were very interested in preserving and examining the interviews with female subjects. We find the interviews with women to be extremely moving and illuminating. Ruth Elias discusses being forced by horrific circumstances to commit infanticide on her newborn baby girl at Auschwitz. Hansi Brand reveals that after her husband, Joel, left for Istanbul, she stood in as negotiator with the Germans, even meeting with Eichmann, against whom she testified in his 1961 trial. Gertrude Schneider, who is interviewed with her mother and sister, talks openly about sex and abortion in the Riga Ghetto.

Finally, there are the *Shoah* location outtakes, so-called because Lanzmann identified them by the location in which they were shot, such as Treblinka, Sobibór, or Wannsee. We initially assigned these materials a low priority because the elements were undescribed, randomly arranged, and of unknown relevance. However, the preservation and digitization of this location footage in recent years has shed new light on important features of Lanzmann's production process, and particularly on his attention to mise-en-scène: his arrangement of the setting and surroundings of an interview or shot of a specific location. In one such reel, shot in Grabów, Poland, Lanzmann physically places a man whom he has decided to interview in a doorway and asks him to take off his coat and hat before beginning the interview. In another take, the camera pans from the interviewee to a crowd of onlookers watching the proceedings; Lanzmann asks one of his crew members to escort a person out of the frame and to replace him with someone different from the crowd.[38] Among the location footage accompanying Lanzmann's interview with Henryk Gawkowski are numerous takes of Gawkowski driving a train back and forth in front of the station sign reading "Treblinka." We also discovered that some of the outtakes designated simply by location in fact contain interviews that are incredibly rich and informative. One such interview was conducted with Polish villagers in the towns near Sobibór, while another takes place on the site of the Grabów Ghetto, from which the Jews of Grabów were deported to Chełmno. Along with hundreds of silent atmospheric shots, which bear can labels like "ambiance," "tournage 3eme," "gare," and "ramp," the locations, too, are important and deserve attention, as they contain images of the places Lanzmann considered at some point in his process as possibilities for illustrating testimonial voices in *Shoah*.

Use of the *Shoah* Outtakes in the Twenty-First Century

Viewing copies of the preserved outtake interviews became available to researchers a decade after the initial acquisition, and, in 2015, we released a complete set of reels as streaming video on Collections Search, the USHMM public online catalog of museum collections.[39] As a result, online discovery and access has soared. In particular, the interviews with Benjamin Murmelstein, Abraham Bomba, Rudolf Vrba, Filip Mueller, and Ruth Elias garner the most views by internet users and exceed even some of the most familiar and sought-after historical film footage in our collection, such as coverage of the liberation of the concentration camps. We are gratified and professionally proud to see people making such diverse and creative use of a film collection that we have worked so hard to preserve and make accessible.

As more people learn of the *Shoah* outtakes or visit the USHMM on months-long fellowships, we are able to respond to their specific interests by pushing select subjects to the top of the preservation queue. For example, Colorlab completed the difficult preservation of the hidden-camera interview with Franz Suchomel, an infamous perpetrator who appears in *Shoah*, for use in the HBO short documentary *Claude Lanzmann: Spectres of the Shoah* (2015).[40] For many years, we chose not to focus attention on this important interview, as it was heavily used in the final film, reasoning that the most significant takes were not part of the outtake rolls. It also required lots of costly handwork by the negative cutter in order to repair tape splices and conform original camera negatives. The producer of the HBO documentary also requested shots of Lanzmann on camera as well as location footage shot in New York and Israel, so we also scanned several of those reels. As Lanzmann no longer managed the unedited *Shoah* materials nor owned copyright after 1996, he also served as a USHMM client. When he needed access to the outtakes to make his later films about Jan Karski, Benjamin Murmelstein, Ruth Elias, Hanna Marton, Paula Biren, and Ada Lichtman, he came to the USHMM to borrow the new, stable preservation film copies as well as high-quality digital versions of his interviews.

Scholars of film and comparative literature have found the archive of outtakes an especially rich source of scholarship, recently writing new analyses or critiques of *Shoah* that in part dispel long-standing myths surrounding the making of the film and shedding light on the lesser-known topics explored in the interviews that were not used by Lanzmann in *Shoah*.[41] Some of the *Shoah* subjects were recorded by other oral historians years after the film, or published their own memoirs, providing historians of memory and others with alternative accounts to compare and study.[42]

Because of the outtakes' public availability, new details have emerged from individuals who were central to the production, including Lanzmann's assistant Irena Steinfeldt, the French-language interpreter Francine Kaufmann, the editor Ziva Postec, and Lanzmann's second wife and translator for Murmelstein, the writer Angelika Schrobsdorff. They have offered details about the film materials or anecdotes about their experiences that help to contextualize the interviews and the circumstances in which they were recorded. For example, Steinfeldt responded to an inquiry from former film archive director Raye Farr, in 2006:

> Much of that period just melted together, and I often find it very hard to isolate this or that part. What I can tell you in general is that I think that the major part of the filming in Poland took place in the summer of 1978 (with some outdoor

shots done in winter a couple of years later), America was towards the end of that year (November-December), Israel was late summer and fall of 1979. . . . The exceptions were Garfunkel and Murmelstein. . . . They were filmed at earlier dates . . . because we were afraid they would die before we would begin the filming. As for Schubert—it wasn't me at the shooting, because I had conducted the preliminary interviews, and Claude didn't want him saying "As I already said last time. . . ." I did most of the preparatory interviews, but was present in very few of the filmed ones. With Claude postponing and postponing the filming, after the American shooting, I . . . didn't feel like running all over the world with a film crew. So I sat in Paris and saw the rushes.[43]

In these few sentences, we learn important information about the mechanics behind the shooting and editing of *Shoah*, including approximations of dates, the organizational work for preliminary meetings with interviewees, and, importantly, memories and impressions from a woman who was, like many others, key to the creation of the film. Recollections from those who worked on *Shoah* offer a fuller and more nuanced history that works to counterbalance Lanzmann's aversion to sharing credit or acknowledging that anyone besides himself participated in the creation of the film. Evidence of the contributions of others, such as those described by Steinfeldt, were absent from the documents we received with the collection in 1996.

Further layers of insight into the making of the film unfold serendipitously in unrelated document and media collections acquired by the USHMM. For example, USHMM Archives collected the papers of Roswell McClelland, who, in addition to the prominent role he played in American responses to the Holocaust, was interviewed for *Shoah*. Within his papers, we discovered a typed formal request for an interview written by Lanzmann on February 16, 1977. He wrote the following to McClelland:

The work is conceived and constructed like an investigation of the Holocaust carried out today, the film traces the development of this investigation, it is this investigation itself, with all its successes and failures, its uncertainties, its contradictions, its impossibilities, its nature of urgency and a race against death. For it is clear—and this feeling is present from the first to the last image, determining the style of the editing, being its very breath—that in a few years from now it will be too late: living History, our History, will have become dead history, just history. The Holocaust will no longer exist in the memory of men. . . . For the young generation, it is already in the nature of a legend, an object less of true knowledge than one of fascination.[44]

From this paragraph, we can speculate that Lanzmann had settled on the central thesis of *Shoah* somewhat early in the production years. Lanzmann's 2013 memoir contains additional valuable information about how the film came into being: some details previously well known, but also some completely new revelations that might seem mundane to the uninitiated but have great value to the USHMM staff and scholars who are working to piece the whole process together.[45] The videotaped Eichmann trial proceedings from 1961 are also accessible at the USHMM and contain early witness testimony from Simon Srebnik, Ada Lichtman, and Abba Kovner, among others. The fact that these individuals were later chosen by Lanzmann as witnesses for his film has led some scholars to argue that the trial, a seminal event in its own right, helped Lanzmann to begin his thinking about possible witnesses to interview for the film.

The availability of the *Shoah* outtakes, details from alternative sources or documents, and assiduous research by scholars have challenged our collective understanding of *Shoah* and Lanzmann's filmmaking process, which, not surprisingly, given his personality and belief in the uniqueness and primacy of his work, he would have much preferred to remain unexplored.[46] Nevertheless, such scholarly work has proven an invaluable tool in helping us to develop our strategies for prioritizing, preserving, cataloging, and providing access to the collection. It has also motivated us to persevere over the past two decades despite this complex, challenging, expensive, and often frustrating endeavor. Recent work on the interviews include the Warsaw Ghetto fighters Simha Rotem and Itzhak Zuckerman, Reichsbahn official Walter Stier, US Ambassador Robert Reams, Kraków survivor Dr. Wiener, American professor Richard Rubenstein, and Faivel Ziegelbaum, who tells the story of his brother Szmuel, who famously committed suicide in 1943 as an act of protest against the refusal of Allied governments to aid Polish Jews.[47] We plan to complete preservation efforts on the *Shoah* outtakes with lab work on the remaining locations and the last bits and trims of negative rolls.

The United States Holocaust Memorial Museum has been deeply committed to preserving the Claude Lanzmann *Shoah* Collection for more than twenty years, and we are proud of our progress. The more accessible this collection becomes, the greater the potential significance the voices of these witnesses hold for scholars, documentary film producers, and the public, among others. The scope, variety, and detail provided in the accounts of these witnesses to the Shoah continue to inform the work of all of us who study Holocaust history, film, memory, testimony, and trauma, and the intersection of these and other academic fields. We encourage you to visit the USHMM's Collections Search catalog online to view and examine the stories shared in the more than 220 hours of outtakes contained in the Claude Lanzmann *Shoah* Collection.

Notes

Epigraph: Claude Lanzmann *Shoah* Collection, interview with Peter Bergson and Samuel Merlin, RG-60.5020, https://collections.ushmm.org/search/catalog/irn1002779 (accessed August 28, 2019), United States Holocaust Memorial Museum (USHMM) and Yad Vashem and State of Israel.

1. Simone de Beauvoir, preface to *Shoah: An Oral History of the Holocaust: The Complete Text of the Film*, by Claude Lanzmann (New York: Pantheon, 1985), x.

2. Roger Ebert, "Reviews," *Chicago Sun Times*, November 24, 1985.

3. Timothy Garton Ash, "The Life of Death," *New York Review of Books* 32, no. 20 (December 19, 1985): 26–40.

4. Patrick Z. McGavin, "'The Ultimate Liberation': *Shoah* on Blu-Ray Reminds Us of Why It Is Essential Cinema," *Balder & Dash*, July 10, 2013, https://www.rogerebert.com/balder-and-dash/shoah-comes-to-blu-ray-and-reminds-us-once-again-why-it-is-essential-cinema (accessed August 27, 2019).

5. Lanzmann claims that 350 hours of footage were shot during the production of *Shoah*. It is unclear if the filmmakers kept an exact record during the long production period, as the project stretched on and on, and funds had to be raised

to complete the film. The USHMM estimate of 220 hours (roughly 185 hours of interview outtakes and 35 hours of location filming) is based on empirical evidence of the outtakes, which we measure precisely as part of the preservation process. We have no reason to believe there is a large cache of film or sound tape somewhere that the USHMM did not receive or hear about. We did not obtain any of the footage used in the completed film and attribute 10 hours at most to that material. It is possible that some footage was lost or destroyed, but likely not 100 hours of it.

6. *Einsatzgruppen* (mobile killing units) were squads composed primarily of German SS and police personnel. Under the command of the German Security Police and Security Service officers, the *Einsatzgruppen* had among their tasks the murder of those perceived to be racial or political enemies found behind German combat lines in the occupied Soviet Union. USHMM Holocaust Encyclopedia, http://www.ushmm.org/wlc/en/article.php?ModuleId=10005130 (accessed August 27, 2019).

7. The Germans established Jewish councils, usually called *Judenräte* (sing., *Judenrat*), during World War II. These Jewish municipal administrations were required to ensure that Nazi orders and regulations were implemented, and therefore remain a controversial subject. Jewish council members also sought to provide basic community services for ghettoized Jewish populations. USHMM Holocaust Encyclopedia, http://www.ushmm.org/wlc/en/article.php?ModuleId=10005265 (accessed August 27, 2019).

8. Raye Farr and Michael Berenbaum to Walter Reich, "*Shoah* Outtakes: Report on Paris Screening, 20–29 February 1996" (memorandum), USHMM, March 4, 1996.

9. Farr and Berenbaum, "*Shoah* Outtakes."

10. The cinematographers enlisted by Lanzmann include Dominique Chapuis, Jimmy Glasberg, William Lubtchansky (whose father was killed at Auschwitz), Caroline Champetier de Ribes, Jean-Yves Escoffier, Slavek Olczyk, and Andrés Silvart.

11. Consult Appendix 1 of the *Shoah* outtakes in this volume, or Collections Search for up-to-date catalog records, streaming video content, and transcripts: https://collections.ushmm.org/search/catalog/irn1000017 (accessed August 27, 2019).

12. Women central to the production of *Shoah* include Hebrew interpreter Francine Kaufmann; Polish interpreter Barbra Janica; Yiddish interpreter Mrs. Apflebaum; assistant directors Corinna Coulmas and Irena Steinfeldt; editors Ziva Postec and Anna Ruiz; and assistant editor Yael Perlov.

13. Lanzmann obtained the following interviews with a *paluche*: Pery Broad, Hans Gewecke, Karl Kretschmer, Eduard Kryshak, Gustav Laabs, Franz Schalling, Walter Stier, and Franz Suchomel. The location outtake called "Camionette" shows footage of the Volkswagen van used to conceal the transmission equipment for these hidden-camera interviews. Interviews with Pery Broad (RG-60.5053), Hans Gewecke (RG-60.5027), Karl Kretschmer (RG-60.5018), Eduard Kryshak (RG-60.5035), Gustav Laabs and Lettre Becker (RG-60.5025), Franz Schalling (RG-60.5034), Walter Stier (RG-60.5064), and Franz Suchomel (RG-60.5046); Camionette footage (RG-60.5058).

14. As Dorota Glowacka points out in her contribution to this volume, in the theatrical release of *Shoah*, the name of the Polish survivor Szymon Srebrnik has been rendered as Simon Srebnik. Given the widespread adoption of the latter spelling in the large body of extant scholarship, this volume, with the exception of Glowacka's chapter, preserves what has become the name's standard presentation.

15. Trims are the hundreds of the bits and pieces "trimmed" out of a completed film during the final stages of editing.

16. It is important to note that the retired Kevin Fallis is deeply committed to this preservation project and continues to work intimately on negative reassembly.

17. For more information about the editing phase of production, refer to the documentary *Ziva Postec: The Editor Behind the Film Shoah*, directed by Catherine Hébert, 2018.

18. Washington University Film & Media Archive similarly tackled a project to digitize and reassemble the interview outtakes from the seminal documentary series *Eyes on the Prize*, a definitive work on the civil rights movement broadcast in the 1980s and 1990s. The archive of 16mm A- and B-rolls and quarter-inch audio amount to just over seventy-five hours of content. Consult this short video for more details: https://www.youtube.com/watch?v=4KsXv7EOFlU (accessed August 27, 2019).

19. See interview with Czesław Borowi (RG-60.5032, Film ID 3348, Camera Rolls 46, 47, 48, 56).

20. Interviews with Abraham Bomba (RG-60.5011) and Ruth Elias (RG-60.5003).

21. This workflow is regularly revisited, given advances in technology or techniques. For example, in order to maximize efficiency and reduce cost, we recently explored alternative workflows to obtaining access files, such as using postproduction software tools to synchronize image scans with digital audio files.

22. Stuart Liebman, "Introduction," in *Claude Lanzmann's* Shoah: *Key Essays*, ed. Stuart Liebman (Oxford: Oxford University Press, 2007), 6.

23. In contrast, an oral history video interview produced by the USHMM or collected from another organization runs two to three hours in length. Interviews with Benjamin Murmelstein (RG-60.5009) and Jan Karski (RG-60.5006).

24. Claude Lanzmann, "Material of *Shoah*," USHMM Accession 1996.166.

25. See note 5 about the difference between Lanzmann's estimates and our own.

26. Interviews with Filip Müller (RG-60.5012), Leib Garfunkel (RG-60.5005), Gertrude Schneider (RG-60.5015), Karl Kretschmer (RG-60.5018), Ruth Elias (RG-60.5003), and Paula Biren (RG-60.5001). Interestingly, the first interviews to be conformed and preserved in 2002 differ from this initial selection and include a selection of interviews with Jan Karski, Sigmunt Forst, Paula Biren, and Herman Landau. In late 2005, the first group of outtakes to be fully cataloged and made available to the public were the interviews with Ehud Avriel (RG-60.5000), Paula Biren, Hansi Brand (RG-60.5002), Ruth Elias, Sigmunt Forst (RG-60.5004), Leib Garfunkel, Jan Karski (RG-60.5006), Herman Landau (RG-60.5007), Hanna Marton (RG-60.5008), and Benjamin Murmelstein (RG-60.5009).

27. Interview with Hansi Brand (RG-60.5002).

28. Interview with Benjamin Murmelstein (RG-60.5009).

29. Interview with Peter Bergson and Samuel Merlin (RG-60.5020).

30. The transcripts of interviews with Polish-speaking individuals through a French interpreter are especially incomplete, as Lanzmann's transcriber did not comprehend the Polish language. See the transcripts for Czeslaw Borowi, Grabów, or the Treblinka railway workers.

31. Consult Collections Search to study and zoom into the transcript pages with an interactive, digital viewer—https://collections.ushmm.org/search/catalog/irn539109 (accessed August 27, 2019).

32. Claude Lanzmann, *The Patagonian Hare: A Memoir* (New York: Farrar, Straus & Giroux, 2013), 449.

33. Lanzmann, *The Patagonian Hare*, 449.

34. Interview with Heinz Schubert (RG-60.5013, Film ID 3219, Camera Rolls 7, 8).

35. Interview with Karl Kretschmer (RG-60.5018, Film ID 3246, Camera Rolls 1–3).

36. Interview with Jan Piwonski (RG-60.5031).

37. In April 2017, Lanzmann directed a new documentary television series called *The Four Sisters*, focusing on the *Shoah* outtake interviews with four women: Paula Biren, Ruth Elias, Hanna Marton, and Ada Lichtman. The series was produced by Synecdoche and Arte for French television.

38. Charlotte Horsey noticed much of Lanzmann's deliberate staging while analyzing and cataloging the outtakes for USHMM as an intern in the fall of 2015.

39. The Claude Lanzmann *Shoah* Collection can be found online at http://collections.ushmm.org/search (accessed August 27, 2019).

40. *Claude Lanzmann: Spectres of the Shoah*, directed by Adam Benzine, HBO Productions, 2015.

41. See works by Sue Vice, "Claude Lanzmann's Einsatzguppen Interviews," *Holocaust Studies: A Journal of Culture and History* 17, nos. 2–3 (2011): 51–74; Brad Prager, "Testimonial Performances on Screen: From the Eichmann Trial to *Kitty: Return to Auschwitz*," in *Lessons & Legacies XIII*, ed. Alexandra Garbarini and Paul Jaskot (Chicago: Northwestern University Press, 2018), 240–63; and Jennifer Cazenave, *An Archive of the Catastrophe. The Unused Footage of Claude Lanzmann's Shoah* (Albany: State University of New York Press, 2019).

42. For example, Ruth Elias, Paula Biren, and Gertrude Schneider, among others.

43. Irena Steinfeldt, email to Raye Farr, October 30, 2006.

44. Claude Lanzmann to Roswell McClelland, February 16, 1977, Roswell and Marjorie McClelland Papers, USHMM Accession 2014.414.1.

45. For example, Lanzmann writes that he holed up in a tiny office at Yad Vashem, where he read Hilberg obsessively and used whiteboards to draw charts, "endlessly erasing and redrawing, which I thought might help me articulate this unthinkable 'thing' that I was discovering." Lanzmann, *The Patagonian Hare*, 413.

46. Lanzmann has expressed disdain about the availability of the outtakes at USHMM. For example, in an interview conducted during the world premiere of *The Last of the Unjust* at Cannes in May 2013, Lanzmann says he returned to work on Benjamin Murmelstein after seeing a public screening of his unedited materials in Vienna: "I was totally outraged! I felt as if I had been robbed," http://www.festival-cannes.com (accessed August 27, 2019).

47. Interview with Simha Rotem and Itzhak Zuckerman (RG-60.5048), Walter Stier (RG-60.5064), Robert Reams (RG-60.5061), Dr. Wiener (RG-60.5078), Richard Rubenstein (RG-60.5062), and Faivel Ziegelbaum (RG-60.5072).

2

Shoah and the Archive

Sue Vice

Reviews of the documentary *A German Life* (Christian Krönes et al., 2016), consisting of interviews with the 105-year-old Brunhilde Pomsel, the wartime secretary to Josef Goebbels, are not unusual in describing it in terms of its editing history. As one reviewer notes, the two-hour film was compiled "from 30 hours of conversation."[1] Such an emphasis on the editing process points to the film's seriousness of both generic and historical purpose, as well as its high standards, since the final version must, it is implied, be a distillation of the best material. In the case of Claude Lanzmann's *Shoah*, invocation of the difference between the 220 hours of the footage shot and the nine-and-a-half hour running time of the 1985 film has extra significance, one that testifies both to its director's extreme commitment to his subject, and to the aesthetic—as much as the documentary—integrity of the final version.

It is this conceptual connection between originary footage and released films that this essay will consider, specifically in relation to nonfiction cinema. It will do so by exploring the concept of a filmic archive, using *Shoah* as a test case. The material held in the *Shoah* collection at the United States

Holocaust Memorial Museum consists of outtakes, in the sense of material that did not make its way into the 1985 film, although some of it has since been included in one of five separate releases: *A Visitor from the Living* (1997), *Sobibór, October 14 1943, 4pm* (2001), *The Karski Report* (2010), *The Last of the Unjust* (2013), and *The Four Sisters* (2018).

In this way, I will attempt to establish what kind of relationship there is between the final version of a film and the material cut from it, or not used in it, but which has been retained. The focus here is the specifically visual component of such an archive as Lanzmann's, since others—for instance, the Ken Loach Archive at the British Film Institute's Reuben Library—consist rather of paper material such as drafted or abandoned scripts and production documents. An investigation of the present kind entails considering the concept of the archive itself, and whether that is the appropriate term in a filmic context, even though it is of course the one used in titling the "collection" of Lanzmann's material at the USHMM's Steven Spielberg Film and Video Archive.

| The Visual Archive

While "the archive" has been the focus of much recent analysis, in the context of both literary and memory studies, the specifically visual archive has not received sustained attention. This is partly due to the fact that the term "archive" in cinema studies is used to refer to a range of different phenomena. For Bhaskar Sarkar and Janet Walker, in their consideration of documentary testimony, the archive is an often virtual "assemblage," one consisting of public collections of expressions of "social suffering."[2] In this sense, the archive is not only generated by, but consists of, shared affronts, including, for example, statements by Hiroshima *hibakushas*, as well as a compilation of "healthcare horror stories" to accompany Michael Moore's film *Sicko* (2007).[3] In a different usage, the archive is invoked in generic rather than ethical terms. Thus "archival footage," of the very kind omitted by Lanzmann from *Shoah* and that makes it in that sense an "anti-archive," in Elisabeth Friedman's phrasing, consists of preexisting historical material as it appears in a later factual or fictional film.[4] For instance, the TV drama series *The Honourable Woman* (Hugo Blick, 2014) concludes with a montage of episodes from Middle Eastern history, as if in representation of its protagonist Nessa Stein's (Maggie Gyllenhaal) "post-traumatic" interiority,[5] while Jeremy Isaacs, the producer of the documentary *The World at War* (1973), notes that the film's researchers avoided wartime newsreel footage, turning instead to "digging through archives to find fresh film" with which to illustrate it.[6] Yet another use of the notion of a filmic archive is a methodological one, in reference to artworks in which meaning is constructed solely through the reediting of anterior material. In this way, Peter Forgács's films rely upon found footage such as home movies and amateur films, and Eyal Sivan's *The Specialist* (1999) consists of repurposed footage from the trial of Adolf Eichmann; as Sivan puts it: "It is made up entirely from these archives."[7] Documentaries whose substance is the exploration of earlier films themselves enact an archiving function, by preserving and presenting the newly uncovered material on which they center, as is the case of Yael Hersonski's *A Film Unfinished* (2010), which explores the making of a Nazi propaganda film of 1942 set in the Warsaw Ghetto. Hersonski's film opens with the visual conceit of a discovery in a basement archive full of film reels, and long sections from the Nazis' unfinished film *The Ghetto* are then shown. *A Film Unfinished* is, as its title suggests, both about and constituted by a visual archive. Lastly, the phenomenon of directors' cuts has the different, but nonetheless archival, function of returning a film to an earlier form, as if taking a documentary perspective on a fiction film. This is the case in the several releases of Ridley Scott's *Blade Runner* (1982), the later versions of which (1992, 2007) include a restored detail that fundamentally alters the plot, by suggesting that the protagonist Deckard (Harrison Ford) is one of the very "replicants" we have seen him hunt down and kill.

Each of these examples relies upon the notion of foregrounding or showcasing archival material, described as such because of its collective, anterior, or historical nature. The present case of Lanzmann's filmic archive is rather different, since it consists of a collection of outtakes which have not been superseded, but rather exist in synchronicity with the final version in an as-yet unedited state. Further even than this, the exact composition of the unedited material itself changes over time, given the later release of five films composed from stock not included in *Shoah*. While the USHMM archive does not house the footage used in *Shoah*'s final version, it does include the entirety of the material from which subsequent releases were formed (thus, for instance, the eleven-hour interview with Benjamin Murmelstein held in the archive includes the four hours that make up *The Last of the Unjust*). Despite the intriguing complexity of notions of excluded and final versions that such a scenario raises, the idea of a collection of filmic outtakes and their circulation around a released film is only infrequently the subject of analysis, in contrast to the widespread commentary on literary variants and drafts and their relation to a published work. The case of *Shoah* and the material held in the USHMM archive assists speculation about why this relative lack of consideration is the case, while exploration of these questions—What is the purpose of this archive, and what ends can it serve? What do we want to find there, and what do we find?—is significant both for the history of Lanzmann's body of work, and for that of Holocaust representation itself.

Among the rare instances of commentary on the filmic archive, as both repository and conceptual field, are two that explore the relationship between discard and final version, albeit in cases that do not follow Lanzmann's practice of later releasing individual feature films drawn from the original body of footage. The first example of this kind is William Fowler's study of the archive of Peter Whitehead, the "documentary filmmaker and counter-cultural force" who directed the film *Wholly Communion* (1965) about a Beat poetry reading at the Albert Hall in London.[8] The second is the case of David Wnendt's film *Look Who's Back* (2015), based on Timur Vermes's 2012 novel, in which Hitler reappears from his bunker seventy years on. This fiction film includes documentary material in the form of unscripted dialogue that arises when members of the public meet the central character as played by Oliver Masucci. The original 380 hours of footage was cut down to the released version's running time of two hours, including some of these vox-pop documentary sequences. Thus, as Kate Connolly puts it, we see "real-life scenes of modern day Germans reacting to seeing [Hitler] walking around," woven "into the fictional scenes."[9] However, as Connolly goes on to speculate, the encounters could equally be artificially staged, by means of the editing. Such a practice is not uncommon—for example, it is evident in Chantal Akerman's *No Home Movie* (2015). As the title implies, the footage of Akerman's conversations with her mother, Nelly, has been carefully constructed to appear as if it took an unedited, domestic form.[10]

These examples show the kinds of issues that the existence of outtakes raises. As Fowler argues, it is possible to gain from Whitehead's archive a practical insight into the methods and materials of his practice of filming, and this is certainly also the case with Lanzmann. In the *Shoah* archive, we are always aware of the existence and implications of eleven-minute sections shot on 16mm film, or with the handheld *paluche* camera for the clandestine interviews. We see, for example, the clapperboard used to start each segment of interview, usually labeled "*Holocauste*," as was Lanzmann's early title for the film; sometimes with other revealing titling. For the interview with Mrs Pietyra, the location given on the clapperboard is "Auschwitz," although it took place rather in the town of Oświęcim: this labeling represents Lanzmann's conflation even at the level of production of town with camp, past with present.[11] Some aspects of the technical context, such as the VW van used to signify the act of secretly filming the interview with Franz Suchomel, are included in *Shoah*, but much more material of this kind is not: the process of Lanzmann being wired up for a secret interview, as we see in the outtakes in relation to the former *Einsatzgruppen* member Heinz Schubert;[12] the audible commentary of the cinematographer Dominique Chapuis, again in the outtakes, on the visual quality of the interview with Pery Broad, who had been an SS officer at Auschwitz;[13] not to mention "silent shots, beginnings of interviews, things that were ruined," as Lanzmann puts it.[14] These examples imply that there exists a continuum, ranging from footage that represents "the actual conditions under which films (and meaning) are produced," to interview material lying in wait to be used.[15]

Fowler argues that, formally speaking, Whitehead's archive shows the "stylistic foundations" of his later work.[16] The *Shoah* archive is distinctive in disrupting such an idea. In contrast to Fowler's argument, the consideration of Lanzmann's outtakes, which relate to a single work undertaken between 1973 and its appearance in 1985, as well as the subsequent releases over the next four decades, registers instead a defiance of what the critic Hans Walter Gabler, in the context of James Joyce's *Ulysses* manuscripts, calls the "teleology of achievement."[17] Lanzmann's archive is a snapshot, albeit one of long duration, rather than the accumulation of a whole career, as in Whitehead's case. The process it represents is not equivalent to that of drafting a novel for the sake of its "improvement," as with *Ulysses*. While collections of annotations and discarded versions in relation to literary drafts—or, indeed, fictional film footage—may be of such interest that they are themselves published or released, these do not usually take the form of alternative versions, but as research aids or curiosities judged to be of secondary value.[18] This distinction arises from referential status rather than medium, since it is nonfiction material specifically which retains its value even outside its aesthetic context.

Rather, it seems that the *Shoah* outtakes are, to draw on Saussure's terminology, a syntagmatic structure, representing the possibility of combination and coexistence and not the differentiation and contrast of the paradigmatic.[19] The choices made by the director are not exclusive ones requiring a definitive choice between different elements, but assume instead the syntagmatic form of a sequence. This is shown by Lanzmann's several releases from the same body of film, as well as the freely accessible nature of the outtake footage: the apparently discarded material can now enter the public realm in its own right, in a variety of forms, ranging from scholarly analyses to extracts used in other documentary films. Such an approach allows us to watch and analyze the outtake material for its own sake, as the very existence of the present collection of essays reveals. If the outtakes are viewed solely in relation to the 1985 film, they are necessarily judged to be inferior due to the very fact of their exclusion, yet those sections included in the separate releases are given unexpected credit. Thus Ronny Loewy uses the expressive term *Abfall*, or rubbish, for the usual conception of outtakes from fiction films; while Mark Lilla claims that Lanzmann's interview with Benjamin Murmelstein, the former "Elder" of the Theresienstadt Ghetto, in *The Last of the Unjust* (2013), strikes "a discordant note" in relation to *Shoah*, implying that the director was correct in his original decision to omit any element of it.[20] Indeed, there is a paradox implicit in attempting to view the outtakes for their own sake: scholars and critics must inevitably regard them in relation to *Shoah* and the other released films, since the former constitutes the frame and auteurist signature by which the extra footage has come to be of such interest. This dialectical tension between outtake and release characterizes even those interviews that are strikingly self-contained or illustrative of particular themes, since it is hard to imagine that they would otherwise have come to public notice. Thus Lanzmann's presence and editorial decisions frame Ruth Elias's three-and-a-half-hour outtake interview, now released in edited form in *The Four Sisters*, in which she describes infanticide in Auschwitz,[21] just as it does Jacob Arnon's discarded two-hour account of his uncle's role in the wartime Jewish Council of Amsterdam,[22] and the almost five-hour encounter between Lanzmann and the poet and partisan Abba Kovner, from which no extract appears in the finished film.[23]

Shoah's Satellites

Lanzmann's releases of material from the Shoah archive—most recently, *The Karski Report* (2010), *The Last of the Unjust* (2013) and *The Four Sisters* (2018)—support the notion of the nonteleological nature of all the 230 hours of footage. Indeed, the box-set that contains all but the last of these films is called "Four Films After *Shoah*," even though some of the footage, most notably that of Benjamin Murmelstein in *The Last of the Unjust*, was one of Lanzmann's earliest interviews. The temporality or succession of the interviews is not their organizing principle. These separate releases show that the outtakes are considered by the director himself as material "for resumption" rather than "ultimate abandonment," in Gabler's phrasing about Joyce.[24] Reviews of this material seem to respond to just this quality of the outtake footage on its separate release, as depending on *Shoah* yet outstripping it in certain respects. While Lilla says of *The Last of the Unjust*, as is true of all but the most recent of the separate releases, that it is a "one-man show" in contrast to the "associative style" of *Shoah*, and therefore, he implies, a lesser work, others view the dialectic between outtake and final film as more productive. Janet Maslin calls *A Visitor from the Living* (1997), about Maurice Rossel's fruitless Red Cross visits to Theresienstadt and Auschwitz, "a transfixing addendum."[25] Of the same film, Godfrey Cheshire notes that, had it been edited into *Shoah*'s "other interviews, [Lanzmann's] conversation with Rossel would merely be interesting. Seen entire, it has a subtle dramatic build that is powerful and revelatory." Similarly, Manuel Köppen argues of the interview with the former prisoner Yehuda Lerner in *Sobibór* (2001) that its individual focus is more successful than *Shoah*'s method of juxtaposition: "The revolt of Sobibór could be not just a moment in *Shoah*: It deserved its own film, it demanded separate treatment."[26] Such phrasing, which acknowledges the primacy of *Shoah* yet argues that its extra footage is "transfixing" when viewed outside but in full knowledge of the released film, brings us into the territory of Jacques Derrida's notion of the "supplement," the "addendum," in Maslin's phrase, or "footnote" in Cheshire's, as a "plenitude enriching another plenitude."[27] These comments show that archival analysis need not always entail hierarchizing comparison, and that, rather, outtake and release depend on each other for their significance.

Doris Toumarkine notes of Lanzmann's *A Visitor from the Living* that "Rossel never expresses any remorse for the fate of the Jews during the Holocaust," and her question "Was such material left on the cutting-room floor?" implies that what seems to be cinematic revelation is in fact an artificially constructed polemic.[28] The outtakes from this encounter do not include material testifying straightforwardly to Rossel's "remorse," although he is shown responding uncomfortably to some of Lanzmann's correctives, including the latter's reading out a letter from 1944 by Paul Eppstein, Murmelstein's predecessor as "Elder" in Theresienstadt, who was killed two days after its composition. Lanzmann's outtakes are valuable in relation to questions of this kind, regarding the material that did make the final cut as well as the footage that remains: that which was excluded but not discarded. David MacDougall argues that "film rushes," in the sense of the entire body of filmed material before any editing has taken place, are "as much a chronicle of a film's production as they are of its supposed subject."[29] This is equally true of Lanzmann's outtakes—that is, those rushes that were edited out of the released films—since the production history of *Shoah* and the other releases is apparent, even in oblique form, as an element of this cinematic meditation on the Holocaust. The films are in part records of their own creation.

This is clear in relation to two opposite tendencies: first, the outtakes point toward the other kinds of film in thematic and conceptual terms that might have emerged from Lanzmann's original hours of footage, had it been edited according to different priorities. The second tendency is the archive's containing extra material from the interviews that are present in *Shoah* itself. For instance, among the outtakes is an extra three hours of footage from Lanzmann's interview with the barber Abraham Bomba, in which the two men sit on a terrace by the sea near Jaffa.[30] Some material from this interview appears in *Shoah*, but in the outtakes, we hear Lanzmann encourage Bomba to talk about his prewar life, his deportation to Treblinka and loss of his family, as well as the difficulty he had in cutting women's hair again after the war. This is not merely material that Lanzmann had to excise for reasons of length. Although the sequence is carefully constructed cinematically, with alternations of close-ups and two-shots as the two men speak, it seems that it is profoundly "preliminary" material, to use Lanzmann's term about other discarded interviews.[31] This is clear in terms of the interview's content and its format: in *Shoah* we do not learn about the biographies of the protagonists, who speak as "witnesses to the deaths of their people," in Lanzmann's phrasing, rather than as individuals.[32] Here, however, Bomba describes his escape from Treblinka (as do Podchlebnik, Glazar, and Zaidel, from Chełmno, Treblinka and Ponary, respectively, in the outtakes of their interviews).[33] In the present case, Lanzmann is shown in shot holding Bomba's hand: this is a gesture that helps the interviewee become accustomed to talking about the past. Yet, because the interviewer is shown to be so close to the subject, that gesture is part of the reason that the footage was judged to be unusable.[34] The clasped hand is a

Abraham Bomba talks about his escape from the Treblinka killing center while Lanzmann holds his hand. Created by Claude Lanzmann during the filming of *Shoah*. (Used by permission of the United States Holocaust Memorial Museum and Yad Vashem, the Holocaust Martyrs and Heroes' Remembrance Authority, Jerusalem.)

striking symbol of the inextricability of production process from subject, in MacDougall's terms: this outtake material is the record of what was necessary to reach the moment of Bomba's breaking down in the barbershop in *Shoah*, in both practical and psychological terms.[35]

Excluded Interviews

In the case of material from which no footage was included in *Shoah*, the relationship between process and subject is necessarily different. One of many possible examples of this kind is an interview remarkable for its existence at all, a fact that overrides its seeming to lack the elements of "reincarnation" or focus on a cinematic "character" that are central to *Shoah*. This is the interview Lanzmann undertook with Tadeusz Pankiewicz, the non-Jewish pharmacist who ran the so-called Kraków Ghetto Pharmacy (its historical name is Under the Eagle) throughout the war, and that is now a museum. Pankiewicz's unrivaled situation as the only "Aryan" who chose to remain behind in the ghetto, where he sheltered many Jews, must have made him seem an ideal witness. Pankiewicz appears in an interview that is designed, like the barbershop scene with Bomba in *Shoah*, to allow the past to reappear: we see him dressed in a chemist's white coat at the reconstructed pharmacy, standing before old-fashioned china apothecary jars.[36] Yet this setting is ironic, since Pankiewicz says several times that he sold food rather than medicine to the ghetto inhabitants. Such re-creation does succeed in provoking a version of reincarnation, in the sense that Pankiewicz's modest persona in the present repeats what he considered to be his unremarkable acts of rescue during the war. Yet despite the pharmacy's vantage point, from which he was an eyewitness to the inhabitants' deportations, Pankiewicz is so low-key and self-effacing that it is hard to imagine him as one of the film's starring "actors," in Lanzmann's phrase.[37] Indeed, his unassuming demeanor has the effect of laying bare the staging, creating a distance between his words and the pharmacy setting to make it seem impassably artificial.

The next example is similarly one about a geographical and conceptual area that does not feature in *Shoah*: that of a Nazi in Lithuania. Despite the material in the released film concerning Ponary Forest, this interview with Hans Gewecke, who was the *Gebietskommissar*, or governor, in Šiauliai,

Lanzmann interviews Tadeusz Pankiewicz, the non-Jewish pharmacist who ran the so-called Kraków Ghetto Pharmacy throughout the war. The pharmacy was reconstructed especially for filming. Created by Claude Lanzmann during the filming of *Shoah*. (Used by permission of the United States Holocaust Memorial Museum and Yad Vashem, the Holocaust Martyrs and Heroes' Remembrance Authority, Jerusalem.)

Lithuania, from 1941 until the war's end, is unique.[38] It might seem that this interview's cinematic revelations are oblique or small-scale in comparison with those of the one-time Nazis Franz Grassler or, in particular, Franz Suchomel in *Shoah*. In his autobiography, Lanzmann concludes with an intriguing ambivalence about Gewecke that he was "not the worst" *Gebietskommissar* in Šiauliai, adding, quite aptly of his interviewee's comportment, that this man in his early seventies seemed "more like a kindly grandfather than a killer." It is, rather, Walter Stier, the railway bureaucrat who scheduled trains to various death camps yet claimed ignorance of the passengers' fates, in a display of unflinching self-exculpation, whom Lanzmann describes as "one of the most despicable Nazis to appear in *Shoah*."[39]

The interview with Gewecke is notable in its unedited form by virtue of its being visually dull and relentless. Much of the interview's scratchy filmic appearance, dependent on the distance of the *paluche* camera from the recording van, makes Gewecke very indistinct, his strikingly deep-set eyes replaced by shadow. But his words, in combination with the look of the image, paradoxically generate revelation: the interview may appear foggy and shrouded in unclarity, but denial of responsibility for actual atrocity emerges sharply nonetheless. In an echo of his trial verdict, that he was an administrator and not (apart from one significant instance) a murderer, we see Gewecke seated at a desk wearing a jacket and tie, holding his spectacles and a sheaf of papers in a pose that might put us in mind of Adolf Eichmann. Gewecke has reconstructed his biography so that he can claim not to have witnessed or ordered any mass killings, but instead to have undertaken magnanimous acts: for instance, he asserts that he let the Jewish Council members sit down when they came to petition him.

This footage reveals more of Gewecke's role than the impression of grandfatherliness that Lanzmann describes, and is, like the interviews with

Lanzmann conducts a clandestine interview with Hans Gewecke, Gebietskommissar in Šiauliai, Lithuania, from 1941 until war's end. The visually dull, unedited footage records Gewecke's denial of responsibility for atrocities. Created by Claude Lanzmann during the filming of *Shoah*. (Used by permission of the United States Holocaust Memorial Museum and Yad Vashem, the Holocaust Martyrs and Heroes' Remembrance Authority, Jerusalem.)

Grassler and Stier in *Shoah*, full of the "excess meaning" described by David MacDougall, which risks getting lost when outtakes are edited into a final version.[40] Gewecke utters what seem to be unconscious admissions of his actual experience and disavowed knowledge. For instance, he discloses, perhaps refreshingly, that, "I was a very convinced National Socialist, and also a great admirer of [Alfred] Rosenberg," the Reich Minister of the Occupied Eastern Territories.[41] After much discussion of the Nazi Rosenberg, Gewecke moves on to a story supposed to demonstrate his own and his hometown's blamelessness: he claims that "in Ratzeburg was just one Jewish business by the name of Rosenberg," the owner of which "was not bothered at all" in November 1938 because there "was no *Kristallnacht*" there, and whose son now "has a business" back in town.[42] Gewecke gives what seems to be a rueful half-chuckle at the irony of this shared name, although what it suggests about a fantasy of racial difference is not made explicit. This is followed by a second example of a detail from the Nazi past that has a tacit relevance to Jewish history, in an unconscious acknowledgement on Gewecke's part of the deeds that he has otherwise denied. Gewecke explains how he came to join the Nazi Party in 1931: "I said to myself: you have to. . . . somehow. . . . Germany lies defeated, 6 million out of work, the Versailles agreement."[43] Yet again, the shared detail, this time the numbers of unemployed and those of the murdered, provokes no overt reflection on the part of Lanzmann's interviewee. And, lastly, Gewecke's wife, who is in the room throughout the recording, describes her feelings on learning that at his trial in Lübeck a death sentence might have been handed down on her husband, as it was for his mentor Alfred Rosenberg: "I was so shaken. My husband has saved all these Jews, and they tried now to bring him to the gallows. That has shaken me."[44] There is a twisting of the truth in Frau Gewecke's comments, and we might in particular wonder who exactly she means by "they." She claims that her husband "saved" Jews, when in fact he ordered their ghettoization and murder.[45] This dark irony is compounded by the fact that, far from Gewecke unjustly facing "the gallows," the one verdict found against him at trial in 1971, resulting in a sentence of four years in prison for manslaughter, was handed down on account of his own role in a hanging: that of a Jewish baker named Mazawetzki, who was condemned to death in 1943 for smuggling food into the Šiauliai Ghetto. The gallows, the threat of which Frau Gewecke deplores on her husband's account, took a very material form on that wartime occasion, having been constructed by slave laborers in the ghetto under Gewecke's command. At the conclusion of his meeting with Lanzmann, it is Gewecke who is eager to keep talking, the former who draws the encounter to a close, perceiving perhaps that continuing to revisit the past in this "grandfatherly" vein would not result in any kind of reincarnation.

My next example seems to possess a clearer rationale for omission, since it is very short and the interviewee never appears. Yet, since the camera has to look elsewhere for its focus, this means that it is an already self-consciously constructed sequence despite its outtake status. Thus this material conveys with remarkable visual and aural symbolism what came across in the dialogue with Hans Gewecke: the notion of the disavowed knowledge of mass murder. In the late 1970s, Lanzmann tried to interview Gustav Laabs, who had been the driver of one of the three gas vans at Chełmno. Laabs was sentenced to fifteen years in prison at trial in Bonn in 1963, reduced on appeal, for his role in the murder of 100,000 people. Lanzmann insists that he was always certain his film would open with the camp at Chełmno, as the very first line of scrolling text in *Shoah* reads: "The story begins *in the present* at Chełmno," establishing a continuous, almost "ahistorical" temporality.[46] Yet it is also clear that the Laabs footage could not be included, as it appears really to show "nothing," to repeat Jean-Luc Godard's verdict on *Shoah*, in his likening the film's eschewal of archive footage to a superstition akin to the Biblical proscription of images.[47]

However, the present interview's significance lies precisely in what it does not show. In the outtake footage, we see that, when Lanzmann arrives at Laabs's apartment, no one answers the door (the USHMM annotation describes Laabs as "refusing" to answer, but it is not clear that he is at home). The sequence opens with a tracking shot (or a traveling shot, as it is aptly called in French), from the vantage point of Lanzmann's filming van, and this is followed by a gradual close-up on Laabs's apartment window, lasting for over 6.5 minutes of the 11-minute reel.[48] This shot echoes that which prefaces the secretly recorded interview in *Shoah* with Franz Schalling; an enigmatic slow zoom onto the curtained window of a modern apartment block in both cases implies both revelation and withholding.[49] The fact that Schalling had been a police guard at Chełmno hints at a preeditorial plan to match his interview with Laabs's, as suggested by Lanzmann's questions to this former Nazi policeman not only about the size, sound, and capacity of the gas vans, but also about their drivers and the drivers' procedure. The interview in *Shoah* with Schalling is followed by one with the survivor of Chełmno, Michael Podchlebnik, to whom Lanzmann also poses questions about what he could see and hear of the vans he then had to unload. Laabs's interview would have constituted a third perspective, allowing the spectator to assemble a spatially and conceptually triangulated image of the gas-van murders at Chełmno from the viewpoints of a guard, a *Sonderkommando* member, and one of the vans' drivers, each with their distinctive role and proximity in relation to the events.[50] In the finished film, the driver's perspective is not included. In its place, in *Shoah* Lanzmann reads from a letter about planned modifications to the vans, addressed to Walter Rauff and signed "Just," a ventriloquist technique that he also uses in the Laabs footage.[51]

In Laabs's case, the slow zoom on to his apartment window reveals "congruence between a visual detail and the textual narrative," in the words of Lanzmann's editor Ziva Postec, one that is "partial" or oblique.[52] Our viewpoint from the back and side windows of the filming van "evokes" the deathly van of the past, from which there was no external view. In his trial testimony, Laabs described seeing corpses from his rearview mirror, while here, in contrast, our backward view is of the streets of 1970s Germany. At the apartment, Lanzmann's reading of the indictment against Laabs at the 1963 Chełmno trial held in Bonn accompanies the ominously slow zoom of the camera itself, on to the window.[53] Such a camera movement implies impending revelation, yet this is not achieved, and indeed is impossible. The window's opacity is more obvious the closer we get, as a reflective rather than a transparent surface that is curtained over. The idea of "nothing to be seen" is just the point of this gradual close-up: since there is no fitting correlative for Laabs's past actions or his response to them, not even the man himself, it is apt that all we see is this unvarying image.

The soundtrack to the Laabs outtakes draws on the historical archive. In the place of a dialogue with his interviewee, as well as reading from the trial judgment, Lanzmann recites a 1942 letter from Dr. Becker, one of the inventors of the gas vans, once more to Walter Rauff.[54] Thus we are reminded of the archival element that exists in Lanzmann's work, despite his repudiation of historical film footage: written texts in the form of timetables, letters and historical works frequently appear in the mise-en-scène or are read aloud.[55] Indeed, *Shoah* has in turn itself taken on the status of an archive, as is apparent in the release of Adam Benzine's documentary *Spectres of the Shoah* (2015) about Lanzmann, in which clips from the released film and outtakes take on the role of illustrative artifacts.

The attempted interview with Gustav Laabs emphasizes the fact that some parts of *Shoah*'s archival material have less of an obviously outtake status than others. It is not always possible to distinguish potential film from those real discards that seem entirely unsuited for inclusion, such as shots of clapperboards or blank frames, and indeed Hersonski includes just such material in her *A Film Unfinished*. An interview such as Laabs's, in which no one appears, acts to straddle the line between the two categories of filmic release and outtake, as Derrida puts it: "But where does the outside commence? This question is the question of the archive. There are undoubtedly no others."[56] In demonstration of this, in the Laabs footage (after nine-and-a-half minutes in the first eleven-minute reel) Lanzmann seems to step out of the realm of filming and into the world of the audience, in addressing the absent interviewee's startled neighbours: "Do you know his history? Don't you know what he did? Do you know what a gas van is?"[57] This is an instance of what MacDougall describes as "rushes [that] seem to unfold in the present tense of a camera running," before being edited into the "past tense" of a finished film. Given that this remains unedited material, it enables us, as viewers of discarded rushes, to "interject [our] own interpretations" into the perpetual present of the outtakes.[58]

My final example is a secretly recorded interview with a Nazi eyewitness to the killings at Auschwitz, the exclusion of which from *Shoah* might seem surprising, given the perpetrator's perspective that it offers as an alternative to those accounts in the final film by the camp's inmates. This encounter with Pery Broad, a former noncommissioned SS officer, was conducted in Germany in 1979 and consists of 2.2 hours of footage.[59] The only part of this interview to have appeared in the public realm takes the form of a few short and easily overlooked moments in *Shoah*. We see Broad's distinctively rangy silhouette in profile, visible on a small screen in the sections of footage taken inside the filming van that accompany the secretly recorded encounter with Franz Suchomel. To viewers of the released film, it seems as if we are witness to the procedure for clandestinely filming Suchomel himself in these interpolated sections. However, familiarity with the out-takes allows us to identify the intercut footage of the filming van as being from quite another secret interview, one with the younger interlocutor Broad, who is shot from a different angle and from a greater distance. Thus, the significance of editorial artistry over documentary illustration is made clear. In *Shoah* the presence of the van to accompany Suchomel's interview has an impressionistic rather than an indexical significance, emphasizing Lanzmann's auteurist interventions.[60]

During the war, the Brazilian-born Broad worked at Auschwitz for three years, principally as a translator and stenographer. Lanzmann's choice of interviewee arises from the fact that, while he was a prisoner of war of the British in 1945, Broad voluntarily wrote an account of what he had witnessed in Auschwitz.[61] As in the case of two other secretly recorded outtake interviews, with the former *Einsatzgruppen* members Heinz Schubert and Karl Kretschmer, whose trial testimony and letters home the director cites, Lanzmann's cinematic and ethical interest was piqued by the written words of a perpetrator.[62]

Broad was sentenced to four years in prison at the Frankfurt Auschwitz Trial of 1965, on the basis of his having been an "accomplice" to murder, for taking part in selections and in the interrogation of political prisoners. Lanzmann's attention to both eyewitness testimony and its written form is clear in the dialogue and the mise-en-scène. Although Broad's book is never visible, and he claims not even to own a copy, other documentary material takes center stage. Indeed, the only time Lanzmann appears in shot occurs when he crosses the room to join Broad in inspecting a map of Auschwitz.[63] In his autobiography, Lanzmann claims that the interview with the "extremely intelligent" Broad did not live up to his hope that the latter would take part in *Shoah* in his guise "as the author of the report" and "repeat for the cameras what he had written of his own accord."[64] Broad's regret at having published the report at all, for the sake of which he says he was even challenged to a duel after the war, meant that he was not willing to be filmed talking on that subject. In her foreword to Bernd Naumann's 1966 account of the Frankfurt Auschwitz Trial, Hannah Arendt argues that the apparently "inexplicable" change of heart in Broad's attitude toward his "reminiscences" arises from the defendants' shared tendency for an extreme sensitization and responsiveness to "the general climate of opinion to which they happened to be exposed."[65] While this had prompted in Broad a willingness to write what Arendt calls his "excellent, entirely trustworthy report" when faced with the British authorities, in the court setting at Frankfurt "among the old 'comrades,'" he was prompted to take up an entirely different kind of "coordination" in denying the guilt he had admitted implicitly in the report, explicitly at his pretrial interrogation.[66] Face to face with Lanzmann in the present interview, as is apparent from the footage itself and emphasized in the director's account of his drink-fueled efforts at persuasion, Broad appears torn between two positions: that of acknowledging his personal significance by going along with his interlocutor's wish to film a discussion of the report, and apprehensiveness about the possibility of being viewed as traitorous in the contemporary "climate of opinion."[67]

It remains possible to imagine some of the material from the Broad interview appearing in *Shoah*, since its focus lies on such subjects of concern to Lanzmann as the layout of Auschwitz and the fate of the Gypsy camp. Yet Broad himself is too disengaged from the topic even to perform a cinematic spectacle of self-deception. Lanzmann frequently tries to get his interviewee to clarify whether he saw or only heard about a particular event, but Broad is invariably uncertain or evasive, leading the interviewer to claim in response that, "Auschwitz is a legend": even if this notion might be said to characterize the postsurvivor era, it is one which does not suit *Shoah* with its focus on the eyewitness.[68] Equally, the interview could constitute a counterpart to Lanzmann's recent release of material for *The Karski Report*, perhaps even called *The Broad Report*, such a title invoking, like that of the Karski film, a document directed at the Allies. As he does in *The Karski Report*, Lanzmann broaches with Broad the cognitive difficulty of comprehending the project of genocide as it was taking place. But, in the present instance, those who had no "presentiment" of this atrocity were the new arrivals, the Hungarian Jews in 1944, who found such a reality "incredible." Broad's explanation of the lack of "violence" during the process of extermination that followed seems to analyze the inmates' submission, yet is in fact a self-concerned description of his own mental state, as he says in implicit comparison of himself with the prisoners: "If . . . you are broken physically, hopeless, absolutely hopeless, then there can't be violence."[69] As well as registering the sense that Broad considered himself to be a victim, one who was "broken physically," any focus in this context on the inability to understand or fight back seems to be uncomfortably critical of the victims, in contrast to the focus on the disavowal of knowledge on the part of Roosevelt and the Allies in *The Karski Report*.

It is the notion of interpretation, arising from Broad's role in Auschwitz and his status as a polyglot—as well as the concept's more symbolic and metaphorical significance—that most strikingly characterizes this encounter. Interpretation and its failures is a multifaceted activity throughout, ranging from the swift changes between German and English that take place during the interview on the part of both Broad and Lanzmann, even within single sentences, to the hesitation over individual words—Broad symptomatically twice says "program" instead of "pogrom"—as well as the effort required of the spectator to make sense of what they see and hear.[70] Due to its secretly recorded nature, the image track to the interview is inconsistent and unstable, showing the indistinct figure of the tall and gangly Broad at home in his apartment, bathed in a flickering blue light. We invariably see Broad from the side, seated on a sofa as he talks to Lanzmann, with Broad's wife and Lanzmann's translator Corinna Coulmas also present. Apart from moments when Broad's wife serves refreshments to the guests, the women are occasionally audible but not visible; the microphone attached to Lanzmann's tie means that his voice is very loud, although he is for the most part not seen, while Broad's words are harder to catch, in a manner that disrupts the relationship of space to sound for the viewer. In this way, the acoustics match the encounter's disorientating ethical and testimonial form.

While Lanzmann does not use the "Dr. Sorel" pseudonym as a protection, as he does with Hans Gewecke, so that we hear Broad address him as "Claude," the interviewer here nonetheless adopts a persona. This is despite the fact that there is surely something of the truth in Lanzmann's claim to Broad that the latter would be an "important" witness in the film for the reason that, in contrast to his viewpoint, "the inmates" at Auschwitz were unable to see the "overall situation, even geographically, even topographically."[71] However, it seems more likely that, had Broad featured in *Shoah*, his perpetrator's perspective would have constituted a secondary and disjunctive contrast to that of an "inmate," just as Suchomel's experience of Treblinka has been edited to stand alongside Bomba's in the released film. Lanzmann asks Broad about such events as the destruction of the Czech family camp, as if already envisaging, before the process of editing took place, that his words might offer a contrast to Filip Müller's account of the same events. Flashes of irony do emerge, for instance, in the director's unexpected exclamation in response to Broad's description of a postwar threat of expulsion from Germany, since he was a foreign national: "A boy from Brazil!" Broad seems oblivious to his interlocutor's reference to Frederick Schaffner's science-fiction thriller *The Boys from Brazil*, which was released in 1978, the year before the present interview took place, and to the satire implicit in this utterance. In Schaffner's film, not only does Broad's native Brazil feature as the location of a group of women who are impregnated with Hitler's offspring, but Josef Mengele's plans for world domination are uncovered by a young man who records and exposes them with the use of a hidden microphone. It is thus fitting that, in this interview with Broad, as in the case of Suchomel in *Shoah*, the moment of Lanzmann agreeing not to record the interview is itself recorded.[72]

Conclusion

In literary and cultural studies, the archive is frequently conceptualized as an agent of malign control and limitation, so that, for instance, Michel Foucault argues it establishes "the law of what can be said."[73] Thus the concept of the archive is often invoked in relation to a totalitarianism that records only to destroy, or uses such records in order to do so, constituting what Carolyn Steedman calls "archives of evil."[74] The case of Lanzmann's outtakes could be said to subvert such estimates of the archive, or to turn archival material against this pejorative view. Where the idea of the archive might seem to shut down debate, that of the outtake enables proliferation. In this regard, Lanzmann's attitude to the outtake material can seem contradictory. It was to assert his ownership of the footage and its reception that he released *The Karski Report* and *The Last of the Unjust*, as an authorial retort to, respectively, Yannick Haenel's account of Karski's *Shoah* interview in his 2009 novel *Jan Karski*, and an unauthorized screening of material from the Murmelstein interview. Yet Lanzmann's decision to deposit the outtakes at the USHMM necessarily makes them publically available. While the outtake material was at first sequestered in an institutional setting, the USHMM's gradual digitization of the footage means that the archive of Lanzmann's outtakes has become a virtual one, offering universal online viewing. Thus, although the outtake material included in Adam Benzine's *Spectres of the Shoah* is described as "never-before-seen," this is true only if the setting is that of a filmic release: almost all the outtake footage was available to view online by the time Benzine's film appeared in 2015.[75]

The relationship between the unedited rushes and released film penetrates down to the smallest unit of film semiotics, according to MacDougall, who argues that the "processes of editing a film from the rushes involve both reducing the length overall and cutting most shots to shorter lengths [and] both progressively center particular meanings," thus shifting the emphasis from viewer to director.[76] Something of the process of "centering" meanings can be divined from the outtakes, in their status as discarded rushes. Although the shift away from the long take is not specifically what takes place in Lanzmann's film, since, as Michael D'Arcy argues, his Bazinian reliance on such an extended shot is evidence of a preference for that over the juxtapositions of montage, it was indeed during the process of editing that *Shoah*'s central focus, on "death in the gas chambers," emerged from the original hours of footage.[77]

It is hardly possible to consider the outtakes without reference to *Shoah*, just as any commentary on, for instance, Joyce's novel *Stephen Hero*, unpublished during his lifetime, must take account of its successor, *A Portrait of the Artist as a Young Man*. Nonetheless, it would be useful to construct a typology of the material in the *Shoah* outtakes, by reference not—or not only—to the possible reasons for its exclusion, but also for the sake of its own attributes. The USHMM online catalog of holdings has initiated something of a typology of this kind, listing the outtakes by surname of interviewee and annotating each in terms of its contents, length, and language, only mentioning *Shoah* or the other releases when a great deal of the material has been used.[78] As well as the examples I have mentioned, the outtake material includes evidence of Lanzmann's interest, at various times during the process of filming, in a wide variety of topics such as Jewish rescue, for instance through American initiatives, and efforts at self-rescue by such figures as Rezső Kasztner and Rabbi Michael Dov Weissmandl, both of whom had died by the time of the filming and so had to be represented by others; members of the *Judenräte* and of the Jewish police, as well as of Jewish resistance groups; and the functionaries who worked on German trains.[79]

Thus in the outtakes a group of "Jewish policemen" from the Riga Ghetto describes being made by the Gestapo to inspect a cache of arms hidden by the resistance underneath a stove;[80] Siegmunt Forst embodies Weissmandl, by acting out the late rabbi's movements and speaking as if in his place;[81] Leib Garfunkel, formerly the deputy leader of the Kovno Ghetto *Judenrat*, is too aged to say much, so the translator Irena Steinfeldt-Levy reads aloud from his book on the ghetto;[82] the German train worker Eduard Kryshak disagrees with Lanzmann about the abbreviation "PJ" on a train schedule: while the director says it must mean "Polish Jews," Kryshak insists that it refers to a passenger train.[83] All of this material and more can be analyzed en masse, individually, thematically, for what it implies about *Shoah*, and in relation to what a future release, edited and spliced together, might look like. By means of Lanzmann's endeavors, the Nazis' genocidal devastation is recorded, since it cannot be offset, by one of archival preservation and dissemination.

Notes

1. Kate Connolly, "Joseph Goebbels' 105-Year Old Secretary: 'No one believes me now, but I knew nothing'" (interview with Brunhilde Pomsel), *Guardian*, August 15, 2016.

2. Bhaskar Sarkar and Janet Walker, eds., *Documentary Testimonies: Global Archives of Suffering* (New York: Routledge, 2010), 1, 5.

3. Sarkar and Walker, *Documentary Testimonies*, 14.

4. Elisabeth R. Friedman, "The Anti-Archive? Claude Lanzmann's *Shoah* and the Dilemmas of Holocaust Representation," *English Language Notes* 46, no. 1 (2007): 111–21.

5. See Joshua Hirsch, *Afterimage: Film, Trauma and the Holocaust* (Philadelphia: Temple University Press, 2004).

6. Jeremy Isaacs and David Elstein, "How We Made *The World at War*," *Guardian*, October 28, 2013.

7. Brian Winston, "*Ça va de soi*: The Representation of Violence in the Holocaust Documentary," in *Killer Images: Documentary Film, Memory and the Performance of Violence*, ed. Joram Ten Brink and Joshua Oppenheimer (New York: Wallflower 2012), 111–13; Eyal Sivan, http://www.eyalsivan.info/index.php?p= elements1&id=51#&panel1-11 (accessed August 27, 2019).

8. William Fowler, "Memory Material and Material Memory: The Film Archive of Peter Whitehead," *Framework* 52, no. 2 (2011): 676–80.

9. Kate Connolly, "David Wnendt on Filming *Look Who's Back*," *Guardian*, October 6, 2015; Duncan Lindsay, "New Comedy *Look Who's Back* follows 'Hitler' in Modern Germany," *Metro*, October 7, 2015.

10. Nick Pinkerton, "Film of the Week: *No Home Movie*," *Sight and Sound*, July 2016.

11. Claude Lanzmann *Shoah* Collection, interview with Helena Pietyra (RG-60.5055, Film ID 3448), US Holocaust Memorial Museum and Yad Vashem and State of Israel.

12. Interview with Heinz Schubert (RG-60.5013, Film ID 3216–19).

13. Interview with Pery Broad (RG-60.5053, Film ID 3437–43, 3672–89).

14. Marc Chevrie and Hervé le Roux, "Site and Speech: An Interview with Claude Lanzmann about *Shoah*," in *Claude Lanzmann's* Shoah: *Key Essays*, ed. Stuart Liebman (New York: Oxford University Press, 2007), 46.

15. David MacDougall, "When Less Is Less: The Long Take in Documentary," *Film Quarterly* 46, no. 2 (1992–93): 36–46.

16. Fowler, "Memory Material," 682.

17. Hans Walter Gabler, "Textual Criticism and Theory in Modern German Editing," in *Contemporary German Editorial Theory*, ed. Gabler et al. (Ann Arbor: University of Michigan Press, 1995).

18. See, for instance, T. S. Eliot, *The Waste Land: A Facsimile and Transcript of the Original Drafts Including the Annotations of Ezra Pound*, ed. Valerie Eliot (New York: Harcourt 1993). Thanks to Katherine Ebury for discussing this with me.

19. Ferdinand de Saussure, *Course in General Linguistics*, trans. Wade Baskin (New York: Columbia University Press [1916] 1959).

20. Ronny Loewy, "Die *Shoah*-Outtakes," in Ronny Loewy and Katharina Rauschenberger, eds, *"Der Letzte der Ungerechten": Der "Judenälteste" Benjamin Murmelstein in Filme 1945–1975*, ed. Loewy and Katharina Rauschenberger (Frankfurt: Campus Verlag, 2011), 11; Mark Lilla, "The Defense of a Jewish Collaborator," *New York Review of Books*, December 5, 2013, https://www.nybooks.com/articles/2013/12/05/defense-jewish-collaborator/ (accessed August 27, 2019).

21. Interview with Ruth Elias (RG-60.5003, Film ID 3112–18).

22. Interview with Jacob Arnon (RG-60.5022, Film ID 3265–9).

23. Interview with Abba Kovner (RG-60.5017, Film ID 3236–45).

24. Gabler, "Textual Criticism," 3.

25. Janet Maslin, "Of One Man Who Saw Evil, and Preferred Not to Focus," *New York Times*, October 7, 1999.

26. Godfrey Cheshire, "*A Visitor from the Living*," *Variety*, October 7, 1999, https://variety.com/1999/film/reviews/a-visitor-from-the-living-1117752225/ (accessed August 27, 2019); Manuel Köppen, "Searching for Evidence Between Generations: Claude Lanzmann's *Sobibor* and Romuald Karmakar's *Land of Annihilation*," *New German Critique* 41, no. 3 (2014): 57–73.

27. Jacques Derrida, *Of Grammatology*, trans. Gayatri Chakravorty Spivak (Baltimore: Johns Hopkins University Press, 1974), 144.

28. Doris Toumarkine, "*A Visitor from the Living*," *Film Journal*, November 2, 2004.

29. MacDougall, "When Less Is Less," 41.

30. Interview with Abraham Bomba (RG-60.5011, Film ID 3197–3204, 3205.1, 3205.2).

31. Claude Lanzmann, *The Patagonian Hare*, trans. Frank Wynne (London: Atlantic, [2009] 2012), 465.

32. Quoted in Jonathan Derbyshire, "Lanzmann: 'There is only life,'" *New Statesman*, March 12, 2012.

33. Interviews with Mordechai Podchlebnik (RG-60.5026, Film ID 3294–7), Richard Glazar (RG-60.5028, Film ID 3314–30), and Motke Zaidel and Itzak Dugin (RG-60.5050, Film ID 3782–92).

34. Lanzmann notes the fading light also meant that the footage could not be used: *The Patagonian Hare*, 431.

35. Interview with Abraham Bomba (RG-60.5011, Film ID 3200, Camera Rolls 7–9).

36. Interview with Tadeusz Pankiewicz (RG-60.5014, Film ID 3220, Camera Rolls 1–2, 3–4, and 5–7).

37. Quoted in Geoffrey McNab, "Return to *Shoah*: Claude Lanzmann's New Film *The Last of the Unjust* Revisits Holocaust Epic," *Independent*, March 15, 2014.

38. Interview with Hans Gewecke (RG-60.5027, Film ID 3298–3309, 3311, 3313).

39. Lanzmann, *The Patagonian Hare*, 457.

40. See Erin McGlothlin, "Listening to the Perpetrators in Claude Lanzmann's *Shoah*," *Colloquia Germanica* 43, no. 3 (2010): 235–71.

41. "Ich war ein sehr überzeugter Nationalsozialist. Ich war außerdem ein großer Verehrer Rosenbergs." Interview with Hans Gewecke (RG-60.5027, Film ID 3298, Camera Rolls 1A, 1B, 2A, 2B).

42. "Dann hat es hier . . . keine Kristallnacht gegeben. . . . In Ratzeburg gab es ein einziges jüdisches Geschäft namens Rosenberg . . . das Geschäft ist in Brand gesetzt worden und dem Juden Rosenberg ist kein Haar gekrümmt worden . . . heute ist der Sohn von Rosenberg als Geschäftsinhaber tätig in Ratzeburg." Interview with Hans Gewecke (RG-60.5027, Film ID 3299, Camera Rolls 3A, 3B, 4A, 4B).

43. "Ich sagte mir, du mußt, du mußt irgendwie . . . Deutschland liegt da nieder— 6 Millionen Arbeitsloser, der Versailler Vertrag." Interview with Hans Gewecke (RG-60.5027, Film ID 3299, Camera Rolls 3A, 3B, 4A, 4B).

44. "Aber ich war nur so erschüttert. Mein Mann hat diese ganzen Juden gerettet, und sie versuchten jetzt ihn so ungefähr an den Galgen zu bringen. Das hat mich so erschüttert." Interview with Hans Gewecke (RG-60.5027, Film ID 3302, Camera Rolls 8A, 8B, 8C).

45. Christoph Dieckman, "The War and the Killing of the Lithuanian Jews," in *National Socialist Extermination Policies: Contemporary German Perspectives and Controversies*, ed. Ulrich Herbert (Oxford: Berghahn, 2004), 240-75; here 261.

46. Lanzmann, quoted in Graham Fuller, "Searching for the Stamp of Truth," *Cinéaste* 36, no. 2 (2011): 16–19: 18, my italics.

47. Godard, quoted in Georges Didi-Huberman, *Images in Spite of All: Four Photographs from Auschwitz*, trans. Shane B. Lillis (Chicago: University of Chicago Press, [2003] 2008), 217.

48. Interview with Gustav Laabs and Lettre Becker (RG-60.5025, Film ID 3824, Camera Rolls 4–7).

49. *Shoah*, directed by Claude Lanzmann, New Yorker Films, 1985, DVD, disc 2, chapter 7.

50. *Shoah*, disc 2, chapter 7.

51. *Shoah*, disc 2, chapter 29.

52. Ziva Postec, "Editing *Shoah*," http://www.postecziva.com/shoah.php (accessed August 27, 2019).

53. Interview with Gustav Laabs and Lettre Becker (RG-60.5025, Film ID 3293 [also called Film ID 3825]).

54. Interview with Gustav Laabs and Lettre Becker (RG-60.5025, Film ID 3383, Camera Rolls 1, 2, 3, 9, 10).

55. See Margaret Olin on Lanzmann's implicit distinction between the misleading indexicality of a photograph and the revelatory metonymy of the document, "Lanzmann's *Shoah* and the Topography of the Holocaust Film," *Representations* 57 (1997): 1-23; here 13.

56. Jacques Derrida, *Archive Fever: A Freudian Impression*, trans. Eric Prenowitz (Chicago: University of Chicago Press, 1995), 8.

57. "Wissen Sie, etwas über seine Vergangenheit? . . . Sie wissen nicht, was er gemacht hat? . . . Wissen Sie, was ist ein Gaswagen?" Interview with Gustav Laabs and Lettre Becker (RG-60.5025, Film ID 3293 [also called Film ID 3825], Camera Roll 5).

58. MacDougall, "When Less Is Less," 49.

59. Interview with Pery Broad (RG-60.5053, Film ID 3437–43, 3672–89).

60. For more detailed discussion of Lanzmann's insertion of the footage of the van used in the Broad interview into the sequences featuring Suchomel in *Shoah*, please see Erin McGlothlin's contribution in this volume.

61. "Reminiscences of Pery Broad," *KL Auschwitz Seen by the SS*, trans. Krystyna Michalik (Oświęcim: Auschwitz State Museum, [1972] 1998).

62. Interviews with Heinz Schubert (RG-60.5013, Film ID 3216–19) and Karl Kretschmer—*Einsatzgruppen* (RG-60.5018, Film ID 3246–47).

63. Interview with Pery Broad (RG-60.5053, Film ID 3441, Camera Rolls 5, 6, 7).

64. Lanzmann, *The Patagonian Hare*, 443, 444.

65. Hannah Arendt, "Auschwitz on Trial," reprinted in *Responsibility and Judgment*, ed. Jerome Kohn (New York: Schocken, 2005), 233. Thanks to Brad Prager for this reference.

66. Arendt, "Auschwitz on Trial," 234. Arendt's argument here echoes something of her well-known thesis on Eichmann's "banal" conformity, yet it needs only slight expansion to suggest that Broad was, with more deliberate agency than she implies, attempting both to curry favour and evade justice with each change of attitude.

67. Lanzmann, *The Patagonian Hare*, 444–45.

68. Interview with Pery Broad (RG-60.5053, Film ID 3682, Camera Roll 16).

69. Interview with Pery Broad (RG-60.5053, Film ID 3441, Camera Rolls 5, 6, 7).

70. Interview with Pery Broad (RG-60.5053, Film ID 3441, Camera Rolls 5, 6, 7).

71. Interview with Pery Broad (RG-60.5053, Film ID 3441, Camera Rolls 5, 6, 7).

72. Interview with Pery Broad (RG-60.5053, Film ID 3441, Camera Rolls 5, 6, 7).

73. Michel Foucault, *The Archaeology of Knowledge and the Discourse on Language*, trans. A. M. Sheridan Smith (New York: Pantheon, 1972), 129.

74. Carolyn Steedman, *Dust: The Archive and Cultural History* (New Brunswick, NJ: Rutgers University Press, 2002), 9.

75. HBO broadcast *Spectres of the Shoah*, and the description is from their website devoted to the film: http://www.hbo.com/documentaries (accessed August 27, 2019).

76. MacDougall, "When Less Is Less," 50.

77. Michael D'Arcy, "Claude Lanzmann's *Shoah* and the Intentionality of the Image," in *Visualizing the Holocaust: Documents, Aesthetics*, ed. David Bathrick, Brad Prager, and Michael D. Richardson (Rochester, NY: Camden House, 2008), 138–61; Lanzmann, quoted in Laura Paull, interview, "Claude Lanzmann, Director of *Shoah*, Turns Literary Lens on the Past," *Huffington Post*, March 15, 2012, https://www.huffpost.com/entry/claude-lanzmann-director-_n_1340719 (accessed August 27, 2019).

78. The catalog is available on the USHMM website: https://www.ushmm.org/online/film/docs/shoahstatus.pdf (accessed August 27, 2019).

79. Pierre Sauvage's film *Not Idly By* (2017) draws on Lanzmann's outtake interview for his documentary portrait of the American activist Peter Bergson.

80. Interview with Society of the Survivors of the Riga Ghetto (New York), former Jewish policemen, and Baer (RG-60.5041).

81. Interview with Siegmunt Forst (RG-60.5004, Film ID: 3119–24, 3823).

82. Interview with Leib Garfunkel (RG-60.5005, Film ID: 3125–32).

83. Interview with Eduard Kryshak (RG-60.5035, Film ID: 3357–61).

3

Composing with Incompossibles

The Jewish Council, the "Kasztner Train," and the Making of *Shoah*

Jennifer Cazenave

It is an important question: What does the audience know?
What does it not know? Up to what point may one preserve
the mystery? Finally I said to myself that I did not have to say
everything, that people ought to ask questions. The film is made
so that people continue to work at it—during the screening, but
also afterward.

Claude Lanzmann

In 1973 Claude Lanzmann embarked on the making of what would become his monumental documentary *Shoah* (1985). In his memoir, *The Patagonian Hare* (2012), he recounts this twelve-year transnational journey, which spanned from the research he first conducted in the archives of Yad Vashem in Jerusalem to the film's premiere at the Théâtre de l'Empire in Paris on April 30, 1985. "*Shoah*," he notes, "is a film impossible to master, offering a thousand ways by which to enter it, so it makes little sense to attempt to recount day by day, year by year, how it came to be made."[1] Rather than proceed chronologically, Lanzmann exposes the filming process by detailing his encounters with the most memorable protagonists in *Shoah*, including "the barber of Treblinka" Abraham Bomba, the "singing child" of Chełmno Simon Srebnik, and the SS officer Franz Suchomel.[2] Conversely, the five-and-a-half-year-long editing phase, which began in the fall of 1979, is encapsulated in a single sentence. "The editing work was a long, serious, delicate, subtle process," recalls Lanzmann, without further detailing the selection undertaken to compose a nine-and-a-half-hour opus from the two hundred and thirty hours of testimonies and location filming he had amassed.[3]

In *The Patagonian Hare*, Lanzmann displaces the narrative of cutting fragments from this vast archive to a previous chapter in which he recounts visiting his mother in Paris in 1942. Coinciding with the implementation of the Final Solution in January of that year and with the Vel' d'Hiv Roundup in the French capital that summer, these wartime recollections are permeated with Holocaust imagery. This narrative strategy is evocative of Alison Landsberg's notion of prosthetic memory: "Privately felt public memories that develop after an encounter with a mass cultural representation of the past, when new images and ideas come into contact with a person's own archive of experience."[4] Accordingly, this chapter of *The Patagonian Hare* opens with a traumatic train ride from the city of Clermont-Ferrand to Paris with false identity papers. "I remember the long wait through the night at the station Vierzon," Lanzmann writes, "the glare of the spotlights on the platforms and the trains, I remember the dogs, the thud of the boots, the brutal way the compartment doors were flung open."[5]

The filmmaker's recollection of this train ride transports the reader to the extermination camps and to the arrival of convoys in the middle of the night. This ritual is not only recounted in *Shoah* by Ruth Elias, who remembers seeing "only SS with dogs and . . . the thousands of lights"; it is also reenacted in fiction features such as *The Last Stage* (1948) by the Polish director and Auschwitz survivor Wanda Jakubowska in a scene Alain Resnais subsequently excerpted in his documentary *Night and Fog* (1955).[6] If Lanzmann recasts his experience "through another's eyes," prosthetic memories of the Holocaust further inform this chapter of his memoir.[7] Visiting a Parisian shoe store in the company of his mother, for instance, an incident occurs that prompts him to unexpectedly and anachronistically reference the process of editing *Shoah*. He writes:

> We went to Chaussures André, a famous emporium—now Aryanized—on the boulevard des Capucines, with an extensive clientele, countless shop assistants and a vast selection of shoes. This, as it turned out, proved to be the source of the problem [*ce fut l'origine du drame*]. Because to choose is to kill. My mother was incapable of choosing, she wanted everything. I'm like her. The title of my dissertation for my philosophy degree was *Possibles and Incompossibles in the Philosophy of Leibniz*, "incompossible" referring to the fact that there are things that cannot coexist. To choose one is to preclude the existence of the other. Any choice is murder, and leaders, apparently, can be defined by their capacity to murder, we call them "decision-makers" and we pay handsomely for it. It is no accident that *Shoah* runs to nine and a half hours. . . . Shoes and boxes piled up around the stool where I sat, trying them on.[8]

Framed in the original French as a *drame*, or tragedy, this episode in *The Patagonian Hare* again transports the reader from Paris to the extermination camps: on the one hand, the systematic selection ("to choose is to kill") when the convoys arrived; on the other hand, the pile of shoes, an iconic image of the Holocaust included in *Night and Fog* that Lanzmann substitutes in *Shoah* for shots of suitcases bearing the name of their owners. Coupled with the epic length of the film and the invocation of the Leibnizian notion of the incompossible ("to choose one is to preclude the existence of the other"), the heap of boxes in the shoe store also invokes the innumerable reels accumulated during the production of *Shoah* as well as the ensuing selection in the editing room between 1979 and 1985.

"To edit [a film]," writes Dominique Villain, "is to choose."[9] Or, to recast Lanzmann's own definition informed by the philosophy of Gottfried Wilhelm Leibniz, to choose a shot, a sequence, or even a testimony is to preclude others from existing—a finality conjured in his memoir through the prosthetic identification with the "decision-makers" and the likening of choice to "murder." The tragic finality he ascribes to the incompossible invokes the notion of "choiceless choice" coined by Lawrence Langer in his analysis of the moral dilemmas that confronted Jewish prisoners in the camps.[10] The theoretical proximity between Langer and Lanzmann attests to the latter's prosthetic identification with the survivors he filmed for *Shoah*, many of whom narrate in the outtakes accounts of survival centered on a "choiceless choice."[11] At the same time, the notion of the incompossible found in *The Patagonian Hare* exceeds Langer's ethics of survival to call our attention to the *ethics of editing*: the selection, over the course of five-and-a-half years, of mere fragments from the vast archive of testimonies the French director had amassed.

In the case of the *Shoah* outtakes, and in spite of Lanzmann's prosthetic framing of the editing phase, selection cannot be equated with elimination. In simultaneously including and excluding outtakes, editing also entails *composing with incompossibles*.[12] In *Theodicy*, his 1710 philosophical investigation into the problem of evil, Leibniz forged the notion of the incompossible to denote the existence of an infinite number of mutually exclusive possible worlds from which God, Leibniz argues, chooses the most just and harmonious one. Likening the divine creator to an architect, he illustrates this concept through the image of a pyramid containing an infinite number of apartments, each constituting a possible world of which only one—situated at the summit—can come into existence.[13] In the second half of the twentieth century, Gilles Deleuze reconfigured this concept to denote not finality but the *coexistence* of incompossibles. In both *The Time-Image* (1985) and *The Fold* (1988), he reframes Leibniz through the lens of Jorge Luis Borges's 1941 short story "The Garden of Forking Paths," whose protagonist, Ts'ui Pen, composes an eponymous novel that moves beyond one alternative to stage all the possible outcomes and ensuing bifurcations of a single event. In *The Patagonian Hare*, however, Lanzmann refutes any Deleuzian coexistence by deploying the incompossible as a metaphor for the at once inevitable and irrevocable selection underlying film editing.

In spite of the analogy between choosing and killing, the two hundred and twenty hours left on the cutting-room floor have returned, like Lazarus, from the dead. Initially scattered between Lanzmann's basement in Paris and the LTC Film Laboratory in the suburb of Saint-Cloud, the outtakes were acquired by the United States Holocaust Memorial Museum (USHMM) in 1996. Since the transfer from Paris to Washington, DC, of nearly three tons of film and sound reels, as well as annotated interview transcripts and summaries, the USHMM has undertaken to create a digital archive of *Shoah*.[14] Consequently, much like Deleuze's refutation of any Leibnizian finality, the finished film and the unused material *coexist*, not only producing new meanings and mobilizations of *Shoah* but also rendering visible "divergences, incompossibilities, discords, dissonances."[15]

Probing Controversial Choices

If the excluded testimonies subsist as a collection of other possible films, they fittingly reveal that Lanzmann first approached the destruction of European Jewry through the lens of a polemic itself haunted by the incompossible. When he began filming in March 1976, he first interviewed Leib Garfunkel in Israel and Benjamin Murmelstein in Italy.[16] The two survivors each had served as members of a Jewish council, or *Judenrat*, an administrative entity established by the Germans in the ghettos. The task of the *Judenrat* was twofold: all the while serving the Jewish community by providing social services, the council was responsible for implementing German orders and regulations, most notably in drafting deportation lists. As the historian Raul Hilberg would explain at a conference held in New York in 1975, "Jewish councils everywhere came face to face with the basic paradox inherent in their role as preservers of Jewish life in a framework of German destruction. They could not serve the Jews indefinitely while simultaneously obeying the Germans."[17] This paradox not only echoes the incompossible, but also intimates the complexity of composing *Shoah*: that is, Lanzmann's difficult editorial selection and his decision to ultimately exclude one of the most controversial episodes of the Holocaust.

Only a decade before Lanzmann embarked on the making of his film, Hannah Arendt had infamously condemned the choices made by these Jewish leaders in her 1963 report on the Eichmann trial. Comparing their compliance to collaboration, she asserted that "if the Jewish people had really been unorganized and leaderless, there would have been chaos and plenty of misery but the total number of victims would hardly have been between four-and-a-half and six million people."[18] Arendt extended her criticism to include Rudolf Kasztner, the director of the Jewish Aid and Rescue Committee in Budapest, also known as the Vaada, to whom Eichmann had proposed the release of one million Jews in exchange for ten thousand trucks.[19] While the so-called trucks for blood deal failed, the negotiations undertaken by Kasztner and his committee resulted in a special transport that carried 1,684 Jews to safety in Switzerland. At the same time, between May and July 1944, nearly half a million Hungarian Jews were deported to Auschwitz.

"The specter of Hannah Arendt haunts every film Claude Lanzmann has made," writes the historian Mark Lilla in his review of Lanzmann's *The Last of the Unjust* (2013), a documentary that includes segments from the Murmelstein interview.[20] Referring here to both Lanzmann's rebuttal of an Arendtian view of the Holocaust as a comprehensible event and to his probing of the role of Jewish councils, Lilla's genealogy is further substantiated by the *Shoah* outtakes, which reveal the existence of filmed interviews with Hansi Brand and Hanna Marton.[21] In 1944, Brand negotiated with Eichmann alongside the director of the Vaada, and Marton was selected as a passenger aboard the so-called Kasztner train.[22] More than Lanzmann's filmography, however, the specter of Arendt haunts the historiographical landscape out of which *Shoah* emerged. In March 1975, Lanzmann attended the conference in New York entitled "The Holocaust—A Generation After," during which Hilberg gave his paper on the Jewish councils. As he recalls in *The Patagonian Hare*, it was there that he met the historian who was to become one of the protagonists of *Shoah*.[23] The publication of the proceedings in the volume *The Holocaust as Historical Experience* (1981) documents a conference devoted to examining—to quote from the book's introduction—"what has become perhaps the most controversial question in the whole field: the issue of the Jewish leadership in Nazi-dominated Europe."[24]

Engaging with both Arendt's controversial generalizations and Isaiah Trunk's subsequent factual study *Judenrat: The Jewish Councils in Eastern Europe under Nazi Occupation* (1972), the contributions consider the varied responses of Jewish leaders across Europe. In his paper, Hilberg focuses on the Warsaw Ghetto and the diary of Adam Czerniaków, the president of the *Judenrat* who committed suicide in 1942 after realizing he could not stop the deportation of children. In *Shoah*, Hilberg provides the sole representation of the Jewish council in reading and commenting on excerpts of Czerniaków's diary, a document originally written in Polish that he coedited with Stanislaw Staroń and Jósef Kermisz for the 1979 English translation.[25] In only retaining Hilberg's affecting account of Czerniaków's growing despair and subsequent suicide in the ghetto by means of a diary penned during the Holocaust, Lanzmann effectively erased in the finished film the moral ambiguities that nevertheless surrounded the issue of the *Judenrat* during the making of *Shoah*, and that he initially probed upon filming Garfunkel and Murmelstein in 1976. At the same time, the representation of a Jewish leader as a deceased protagonist, bestowed with the historian's voice who incarnates him—without ever passing judgment—in front of the camera in January 1979 differs by sheer physical presence alone from Lanzmann's interviews with the two surviving *Judenrat* members nearly three years earlier.

Describing in his memoir the initial research conducted for *Shoah*, Lanzmann emphasizes above all the scope of his ignorance. "I later learned that one needs a vast body of knowledge before questioning [someone]. At the time I really didn't know enough," he observes.[26] It is not surprising that, when they were recorded for *Shoah*, both Garfunkel and Murmelstein communicate knowledge of the catastrophe the filmmaker himself does not possess—as manifested by the fact that Lanzmann's notes are visible in the Garfunkel outtakes and during Murmelstein's testimony. In the case of the former, this lack of historiographical mastery can be attributed to a sense of urgency insofar as Garfunkel was nearly eighty years old at the time of the interview and passed away shortly after.

While acting as vice-chairman of the Kovno *Judenrat* in central Lithuania, Garfunkel—like Czerniaków—secretly kept a diary wherein he recorded detailed accounts of several important events in the history of the ghetto: its establishment in 1941; the so-called Great Action on October 28 of that year during which the Germans murdered 9,200 Jews; the transports to the death camps beginning in 1943. Garfunkel was later deported to Kaufering, a subcamp of Dachau whose inmates were used as forced labor in fighter aircraft production. He survived and emigrated to Israel in 1948. A decade later, he drew on his wartime diary to write a historical monograph in Hebrew entitled *The Destruction of Kovno's Jewry*, which was published in 1959. Rather than the survivor's testimony, this book becomes the centerpiece of Lanzmann's two-and-a-half-hour-long inter-view with Garfunkel a year after attending the New York conference. Cou-pled with the question of the *Judenrat*, the centrality of this paper memory approximates the representation in *Shoah* of Czerniaków who—as Hilberg and Staroń speculate in their introduction to the English translation of the diary—possibly chronicled the quotidian reality of the ghetto "with a view to writing a book later on."[27]

"I would like Irene [*sic*] to read a part of your book," begins Lanzmann. Sitting in Garfunkel's living room, he is assisted by Irena Steinfeldt during the interview.[28] Unlike Francine Kaufmann, the Hebrew interpreter in *Shoah*, who remains off-frame in both the outtakes and the finished film, Steinfeldt translates aloud into English several lengthy passages from *The Destruction of Kovno's Jewry*. Garfunkel, with the book balanced on his knees and his appearance frail, interrupts her from time to time, either by briefly commenting or by turning toward the filmmaker, nodding his head in silence to highlight the importance of certain facts as they are being cited. Lanzmann does not have a copy of *The Destruction of Kovno's Jewry*. Instead, he listens to both the interpreter and the survivor, at times writing down notes. This is a gesture that appears less performative than indicative of the relative lack of historiographical knowledge Lanzmann would later describe in his memoir. Along with his papers scattered over the coffee table in Garfunkel's living room, his note-taking illustrates "the position of an attentive listener" he first adopted when he began filming *Shoah*.[29] Suggestive of the auteur he would become over the following years, there remains no visible trace of this position by the end of the shooting phase or in the finished film where he assumes the role of a largely off-screen interlocutor.

The distinct mise-en-scène underlying the Garfunkel outtakes exposes a method that, in 1976, is still in the making. Oscillating between Steinfeldt's translation of *The Destruction of Kovno's Jewry* and Garfunkel's factual memories of the ghetto, this unedited material offers a significant variation to both the centrality of filmed speech in *Shoah* and to the excavation of deep memory exemplified in the testimonial performances of protago-nists such as Simon Srebnik returning to Chełmno and Abraham Bomba in the Tel Aviv barbershop. In 1976, the camera thus captures—to borrow the distinction of Auschwitz survivor Charlotte Delbo—not sensory but

Claude Lanzmann, as he takes notes while interviewing Leib Garfunkel
with Irena Steinfeldt. Created by Claude Lanzmann during the filming of
Shoah. (Used by permission of the United States Holocaust Memorial Museum
and Yad Vashem, the Holocaust Martyrs and Heroes' Remembrance Authority,
Jerusalem.)

external memory.[30] This narrative distanciation is further accentuated by the
presence of Steinfeldt, who mediates Garfunkel's account of the catastrophe. In turn, between each translated passage, Lanzmann discusses with
the survivor particular factual events, including the first massacre in the
forts around Kovno committed by the *Einsatzgruppen*. When Garfunkel
responds, slightly out of breath and speaking slowly and quietly in English,
the camera moves from a medium long shot detailing the interviewee's living room, Lanzmann and Steinfeldt to either side of him, toward a close-up
of Garfunkel's face. In accentuating his frailty, the juxtaposition between the
domestic space and Garfunkel's face shifts the focus away from the moral
ambiguities surrounding the role of the *Judenrat* to the imminent passing of
Holocaust survivors.

Although the interview with Garfunkel was filmed merely a year after
the Holocaust conference in New York, the controversial role of the *Judenrat* is itself broached only briefly when the two men discuss a dilemma

A close-up of the survivor. Created by Claude Lanzmann during the filming of *Shoah*. (Used by permission of the United States Holocaust Memorial Museum and Yad Vashem, the Holocaust Martyrs and Heroes' Remembrance Authority, Jerusalem.)

faced by the council in September of 1941: to follow or not German orders by selecting five thousand artisans who would be spared during the liquidation of the ghetto. Without directly evoking Arendt, Lanzmann asks Garfunkel whether the Jewish council should have refused to comply or tried to save whatever lives they could. Opting for the latter, the survivor emphasizes the tragedy of choice inherent to the role of the *Judenrat* in the Kovno Getto. "It's a terrible thing to have to decide: this man is entitled to live, this man is not entitled to live," he says to Lanzmann who himself remarks succinctly: "It is an impossible dilemma."[31] Garfunkel concludes this discussion by comparing the Jewish council's situation to that "of a captain of a sinking ship."[32] Incidentally, in a passage from Czerniaków's diary that Lanzmann evokes in *Shoah*, the *Judenrat* chairman deploys the same image of "a sinking ship" to describe his tragic position or confrontation with the incompossible in the Warsaw Ghetto.

More than a representation of "the most controversial question" in Holocaust studies at the time, this interview records a memory on the verge

this |extraordinary| passage from your book about
the Lebensscheine. And how the German cracked
completely the Jews with these life certificates.
It was the same everywhere in the ghettos in
Lithuania, in Vilna.

G.   I think they were yellow Scheine...

C.L. And these ones were white.

I.   "On 15th September 1941 in the evening Kominsky
came to the office of the Ältesten Rat and delivered
a written order from the Gebietskommissar of
Kovno together with 5000 white certificates. On
each certificate it was written in German: 'A
certificate for Jewish artisans. Gebietskommissariat,
Kovno. Signed Jorgan S.A. Hauptstürmführer.'" By
the order of the Gebietskommissar it was said that
the Ältesten Rat has to distribute these certificates
among the artisans of the ghetto and their families;
all this in one day, 16th September. When
Kominsky was asked what these certificates meant
he answered that there would be certain advantages
for the people who had the certificates and that
on the whole the economic situation would improve."

G.   He knew everything.

C.L. He knew everything?

G.   He knew, Kominsky, that a big action would destroy

An annotated page from the Leib Garfunkel transcript. Created by Claude Lanzmann during the filming of *Shoah*. (Used by permission of the United States Holocaust Memorial Museum and Yad Vashem, the Holocaust Martyrs and Heroes' Remembrance Authority, Jerusalem.)

of disappearance. While the footage opens with a passage from Garfunkel's monograph, it closes with black and white photographs of the Kovno Ghetto, which the survivor shows to the filmmaker. Given that Lanzmann claims to have known very early on that there would be no archival images in *Shoah*, the act of filming these photographs in 1976 refutes his oft-cited discourse on the unrepresentable—revealing instead an ethical paradigm and auteur largely still in the making. Unlike the centrality of testimony privileged in the finished film, this first interview for *Shoah* appears, in fact, entirely made out of paper. From Garfunkel's book to Lanzmann's note-taking to the closing shots of the black and white photographs, these epistemic objects articulate a narrative frame that is not centered on the voice of the witness but on paper knowledge.

Another documentary trace further evidences this testimonial displacement: the forty-eight-page transcript from which Lanzmann initially worked while editing *Shoah*. Bearing witness to the process of composing a film from his monumental archive of testimonies, this document contains notes in French specifying historical facts and visual details from the interview, as well as bracketed passages from both the translated excerpts of *The Destruction of Kovno's Jewry* and Garfunkel's fragmentary account in front of the camera. It also reveals an enduring interest in the testimony of a *Judenrat* member during the editing phase, notably exhibited by a section of the transcript that alludes to the impending selection of the aforementioned five thousand artisans from the ghetto.

By way of scribbles representing the survivor and the interpreter and by way of the annotations "off" and "GP" (*gros plan,* or close-up), Lanzmann's handwritten notes on this Steinfeldt-translated passage of Garfunkel's book suggest a possible juxtaposition for the finished film between her voice-over and a close-up of his face.[33] In line with Lanzmann's relative visual absence in *Shoah*, the cropping intimated by the scribble displaces him, along with his notes scattered on the coffee table, to the off-frame. The juxtaposition of the interpreter's voice and the survivor's face bears witness to the process of editing, between September 1979 and April 1985, around the controversial choices of Jewish councils—namely, how to represent the dilemmas they faced without passing moral judgment. If Lanzmann chose to exclude this interview from *Shoah*, the prominence of both Steinfeldt's voice and Garfunkel's book in the annotated transcript approximates Hilberg's own reading of Czerniaków's Warsaw Ghetto diary, a paper memory that constitutes the only representation of the *Judenrat* in the finished film.

Akin to their brief evocation in the Garfunkel interview, the Jewish councils are referred to just once in *The Patagonian Hare*. Recalling his search for members of the *Sonderkommando*, Lanzmann proceeds to dismiss the Eichmann trial where several of these men, including *Shoah* protagonist and Chełmno survivor Simon Srebnik, had previously testified. He laments in particular how "the shocking way in which [it] was directed unjustly put much of the responsibility and the blame for the extermination on the *Judenräte*." This aspect of the 1961 trial, Lanzmann reminds his readers, "became the subject of a bitter dispute between Gershom Scholem and Hannah Arendt, who . . . in her book *Eichmann in Jerusalem*, showed a partiality, a lack of compassion, an arrogance and a failure of comprehension for which he was right to reproach her."[34] This allusion to the disagreement between Scholem and Arendt that eventually ended their friendship obscures for the reader not only their correspondence spanning nearly a quarter of a century, but also Scholem's condemnation in a letter dated June 23, 1963, of Murmelstein who, he writes, "deserves to be hanged by the Jews."[35]

Lanzmann himself quotes this phrase in a segment of the Murmelstein interview included in the final moments of *The Last of the Unjust*. Conversely, he never once mentions in his memoir the Garfunkel and Murmelstein interviews. The latter, along with the making of *Shoah*, surfaces instead in *When Memory Comes*, the 1978 autobiography of Saul Friedländer, who also attended the conference in New York. "The conversation with Claude is hard to forget," he writes in an entry dated September 20, 1977. "He told me about his film. The last sequence finished was with a former SS officer at Treblinka. . . . The notorious Perry Broad of Auschwitz tells his story in the film, too, as does Murmelstein, old Murmelstein, whom we still consider to be a traitor, the chief of the Jewish council of Theresienstadt; he, too, tells his story beneath a soft spring sky, in Rome."[36] As both Scholem's verdict and Friedländer's portrayal (the latter being framed in terms of an unspecified collective "we," itself conjugated in the present tense) attest, Murmelstein, who was the only surviving chairman of any Jewish council, remained a figure of controversy until his death in 1989.

Deported in 1943 from Vienna, where he had worked in the Office of Jewish Emigration established by Eichmann in 1938, Murmelstein was first appointed as a member of the Theresienstadt Jewish council before becoming its last chairman in 1944. At the end of the war, the Czech authorities arrested him; he spent a year and a half in prison awaiting trial before all charges of collaboration against him were dropped. Exiled to Rome in 1947, he was never summoned to testify at the Eichmann trial in Jerusalem. In early 1976, he told his story in German to Lanzmann over the course of a nearly twelve-hour-long interview, a length that itself exceeds the finished film. Beyond its proportions and inclusion nearly forty years later in *The Last of the Unjust*, the significance of the Murmelstein interview is further confirmed by Lanzmann's brief description in a document titled "Material of *Shoah*," drafted in 1994 when he first approached the USHMM regarding the acquisition of the outtakes. "One full week shooting in Rome," he writes about the unedited footage with Murmelstein before adding: "Unique. He never talked before and after. He is now dead."[37]

Murmelstein did speak again. In 1977, he was interviewed and recorded on audio cassette by Edith and Leonard H. Ehrlich as part of their research for a monograph on the dilemmas faced by Jewish leaders.[38] In this recording, Murmelstein recounts Lanzmann approaching him, bringing with him a reference letter from the historian Yehuda Bauer. After a first meeting and a lengthy "back and forth, back and forth," Lanzmann convinced him to "represent his side of history," supposedly even proposing to pay him (an offer the survivor declined). Murmelstein situates the interview in February 1976, at the end of which he entrusted Lanzmann with a secret manuscript from Theresienstadt to be given to Bauer. Talking to the Ehrlichs, he now regrets this transaction, since he never received the transcript of his interview Lanzmann had agreed to send him.[39]

If *The Last of the Unjust* exposed Lanzmann's probing for *Shoah* of postwar accusations leveled against Jewish councils, the Murmelstein outtakes render visible—much like the interview with Garfunkel—a method still in the making. First, the epic length of the interview (the longest in the archive, it is even longer than *Shoah*) and its circular structure (the unedited reels open and close with shots of Rome) give the impression of a film in its own right. As Lanzmann himself observes on the final day of shooting, "You know, this is very surprising, we have been talking for four days and I think I am quite mad, because I am making a film not about the Shoah, the Holocaust, but about Dr. Murmelstein."[40] More than the lack of historiographical mastery exhibited in the Garfunkel interview by Lanzmann's note-taking, however, these outtakes gradually unfold not only the filmmaker's fascination with the controversial *Judenrat* chairman; the material also recovers the immense gap between Lanzmann's own, acquired "bookish, theoretical . . . second-hand knowledge" and Murmelstein's personal experiences and recollections.[41] Comparing himself to the first-century Jewish historian Flavius Josephus and continuously referencing legends and folktales, the Theresienstadt survivor constructs an endless account of the past in front of the camera that reproduces the complexity of a mythological narrative.

The encounter reveals a distance between the filmmaker's research and the survivor's "side of history," a distance underscored by the fact that, following Murmelstein's own affectation, they often speak of him in the third person singular as though he were, effectively, a literary figure (it is he that self-designates during the interview as "the last of the unjust," inversing the title of André Schwarz-Bart's postwar Holocaust novel).[42] Yet, a few weeks after the interview with Garfunkel, the conversation with Murmelstein in the outtakes also registers a first shift in Lanzmann's approach to representing the catastrophe. Indeed, toward the end of the interview, he asks Murmelstein whether it is even possible to write the history of the Holocaust solely from documents, in which case the Theresienstadt survivor would only be represented as a collaborator (this question itself intimates the centrality, to come, of eyewitness testimony in the finished film). In the Murmelstein outtakes, a certain initial historiographical distance is progressively undone through the growing friendship between the two men, which culminates in their respective decision to wear a suit on the last day.

"You are very elegant today," begins Lanzmann. "Oh, in honor," replies Murmelstein, "because we say good-bye today."[43] This moment of mimesis crystallizes the unconventionality of Murmelstein's testimony. Set against the backdrop of Scholem and Friedländer's judgment and of Murmelstein's absent voice during the 1961 trial in Jerusalem, the filmed interview takes the form of a dialogue over the course of which the survivor weaves his defense. At the same time, the very length of these outtakes confirms Lanzmann's growing awareness that, in capturing Murmelstein's "side of history," he could possibly rehabilitate the controversial *Judenrat* chairman. Two decades later, a sense of guilt transpires in Lanzmann's interview synopsis penned for the USHMM through his evocation of Murmelstein's passing

("He is now dead"). This guilt further attests to the fact that Lanzmann, once at the LTC editing room, was not capable of composing around the controversial choices of the *Judenrat*.

An Impossible Selection

Murmelstein's survival inevitably fueled a controversy concerning his wartime activities—a controversy itself equaled in scope and violence only by the one surrounding Rudolf Kasztner. Lanzmann describes the so-called Kasztner train in his interview with Hanna Marton as "a unique matter in the history of the Holocaust."[44] This controversy also marked a first turning point, several years before the Eichmann trial, for the emergence of the memory of the catastrophe in Israel, where Kasztner had settled in 1947. In a pamphlet published in 1953, Malchiel Gruenwald, a Hungarian Jew who had emigrated to Palestine before the war, accused Kasztner of having collaborated with the Nazis and keeping silent about the fate that awaited the Jews of Hungary at Auschwitz. Kasztner sued Gruenwald for defamation, but the libel case became known as the "Kasztner trial" after the defense sought to prove that the former director of the Vaada was in fact guilty of collaboration.

This "first great Holocaust trial held in Israel" opened in early January 1954 in the small Tel Aviv courtroom of Benjamin Halevy, who would later serve as one of the three presiding judges of the Eichmann trial. In this high-profile case, Shmuel Tamir defended Gruenwald and famously cross-examined Kasztner, who took the stand eleven times to detail the steps leading up to the destruction of Hungarian Jewry. Intent on proving the collaboration of the Vaada director, the young defense attorney argued that he had concealed his knowledge of the extermination in 1944 in exchange for the transport to Switzerland. Tamir also placed significant emphasis on how the passengers of this special train had been chosen. "Kastner [*sic*]," Tom Segev writes in *The Seventh Million*, "now looked like the 'doctor' who had stood on the train platform at the death camps and, with a wave of his finger, performed the selection—who would be sent to work, who to the gas chamber."[45] As Hilberg himself remarks in an excluded segment of his interview for *Shoah*, Kasztner was never forgiven for "playing God" and for choosing who would survive and who would perish—a formulation that approximates the notion of the incompossible.[46]

On June 22, 1955, Halevy delivered his verdict: finding Gruenwald innocent of the majority of the libel charges, he ruled that Kasztner had collaborated with the Nazis and even "sold his soul to the devil"—a dramatic verdict that would reverberate throughout Israeli society well into the late eighties and thus beyond the making of *Shoah*.[47] In Lanzmann's archive of the catastrophe, the legacy of Halevy's phrase is evidenced in the excluded interview he filmed in 1979 with Tamir, who likens Kasztner in his closing words to "a man whose soul was burned in Auschwitz."[48] Following the trial, Kasztner appealed the verdict, which the Supreme Court eventually overturned in early 1958. The Court's decision came too late: in March 1957, Kasztner was assassinated in front of his home in Tel Aviv.

In the outtakes, Hilberg effectuates a parallel between the fates of Czerniaków in Warsaw and Kasztner in Budapest: both men witnessed the destruction as it was unfolding and tragically paid for it with their lives.[49] This comparison encapsulates Lanzmann's parallel investigation of the two deceased Jewish leaders' choices, only one of whom he retained as a protagonist of *Shoah*. "The question of the rescue of the Hungarian Jews will be one of the major topics of my film," he declared in a 1977 introductory letter to Roswell McClelland, the representative of the War Refugee Board in Switzerland who had been informed of the "Blood for Goods" deal in 1944 (Lanzmann filmed McClelland for *Shoah* in the fall of 1978 but eventually excluded his testimony).[50] Years later, however, the filmmaker chose to leave on the cutting-room floor this unique episode in the history of the Holocaust that, beyond epitomizing the leitmotif of the incompossible, also bears witness to both memory politics in Israel and *Eichmann in Jerusalem*.

In her report of the trial, Arendt bitterly summarizes the incompossible underlying the "Kasztner train." "Dr. Kastner [*sic*]," she writes, "saved 1,684 people with approximately 476,000 victims."[51] In 1961, two members of the committee in Budapest were called to the witness stand to recount these rescue efforts: Joel and Hansi Brand. Joel Brand had traveled to Istanbul in the midst of the "Blood for Goods" negotiations where he desperately appealed for help from the local Jewish Agency. Arrested by the British authorities, he never returned to Hungary. Hansi Brand, who initially refused to testify at the 1961 trial, played an active role in the Vaada. Serving as the committee liaison after her husband's departure, she partook in the negotiations with Eichmann, sometimes alone sometimes with Kasztner, and in the selection of the train's passengers.[52]

Nearly two decades after the trial, Lanzmann recorded Hansi Brand at home in Tel Aviv during the final weeks he spent shooting *Shoah* in Israel. First evoking her reluctance to be interviewed for his film, he quickly reveals his intention to speak with her in lieu of both the director of the Vaada and her late husband, who had passed away in 1964. "Hansi Brand was the wife of Joel Brand and the collaborator of Rezső Kasztner, the two men who were the most important in the negotiations about the fate of the Hungarian Jews," he explains to the Hebrew interpreter in the opening moments of the interview, thereby displacing to the off-frame the woman survivor's own participation in the negotiations.[53] In spite of this introduction, Hansi Brand bears witness throughout her testimony to the significant role she played as the committee liaison, even remarking: "I want to add that some people on our committee protested against [my role], saying that a woman can't represent Jewish concerns by herself."[54]

In Lanzmann's archive of the catastrophe, the excluded interview with the former Jewish Aid and Rescue Committee liaison recovers a sense of urgency in capturing for *Shoah* the moral dilemmas faced by the Jewish leaders in Hungary. "Hansi," Lanzmann says halfway through the interview, suddenly addressing her by her first name, "really now, you have to help me. I want to understand and to see [the situation] and not just for myself, but for the people who will see this film. What was your situation from a human point of view, and the situation for Kasztner?"[55] In spite of this intimation of familiarity, the dynamics between the filmmaker and the survivor offer a stark contrast to the interviews recorded in 1976 with members of the *Judenrat*, above all Murmelstein.

Unlike the chairman of Theresienstadt, who defended himself over the course of four entire days, Hansi Brand's unedited testimony is marked by brevity, totaling a mere one hour and forty-two minutes. In this unused footage contemporaneous with the Tamir interview, Lanzmann's questions are themselves reminiscent of the ones the defense attorney had posed during his famous cross-examination in the 1954 trial where "Kastner [*sic*] lost his temper, shouted, became flustered."[56] Not surprisingly, Lanzmann's conversation with Brand for *Shoah* quickly shifts to a confrontation unparalleled in any of the omitted material. The tensions permeating the footage are first hinted at by the linguistic change that, unexpectedly and without any visible explanation, occurs early in the interview. Aided by an interpreter, Brand begins in Hebrew and Lanzmann in English. In take five, however, they abruptly switch to German, their sole common tongue, which they speak for the remainder of the interview. More than the language in which Brand had negotiated with Eichmann and later asked to testify at the witness stand in 1961, this linguistic change permits the interviewer and interviewee to address or, rather, confront each other directly.

Echoing the "Kasztner trial" and Arendt's own verdict in *Eichmann in Jerusalem*, Lanzmann probes the contentious rescue efforts that resulted in the special convoy of 1,684 Jews by way of three questions: First, given that Kasztner was accused of not having warned the Hungarian Jews about Auschwitz, had people in fact known of the extermination in 1944? Second, was it fair that Kasztner had included his own family among those selected for the transport to Switzerland? Third, how were the remaining passengers chosen? Upon answering the first question, Brand evokes Rudolf Vrba's report following his escape from Auschwitz, in which he detailed the extermination process. Unbeknownst to Brand is the fact that Lanzmann had already discussed with Vrba the negotiations that resulted in the "Kasztner train," having filmed him for *Shoah* in November 1978. Akin to his silence in the Brand interview, Lanzmann carefully edited around Vrba's testimony for the finished film in order to exclude the segments pertaining to the committee's rescue deal with Eichmann. In the outtakes, Vrba deems Kasztner a "traitor" who, rather than warn Hungarian Jewry, preferred to carry on with his negotiations in order to ensure not only his survival, but also that of "a small community of his own choice."[57]

In her filmed testimony, Brand utilizes Vrba's report as proof that "people knew" of the reality of Auschwitz when the deportations began. She also observes that, even prior to his report, knowledge of the extermination was widespread in Hungary where many Polish and Slovak refugees were living. "For God's sake, how can anyone maintain that in 1944, that no one knew what was going on in the German areas?" she tells Lanzmann, who continues to probe the question of whether "ordinary Jews" had knowledge of the extermination. Brand, however, interrupts him by ultimately shouting: "People knew!" (Man hat gewusst!)[58] Then, turning to the selection of the passengers and, in particular, the inclusion of Kasztner's family members, she once more reframes the interviewer-interviewee dynamics by posing the question to Lanzmann. "If you were in the same situation, wouldn't you be thinking about your own family?" she asks. "That's a very good answer," Lanzmann concedes.[59]

This 1979 interview with Hansi Brand differs from the interview Tom Segev would conduct with her a decade later when the controversy had begun to subside in Israel. "After almost fifty years, Han[s]i Brand is no longer angry," he writes in *The Seventh Million*, recounting their exchange in which she evokes the twofold incompossible, unvoiced in the *Shoah* outtakes, that ultimately defined the 1944 rescue deal. If Kasztner was never forgiven for having chosen several hundred Jews for survival, "those who were put on the train never forgave him either. . . . Every morning, when they woke up, they knew that they were living at the expense of those who had not boarded the train."[60]

Also filmed for *Shoah* in 1979, Hanna Marton describes how she lives with the guilt, unabated, of having been selected for the transport, which Kasztner had nicknamed "Noah's Ark." After Tamir and Brand, Lanzmann attempts to capture the perspective, past and present, of a passenger chosen in 1944 by the director of the Vaada. Assisted by the interpreter Francine Kaufmann, Marton narrates her story of choice and survival in accented Hebrew, evidencing her postwar emigration to Israel. At the same time, she translates excerpts from the diary that her late husband, Ernst Marton, kept during the 1944 journey to Switzerland.

This mise-en-scène centered on a document contemporaneous with the events is evocative of Hilberg's methodology. In his discussion of the controversial rescue deal with Lanzmann, the historian declares: "I only try to understand from the writings left behind, from the diaries and the reports and the testimonies of these people, what it is they were thinking."[61] Similarly, the Marton material calls to mind Leib Garfunkel's 1976 filmed testimony, during which Steinfeldt translates out loud the former *Judenrat* member's monograph, based on his own wartime diary. Staged at the very beginning of the shooting phase and again several weeks before Lanzmann would begin editing *Shoah* in the fall of 1979, these mise-en-scènes are testament to Lanzmann's privileging of paper memory as a framing device for postwar debates surrounding the choices of Jewish leaders during the Holocaust. In the finished film, Czerniaków's diary read by Hilberg subsists as the sole trace of this authorial preference. Unlike the Garfunkel outtakes, where the survivor seldom bears witness to his personal experience in the Kovno Ghetto, however, Marton's testimony renders visible a shift from the paper memory to the present-day testimony of a woman rescued as a result of Kasztner's deal with Eichmann.

As a passenger removed from the negotiations, her account differs from the one given by Brand, particularly regarding the crucial question, in Lanzmann's investigation, of what exactly the Jews in Hungary knew in 1944. Marton claims to never have heard of Auschwitz when the deportations began that year. She then adds that, even if people had known of the destruction of European Jewry, it was too late to escape. Paradoxically, one of the episodes chronicled in Ernst Marton's diary and read out loud by the survivor suggests that those selected for the "Kasztner train" had in fact known of the extermination camp. During the journey, one of the passengers mistakenly heard the convoy was headed to Auschwitz—instead of the Moravian town of Auspitz—causing everyone aboard to panic. In spite of this anecdote, Marton affirms that the word "Auschwitz" did not signify death in 1944. Nevertheless, she acknowledges that, at the time, such ignorance was perhaps a defense mechanism that allowed the passengers of "Noah's Ark" to not admit to themselves that, unlike the Jews who were being deported en masse to Auschwitz, they had been chosen to survive.[62]

Much like the excluded footage with Brand, these outtakes reveal that it is impossible to discuss this unique episode in the history of the Holocaust without evoking the ethical implications of Kasztner's "selection," which fueled accusations of collaboration for decades in Israel. As Marton's testimony moves beyond the memory of the special convoy to address its present-day legacy, she remarks that the so-called Kasztner trial was one of the worst events she had to live through after the Holocaust. For her, in portraying the Vaada director as a collaborator, the trial minimized his rescue of 1,684 Jews and erased the very context out of which his negotiations with Eichmann arose. "What bothers me in this story," she explains, "it's that one always forgets the origin of this horror, that is to say the Nazi horror; it's the Nazi system which forced people to choose, rather than those who were put in the position of being forced to choose who should live and who should die."[63] A few instants later, Lanzmann reframes the survivor's poignant observation and indirect refutation to Arendt's controversial claim through a paradigm once again reminiscent of Lawrence Langer's notion of "choiceless choices" and intended to encapsulate the Holocaust as a whole: the tragedy of choice. "The dilemma of Kasztner," he remarks, "the tragedy of Kasztner, the tragedy of choice . . . it was not the case only with Kasztner, I mean, this happened generally throughout the Holocaust."[64]

Seemingly prompted by Lanzmann's confrontation, after Tamir and Brand, with a survivor of the "Kasztner train," this nuanced conclusion to his extensive probing of the 1944 negotiations obscures his own difficulty, evidenced throughout the making of *Shoah*, of coming to terms with the fact that Kasztner had accepted the Faustian bargain of selection. "I would never dare to judge, but we are obliged to go on with this question," he tells Hilberg during their discussion, excluded from the finished film, of the selection of the passengers aboard "Noah's Ark."[65] A single question raised in the immediate postwar period permeates his investigation in the late seventies: Should there have been an ethical limit to negotiations with Nazis and should this limit have been to *not* choose who would live and who would die?[66] While filming Tamir the following year, he concedes in anticipation of his own paradigm: "I agree with you the tragedy is the selection."[67] In the end, Lanzmann would produce a "cut" that inscribed within the finished film an ethical limit—a cut separating the suicide of Czerniaków in Warsaw from the selection of Kasztner in Budapest. "Do you think Czerniaków would have behaved like him?" Lanzmann asks Hilberg toward the end of their discussion in the outtakes. "No," the historian responds. "Different person. Different personality."[68]

The Ethics of Editing

Recorded on October 10, 1979, the excluded footage with Marton was one of the very last testimonies Lanzmann captured for *Shoah*. As his comment in the closing moments of the interview suggests, he had already accumulated the near entirety of an archive of the catastrophe that would, time and again, bear witness to "the tragedy of choice." In 2017, Lanzmann retrieved this interview and included parts of it in *The Four Sisters*, his final documentary made from outtakes.[69] The film draws on the testimonies of four Jewish women (Ruth Elias, Paula Biren, Ada Lichtman, and Hanna Marton) whose respective tales of survival invoke the leitmotiv of "choiceless choice[s]." Titled "Noah's Ark," the hour-long edited interview with Marton recovers the controversial selection of passengers undertaken by Kasztner in 1944, an episode that itself anticipates the notion of the incompossible. "Because to choose is to kill," Lanzmann writes in his memoir, seemingly recasting his own selection for *Shoah* through the prosthetic memory of the selection of the "Kasztner train" passengers.

In light of the Arendt controversy and of the interviews with Garfunkel, Murmelstein, Brand, and Marton, the transposition of the incompossible to Lanzmann's editing choices ultimately recovers an ethical dimension underlying the making of *Shoah*: the exclusion of the members of the *Judenrat* as well as of the Aid and Rescue Committee in Budapest from the finished film—the exclusion, that is, of survivors who problematize Arendt's controversial claims of complicity. If the preservation of these unedited testimonies by the USHMM opens the possibility, as Lanzmann had proposed during an interview with the *Cahiers du cinéma* following the film's release in 1985, for "people to continue to work at [*Shoah*]," the return of the unused footage in the twenty-first century reframes this contentious episode of Holocaust history through the voices of survivors, which, captured by the camera between 1976 and 1979, would be silenced in the editing room.

Notes

Portions of this chapter previously appeared in my monograph *An Archive of the Catastrophe: The Unused Footage of Claude Lanzmann's* Shoah (Albany: State University of New York Press, 2019). They are reproduced here with the permission of the publisher.

Epigraph: Quoted in Marc Chevrie and Hervé Le Roux, "Site and Speech: An Interview with Claude Lanzmann about *Shoah*," in *Claude Lanzmann's* Shoah: *Key Essays*, ed. Stuart Liebman (Oxford: Oxford University Press, 2007), 37–49; here, 48.

1. Claude Lanzmann, *The Patagonian Hare: A Memoir*, trans. Frank Wynne (New York: Farrar, Strauss & Giroux, [2009] 2012), 423.

2. Lanzmann, *The Patagonian Hare*, 426, 439.

3. Lanzmann, *The Patagonian Hare*, 490.

4. Alison Landsberg, *Prosthetic Memory: The Transformation of American Remembrance in the Age of Mass Culture* (New York: Columbia University Press, 2004), 19.

5. Lanzmann, *The Patagonian Hare*, 70.

6. See Ruth Elias in *Shoah* (1985), directed by Claude Lanzmann, Criterion Collection, 2013, DVD. For an account of the use of *The Last Stage* in Resnais's documentary, see Sylvie Lindeperg, *Night and Fog: A Film in History*, trans. Tom Mes (Minneapolis: University of Minnesota Press, 2014), 102–3.

7. Landsberg, *Prosthetic Memory*, 148.

8. Lanzmann, *The Patagonian Hare*, 75.

9. Dominique Villain, *Le montage au cinéma* (Paris: Cahiers du cinéma, 1991), 53; translation mine.

10. Lawrence Langer, *Versions of Survival: The Holocaust and the Human Spirit* (Albany: State University of New York Press, 1982), 72–73.

11. The story of Ruth Elias recovered in the outtakes epitomizes Langer's notion of "choiceless choice": in order to survive, she had to kill her newborn at Auschwitz. For a detailed analysis of this motif in her testimony, see my book, *An Archive of the Catastrophe: The Unused Footage of Claude Lanzmann's* Shoah (Albany: State University of New York Press, 2019), 140–51.

12. I would like to thank Samuel Weber for suggesting the phrase "to compose with the incompossible."

13. Gottfried Wilhelm Leibniz, *Theodicy: Essays on the Goodness of God, the Freedom of Man, and the Origins of Evil* (1710), trans. E. M. Huggard (Chicago: Open Court, 1998), 242–43.

14. For a detailed account of the restoration and digitization of the *Shoah* outtakes, see in this volume Lindsay Zarwell and Leslie Swift, "Inside the Outtakes: A History of the Claude Lanzmann *Shoah* Collection at the United States Holocaust Memorial Museum."

15. Gilles Deleuze, *The Fold: Leibniz and the Baroque* (Minneapolis: University of Minnesota Press, 1989), 81.

16. Claude Lanzmann *Shoah* Collection, interview with Leib Garfunkel (RG-60.5005, Film ID 3125, Camera Rolls 1–3; Film ID 3126, Camera Rolls 4–6; Film ID 3127, Camera Rolls 7, 8, 8/2; Film ID 3128, Camera Rolls 9–12; Film ID 3129, Camera Rolls 13–16, 19–20; Film ID 3130, Camera Rolls 17–18; Film ID 3131, Camera Roll 2; Film ID 3132, Camera Roll 21A), US Holocaust Memorial Museum and Yad Vashem and State of Israel; interview with Benjamin Murmelstein (RG-60.5009, Film ID 3158, Camera Rolls 22, 23, 24, 26A; Film ID

3159, Camera Rolls 27–29; Film ID 3160, Camera Roll 30; Film ID 3161, Camera Rolls 31–32; Film ID 3162, Camera Rolls 33–34; Film ID 3163, Camera Rolls 35–36; Film ID 3164, Camera Roll 37; Film ID 3165, Camera Rolls 38–39; Film ID 3166, Camera Rolls 40–41; Film ID 3167, Camera Rolls 42–43; Film ID 3168, Camera Rolls 44–45; Film ID 3169, Camera Rolls 46–47; Film ID 3170, Camera Rolls 48–49; Film ID 3171, Camera Rolls 50–52; Film ID 3172, Camera Rolls 53–54; Film ID 3173, Camera Rolls 55–56; Film ID 3174, Camera Rolls 57–58; Film ID 3175, Camera Rolls 59–60; Film ID 3176, Camera Rolls 61–62; Film ID 3177, Camera Rolls 63, 65; Film ID 3178, Camera Rolls 63A, 64, 64A, 65AM; Film ID 3179, Camera Rolls 66–67; Film ID 3180, Camera Rolls 68–69; Film ID 3181, Camera Rolls 65A, 62AM, 69A; Film ID 3182, Camera Rolls 71–72; Film 3183, Camera Rolls 73–74; Film ID 3184, Camera Rolls 75–76; Film ID 3185, Camera Rolls 77–79; Film ID 3186, Camera Rolls 80–82; Film ID 3187, Camera Rolls 83–87; Film ID 3188, Camera Rolls 88–92; Film ID 3189, Camera Rolls 93–96; Film ID 3190, Part 1, Camera Rolls 21B, 21D, 64B; Film ID 3190, Part 2, Camera Rolls 21, 26A, 69A, 27; Film ID 3190, Part 3, Camera Roll 26A; Film ID 3190, Part 4, Camera Roll 34A; Film ID 3190, Part 5, Camera Roll 30A). As indicated in subsequent notes, all transcriptions from the outtakes are taken from either the original English transcripts used by Lanzmann during the editing phase or the English translation of French and German interviews into English by the USHMM.

17. Henry Feingold, Isaiah Trunk et al., "Discussion: The *Judenrat* and the Jewish Response," in *The Holocaust as Historical Experience: Essays and a Discussion*, ed. Yehuda Bauer and Nathan Rotenstreich (New York: Holmes & Meier, 1981), 223–71; here, 268.

18. Hannah Arendt, *Eichmann in Jerusalem: A Report on the Banality of Evil* (New York: Penguin, 2006), 125.

19. See Yehuda Bauer, *Jews for Sale? Nazi-Jewish Negotiations, 1933–1945* (New Haven, CT: Yale University Press, 1996), 145–95.

20. Mark Lilla, "The Defense of a Jewish Collaborator," *New York Review of Books*, December 5, 2013, https://www.nybooks.com/articles/2013/12/05/defense-jewish -collaborator/ (accessed February 17, 2019); Benjamin Murmelstein in *The Last of the Unjust* (2013), directed by Claude Lanzmann (Cohen Media Group, 2014). On this film, see in this volume Tobias Ebbrecht-Hartmann, "Double Occupancy and Delay: *The Last of the Unjust* and the Archive."

21. For Lanzmann, the Holocaust as an ungraspable experience is most accurately summarized in the phrase "Here there is no why" pronounced by an SS guard at

Auschwitz and retold by Primo Levi *in Survival in Auschwitz: If This Is a Man*. See Claude Lanzmann, "Hier ist kein Warum," in *Claude Lanzmann's Shoah*, 51–52.

22. Interview with Hansi Brand (RG-60.5002, Film ID 3109, Camera Rolls 1–5; Film ID 3110, Camera Rolls 6–8; Film ID 3111, Camera Rolls 9–13); interview with Hanna Marton (RG-60.5008, Film ID 3148, Camera Rolls 1–5; Film ID 3149, Camera Rolls 6–8; Film ID 3150, Camera Rolls 9–11; Film ID 3151, Camera Rolls 12–14; Film ID 3152, Camera Roll 15; Film ID 3153, Camera Roll 16; Film ID 3154, Camera Roll 17; Film ID 3155, Camera Rolls 18–19; Film ID 3156, Camera Rolls 20–21; Film ID 3157, Camera Rolls 5A, 1A-B, 21A–C, 19A, 9A–B, 13A–C, 15A, 18A–B).

23. Lanzmann, *The Patagonian Hare*, 426.

24. Yehuda Bauer and Malcolm Lowe, "Introduction," in *The Holocaust as Historical Experience. Essays and a Discussion*, vii–xiv; here, xi. Of the ten articles included in this volume, seven deal with Jewish leadership.

25. See Raul Hilberg's account of Czerniaków in both the finished film and the outtakes; see, as well, Raul Hilberg, Stanislaw Staroń, and Jósef Kermisz, eds., *The Warsaw Diary of Adam Czerniaków: Prelude to Doom* (Chicago: Ivan R. Dee, 1999).

26. Lanzmann, *The Patagonian Hare*, 419.

27. "Introduction," in *The Warsaw Diary of Adam Czerniaków*, 67.

28. Interview with Leib Garfunkel (RG-60.5005, Film ID 3125, Camera Rolls 1–3); transcript, 1.

29. Lanzmann, *The Patagonian Hare*, 419.

30. On the distinction between deep and common memory, as well as sensory and external memory, see Charlotte Delbo, *Days and Memory*, trans. Rosette Lamont (Evanston, IL: Marlboro Press/Northwestern, [1985] 1990), 1–4. See, as well, Lawrence Langer, *Holocaust Testimonies: The Ruins of Memory* (New Haven, CT: Yale University Press, 1991), 1–38.

31. Interview with Leib Garfunkel (RG-60.5005, Film ID 3128, Camera Rolls 9–12); transcript, 29–30.

32. Interview with Leib Garfunkel (RG-60.5005, Film ID 3128, Camera Rolls 9–12); transcript, 31.

33. I thank Corinna Coulmas for identifying Lanzmann's handwriting.

34. Lanzmann, *The Patagonian Hare*, 425.

35. Marie Louise Knott, ed., *The Correspondence of Hannah Arendt and Gershom Scholem*, trans. Anthony David (Chicago: University of Chicago Press, 2017), 203.

36. Saul Friedländer, *When Memory Comes*, trans. Helen R. Lane (Madison: University of Wisconsin Press, [1978] 2003), 116–17.

37. Claude Lanzmann, "Material of *Shoah*," USHMM, Film Archive Administrative Files, uncataloged, 7.

38. Their research on Murmelstein was published posthumously under the title *Choices under Duress of the Holocaust: Benjamin Murmelstein and the Fate of Viennese Jewry, Volume I: Vienna* (Lubbock: Texas Tech University Press, 2018).

39. "Oral History Interview with Benjamin Murmelstein," Oral History Interviews of the Leonard and Edith Ehrlich Collection, USHMM, RG-50.862. I thank Anatol Steck for sharing and discussing the Ehrlich interviews with me.

40. Interview with Benjamin Murmelstein (RG-60.5009, Film ID 3185, Camera Rolls 77–79); transcript of the *Shoah* interview with Benjamin Murmelstein, translated into English by Lotti Eichorn, USHMM, part 2, 247.

41. Chevrie and Le Roux, "Site and Speech," 38.

42. André Schwarz-Bart, *The Last of the Just*, trans. Stephen Becker (New York: Overlook, [1959] 2000).

43. Interview with Benjamin Murmelstein (RG-60.5009, Film ID 3185, Camera Rolls 77–79); translated transcript, part 2, 247.

44. Interview with Hanna Marton (RG-60.5008, Film ID 3156, Camera Rolls 20–21); transcript of the *Shoah* interview with Hanna Marton, translated into English by Deborah S. Droller, USHMM, 35.

45. Tom Segev, *The Seventh Million: The Israelis and the Holocaust*, trans. Haim Watzman (New York: Owl, [1991] 2000), 271.

46. Interview with Raul Hilberg (RG-60.5045, Film ID 3777, Camera Rolls 33, 43, 44).

47. Yehuda Bauer, *Jews for Sale?*, 145.

48. Interview with Shmuel Tamir (RG-60.5040, Film ID 3398, Camera Rolls 7–8).

49. Interview with Raul Hilberg (RG-60.5045, Film ID 3777, Camera Rolls 33, 43, 44).

50. Claude Lanzmann, "Letter to Roswell McClelland dated February 16, 1977," USHMM, 2014.500–Roswell and Marjorie McClelland Papers, series 6, folder 10, file 3.

51. Arendt, *Eichmann in Jerusalem*, [2001] 118.

52. Hanna Yablonka, *The State of Israel vs. Adolf Eichmann*, trans. Ora Cummings with David Herman (New York: Schocken, 2004), 96.

53. Interview with Hansi Brand (RG-60.5002, Film ID 3109, Camera Rolls 1–5); transcript of the *Shoah* interview with Hansi Brand, translated into English by Uta Allers, USHMM, 2.
54. Interview with Hansi Brand, transcript, 5.
55. Interview with Hansi Brand (film ID 3111, Camera Rolls 9–13); transcript, 21.
56. Segev, *The Seventh Million*, 271.
57. Interview with Rudolf Vrba (RG-60.5040, Film ID 3234, Camera Rolls 135–37).
58. Interview with Hansi Brand (Film ID 3110, Camera Rolls 6–8); transcript, 16.
59. Interview with Hansi Brand (Film ID 3111, Camera Rolls 9–13); transcript, 29.
60. Segev, *The Seventh Million*, 469–73.
61. Interview with Raul Hilberg (RG-60.5045, Film ID 3777, Camera Rolls 33, 43, 44).
62. Interview with Hanna Marton (RG-60.5008, Film ID 3152, Camera Roll 15); transcript, 24.
63. Interview with Hanna Marton (Film ID 3155, Camera Rolls 18–19); transcript, 35.
64. Interview with Hanna Marton (Film ID 3155, Camera Rolls 18–19); transcript, 35.
65. Interview with Raul Hilberg (RG-60.5045, Film ID 3777, Camera Rolls 33, 43, 44).
66. Thus Yehuda Bauer summarizes in *Jews for Sale* the issues raised by the episode of the "Kasztner train": "Was it justifiable to conduct negotiations with the Nazis to save Jews? And if it was, what were the limits to such contacts?" (145).
67. Interview with Shmuel Tamir (RG-60.5040, Film ID 3397, Camera Rolls 4–6); transcript, 25.
68. Interview with Raul Hilberg (RG-60.5045, Film ID 3777, Camera Rolls 33, 43, 44).
69. See Hanna Marton in *The Four Sisters*, directed by Claude Lanzmann (2018).

4

"The dead are not around"

Raul Hilberg as Historical Revenant in *Shoah*

Noah Shenker

In his approach to making *Shoah* (1985), Claude Lanzmann draws heavily from his on- and off-screen exchanges with the Holocaust scholar Raul Hilberg, evoking the latter's method to researching history:

> In all of my work I have never begun by asking the big questions, because I was always afraid that I would come up with small answers; and I have preferred to address these things which are minutiae or details in order that I might then be able to put together in a *gestalt*, a picture which, if not an explanation, is at least a description, a more full description, of what transpired.[1]

Both Lanzmann and Hilberg approach their interviews with witnesses and engagement with historical sources, respectively, with minute rather than broad questions in order to represent a "*gestalt*, a picture" of the Holocaust. For Hilberg, his conception of gestalt is akin to creating a "historical representation" of the Holocaust—one that can piece together not only individual experiences but also larger collective and structural aspects of the past.[2] Lanzmann further echoes many of Hilberg's views, writing in his memoir:

> I became convinced that there would be no archive footage, no individual stories, that the living would be self-effacing so that the dead might speak through them, that there would be no "I," however fantastical or fascinating or atypical an individual fate might be; that, on the contrary, the film would take a strict form—in German a *Gestalt*—recounting the fate of the people as a whole, and that those who spoke for them, forgetting themselves and supremely conscious of their duty to pass on their memories, would naturally express themselves in the name of all, considering the question of their own survival almost as anecdotal, of little interest, since they too were fated to die—which is why I consider them as "revenants" rather than as survivors.[3]

However, Hilberg and Lanzmann's visions of a gestalt are not value-neutral, but rather reflect their particular dispositions toward interview methodologies and the worth assigned to individual survivor accounts, among other considerations. And each of their formulations of gestalt are subject to change, as revealed through the messy and contested dialogues between interviewers and witnesses that Lanzmann leaves on the cutting-room floor as outtakes, or in the perpetrator documents that Hilberg privileges over testimonies of survivors in the course of his research. Both Lanzmann and Hilberg set out to create definitive works on the Holocaust, and yet despite the foundational stature of their respective contributions, Lanzmann's *Shoah* and Hilberg's multiple editions of *The Destruction of the European Jews* (1961, 1985, 2003), are "always in motion," subject to new discoveries, revisions, and editions that extend beyond their original authorial intentions.[4]

This essay examines those multiple iterations, in particular the *Shoah* outtakes from the extended interviews between Lanzmann and Hilberg, to reveal some of the structuring presences and absences in the finished film. Those fragments, now accessible through the collection of the United States

Holocaust Memorial Museum (USHMM), illuminate the ways in which Lanzmann's and Hilberg's representational and historiographical approaches both converge and depart from one another in ways that can reshape critical interpretations of *Shoah*. Hilberg appears in only three scenes of the film. And yet, the profound influence of his book *The Destruction of the European Jews*; the six hours of film footage (including outtakes) capturing his dialogues with Lanzmann; and Hilberg's masterful, commanding, but also emotionally charged performance all provide historical anchorage and a new conceptual lens through which to reinterpret Lanzmann's film. Just as Hilberg's discovery of perpetrator documents serve as a Rosetta stone, or a key for him in uncovering what occurred during the Holocaust, the recent accessibility of the *Shoah* outtakes enables us to excavate how Lanzmann, in conversation with Hilberg, negotiates the intersections of history and memory, thereby revealing a gestalt—or, according to Hilberg's definition, "a more full description, of what transpired" during the making of *Shoah*.

Lanzmann's labors were no doubt exhausting and exhaustive—spanning more than ten years, creating over two hundred hours of footage shot across fourteen different countries with over four years of editing, not to mention physical danger and serious injury—all directed toward creating a work that could take only one shape in the filmmaker's conception of the project.[5] At the heart of his editing process is Lanzmann's focus on the small questions, with resulting shots that "seem both clear and sometimes deliberately arbitrary, focusing on a detail which is striking or concrete rather than historically central."[6] While Lanzmann crafts *Shoah* in such a way to invoke that sense of elusiveness, there is nonetheless a clear structuring methodology—one that comes about through acts of coidentification and collaboration. While it is hardly breaking new ground to point out that *Shoah* is a constructed film project like any other, the preservation and digitization of the 220 hours of *Shoah* outtakes afford scholars a unique opportunity to examine its architecture in richer detail and to investigate how Lanzmann interweaves, and in several instances, excludes, competing historiographical and representational elements in his film. In opposition to Lanzmann's expressions of his deep wish to destroy the unused footage of his film in order to "prove that *Shoah* is not a documentary," the outtakes remain as traces of the shared labor between him and his subjects.[7] They serve as more than traces: they constitute a form of paratextual commentary on the film, an index and catalog of *Shoah* as an archive of its conceptualization and production.

Furthermore, they reveal the extent to which the interviews in *Shoah* are "cumulative but often contradictory."[8] That is to say, the exchanges with survivors, bystanders, perpetrators, and historical experts in that film often clash in ways that contrast with the uses of survivor interviews employed in more traditional documentaries, such as *The Last Days* (James Moll, 1998), in which survivors' stories are assembled in a manner to suggest historical unity and correspondence. There, are, however, moments when even a narratively cohesive documentary like *The Last Days* can be read against the grain in search of its antirealist or less unifying aspects.[9] I would take that point even further and contend that it is also possible to read against the grain of the more fragmentary, high-modernist elements of *Shoah* in search for unifying elements of a rationalist historical methodology.[10]

A "Privileged Source": *The Destruction of the European Jews*

The outtakes of Claude Lanzmann's interviews with Raul Hilberg reveal moments of transference and overidentification between the two men. And they show the formation of a historiographical template for piecing together a gestalt that shapes the construction of history within *Shoah*. It has been well established that Hilberg's groundbreaking first edition of *The Destruction of the European Jews* served as "the master narrative" for Lanzmann's research into and construction of his film.[11] Lanzmann recalls "the luminous afternoon of the summer of 1974" when he first received Hilberg's tome and notes that it "would change my [his] life."[12] It was the filmmaker's "privileged source," one that he would reread over many years, "not for the purpose of storing knowledge but in the pursuit of a concrete goal, with the perspective of a work to be realized or in the process of being realized."[13] *The Destruction of the European Jews* would help launch Lanzmann's "insane pursuit" to make *Shoah* and he was inspired by and in many respects emulated the book's monumental breadth and depth and its nonchronological structure.[14] He also gravitates toward its largely static analytical categorization of victims, perpetrators, and bystanders—classifications that often lack ethical and historical nuance in Hilberg and Lanzmann's depictions of non-Jewish Poles.

It also initially appears that Lanzmann and Hilberg are bound by their commitment to investigating the "how" questions that shape the destruction processes of the Holocaust. While Hilberg's groundbreaking book was central to the formulation of those "how" questions in Holocaust history, so too was his essay "German Railroads/Jewish Souls," originally published in 1976.[15] *The Destruction of the European Jews* does document the railway infrastructure and its role in the deportation and extermination process, but the 1976 essay expands on new research into that area, shedding light on how the German railways "became the live organism which acted in concert with Germany's military industry, or SS, to make German history."[16] The research for that essay enables Hilberg to investigate, and subsequently include in his interviews with Lanzmann, a more detailed and evocative discussion of the specialized nature and handling of railway documents. His interpretation of such sources, as discussed later in this essay, as well as the notion of the railway system as a "live organism," will ultimately become central features and tropes of the finished film, including its closing shot of a freight train in motion.

There are critical points of departure, however, between Hilberg and Lanzmann in their positions on addressing the central question: "Why were Jews killed?" I will explore those distinctions on the "why" questions in more detail later on. For now, I draw attention to Hilberg and Lanzmann's shared investment in process-oriented details of the Holocaust that shape their handling of material documents and interviews. As mentioned earlier, both figures espouse the illuminating power of a gestalt, "a picture which, if not an explanation, is at least a description, a more full description, of what transpired" during the course of the Holocaust.[17] For Hilberg, history is a matter of representation, though with limits and parameters set in place in order to avoid its manipulation.[18] Authenticity is crucial to Hilberg's historical endeavors, vested as he is in being able to conjure a connection, albeit incomplete, with the historical real through his use of proper and rigorous techniques of handling and interpreting artifacts and sources. Lanzmann's approach to conducting interviews with his subjects largely reflects Hilberg's aversion to "big questions," instead preferring to address the "minutiae or details" of their experiences. Scholars and critics have praised Lanzmann's film for privileging its representation of the "traces of traces" left behind by the Holocaust, rather than presenting a redemptive or "totalizing narrative" arc of the events.[19]

However, the interview outtakes of Hilberg and Lanzmann reveal the degree to which careful filmic assemblage positions Hilberg's canonical book and his sacred status as "the" historian in *Shoah*, as grounding and centering forces in an ostensibly elusive and decentered film.[20] With some critical exceptions, Hilberg represents to many Holocaust historians the figure of a "documents man"—the historian toiling within the archive, working obsessively with sources—primarily those in written form and created from the perspective of perpetrators.[21] It has been widely discussed in Holocaust studies that Hilberg was, for most of his career, reluctant to work with oral histories of the Holocaust.[22] While testimonies of survivors could be imbued with "sacred value," he nonetheless sees them as unreliable in part because of the passage of time, the nature of questions asked, and the frailty of individual recollection. For Hilberg, working with the written documents, decoding and composing their meaning through his archival expertise, is a more rigorous albeit incomplete task akin to the challenges of a "jigsaw puzzle."[23] Hilberg acknowledges that the particular puzzle of the Shoah can never be rendered complete and that, far from being the work of history, the search for complete answers resides in the sphere of theory:

> A theorist stakes everything on coming up with a perfect answer. That is an all-or-nothing wager with no real reward for an incomplete achievement. Those on the other hand who ask the small questions clearly move in the opposite direction, investing a great deal of effort and inevitably producing a partial response.[24]

For Hilberg, the "explanatory power" of sources emerges from the partial reconstruction of what can be ascertained from documents.[25] Yet, as Frederico Finchelstein argues, Hilberg's approach is not devoid of theory in that, however hard he tries to objectify his sources, his "small questions" and focus on the minutiae do in fact constitute frameworks and theories of knowledge.[26] Those written sources are mediated through historiographical approaches just as interviews and testimonies are shaped by filmic and archival practices. According to Finchelstein, Hilberg's methodology seems to "invert the value of his gestaltic approach," and he is unable to work with those minutiae that reside within the traumatized psyches of survivors—psyches that cannot always be easily integrated into rational, objectivist approaches to history.[27]

The outtakes call that assessment into question. Lanzmann was drawn to Hilberg as his chief historical expert precisely because he identified in him the ability to master a delicate balancing act: to convey both pathos and sobriety, objectivity and subjectivity.[28] Lanzmann attended the "International Scholars Conference on the Holocaust—A Generation After" in New York in 1975—a conference also attended by the likes of Yehuda Bauer, Saul Friedländer, and Raul Hilberg—and the filmmaker was immediately struck by how Hilberg "stood out against the others [academics]" with their more sterile delivery and tone, noting in contrast to Hilberg's "metallic and warm" voice and the "way he carried his body . . . his body itself spoke."[29] According to Lanzmann, he not only was heavily indebted to Hilberg's rationalist historiographical approach, but was also in awe of his innate ability to perform and transmit the history of the Shoah: "Hilberg literally embodied and accepted the essential dare that the Holocaust makes to all who seek to bring it to life."[30]

That adeptness at bringing the Holocaust to life rested not only with Hilberg's archival and historical expertise with documents, but also with his conception of written sources as requiring both preservation and reembodiment. In Hilberg's capacity as a member of the USHMM's Content Committee, he once argued, "We need archives—documents are the last surviving witnesses and will endure long after the last survivor has perished."[31] Those words are an echo of his comments in *Shoah*, that "when I hold a document in my hand, particularly if it's an original document, then I hold something which is actually something that the original bureaucrat held in his hand. It's an artifact. It's a leftover. It's the only leftover there is. The dead are not around."[32] For Hilberg, the archive can speak, but only if its constituent sources are given the proper incantation by an expert scholar with the right historical method. In that sense, both he and Lanzmann are creators who substitute texts, images, words, and other traces for a fading history. However, their acts of incantation are circumscribed; not all archival materials, not all artifacts, hold the same value. Whether it is video or other forms of testimonies for Hilberg, or archived still and moving images for

Lanzmann—certain artifacts are off-limits. For Hilberg, video or other formats of survivor testimony lack precision and he largely steers clear of them due to their subjective biases and the fact that many testimonial methodologies avoided detailed questions concerning the names, places, and dates of particular events. According to Hilberg, they are at best "self-portraits" of survivors.[33]

"It's the Only Leftover There Is": Hilberg and the Uses of Documentary Evidence

The six hours of footage documenting the interviews between Lanzmann and Hilberg (recorded at some point between 1978 and 1979, forty-five minutes of which are included in *Shoah*) reveal the extent to which both figures were dedicated to giving embodiment not only to historical actors invoked in the film, but also to the artifacts left behind. Thus, it seems unfounded to suggest that Hilberg's presence in *Shoah* was a "mistake" for having inserted his "mood of knowingness" and "distance" in "contradiction to the film." Rather, Hilberg's knowingness is actually coupled with an often somber, at times even emotive tone, that is a central asset to the film.[34]

That is evident in the scene much discussed in scholarship in which Hilberg handles and interprets the *Fahrplananordnung 587* documenting the rail transport to Treblinka. Hilberg provides a "lesson in reading, in the semiotics of historical analysis" but also in the mentality and process that governed the individual functionary's encounter with the document.[35] It is a textual, visceral, as well as an intellectual interpretation. And, while it comes relatively late in *Shoah*, it is nonetheless formative, for it helps to provide retrospective methodological anchorage to the film. For Hilberg, finding documents such as the *Fahrplananordnung 587* is akin to being present at the moment of "creation," for it revealed singular insights into the language and logic of the Nazi bureaucratic apparatus.[36] Again, as Hilberg states, in a fashion that seemingly bestows him with heroism as an archival investigator, "It's the only leftover there is. The dead are not around."[37] The document carries the analytical and corporeal charge of the functionary but also the documentation of what happened to victims. Hilberg's position reflects his initial dismissal of the uses of oral histories as sources for historical inquiry, considering them as lesser in value than the artefactual leftover. But, whereas Hilberg largely dismisses testimonies as the work of mediated, collected memory, documents such as the *Fahrplanan-ordnung 587* are "pure texts" that require a correct and rigorous mode of analysis—they have to be brought to life through an objective re-creation of the thought processes of those who authored them. Therein lies one of the contradictions of Hilberg's position, as his search for objectivity ultimately requires the re-creation of subjective interpretation. Although Hilberg suggests that the words written in a recovered document will take the place of the past—the notion that the words rather than the events themselves will be remembered—he nonetheless stresses that those words can only be made legible through subjective, hermeneutics-based practices.

Throughout Lanzmann's interviews with Hilberg, the former, in the presence of the master, often sits or leans diligently toward his subject, attentively listening to the historian as an expert and conduit to history rather than adopting the position of "inquisitorial distance" that Lanzmann exhibits with some of his other subjects in the final cut of his film.[38] Throughout what appears to be three days of interviews, in both the included and excluded footage, Lanzmann is always in close proximity to Hilberg—just by his side or behind him as he sits at his desk or table in the latter's home in Vermont. Lanzmann is often within the frame, shown looking on at Hilberg with deference, his chin frequently resting on his hands as he listens. One reel from the outtakes includes a series of reaction shots taken of Lanzmann in anticipation of the editing process. In several shots, Lanzmann is shown with a glow in his face, nodding in approval toward Hilberg and frequently smiling, or fixed in an intense gaze.[39] There is an evident sense of the filmmaker's reverence for Hilberg's expertise, technique, and his character. Perhaps, just as Michael Renov has commented on Lanzmann's choice to record and stage Abraham Bomba "as he works" as a barber in order to "unleash memory," Lanzmann asks Hilberg to conduct his labor as a historian, handling and interpreting documents in order to unleash history.[40]

While other contributions to this volume illuminate the structuring presences and absences of women unleashing history and memory in *Shoah*, it is important to note here the gendered dimensions of Lanzmann's approach toward Hilberg. Lanzmann's identification with and clear affection for Hilberg exemplifies Marianne Hirsch and Leo Spitzer's invocation of the "Orphic creation" of knowledge—the "masculine collaboration

Reaction shot taken of Lanzmann during the interview with Raul Hilberg. Lanzmann's glowing smile indicates reverence for the historian's expertise, technique, and character. Created by Claude Lanzmann during the filming of *Shoah*. (Used by permission of the United States Holocaust Memorial Museum and Yad Vashem, the Holocaust Martyrs and Heroes' Remembrance Authority, Jerusalem.)

and historical creation, dependent on the intermediary role of women."[41] Nowhere is that more evident than in Hilberg's recitation of Adam Czerniaków's diary, discussed later in more detail, during which the historian stands in for both the chairman of the Warsaw *Judenrat* and the helpless members of his community, particularly women and young children.[42] It has been argued that Hilberg, through his performance of the diary, reincarnates Czerniaków, taking "the masculine role of responsible paternity extremely seriously."[43] Hilberg, in conversation with Lanzmann, is able to "give birth" to stories never intended for discovery.[44] And yet Hilberg is not the only historian whom Lanzmann interviewed for his film. In addition to Yehuda Bauer, Lanzmann recorded an interview with Gertrude Schneider, a Jewish survivor of the Riga Ghetto. After the war, she became a historian, driven in large part by her desire to anchor her experiences and those of other survivors in rigorous historiographical terms and to commemorate

Lanzmann interviews Gertrude Schneider, a Jewish survivor of the Riga Ghetto and a historian of the Holocaust. Created by Claude Lanzmann during the filming of *Shoah*. (Used by permission of the United States Holocaust Memorial Museum and Yad Vashem, the Holocaust Martyrs and Heroes' Remembrance Authority, Jerusalem.)

the experiences of victims, often by drawing from eyewitness testimony. Ultimately, Lanzmann chooses to include her as a singer rather than as a historian, thereby excluding her from "giving birth" to her particular historical accounts and consequently limiting the film's perspectives on gender and the Holocaust.[45]

This is underscored by the ways in which Lanzmann repeatedly asks Hilberg to perform not only as a historian or actor—he is not just simply another witness or character—but also as a gatekeeper of knowledge whom the filmmaker idealizes thorough a process of transference. More specifically, the outtakes reveal moments in which Lanzmann overidentifies with Hilberg, his methodological approach, his demeanor, and his perspectives, without adequately drawing attention to his transferential bond. Furthermore, they illuminate the ways in which Hilberg the rationalist seems to identify with the methodologies though certainly not the moral perspectives or ideologies of the functionaries who created the documents he analyzed. While I concur with the criticism presented by Janet Walker and others that Dominick LaCapra placed far too much emphasis on transference as marking the crucial link between Lanzmann and the survivors whom he interviewed, that transferential dynamic nonetheless seems much more evident in the relationship forged with Hilberg; one that is marked by his overidentification with the subject absent of analytical distance or self-reflexivity.[46] Whereas with several witnesses Lanzmann sparks the reenactment of their own past experiences in the present, with Hilberg he uses the historian to handle and narrate documents in order to make the words of others come alive. As I described earlier, Lanzmann saw something in Hilberg that distinguished him from other historians. More specifically, the ways in which Hilberg eschews large questions in favor of small questions; his apparent shared aversion with Lanzmann to "why" questions (though not as extreme as Lanzmann's); their emphasis on piecing together a similar notion of a gestalt; and his embodiment of the "essential dare that the Holocaust makes to all who seek to bring it back to life" could just as easily describe Lanzmann's core approach to filmmaking.[47]

However, the two men depart from one another in key respects that Lanzmann leaves out of the final cut, with the effect of underscoring the appearance of an even closer affiliation of Lanzmann with Hilberg. The deviations between them are particularly evident as they regard the "why" questions that emerge during the outtakes of the interview process, otherwise largely absent from the final version of the film. For example, at one point, Lanzmann asks Hilberg about the crucial moment, the gap when perpetrators had to decide between established measures and going beyond those steps and toward annihilation. For Hilberg, ideology was not a sufficient motivation, because "the Final Solution cannot be divorced from the war."[48] Hilberg comments on the parallels between the endeavors of war and those of genocide; in his findings, there was a lack of clarity in achieving both ends. He remarks on the absence of planning regarding what was to be done with the Jewish populations held under control through Operation Barbarossa. There were no clear orders in place for the *Einsatzgruppen* operating in those territories. At best, Hilberg commented, there was an "amorphous" set of directives. The system operated on understandings rather than prescriptions. Hilberg proceeds to concur with Lanzmann's contention that "the Final Solution was a product of everybody."[49]

Although those discussions of *why* the Nazis filled in the "gaps" required to commit genocide can coexist with the very "how" questions that are central to both men's work, Lanzmann largely removes the former from his finished film. In effect, Lanzmann's editing strategy focuses on the process-oriented aspects of the destruction rather than examining *why* perpetrators may or may not have taken certain actions. In several ways, Hilberg's work—his detailed questions and categories of bystanders, perpetrators, and victims—has provided points of entry for exploring why certain actions were taken.[50] Some scholars, such as Allan Megill, argue that the big, "almost unanswerable questions ought to be asked of history"—that there is an ethical obligation on the part of the historian to make sense of the past for us and not just set out what happened. Hilberg, who avoids invoking clear and reductive ideological motivations that drove the destruction of European Jewry, nonetheless creates a representation, however incomplete, of structures that could facilitate engagement with questions of the "why." Hilberg's use of the term gestalt reflects a historical aim to create a partial image of the past through an interpretative and narrative framework, "embracing but also going beyond the specific details being recounted."[51] In order to go beyond the specific details however, one must be able to address at least the conditions of possibility for individual and collective actions, experiences, and interpretations. That positivistic gap must be filled with subjective interpretations and re-creations of historical experiences. The reconstruction of that past may be fragmented, but "the larger structures eventually take on a gestalt" with "explanatory power."[52] In that sense, Hilberg's approach, while not totalizing, is nonetheless hinged on selective, privileged forms of historical re-creation that he often attempts to efface in his work.

"I think it is necessary to role-play": Hilberg's Reembodiment of Adam Czerniaków

Historical re-creation is central to Hilberg and Lanzmann's discussions of Adam Czerniaków, the former chairman of the Warsaw Ghetto *Judenrat*. In his autobiography, Hilberg speaks of being drawn to that historical figure and of having "spent about six years with Czerniaków" by going through his diaries.[53] Hilberg, the aforementioned "documents man" with an aptitude for analyzing institutional and state bureaucracies, sees in Czerniaków the parallel figure of an "organization man." The ghetto leader was someone who served a functionary role that, while different from that of the Nazi perpetrators, is nonetheless recognizable to Hilberg as a political scientist, as a someone working within a system, under institutional constraints.[54] And Czerniaków was determined to keep detailed records and write in a matter-of-fact style not dissimilar to Hilberg's. As Hilberg remarks to Lanzmann in the final cut: "He [Czerniaków] left a record . . . and because he wrote in such a prosaic style, we know now what went on in his mind, how things were perceived, recognized, related to."[55]

Just as Lanzmann had gravitated toward Hilberg as someone who "literally embodied" the task of grappling with the Holocaust, Hilberg was drawn to Czerniaków as a fellow "documents man" who attempted to record as many details as possible. During his interviews with Lanzmann (both those included and excluded from the final version of the film), Hilberg inhabits the diary and was so successful in his performance that Lanzmann declared to Hilberg, "you were Czerniaków."[56] Daniel Listoe notes that Hilberg's reciting of the Czerniaków diary in *Shoah* allows Lanzmann to insert a Jewish voice after the Jan Karski interview and before the encounter with Franz Grassler, thereby providing a more interior perspective of a victim rather than limiting the dialogue to that between a bystander and perpetrator.[57] Listoe suggests that Hilberg was featured as an actor who can "feel the past as it unfolds in the present."[58] And Hilberg himself comments in his autobiography on how the diary allowed him to be a "voyeur, a ghost inside Czerniaków's office, unobserved."[59] He can witness Czerniaków and then embody his first-person perspectives in the reading of his diary. However, as Listoe argues, "if Czerniaków's diary has, in its bookish heft, a testimonial presence, Hilberg's performance of it complicates that quality."[60] In opposition to Listoe, I am inclined to look at Hilberg's particular performance—his evident, albeit measured, pathos coupled with his commanding demeanor—as carrying precisely that kind of testimonial presence. The juxtaposition between Dr. Franz Grassler (the deputy to the Nazi commissioner of the Warsaw Ghetto) and Czerniaków does not simply fill in "profound gaps" in Grassler's interview, but also creates a dialogue between two historical subjects, using Hilberg as a surrogate for Czerniaków.[61]

Even though Lanzmann had recorded the perspective of a ghetto official through his extensive interviews with Benjamin Murmelstein, the
former chairman of the Theresienstadt *Judenrat*, Shoshana Felman notes
that, in Hilberg, Lanzmann had found the ideal subject, allowing him to
have "taken a historian so that he will incarnate a dead man, even though
I [Lanzmann] had someone alive who had been a director of the ghetto."[62]
Hilberg is not only providing a voice of objective analysis, but also enacting
a mode of interpreting and performing the diary in a way that allows that
text to re-create a fragment of Czerniaków's subjectivity. While "the dead
are not around," the documents cannot speak for themselves until given a
sensitive and attentive historiographical reading. The outtakes with Hilberg
reinforce this point when he comments on putting himself in the place of
Czerniaków, trying to imagine, via the act of role-playing, what it would
have been like to be in his shoes.[63] This is evident in the following exchange
that is ultimately left out of the finished film:

LANZMANN: What do you think of the people who have a definite attitude on the Jewish councils? That they say, they were collaborators?
HILBERG: All sorts of people say all sorts of things. They have done it
   without much study. They have done it without deep penetration into
   the problem areas that these very people had. I think it is necessary
   to role-play. It is necessary to put oneself, to some extent, in someone
   else's place. Invariably and inevitably I did this, living five years with
   this diary. And beginning to think, somewhat, the thoughts which
   Czerniaków had. In that sense, of course, one enters into the mind of
   the person and begins to see the parameters, the limits, much as they
   were seen then. There was no such thing as collaboration, as such, in the
   Jewish community, because there is no Jewish leader who even in
   the remotest, identified with or wanted to help the German cause.[64]

Hilberg comes across as sympathetic to and empathetic with Czerniaków,
noting his loyalty and steadfastness, and the absence in him of a thirst for
power, the latter of which he associates with Murmelstein. Hilberg states
that based on his immersion into the details of Czerniaków's diary and trying to put himself in his perspective, he was able to determine that resistance
was unthinkable in the mind of the chairman. According to Hilberg, the

Jews did not resist because, unlike the historians who have the benefit of hindsight, they could not see the "gestalt."[65] It is futile, according to Hilberg, to expect Jews and their leaders to clearly see the writing on the wall, as the situation was "fraught with too many dangers," and the larger picture of what was to occur could not be viewed at that time—only in retrospect.[66]

Hilberg performs a close historical reading of the text, but also an act of reembodiment—or, to use Felman's terms, an attempt to "reverse the suicide" of Czerniaków based on a deeply personal identification with him that appears to have been cultivated during his years editing and writing an introduction for the ghetto leader's diary.[67] That is not to suggest a comparison between Hilberg and the firsthand survivors, bystanders, and perpetrators whom Lanzmann interviews for this film. However, Hilberg is not simply an authoritative talking head providing sober insights from an analytical remove. Rather, as the outtakes reveal, he negotiates the terrain of being objectively and rationally engaged in his textual sources, while also attempting to inhabit a position of psychic proximity to Czerniaków. He is both a political scientist searching to understand the parameters of state and communal systems and a humanist attempting to inhabit the worldview of a historical subject. By turning to the unused footage from *Shoah*, we can discover a Hilberg who speaks not only of Czerniaków as a figure who "left us a window through which we can observe a Jewish community"—a somewhat detached metaphor that he employs in the final cut of the film—but also as a complex human being placed under tremendous pressures.[68] Hilberg is only able to glean that insight from having projected himself, in part, into Czerniaków's mindset. That intersubjective process unsettles the critique that Hilberg was unable to work with the "traumatized psyches" of historical subjects. While that is largely the case with Hilberg's work (or lack thereof) with survivor oral histories, it less neatly applies to his engagement with the traumatic resonances left behind in victims' written sources.

Furthermore, Hilberg's performance of the diary reading reflects his evolving, albeit conservative, position as a scholar, particularly on matters pertaining to the *Judenräte*. While he had been far more critical of the actions of the councils in the first edition of *The Destruction of the European Jews*, by the time of his interview with Lanzmann he not only had begun work editing Czerniaków's diary but had also reviewed the book

Judenräte by Isaiah Trunk in 1972, detailing life in the ghettos in Nazi Eastern Europe. Within that review, Hilberg writes of the restrictions, pressures, and constraints placed on Jewish ghetto authorities, noting that they were "totally subordinate to the Germans" and that, in turn, the Jewish inhabitants were at the mercy of the councils.[69] The *Judenräte* could not both obey the Germans and serve their Jewish constituents. Furthermore, by the time Lanzmann interviewed Hilberg, the latter had started work on what would become the 1985 edition of *The Destruction of the European Jews*, in which he would provide a more tempered view of the *Judenräte* compared to the first edition, one that attributed the actions of the councils to perceptual rather than moral failures.[70] At one point, in an exchange that is not included in the final edit of the film, Lanzmann asks Hilberg about how his views on the councils might have evolved:

LANZMANN: Did you change your mind since you wrote *The Destruc-tion of the European Jews* . . . on this particular point, as I have the feeling that you were much more harsh, severe towards these people when you were writing the book than you are now?

HILBERG: Well, of course in the first version . . . I was very brief, I was very, very brief about the roles of the Jews in their own destruction. And the very brevity of the words made them harsh. It isn't the tone, it isn't the adjectives, but rather it is the sheer brevity, the simple statement that the Jews were aiding their own destruction. . . . And to say this, as I have just said at this minute, so briefly, in a single paragraph is to be very harsh, because a single paragraph does not tell what happened in the process of doing these things, what thoughts, what pain, occurred during that time. Now of course, then we did not have the diary of Adam Czerniaków, we did not have a lot of other documents. Today, we do. So today, while not really changing the conclusion, I certainly tell the story at a much more elaborate, and hence, perhaps more consoling fashion.

LANZMANN: Human?

HILBERG: Perhaps a more human fashion. This is not to say that I now believe that the councils were not a disaster . . . but one can see the mechanisms. One can see the step-by-step process not only on the German side but on the Jewish side.

The Hilberg whom we encounter in the final version of *Shoah*, while sensitive to the demands placed on Czerniaków, does not reveal, as he does in the outtakes, the extent to which he identifies with and inhabits the perspectives of the ghetto leader. And across both the final cut and outtakes of the film, Hilberg is by no means as open to forms of Jewish agency and resistance within the ghettos as his peer and frequent foil, the Israeli historian Yehuda Bauer. In his own scholarship, Bauer had underscored the importance of various acts of resistance that extended beyond armed combat to include the preservation of cultural and religious practices, among other areas. He had sharply critiqued Hilberg as being "historically inaccurate" for having been single-mindedly concerned with locating armed resistance as the only legitimate form of defiance, rather than taking a more inclusive view of Jewish resistance as "any *group* action consciously taken in opposition to known or surmised laws, actions, or intentions directed against the Jews by the Germans and their supporters."[71] And yet it is Hilberg's perspectives on the *Judenräte* and resistance, and not those of Bauer, that make their way into Lanzmann's finished film.

Lanzmann had in fact interviewed Bauer for *Shoah* for over six hours at the historian's home in Israel at some point between 1978 and 1981. Although none of the recorded footage with Bauer makes its way into the final cut, those outtakes reveal the performative and historiographical distinctions between Hilberg and Bauer. In contrast to the more formal mise-en-scène of Hilberg's interview, with him frequently sitting at a table with piles of sources before him, Bauer is filmed sitting rather casually in a beach chair in Israel in what appears to be his backyard, complete with a dog and a toddler straggling across the background at various points. Wearing a beige shirt (which eventually gets covered by a cardigan as day turns to night), Bauer sits framed in the single shot, never appearing on camera with Lanzmann. There appears to be a spatial and inquisitorial distance between them, and there are no reels containing reaction shots of Lanzmann listening to or watching Bauer. Throughout the daylong interview Lanzmann and Bauer never develop anything resembling a rapport. Bauer is more reserved in contrast to Hilberg. Unlike the latter, who avoids talking about his fears or anxieties associated with his work, Bauer speaks openly about being "scared" and emotionally taxed by the process. He remarks that his work is done not simply to uncover the past, but to provide important lessons to humanity. Bauer attests that his work carries value only if it can "mean something for the next generation."[72] Throughout these and other exchanges between Lanzmann and Bauer, you can hear the filmmaker sigh with frustration or impatience with his interlocutor. At one point, on the topic of Chaim Rumkowski, the chairman of the Łódź *Judenrat*, Lanzmann presses Bauer, "We must try to go deeper."[73] Bauer attempts to provide a broader context for Rumkowski and the ghettos more generally, asserting that the *Judenräte* were part of a larger bureaucracy and ostensibly had their hands tied. Lanzmann seemingly grows frustrated, failing to show anything resembling the deference he exhibits toward Hilberg. At other points, Lanzmann interrupts Bauer to challenge his conclusions and assert his own knowledge based on his own research for the film. Bauer diverges from Hilberg in terms of both content and performance. He rarely strays beyond a mild-mannered, rather uninspired academic analysis, which contrasts with Hilberg's more charismatic recitations. Bauer is also more sensitive and inclusive compared to Hilberg and Lanzmann on issues pertaining to the *Judenräte* and notions of Jewish resistance, and his absence from the final cut of *Shoah* obscures more nuanced historiographical debates regarding Jewish agency under the Nazi regime.

Conclusion

As the outtakes reveal, Raul Hilberg holds a privileged role in *Shoah* as both "the" historian and as a revenant of Adam Czneriakow, who creates a bridge between the past and those who were not present at the Nazi destruction but who will nonetheless inherit both the testimonies and documents left behind by victims, survivors, bystanders, perpetrators, and others. Hilberg's performance in *Shoah* is tied to his unique persona and historiographical approach, which includes his conception of gestalt—a conception that is largely congruent with Claude Lanzmann's. Just as Lanzmann is singularly invested in interviewing the last of the living in order to capture their reenactment of the past, Hilberg's is devoted to preserving documentary evidence in ways that can preserve the legacies of the dead.

Lanzmann and Hilberg are particularly bound by their commitment to small, detailed questions in order to produce a "gestalt image" with "greater force than the pure reproduction of the actual."[74] That shared commitment

Lanzmann interviews historian of the Holocaust Yehuda Bauer, whose mild-mannered, academic analysis of issues pertaining to the *Judenräte* and notions of Jewish resistance contrasts with Raul Hilberg's more charismatic recitations in his interview. Created by Claude Lanzmann during the filming of *Shoah*. (Used by permission of the United States Holocaust Memorial Museum and Yad Vashem, the Holocaust Martyrs and Heroes' Remembrance Authority, Jerusalem.)

is not only methodological but also transferential in nature, creating a chain of identification between Lanzmann, Hilberg, and Czerniaków. The *Shoah* outtakes illuminate a more complex picture of both Lanzmann and Hilberg. They reveal Lanzmann not only as a modernist filmmaker who eschews a historical center, but also an investigator who is, in part, looking to address certain "why" questions that can ground his inquiry. Hilberg serves as the conceptual anchor for that investigation, giving historical authority and legibility to witnesses' and victims' accounts. But Hilberg's role extends beyond that of an objective analyst of sources, as is evident in his viscerally charged attempts to partially inhabit the subjective position of Czerniaków. Ultimately, the Hilberg outtakes reveal how Lanzmann tries to smooth over what he perceives to be the tensions that mark the intersection between objective historical investigation and the subjective aspects of firsthand sources. They provide us with an invaluable opportunity to excavate the "presence of commentary" left behind in the archives of Lanzmann's unused footage.[75] And, in doing so, they allow us to interpret Lanzmann's and Hilberg's respective works in ways that go against the grain of their preferred representational and historiographical frameworks.

Notes

1. Claude Lanzmann, *Shoah: An Oral History of the Holocaust* (New York: Pantheon, 1985), 70. The word *gestalt*, which would normally be capitalized in German, is lowercase in published editions of the film's transcript. We have followed that convention here. Both Shoshana Felman and Dominick LaCapra have noted the similarity between Lanzmann and Hilberg with regard to avoiding "big questions" in their respective approaches to representing and documenting the Holocaust. See Shoshana Felman and Dori Laub, *Testimony: Crises of Witnessing in Literature, Psychoanalysis, and History* (New York: Routledge, 1992), 216, and Dominick LaCapra, "Lanzmann's *Shoah*: 'Here There Is No Why,'" *Critical Inquiry* 23, no. 2 (1997): 261–62. This essay develops those observations further by going beyond the on-camera exchanges between Hilberg and Lanzmann to examine the ways in which their interactions preserved in the *Shoah* outtakes reveal a transferential relationship between the two figures.

2. Allan Megill, "Two Para–Historical Approaches to Atrocity," *History and Theory* 41, no. 4 (2002): 117.

3. Claude Lanzmann, *The Patagonian Hare: A Memoir* (New York: Farrar, Straus & Giroux, 2013), 423–24.

4. Christopher Browning describes Hilberg's *The Destruction of the European Jews* as "always in motion," continually revised by the author as he discovered new sources. "The Three Editions of *The Destruction of the European Jews* (1961, 1985, 2003)," paper presented at the conference "Raul Hilberg und die Holocaust-Historiographie," Berlin, Germany, October 2017. As with Hilberg's work, Lanzmann's *Shoah* has several afterlives, including the films *The Last of the Unjust* (2013) and *The Four Sisters* (2018). As discussed later in this essay, the various iterations of Lanzmann's and Hilberg's work evolve to explore, with varying success, such issues as gender, survivor testimony, and the role of the Jewish Councils.

5. During his hidden-camera interview with the former *Einsatzgruppen* member Heinz Schubert in Germany in 1976, the filmmaker was physically attacked

and severely injured by Schubert's family. For a more detailed account of that incident, see Sue Vice, "Claude Lanzmann's Einsatzgruppen Interviews," *Holocaust Studies* 17, nos. 2–3 (2011): 51–74.

6. Sue Vice, *Shoah* (London: Palgrave Macmillan, 2011), 37.

7. Claude Lanzmann, "Seminar with Claude Lanzmann, 11 April 1990," *Yale French Studies*, no. 79 (1991): 96.

8. Janet Walker, *Trauma Cinema: Documenting Incest and the Holocaust* (Berkeley: University of California Press, 2005), 142.

9. Walker, *Trauma Cinema, 142.*

10. For debates regarding *Shoah* and cinematic tropes of realism and modernism, see Miriam Bratu Hansen, "*Schindler's List* Is Not *Shoah*: The Second Commandment, Popular Modernism, and Public Memory," *Critical Inquiry* 22, no. 2 (1996): 292–312; and Michael D'Arcy, "Claude Lanzmann's *Shoah* and the Intentionality of the Image," in *Visualizing the Holocaust: Documents, Aesthetics, Memory*, ed. David Bathrick, Brad Prager, and Michael D. Richardson (Rochester, NY: Camden House, 2008).

11. Federico Finchelstein, "The Holocaust Canon: Rereading Raul Hilberg," *New German Critique*, no. 96, Memory and the Holocaust (Fall 2005): 7. Robert Skloot also discusses the foundational influence that Hilberg's scholarship had on Lanzmann, giving the filmmaker a "seal of approval" of a preeminent Holocaust scholar and providing Lanzmann with categories of victims, perpetrators, and bystanders through which he could address his subjects. See Robert Skloot, "Lanzmann's *Shoah* after Twenty-Five Years: An Overview and a Further View," *Holocaust and Genocide Studies* 26, no. 2 (2012): 261–75; here, 266–69.

12. Claude Lanzmann, "Raul Hilberg, Actor in *Shoah*," in *Perspectives on the Holocaust: Essays in Honor of Raul Hilberg*, ed. James S. Pacy and Alan P. Westheimer (Boulder, CO: Westview, 1995), 185. In one of the outtake reels there is a pan-and-scan shot of Hilberg's table in Vermont on which rests German railway documents and a copy of Hilberg's *The Destruction of the European Jews*, complete with the cover image photograph of three deportees peering out of a barbed-wired window of a cattle car. That image is one among other photographs from the time of the Holocaust that were recorded for the film yet are publicly and famously disparaged by Lanzmann and kept out of the final cut. It can be found in Claude Lanzmann *Shoah* Collection, interview with Raul Hilberg (RG-60.5045, Film ID 3770, Camera Rolls 7–8), US Holocaust Memorial Museum and Yad Vashem and State of Israel.

13. Lanzmann, "Raul Hilberg," 185.

14. Lanzmann, 185.

15. Raul Hilberg, "German Railroads/Jewish Souls," *Society* 14, no. 1 (1976): 60–74.

16. Hilberg, "German Railroads/Jewish Souls," 60.

17. Lanzmann, *Shoah*, 70.

18. Michael Dintenfass, "Truth's Other: Ethics, the History of the Holocaust, and Historiographical Theory after the Linguistic Turn," *History and Theory* 39, no. 1 (2000): 17.

19. LaCapra, "Lanzmann's *Shoah*," 239. Here LaCapra invokes the words "traces of traces" to describe the laudatory terms invoked in scholarship about the film in contrast to his own, more critical assessment of *Shoah*.

20. Frederico Finchelstein makes that characterization of Hilberg as "the" historian in *Shoah* in Finchelstein, "The Holocaust Canon," 37. While Hilberg received his training and ultimately his professorial appointment in political science, his research spans other disciplines, including history. As this chapter will explore, it is precisely the combination of those two areas of training and practice that shape Hilberg's particular approach to handling primary sources.

21. For this description of Raul Hilberg as a "documents man," see Browning, "The Three Editions of *The Destruction of the European Jews*." Browning elaborates upon this term to characterize Hilberg as a scholar who revised his multiple editions of *The Destruction of the European Jews* based not on new debates within academia, but rather on his discovery and analysis of text-based documents (as opposed to other sources such as video testimonies).

22. Finchelstein, "The Holocaust Canon," 35–37.

23. Interview with Raul Hilberg (RG-60.5045, Film ID 3768, Camera Rolls 1–3).

24. Finchelstein, "The Holocaust Canon," 15.

25. Finchelstein, 15.

26. Finchelstein, 15.

27. Finchelstein, 39.

28. Lanzmann, "Raul Hilberg," 187.

29. Lanzmann, 187.

30. Lanzmann, 187.

31. Minutes of the Meeting of the Museum Content Committee, 21 October 1987. USHMM; Institutional Archives; Research Institute; Michael Berenbaum's Committee Memoranda and Reports Dates: 1986–96; 1997–016.1; Box 1; Content Committee, October 21, 1987.

32. Lanzmann, *Shoah*, 131.

33. Raul Hilberg. *The Politics of Memory: The Journey of a Holocaust Historian* (Chicago: Ivan R. Dee, 1996), 133.

34. L. Leon Wieseltier, "*Shoah*," in *Claude Lanzmann's* Shoah*: Key Essays*, ed. Stuart Liebman (New York: Oxford University Press, 2007), 89–93.

35. Paula Rabinowitz, "Wreckage Upon Wreckage: History, Documentary, and the Ruins of Memory," *History and Theory* 32, no. 2 (1993): 134.

36. Hilberg, *The Politics of Memory*, 75.

37. Hilberg, 75.

38. Michael Renov, *The Subject of Documentary* (Minneapolis: University of Minnesota Press, 2004), 126.

39. Interview with Raul Hilberg (RG-60.5045, Film ID 3781, Camera Rolls 24, 25, 52, 53, 54).

40. Renov, *The Subject of Documentary*, 127.

41. Marianne Hirsch and Leo Spitzer, "Gendered Translations: Claude Lanzmann's *Shoah*," in Liebman, *Claude Lanzmann's* Shoah, 186.

42. Hilberg had spent a great deal of time working through Czerniaków's diary in the course of editing its publication, which was released shortly after Hilberg's interview with Lanzmann. See *The Warsaw Diary of Adam Czerniakow: Prelude to Doom*, ed. Raul Hilberg, Stanislaw Staron, and Josef Kermisz; trans. Staron and the staff of Yad Vashem (New York: Stein & Day, 1979).

43. Hirsch and Spitzer, "Gendered Translations," 177.

44. Hirsch and Spitzer, 186.

45. Doris Bergen points out the ways in which Raul Hilberg had been taken to task by certain scholars for failing to adequately incorporate gender as a category of analysis in his research. In that sense, it could potentially be argued that both Hilberg and Lanzmann eschew female perspectives in their work. However, Bergen aptly complicates that critique by pointing out the ways in which Hilberg—while far from being a feminist scholar who adequately acknowledges female agency—nonetheless delves into women's experiences and draws from women's sources in some depth in his research. In that sense, at least in the final cut of *Shoah*, Lanzmann diverges from Hilberg. See Doris Bergen, "'Much is Unsaid': Women in Hilberg's Work and Life," paper presented at the conference "Raul Hilberg und die Holocaust-Historiographie," Berlin, Germany, October 2017. Similarly, other essays in this edited volume will explore how Lanzmann's representation of female subjects is more complicated than previous critiques suggest.

46. For an example of that critique, see Walker, *Trauma Cinema*, 131.

47. Lanzmann, "Raul Hilberg," 187.

48. Interview with Raul Hilberg (RG-60.5045, Film ID 3773, Camera Rolls 16–18).

49. Interview with Raul Hilberg (RG-60.5045, Film ID 3773, Camera Rolls 16–18).

50. Bernd Hüppauf, "Emptying the Gaze: Framing Violence through the View-finder," *New German Critique* 72 (1997): 11.

51. Megill, "Two Para-Historical Approaches to Atrocity," 117.

52. Finchelstein, "The Holocaust Canon," 15.

53. Hilberg, *The Politics of Memory*, 187.

54. Hilberg, 187.

55. Lanzmann, *Shoah*, 177.

56. Hilberg, *The Politics of Memory*, 187.

57. Daniel Brian Listoe, "Seeing Nothing: Allegory and the Holocaust's Absent Dead," *SubStance* 35, no. 2 (2006): 64.

58. Listoe, "Seeing Nothing," 64.

59. Listoe, 64.

60. Listoe, 64.

61. Erin McGlothlin, "Listening to the Perpetrators in Claude Lanzmann's *Shoah*," *Colloquia Germanica* 43, no. 3 (2010): 253.

62. Shoshana Felman attributes that quote from a private conversation with Lanzmann held in Paris in 1987. See Felman and Laub, *Testimony*, 216. Lanzmann would later repurpose the Murmelstein footage for *The Last of the Unjust* (2013).

63. Interview with Raul Hilberg (RG-60.5045, Film ID 3775, Camera Rolls 27–29).

64. Interview with Raul Hilberg (RG-60.5045, Film ID 3775, Camera Rolls 27–29).

65. Interview with Raul Hilberg (RG-60.5045, Film ID 3775, Camera Rolls 27–29).

66. Interview with Raul Hilberg (RG-60.5045, Film ID 3775, Camera Rolls 27–29).

67. In Hilberg's introduction to the edited diary he attempts to piece together not only Czerniaków's activities, but also the nature of his character, asking, "What sort of man was he?" Though his cinematic evocations of Czerniaków are far more dramatic, underscored as they are by Hilberg's acumen as a performer on camera, his written account of the man indicates a deep immersion in reconstructing his persona. See *The Warsaw Diary of Adam Czerniakow: Prelude to Doom*, ed. Raul Hilberg, Stanislaw Staron, and Josef Kermisz; trans. Staron and the staff of Yad Vashem (Chicago: Elephant Paperback, 1999), 25. Felman describes the attempt to "reverse the suicide" of Czerniaków in Felman and Laub, *Testimony*, 216.

68. Lanzmann, *Shoah*, 177.

69. Raul Hilberg, "The Ghetto as a Form of Government," in *The Annals of the American Academy of Political and Social Science* 450 (July 1980): 101.

70. Browning, "The Three Editions of *The Destruction of the European Jews*."

71. Yehuda Bauer, *The Jewish Emergence from Powerlessness* (Toronto: University of Toronto Press, 1979), 151; italics in original.

72. Interview with Yehuda Bauer (RG-60.5049, Film ID 3793, Camera Rolls 1–3).

73. Interview with Yehuda Bauer (RG-60.5049, Film ID 3793, Camera Rolls 1–3).

74. Listoe, "Seeing Nothing," 60.

75. Saul Friedländer, "Trauma, Memory, and Transference," in *Holocaust Remembrance: The Shapes of Memory*, ed. Geoffrey Hartman (Cambridge, MA: Blackwell, 1994), 261.

5

"Traduttore traditore"

Claude Lanzmann's Polish Translations

Dorota Glowacka

Poland contra Lanzmann

Since the release of Claude Lanzmann's *Shoah* on April 25, 1985, the film's reception in Poland has undergone many transformations. These tribulations of *Shoah*'s presence in the country's social imaginary have run parallel to the changes in the country's social and political landscape, particularly in relation to the various stages of the debate about Polish-Jewish relations. What has remained constant, however, throughout the different phases of the film's reception is an antagonistic model of memory, which emphasizes the conflict between Poles' memory of the fate of their Jewish neighbors during the Holocaust and the Jewish recollection of the betrayal on the part of the Poles.

In this chapter, I will summarize Polish responses to *Shoah* and then examine the scenes that feature Polish witnesses in both the film and the outtakes. I will argue that a reexamination of Polish sequences in the film and careful attention to some of the interviews that were excluded from the final version allow us to detect a unique form of bearing witness, to which I refer as co-witnessing. Although these exchanges are recorded by the camera and on the soundtrack, they often escape the attention of the participants—the director's as well as his interviewees'—despite Lanzmann's effort to maintain control over all aspects of the filming process. I will focus specifically on the uses of the Polish language in Lanzmann's interviews with Polish witnesses and comment on what I perceive as the director's contempt for their native tongue; on the interviewees' peculiar expressions in that language; and on the translator's efforts to navigate this rough linguistic terrain. By focusing on the uses of Polish in the film and detecting moments of co-witnessing, this inquiry thus aims to move beyond accepted interpretations that *Shoah* stages the conflict between Polish and Jewish memories of the Holocaust and to rethink the meaning of the film as an exemplary *lieu de mémoire*.

Shoah's debut in Paris in April 1985, which was accompanied by French media coverage that highlighted Polish antisemitism, was greeted in Poland with a chorus of voices that condemned Lanzmann for besmirching the nation's good name.[1] It was not until October 30, 1985, however, that the truncated version of the film, which amounted to about two hours of footage that focused almost exclusively on Polish witnesses, was shown on Polish TV. Although few authors of over fifty articles that appeared in the first two months after the film's release in Paris had actually seen it, they expressed indignation that "the most hideous calumny was thrown in the face of our nation, accusing us of criminal deeds in the eyes of the entire world."[2] The complaints focused on Lanzmann's silence about the Polish Righteous Among the Nations; his choice of illiterate peasants as the only Polish witnesses; his lack of acknowledgement of Polish resistance efforts; his disregard for the ethos of Polish victimhood and for the common fate of Poles and Jews under the Nazi occupation; and his manipulation of anti-Polishness as a smokescreen to cover up French collaboration under the Vichy regime and the Allied powers' unwillingness to come to the rescue of European Jews.[3] Allegations also emerged that, by putting the blame for the extermination of European Jews on Polish shoulders, the film exonerated fascist Germany in order to court the West German government in Bonn as a powerful NATO ally against the Soviet Union.[4] In the words of Polish patriot Stefan Korboński, Lanzmann's film amounted to hostile propaganda, which purposefully omitted references to "Polish immense resistance effort and Poland's perseverance in the struggle against the Nazi invader."[5] Notably, representatives of Jewish organizations in Poland, such as the Religious Association of Mosaic Faith and the Jewish Social and Cultural Society, also voiced their protest against Lanzmann's "provocation and anti-Polish campaign."[6] Lanzmann's alleged portrayal of Polish people as Nazi collaborators who had been partly responsible for the fate of Polish Jews provoked outrage, since it was perceived not only as disastrous for Poland's international reputation but also as a serious threat to Polish national identity, which had been supported by the martyrological narrative of World War II.[7] As Grzegorz Niziołek has observed, these Polish responses to *Shoah* were different from French and American discussions about the crisis of post-Auschwitz aesthetics and the impossibility of witnessing trauma. The debates about the film in Poland reflected social and political upheavals and focused on the questions of justice and historical truth.[8]

According to Ewa Ochman, the maelstrom of public discontent in Poland was deliberately fueled by Wojciech Jaruzelski's hard-line regime, which came into power on December 13, 1981, after a military coup, and imposed the martial law that lasted for a year and a half. Amid the deepening economic and political crisis and growing public discontent, the regime relied on an "old and well-tried method, often used in the past to gain public support for the current political system: the so-called 'Jewish question.'"[9] Familiar antisemitic motifs of Polish Jews' lack of loyalty and patriotism were being evoked in order to gain legitimacy, stem the opposition, improve Poland's image abroad, and unify the nation under the banner of patriotism and sacred national values.[10] In August 1985, however, two writers, Jerzy Urban (writing under the pen name "Jan Rem") and Artur Sandauer, who actually had seen the film, sounded a slightly different note in the official communist press.[11] Urban, the spokesperson for Jaruzelski's government, who initially had been at the forefront of the anti-Lanzmann campaign, expressed guarded admiration for the French director's achievement, although he also repeated the accusations that Lanzmann had "perfidiously falsified" Polish war history.[12] Sandauer, a well-known Polish literary critic, was more overtly laudatory: he described his experience of watching the film as "shattering" and acknowledged that *Shoah* was a cinematic tour de force.[13] Both writers focused on Lanzmann's criticism of the Catholic Church's role in fomenting antisemitism in prewar Poland, the line that de facto played into the regime's agenda of trying to undermine the moral authority of the Church in Polish society.[14]

The TV broadcast of the excerpts from *Shoah* in October 1985 spurred another wave of accusations against Lanzmann, although dissenting voices also could be heard. In a review in the official weekly magazine *Polityka*, maverick film critic Zygmunt Kałużyński disagreed with the prevalent opinion that Lanzmann's film was obsessively focused on Polish antisemitism and the Poles were uniformly shown as indifferent or pleased with the disappearance of their Jewish neighbors. He drew attention to the moments in the film when Polish witnesses expressed sadness over the fate of the Jews.[15]

The reviews that appeared in oppositional and Catholic publications repeated a litany of accusations similar to those in the official press. In May 1985, however, Konstanty Gebert (writing under the pen name "Dawid Warszawski") countered the negative responses to the film in an underground publication of the Committee for Social Resistance (KOS), and he urged Poles to undertake a public discussion on the difficult and painful subject of Polish-Jewish relations.[16] After the October screening, Jacek Kuroń, one of the leaders of the opposition and a cofounder of the underground organization KOR (the Committee for the Defense of the Workers), writing for the underground publication *Tygodnik Mazowsze*, challenged the prevalent view that "Poles were next in line for the ovens" by emphasizing the differences between the Jewish and Polish fates during the war.[17] Another notable contribution was a review by the prominent journalist Jerzy Turowicz, in the Catholic journal *Tygodnik Powszechny*. Contesting the Polish posture of defensiveness and wounded national pride, Turowicz described *Shoah* as a masterpiece that was "shattering in its description of the tragedy of European Jews." He also issued a call for a national "examination of conscience" and a reckoning with the legacy of Christian antisemitism, although he was also critical of what he saw as the French director's attempt to implicate Poles in coresponsibility for the Final Solution. Importantly, Pope John Paul II, whose moral authority in Poland had always been uncontestable, in a meeting with former Belgian and French resistance fighters expressed his admiration for Lanzmann's effort to shake the conscience of the world.[18] On the whole, however, the Catholic and oppositional press in Poland shied away from the subject of

Polish antisemitism and defended the Church's record in saving Polish Jews during the war.[19]

Generally speaking, although it was limited in scope and politically opportunistic, the screening of *Shoah* in Poland in 1985 spurred a public debate about Polish-Jewish relations and Polish complicity in the extermination of Polish Jews during World War II. There is therefore more than a grain of truth in Lanzmann's boastful remark, in his autobiography *The Patagonian Hare*, that his film inaugurated "an examination of conscience that was to encompass all of Poland, one that would go on for years."[20] Moreover, these charged conversations were taking place against the backdrop of growing interest in Jewish culture and history, and works such as Hanna Krall's long interview with Marek Edelman, one of the leaders of the Warsaw Ghetto Uprising (*Zdążyć przed Panem Bogiem*, 1977); director Jerzy Kawalerowicz's film *Austeria* (1982), based on the novel by Polish Jewish writer Julian Stryjkowski; and the theatrical interpretation of Isaac Bashevis Singer's novel *The Magician of Lublin*, directed by Jan Szurmiej (1986), were gaining in popularity. Yet when *Shoah* was finally screened in its entirety in 1986 in selected movie theaters in Warsaw, Kraków, and Lublin, the attendance was scant.[21] Thus, at best, the early responses to Lanzmann's film, in Piotr Forecki's words, "revealed the empty spaces of Polish memory and sketched a map of the repressed content in the memory of Polish witnesses to the Shoah."[22]

Act two of Poland's dispute with Lanzmann followed Shoah's premiere in the postcommunist Republic of Poland. In 1997, the entire film was broadcast on Canal + on the initiative of its owner, the media mogul Lew Rywin.[23] Unlike in the early responses, the sentiments expressed in the late 1990s were mitigated by what had become a passionate interest in Jewish culture and history—at least among certain segments of Polish society—and by the onset of the debate on the subject of Poles' complicity in the wartime fate of their Jewish neighbors. Thus, the reactions to *Shoah* became eventually intertwined with stormy public discussions that had been unleashed by the publication, in 2000, of Jan Tomasz Gross's *Sąsiedzi* (Neighbors), about the murder of the Jewish inhabitants of Jedwabne in July 1941, and by former president of Poland Aleksander Kwaśniewski's public apology for the crime, which he delivered the following year, on the occasion of its sixtieth anniversary.[24] The controversy was reignited in 2008 by the

Polish language publication of Gross's *Fear*, about the 1946 pogrom on Jewish survivors in Kielce.[25] In the first decade of the twenty-first century, dynamic Polish scholars (such as Joanna Tokarska-Bakir, Anna Bikont, Jan Grabowski, Jacek Leociak, and Barbara Engelking) continued to expose the fallacies of the nationalist posture in defense of Polish honor, calling for a reappraisal of Poland's war history in light of its "Jewish question."[26] This radical critique of the official Polish narrative of World War II was bolstered by numerous initiatives aimed at recovering Jewish history and culture in Poland. A notable example was Joanna Dylewska's film *Po-lin* (2008), which featured positive, albeit nostalgic, recollections by Polish witnesses about their Jewish neighbors.[27]

This changing ideological climate in "new Poland," at least within the progressive ranks, paved the way for the third stage of Polish responses to *Shoah*, which culminated in a celebration of the film on the twenty-fifth anniversary of its release, with public screenings and events, conferences, and a significant number of scholarly publications. Lanzmann was invited as the keynote speaker and guest of honor at the second Joseph Conrad Festival, held in Kraków in 2010 (where he engaged in "a heated and emotional discussion" with Konstanty Gebert), and he had several speaking engagements in other Polish cities.[28] Lanzmann's autobiography, *The Patagonian Hare*, was translated into Polish in 2010, predating the English translation by two years. The translator was Maryna Ochab, whom Lanzmann had initially hired in 1978 as the interpreter for the interviews with Polish witnesses, but then decided in favor of Barbara Janicka. For the most part, the book met with critical acclaim, and Polish reviewers were reluctant to criticize Lanzmann, possibly for fear of being accused of antisemitism, although some were taken aback by the author's self-adulation.[29] The exception was a brilliantly candid review by Tokarska-Bakir, who lampooned Lanzmann's megalomania, buffoonery, heroic posturing, and terrible writing style. The Polish scholar was especially unforgiving of Lanzmann's self-indulgent misogyny toward many women he reminisced about in the book, including Simone de Beauvoir. Tokarska-Bakir concluded that "Claude Lanzmann, the way he is in this book, does not deserve to be discussed in the context of such a masterpiece [his film *Shoah*], even though it is his own masterpiece."[30]

At the time of *Shoah*'s twenty-fifth anniversary, a new generation of Polish Holocaust scholars began to draw on the film as a crucial resource for thinking about representations of traumatic history, in contexts no longer limited to the Polish problematic.[31] This striking about-face in the reception of *Shoah* in Poland corresponded closely to positive transformations in the area of Polish-Jewish relations, culminating in the opening, on April 19, 2013, of POLIN, the Museum of the History of Polish Jews in Warsaw. These developments, whereby Polish overtures to Lanzmann mirrored the strengthening of the Polish-Jewish dialogue, nevertheless ran parallel to the unabated hostility of Polish ethnonationalists, who continued to point an accusatory finger at the French director. The hospitable tide was indeed reversed when the right-wing Law and Justice government, known for instigating xenophobic and antisemitic sentiments, came to power in October 2015.[32] This divided history of the Polish reception of Lanzmann's film points to a need for developing a way of thinking about the Polish sequences in *Shoah* that would depart from an adversarial model of history and memory. In this context, the significance of the outtakes, which became available for viewing on the United States Holocaust Memorial Museum (USHMM) website, for the task of rethinking *Shoah*'s Polish narrative is inestimable.

Lanzmann contra Poland

In numerous interviews and symposia following the release of the film in 1985, Lanzmann was unapologetic in response to the charges that he had presented a woefully distorted view of Poland. At the symposium held at the Institute for Polish-Jewish Studies in Oxford, in September 1986, he claimed that he had shown "the real Poland . . . the deep Poland."[33] He also insisted that "*Shoah* was not an anti-Polish film" and considered the accusations to be highly exaggerated and ideologically motivated.[34] Following the Oxford symposium, writer and artist Ewa Kuryluk and scholar Jean-Charles Szurek, both of Polish Jewish descent but living in France, wrote insightful critiques of Lanzmann's posture with respect to Poland, while acknowledging the uniqueness and artistry of the film and its momentous role in the debates about Holocaust memory. British historian Timothy Garton Ash concluded that although the director's focus on Polish antisemitism was disproportionate, Lanzmann showed Poles as "so much more human" than the "civilized Germans who would not dream of laughing on camera about death camps."[35]

Following the screening of the film in its entirety on Canal+ in 1997, Lanzmann's comments regarding Polish antisemitism began to sound somewhat more conciliatory than in the past. In an interview with Anna Bikont, for instance, he admitted that he had been unfairly aggressive toward one of his Polish witnesses ("pot-belly" Czesław Borowy) and added, "If I had been a peasant who was born near Treblinka, I would have probably behaved in the same way."[36] On the other hand, he reiterated his conviction that Polish antisemitism was a decisive factor in the Nazi decision to locate the death camps on Polish territory: "Poland was the place where the final solution was possible."[37] Such views, vehemently disputed by Polish scholars (often on the occasion of protests against the expression "Polish concentration camps," used in the Western media) had always been a catalyst in deepening the divide between Polish and Jewish narratives of the Holocaust.

There is no indication that public reckoning with the legacy of antisemitism and tectonic shifts in Polish perceptions of Jewish history and culture in the first decade and a half of the twenty-first century resulted in Lanzmann's change of heart with respect to Poland. However, in *The Patagonian Hare*, his portrayal of the country and of his interactions with Poles was somewhat more subtle, expressing sympathy for many of his Polish witnesses (such as Bronisław Falborski from Koło, near Chełmno; Jan Piwoński from Sobibór; and Henryk Gawkowski, the driver of the Treblinka locomotive). In the outtakes, the director's attitude toward these individuals appears to be quite friendly, although this is difficult to discern in the film. Despite these nuances and the fact that *Shoah* indeed was not primarily intended as an anti-Polish film, it is obvious that Lanzmann had never been a great fan of Poles and Poland, and to the Polish ear his comments will always sound, if not overtly hostile, then at least condescending.

In *The Patagonian Hare*, Lanzmann presents himself as a French patriot, entirely secular in his views, yet proud of his Jewish roots and fiercely loyal to Israel. According to Simone de Beauvoir, in her account of their relationship in *Tout compte fait* (1972), Lanzmann was obsessively focused on his Jewishness: "A deep scar of otherness, which he kept for life."[38] As

Lanzmann confirmed in a 2017 interview in *Paris Match*, "Being Jewish, in my own way [d'être juif, à ma façon], is one of the great pleasures of my life. . . . I don't speak Hebrew, I don't know the prayers, I don't observe the customs. But being Jewish has conditioned my existence."[39] Lanzmann's Polish translator, Barbara Janicka, reminisced that, during their first meeting in 1978, Lanzmann's first words of introduction to her had been: "I am a Jew. A French Jew, but still a Jew."[40] During an interview with Polish journalist Maciej Nowicki in 2011, Lanzmann started the conversation in a similar vein: "Do you realize that I am a Jew? Do you know that?"[41]

In the *Paris Match* interview, Lanzmann made an additional claim that being Jewish taught him audacity and unconditional courage, allowing him to become a fearless resistance fighter during the war and then to carry that attitude for life. In *Shoah*, he approached the task of telling the story of the extermination of European Jews with equal audacity and guerilla tactics. In the director's view, a part of that task was to unmask Polish prejudices and hostility toward the Jews. As I hope to show, one of his aggressive strategies was a linguistic one, aimed at the Polish language as the carrier of Polish national values and attitudes, which included a centuries-old legacy of antisemitism.

Describing Lanzmann's self-presentation in the film, Polish sociologist Magdalena Nowicka argues that the director constructed his persona as a Jewish intellectual based on the tropes of Jewish nonbelonging and persecution. This posture was instantiated by Lanzmann's overidentification with the Jewish victims, who had been abandoned by their neighbors and by the world at large.[42] I would argue that Lanzmann's performance in *Shoah* was also staged in opposition to what Shoshana Felman, in her seminal essay on Lanzmann's film, referred to as Polish "false witnessing."[43] The director thus used Polishness as a foil, reenacting his "Jewishness" in the encounters with his interviewees (as well as in the debates that followed the release of the film).

What's in a Name? Lost in (Lanzmann's) Translation

As Nelly Furman has noted, one of the unique effects of Lanzmann's *magnum opus* lies in its multiplicity of languages: "*Shoah* enacts the rebuilding of the shattered Tower of Babel in an obsessional attempt at grasping the event beyond human imagination, beyond the communicative powers of language."[44] Lanzmann's witnesses testify in many languages, though none of them speaks French, and only one of the survivors featured in the film, Mordechaï Podchlebnik, speaks in his mother tongue (Yiddish), while all the others can be heard in their second or even third language, often with heavy accents. Three main interpreters, all them female, play a prominent role in the film, although only the Polish interpreter, Barbara Janicka, is visible on the screen, while the voices of the other two, translating from Hebrew and Yiddish, can be heard in long translation sequences. Despite the difficult choices he had to make about what to include in the final version of the film, the director opted for consecutive translation, intended to appear on the soundtrack, while the subtitles were synchronized with the oral translation into French, however imperfect or inaccurate, rather than with the witnesses' actual speech. In the opinion of Lanzmann's translator from Hebrew, Francine Kaufmann, the duties he assigned the three women were difficult: on the spot, they had to render into French conversations that were often affectively charged and fast paced, without being able to prepare, take notes, or verify the content for accuracy. The interpreters were the first recipients of traumatic stories with highly disturbing content, for which they were not emotionally prepared.[45]

In Shoshana Felman's influential interpretation, informed by Freudian and Lacanian conceptualizations of trauma, "The incommensurability between different testimonial stances [in the film] is amplified and duplicated by the multiplicity of languages in which testimonies are given."[46] According to Felman, the process of translation is integral to the film: the foreignness of the film's languages and their inaccessibility to any one viewer stand as a metaphor for the radical inscrutability of the events.[47] Like Felman, I am interested in the complicated relations between the performance of language, translation, and testimony in the film. In contrast to Felman's dismissal of Polish testimony, however, I give credence to Polish villagers' desire to bear witness to what happened to the Jews, even though their testimony is sometimes hostile and overlaid with antisemitic prejudice. I argue that what emerges in polyvalent exchanges between Polish witnesses and Holocaust survivor Szymon Srebrnik is a complicated event of co-witnessing, which escapes Lanzmann's effort to control and even suppress

Polish testimony.[48] It occurs in the intersubjective, relational space that may be impossible to map in terms of individual acts of testimony and memory.

An attempt to reconceptualize the function of Polish witnessing in *Shoah* must take into account a preponderant presence of the Polish national narrative in the speech of Lanzmann's Polish interlocutors—the narrative that, as I have noted earlier, also played a central role in the perceptions of the film by Polish audiences. The martyrological myth emerged in Poland toward the end of the nineteenth century, in the wake of failed national uprisings against the three occupying powers. According to historian Joanna Michlic, this dominant narrative was founded on the exclusion of the national community's "threatening Other," the figure epitomized in the history of Poland by the Jewish stranger. During the period of over a hundred years of foreign occupation of Poland, this antisemitic topos served to forge a sense of cultural, linguistic, and historical cohesion. When Poland regained independence in 1918, it also became "a powerful tool in nation building."[49] During World War II, the stereotype of unpatriotic Jews often served as a unifying element in the nation's struggle against the German invader. After the war, the myth of Jewish treachery was used to rally Polish people's resistance to the Soviet regime, although it was also deployed by the communist government to fight political opposition. In postcommunist Poland, the efforts to redefine the country's emergent national identity once again became twinned with the idiom of the "Jewish menace." In its more malignant form, nostalgia for national essence has led to renewed calls for ridding Poland of un-Polish and un-Catholic elements.[50]

The myth of heroic sacrifice at the altars of history, albeit in a simplistic form, surfaces in Lanzmann's interviews with Polish witnesses, both in the film and in the outtakes, and it is always inseparable from the phantom of the Jewish Other. Whenever the villagers evoke the theme of the Polish struggle against the German occupier, they immediately contrast it with Jewish cowardice. Throughout the long passages of the interviews with Borowy, Piwoński, and the inhabitants of Grabów and Włodawa, as well as in Srebrnik's conversations with the Poles in the outtakes, Poles invariably condemn Jewish passivity and assert that Polish people would have never allowed "that" to happen to them. These beliefs are crudely conveyed by Borowy, the witness whom Lanzmann finds particularly distasteful:

No wzięli się za Żydów, i te Żydzi się nie bronią . . . bali się, tchórzostwo byli i więcej nic . . . bo Polacy by sobie na to nie pozwolili.

(They started with the Jews because these Jews don't defend themselves. They were afraid, they were cowards and nothing else. . . . Because Poles would have never allowed that.)[51]

Mr. Piwoński, the Polish witness whom Lanzmann found to be likeable because of his eloquence and knowledge of local history, conveys similar sentiments:

Na tym polegała niezrozumiałość dla nas obserwujących te sceny, ta niesłychana bierność tych Żydów. . . . Poza tymi faktami ucieczek z transportów . . . ogólnie panowała bierność, bierność, która jakoś tak chyba różniła w tym przypadku Żydów of społeczeństwa polskiego.

(This is what the incomprehensibility for us, who were observing these scenes, consisted in, this incredible passivity of those Jews. . . . With the exception of the facts of the escapes from transports . . . , generally there was passivity, the passivity that somehow seemed to distinguish the Jews from the Poles.)[52]

Although Mr. Piwoński is a sympathetic witness, his carefully crafted locutions mask his deep-seated prejudices. Furthermore, to the Polish ear, his expressions and tone of voice are stilted, "teacherly," and rendered strange by the excessive use of passive voice, which allows him to circumvent any references to individual actions. Perhaps this grammatical ruse betrays a certain transferential dynamic with respect to "Jewish passivity" that Piwoński finds so "incomprehensible": projecting passivity onto Jewish victims stems from the Poles' inability to accept that they were also helpless against the German occupier. The myth of heroism that Lanzmann's Polish interlocutors are trying to salvage is augmented with the accounts of their efforts to help the Jews. In several sequences, we hear stories about the villagers who, on the pain of death, were passing water to the people crammed in cattle cars near Treblinka, or smuggling bread and even cucumbers to the victims locked up in the church in Chełmno.

In one of the outtakes, Lanzmann, who prides himself on his past experiences as a resistance fighter, pressures Borowy to explain what he means by "Jewish cowardice," until the man's answers become convoluted and almost fantastical. He claims that if Poles had been in the same situation, they would have cut through the doors and windows of the cattle cars and killed the German guards.[53] By cornering Borowy and reducing his testimony ad absurdum, Lanzmann discredits the villagers' accounts of Polish heroism. Yet a much more persuasive refutation of the juxtaposition between Jewish passivity and Polish heroism is carried out not by Lanzmann but by Szymon Srebrnik, although it can only be heard in the outtakes. The survivor of Chełmno is standing at the site of the former extermination camp (the location that is not shown in the film), talking to a group of Polish workers. When one of the men repeats the cliché of Jewish cowardice and Polish courage: "Żydzi się bali, Żydzi byli bardziej tchórzliwi" (The Jews were afraid, the Jews were more cowardly), Srebrnik becomes argumentative and retorts, "Moje zdanie jest inne. . . . Ja, ja mówię coś innego, stale coś innego" (I have a different opinion. . . . I, I am saying something different, always something different), explaining in halting detail why it would have been impossible for the Jews to escape, including the fact that they would not have been able to count on Poles to hide them.[54] Srebrnik also challenges his interlocutors to explain why, if they were so brave, they did not come to the rescue of Polish priests incarcerated at Chełmno. He also reminds the men of his own bravery, when, despite having been shot and left for dead, he not only escaped from the camp but also had the presence of mind to break the lights of a German van, in order to thwart the manhunt. This sequence, in which Srebrnik, speaking in fluent Polish, attests to his agency, courage, and capacity to bear witness, contrasts markedly with the episode included in the film in which he appears to be standing passively and silently in front of the church in Chełmno. As we recall, Felman explains that "Sreb[r]nik's silence in front of the church, in the middle of the talkative, delirious, self-complacent Polish crowd" is a defense mechanism, which shields him from being revictimized by a virulently antisemitic mob.[55]

Although the outtakes show Srebrnik speaking Polish animatedly and at length, only his silence "in Polish," amid the antisemitic cackle in front of the church is foregrounded in the film. In fact, even in that scene, Srebrnik is hardly silent, since he is exchanging comments with those around him, but his words are for the most part inaudible and remain untranslated. Lanzmann does not allow Srebrnik's words in Polish to be heard, although elsewhere in the film the survivor gives long testimony in German. In fact, Srebrnik becomes a valuable witness for Lanzmann the moment the exchanges between him and the film director switch from communicating in Hebrew, via a translator (long sequences not included in the film), to a direct conversation in German. Srebrnik is the only eyewitness who can identify the site of mass murder: looking at the empty field covered with grass, he says, "Ja, das ist das Platz" (This is the place).[56]

Lanzmann's disregard for the Polish language is exacerbated by misspellings of Polish proper names, both in the English subtitles and in *Shoah: The Complete Text of the Acclaimed Holocaust Film*. Throughout the film and in the outtakes, Szymon Srebrnik's name is misspelled as "Simon Srebnik," the error that has been duplicated in all the English and French language interpretations of the film.[57] It is likely that the mistake did not originate with Lanzmann; yet in a number of postwar court documents, both Polish and Israeli, which the director probably consulted when he was searching for survivors, the witness's name was spelled as "Srebrnik," and he clearly introduced himself as "Srebrnik" as late as in his 1997 Shoah Foundation oral interview.[58] Polish witnesses' names are routinely misspelled: Czesław Borowy's name appears as "Borowi" and Henryk Gawkowski becomes "Henrik."[59] The Polish place names are skewered by bizarre misspellings (such as "Orkrobek" instead of what, to the Polish ear, clearly sounds like "Orchówek," or "Myndjewice" instead of "Międzyrzecz"), and all diacritical marks, which are specific to that language (in the names such as Sobibór, Chełmno, Łódź, and Oświęcim), are omitted.[60] In fact, the name of the town of Oświęcim appears in the subtitles and in *Shoah: The Complete Text of the Acclaimed Holocaust Film* only once, misspelled as "Oswiecin (Auschwitz)."[61] These flagrant distortions of Polish proper names may appear to a Polish eye as a weapon of linguistic revenge; in the case of place names, it is wrought on the locations that, in the past, bore silent, indifferent witness to the suffering of the Jews. The errors infract the fundamental rules of Polish orthography, in contrast to the correct spelling, including the *Umlaute*, of the German names used in the film.

These glaring errors also underscore that, for Lanzmann, Poland is not a land of the living but a vast and ghastly cemetery, or, in Lanzmann's words, "a non-site of memory."[62] The director often tells an anecdote about unexpectedly coming across the road sign, in the middle of the Polish countryside, bearing the name of Treblinka: "Then I arrived at Treblinka, and I saw the camp and these symbolic commemorative stones. I discovered that there was a train station and a village called Treblinka. The sign for 'Treblinka' on the road, the very act of naming it, was an incredible shock for me."[63] The director conveys similar astonishment in the film and in the outtakes by using long, unmoving shots of other signs with place names, such as "Treblinka," "Sobibór" and "Grabów." They mark these sites as places of life and thus puncture Lanzmann's topography of death, in which they have no right to exist other than in direct relation to the gas chambers.

Lanzmann is not unaware of the politics of naming and of the historical and political consequences of the Germanization of proper names: in the opening text of the film, he notes that, by a Nazi decree, Polish names of the towns were changed ("Chelmno to Kulmhof, Lodz to Litzmannstadt, Kolo to Warthbrücken").[64] The names of Polish villages and towns, some of them Germanized, can also be seen on the German train schedule document (*Fahrplananordnung* no. 587), displayed by Hilberg, which is one of the very few documents included in the film. For Tokarska-Bakir, the episode when Lanzmann sees the sign and discovers the village of Treblinka is symptomatic of Lanzmann's posture of colonial superiority with respect to Poland: "The demon of colonialism appears fully when Lanzmann finds out that Poland actually exists."[65] Although it is construed as a desire to re-create the past in the present, the gaze that the director casts upon Poland imposes colonial cultural norms and allows him to present Polish witnesses as a backward, exotic Other, and Poland as an empty, unchanging, archaic landscape. Contempt for the language of the natives and replacing it with a more civilized tongue have always been a part of a colonial mindset.

It seems that, throughout the Polish translation sequences, the Polish language itself, indelibly marked by the trauma of the extermination of Polish Jews, is put on trial before the camera. According to Kuryluk, the Polish villagers' lack of linguistic mastery exposes their prejudices: unlike Jan Piwoński, they cannot hide behind polite, euphemistic locutions.[66] The translator, Barbara Janicka, whom Lanzmann describes as being of "good Catholic stock," tries to mitigate both the antisemitic undertones in witnesses' remarks as well as Lanzmann's evidently anti-Polish sarcasms.[67] Polish commentators have pointed out Janicka's frustration with Lanzmann's disdain for Polish-speaking witnesses and his manipulation of the interviewing process. Indeed, in interviews after the release of the film, Janicka talked about the difficulties of working with Lanzmann and her discomfort with his brash interviewing tactics, such as asking the same question over and over again and ignoring the interviewees' answers. On at least two occasions, when asked the same question for the tenth time, the interlocutor became agitated and laughed, yet only the moment of laughter was included in the film.[68] Janicka is the only translator shown on screen, and her uneasiness is perceivable. The microphone records the hesitation in her voice, instances in which she sighs heavily or chokes up, and euphemisms she employs to translate offensive content, for which Lanzmann calls her out several times. Yet, in the same interviews, Janicka also expressed her admiration for Lanzmann's unrelenting effort to elicit testimony from witnesses for the sake of historical record and for his "painful sense of his own mission"; she also vouched for Lanzmann's honesty in his interactions with Polish witnesses.[69]

What emerges in the film is a tacit hierarchy of languages, with French as the master tongue that imposes order on a mass of linguistic fragments, although none of the witnesses speak it. Lanzmann's contentment with his growing competence in German is noticeable, and it turns into triumph in his cunningly extorted interview with Franz Suchomel.[70] He is respectful toward English, in consideration of its eminent status as the repository of scholarly knowledge about the Shoah, as exemplified in Raul Hilberg's expertise, although this neutrality of English is put to test in the emotionally charged interview with Abraham Bomba. He is reverent with respect to Hebrew, which he never learned, but that is the language of the Jewish homeland, where the idea to create *Shoah* gestated. The elevated status of Hebrew is also indicated in the choice of the Hebrew word for the title of the film. Yet the director is patronizing, occasionally disdainful, and sometimes hostile toward Polish, clearly an inferior language in the linguistic universe of the film. Although the director seems to take pride in his ability to speak foreign languages and claims, in *The Patagonian Hare*, that after hundreds of hours of filming in Poland he could understand the language quite well, only once can he be heard uttering Polish words. In one of the outtakes, in a conversation with a woman in Grabów, he says, *Dziękuję bardzo* (Thank you very much).[71]

Found in Translation: From False Witness to Co-witnessing

Protracted translation sequences in Lanzmann's *Shoah* often reveal the extent to which language itself is implicated in symbolic violence. As Tokarska-Bakir explains in *Legendy o krwi: Antropologia przesądu* (Blood libel myths: an anthropology of prejudice, 2008), negative stereotypes about Jews have been woven into the fabric of the Polish language in the form of linguistic fossils and dead metaphors, whose forgotten roots reach deep into the past. Such linguistic acts of negative valuation of the Jewish Other occur "naturally" and are not registered by language users since they originate in sources that may not be consciously grasped and acknowledged.[72] As has been frequently noted, Polish villagers in Lanzmann's film use the derogatory term "Żydki," which is a diminutive form of the word "Żydzi" (Jews), and its literal meaning is "little Jews." The word "Żydki" stands in contrast to a strange expression used by Mr. Piwoński, a relatively sophisticated speaker, who says "więźniowie narodowości żydowskiej" (the prisoners of Jewish nationality) instead of "Jews." Possibly, he chooses a euphemism because he is aware that the word "Jews" is often used in Polish as an invective; in the words of Polish philosopher Leszek Kołakowski, it has always functioned in the Polish language as "an abstract negative symbol."[73]

In the Srebrnik episode, however, another diminutive form is also frequently mentioned—namely, the Poles interacting with Srebrnik in front of the church refer to him as "pan Szymek," which is an affectionate form of the Polish proper name "Szymon," normally used to address children rather than adult men. In this case, the use of the diminutive indicates that, in the present time of the interview, Srebrnik's entourage is still interacting with the "boy singer" from the past, as if unable to accommodate the presence of an adult witness in their midst. The grammatical form of Srebrnik's first name thus carries the trace of the villagers' memory of the past. Lanzmann has often described his film as an attempt to resuscitate the past and to relive it in the present through the process of giving testimony. Whether he intended it or not, this act of "resuscitation" also refers to the way his soundtrack brings back the past uses of the Polish language. In these performative speech acts, accented, misshapen, or idiomatically marked words become arcs into the past. It is also in that sense that, to quote Felman, "The film speaks in the multiplicity of voices that, like Sreb[r]nik's, all transmit *beyond* what they can say in words."[74]

In light of Lanzmann's disparaging attitude toward the Polish language and his silencing of the testimony in Polish, I would like to draw attention to a different kind of "beyond what can be said in words"—or, rather, to what transcends the words that have been translated in the official version of the film and thus heard by the viewers and interpreters. I would argue that what transpires in the apertures of the film's translatory exchanges are moments of rapprochement between Polish and Jewish witnesses. These events of co-witnessing, which can be recovered from the director's own footage, are only liminally registered by his camera and microphone and therefore escape not only the director's but also the witnesses' attention and linguistic competence.

In the interviews with Polish witnesses, the imposition of Lanzmann's French is a means of exerting mastery over the narrative sequence. What eludes the director's supervision, however, is a variegated chorus of background voices, including direct exchanges between Polish-speaking participants, all of which are muted by the single-track communication in French between Lanzmann and the translator. As mentioned before, in the episode in front of the church in Chełmno, the translation into French glosses over the exchanges in Polish between Srebrnik and several people standing in the crowd. One of the women, for instance, tries to verify her memories by addressing questions to Srebrnik directly: "Ale założone były deski na schody?" (But did they put wooden planks on the steps?), to which he responds and then encourages her to speak for the camera: "Niech pani to powie!" (Please say it!). Some members of the group standing around Srebrnik give contradictory answers to Lanzmann's questions: "Wiedzieliśmy!" and "Ja nie wiedziałem!" (Yes, we knew; No, I didn't know), and they continuously vie to correct one another. One man interjects impatiently, "Państwo tłumaczą źle" (You are explaining it all wrong). By necessity, the translation belies the complexity of these verbal transactions, and it obscures occasional moments of camaraderie between Srebrnik and the Polish participants, as well as the survivor's agency in orchestrating this event.

A similar cacophony of voices can be heard in other episodes, such as in Lanzmann's interviews with the inhabitants of Grabów near Chełmno. This discordant multiplicity is impossible to approximate in a translation that channels it into a homologizing medium of the French language. We hear untranslated fragments of conversations, in which the Poles argue about the details of the events they witnessed and seek to confirm their recollections. It has been noted that Lanzmann's interlocutors in Polish villages and small towns are not highly articulate. Indeed, their answers to Lanzmann's questions often come out in garbled Polish, although each ungrammatical phrase immediately becomes corrected in the French translation: for instance, the grammatically incorrect "Tu jest taka morderstwo" (Here is such a murder) instantly becomes "Il était un meurtre" (It was a murder).[75] These errors, however, are sometimes so unusual that one hesitates to attribute them solely to low levels of literacy among the villagers. Rather, some of the Polish witnesses visibly struggle to bring to speech the memory of the events that have been encrusted by several decades of silence, the difficulty highlighted by constant (untranslated) repetitions: "To było coś okropnego, coś okropnego" (It was something horrible, something horrible). . . . "Ja to przeżywałem, przeżywałem!" (It was really hard for me, really hard for me!). In another sequence, Mr. Gawkowski, the driver of the locomotive, explains that he is sad because he saw so many people going to their deaths, and he keeps repeating, "Tak, tak, tak . . . tak, tak," the sound that in Polish, incidentally, is an onomatopoeia that imitates the sounds of the moving train.[76] Lanzmann's camera accidentally captures the affective charge of the witnesses' distress, as it has been conveyed in the use of language.

The effect of the intertwining of voices is amplified in the outtakes: in a long sequence at the site of the former camp in Chełmno, one of the Polish workers is particularly interested in Srebrnik's recollection because, at that time, he was a forced laborer, and he often worked together with the Jewish prisoners. Srebrnik and the man begin to reminisce together: the man is helping Srebrnik find the right words in Polish, while Srebrnik has a better recall of what actually happened and corrects the man's version of events several times, to which his interlocutor responds, "Tak, pan ma rację . . .

słusznie pan mówi" (Yes, you are right . . . you are saying it right). They even finish each other's sentences, and, as their memories coalesce, they turn to face each other and repeatedly nod their heads.[77] One of the episodes that they both witnessed and are now trying to re-create is the accident when one of the gassing vans transporting the Jewish inmates from the castle to the forest slid on the snow and hit the ditch, spilling its gruesome cargo onto the road. The two men saw the accident from very different vantage points: the Polish worker was watching from a distance (the Germans chased Polish onlookers away to a nearby forest), while Srebrnik was brought in from the camp with a work detail to clean up and load the bodies back into the van. Eventually, to Lanzmann's question whether there was only one driver in the van, Srebrnik and the man reply in unison: "Jeden był" (There was one).[78]

In the same conversation with the Polish workers, Srebrnik inquires about the family named Król. What he really seems interested in, however, is whether raspberry bushes are still growing in the vicinity, and he keeps

Simon Srebrnik in conversation with a Polish worker. Created by Claude Lanzmann during the filming of *Shoah*. (Used by permission of the United States Holocaust Memorial Museum and Yad Vashem, the Holocaust Martyrs and Heroes' Remembrance Authority, Jerusalem.)

returning to the question about "maliny" (including in the sections of the interview when he is conversing with Lanzmann in German, though he interjects the Polish word "maliny," for which he does not know the German equivalent). Srebrnik's fluent but ungrammatical Polish bespeaks his nonbelonging, but it also conveys his attachment to the place "tam gdzie rosły maliny" (with raspberry bushes). It seems that it is the raspberries that have truly "stayed in [Srebrnik's] memory" ("w mej pamięci tkwi") rather than the song about "mały biały domek" (the little white house) he was forced to sing on the river and that Lanzmann asks him to reenact.[79] Thus Srebrnik's return to Chełmno is a return to his native tongue, whose taste he remembers, literally, on his tongue through the recollection of "maliny" and that triggers the recollection of the past. The relation between Srebrnik's return to Poland and the word connoting nourishment is not coincidental: both in the film and in the outtakes, he recalls the unbearable hunger that he experienced in the Łódź Ghetto. He says that hunger made him indifferent to death and stunted his ability to experience grief for the dead and dying relatives; in comparison with hunger, everything else was "ganz egal" (all the same). In the outtakes, while he answers the questions about what happened in Chełmno, Srebrnik keeps circling back to the memory of hunger. When asked if he was thinking about his mother, who had been murdered in Chełmno, he gives what sounds like a callous answer: "Kto myślał o matce, każdy myślał zjeść coś, kawałeczek chleba" (Who thought about the mother if everyone only thought to eat something, a little piece of bread).[80] Lanzmann, however, has no interest in Srebrnik's recollections from the ghetto; in fact, he refused Srebrnik's request that they also travel to Łódź, where Srebrnik was hoping to find Marynia, the daughter of Mr. Miszczak, who, after his escape from Chełmno, found him in a pigsty and nursed him to health.[81] Is there a connection, perhaps, between Srebrnik's mother tongue, the language of hunger that he spoke in Łódź, and his sudden recollection of his mother's purse, containing documents and family photographs, which he found in a pile of victims' effects? It is not coincidental that this memory imposes itself together with the recollection of "maliny," though he says he felt "nothing" about his mother's death.

Most likely, Polish was not Srebrnik's only mother tongue. Yiddish was also spoken in the Łódź Ghetto; in fact, Chaim Rumkowski, the chairman of the Łódź *Judenrat*, had a vision to make Yiddish an official language of his "kingdom," and the teachers were being trained to implement it in schools.[82] Lanzmann feels no connection to the vanished world of Eastern European *Yiddishkeit*, which Rumkowski, however misguided his rule in the ghetto may have been, was trying to preserve. In "The Languages of Pain in *Shoah*," Nelly Furman comments on Lanzmann's exclusion of Yiddish, the language of the majority of the Ashkenazi Jews, even though it keeps appearing, often unexpectedly, throughout the film. In Furman's view, "Yiddish provides the audible axis, the sonorous vortex of the deaths being evoked" in the film, and it striates the sound track with "the faint murmur of the language of the majority of those who died."[83]

In the Polish sequences, several Polish witnesses recall the sounds of "Jewish," though most of these resurfacings of Yiddish in their accounts are pejorative: Borowy, for instance, mimics the sounds of Yiddish as "ra, ra, ra" and "ay vey or oyey," and as the sounds of the fiddles and the honking of the geese.[84] A man in Grabów, however, sitting on the doorstep of a formerly Jewish house, claims that he was fluent in Yiddish when he was a child since most of his friends were Jewish. On Lanzmann's request, he says a few words in Yiddish, but the director discredits his knowledge because he doesn't know the word "shtetl." After pronouncing the Yiddish words, the man wipes his eyes; he also keeps repeating, "Ja byłem obecny przy tym, wszystko widziałem . . . Tak, ja tam byłem!" (I was present at that, I saw everything, yes, I was there!).[85] The traces of Yiddish, the language that, before the war, was woven into the fabric of colloquial Polish, also crop up in witnesses' speech. Mr. Gawkowski, for instance, the driver of the locomotive, when describing his memories of Treblinka, uses the word "sztynk" to describe the terrible smell of decomposing bodies.[86] In diametrically opposed ways, the sounds of Polish for Srebrnik ("maliny") and the sounds of Yiddish ("ra, ra, ra") for Polish witnesses function as acoustic traces of the past, the traces that are released in these often untranslated sequences. As we have seen in frequent references to smell and food, these words and sounds also carry olfactory and even gustatory sense memories.

A peculiar quid pro quo occurs when Lanzmann asks whether Polish inhabitants of Grabów knew where the synagogue was located, and since they do not know the word "synagoga," the translator explains that the word meant "the Jewish church" ("żydowski kościół"). The same interlocutors, however, later make references to "bóżnica" (misspelled in *Shoah: The Complete Text of the Acclaimed Holocaust Film* and in the subtitles as "buzinica"), a common Polish word for the Jewish place of worship.[87] This instance of mistranslation, this time between Polish witnesses and Lanzmann and his Polish translator, who also keeps using the word "synagoga," is used by the director to emphasize the villagers' ignorance of Jewish customs. This effect is amplified in the preceding episode, in which Lanzmann himself performs a unique act of surrogate witnessing in front of the building that used to be the Grabów synagogue and is now a furniture warehouse. The director, alone before the camera, reads a letter, written in January 1942 by Jakub Szulman, the rabbi of Grabów, to his friends in Łódź, in which Szulman described, in sentences brimming with despair and horror, mass executions taking place in Chełmno (about which he had learnt from an escapee).[88]

Lanzmann's reading of the letter, in which he takes the place of the murdered rabbi, is a dramatic attempt to reenact in the present the abysmal desolation and the horrifying death of the victims of Chełmno. Yet the scene also functions as a somber indictment of Poles' forgetting and desecration of Jewish culture and religion. We learn from the outtakes that Lanzmann shot this scene multiple times, which intensifies the effect of a sacred ritual and confers on the director the status of the witness par excellence to the suffering of the Jews. Lanzmann thus rescues the rabbi's testimony from the unworthy and backward Polish eyewitnesses, some of whom knew him in person, and purifies it in the solemn ritual of reading. In ventriloquizing the rabbi, however, Lanzmann also makes him speak in French, thus erasing further the original Yiddish of Szulman's searing testament, the language of the majority of the victims who perished at Chełmno.[89]

Conclusions: *Shoah* and the Unwitnessed Cotestimony

While Lanzmann has repeatedly stated that his intention in the film was to create a chorus of voices, his interviewing style, his discomfort with Polish witnesses, and his contempt for the Polish language act to suppress the plurality of voices in Polish, the plurality that he himself has summoned into existence. As I have attempted to show through examples of the exchanges in Polish between Srebrnik and Lanzmann's Polish witnesses, the director's representations of Poland as a landscape of death have obliterated the fleeting yet poignant moments of co-witnessing that occasionally transpire between the survivor and his Polish interlocutors.

In his notes from the first trip to Poland in 1978, Lanzmann expressed his outrage at Polish witnesses' indifference: "30 mln witnesses, deaf, dumb and blind."[90] In response, Jean-Charles Szurek asked Lanzmann to consider what it meant to live in the country marked by the trauma of the genocide, which its inhabitants "bore witness to but didn't see,"[91] while Jacek Kuroń remarked that "all of us, who lived there, in that valley of death, were in a way mutilated, and *Shoah* lays bare these ravages of the Polish spirit."[92] In one of the outtakes, Mr. Gawkowski speaks with great sadness about the horrors he saw from the small window of his locomotive: "Widziałem na własne oczy, nigdy się nie zaprę. . . . przeżywam do dzisiejszego dnia" (I saw with my own eyes, I will never deny it. . . . I am still reliving it today).[93] In Polish, the expression "nigdy się nie zaprę" (I will never deny it) brings to mind the New Testament episode when Christ's disciple Simon Peter boasts that he would never forsake the Lord, even if everyone else did (Matthew 26:33), and then later denies three times that he even knew the Lord (26:70–74). Gawkowski's expression therefore grounds his witnessing to the murder of the Jews in his Christian faith, underscoring its gravitas.[94] By no means is this avowal sufficient to counter the poison of Christian antisemitism that permeates the words of Polish witnesses, but it bespeaks the deep need of many of them to affirm their own existence as Polish Christians by bearing witness to what happened to the Jews.[95]

The potential for Polish witnessing to the suffering of the Jews, both during and after the war, was undermined in multiple ways: first, by Germany's brutal occupation of Poland, which Hitler saw as the "wild east" to be stripped of existing culture and history and resettled with non-Poles. Second, it was mutilated by Polish antisemitism, which was twinned with the nationalist ethos of heroic struggle against the oppressor, and which sometimes turned murderous. Last, it was smothered by the official communist narrative of World War II, in which the extermination of Polish Jews was assimilated into the narrative of Polish victimhood. Yet that witness did happen, and it must be drawn out of the black hole of Lanzmann's (mis)translations. Such recovery, which the study of the outtakes has now made possible, will allow us to restructure the testimonial force field in the film and open up a space for Polish and Jewish co-witnessing, the phenomenon that both the director and many of the commentators of the film have foreclosed.

The outtakes have now become a part of the testimonial archive, and their availability has disrupted Lanzmann's narrative of the Holocaust and reshaped his artistic vision. As a result, we can now participate in the past's uncanny return, even against Lanzmann's intention. On the margins of his elaborately crafted narrative, and in numerous instances in the outtakes, his camera and microphone recorded the plurality of languages and voices that used to coexist in Poland.

Lanzmann described his film as a meeting place: "Nobody meets anyone in *Shoah* . . . , but there is a corroboration in spite of this—I make them meet."[96] Important encounters, often face to face, also occur between at least one of the survivors and Polish witnesses, and even between Polish witnesses themselves, within, outside, and in between the frames of the film's theatrical release—encounters which, to Lanzmann's inestimable credit, he himself made possible. Among the Babelian scattering of languages in the film, these fleeting exchanges between the witnesses escape the mastery of French, English, and German as the languages in which to tell the history of the Shoah in Poland. Henryk Szlajfer, in his book *Polacy/Żydzi: zderzenie stereotypów* (Poles/Jews: a clash of stereotypes) argues that we must find a way to forge a "a rift in the space of silence" (wyłom w przestrzeni milczenia) that the "clash of stereotypes" has imposed on the memory of the Shoah in Poland.[97] Perhaps recovering the moments of Polish-Jewish co-witnessing and listening to the performance of the Polish language in the film, in the outtakes as well as in the responses to Lanzmann in Poland, would finally bring about such a "rift," as well as facilitate a rapprochement between Polish and Jewish memories of the Holocaust, against the myths founded on the mechanisms of exclusion. Perhaps this would be Act Four and a satisfactory denouement of the dramatic itinerary of the reception of Lanzmann's film in Poland. No, Poland is not yet done with this film.

Notes

1. French daily newspaper *Libération*, for instance, published a headline article entitled "La Pologne au banc des accusés," which was frequently cited in Poland as proof of an anti-Polish campaign in France. *Libération*, April 25, 1985.

2. This statement was made at the nineteenth plenary of the KC PZPR (the Central Committee of the Polish United Workers' Party). See Ewa Ochman, "Próby legitimizacji władzy w Polsce po zniesieniu stanu wojennego: przypadek *Shoah* Lanzmanna," in *Pamięć Shoah: Kulturowe reprezentacje i praktyki upamiętniania,* ed. Tomasz Majewski and Anna Zajdler-Janiszewska (Łódź: Oficyna, 2011): 337–60; here, 348–49. All the translations of the passages from the Polish sources are mine unless indicated otherwise.

3. Lanzmann did not include the footage from his interview with Władysław Bartoszewski, the founding member of Żegota (Council for the Aid to the Jews) and a Polish Righteous among the Nations. According to Lanzmann, Bartoszewski was "incapable of re-living the past" and therefore useless as a witness. See Dominick LaCapra, "Lanzmann's *Shoah*: 'Here There Is No Why,'" in *Claude Lanzmann's* Shoah: *Key Essays,* ed. Stuart Liebman (Oxford: Oxford University Press, 2007), 191–229; here, 213.

4. See Anson Rabinach's review of *Shoah* in the *Nation*, March 15, 1986, 313–17.

5. Stefan Korboński, *The Jews and Poles in World War II* (New York: Hippocrene, 1989). During the war, Korboński was a resistance fighter for the Home Army and a prominent member of the Polish Secret State. In his book, he expressed the sentiments of the Polish North American émigré community, which protested against Lanzmann's "calumnies."

6. Anna Bikont, "A on krzyczał: 'Wszyscy jesteście kapo!'" *Gazeta Wyborcza*, October 4, 1997, 3.

7. Ochman, "Próby legitimizacji władzy," 344.

8. Grzegorz Niziołek, "Lęk przed afektem," *Didaskalia* 116 (2016): 9–17; here, 9.

9. Ochman, "Próby legitimizacji władzy," 339.

10. Ochman, 337.

11. According to Ochman, this was the first time that opinions about *Shoah* were publically expressed by individuals who had actually seen Lanzmann's film ("Próby legitimizacji władzy," 351).

12. Jan Rem, "Szpetni i dzicy," *Polityka*, August 3, 1985.

13. Artur Sandauer, "*Shoah* a sprawa polska," *Polityka*, August 3, 1985.

14. Ochman, "Próby legitimizacji władzy," 357.

15. Zygmunt Kałużyński, "Odmawiam przebaczenia," *Polityka*, December 7, 1985.

16. Dawid Warszawski, "Historia i fałszerze," *KOS*, the publication of Komitet Obrony Społecznej (Committee for Social Resistance), May 19, 1985. Konstanty Gebert is a prominent member of the Jewish community in Poland and the founder and coeditor of the journal *Midrasz*.

17. Jacek Kuroń wrote, "What was the difference between Poles and Jews during the German occupation? Well, the difference was that, on my way to the swimming pool, I was taking a tram ride through the ghetto, and I saw people die on the other side of the wall." "O filmie *Shoah*," *Tygodnik Mazowsze*, November 7, 1985.

18. Turowicz, "*Shoah* w polskich oczach," *Tygodnik Powszechny*, November 10, 1985.

19. The exemplary story of Father Maksymilian Kolbe, who volunteered to be executed in Auschwitz in place of another man, was often brought up, as well as the fact that many Jewish children were hidden in Catholic convents.

20. Claude Lanzmann, *The Patagonian Hare: A Memoir*, trans. Frank Wynne (New York: Farrar, Straus & Giroux, 2012), 496.

21. Bikont, "A on krzyczał," 1. One of the reasons for poor attendance at the screenings was the fact that they were not advertised or announced in the designated movie theaters' repertoires.

22. Piotr Forecki, *Od* Shoah *do* Strachu: *Spory o polsko-żydowską przeszłość i pamięć w debatach publicznych* (Poznań: Wydawnictwo Poznańskie, 2010), 149.

23. In interviews immediately following the screening and later in *The Patagonian Hare*, Lanzmann expressed his indignation about Rywin's "treacherous ways" and broken promises, through which the latter had allegedly secured the director's consent to broadcast the film in Poland (even though Lanzmann initially liked Rywin, whom he had immediately recognized as a Polish Jew).

24. Jan Tomasz Gross, *Sąsiedzi: historia zagłady żydowskiego miasteczka* (Sejny: Fundacja Pogranicze, 2000). A year later, Gross published the English version of the book, *Neighbors: The Destruction of the Jewish Community in Jedwabne, Poland* (Princeton, NJ: Princeton University Press, 2001).

25. Jan Tomasz Gross, *Fear: Antisemitism in Poland after Auschwitz: An Essay in Historical Interpretation* (New York: Random House, 2006). Two years later, Gross published a Polish version of the book, *Strach: antysemityzm w Polsce tuż po wojnie. Historia moralnej zapaści* (Kraków: Znak, 2008).

26. Some of the seminal works include: Anna Bikont, *My z Jedwabnego* [(We, from Jedwabne) Wołowiec: Wydawnictwo Czarne, 2004]; Jan Grabowski, *Juden-jagdt: Polowanie na Żydów. Studium dziejów pewnego powiatu* (Warszawa: Stowarzyszenie Centrum Badań nad Zagładą Żydów, 2011); *Hunt for the Jews: Betrayal and Murder in German-Occupied Poland* (Indianapolis: Indiana University Press, 2013); Barbara Engelking's *Jest taki piękny słoneczny dzień . . . Losy Żydów szukających ratunku na wsi polskiej 1942–1945*. Warszawa:

Stowarzyszenie Centrum Badań nad Zagładą Żydów, 2011 [(Such a beautiful, sunny day. . . . Jews seeking refuge in the Polish countryside, 1942–1945) Jerusalem: Yad Vashem, 2016]; Jan Grabowski et al., *Dalej jest noc. Losy Żydów w wybranych powiatach okupowanej Polski* [(It is still night: The fate of Jews in selected counties in occupied Poland) Warsaw: Stowarzyszenie Centrum Badań nad Zagładą Zydów, 2017]; Joanna Tokarska-Bakir, *Okrzyki pogromowe [(Pogrom cries)* Wołowiec: Wydawnictwo Czarne, 2012]; and *Pod klątwą. Społeczny portret pogromu kieleckiego. Warszawa: Wydawnictwo Czarna Owca, 2017* [(Accursed: a social portrait of the Kielce Pogrom) Warsaw: Czarna Owca, 2018].

27. The film, narrated by well-known Polish actor Piotr Fronczewski, included numerous quotations from Hanna Krall's *Dowody na istnienie* (Proofs of existence, 1995), a series of literary reportages about Jewish life in Poland before and during the war. In Sue Vice's view, *Po-lin* was "an implicit riposte to *Shoah.*" See Vice, *Shoah* (London: Palgrave Macmillan, 2011), 75.

28. "'This is not an anti-Polish film at all'—A Meeting with Lanzmann to End the 2nd Joseph Conrad Festival," November 8, 2010, http://en.conradfestival.pl/a/ 880,this-is-not-an-anti-polish-film-at-all-a-meeting-with-lanzmann-to-end -of-the-2nd-conrad-festival (accessed August 27, 2019).

29. See Anna Napiórkowska, "Pocięte świadectwo," *Gazeta, Wyborcza,* March 24, 2010; Anna Kałuża, "Dylematy sztuki i moralności," Witryna Czasopism.pl., May 22, 2003; Wojciech A. Wierzewski, "Opcja na prawo: a conversation with Natalia Dueholm," *Niezbędny dialog,* December 7, 2010; and Sebastian Smoliński, "Dokument czy ikona," *Kultura Liberalna,* February 12, 2013.

30. Joanna Tokarska-Bakir, "Spowiedź farmazona," Dwutygodnik.com, December 2010, http://www.dwutygodnik.com/artykul/1706-spowiedz-farmazona.html (accessed August 27, 2019).

31. See, for example, Tomasz Majewski, "Sub specie mortis: Notes on Claude Lanzmann's *Shoah*" (*Kultura Współczesna,* no. 4, 2003), and "Dyskurs publiczny po Shoah" in *Pamięć Shoah: Kulturowe reprezentacje i praktyki upamiętnienia,* 237–44; Sonia Ruszkowska, *Każdemu własna śmierć: o przywracaniu podmiotowości ofiarom Zagłady* (Warsaw: Instytut Badań Literackich PAN, 2014); and Katarzyna Liszka, *Etyka i pamięć o Zagładzie* (Warsaw: Instytut Badań Literackich PAN, 2016).

32. In February 2018, the Polish government passed a law criminalizing any activity or publication that besmirched Poland's honor. Following an international outcry, the law was partly reversed in June 2018.

33. Timothy Garton Ash, "'The Life of Death': *Shoah*—A Film by Claude Lanzmann," in Liebman, *Claude Lanzmann's* Shoah, 135–47; here, 137.
34. Interview with Claude Lanzmann, *Cineaste*, Spring 2011, 4.
35. Garton Ash, "The Life of Death," 143.
36. See comments elsewhere in this chapter regarding the spelling of Czesław Borowy's last name.
37. Bikont, "A on krzyczał," 6–9.
38. Quoted in a review of *Shoah* in *Długi Montaż*, 19.
39. Claude Lanzmann, "L'extrême droite au pouvoir, c'est une fausse peur," *Paris Match*, March 5, 2017; translation mine.
40. Anna Matałowska, "Ludzie garną się do skandalu" (interview with Barbara Janicka), *Polityka*, May 11, 1985, 1–4; here, 1.
41. See Maciej Nowicki, "Rachunek krzywd po Auschwitz" (A calculation of wrongs after Auschwitz), interview with Claude Lanzmann in *Newsweek*, January 27, 2011, http://polska.newsweek.pl/rachunek-krzywd-po-auschwitz,71020,1,1.html (accessed August 27, 2019).
42. Magdalena Nowicka, "Żyd, czarownica i stara szafa: O konstruowaniu żydowskości autorów piszących o 'trudnej' przeszłości," *Teksty Drugie* 4 (2012): 251–66; here, 251 and 258.
43. Shoshana Felman, "In an Era of Testimony: Claude Lanzmann's *Shoah*," *Yale French Studies* 79 (1991): 38–81.
44. Nelly Furman, "The Languages of Pain in *Shoah*," in *Auschwitz and After: Race, Culture, and the Jewish Question in France*, ed. Lawrence D. Kritzman (New York: Routledge, 2014), 299–312; here, 299.
45. Kaufmann describes her feelings of frustration, disorientation, and shock when, on the spot, she had to translate horrifying stories that "hit her like a fist in the stomach." See Francine Kaufmann, "Interview et interprétation consécutive dans le film *Shoah*, de Claude Lanzmann," *Meta: Journal des traductions* 39, no. 4 (1993): 664–73; here, 665.
46. Felman, "In the Era of Testimony," 45.
47. Anny Dayan-Rosenman writes that central to Lanzmann's film is "the necessity to translate, the urgency to transmit, and at the heart of all this work, the certainty that there exists a core that resists all translations, all effort to transmit it." See "L'écho du silence," in *Au sujet de* Shoah: *le film de Claude Lanzmann*, ed. Bernard Cuau et al. (Paris: Belin, 1990), 193; translation mine. According to Gabriela Stoicea, the multiplicity of languages in *Shoah* is "emblematic of the radical foreignness of all traumatic experience, even to its own participants."

See Stoicea, "The Difficulties of Verbalizing Trauma: Translation and the Economy of Loss in Claude Lanzmann's *Shoah*," *Journal of the Midwest Modern Language Association* 39, no. 2 (2006): 43–53; here, 45.

48. See comments elsewhere in this chapter regarding the spelling of Szymon Srebrnik's name.

49. Joanna Beata Michlic, *Poland's Threatening Other: The Image of the Jew from 1880 to the Present* (Lincoln: University of Nebraska Press, 2006), 1.

50. Although anti-Muslim and anti-immigrant sentiments now appear to be stronger in Poland than antisemitic attitudes, the term "Jews" continues to epitomize strangeness in the Polish xenophobic imaginary. This figurative substitution became apparent when, at an antirefugee rally in Wrocław in November 2015, participants burnt an effigy of the Orthodox Jew.

51. Claude Lanzmann, *Shoah* Collection, Interview with Czesław Borow[y] (RG-60.5032, Film ID 3348, Camera Rolls 46–48, 56; Film ID 3349, Camera Roll 49; Film ID 3350, Camera Rolls 50–52; Film ID 3351, Camera Rolls 53–55, US Holocaust Memorial Muse and Yad Vashem and State of Israel. Here, Film ID 3349, Camera Roll 49). All translations of the excerpts from the outtakes are mine.

52. Interview with Jan Piwoński (RG-60.5031, Film ID 3339, Camera Rolls 7–8; Film ID 3340, Camera Rolls 9–11; Film ID 3341, Camera Roll 12; Film ID 3342, Camera Rolls 13; 15–20; Film ID 3343, Camera Roll 14: Film ID 3344, Camera Rolls 20–21; Film ID 3345, Camera Rolls 22–24; Film ID 3346, Camera Rolls 25–27; Film ID 3347, Camera Rolls 31–32); here, Film ID 3345, Camera Rolls 22–24.

53. Interview with Czesław Borow[y] (RG-60.5032, Film ID 3349, Camera Roll 49).

54. Interview with Simon Sreb[r]nik (RG-60.5024, Film ID 3278, Camera Rolls 1–3; Film ID 3279, Camera Rolls 4–7; Film ID 3280, Camera Rolls 45–48A; Film ID 3281, Camera Rolls 49–50; Film ID 3282, Camera Rolls 51–55: Film ID 3283, Camera Rolls 56–59; Film ID 3284, Camera Rolls 60–63; Film ID 3285, Camera Rolls 70–82; Film ID 3286, Camera Rolls 83–85; Film ID 3287, Camera Rolls 86; 102–5; Film ID 3288, Camera Rolls 106–9; Film ID 3289, Camera Rolls 111–12; 116; Film ID 3290, Coupe Soul + Fin Chełmno II Montage; Film ID 3291, Camera Roll 112A; Film ID 3292 Coupes); here, Film ID 3282, Camera Rolls 51–55.

55. Felman, "In an Era of Testimony," 67. Other interpreters have followed suite; Michel Deguy, for instance, also writes of Srebrnik as "silent and smiling, in Chelmno among the Polish parishioners." See *Au sujet de* Shoah, 21.

56. The correct grammatical form in German is "der Platz."

57. Polish scholars writing about Lanzmann's film automatically have been correct-
ing the spelling to "Srebrnik," since it is a derivative of a common Polish word
"*srebro*" (silver).

58. Srebrnik's name is spelled as "Srebrnik" in the protocols of Chełmno trials in
Łódź, in June 23, 1945 (http://www.holocaustresearchproject.org/survivor/
srebrnik.html, accessed August 27, 2019), in the protocols of Chełmno trials in
Bonn 1959–1960 (see USHMM archive collection, RG-14.110m, files 3243–52),
and in the transcripts of the witness testimony from the Eichmann trials (see
the English translation of the transcripts, *The Trial of Adolf Eichmann Record of
Proceedings in the District Court of Jerusalem*, vol. 3 [State of Israel Ministry
of Justice, Jerusalem, 1993], 1197–2001).

59. I would like to thank Roma Sendyka for pointing out the misspelling of
Borowy's name.

60. Claude Lanzmann, *Shoah: The Complete Text of the Acclaimed Holocaust Film*
(New York: Da Capo, 1995), 15 and 89.

61. Lanzmann, *Shoah*, 12.

62. Marc Chevrie and Hervé le Roux, "Site and Speech: An Interview with Claude
Lanzmann about *Shoah*," trans. Stuart Liebman, in *Claude Lanzmann's* Shoah,
37–49; here, 39.

63. Chevrie and le Roux, "Site and Speech," 43.

64. Lanzmann, *Shoah*, 1.

65. See Tokarska-Bakir, "Spowiedź farmazona." See also Niziołek, "Lęk przed afektem," 14.

66. Ewa Kuryluk, "Memory and Responsibility: Claude Lanzmann's *Shoah*," *New
Criterion,* November 1986, 14–20; here, 17. Jean-Charles Szurek comments
that "however important it is to comprehend their relationship with the Jews,
when their words are translated, they have been emasculated as they cross the
language barrier." See Szurek, "From the Jewish Question to the Polish Question," in Liebman, *Claude Lanzmann's* Shoah, 149–69; here, 153.

67. Lanzmann, *The Patagonian Hare*, 481.

68. Quoted in Jerzy Płażewski, "Jak się pan czuje w tym pożydowskim sklepie?"
Magazyn Filmowy SFP 27 (2013): 80.

69. Matałowska, "Ludzie garną się."

70. See Erin McGlothlin, "Listening to the Perpetrators in Claude Lanzmann's
Shoah," *Colloquia Germanica* 43, no. 3 (2019): 235–71.

71. Short interviews near Grabów (RG-60.5039, Film ID 3386, Camera Rolls CH
18, 19, 21; 90 Maisons Grabów Part 1; Film ID 3387, Camera Rolls CH 18, 19,

21; 90 Maisons Grabów Part 2; Film ID 3388, Camera Rolls CH 1–6 Grabów Moulin [White 24] Part 1; Film ID 3389, Camera Rolls CH 1–6 Grabów Moulin [White 24] Part 2; Film ID 3390, Grabów Village No. 30 [White 25]: Film ID 3391, Grabów Village No. 30 [White 26]; Film ID 3392, Grabów Synagogue [White 27]; Film ID 3393, Grabów Le Marche [White 28]; Film ID 3394, Grabów Le Paille [White 29]; Film ID 3395, Repiquage Denteile eglise Grabów); here, Film ID 3386, Camera Rolls CH 18, 19, 21; 90.

72. Joanna Tokarska-Bakir, *Legendy o krwi: Antropologia przesądu* (Warsaw: Wydawnictwo WAB, 2008), 39–47.

73. Quoted by Tokarska-Bakir in *Legendy o krwi*, 43.

74. Felman, "In an Era of Testimony," 77 (emphasis mine).

75. In the subtitles and in *Shoah: The Complete Text of the Acclaimed Holocaust Film*, the sentence is translated into English as "because what happened here . . . was a murder" (2). The grammatical error is very uncommon in Polish, since the man uses the feminine form of the adjective ("taka") to qualify a noun that is gender neutral ("morderstwo")," though it is possible that the word he had in mind was a feminine noun "zbrodnia" (crime) but replaced it at the moment of the utterance. It is also unusual that the man says "Tu jest" (Here is) instead of "To było" (It was), which perhaps indicates the immediacy of this recollection in the present time and place.

76. See the interview with Henryk Gawkowski and Treblinka railway workers (RG-60.5036, Film ID 3362, Camera Rolls 4–7; Film ID 3363, Camera Rolls 8–10; Film ID 3364, Camera Rolls 11–13; Film ID 3365, Camera Rolls 14–16; Film ID 3366; Camera Rolls 17–18; Film ID 3367, Camera Rolls 19–21; Film ID 3818; ID 3743, Treblinka 18; Film ID 3744, Treblinka 19; Film ID 3368, Camera Roll 71; Film 3370, 3 int. loco; Film ID 3371, 3bis entre engage train; Film ID 3372, 3ter derrière le loco); here, Film ID 3818 and Film ID 3368, Camera Roll 71. For the onomatopoeic imitation of the sounds of the moving train, see one of the most popular poems for children in the Polish language, Julian Tuwim's *Lokomotywa* (Locomotive).

77. Nicholas Chare analyzes the language of gestures in *Shoah* and concludes that Lanzmann provides a space "in which the binding of gesture and speech, their co-emergence, can be fostered." See Nicholas Chare, "Gesture in *Shoah*," *Journal for Cultural Research* 19, no. 1 (2015): 30–42; here, 38.

78. Interview with Simon Sreb[r]nik (RG-60.5024, Film ID 3283, Camera Rolls 56–59). Only fragments of these exchanges are recorded in Lanzmann's transcripts of Srebrnik's conversations with the Polish workers.

79. As we learn from the outtakes, Lanzmann asked Srebrnik to sing the song over and over again, which, in a way, paralleled his request to Suchomel that he sing a song about Treblinka numerous times.

80. Interview with Simon Sreb[r]nik (RG-60.5024, Film ID 3286, Camera Rolls 83–85).

81. Lanzmann did make a trip to Łódź, however, and he included a prolonged shot of the Jewish cemetery in the film, to accompany survivor Paula Biren's testimony.

82. I would like to thank Ewa Wiatr, one of the coauthors of *Encyklopedia getta: Niedokończony projekt archiwistów z getta łódzkiego* (Wydawnictwo: WUŁ–Uniwersytet Łódzki, 2014), for providing me with this information.

83. Furman, "The Languages of Pain," 307 and 308. In one of the outtakes, Lanzmann actually asks Srebrnik whether he also sang songs in Yiddish while in Chełmno, to which he replies that he did not.

84. Interview with Czesław Borow[y] (RG-60.5032, Film ID 3351, Camera Rolls 53–55).

85. Short interviews near Grabów (RG-60.5039, Film ID 3386, Camera Rolls CH 18, 19, 21, 90).

86. From Yiddish: "sztynken" (sztinken), to "stink." I would like to thank Karolina Szymaniak for her help with establishing the etymology of this word.

87. Lanzmann's Polish interlocutors in Włodawa, on the other hand, are familiar with the word "synagoga," although they use the familiar term "bóżnica."

88. Short interviews near Grabów (RG-60.5039, Film ID 3392, Grabów Synagogue [White 27]).

89. Lanzmann came across rabbi Szulman's letter in Léon Poliakov's book *Bréviaire de la haine* (1951), from which he seems to be reading in the film. The book was translated into English as *Harvest of Hate* (New York: Stratford, 1954), and the letter can be found on pages 153–54. See a photograph of the original of the letter, written in Yiddish, at https://issuu.com/remybesson/docs/grabow/ 7 (accessed August 27, 2019). I would like to thank Rémy Besson for his help with establishing the provenance of the letter.

90. Quoted in Bikont, "A on krzyczał," 9.

91. Szurek, "From the Jewish Question," 62.

92. Kuroń, "O filmie *Shoah*."

93. Interview with Henryk Gawkowski and Treblinka railway workers (RG-60.5036, Film ID 3368, Camera Roll 71).

94. Dominick LaCapra perceives Gawkowski's demeanor very differently, interpreting his "sigh of sorrow for dead Jews [as] feigned and histrionic." LaCapra, "Lanzmann's *Shoah*," 213.

95. In one of the outtakes, Lanzmann interviews a priest in Chełmno. The priest's answers to Lanzmann's questions about how much he knew about what had happened to the Jews of Chełmno are evasive and contradictory, yet he also states, several times, that "to nie była ich wina" (it was not their fault) that they were locked up in the church and then murdered. The priest is clearly familiar with the teachings of Vatican II, and in a clumsy way is trying to counter the canard, expressed in the infamous church episode by Kantorowski (and then later also by Borowy) that Jews were being punished for the crime of deicide. To Lanzmann's question why it was the Jews that were targeted, he answers that it happened as a result of Hitler's ideology, which he had developed in *Mein Kampf*. Interview with Simon Sreb[r]nik (RG-60.5024, Film ID 3284, Camera Rolls 60–63).

96. Claude Lanzmann, "Seminar with Claude Lanzmann," *Yale French Studies* 79 (1991): 82–99; here, 84.

97. Henryk Szlajfer's expression "wyłom w przestrzeni milczenia" is quoted by Piotr Forecki in *Od* Shoah *do* Strachu: *Spory o polsko-żydowska przeszłość i pamięć w debatach publicznych* (Wydawnictwo Poznańskie: Poznań, 2010), 116.

6

Yehuda Lerner's Living Words

Translation and Transcription in *Sobibór, October 14, 1943, 4 p.m.*

Gary Weissman

An Impossible Book

In a 2006 interview in which Claude Lanzmann discusses "the logic of creativity" that informs the choices he made while filming *Shoah*, his interviewer, Jean-Michel Frodon, suggests that these choices were specific to cinematography:

> *If you had chosen to make a book of* Shoah, *it would also have been creative, but you would have made other choices . . .*
> A book? What a crazy idea! *Shoah* is not a book, it is a film. It would be impossible for it to be a book.
> *Why?*
> Because . . . the faces. [Claude Lanzmann hesitates] The face is something that is totally incompatible in any other context.[1]

What Lanzmann declares impossible is belied by the fact that the very idea he dismisses as "crazy" had already been realized by the filmmaker himself. In 1985, the same year as his film's release, a book authored by Lanzmann and titled *Shoah* was published by Éditions Fayard in France, as well as in English translation by Pantheon Books in the United States, under the title *Shoah: An Oral History of the Holocaust: The Complete Text of the Film*. A description on the copyright page of the Pantheon edition reads: "Transcription of English subtitles to 1985 French film *Shoah*."[2] Lanzmann was apparently invested enough in the book made of *Shoah* that a new edition—"extensively corrected and revised by Claude Lanzmann in order to conform more closely to the original film"—was published in 1995 by Da Capo Press with the revised title *Shoah: The Complete Text of the Acclaimed Holocaust Film*.[3]

The "impossible" book thus exists. While Lanzmann may be faulted for denying its existence, he is justified in saying that such a book cannot capture or communicate what the film does. Although the Pantheon edition contains several film stills of interviewees, these hardly render the information conveyed by the faces in his film. The small black and white images do not convey the witnesses' ever-changing expressions, hand gestures, and postures, not to mention the sounds of their voices, their cadences, and their intonations—all that is communicated, verbally and nonverbally, through their bodies. Yet pointing to this deficit only begins to address what is lost when *Shoah* is boiled down to its English subtitles.

Commenting on the title of the Pantheon edition, André Habib remarks that "a paradox certainly lies in the expression an 'Oral History of the Holocaust' since it refers to a text, and what's more, a text that does without one of the defining features of the 'orality' *of* the film: its multilingualism."[4] This multilingualism includes the French spoken by Lanzmann, the various languages spoken by the interviewees, and the translation work done by his three interpreters. The book flattens out the film's multilingualism if for no other reason than expediency, virtually creating the impression that only one language is spoken in *Shoah*. Habib writes, "Reading the *text of the film*, it is impossible to know what is the language each person originally spoke in the film (since certain Polish or Czech speakers decide to speak German, English, Yiddish, Hebrew, etc.)."[5] Remarkably, it is also impossible to know which words were spoken not by the interviewees, but by the interpreters who translated what they said into French for Lanzmann. The book provides little to no indication of the interpreter's presence. The name of the interviewee appears above a block of text, with questions, presumably asked by Lanzmann, set apart in italics. The text might have been presented as a translation of a translation—an English translation of an interpreter's French translation of what a witness said in Polish, German, Hebrew, or Yiddish—but the reader would have no way of knowing this.

The book fails to convey the film in at least one more way worth noting. Whereas "the complete text of the film," comprising two hundred or fewer pages, might be read in one sitting, the film is exceptionally long. Indeed, no aspect of *Shoah* is more frequently noted than its running time, which appears central to nearly all commentary on the film. Indeed, it is customary to append the running time to the film's title and to write about "the nine and one-half hour film *Shoah*" as though it were an endurance test. The film's epic length, it is repeatedly held, only befits the enormity of the Holocaust. "The standard two-hour feature format is something to which we are all accustomed," writes Fred Camper, whereas "a very long film, even one of only four or five hours (*Shoah* is generally shown in two parts, though I prefer to see both parts together, in order, on the same day), carves a significant space out of one's temporal field. We attend to it differently; it intrudes more directly into our thoughts and lives, an intrusion thoroughly appropriate to *Shoah*'s subject."[6] Similarly contrasting the film to standard cinema in a piece that begins "Claude Lanzmann's *Shoah* is more than nine hours long," Leon Wieseltier states that "*Shoah* has the duration not of spectacle, but of experience"—namely, the experience of being "taken to the catastrophe and left there for nine hours."[7]

As exceptional as the film's running time may be, that number is dwarfed by the approximately two hundred hours of footage that Claude Lanzmann shot over six years and then spent five years editing, producing a film eleven years in the making.[8] Recognition of this prolonged filmmaking process has only bolstered conceptions of the film's magnitude. "What emerged from this long process," writes Stuart Liebman in his introduction to the volume *Claude Lanzmann's* Shoah: *Key Essays*, "was one of the longest and most demanding films ever released, the nine and one-half hour *Shoah*."[9] The film is "most demanding" because it involves viewers in an extended confrontation with a most "immense and devastating historical topic": the

Nazi extermination of Europe's Jews.[10] But, quite aside from its disturbing content, the film's form, sheer length, and slow pace may deter viewers. "Not all spectators prove up to the challenge," writes Liebman.[11]

As Liebman has it, two aspects of *Shoah* try viewers' patience. Firstly, "some viewers are put off by the delays in translating comments from Polish, Hebrew, or Yiddish into French, because these extend the film's length"; and, secondly, "lengthy takes of boxcars in motion or extending tracking shots down rail beds leading to former sites of destruction" and "extended takes that are not necessarily thematically motivated—long shots of empty forests and fields—can be frustrating to those who prefer to get on with the story."[12] Both objections found their most infamous expression in Pauline Kael's review of the film for the *New Yorker*, in which she comments: "I found *Shoah* logy and exhausting right from the start, and when it had been going on for an hour or longer I was squirming restlessly, my attention slackening."[13]

Kael objects to how Lanzmann extends his film with long camera movements that scan the countryside and railroad tracks that lead to the camps and with a similarly protracted translation method that she describes as follows: "Lanzmann speaks French, German, and English, but he doesn't speak Polish, and so for much of the time he asks questions in French and a woman translator puts them into Polish; the subject replies in Polish and the translator puts the answers into French for Lanzmann while we read the English subtitles. (A translator is also required when those interviewed speak Hebrew or Yiddish.)" This method, she writes, slows down and stretches out the interviews "almost languorously," making the process of translation part of the film's taxing duration.[14]

Although Lanzmann's own fluency in German has been the subject of some discussion, he generally needs no interpreter for sequences featuring witnesses who speak French, German, or English.[15] In those sequences "foreign languages" are transcribed and inscribed on the film: French subtitles accompany spoken German and English in the film made for French audiences, whereas English subtitles accompany spoken French and German in the version distributed in the United States. In contrast, subtitles do not appear on screen when witnesses speak Polish, Hebrew, or Yiddish. Where the filmmaker relies on an interpreter to translate his questions into another language and the witness's responses into French, the witness's spoken words are not subtitled. Instead, viewers are expected to rely on the interpreter and wait for testimonies to assume their French form—and, for viewers of the American version, corresponding English form in subtitles. Time passes, and viewers are presented with the subjects' faces—whether they are listening attentively, staring into space, or taking the opportunity to light a cigarette—during the intervals.

It is precisely these delays in transmission that I will be discussing in relation to another film by Lanzmann, one largely comprised of footage shot for, but not featured in, *Shoah*. Unlike *Shoah*, with its many hours of interwoven interviews with multiple subjects, *Sobibór, October 14, 1943, 4 p.m.* (*Sobibór, 14 octobre 1943, 16 heures*, 2001) features the testimony of a single survivor named Yehuda Lerner, who speaks of his role in the prisoner uprising at Sobibór that led to the death camp's immediate closure. The film is unlike *Shoah* in other ways. In the film's prologue Lanzmann states, "The Sobibór uprising could not be a mere moment in *Shoah*. It deserved its own film, individual treatment." Whether or not Lanzmann had long planned to make a film about the uprising, his interview with Lerner did not fit his conception of *Shoah* and was most likely excluded on those grounds.

Asked by Frodon how he chose which people to include in *Shoah*, Lanzmann replies, with respect to the Jewish witnesses, "*Shoah*, as I've said a thousand times, is not a film about survival: it is not, in particular, a film about their survival, their personal survival. And it is not of themselves that they speak in the film. They never say 'I,' they are never telling us their personal story, or how they escaped."[16] While questionable as a description of the Jewish witnesses who appear in *Shoah* (many of whom do say "I" and tell personal stories), this characterization is most inapplicable to Lerner, whom Lanzmann identifies in the film's prologue as the uprising's "emblematic hero, an astonishing figure," and "a man of tireless and indomitable courage" who, in six months, escaped from eight camps—and then escaped from Sobibór.[17]

Despite being a film about survival that features one witness's personal story, *Sobibór* is indicative of *Shoah* in its construction and presentation of oral testimony provided by an interviewee for whom Lanzmann required an interpreter during filming. Through an examination of Lanzmann's staging of Lerner's story, this chapter seeks to show that the presentation of witness testimony in the book version of *Shoah* represents the reductio ad absurdum of how witness accounts conveyed through interpreters are presented in both *Sobibór* and *Shoah*. Rather than betraying the film's multilingualism, the book—in both replacing multiple tongues with a single language and negating the central role of the interpreter—manifests in extreme form the proclivities that shape how eyewitnesses' spoken words are treated in *Shoah* and in the films Lanzmann composed from its outtakes.

Viewers struck by the multiplicity of voices in *Shoah*, by the number of witnesses interviewed, and by the variety of languages they speak, may be less prone to observing ways in which many of these voices are compromised and displaced by the film's construction. Such treatment of the witness's words may be more readily observed in Lanzmann's comparatively succinct film featuring only Lerner's story. In *Sobibór* as in another "impossible" book authored by Lanzmann—*Sobibor, 14 octobre 1943, 16 heures*, the book made of his 2001 film and published by Cahiers du Cinéma to correspond with its release—the conflated voices of the witness and the interpreter call for critical examination.[18]

| The Living Words

Filmed in Jerusalem in October 1979 and speaking in Hebrew, Lerner tells of being deported in July 1942 from the Warsaw Ghetto to Belarus, where he escaped from eight camps, and of being sent to the Sobibór extermination camp, where he took part in the prisoner revolt of October 14, 1943—an uprising in which three hundred prisoners, more than half of the prisoner population, fled the camp. Most were killed shortly after their escape; Lerner is one of fifty-eight known survivors of the prisoner revolt.

The revolt involved summoning German soldiers to various workshops, where prisoners served as craftsmen, and killing them there with axes. At Lanzmann's prompting, Lerner repeatedly describes how he split the skull of an exceptionally large and monstrous German SS officer, and then briefly recounts his escape from the camp into the forest, where he collapsed. At that point Lanzmann's voice-over intrudes, translated into English subtitles that appear over the image of trees silhouetted against the night sky. They read as follows: "We'll stop here. It's so beautiful when he collapses in the forest. The rest is an adventure of freedom." This remark in the 2001 film is similar to but altered from what Lanzmann actually said near the end of the interview in 1979, in a remark he directed not at the viewer but at his interpreter, Francine Kaufmann: "Dis-lui, qu'on arrête là, je veux pas qu'il me raconte la suite, parce que c'est trop beau d'arrêter quand il dit qu'il s'est effondré dans la forêt; les histoires de partisans, c'est un autre chapitre" (Tell him, stop there, I don't want him to tell me what follows, because it is so beautiful to stop when he says he collapsed in the forest; the history of the partisans, it's another chapter).[19] Lanzmann had already decided, long before entering the editing room, that this would be the perfect note on which to end Lerner's story, and he here gives himself the last word, re-creating that moment of decision-making with a more poetic turn of phrase.

And yet the account does not stop here. Lerner reappears on screen in a close-up shot, silently and idly looking about as if waiting patiently during a break. This shot is accompanied by a voice-over in which Lanzmann tells of what happened to the death camp following the prisoner revolt. The accompanying subtitles read: "The extermination devices and gas chambers were demolished by the Germans immediately after the uprising. No more convoys arrived at Sobibór station. There, at least, the extermination had been stopped." The story thus ends not when Lerner collapses in the forest,

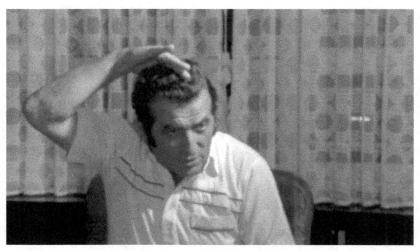

Yehuda Lerner describes how he split the skull of a German SS officer. DVD capture from *Sobibór* (2001), directed by Claude Lanzmann. Released by Criterion.

but rather when Lanzmann, speaking in terms that move beyond "personal survival," merges his voice with the face of the uprising's "emblematic hero."

Sobibór was culled from two-and-one-half hours of interview material. At ninety-five minutes, Lanzmann's film provides us with a highly abridged version, and, as with *Shoah*, issues of temporality loom large. Indeed, their centrality is inscribed in the film's very title, which, in its French and English versions, calls attention to the moment of the uprising in unusually precise terms, identifying the minute at which SS officer Siegfried Graetschus entered the workshop where he would be killed. This precision extends to Lerner's description of the camp and the revolt. Viewers reading the film's English subtitles learn that in the camp things ran "just like clockwork" and that the prisoners' plan, which "worked like clockwork," "only succeeded because Germans are so punctual."[20] It also succeeded because Jewish prisoners involved in the revolt moved very quickly to keep to the Germans' schedule and retain the element of surprise. Lerner states, via the subtitled English translation of Kaufmann's French translation, that "everything depended on German punctuality and our own rapidity."[21] This rapidity extends to Lerner's act of striking Graetschus in the head with an ax, which the subtitles describe as "so rapid that I can't even say."[22]

The precise synchronization and rapidity emphasized in Lerner's testimony—a story of rapid-fire decision-making and action—are dramatically offset by the typically extended duration and delay that characterize Lanzmann's filmmaking. An unhurried, even languid, pace is set by a five-minute prologue comprised of vertically scrolling white text against a black background, accompanied by Lanzmann's voice-over delivery. After providing a good deal of expository information, it concludes: "But museums and monuments instill forgetfulness as well as remembrance. Now we'll listen to Yehuda Lerner's living words [la parole vive]."[23] A series of slow panning shots of Warsaw, filmed in 2001, immediately follow. An aerial view of the cityscape is followed by a shot of the square containing the Warsaw Ghetto Monument, which is followed by a shot of a tram passing along a city street. This last panning shot comes to rest on the Umschlagplatz Monument, which marks the holding area from which over three hundred thousand Jews were transported to Treblinka and other camps. Viewers then hear "Yehuda Lerner's living words" in voice-over, but, unless they speak Hebrew, they cannot *listen* to them—not if listening here involves not just hearing sound, but deciphering words and making sense of them. Given the importance Lanzmann has just placed on these "living words" in his film's prologue, viewers may well wonder why no English subtitles accompany them.

Simply put, Lerner's words are not subtitled because they are spoken in Hebrew rather than French. The French filmmaker's utterances are subtitled in English, as is the French spoken by his interpreter, Francine Kaufmann. But the remarks she makes to Lerner in Hebrew, and the surviving witness's own "living words," are not accompanied by English subtitles, and so, for viewers who do not speak Hebrew, Lerner's testimony remains opaque, impenetrable. These viewers watch Lerner speak at length in Hebrew and then watch him sitting patiently as he waits for Kaufmann to convey to Lanzmann, in her own words, what he has said. Or, in the case of Lerner's opening voice-over, they hear him speak a language they do not understand and wait for English subtitles, only to find that they accompany not his words but the French spoken by his interpreter.

While watching *Sobibór*, we witness stages of the laborious translation process described by Kael: Lanzmann asks questions in French, and his translator puts them into Polish; the subject, Yehuda Lerner, replies in Polish, and the translator puts the answers into French for Lanzmann while we read the English subtitles. Kael writes that "this method of questioning inflates the scale of the film."[24] And yet anyone watching the entire interview with Lerner in the outtakes restored and held by the USHMM will notice that in *Sobibór* the scale of the interview has, in fact, been radically reduced through editing. In fact, in matching the words spoken in *Sobibór* to the transcript of the full interview with Lerner, one finds that the story Lerner appears to tell in the film—particularly in its first half, which concerns events prior to his arrival at Sobibór—is comprised of small segments that have been excerpted from the larger whole, reordered, and pieced together like a jigsaw puzzle. Lanzmann is able to present this assemblage as a seamless narrative through the use of long shots of city streets and the countryside. That is to say, footage Lanzmann shot in Poland and Belarus in 2001 serves to cover over his radical editing of oral testimony recorded in 1979. When Lerner is not shown speaking, his words and those of his interpreter can be reshaped to serve the film's narrative.

Lerner's story is streamlined at the cost of misrepresenting the process through which it gets told. Whereas in the film Lerner's story is presented as a succinctly told narrative, in the unedited interview his stories are sometimes repeated with small variations, owing to Lanzmann's interruptions and objections. Most if not all the nuance that comes of this telling and retelling is unaccounted for in the French- and English-language transcripts of the outtakes provided by the USHMM, as these oddly mimic the format of the *Shoah* book—firstly, by including text only for what is spoken in French; and, secondly, by attributing the interpreter's words to the interviewees. We see this, for instance, in a passage from the transcript in which the working relationship between the filmmaker and his interpreter grows combative; at issue is a substantial disputation over Kaufmann's translation of a term for a concentration camp's "director." Lanzmann badgers Kaufmann for the precise translation of the rank of the man mentioned in Lerner's Hebrew language account:

LANZMANN: Oh, écoute, le directeur, enfin . . . merde . . . le directeur, le directeur, le directeur du camp, qu'est-ce que ça veut dire, le directeur, enfin . . . !! (Oh, listen, the director, finally . . . shit . . . the director, the director, the director of the camp, what does that mean, the director, after all . . . !!)

LR: J'ai traduit, qu'est-ce que vous voulez . . . moi, je sais rien de cette période . . . j'ai traduit . . . écoute! (I translated, what do you want . . . me, I know nothing of this period . . . I translated . . . listen!)[25]

The transcript indicates that it was Lerner speaking here ("LR"), but it is, of course, Kaufmann who responds to Lanzmann. As if following the method set by Lanzmann in the book version of *Shoah*, the transcriber appears limited to attributing any and all spoken words either to the filmmaker or to his interviewee; the presence and participation of the interpreter are not acknowledged, even when Lanzmann and Kaufmann address each other directly, sometimes heatedly. This is not infrequently the case, as Lanzmann's own grasp of matters occasionally displaces Lerner's story as the focus of attention.

At one point Lanzmann, confused by Kaufmann's account of what Lerner has said about being brought from the Minsk Ghetto to a camp holding Jewish Red Army POWs, says: "Je comprends pas; qu'il raconte cette histoire mieux que ça, parce que je comprends rien" (I don't understand; [if] he is telling this story better than this, because I am understanding nothing). Suggesting that the story was both poorly told by Lerner and poorly translated by Kaufmann, he tells her, "Qu'il recommence à zero cette histoire; et puis, toi, s'il te plaît, traduis comme il faut. Allez, vas-y . . ." (Let him start this story again from zero; and then, you, please, translate it as it should [be]. Come on, go . . .).[26] At another point, Lanzmann once more presumes that Kaufmann's translation is inadequate, remarking, "J'imagine qu'il a dit un peu plus que ce que tu dis" (I imagine that he said a little more than what you said).[27] At such moments Lanzmann makes his irritation evident for the camera. The focus is on his urgent and immediate need to understand the survivor who speaks in a language he does not know, and Lerner and Kaufmann are often compelled to attend to it.

| Lost in Transcription

Whereas the first half of *Sobibór* is a mosaic of pieced-together sound clips, talking-head shots, and long panning and tracking shots of landscapes and cityscapes, the second half is largely free of cutaways from the filmed interview with Lerner. It is as if Lerner earns the film's full attention only in arriving at that part of his story set at Sobibór and nearing the titular moment of 4 p.m. on October 14, 1943. In what can rightly be called the film's climax, Lerner recounts how he and another prisoner, posing as tailors in a workshop and concealing axes under the coats they were pretending to sew, sat waiting for the opportunity to kill the monstrously huge SS officer Graetschus. The plan was for the other prisoner, a Jewish Soviet POW, to kill Graetschus, because he was a soldier, whereas Lerner had never killed anyone. But it so happened that Graetschus stood closer to Lerner than to the other prisoner.

Turning to the book version of *Sobibór*, we can see how this part of Lerner's story appears when rendered in the same manner that *Shoah* is depicted on the page in *The Complete Text of the Film*—that is, with nearly all markers of multilingualism and translation effaced. At its start, the book attributes the italicized text to Lanzmann and the nonitalicized or roman text to Lerner, expunging both spoken Hebrew and Kaufmann from the exchange. With added English translations of the French text, the passage reads:

Oui, il était à un mètre, un mètre et demi à peu près de moi, il avait donc été convenu que lorsque le tailleur essayerait le manteau, marquerait, indiquerait l'endroit des boutons et s'inclinerait, mon ami devrait s'approcher, mais puisque c'était moi le plus proche, je me suis levé, j'avais le manteau qui recouvrait mes mains et la hache sous le manteau, alors je me suis levé, j'ai laissé tomber le manteau, j'ai pris la hache, j'ai fait un tout petit pas vers lui et tout a duré peut-être un millième de seconde . . . C'était même . . . tellement rapide que je peux même pas vous . . . Imaginez, c'était un quart de millième de millième de seconde et tout s'est finis, j'ai pris la hache, et il a laissé échapper un grand cri et il est tombé, et j'avais levé la hache et je l'avais abattue sur sa tête d'un coup, la hache, tout la hache sur sa tête d'un coup.

[Yes, he was a meter, a meter and a half from me, it had been agreed that when the tailor tried the coat on him, marked the spot for the buttons and bent down, my friend would step forward, but since I was the closest, I stood up, I had the coat covering my hands and the ax under the coat, so I stood up and dropped the coat, I gripped the ax, I took a small step towards him and it all lasted perhaps a thousandth of a second . . . It was so . . . so fast that I cannot . . . Imagine, it was a quarter of a thousandth of a thousandth of a second and everything ended, I took the ax, and he let out a loud cry and he fell, and I had raised the ax and I had struck him on his head with one blow, the ax, the whole ax on his head in one blow.]

Il a frappé sur le crâne?
[*He struck his skull?*]

La hache est entrée exactement au milieu de son crâne, je peux dire que je lui ai coupé le crane en deux, exactement . . . Je sais même pas comment ça s'est passé, c'est comme si j'avais fait ça toute ma vie, si j'avais été spécialiste, j'ai coupé exactement à cet endroit et j'ai réussi.

[The ax went right into the middle of his skull, I can say that I split his skull in two, exactly. . . . I don't know how it happened, it's like I've been doing it all my life, as if I was a specialist. I hit exactly on this spot and I succeeded.]

Vous lui aviez complètement fendu le crâne?
[*You had completely split his skull?*]

Complètement, il est tombé . . . Mon camarade est venu . . . ça a duré vraiment un quart de seconde, donc j'ai frappé, il a faibli, il s'est écroulé, il est tombé et mon camarade est venu, il a donné un deuxième coup, et à ce moment-là, les gens qui travaillaient dans l'atelier sont venus pour essayer de retirer le cadavre, puisque nous savions qu'un deuxième Allemand devait entrer immédiatement après.

[Completely, he fell . . . My comrade came over . . . it lasted really a quarter of a second, so I hit him, he weakened, he slumped down, he fell and my comrade came over, he hit him a second time, and at that moment, the people who worked in the workshop came to try to remove the body, since we knew a second German would arrive immediately after.][28]

In this rendering the only indication of the interpreter's presence and participation as an intermediary is the odd appearance of the pronoun "he" ("il"). "He struck his skull?" ("Il a frappe sur le crâne?") Lanzmann asks, and not "You struck his skull?" The phrasing of his next question corrects this disjunctive sign that his words were directed at Kaufmann rather than Lerner by replacing "he" with "you" ("vous"), although Lanzmann can be heard on film asking not "Vous lui aviez complètement fendu le crâne?" (You had completely split his skull?) but only "Complètement fendu?" (Completely split?). Here, as elsewhere in the *Sobibor* book, the omission of the Hebrew and elaboration of the French foster the illusion of communication unmediated by a translator. To judge from the written text, it is as though the filmmaker and his witness were speaking the same language, addressing their words directly to one another.

Basing one's scholarship on a translation and transcription of this sort would be misguided; it elides both the details of the testimony and the process by which it was obtained. And yet, as Kaufmann notes in her essay

"The Ambiguous Task of the Interpreter in Lanzmann's Films *Shoah* and *Sobibór*," doing so is the norm. Readers of "the book of *Shoah*," she writes, "can never know whether the words are those of the interpreter (oral translation) or those of the subtitles (written and abridged translation)"; nor can they know "the real words of the witnesses" if they turn to these French translations—or to translations of these translations. She notes that the "original" version of *Shoah* is the French film, and that "this French version is translated for other countries, analyzed and quoted by researchers, while the real words of the witnesses have never been transcribed and examined."[29] Nor, for that matter, have these "real words" been translated through more reliable means than that provided by film subtitling and consecutive interpreting without taking notes, a method Kaufmann describes as "perilous" and likely to produce errors.[30]

What might the transcript of this roughly four-minute section of film look like if we were to include a multilingual transcription of the words spoken by the witness, the interpreter, and the filmmaker? Consider how much the version containing "the text of the film" differs from the following one, which includes Lerner's words in Hebrew; Kaufmann's words in French and Hebrew translation; Lanzmann's words in French; and, in brackets, the film's English subtitles:

LERNER: ואז באמת כבר הגענו למצב. וקבענו עם החייט

KAUFMANN: Il avait donc été convenu—

[It had been agreed—]

LERNER: שהוא יכרע ברך באותו הזמן שהוא יתחיל לסמן לו את החורים לכפתורים צריכים להתחיל לתת לו מכה. ואז הוא עמד יותר אליי עם הגב. וכשעמד ככה ואני רואה שהחייט כבר מתחיל לקחתי את המעיל על הידיים שלי עשיתי כאילו שאני קם. אבל מה? לקחתי את המעיל עם הגרזן ביד ונתתי פסיעה אחת אליו. המעיל נפל מעליי, יישרתי את הידיים, הרמתי את הגרז—זה לקח פסיק של אלפית שנייה—והגרזן הייתה בראש שלו. וממש בכל הראש. הגרזן נכנס והוא כרע במקום.

KAUFMANN: Il était à un mètre, un mètre et demi à peu près de moi, il avait donc était convenu que lorsque le tailleur essayerait le manteau, marquerait, indiquerait l'endroit des boutons et s'inclinerait, mon ami devrait s'approcher, mais puisque c'était moi le plus proche, je me suis levé. J'avais le manteau qui recouvrait mes mains et la hache sous le manteau, alors je me suis levé, j'ai laissé tomber le manteau, j'ai pris la hache, j'ai fait un tout petit pas vers lui et tout a duré peut-être un millième de seconde.

[He was about three or four feet from me, and we'd arranged for when the tailor tried the coat on him, marked the spot for the buttons and bent down, my friend would step forward, but since I was now the closest, I stood up. The coat covered my hands and the ax. I stood up, I dropped the coat, gripped the ax and took a tiny step towards him. It all took one one-thousandth of a second.]

LERNER: אה . . . זה . . . זה הלך זה פסיק של—של—אני לא יודע איך
להגיד כמה שניות.

KAUFMANN: C'était même . . .

[It was even . . .]

LERNER: ו . . . זהו זה.

KAUFMANN: tellement rapide je peux même pas vous. Imaginez: c'était un quart de millième de millième de seconde et tout s'est finis. J'ai pris la hache,

[so rapid that I can't even say—It was over in a quarter of a millionth of a second. I gripped the ax,]

LERNER: והוא עשה—"וְרֶה!"—ונפל.

KAUFMANN: et il a laissé échapper un grand cri et il est tombé, et j'avais levé la hache et je l'avais abattue sur sa tête d'un coup, la hache, tout la hache sur sa tête d'un coup.

[and he gave a loud cry, and he fell. I raised the ax and slammed it down on his head. In one blow, the whole ax went into his head.]

LANZMANN: Il l'a frappé sur le crane?

[He struck him in the skull?]

KAUFMANN: על הגלגולת?

LERNER: על הראש, ממש, לחצי !הגרזן נפל לו בדיוק בחצי הראש! כל הראש נפתח ממש.

KAUFMANN: La hache est entrée exactement au milieu de son crane. Je peux dire que je lui ai coupé le crane en deux.

[The ax went right into the middle of his skull. I split his skull in two.]

LERNER: ממש! זה היה . . . אני לא יודע איך זה קרא אבל זה היה באמנות ממש כאילו שהייתי מומחה לזה. זה . . . הצלחתי!

KAUFMANN: Je sais même pas comment ça s'est passé. C'est comme si j'avais fait ça toute ma vie, si j'avais été spécialiste. J'ai coupé exactement à cet endroit et j'ai réussi.

[I don't even know how. It was like I'd been doing it all my life. Like a specialist, I hit exactly the right spot. I succeeded.]

LERNER: ואז הבחור—

LANZMANN: Complètement fendu?

[It split his skull?]

LERNER: Complète! ממש! נפל!

KAUFMANN: Complètement! Il est tombé.

              [Completely! And he fell.]

LERNER: —קרא, אמר: "וֹרֶה!" ונפל. ואז הבחור השני

KAUFMANN: Mon camarade est venu—

              [My comrade came over.]

LERNER: קם וגם כן נתן לו מכה עם הגרזן. וידענו שצריך—בעוד כמה
              דקות צריך להכנס שני. תקף האנשים שעבדו שמה לקחו את
              הגופה וזרקו אותה—היה שמה שולחן גדול, איפה שהחייטים
              היו מגהצים הכל. והיה להם הרבה מעילים של הגרמנים מתחת
              לשולחן. זרקו את הגופה, וכיסו אותה עם המעילים של הגרמנים.

KAUFMANN: Ça a duré vraiment un quart de seconde, donc j'ai frappé,
              il a faibli, il s'est écroulé, il est tombé et mon camarade est
              venu. Il a donné un deuxième coup, et à ce moment-là
              les gens qui travaillaient dans l'atelier sont venus pour
              essayer de retirer le cadavre, puisque nous savions qu'un
              deuxième Allemand devait rentrer immédiatement après.

              [It lasted a fraction of a second. I hit him, he slumped
              down and fell. My comrade came over. He struck him
              again. Then the people in the workshop helped us move
              the body because we knew a second German would arrive
              immediately after.]³¹

Still more important information, of course, comes to light when readers
who do not know Hebrew are provided an English translation, and the
French is translated with a bit more care. Here the translated French is
distinguished from the translated Hebrew by italics:

LERNER: Then really, we got to the situation. We arranged with the tailor that he will kneel.
KAUFMANN: *It had been agreed*—
LERNER: At the same time that he will start marking the spots for
the buttons we have to start striking him. And then he stood more

towards me with his back. As he stood there I saw that the tailor was starting. I took the coat over my arms and pretended I was getting up, but I took the coat with the ax in my hand and I took one step towards him. The coat fell off my arms, I straightened my arms, I lifted the ax, it took a fraction of a thousandth of a second, and the ax was in his head! And then, really, the ax entered his entire head and he collapsed on the spot.

KAUFMANN: *He was one meter away, a meter and a half from me, so it was agreed that when the tailor would try the coat on him, mark, indicate the spot for the buttons and bend down, my friend should step forward. But since I was the closest, I stood up. I had the coat that covered my hands and the ax under the coat, so I stood up, I dropped the coat, I took the ax, I took one short step towards him and it all lasted perhaps a thousandth of a second.*

LERNER: Ah, it took a fraction of a second. I don't know how to tell you how many seconds.

KAUFMANN: *It was even . . .*

LERNER: And that's it.

KAUFMANN: *so rapid that I can't even say—It was over in a quarter of a millionth of a second. I gripped the ax,*

LERNER: And he went "wrah," and he fell.

KAUFMANN: *and he gave a loud cry, and he fell. I raised the ax and slammed it down on his head. In one blow the whole ax went into his head.*

LANZMANN: *He struck him in the skull?*

KAUFMANN: On the skull?

LERNER: On his head, really, in half! The ax fell exactly in the middle of his head. The entire head split open, really!

KAUFMANN: *The ax went exactly into the middle of his skull. I can say that I split his skull in two.*

LERNER: Really! It was, I don't know how it happened, it was theatric, really, like I was an expert. And I succeeded.

KAUFMANN: *I don't even know how. It's like I've been doing this all my life, if I'd been a specialist. I cut exactly here and I succeeded.*

LERNER: And then he was dead.

LANZMANN: *Completely split?*

LERNER: Completely, really, he fell.

KAUFMANN: *Completely! And he fell.*

LERNER: It happened. He went "wrah!" and he fell. And then the other guy—

KAUFMANN: *My comrade came over.*

LERNER: got up and also hit him with the ax. And we knew that in a few minutes the second one is going to enter. Soon people who worked there took the body and threw it. There was a big table where the tailors would iron everything, and they had many coats of the Germans under the table where they threw the body and covered it with the German's coats.

KAUFMANN: *It really lasted a quarter of a second, so I hit him, he faltered, he slumped down, he fell and my comrade came over. He hit him a second time, and at that time the people working in the workshop came to try to remove the body, since we knew that a second German would arrive immediately afterwards.*

Bearing in mind that the above transcriptions include translations and are thus interpretations, they reflect an effort to come significantly closer to understanding what was actually said. Viewers of the sequence in Lanzmann's *Sobibór* who do not speak Hebrew will watch Lerner speak and gesticulate without comprehending his words, and then gaze at a close-up of Lerner's face as he waits for Kaufmann to recall what he has said and paraphrase his testimony in French for Lanzmann. The fact that spoken Hebrew is not subtitled in the French version of *Sobibór*, and that only spoken French is subtitled in the film's American version, indicates the different value accorded the "living words" of the three persons involved in this exchange.

The duration of the scene is, on several levels, essential to Lanzmann's project. After Kaufmann says that the whole ax went with one blow into Graetschus's head, Lanzmann asks, "Il l'a frappé sur le crane?" (He hit him on the skull?). Shortly thereafter he asks, "Complètement fendu?" (Completely split?). Here Lanzmann has Lerner repeat himself not only to induce his subject to dwell on the details and to approach the memory anew, but also to reduce the interval separating what Lerner says from what the filmmaker understands. Speaking in Hebrew, Lerner augments his account with dramatic body language. He mimics the tailor's act of marking the spots for the buttons on his own shirt, gathers his arms together when telling about having the coat over his arms, grips his hand as if holding the ax, enacts the coat falling off his arms, and repeatedly swings his open hand to mimic the ax. While Kaufmann interprets his account in French for Lanzmann, Lerner sits idly by, silent and still as he waits. He then bursts back to life, swinging his arms as he describes how quickly it all happened and retells how Graetschus went "wrah" and fell. Lanzmann's questions cause Lerner to repeat himself twice more, allowing Lanzmann to reduce the gap between the survivor's body language and the non-Hebrew speaker's grasp of what he might be saying.

While Lanzmann seeks to *reduce* the temporal distance separating Lerner's physical and verbal utterance from the meaning of his words, he also *extends* the skull-splitting moment with questions that require Lerner to recount it anew. The skull-splitting moment captures what Lanzmann, in the film's introductory scroll, calls "the re-appropriation of power and violence by the Jews." The Sobibór revolt involved many prisoners, most notably Jewish Red Army officers, and it resulted in the killing of several German officers and Ukranian guards. But it is Lerner whom Lanzmann regards as the uprising's "emblematic hero," because it is through his account that the filmmaker draws himself closer to this heroic moment of violence.[32]

In the parts of the film that deal with events prior to the prisoner uprising at Sobibór—those that are at a remove from the act of violent rebellion—the interactions and translations are handled quite differently. For most of this section, essentially the film's first fifty minutes, Lerner's image is replaced by long tracking shots of cityscapes and the countryside. At times his voice disappears and Kaufmann's voice can be heard recounting the story in its absence. That is, the interpreter continues to tell Lerner's story in the complete absence of his spoken words. It is a surprising elision of the testimonial voice: when the Hebrew not only goes untranslated in the subtitles but is cut from the soundtrack, it is as though the precise text of Lerner's Hebrew-language testimony and his particular vocal inflections are less integral than Kaufmann's speech, which, by virtue of being translated and subtitled, comes across as comparatively authoritative.

For example, about twenty-two minutes into the film Lerner is shown telling how, when he was caught after escaping a camp, he was lucky to be taken to another camp rather than returned to the one from which he had escaped, as he would have been shot there. Lanzmann remarks that Lerner was incredibly lucky not to be shot. After Kaufmann translates his sentiment, Lerner responds in Hebrew, in words that might be translated as follows: "That's right! When you have the luck to live, everything works out. But when you have no luck, nothing will help." His remark, which he says with a nod and a smile, is not subtitled in English. Instead, the image cuts from the close-up shot of Lerner to a tracking shot of trees silhouetted against the sky at dusk. Kaufmann's spoken French is heard on the soundtrack as English subtitles appear over the fleeting landscape: "That's true. If you've got a lucky star, you'll live. I must have been lucky. If I'd been caught by the Germans in charge of fugitives, or one of the camps, they'd have simply hung me like all the rest. All captive fugitives were brought back and hung. But my luck always held. I was always caught by Germans passing by chance, and I'd wind up in another camp."[33]

Kaufmann's translation clearly extends beyond what Lerner has said, but viewers who do not speak Hebrew are unlikely to notice this. When I watched the film with an Israeli friend, he drew my attention more than once to such passages where Lerner's words are cut from the film altogether, replaced entirely by Kaufmann's paraphrased translation. At one point he said to me: "I'd love to hear all this from him. Those are pretty important pieces of the story." The film's treatment of those "pieces" of Lerner's story that precede the events of October 14, 1943, suggests otherwise.

Mistranslation as Metaphor

Lanzmann's treatment of Lerner's testimony matches, for the most part, what we see in much of the American version of *Shoah*: an interpreter present at the filmed interview translates into French what a witness says in Polish, Hebrew, or Yiddish, and the interpreter's words, rather than those of the witness, are presented in English translation through subtitles. Those words are the ones canonized in the book versions of the films and in the ensuing scholarship, although the translations performed on-site by an interpreter working under time pressure often contain mistakes. Kaufmann, who frequently worked as Lanzmann's interpreter during this period, recognized as much. Her work is remarkable, particularly where she moves back and forth with agility between Lanzmann and his witnesses, often contending with his demands and interruptions. Still, translation is a process, and accuracy is never absolute.

In a 1993 essay Kaufmann recalls that "Lanzmann demanded a consecutive interpreting without 'note taking'" and without, as she puts it, "the possibility of interrupting the speech to conduct a verification, to request a reminder or an explanation, this to guarantee the accuracy and fidelity of that speech."[34] Disallowed from taking notes or asking the witness to pause, she "would have to mentally memorize while listening" to him speak at length. Kaufmann naturally worried that this method would invite omissions, inaccuracies, and other errors:

> The method seemed perilous [périlleuse], even impractical for long narrative spans. But I believe that internally I reassured myself by telling myself that in the end Lanzmann would give up on his project while watching the rushes. Indeed, I started with the assumption that, if Lanzmann resorted to an interpreter, it was because he did not understand the language of witnesses and could interview them only through this technical crutch. Once filming was completed, the crutch had (in my eyes) no more reason to be and could be removed. My sense of logic whispered to me that Lanzmann would then resign himself to captioning, or even to re-doing during mixing, a *voiceover* translation, precise and made only of the sequences selected during editing.[35]

Of course, what Kaufmann told herself did not come to pass. What, then, has been made of the inevitable mistranslations that found their way into Lanzmann's film?

Scholarly response to Lanzmann's "perilous" method has largely treated his process as a metaphor for the Holocaust's unrepresentability, following Lanzmann's insistence on "the impossibility of telling this story even by the survivors themselves."[36] "It is a metaphor of the film that its language is a language of translation," states Shoshana Felman in an influential 1991 essay. She writes, "The palpable foreignness of the film's tongues is emblematic of the radical foreignness of the experience of the Holocaust, not merely to us, but even to its own participants."[37] Indeed, Felman contends that "the prolonged *delay* incurred by the translation" of the witness's words places *Shoah*'s viewers in "the position of the witness," who, during the Holocaust, could not understand the significance of what he saw and heard.[38] Survivors' actual words are important, but, seen in these terms, it is almost as though every utterance of every survivor is akin to the noise—the "wrah" sound—made by Graetschus when he was struck; Kaufmann translates this sound as "un grand cri" (a loud cry), because one has no hope of actually "translating" a cry of anguish.

Taking cues from Felman's essay, which she cites, Kaufmann adopts her thinking to make sense of an experience that had troubled her while working as an interpreter for Lanzmann. "During the filming," she writes, "I was aware that I was being placed in a borderline situation, which was unlike any of the potential situations taught in schools. Each sequence left me frustrated and confused, unable to use familiar criteria to judge if I had or not done what the director really expected of me."[39] Adopting Felman's notion of translation as metaphor, Kaufmann writes that

> even the inaccuracies, infidelities, errors, and omissions of translation are meant to play a role in the film, and this is why they are kept in the filming. The infidelity of translation is a metaphor for the infidelity of memory and the infidelity of listening, even carefully, on the part of an observer who can only stay an outsider to planet Shoah. All that which during the filming of *Shoah* preoccupied me, worried me, seemed to me a cumbersome obstacle to communication and to the faithful transmission of information, was the result of a deliberate cinematic process.[40]

One might question the idealization that attends this metaphor, given that most viewers have no recognition of "the inaccuracies, infidelities, errors, and omissions of translation" that Kaufmann describes. The metaphor would be far better served if subtitled translations were included for *all* "foreign languages" spoken in *Shoah* and *Sobibór*, so that viewers might observe discrepancies between the interviewee's spoken words and the interpreter's consecutive translation.

To be sure, the amended transcripts above do not give us *direct* access to Lerner's "living words." Still, they bring us closer to an understanding of those words as they are produced through interlingual dialogue. Had the English-language version of *Sobibór* subtitled the Hebrew as well as the French, we as viewers would be able to match the tone of Lerner's voice and his body language with the meaning of his utterances, with the result that the survivor would appear to speak for himself rather than to be spoken for. Furthermore, we would be better positioned to adjudicate for ourselves the layers of mediation that separate not only the viewer but also the film-maker from events as they are recounted by Lerner. One should always be cautious in providing one's own words in the place of those of a witness. In *On Listening to Holocaust Survivors,* Henry Greenspan remarks that "we follow recounting best when we follow it as a process: when we are able to enter into survivors' struggles for words rather than receiving those words as finished texts."[41] In *Sobibór* as in *Shoah*, the viewer's ability to follow this process is hindered by a method of delay that places paraphrase above living words and preserves it in *The Complete Text of the Film.*

Kaufmann's notion that inaccuracies in her translations of Hebrew-speaking witnesses were intended as "a metaphor for the infidelity of memory" finds little support in commentary that suggests Lanzmann got the "real" story from his interviewees through obsessive, steely persistence, if not ethically dubious insistence. Viewers of *Sobibór* will be surprised to learn that Arkady Wajspapir, the Jewish Soviet POW who was sent with Lerner to the workshop on October 14, 1943, to kill Germans with axes, offers a markedly different account of how Graetschus was killed. In a videotaped 1984 interview, he provides an account in Russian that is subtitled in English as follows:

> I was paired with a Polish Jew who had also come from Minsk. His name was Lerner. We were both sent to the workshop. I don't remember if it was the shoemaker's or the tailor's. In any case, we had to go to the workshop. Once there, we pretended we were repairing a table. We were standing there together. I didn't know which German was supposed to come in. The boss of the workshop probably did not know who it was. He told us where we were supposed to

stand. And where we should wait for the German who was about to come in. A little later, the German showed up. He came in and stood close to the door. Something was measured for him. The boss of the workshop went to talk to him. But he stayed over near the door. That's why I walked in his direction. I acted like I was leaving, but turned around and hit him with my ax. He let out a scream as he fell down. Then Lerner jumped forward and axed him to death. We then dragged him to the side, out of view. Some others covered the German with rags.[42]

Wajspapir not only says that it was he and not Lerner who first struck Graetschus with an ax, but he also describes the uprising as a far more haphazard undertaking; here nothing "worked like clockwork." Wajspapir states that the second German who entered was so unexpected that all the prisoners normally assigned to the workshop did not know what to do and left one after the other. The room was a mess, and the German asked about the pile of rags covering the body. "When he bent down over the rags, I struck him with my ax," Wajspapir says. "Lerner helped me and we killed the second German." Only in the woods after escaping the camp did Wajspapir learn that the first German he had killed was Graetschus, from papers he had taken off the body.

Wajspapir's recounting of what he and Lerner did during the prisoner revolt is notably less captivating in its telling and certain in its details than the story told by Lerner in Lanzmann's film. My point is not that inconsistencies between their accounts should lead us to question Lerner's story, but rather that they should lead us to question why Lanzmann's presentation of Lerner's story makes it seem unquestionable. Like *Shoah*, *Sobibór* does not suggest "the infidelity of memory." Instead, it suggests the truthfulness of memories that Lanzmann can "revive" through sheer power of will, as well as through the art of shooting and editing film.[43] Wajspapir's account is far less visually compelling, thematically organized, performatively told, and dramatically shaped than Lerner's. It is brief and marked by the vagaries of memory, whereas Lerner's recounting takes "traditional story form: with identifiable actors, a specific place and time, and a coherent unfolding of action, reaction, and development."[44] Beyond this, Wajspapir's account cannot compete, because Lerner's story is authorized by Lanzmann, the foremost filmmaker of "Holocaust cinema."

Lanzmann's authority is not only born of *Shoah*; it is inscribed in that very film—in what does and does not bear inscription. Because Lanzmann knows German, the words in *Shoah* spoken in German by a surviving victim or Nazi officer are subtitled. But because Lanzmann does not know Hebrew, subtitles do not accompany the words of a Hebrew-speaking survivor. If viewers understood these words before they passed through French translation, their understanding would exceed Lanzmann's at the time of filming, and the image of the process through which the filmmaker acquired his mastery—the basis of the authority by which he declares the obscenity of others' efforts to understand the Holocaust—might be compromised. Lanzmann has famously asserted that to seek certain knowledge of the Holocaust is to engage in "the obscenity of the project of understanding," and that the Holocaust "created a circle of flame around itself, a boundary not to be crossed, since horror in the absolute degree cannot be communicated."[45] Ultimately, however, it is not the Holocaust's limits but rather those of Lanzmann's own understanding that mark the boundary of communication he would not have us cross.[46]

Lanzmann was once asked about why he chose the title *Shoah*. Kaufmann claims that "he had first intended to entitle his work *Holocaust*, but the worldwide broadcast of the American series for NBC in 1978 was forcing him to seek another title. He fulminated."[47] Without mentioning this, Lanzmann answered that he titled his film *Shoah* "because I don't understand Hebrew and because it was very short, because it was opaque and a little unbreakable, like an atomic nucleus. For the first screening of the film at the Empire Theater, George Cravenne asked me: 'What is the title of the film?' '*Shoah*.' 'What does it mean?' 'I don't know.' 'But how, you must translate it! No one will understand!' And I said: 'It's what I want, that no one understands.'"[48] Lanzmann became well known for this resistance to translation, which is also his resistance to understanding. It is the basis on which innumerable critics have praised the film; Carles Torner, for example, writes that "for the entire length of the film, translation becomes a figure in the chain of transmission and its consubstantial incompletion. The noun 'Shoah,' a Hebrew word become a French one, whose opacity begs unending inquiry, remains a powerful image of a translation-transmission continually falling short."[49] A subtext of this story, however apocryphal it may be, is that if Lanzmann does not understand a word of Hebrew, viewers of his film should not either.

Of course, the word "Shoah" is not inherently opaque. Rather, a kind of willful ignorance makes it so by withholding its translation from the Hebrew. Henri Meschonnic, who translated the Hebrew Bible into French, deems "Shoah" to be as inadequate a term for the Nazi genocide of the Jews as "Holocaust," given that "the thirteen occurrences of the term in the Bible all refer to natural disasters, never man-made catastrophes."[50] For this reason, some commentators prefer the Hebrew word "Hurban" (alternately anglicized as "Churban" or "Hurbn"), meaning "man-made destruction, ruin."[51] This Hebrew must be suppressed if what is lost in translation is to serve as a metaphor for the incommunicability of the Holocaust. A problem with this metaphor is that it makes a virtue of mistranslation. Few would justify a poor translation of a Holocaust memoir on the grounds that it artfully speaks to the impossibility of a survivor telling her or his story, yet Lanzmann's method has been valorized on just such grounds—grounds that, in this case, oddly make the Hebrew language a figure for the Holocaust's incomprehensibility. Even the most laudable translation, of course, will differ considerably from its source material. It will fail to *be* that material as surely as that material will fail to *be* the event it recounts. But to idealize translation as a metaphor for the failure of communication and comprehension with regard to the Holocaust is to disregard it as a complex process through which communication and comprehension do, in fact, occur.

Notes

I thank Jason Schapera for transcribing and translating the Hebrew in this chapter, Rami Levinthal for piquing my interest when he provided an earlier translation of the Hebrew, and Thérèse Migraine-George for her generous work in translating the French. I am grateful to Brad Prager for contributing to this essay in ways above and beyond the call of duty.

1. Jean-Michael Frodon, "The Work of the Filmmaker: An Interview with Claude Lanzmann," *Cinema and the Shoah: Art Confronts the Tragedy of the Twentieth*

Century, ed. Jean-Michael Frodon; trans. Anna Harrison and Tom Mes (Albany: State University of New York Press, 2010), 99; brackets in original.

2. Claude Lanzmann, *Shoah: An Oral History of the Holocaust: The Complete Text of the Film* (New York: Pantheon, 1985), iv. This page notes "English subtitles of the film by A. Whitelaw and W. Byron," but does not identify the translator of Simone de Beauvoir's preface or Lanzmann's introduction.

3. Claude Lanzmann, *Shoah: The Complete Text of the Acclaimed Holocaust Film* (New York: De Capo, 1995), ii.

4. André Habib, "Delay, Estrangement, Loss: The Meanings of Translation in Claude Lanzmann's *Shoah* (1985)," *SubStance* 44, no. 2 (2015): 108–28; here, 112; italics in original.

5. Habib, "Delay, Estrangement, Loss," 112; italics in original.

6. Fred Camper, "Shoah's Absence," *Claude Lanzmann's Shoah: Key Essays*, ed. Stuart Liebman (New York: Oxford University Press, 2017), 103–11; here, 104.

7. Leon Wieseltier, "Shoah," in Liebman, *Claude Lanzmann's Shoah*, 89–93; here, 89, 91.

8. Austin Guy, *Contemporary French Cinema: An Introduction* (New York: Manchester University Press, 1996), 24. The website for the Claude Lanzmann *Shoah* Collection at the US Holocaust Memorial Museum (USHMM) refers to "185 hours of interview outtakes and 35 hours of location filming." "Claude Lanzmann Shoah Collection," United States Holocaust Memorial Museum, July 5, 2018, https://collections.ushmm.org/search/catalog/irn1000017 (accessed August 27, 2019).

9. Stuart Liebman, "Introduction," *Claude Lanzmann's Shoah*, 3–24; here, 4.

10. Liebman, "Introduction," 3.

11. Liebman, 17.

12. Liebman, 17.

13. Pauline Kael, "Sacred Monsters (December 30, 1985)," in *Hooked* (New York: E. P Dutton, 1989), 76–88; here, 84.

14. Kael, "Sacred Monsters," 84.

15. On Lanzmann's movement between languages, see Nelly Furman, "The Languages of Pain in *Shoah*," in *Auschwitz and After: Race, Culture, and "the Jewish Question" in France*, ed. Lawrence Kritzman (New York: Routledge, 1995), 299–312; and, specifically on Lanzmann's use of German, see Erin McGlothlin, "Listening to the Perpetrators in Claude Lanzmann's *Shoah*," *Colloquia Germanica* 43, no. 3 (2010): 235–71.

16. Frodon, "The Work of the Filmmaker," 96.

17. All English subtitles are taken from the version of *Sobibór, 14 octobre 1943, 16 heures* included in the *Shoah* Criterion Collection DVD box set, released in 2013; here from timecode 1:59–2:02. These English subtitles occasionally differ from those in the American version of *Sobibór* released on DVD in 2001.

18. Claude Lanzmann, *Sobibor, 14 octobre 1943, 16 heures* (Paris: Cahiers du Cinéma, 2001). This book omits the Polish diacritical mark from the word "Sobibór." For purposes of consistency, I have omitted that diacritical mark in all references to the book's title.

19. This is based on the outtakes at the USHMM. See the French transcript of Lerner's interview on the USHMM website, https://collections.ushmm.org/film _findingaids/RG-60.5030_01_trs_fr.pdf (accessed August 27, 2019); here, 41. To watch the outtakes, and for links to the French and English transcripts, see "Yehuda Lerner–Sobibór," United Holocaust Memorial Museum, April 26, 2018, https://collections.ushmm.org/search/catalog/irn1004204 (accessed August 27, 2019).

20. *Sobibór, Shoah* Criterion Collection, timecode 1:09:10, 1:20:26, 1:09:28. The French for "like clockwork" is "comme une montre," like a watch. See Lanzmann, *Sobibór*, 36, 40; or the USHMM French transcript of Lerner's interview, 32, 35.

21. *Sobibór*, timecode 1:20:20.

22. *Sobibór*, timecode 1:16:02. Kaufmann's French reads: "C'était même . . . tellement rapide que je peux même pas vous . . ." See Lanzmann's book *Sobibor*, 36, and the USHMM French transcript of the Lerner interview, 34.

23. *Sobibór, Shoah* Criterion Collection, timecode 05:09–05:13.

24. Kael, "Sacred Monsters," 88.

25. USHMM French transcript of Lerner interview, 19. The English is altered from the USHMM transcript of the *Shoah* interview with Yehuda Lerner, translated by Caitlin N. Kelly, October 2008, https://collections.ushmm.org/film _findingaids/RG-60.5030_01_trl_en.pdf (accessed August 27, 2019).

26. Claude Lanzmann *Shoah* Collection, interview with Yehuda Lerner (RG-60.5030, Film ID 3335, Camera Rolls 4–6), US Holocaust Memorial Museum and Yad Vashem and State of Israel. The comment comes at 2:10:30, near the end of reel 4. See also the USHMM's French transcript of Lerner's interview, 15; and Kaufmann's own comments on this exchange in Francine Kaufmann, "The Ambiguous Task of the Interpreter in Lanzmann's Films *Shoah* and *Sobibór*: Between the Director and Survivors of the Camps and Ghettos," *Interpreting in Nazi Concentration Camps*, ed. Michaela Wolf (New York: Bloomsbury, 2016), 161–79; here, 174.

27. See USHMM French transcript of Lerner interview, 26.

28. See Lanzmann, *Sobibor*, 38–39. This English translation is based on the subtitles in *Sobibór* but altered to better match the French text in the *Sobibor* book.

29. Kaufmann, "The Ambiguous Task of the Interpreter," 166n10.

30. Francine Kaufmann, "Interview et interprétation consécutive dans le film *Shoah*, de Claude Lanzmann," *Meta: journal des traducteurs* 38, no. 4 (1993): 664–73; here, 664.

31. *Sobibór, Shoah* Criterion Collection, timecode 1:14:18–1:18:08.

32. Some interpreters have enfolded that aspect of the story into a Zionist narrative wherein the legitimacy of Lerner's behavior at Sobibór becomes the legitimacy of Israel's contemporary behavior. See, for example, Laurence Giavarini, "Sur les héros de Sobibór: Le Dernier Film de Claude Lanzmann et la représentation de la Shoah," *Cahiers du Cinéma* 565 (February 2002): 46–48.

33. *Sobibór, Shoah* Criterion Collection, timecode 23:22–24:10.

34. Kaufmann, "Interview et interpretation consecutive," 664, 666.

35. Kaufmann, 664–65.

36. See Marc Chevrie and Hervé Le Roux, "Site and Speech: An Interview with Claude Lanzmann about *Shoah*," in Liebman, ed. *Claude Lanzmann's* Shoah, 37–49; here, 39. For the French original, see "Le lieu et la parole," *Cahiers du Cinema* 374 (July–August 1985): 18–23; here, 19.

37. Shoshana Felman, "In an Era of Testimony: Claude Lanzmann's *Shoah*," *Yale French Studies* 79, Literature and the Ethical Question (1991): 103–50; here, 111.

38. Felman, "In an Era of Testimony," 110.

39. Kaufmann, "Interview et interprétation," 666.

40. Kaufmann, 669.

41. Henry Greenspan, *On Listening to Holocaust Survivors: Beyond Testimony* (St. Paul, MN: Paragon House, 2010), 209.

42. "Interview with Arkady Wajspapir (Russian), 1984 (Rostov)." Sobiborinterviews .nl, November 6, 2010, https://www.Sobiborinterviews.nl/en/search-interviews ?miview=ff&mizig=317&miaet=14&micode=804b&minr=1412884 (accessed August 27, 2019).

43. For example, Manuel Köppen writes that "Lanzmann repeatedly insists on having the act of killing described" by Lerner for this reason: "The technique of questioning has as its goal the revival of memories." See Köppen, "Searching for Evidence between Generations: Claude Lanzmann's *Sobibór* and Romuald Karmakar's *Land of Annihilation*," *New German Critique* 41, no. 3 (2014), 57–73; here, 65–66.

44. Greenspan, *On Listening to Holocaust Survivors*, 21.

45. Claude Lanzmann, "From Holocaust to 'Holocaust,'" in Liebman, *Claude Lanzmann's* Shoah, 27–36; here, 30.

46. Kaufmann's experience of sending Lanzmann a draft of her 1993 essay on *Shoah* is telling in this regard. She writes, "I asked him for comments, explanations, and corrections, but Lanzmann did not answer. When I phoned him, he just said that I overestimated the function of interpretation in the film" ("The Ambiguous Task of the Interpreter," 176). So much for the film's very language being a language of translation: when the interpreter threatens to approach the filmmaker in understanding, Lanzmann downplays the meaningfulness of interpretation in *Shoah*.

47. Kaufmann, "Interview et interprétation consecutive," 665.

48. Quoted in Habib, "Delay, Estrangement, Loss," 108, from Sorj Chalando, "La chose," *Libération*, January 24, 2005.

49. See Carles Torner, "The Silence of Abraham Bomba," Words Without Borders, July 2009, https://www.wordswithoutborders.org/article/the-silence-of-abraham-bomba (accessed August 27, 2019).

50. Habib, "Delay, Estrangement, Loss," 110.

51. Habib, 109.

7

Double Occupancy and Delay

The Last of the Unjust and the Archive

Tobias Ebbrecht-Hartmann

When Claude Lanzmann's *Shoah* (1985) was first released it impressed the audience with its specific notion of "presentness."[1] Based almost solely on testimonies of surviving victims, bystanders, and perpetrators, the film created situations that evoked the unprecedented crimes committed during the Holocaust in the very present. By this means, through the immediate presence of voices and places, Lanzmann precluded any comforting temporal distance that would have been able to mitigate the gaps between the atrocious past and the present. But *Shoah*, soon celebrated as an outstanding masterpiece, had its own history that began—shortly after the idea for the film was suggested to Lanzmann by Alouf Hareven, a division head in the Israeli foreign ministry—at an archive, a significant threshold between past and present. In the summer of 1973 Lanzmann started working on his project at the archives of Yad Vashem, the Holocaust memorial in Jerusalem, where he moved into a small office filled with files and books.[2]

Although, on the one hand, the archive as actual place of preserving knowledge about the past obviously contributed to what later became *Shoah*, on the other hand Lanzmann radically excluded the archive of photos and visible documents pertaining to the Holocaust from his film. Despite minor exceptions—such as an SS photograph, pictures in the Thessaloniki sequence, a schedule for a deportation train, or a display at the Ghetto Fighters' Kibbutz in Israel—archival sources are consciously absent in *Shoah*. This chapter intends to shed light on Lanzmann's complex and controversial relationship with the archive. In doing so, my intention is not to assess the value of archival footage from the Nazi past (which, however, is a very important subject that has been discussed elsewhere).[3] Rather, I am interested in following the indiscernible thread of the archive in Lanzmann's works by discussing *Shoah* in conjunction with his later work, *The Last of the Unjust* (2013), which could be interpreted as Lanzmann's first "archival film," owing to the fact that it draws on interviews from different time periods and that it includes Nazi propaganda footage as well as clandestine drawings from inmates of the Theresienstadt Ghetto. Thereby I intend to reevaluate *Shoah*'s temporal notion of "presentness" by analyzing how *The Last of the Unjust* introduces a different temporal concept that is based on the notion of delay, a temporality characterized by an interaction of different time layers that respond to resonances from the archive.

Following my introduction on the presence and nonpresence of archives in Lanzmann's films, I situate the interview with Benjamin Murmelstein, on which *The Last of the Unjust* is primarily based, within Lanzmann's body of work. Then I identify key issues in the original interview, particularly the double occupancy of Murmelstein as historical actor and historian, before exploring what I describe as multilayered temporality that characterizes *The Last of the Unjust*.

Principle of Nonarchiving

Quite early in the process of making *Shoah*, Lanzmann decided not to integrate any archival film footage or images into his film. Previous films about the Holocaust, such as *Le Temps du ghetto* (1961) by Frederic Rossif, had made him question the use of footage such as that shot in the Warsaw Ghetto by German cameramen in 1942 for a propaganda film that was left unfinished.[4] Lanzmann was convinced that actual footage from the Holocaust, including visual evidence of killings and anti-Jewish atrocities, would be "images without imagination."[5] Speaking about a two-minute-long film by the German naval soldier Reinhard Wiener, who had shot footage of a killing site close to the Latvian town Liepaja with his private camera in the summer of 1941, Lanzmann rejected such archive films as "only images, without signification," which means images that cannot present anything that would help getting closer to an understanding of the Holocaust.[6]

Instead, and in response to his encounters with witnesses and the sites of atrocities, respectively, both functioning for Lanzmann as media that in contrast to the films and pictures preserved from the past provided access to the inaccessible, Lanzmann intended to create a different aesthetic approach than earlier films. His mediation of memories departs from experimental situations, a mode that transports the past through commemoration and a specific version of reenactment into the present.[7] Gertrud Koch has emphasized that this is not a pure documentary approach. According to Koch, the witnesses perform as actors, they reenact what they experienced.[8] This results in a process of imagination on the part of the audience, which in fact is the imagination of what is not present in the images and maybe even cannot be represented: the inaccessible core of destruction. Hence, Koch points out that *Shoah* creates a "gap" (*Aussparung*) by avoiding any pictorial representation of the mass murders, even that "ghostly" documentary footage that characterizes most other nonfiction films about the Holocaust.[9] This gap delineates the border between what we can imagine and what marks the unimaginable dimension of the crimes. This results, according to Koch, in a dialectical relationship in which the gap—or better, the suspension of concrete imagination—allows viewers to imagine the unimaginable.[10]

Lanzmann's method introduced a particular temporal structure into the film. *Shoah* contains two time levels: the present of Lanzmann's journeys and interviews—footage that was shot over the course of several years—and the experiences of the past that are evoked through the testimonies of the witnesses. In addition, the constantly changing temporality of watching the film means that it is framed in a variety of ways: from the impactful contact with survivors' testimonies by a generation that predominantly had learned about the Holocaust through the shocking footage displayed in films such as Alain Resnais's *Night and Fog* (1955) or Erwin Leiser's *Mein Kampf* (1960) to reencounters with *Shoah* after Lanzmann's criticism of Steven Spielberg's *Schindler's List* (1993) or the publication of Lanzmann's autobiography in 2009. The growing temporal distance from the Holocaust itself and the significant changes in its medial representation (from a dominance of visual evidence in the early postwar decades to the authoritative role of testimonies in the "era of the witness") result in shifting temporalities of spectatorship and affect our mediated memories of the Holocaust.[11] In that it is constantly reframed, *Shoah* retains a degree of pressing "presentness."[12]

Through its multiple layers the temporal structure of *Shoah* resembles what Lawrence Langer has described as the "durational time" of testimony, which refers to the experience of a "death that has not been preceded by a life connected to such an end, followed by a temporal void," a temporal experience that resists any "foreclosure toward the past."[13] While chronological time, in contrast, presumes a consistency of temporal experience (a before, a during, and an after), durational time is based on the persistent experience of presence. It renders impossible any closure of the past and evokes the impression of an enduring "now," because closure of the traumatic memories is not possible without processing. However, processing would mean domesticating the unspeakable. Langer's concept of durational time thereby responds to the temporal structure of trauma.

According to Langer, the enduring presence is the temporal mode of survival. This mode of the constant reexperiencing of experiences, which is, strictly speaking, an enduring mode of delay, is characteristic for witnesses of the Holocaust in general as well as for his or her testimony. Hence, this variant of witnessing is a mode of repeating rather than of remembering, a notion that is clearly expressed in Lanzmann's film.[14]

Shoah's stylistic equivalent of "durational time" is a significant (and sometimes exhausting) temporality of endurance. Long takes as well as long, panning, and tracking shots dominate the film's style, which is augmented by the faces and/or voices speaking at length into the camera. Consequently, the dominant narrative mode of *Shoah* is one of openness, which is based on Lanzmann's technique of creating situations for reimagining memories. An example would be the opening sequence depicting Simon Srebnik singing on a boat. The interplay of the artificial situation with Srebnik's singing voice establishes an open space for the audience's imagination that introduces at the same time the aesthetic concept of the film. Similarly, by use of a circling camera and reflecting mirrors, the most famous and controversial sequence with survivor Abraham Bomba in the barber shop functions as a situative arrangement that opens a perceptive space for recollection and an uncomfortable encounter with the survivor's trauma.

Several studies have discussed this controversial approach of letting survivors "reenact" their experiences as well as the ethical implication of this form of retraumatization.[15] Without question, *Shoah* contains some of the most evocative and disturbing accounts of the Holocaust, especially because of embodied memories such as Abraham Bomba's.

However, subtly—in particular because *Shoah* introduced a new paradigm ·
into the cinematic discourse about the Holocaust—Lanzmann's unique film itself virtually transformed into a kind of a new archive. *Shoah* became a crucial reference point for commemorating the Holocaust and effectively also an "archive" for subsequent films that displace the documentary's "mental" images, which are mainly evoked in the imagination of the viewers in response to the oral testimonies and embodied memories of the witnesses. Later films transformed these "mental" images into graphic representations of the past, which is exemplarily illustrated in a key sequence in Spielberg's *Schindler's List* in which a group of Jewish women is mistakenly taken to Auschwitz. On their journey, they notice a Polish boy making a notorious gesture of cutting his throat, a depiction that refers to an emblematic gesture made by several witnesses in *Shoah*. Lanzmann has once described this gesture as "an open sign."[16] Although the gesture seems to self-evidently signal that the addressee is going to die, survivors such as Richard Glazar testified in *Shoah* that they were not able to decode the meaning of the gesture at that time because they could not imagine the destination of their journey. Spielberg, by introducing this open sign into the narrative of his film, transforms it into an iconic image. Thereby he fixes the gesture's meaning as self-evident. Such emulation tends toward closure where there should be openness; it suggests a fixed meaning where there should be hermeneutic complexity.[17] In result, openness is replaced with closure and durational time is replaced with the "chronological time" of a historical narrative that looks back from a position where one already knows about the fatal consequences of the Holocaust, not to mention its equivalent—the chronological time of classical cinematic narration and suspense.[18] In this way, *Schindler's List* produces a cinematic monument intended to substitute the temporal emptiness left by mass murder. For Lanzmann, the film thus

became a "fabricated archive" that provided bearable images and narratives in contrast to the abyss left by mass extermination.[19]

Film Generated Archives

But Spielberg's *Schindler's List* not only used *Shoah* and other films as a virtual archive that attempted to produce a universally accepted representation of "the" Holocaust.[20] *Schindler's List* actually also became the starting point for another, increasingly influential archive. Following the success of his film, Spielberg decided to establish the USC Shoah Foundation for Visual History and Education, which began to record, collect, and make available interviews with survivors of the Holocaust. This collection became a powerful visual source for new documentaries as well as for educational purposes and the basis for an online archive with worldwide accessibility.

The same year *Schindler's List* was released—and was met with critical remarks from Lanzmann—the director of *Shoah* himself decided to hand over the outtakes of his own landmark film to the archive of the newly established US Holocaust Memorial Museum (USHMM). One year after the museum opened its doors in Washington, DC, Lanzmann approached the Holocaust historian Raul Hilberg, who had participated in the making of *Shoah* as an expert witness and interview partner.[21] As such, he is thus one of the few participants in the film who does not relate to his actual experiences during the period of destruction. While the other interviewees either speak from the position of surviving witnesses or are former perpetrators or local bystanders, Hilberg appears in his role as a historian, even though he also personally experienced the rise of National Socialism in Vienna and fled from Austria with his family in 1939, first to France and then to the United States. In *Shoah* Hilberg also acts as the custodian and interpreter of the archive. He is the one who provides archival material in the film and assists in reading and deciphering it. In a significant scene in the film, he explains the meaning embedded in a train schedule for a deportation transport, thereby performing an exploration and mediation of the archive and its records for the camera, while at the same time he is also testifying. Hence, Hilberg's presence is simultaneously testimonial and evidentiary, and to a certain extent he implicitly "represents" the otherwise absent institution of the archive in Lanzmann's film.

Therefore, it is coherent that Hilberg became the messenger who would pave the way for the acquisition of the 220 hours of unedited material by the USHMM's film and video archive that was not included in Lanzmann's "condensate of this cinematic research."[22] In March 1994, Hilberg sent a letter to the USHMM proposing Lanzmann's idea to allocate the *Shoah* outtakes to the museum. After twelve years of negotiations, the Claude Lanzmann *Shoah* Collection was established, which, in addition to the outtakes of those interviews that were edited into the film, includes more than forty interviews that were not included in *Shoah* at all.[23]

The 16mm outtakes were then digitized, and a selection of the footage was published on the DVD *Shoah: The Unseen Interviews*. However, with its digitization, the "historiographical quarry" of material that was originally not intended for public release also entered a "new media form of existence."[24] Today the outtakes constitute a complex digital archive that is accessible online on the USHMM website. This "archive" represents, as Simon Rothöhler has emphasized, an additional intersection of *Shoah* as an open artwork.[25] The film thus started meandering through its multiple remnants and variants that correspond the palimpsestic character of the archive. As accessible archival sources, the outtakes now contribute different versions and approaches to *Shoah*. In this way, it becomes possible to unlock, on the one hand, the distinct composition of Lanzmann's film, an operation that also responds to its unsettled nature as constantly changing. On the other hand, because the outtakes of *Shoah* have been stored in an archive and made accessible in the present and for the future, Lanzmann's own material effectively has been turned into archival footage. As such, it permits us to revisit *Shoah* from the perspective of unrealized possibilities and previously untold stories that withstand the tendency of the fabricated archive to finally settle the past by transforming it into a fixed narrative. This is precisely the case of those outtakes that contain Lanzmann's interview with Benjamin Murmelstein.

| Return to the Archive

The meeting with Murmelstein was among the first interviews that Lanzmann conducted for his acclaimed masterpiece. However, like other outtakes, this interview was omitted from the released version of the film. It fit neither the film's "organizing principle" nor its notion of radical presence.[26] Vice reminds us that this was because *Shoah* focused on the topics of "death" and the "process of extermination." According to Lanzmann and his editor, this explains why the Murmelstein interview with its reflexive metahistorical references and its discourse on the "pretense of life" in Theresienstadt did not fit into the final film.[27]

However, the outtakes of the interview reveal an intensive encounter with the survivor and self-proclaimed historian Murmelstein that touched several sensitive issues regarding the history and historiography as well as the memory and legacy of the Shoah. In late 1975, Lanzmann had managed to meet Murmelstein, the only surviving Jewish "Elder" of a ghetto created and administered by the Nazis, at his new home in Rome. At that time Lanzmann and his wife, the writer Angelika Schrobsdorff, two travelers from Jerusalem, talked with the "exiled" Murmelstein about his experiences face to face with Nazi perpetrators at the Jewish Community in Vienna and at Theresienstadt. After the war Murmelstein was accused of collaboration, and although he was found not guilty by a Czech court, he was treated as a traitor, shunned by Jewish intellectuals and religious authorities, and—as he states in the interview—prevented from moving to Israel. In particular, certain Jewish historians, such as Gershom Scholem and Raul Hilberg, together with Hannah Arendt (in her book *Eichmann in Jerusalem*), claimed that the Jewish councils cooperated with the Nazis instead of resisting their requests.[28] Although Murmelstein and Lanzmann are explicitly addressing this issue, the controversy on the role of the Jewish councils was later excluded from *Shoah*. Only Raul Hilberg, who evokes Chaim Rumkowski, the leader of the Jewish Council in the Warsaw Ghetto, implicitly refers to it in a brief sequence of the finished film.[29]

Murmelstein soon became the prototype of the Jewish Nazi collaborator. H. G. Adler, the historian of the Theresienstadt Ghetto, continued to accuse him harshly even after Adler had turned away from the critical notion of collaboration: "There were four Elders of the Jews [in Terezin]—Edelstein, Zucker, Eppstein and Murmelstein, so different from each other, yet each in his own way wanted to save Jews. The first three failed in different ways, as they were bound to fail, while the fourth acted in ways hardly compatible with human dignity."[30]

Murmelstein, who had worked in Vienna as a rabbi before the Anschluss of Austria to the Third Reich, had already come into contact with Nazi officials like Adolf Eichmann because of his activities in the Viennese Jewish community. Initially the forced emigration of Austrian Jews and then the beginning of their deportation to the death camps involved him more deeply in the Nazi machinery of destruction. Finally, after his tenure as Jewish 'Elder' in Theresienstadt, he was the only remaining Jewish head official of a ghetto who survived the Holocaust. Not least because of this, accusations of collaboration and complicity focused on him.

However, according to Doron Rabinovici, Murmelstein did not want to be a mere object of history. Instead, he demanded to be seen as a subject and refused to be acknowledged only as a victim.[31] Murmelstein's demand to participate in writing his own history is also obvious in the outtakes from *Shoah*. Lanzmann's interview and his prospective film were another medium in which Murmelstein attempted to posit his version of the historical events, thereby reaching beyond his perspective as a witness. However, this message only arrived after a delay, because Lanzmann did not include the interview in his film. Accordingly, Rabinovici, who also emphasizes the fragmentary character of the outtakes that constantly remind the viewer of its status as source, describes the interview as a "remnant" (*Überbleibsel*)—a "message in a bottle" that, like an archive, is addressed to an undefined future.[32]

According to the transcripts of the interview, the filming began with a conversation between Lanzmann and Murmelstein about Rome. Lanzmann emphasizes the beauty of the city, an opinion with which Murmelstein agrees. This motivates Lanzmann to dig more deeply and ask about Murmelstein's perception of Rome, a question that the latter hesitates to answer. Murmelstein instead emphasizes that he is neither an architect nor an art expert.[33] Although when he met with Murmelstein Lanzmann had not yet developed his concept of using specific places for the evocation of memories, this early interview departs already from a similar objective. Rome functions as a "third space," a place of exile, as Murmelstein characterizes the city after telling Lanzmann when and how he came to it following his liberation. This place of exile, itself a city that is significantly shaped by a multitude of overlapping historical layers, becomes the starting point of "looking back," as Lanzmann describes the objective of the conversation.

Murmelstein replies with a reference to the myth of Orpheus and Eurydice, a significant metaphor for the ambivalence of memory and historiography: "First of all you talked me into it and now you are asking me. You know [Murmmelstein mumbles] it is difficult to look into the past. So, let me get back to something which is removed from our subject, but closer to my specialty, mythology. There is the myth of Orpheus and Eurydice . . . who escaped from the realm of the dead, or let's say they almost escaped, but she looked back and then had to stay there. Sometimes it is good not to look back. On the other hand, you have convinced me that this retrospective is necessary and it is not my way . . . to recoil. It never was my way to recoil from a possible danger. Let's hope that it will end well."

With this statement Murmelstein unfolds his historiographical concept. The past is described as a dangerous territory, still affected by the experience of death, a descriptor that is in a similar way true for Lanzmann's *Shoah*, which he often described as attempt to get closer to the essence of the Holocaust: destruction and death. However, Murmelstein's reference to Orpheus and Eurydice can also be interpreted as a reference to the archive that contains and buries the remnants of the past. Although looking back in time is dangerous, because it can question and challenge what we perceive as history, the process of recollection is necessary in order to transform past experiences into history. Hence, it is Eurydice who becomes the model for the joint journey of Murmelstein and Lanzmann into the past of Theresienstadt and the Shoah. However, it is the interrelation of history and mythology, the combination of recollection and narration, that characterizes the historiographical concept offered by Murmelstein. Thereby, Murmelstein blurs the boundaries between myth and history. Storytelling, which was already the strategy of survival in Theresienstadt, where the ghetto transformed into a mock-up of an ordinary city, is an essential part of this mode of historiography.[34] Hence, Murmelstein takes an ambiguous point of view. He is a transformative messenger (intertwining the position of the witness and of the archive) and storyteller (historian).

This is illustrated by the actual beginning of the first reel. Before the camera pans over the panorama of Rome from the balcony of Murmelstein's apartment, it records a series of quite different frames. Placed on the floor, the camera focuses on fragmented body parts, legs, shoes, and parts of furniture. The exemplary top-down perspective of the historian, which

Benjamin Murmelstein, Claude Lanzmann, and Angelika Schrobsdorff view the panorama of Rome from Murmelstein's residence in *The Last of the Unjust* (2013). Directed by Claude Lanzmann. Released by Cohen Media Group. DVD still.

is expressed through the significant framing of the conversation above the city of Rome, is contrasted with the bottom-up perspective of the archive. Hence, the fragmentary and contingent film footage accidently resonates its later status as archival source.

Within the interview itself, the archive as a place that stores the remnants of the past plays only a minor role. However, it is addressed several times as a reference for historical authentication. Murmelstein first mentions archives in the context of a speech given by Adolf Eichmann at the train station in Nisko. After the German invasion of Poland, Eichmann had set up a transit camp at the Southern Polish town, through which over ninety thousand Polish Jews were deported. However, the wider context of this reference is the Eichmann trial in Jerusalem and Arendt's report about this trial. Murmelstein adds: "In addition in the archives or I don't know where, is a book in which the speech is described. The first chapter of my book 'Theresienstadt' carries the title 'Altimenti cioè morir'—'Otherwise there is death.' But they [the investigators preparing the Eichmann trial] did not even look at the table of contents." The archive serves as general reference point for Murmelstein's statement. Murmelstein even admits that he does not actually know where the speech is preserved. In fact, the controversy over the historiographical shortcomings of the Eichmann trial is about something different that can be described as hidden or suppressed historical knowledge. Murmelstein uses the archive as a metaphor for this rejected knowledge, which is then contrasted with his overlooked—or, in Murmelstein's perception, ignored—study, in which he portrays Theresienstadt based on an interplay of his own experiences and historical sources. His book was published in 1961 in an Italian version, but disregarded by historians at that time; a German edition only came out in 2014. By referring to his book, Murmelstein frames himself as an unheard historian of the ghetto, Orpheus, the archivist of the Holocaust, thus multiplying his speaking position. He is both: an actor (participant) in the course of history and its historian. Accordingly, Rabinovici compares Murmelstein, the last Elder of the Jews in Theresienstadt, with the task of the modern historian to understand the actions of different groups of perpetrators as well as the differences between them.[35]

The double role of Murmelstein as a historical actor and as a historian is obvious as well in other parts of the interview in which archives are mentioned. Murmelstein refers, for instance, to weekly reports, which he had to write on request of Eichmann, suggesting that Lanzmann should look for them in archives in Vienna. Here, Murmelstein appears as both originator and interpreter of these historical records. As mentioned earlier, in the final version of *Shoah* it is Hilberg who bears the interpretative voice of the historian. Obviously, Lanzmann decided to separate both positions: the historical actors (embodied in the two clearly differentiated positions of the surviving witnesses and the perpetrators), and the historian's authority.

However, Murmelstein evokes the archive with its ambiguous temporality to "resolve" the contradiction between the historical actor and the historiographer. Accordingly, he refers to it as being simultaneously both: a place, in which the unsettling past continues to exist as trace, and as an institution that preserves a distinct historical record.

This interplay is illustrated in two sequences (again, excluded from *The Last of the Unjust*) that refer to archives as places of revelation. One, referring to the archives of the American Joint Distribution Committee, evokes the historian Murmelstein offering a counterversion to the dominant and incomplete historiography (of his own involvement in the history of

Theresienstadt), which he supports with evidence from the archive: "Yes, there are documents, yes. But when you read documents based on reports which I have written, or one takes the documents . . . documents of the International Red Cross, the protest documents, documents of the Archives of the American Joint Distribution Committee . . . there are documents by the Council of British Jewry, etc. then you will get a totally different impression. I hope."[36] Murmelstein thus assumes that the archive will reveal a different version of his history that will also reunite the two disparate "Murmelsteins": the historical actor and the historian.

The second sequence refers to Scholem's criticism of Murmelstein's actions. Here again, Murmelstein attributes to archives the power of revealing historical truth and establishing historical justice. Murmelstein contrasts Scholem's authority as a scholar of Jewish history with the authority of the archive: "Because [Scholem] was such a big scholar, who had to research scholarly systems and sources. And there are sources regarding Murmelstein. The archives of the Red Cross, the Rahm trial, the Murmelstein trial. And very obviously, the Eichmann trial." This argument characterizes "the archive" as an account of a counternarrative to the official rejection of his person by Scholem and others.

This specific part of the conversation between Murmelstein and Lanzmann is situated in front of the Arch of Titus, which symbolizes the Roman victory over the Jewish resistance in Judea and the destruction of the Second Temple in Jerusalem, and refers to another ambiguous Jewish historian, Josephus Flavius. Flavius, a Roman Jew who, like Murmelstein, acted as both historical participant and historiographer, was the only one who preserved the lost Jewish memory of the destruction of ancient Judea. Correspondingly, Zdenek Lederer would later compare Flavious to Murmelstein, who was simultaneously participant and historiographer of Theresienstadt, a comparison that Murmelstein nevertheless questioned in his conversation with Lanzmann.[37]

The appearance of archival sources on the visual level correspondingly contributes to Murmelstein's self-representation as playing a double role. At some point the camera focuses on a book that contains a photograph of Murmelstein at a meeting of the Jewish council in Theresienstadt. Lanzmann holds the book toward the camera, which then zooms in on the photograph and hence enlarges the face of a younger Murmelstein, who is looking up to his predecessor, Dr. Epstein. Then the camera zooms back again and refocuses on the face of the older Murmelstein. Without any cut, this single camera movement, which is even repeated in the footage several times, thus captures the two different versions of Murmelstein, the historical actor and the historian, in two distinct temporalities.[38]

Rediscovery of the Haunting Archive

In hindsight, the meeting with Murmelstein marks another point of origin of *Shoah,* but, because the interview was left out, this origin is invisible in the completed film. After its release, Lanzmann retained the ten-hour conversation among the other outtakes and later handed them over to the USHMM archives. But the Murmelstein interview remained an open account that, in Lanzmann's words, has "continued to dwell in my mind and haunt me."[39] The primary reason for Lanzmann's decision to finally return to the interview was its first public screening at the Vienna Film Museum in October 2007.[40] When parts of the unedited footage, by then transformed into an archival source, were presented there, Lanzmann, who was present at that screening, felt "robbed" of his filmmaking work.[41] In his perception, the participants at the screening spoke about the footage as if it was theirs: "I was incensed. It is my work, my face, my voice."[42] At that moment, he decided to make a film from the unedited footage. The impression of a detached usage of the material by scholars and historians thus provoked Lanzmann to reenter "his" archive and to integrate unused fragments from *Shoah* into his first "archival film," *The Last of the Unjust.*[43]

On many levels, this film turned out to be very different from *Shoah.* If *Shoah* is about death, then *The Last of the Unjust* might be seen as a film about life. *Shoah* evokes the presence of the absence of the murdered European Jews, whereas in *The Last of the Unjust* Lanzmann attempts to show the continued existence of Jewish life—for example, when visiting a Viennese synagogue.[44] While *Shoah*'s mode of address is a radical presence, and the concise editing of the film serves this present tense, *The Last of the Unjust* edits together different sources from different periods of time, such as film footage from the 1944 Theresienstadt propaganda film; photographs and paintings originating from the Theresienstadt Ghetto; footage from the interview with Murmelstein from the mid 1970s; and contemporary footage of Lanzmann visiting Vienna and the remnants of the ghetto at the Theresienstadt memorial site. The film thereby creates another form of an open narrative that is based, as I will demonstrate, on the specific interplay and friction of these materials as well as on a layered interplay of different temporal frames defined by these archival sources. Finally, while *Shoah*, through the voices of the witnesses, established a specific form of cinematic history of the Holocaust, the interview with Murmelstein constantly reflects the ambivalences of writing history and reveals the double role of the protagonist as actor/witness and historian.

However, at the same time, *The Last of the Unjust* still remains a supplement to *Shoah*, another—belated—way of trying to approach the experience of mass destruction. But in this case the dominant temporal mode of duration in *Shoah* is replaced by a different form of temporality. Durational time is complemented by the temporality of delay. This is illustrated in the three different time frames that characterize *The Last of the Unjust* and correspond to its multifaceted protagonists. Lanzmann has emphasized that his film contains three protagonists: Murmelstein; Lanzmann at the age of fifty interviewing Murmelstein; and Lanzmann at the age of eighty-seven, making his film about Murmelstein.[45] But, in fact, as demonstrated above and also emphasized by Vice, Murmelstein also appears in the film twice, as the seventy-year old historian talking with Lanzmann about his experiences, and as the young man the older one evokes in his descriptions of his time in Vienna after the Anschluss and in Theresienstadt during the Holocaust.[46] Correspondingly, Koch proposes to "enlarge the group portrait by suggesting that the film contains two self-portraits, one of Murmelstein and the other of Lanzmann (in addition to the portrait of Murmelstein by Lanzmann). And in many respects one could even say that the men mirrored each other in their admiration for action—even if the action ranged from minimal to none."[47] This mirroring structure can also be related to the writing of (self-) history and the role of the archive. Similar to Murmelstein, who appears as historical actor and historian in the film, the "two" Lanzmanns represent two different perspectives—the younger critical investigator (actor) and the older historian who evokes the rejected history of Murmelstein but implicitly also digs out his own archive in order to define his legacy. Hence, *The Last of the Unjust* is also an autobiographical movie that is significantly shaped by the ambivalent and partly contradictory speaking positions of the narrating and the narrated "I."

The multifaceted protagonists echo the three dominant time frames in the film: the period between 1938 and 1945, the meeting between Lanzmann and Murmelstein in the mid-seventies, and the making of the later film in 2011 and 2012. Moreover, these temporal levels correspond to the three different types of footage. With that, the archive and its temporality significantly structure the temporality of the film and its composition.

The Last of the Unjust opens with a prologue. Like many of Lanzmann's films, the director uses the written word, scrolling on the black screen, to contextualize what we will later see. The prologue refers to Murmelstein and Theresienstadt, the historical reference points of the film. But it also identifies different archival sources: his filmed interview with Murmelstein, of course, but also Murmelstein's 1961 book *Terezín, il Ghetto Modello di Eichmann* and the unique drawings made by a group of painters around Bendrich Fritta and Leo Haas, who were forced to work in the technical office of the Theresienstadt Ghetto. But Lanzmann also identifies his own position in relation to the archive, describing himself as a "custodian of something unique," hence inhabiting the role of the archivist and gate-keeper who is at the same time irrevocably bound to the material that has continued to haunt him. This is precisely the role of the aging auteur film-maker. He revisits his own filmmaking past by framing and structuring the outtakes from the archives with his authenticating presence at the historical places. In addition, he gives voice to his fellow "actor" Murmelstein by reading passages from his writings and thereby completing the palimpsest of temporal layers of the film.

This approach is already introduced in the first sequences of the film. It opens with a shot of a train station. Claude Lanzmann, the eighty-seven-year-old director, stands on a train platform that is marked by a sign reading "Bohušovice." It is a new, modern train station, although the main building on the left side of the frame may be a remnant of an earlier time. Despite the apparent newness of the train station, however, Bohušovice is a historical site. Beginning in 1942 and continuing until the end of the war, Jews arrived here first from Prague, then from cities of the German Reich, to be imprisoned in the Theresienstadt Ghetto. Lanzmann begins to explain this

Claude Lanzmann at the train platform at Bohušovice in *The Last of the Unjust*. DVD still.

hidden connection between past and present ("Nobody in the world knows the name of Bohušovice and its train station"), thus transforming the place into a threshold to a chapter of the Holocaust that was not included in *Shoah*.

However, *Shoah* is still present in this opening sequence. Suddenly, the noise of a freight train interrupts Lanzmann's opening words when it rushes through the image. The train resonates with those trains that inhabit *Shoah* as its central visual trope. Hence, the train in the present evokes two additional temporal layers: the time of the deportations during the Shoah and the time of the film *Shoah*. Furthermore, the shot of Lanzmann and the trains in Bohušovice is characterized by its duration, expressed through the cinematic device of the long take, which had already characterized the visual style of *Shoah*. Several trains are shown moving through the station, while the camera rests on Lanzmann as narrator of the story, historian, and custodian of the archival traces, who has to resist the noisy restlessness of the present: "We cannot control the traffic," Lanzmann states. The audience has to wait until the film can continue on the narrative level, because the interruptions postpone Lanzmann's reading. Hence, two significant temporalities are introduced in the opening sequence—duration and delay. In this way, both the durational time of the witness and the temporal mode of delay as central mode of the archive are intertwined.

Lanzmann's presence at the places of Murmelstein's life is, however, a lonely one. While, in *Shoah*, the witnesses and their voices resonated at the sites of destruction in *The Last of the Unjust*, Lanzmann appears as the last remaining custodian of the preserved testimonies. Hence, along with his own presence at the historical sites, Lanzmann edits fragments from the archive, his original interview footage. Both materials, the present footage and the outtakes, are connected through another archival element, Murmelstein's book *Terezin, il Ghetto Modello di Eichmann*, from which Lanzmann reads passages translated into French. Thus the film creates associative resonances between the different pasts that illustrate the impossibility of "immediate" access and emphasize the moment of delay. On the one hand, Murmelstein was forced to create delay in his position as Jewish Elder in Theresienstadt by continuously inventing the tale of the ghetto as a "pleasant" place. On the other hand, Lanzmann brought Murmelstein's memories to the public's attention only after a delay, although it was supposed to be included in *Shoah* and may have restored Murmelstein's reputation if it had been. Because it wasn't, *The Last of the Unjust* is itself a delayed film. In contrast to Murmelstein's authorative approach to the archive as a place of revelation, both aspects of delay also refer to the fictive character of the archive, which in fact does not contain historical truth but fragmented remnants and ambiguous traces. Hence, a notion of "truth" can be achieved only through colliding encounters with different archival materials and multilayered voices.

This attempt to establish a palimpsest-like interplay of different archival materials and multilayered voices characterizes the composition of *The Last of the Unjust*. Murmelstein in his double function as historical actor and his own historian only appears on-screen in person after twenty-two minutes. This first appearance is quite significant, because its montage aligns and combines different archival sources. The first archival sequence that is used in *The Last of the Unjust* is the panning shot from the first reel of the outtakes. The camera pans the panorama of Rome while from off-screen Murmelstein's voice can be heard. He speaks about the beauty of the city and his exile, when Lanzmann refers to the strange fact that they look back to a past, which now seems as ancient as ancient Rome. Murmelstein has turned his back to the camera. Then, when talking about the repercussions in present-day Europe of the extermination of the Jews, he slowly turns his face to the camera. It seems as if Murmelstein in this movement toward the camera literally turns his gaze to the past, which is even emphasized when then he explicitly refers to Orpheus and Eurydice. Hence, with this cinematic movement Lanzmann attributes to Murmelstein, as I have already described above, the part of Eurydice, while Murmelstein himself might have identified earlier with Orpheus, who is able to transgress the threshold between death and life. Only now does Murmelstein accept the necessity of looking back in time. However, he describes this as an act of courage, because he had never let danger hold him back. In this way, he implicitly interrelates his time-transgressing position as witness of the Nazi past with his past role as Elder in Theresienstadt. This illustrates his attempt to reframe his own past and the history of the ghetto in a new way, as he openly states in his next statement: "I consider our talk today a delayed epilogue to my former work. For this reason, I overcome this sentiment of danger and put myself at your disposal." Interestingly, Murmelstein already includes in this self-positioning as a historian the notion of delay.

The archival footage with the panning shot over Rome and Murmelstein's significant movement toward the camera follows another important sequence that resonates in Murmelstein's words about the loss of European Jewry. In these previous shots we see Lanzmann in the buildings of the former Theresienstadt Ghetto, standing in front of a crematorium oven and reciting Murmelstein's description of the ghetto life and—foremost—the everyday experience of death. The reading is interrupted by several drawings, created by Otto Ungar, Ferdinand Bloch, and Bedrich Fritta, all of them inmates from the ghetto, who clandestinely produced these images during their imprisonment. These drawings, clearly not pretending a realist or documentary style, correlate with the description of the ghetto as a "world upside down." The pictures reappear as ghosts (accordingly, the reading is referring to Theresienstadt as a "ghost ship") from a secret archive, which the artists had addressed to an indefinite future. But in *The Last of the Unjust* the paintings bear witness as historical records precisely because they are no "pure" documents. The artistic drawings from the ghetto prisoners thereby contradict another visual source that appears shortly after: moving images from propaganda footage that "documented" in 1944 the fiction of the ghetto as a pleasant and comfortable place. At first, however, before film extracts from the movie *Theresienstadt—Ein Dokumentarfilm aus dem jüdschen Siedlungsgebiet* appear on-screen, *The Last of the Unjust* inserts the photograph showing Murmelstein sitting next to Epstein, which is described as a production still from the shooting.[48] With a sarcastic undertone, Murmelstein refers to this image as the "first time" when he was standing in front of a movie camera. This "first time" is contrasted to the second time when he is now approaching Lanzmann's camera. While in the propaganda film he appeared as an "actor," he describes his appearance in Lanzmann's film as "epilogue" (hence as commentary from hindsight) to his "active" part in history.

Vice is obviously right when she emphasizes, regarding the appropriation of Nazi propaganda footage and clandestine drawings, that "what we see is not given the status of documentary imagery." Indeed, the "film extracts and drawings are clearly marked as representations."[49] But as archival sources they also introduce a different temporality, and this temporality of the archive creates frictions and resonances that result in the fragmentary character of the film. The different materials (drawings, recitation, outtakes and propaganda footage) are related to each other through the montage neither to the effect of creating a coherent argument (in the sense of warranting) nor to the offering of a chronological narrative.

Instead, the editing of *The Last of the Unjust* emphasizes the double appearance of Murmelstein as younger and older man, as a prisoner in Theresienstadt and as an exile in Rome. Furthermore, it relates this double occupancy to different temporalities, the historical time of the Holocaust and the experienced time of the witness as they are approached in the mode of delayed time. Hence, *The Last of the Unjust* adds to the notion of an inaccessible past in *Shoah* the temporal mode of an infinite deferral. This emphasizes the impression of ambiguity, which corresponds to Murmelstein's double role as actor and historian in the outtake footage. This is clearly a result of the meandering of *Shoah* into its delayed successor, on the one hand, and the collision of archival sources in *The Last of the Unjust*, on the other.

| Temporality of the Archive

For that reason the different temporal layers and materials in *The Last of the Unjust* prevent any final balancing of past and present. A temporal reconciliation that might finally turn the experience of the Holocaust into a bygone past is blocked by both: the durational mode of the testimony and the archival mode of delay. Such an attempt to "restore the balance" is, in contrast, according to Langer, the domain of memory culture, which is illustrated in *The Last of the Unjust* by numerous plates and memorials.[50] These memorials represent the opposite not only of "durational time" but also of archival time, and although Lanzmann himself seems to have sympathy for the attempts to come to terms with the past illustrated by these memorials, his film and its heterogeneous temporality withstand any coherent and consistent interpretation, in particular because of its fragmentary nature. The past still persists and continues to live on in haunting resonances and the archival time of delay.

In contrast to the—maybe too easy—conclusion that *The Last of the Unjust* could be interpreted as a revision of Lanzmann's approach in *Shoah* and as a rehabilitation of the archive, I conclude that the usage of the postponed archival outtakes from *Shoah*; Murmelstein's double occupancy as historian and historical actor; the presence of (the older) Lanzmann in context of the twenty-first century's culture of memory; and the distorted "then" of the Nazi propaganda archive add a reflection of archival time to *Shoah*'s preoccupation with the "durational time" of the testimony. Therefore, and in addition to the experience of duration within the cinematic reflection of the Holocaust's infinite deferral, *The Last of the Unjust* emphasizes a moment of delay that is already inscribed in the outtakes of the Murmelstein interview.

| Notes

1. Stella Bruzzi, for instance, observes the "physicality and presentness of Lanzmann's pursuit of personal recollection," particularly in the interviews with Jan Karski and Abraham Bomba. See Bruzzi, *New Documentary: A Critical Introduction* (London: Routledge, 2000), 107. Michael D'Arcy emphasizes the contrast between Bazin's concept of presentness and Lanzmann's approach. Lanzmann, according to D'Arcy, "is not locating his film's experience of presentness in the cinematic image of the Holocaust but rather in the viewer's imagination." See D'Arcy, "Claude Lanzmann's *Shoah* and the Intentionality of the Image," in *Visualizing the Holocaust: Documents, Aesthetics, Memory*, ed. David

Bathrick, Brad Prager, and Michael David Richardson (Rochester, NY: Camden House, 2008), 138-61; here, 148.

2. Claude Lanzmann, *Der patagonische Hase: Erinnerungen* (Reinbek: Rohwolt, 2010), 531.

3. See Brad Prager, "The Warsaw Ghetto, Seen from the Screening Room: The Images That Dominate *A Film Unfinished*," *New German Critique* 41, no. 3 (2014): 135–57; Tobias Ebbrecht-Hartmann, "Echoes from the Archive: Retrieving and Re-viewing Cinematic Remnants of the Nazi Past," in *Archive and Memory in German Literature and Visual Culture: Edinburgh German Yearbook 9*, ed. Dora Osborne (Rochester, NY: Camden House, 2015), 123–39; and Tobias Ebbrecht-Hartmann, "Trophy, Evidence, Document: Appropriating an Archive Film from Liepaja, 1941," *Historical Journal of Film, Radio and Television* 36, no. 4 (2016): 509–28.

4. Lanzmann, *Der patagonische Hase*, 532.

5. Claude Lanzmann, "Der Ort und das Wort: Über *Shoah*," in *"Niemand zeugt für den Zeugen": Erinnerungskultur nach der Shoah* (Frankfurt/M.: Suhrkamp, 2000), 101–18; here, 107.

6. Lanzmann "Der Ort und das Wort," 107.

7. See Christoph Hesse, Doron Rabinovici, and Gerhard Scheit, "Der letzte der Ungerechten: Eine Diskussion zum Werk Claude Lanzmanns," *sans phrase* 4, no. 1 (2014): 211–20; here, 212.

8. Gertrud Koch, "The Aesthetic Transformation of the Image of the Unimaginable: Notes on Claude Lanzmann's *Shoah*." *October* 48 (1989): 15–24; here, 20; and Koch, *Die Einstellung ist die Einstellung: Visuelle Konstruktionen des Judentums* (Frankfurt/M: Suhrkamp, 1992), 148.

9. Koch, *Die Einstellung ist die Einstellung*, 149.

10. Koch, 152.

11. Annette Wieviorka, *The Era of the Witness* (Ithaca, NY: Cornell University Press, 2006).

12. See, for example, the tribute to Lanzmann at the Berlinale in 2013, the retrospective of his films about the Holocaust at the Haifa Film Festival in 2015 and festival screenings of Lanzmann's oeuvre at the This Human World Festival in Vienna. Tobias Ebbrecht-Hartmann, "*Tsahal* zwischen *Shoah* und *Sobibór*: Über Vermittlung und Resonanz bei Claude Lanzmann," in: *Le Regard du Siècle: Claude Lanzmann zum 90. Geburtstag*, ed. Susanne Zepp (Baden Baden: Tectum), 175–92.

13. Lawrence Langer, "Memory's Time: Chronology and Duration in Holocaust Testimonies," in *Admitting the Holocaust: Collected Essays* (Oxford: Oxford University Press, 1995), 53–67; here, 14 and 20.

14. I thank Yonatan Kay and my course The Holocaust, Collective Memory and Cinema at the Hebrew University of Jerusalem 2016/17 for inspiring and fruitful discussions about Langer's concept of durational time.

15. See, for example, Dominick LaCapra, "Lanzmann's *Shoah*: 'Here There Is No Why,'" *Critical Inquiry* 23, no. 2 (1997), 231–69; here, 256–57; and also Ora Gelley, "A Response to Dominick LaCapra's 'Lanzmann's *Shoah*,'" *Critical Inquiry* 24, no. 3 (1998): 830–32.

16. Claude Lanzmann, "Seminar with Claude Lanzmann 11 April 1990," *Yale French Studies* 79 (1991): 82–99; here, 87.

17. Tobias Ebbrecht, *Geschichtsbilder im medialen Gedächtnis: Filmische Narrationen des Holocaust* (Bielefeld: transcript, 2011), 194–95.

18. Among others Miriam Hansen has convincingly challenged the binary juxtaposition of *Schindler's List* and *Shoah* in her seminal article "*Schindler's List* Is Not *Shoah*: Second Commandment, Popular Modernism, and Public Memory," in: *Spielberg's Holocaust: Critical Perspectives on* Schindler's List, ed. Yosefa Loshitzky (Bloomington: Indiana University Press, 1997), 77–103. Therefore, it is important to emphasize that my juxtaposition of both films is not based on the presumption of a singularity of the Holocaust or a general impossibility of representing the mass murder of the European Jews. Rather, corresponding with Hansen's view, I understand the Holocaust as fundamentally challenging our ideas of representation, temporality, and history (82). The ability of imagination is a crucial precondition for confronting this challenge as well, as are multisensory modes of experience and the often-overlooked "dimension of the acoustic" (85); narrative cinema—proven, for instance, by a film such as *Son of Saul* (2015)—is perfectly capable of establishing an equally resonant mode of representation. Furthermore, especially because it integrated *Shoah* into its visual (and narrative) structure, *Schindler's List*, as I will show, preserves, as a cinematic archive, yet another access point to *Shoah* and through *Shoah*. The films are not opposing each other, but are instead bound together in an entangled relationship.

19. Claude Lanzmann, "Ihr sollt nicht weinen: Einspruch gegen Schindlers Liste," in: *"Der gute Deutsche": Dokumente zur Diskussion um Schindlers Liste in Deutschland*, ed. Christoph Weiss (St. Imbert: Rohrig Universitätsverlag, 1995), 173–78; here, 175–76.

20. See Tobias Ebbrecht-Hartmann, "Preserving Memory or Fabricating the Past? How Films Constitute Cinematic Archives of the Holocaust," *Cinéma & Cie* 15, no. 24 (2015): 33–47.

21. Ronny Loewy, "Die Shoa-Outtakes," in *"Der Letzte der Ungerechten": Der "Judenälteste" Benjamin Murmelstein in Filmen 1942–1975*, ed. Ronny Loewy and Katharina Rauschenberger (Frankfurt/M: Campus Verlag, 2011), 11–14; here, 13.

22. Simon Rothöhler, "*Shoah*-Compilation im Netz: Das Pop-up-Fenster samt Zeitzeugen," *tageszeitung*, March 22, 2012, https://taz.de/!5097895/ (accessed August 27, 2019).

23. See Loewy, "Die Shoa-Outtakes," 13. See also the chapter by Zarwell and Swift in this volume.

24. Rothöhler, "*Shoah*-Compilation im Netz," n.p.

25. Rothöhler, n.p.

26. Sue Vice, "Supplementing *Shoah*: Claude Lanzmann's *The Karski Report* and *The Last of the Unjust*," in *Holocaust Cinema in the Twenty-First Century*, ed. Gerd Bayer and Oleksandr Kobrynskyy (London: Wallflower, 2015), 41–75; here, 44.

27. Gertrud Koch, "'Madagascar, Nisko, Theresienstadt, Auschwitz': On the Visibility of Sites in Claude Lanzmann's *The Last of the Unjust* (2013)," *Apparatus. Film, Media and Digital Cultures in Central and Eastern Europe*, nos. 2–3 (2016): http://dx.doi.org/10.17892/app.2016.0003.49 (accessed August 27, 2019).

28. Lisa Hauff, "'. . . zwischen Hammer und Amboss': Selbstwahrnehmung und Zuschreibung bei Benjamin Murmelstein," in *"Der Letzte der Ungerechten,"* 53–74; here, 56.

29. Vice, "Supplementing *Shoah*," 39.

30. H. G. Adler, "The 'Autonomous Jewish Administration of Terezin,'" in *Imposed Jewish Governing Bodies Under Nazi Rule: Yivo Colloquium, December 2–5, 1967*, ed. Yivo Institute for Jewish Research (New York: Yivo Institute for Jewish Research, 1967), 70–82.

31. Doron Rabinovici, "Benjamin Murmelstein, 'Der letzte der Ungerechten': Elemente und Folgen totaler Ohnmacht," in *"Der Letzte der Ungerechten,"* 35–52; here, 50.

32. Rabinovici, "Benjamin Murmelstein," 52.

33. I thank Lindsay Zarwell and the USHMM film and video archive for providing me with the transcripts and translations of the *Shoah* interview with Murmelstein and information about those parts of the interview that were used in

Lanzmann's *The Last of the Unjust*. The outtakes as well as the transcripts contain several repeated takes. This is also the case with the opening scene, which was shot several times in different versions.

34. See Koch, "Madagascar, Nisko, Theresienstadt, Auschwitz," n.p.

35. Rabinovici, "Benjamin Murmelstein," 50.

36. Claude Lanzmann *Shoah* Collection, interview with Benjamin Murmelstein (RG-60.5009, Film ID 3189, Camera Rolls 93–96), US Holocaust Memorial Museum and Yad Vashem and State of Israel.

37. Hauff, ". . . zwischen Hammer und Amboss," 64.

38. This double role is similar to the basic narratological structure of autobiographies or memoirs with a "narrating I" and a "narrated I," which also indicates the blurred genre boundaries of Murmelstein's book, on the one hand, and the interview with Lanzmann, on the other. His book presents itself as a historical study but is simultaneously a biographical account. The interview is intended as a testimony but Murmelstein also uses it to present his own historiography of the Theresienstadt Ghetto.

39. See Geoffrey Macnab, "Return to *Shoah*: Claude Lanzmann's New Film *The Last of the Unjust* Revisits Holocaust Epic," *Independent*, March 14, 2014. Correspondingly, Lanzmann also mentions in the opening titles of *The Last of the Unjust* this continuing persistence of his encounter with Murmelstein as one of his motivations to make the film.

40. For details, see the respective note on the homepage of the Vienna Film Museum: https://www.filmmuseum.at/jart/prj3/filmmuseum/main.jart?rel=en&reserve -mode=active&content-id=1219068743272&schienen_id=1215680368518& ss1=y (accessed July 13, 2017).

41. Vice, "Supplementing *Shoah*," 45.

42. See Jürg Altwegg, "Die Marionette konnte die Fäden ziehen: Ein Gespräch mit dem französischen Regisseur und Produzenten Claude Lanzmann," *Frankfurter Allgemeine Zeitung*, May 27, 2013, 27. For Lanzmann's quotation, see Macnab, "Return to *Shoah*."

43. However, it should be mentioned that this was not Lanzmann's first return to the outtakes from *Shoah*. Lanzmann had already based previous projects—most notably *Sobibór, Oct. 14, 1943, 4 p.m.* (2001) and *The Karski Report* (2010)—on footage that was originally shot for *Shoah*. Nevertheless, *The Last of the Unjust* is the first of these films that explicitly reflects the archival dimension of the outtakes, combines them with other archival sources, and integrates them in a complex network of different temporalities. Recently, Lanzmann worked on

another film that was edited from the outtakes. *The Four Sisters* (2018) focuses on some of the female witnesses he interviewed for *Shoah*: Paula Biren, Ruth Elias, Ada Lichtman, and Hanna Marton.

44. Richard Brody, "Claude Lanzmann's *The Last of the Unjust*," *New Yorker*, September 27, 2013, https://www.newyorker.com/culture/richard-brody/claude-lanzmanns-the-last-of-the-unjust (accessed August 27, 2019).

45. Claude Lanzmann, "Den Deutschen war egal, wer zur Vernichtung fuhr," interview with Max Dax, *Spiegel Online*, February 14, 2013, http://www.spiegel.de/kultur/kino/interview-mit-claude-lanzmann-zum-goldenen-ehrenbaeren-der-berlinale-a-883167.html (accessed July 13, 2017).

46. Vice, "Supplementing *Shoah*," 45.

47. Koch, "Madagascar, Nisko, Theresienstadt, Auschwitz," n.p.

48. According to Murmelstein, the actual film scene showing him next to Epstein was left out of the film's "final" version.

49. Vice, "Supplementing *Shoah*," 45.

50. Langer, "Memory's Time," 14.

8 | In Search of Suchomel in *Shoah*

Examining Claude Lanzmann's Postproduction Editing Practice

Erin McGlothlin

The recent availability of the roughly 220 hours of outtakes in the Claude Lanzmann *Shoah* Collection held by the United States Holocaust Memorial Museum (USHMM) and Yad Vashem not only allows researchers to discover new facets of Lanzmann's massive cinematic project, to explore the previously unseen testimony of witnesses, and to learn about aspects of the Holocaust not directly addressed in *Shoah*; but it also has the capacity to alter significantly the scholarly consensus on Lanzmann's filmmaking practice. Particularly for those of us who researched and wrote about *Shoah* before the outtakes were fully digitized and widely accessible, this new archive of material bears the unsettling potential to challenge and even upend what we thought we knew about the film and the interpretations we developed based on that knowledge. At the same time, the *Shoah* outtakes also present a singular opportunity to retrace territory already traversed in an effort to glean new insights and critical conclusions, to reexamine outdated assumptions that were based on the partial information available at the time, and to rethink outmoded categories, frameworks, and analyses. In short, the outtakes entreat us to review and revise scholarly conclusions that we once asserted as immutable; they compel us to acknowledge as provisional arguments that we once framed as invariable. This is true of my own work on the film. As the following will demonstrate, my encounter with the outtakes has required me to engage in a productive and illuminating exercise of reevaluation by obliging me to reconsider and to amend the conclusions of my prior research on Lanzmann's representation of the perpetrators in *Shoah*, particularly as it regards one of the film's central figures.

Lanzmann's Interview with Franz Suchomel in *Shoah*

Of all the disquieting scenes of testimony that appear in the theatrical release of Claude Lanzmann's nonfiction masterwork *Shoah*—testimony that has disparately devastating effects on the viewer, depending on whether the witness is a Holocaust survivor, perpetrator, or bystander—the scenes with Franz Suchomel, the former SS guard at Treblinka, are arguably among the most difficult for the viewer to digest. Filmed with a hidden camera and organized into five separate sequences distributed throughout the film, Lanzmann's interview with Suchomel reveals in horrific detail the inner workings of Treblinka, thereby contributing not insignificantly to historical knowledge about the killing center at which nearly a million Jews were murdered and for which there is relatively scant survivor testimony and primary documentation. The scenes with Suchomel in *Shoah* are troubling above and beyond their historical import, however; they also give the viewer a disturbing glimpse into the mind of a perpetrator who, though voluble about his participation in the genocide that occurred at Treblinka, appears to be shockingly at ease with the ethical implications or moral dimensions of his role there. His astonishing forthrightness about the operations of the mass murder in which he himself played a part disaccords with his apparently untroubled conscience; although he claims to have been plagued by moral qualms at the time of his service in Treblinka, during his conversation with Lanzmann he displays few signs of remorse. The antithetical character of Suchomel's testimony is best exemplified in a notorious moment that occurs just after he has reproduced vocally the infamous camp anthem of Treblinka, the so-called "Treblinkalied."[1] After singing, he pauses and says to Lanzmann, "Sind Sie zufrieden? Das ist ein Original. Das kein kein Jude heute mehr" (Are you satisfied? That's an original. No

Jew today can [sing] that any longer).[2] With this response, Suchomel does not disavow knowledge of the Holocaust or deny his role in it (as do other perpetrators featured in the film); rather, he appears strikingly unperturbed by the memory of his participation in it.

Such moments that emphasize the seemingly contradictory quality of Suchomel's testimony in *Shoah*, which is extraordinarily frank and at the same time dissembling and morally obtuse, were made possible by Lanzmann's particular practice as both interviewer and filmmaker, which was fervent, uncommonly courageous, uncompromising in its aims, and at times unorthodox. As Shoshana Felman, Sue Vice, and others have argued, Lanzmann self-consciously staged all of the interviews in *Shoah*, deliberately constructing conditions and a mise-en-scène in which the witnesses are provoked or even forced to "reenact" or "reincarnate" the past.[3] According to Felman, Lanzmann's particular achievement in the film was "to elicit from the witness . . . a testimony which is inadvertently no longer in the control or the possession of the speaker."[4] Dominick LaCapra has connected Lanzmann's methodology, whereby he incited his witnesses—whether survivor, perpetrator, or bystander—to relive through performative reenactment especially arresting moments of the Holocaust past, to his "absolute refusal of the *why* question and of understanding," meaning that *Shoah* exhibits "a tendency to sacralize the Holocaust and to surround it with taboos."[5]

Lanzmann's stated objective to not elicit or provide any understanding applies in particular to his interviews with the perpetrators that appear in *Shoah*, especially Suchomel. Rather than pursue a "purely psychological" approach in his interviews with former perpetrators, a method he attributed (not admiringly) to Gitta Sereny and her penetrating interview with the former Treblinka commandant Franz Stangl as chronicled in her 1974 book *Into That Darkness: An Examination of Conscience*, Lanzmann adamantly refused, as he insists in his 2009 autobiography, *The Patagonian Hare*, to "think about evil, to understand how a husband and father can calmly take part in mass murder."[6] Contrasting his approach with Sereny's method, which he sees as naïvely empathetic and perilously indulgent of the perpetrator's mindset, he writes, "I buttressed with all my might the refusal to understand."[7] In other words, Lanzmann expressly declined to psychologize the perpetrators or to investigate their actions as stemming from explicable attitudes, ideologies, or motivations. His interviews with the perpetrators featured in the theatrical release of *Shoah* were thus designed not to illuminate these men as human beings, but rather to incite them to reenact in the present day their personas as perpetrators, thereby exposing the evil core that persisted behind their postwar façade.[8] Much of the scholarship on *Shoah*, as I argued in a 2013 article that analyzed the representation of perpetrators in the film, has tended to follow Lanzmann's approach to the perpetrators, "stressing their opaqueness and their resistance to conventional structures of comprehensibility and representation."[9] Critics have focused in this regard chiefly on the film's depiction of Suchomel, who, as I argued, functions as the "the ideal 'other' onto which they can project their discomfort about the testimony of the former Nazis," in particular in the notorious third sequence of the interview, which occurs at the beginning of the second half of the film and in which Suchomel is depicted singing with gusto the "Treblinkalied."[10] My 2013 analysis of the interviews with Suchomel and the other perpetrators in *Shoah* acknowledged that Lanzmann, with his production of a particular mise-en-scène, his interviewing style (which includes his purposeful employment of faulty German), and his stroking of the perpetrators' egos, did much to sustain such a view of these perpetrators as evil others. On the other hand, I maintained that "*Shoah* offers a much more complex picture of the perpetrators than Lanzmann perhaps envisioned or that is maintained by his absolutist methodology" by exposing, inadvertently or at least contra to Lanzmann's stated objectives, the perpetrators' contradictory relationship to their experience in the Holocaust.[11] Moreover, by revealing the myriad responses the perpetrators employed when crafting a narrative of their participation in violence—ranging from obstinate refusal to acknowledge more than surface culpability to earnest if ultimately self-justifying attempts to render the events of the Holocaust through their own perspective—*Shoah* makes possible, I contended, a much more differentiated depiction of perpetrators than the scholarship on Lanzmann's film acknowledges.

The antithetical character of Lanzmann's interviews with former perpetrators in *Shoah* is particularly at play in the sequences that feature Suchomel, which, with their forthright and compliant character, are anomalous not only in the context of *Shoah* itself but also for perpetrator testimony in general. In this, the interview with Suchomel—as to a lesser extent the scene with Franz Schalling—contrasts sharply with the interviews Lanzmann conducts with other perpetrators in the finished film, who either prevaricate about their function in the implementation of the Holocaust, deny having any knowledge of the genocide at the time, or remain altogether mute about it. Astonishingly, the Suchomel we encounter in the film appears eager to impart to Lanzmann his extensive knowledge of Treblinka, a fact that many critics of *Shoah*, who focus on Suchomel's supposed intrinsic evil, either overlook or reflexively attribute to what they see as Suchomel's "enthusiasm [to] reliv[e] his past glory," his "obvious pride" in his testimony, or his nostalgic wallowing in "the happy memories of *Heimat*."[12] However, as I have argued, Suchomel's extraordinary openness in *Shoah* about the operations of Treblinka is not accompanied by an equally exceptional awareness of their moral dimensions. Indeed, by virtue of assuming a didactic posture of self-importance, perversely secure in the knowledge that Lanzmann needs him for his expert testimony, Suchomel is able to displace acknowledgment of culpability for the genocide that he played a role in perpetrating there.

My assessment of the ways in which Lanzmann, by massaging the tensions between Suchomel's remarkably candid historical account and his ethical stolidity, facilitated a contradictory representation of the perpetrator was predicated entirely on careful viewing of the long scenes in the theatrical release of *Shoah* in which Lanzmann questions him (and which, along with the published German- and English-language transcripts of the film, were the sole form of the interview available at the time). Yet these scenes collectively constitute only a small part of the longer interview that Lanzmann conducted with Suchomel, a fact of which I was aware as I wrote the article, since Lanzmann asserts in *The Patagonian Hare* that he met with Suchomel for almost an entire day.[13] However, even though I speculated that the longer filmed interview, which at that time was not available to researchers, likely contained additional illuminating moments in Suchomel's testimony, I assumed that Lanzmann had distilled the essence of it with the parts that he included in the finished film.

Reassessing the Suchomel Interview Through Lanzmann's Postproduction Editing Practice

When the preserved digitized outtakes of this interview were made publicly available in 2015 by the Spielberg Film and Video Archive at the USHMM, I approached them with the expectation that they would reinforce and perhaps even augment my original assessment of Suchomel's testimony. Instead of confirming the conclusions I had developed in my close study of the scenes in *Shoah*, however, my encounter with the recently restored footage of the entire interview calls into question some of the most basic premises I had assumed in my analysis. Indeed, far from aligning with my original assessment, my examination of the outtakes requires me to thoroughly reevaluate key aspects I had identified in the Suchomel scenes in the theatrical release of *Shoah*, including Lanzmann's performance as interviewer in them, Suchomel's responses to Lanzmann's questioning, and the nature of Suchomel's more comprehensive testimony. Most important, my review of the outtakes necessitate that I more carefully and comprehensively consider the ways in which they illuminate Lanzmann's deliberate, extensive, and artful postproduction editing of the Suchomel interview into the five sequences we see in the film, and, by virtue of that, his deliberate shaping of Suchomel's ethical relationship to his past as we see it unfold on screen.

The particular characteristics and precise details of Lanzmann's editing practice are an aspect of his filmmaking that has mostly been neglected by the scholarship on *Shoah* (including my previous work), which limits the discussion of editing to observation about how Lanzmann reduced the hundreds of hours of footage filmed for *Shoah* into a mere nine-and-a-half hours and consideration of the ways in which entire sequences of interviews with various witnesses were edited into the film's larger narrative trajectory, rather than analysis of how specific scenes from individual interviews were constructed. Critics have tended to assume that those individual sequences themselves closely resemble and in the main reflect the entire interviews from which they were culled; in this way we have naturalized the film's presentation as an authentic and authoritative depiction of both its witnesses and the interviews Lanzmann conducted with them.[14] Such a position is enabled by Lanzmann's public performance as both auteur *of* and cinematic subject *in Shoah*, which encouraged viewers and critics alike to conflate his extradiegetic function as filmmaker with his intradiegetic role as interviewer and consequently discouraged them from attending to the ways in which the apparently self-understood character of the latter is a construction of the former. Indeed, Lanzmann himself claimed, "I inhabit *Shoah*," a statement that erases the distinction between these two roles.[15] The predominant focus on Lanzmann's craft during the production process through his performance as interviewer and his creation of the mise-en-scène as director thus results in a certain critical inattention to aspects of his filmmaking, such as his postproduction editing practices, that relate less directly to the ways in which he provoked and recorded traumatic reenactment in his witnesses. Moreover, as LaCapra has argued, the scholarship on *Shoah*—at least in its initial manifestations—has tended to adopt as its analytical paradigm Lanzmann's own framework for understanding the film.[16] With regard to the role that editing played in the creation of *Shoah*, this means that critics have largely accepted his declarations of editorial transparency and his claim to have minimized postproduction editorial intervention (a curious deemphasis on Lanzmann's part, given that he spent, as he informs us in *The Patagonian Hare*, as many as five years editing the film).[17] In a discussion with Jean-Michel Frodon about some of the technical aspects of the making of *Shoah*, Lanzmann gives his view on the practice and ethics of editing:

> I absolutely refused to add sound that had not been recorded at the same time as the image, so as not to introduce any doubt regarding the rapport of image to sound. There are ethics to filming and there are ethics in editing. Nowadays, there is absolute immorality, when you see how an interview or a debate is made for television. The use of video cameras is in itself potentially a bearer of great changes, but when you use four or five cameras, it is the temporality of the spoken word that you kill. There is no continuity, there is contiguity, a series of "appearances," coordinated through various tricks—among others, "continuity shots." To each his own circus. . . . There is also a tendency to make fiction in this way, nowadays. This seems deeply immoral to me. . . . It is the

killing of time that is immoral! It is the loss of the relationship to the real word, sacrificing it for spectacular compla-
cent advantages. This is a misadventure that has happened
to me often: to participate in a filmed debate and discover
that after editing everything has changed. The beginning is
at the end, everything is chopped up . . . a meeting between
two people is transformed into a series of appearances. Time
is dead! Reality is dead. That is the ethical crime.[18]

Lanzmann indicates with this statement that, in the process of making
Shoah, he avoided what are broadly considered standard editing conventions in fiction as well as nonfiction film. However, as will become clear in
the following review of the Suchomel outtakes, he, along with his editing
team (in particular the chief editor of *Shoah*, Ziva Postec), violated in a
number of ways his stated code of editorial ethics in the postproduction
editing of the Suchomel interview for *Shoah*: with his predilection for the
principle of "contiguity" over that of "continuity"; with his violation of
"the temporality of the spoken word"; with his disruption of "the rapport
of image to sound"; and with his "chopp[ing] up" of filmed material. But by
so vehemently disavowing the employment of such commonly used conventions, which he somewhat disingenuously associates with television and its
allegedly "immoral" use of multiple video cameras (as if one could not also
achieve the same effect—as he turns out to have done—by editing footage
from a single 16mm film camera), he signals to scholars that, in the creation
of *Shoah*, he employed minimal postproduction editorial techniques—and
that those he did utilize were applied in ethically correct ways.

By adopting Lanzmann's own characterization of his process in our
assessment of the interviews in *Shoah* and by neglecting to attend to the
postproduction mechanisms of shaping them, we critics have thus made one
of the gravest mistakes an interpreter of a cultural text—especially a nonfiction film—can make: we have assumed that what we see on screen closely
corresponds to and reflects off-screen reality, which in this case means the
reality not only of Lanzmann's encounters with the witnesses but also of
the raw footage that he recorded of them. While we have been attentive
to the ways in which Lanzmann manipulated the content and staging of the
interviews through his method of provoking traumatic reenactment and

his careful composition of the mise-en-scène, we have failed to acknowledge fully the artistic, technical, and material postproduction strategies employed to further construct these scenes. In my 2013 article I took pains to distinguish the Suchomel I saw in *Shoah* from the historical person by highlighting the ways in which the interviewer Lanzmann compelled him to perform particular roles, but I neglected to consider the ways in which Lanzmann and Postec, through deliberate and sophisticated editing practices, may have constructed a version of the interview for *Shoah* that is incongruent with or even misrepresents aspects of the raw footage of his full conversation with Suchomel and instead constitutes a contradistinctive narrative crafted particularly in accordance with Lanzmann's goals for the finished film. My discussion here aims to correct this oversight by focusing both on the aspects of the Suchomel interview that Lanzmann incorporated into his film and on important elements in the interview that he left to languish in the outtakes. After providing a little background on Suchomel and on the interview, I will examine the methods Lanzmann and Postec employed to create the interview we see in *Shoah,* a process I was able to reconstruct by painstakingly comparing the outtakes to the finished film. I will then discuss two fascinating moments from the interview that did not make it into the finished film but that stand in uncomfortable tension with the portrait of Suchomel that is postulated in *Shoah.* My juxtaposition of the outtakes with the theatrically released version of the film compels us to reconsider our relationship to this famous cinematic portrait of a perpetrator that we have known for over thirty years.

Conceptual and Narratological Frameworks for Reassessing the Suchomel Interview

Before I contextualize Lanzmann's interview with Suchomel, however, I find it necessary to clarify the relationship of the Suchomel outtakes to the scenes in the finished film in conceptual and narratological terms. For the purpose of the former, it is useful to adopt the framework of "the three overlapping references sets" of filmed material that Brad Prager and I develop in the introduction to this volume. In the case of the Suchomel interview, the first set refers to the sequences that feature Suchomel in the theatrical release of *Shoah*; the second set is the restored and digitized outtakes owned by the

USHMM and Yad Vashem (i.e., "the filmed material and audio recordings that Lanzmann abandoned on the cutting room floor");[19] and the third set is the unedited video and audio record of the entire interview, which in principle "exists only as an abstract, virtual idea,"[20] because, as part of the institutional agreement with Lanzmann, the USHMM and Yad Vashem hold rights only to the footage that was *not* included in *Shoah*, meaning those scenes "that were shot in the course of making *Shoah* but that were not used in the final version."[21] However, in the case of the Suchomel interview, there *is* extant one important part of the third reference set—namely the full, unedited audio track of the entire interview, which archivists at the USHMM made available to me prior to the full restoration, synchronization (or, in film technical vocabulary, "conformation"), and digitization of the outtakes (both audio and video). I thus had at my disposal an uninterrupted audio record of the interview, which was of particular value as a point of reference for determining how the sequences in *Shoah* had been edited. In addition, a fourth reference set—and one that was also of particular use—is constituted by the original transcripts of the interviews (in the original German of that encounter) prepared by Lanzmann's team. By correlating and cross-referencing these four reference sets (scenes from the Suchomel interview in the DVDs of the theatrically released *Shoah*; the archive of synchronized audio and video outtakes; the raw, unedited audio track of the interview; and Lanzmann's German-language transcript of the interview, the latter three of which were made available by the USHMM), I am able to infer the content and structure of the third, virtual set: that is, the original, uncleaved footage of the full interview. In so doing, I am able to evaluate how the original interview was edited for *Shoah* and make conclusions about the editorial practices of Lanzmann and his team.

In narratological terms, it is useful to distinguish between the full interview itself (i.e., the third, virtual set) and the portions of that interview that appear in the theatrical release of *Shoah* (the first set). For this, the narratological distinctions between *fabula* and *discourse* are helpful. Simply put, a narrative's fabula (also known as its *story*) is the event or sequence of events on which the narrative focuses; it is what H. Porter Abbott terms "the raw flux" of phenomena or happenings.[22] A narrative's discourse, on the other hand, is how those events are shaped formally through representation, including how they are selected, ordered, and emphasized, and from which perspective they are presented.[23] With regard to the narrative relayed *within* the Suchomel interview, the fabula is Suchomel's experience as an SS guard at Treblinka, while the discourse is Suchomel's account of that event as he narrates it in dialogue with Lanzmann. With regard to the narrative *of* the interview, which takes place on a different narrative level and frames the story that Suchomel tells, one can view the fabula as the event of the full interview (an event that includes its recording by a hidden camera) and the discourse as the selected, ordered, emphasized, and perspectivized presentation of that event in the theatrical release of *Shoah*. In other words, the fabula is Lanzmann's complete raw footage of the interviewing situation constituted by the third reference set, while the discourse is Lanzmann's edited representation of the interview in the scenes featured in the first reference set, *Shoah*. Conceiving of the relationship between the original interview and its edited presentation in *Shoah* allows us to better understand the connection between the two. Moreover, it also permits us to recognize moments in which this apparently clear division is breached through what is known as metalepsis, or the deliberate transgression of the boundaries between fabula and discourse. As will become clear in my analysis, the metaleptic moments revealed by examination of the outtakes of the Suchomel interview provide a framework for more fully understanding the ways in which Lanzmann constructed a particular perspective on Suchomel in the discourse of *Shoah*.

Contextualizing the Suchomel Interview

Franz Suchomel, who died in 1979, three-and-a-half years after he met with Lanzmann five-and-a-half years before *Shoah* was released, is without question the most prominently featured perpetrator to appear in Lanzmann's film. However, although arraigned and sentenced in West Germany during the first Treblinka trial (1964–65), he has not been considered a major perpetrator by either the West German courts or historians of the Holocaust (even if Lanzmann's framing of him in *Shoah* implies as much).[24] Born in Bohemia in 1907 and trained as a tailor, Suchomel was a member of the pro-Nazi Sudeten German Party until the Sudetenland was incorporated into the Third Reich in 1938; thereafter he was a member of the National Socialist Motor Corps (but not the Nazi Party itself).[25] At the beginning of the war he served in the Wehrmacht as a tailor, but in March 1941 he was summoned to Tiergarten 4 in Berlin, the offices of the chancellery responsible for the notorious T-4 euthanasia program. There and later in the T-4 euthanasia institute Hadamar, he worked as a clerk filing photographs and documents pertaining to the mentally ill "patients" in the program.[26] In July 1942, almost a year after the euthanasia program had been nominally halted in late summer 1941 due to pressure from the German public, Suchomel, along with other T-4 personnel from the six German euthanasia centers, was put into service in the Aktion Reinhard extermination program, which undertook the murder of 1.7 million Jews at the three gassing facilities Bełżec, Sobibór, and Treblinka, all of which became operational in the spring and summer of 1942. He was sent to Treblinka at the end of August 1942, where he was employed at the receiving ramp and in the women's undressing barracks before being made supervisor of the so-called *Goldjuden*, the Jewish prisoners who were forced to collect and sort the valuable material effects of the murdered deportees for shipment to the Reich. With the rank of *Scharführer*, Suchomel was among the lower-level SS personnel at the camp; moreover, while he was known to have exercised violence toward the deportees at Treblinka, he was also characterized as much less brutal than some of the other SS and the Ukrainian auxiliary guards, especially in his interactions with the *Goldjuden* who worked under him.[27] At the end of October 1943, a couple of months after the Treblinka revolt and shortly after the Sobibór uprising, he was posted briefly at Sobibór; in late 1943 he was dispatched with other T-4 and Reinhard personnel to Trieste, where he was charged with fighting partisans and confiscating Jewish-owned property. After the war, he was briefly held in a US prisoner-of-war camp; in 1949 he settled in Bavaria, where he was arrested in 1963. At the first Treblinka trial, held in Düsseldorf in 1964–65, Suchomel was convicted not as an accomplice to murder but as an accessory; he was sentenced to six years imprisonment but was released in 1969.[28] In terms of the implementation of the Final Solution, Suchomel's role was thus that of a foot soldier rather than that of an originator, organizer, or administrator. The value of his testimony lies less in matters of his own responsibility for the Holocaust (which, though secondary, was certainly not inconsequential) and more in his ability—and his willingness—to give detailed information about the daily operations of a camp for which at the time there was relatively little historical knowledge.

Lanzmann's interview with Franz Suchomel took place in March 1976 in Braunau am Inn in Austria, about thirty-five kilometers from Suchomel's home across the border in Altötting, Bavaria.[29] It lasted just over four-and-a-half hours and was one of the first interviews that Lanzmann recorded for the *Shoah* project; it was also the first encounter that was shot clandestinely using a secret camera, a then–brand-new device known as the *paluche*, which, rather than recording directly to film, transmitted a signal that could be received within a specific distance and recorded onto videotape.[30] As Lanzmann writes in his autobiography, the technical possibilities of the *paluche* made possible both the Suchomel interview and interviews with further perpetrators; it changed "radically the conditions in which I could film in Germany and led me to choose the path of deception, subterfuge, secrecy and maximum risk."[31] Suchomel willingly agreed to the interview, believing that he was being audiotaped but not aware that he was being filmed; he further requested that his name and identity not be revealed in the interview, a condition to which Lanzmann verbally agreed but then of course violated by his inclusion of the interview and his naming of Suchomel's identity in *Shoah*. Lanzmann furthermore implicated himself in this breach of the oral contract by including his promise to Suchomel in the finished film, a nuanced act that can be seen in a number of ways: as a statement of transparency about his process, as an admission of the problematic lengths to which he was willing to go in his quest for knowledge and filmic evidence, and as an acknowledgement of his own ethical ambivalence as both interviewer and filmmaker.[32] Lanzmann's cinematographer, William Lubtchansky, posed as the sound engineer for the ostensibly audiotaped interview and by virtue of this stratagem was able to operate the hidden camera. According to Lanzmann,

> We had commissioned a large leather bag with two side pockets. When opening the bag, one could see only a Nagra, the standard professional sound-recording equipment. The Paluche lay in one of the pockets, with a hole cut in the leather for the lens. However, William made a foam cover to

make the lens look like a microphone. In the other pocket was a tiny video monitor, allowing him to frame the shot. We left for Braunau two days before the scheduled meeting; I rented rooms at the Hotel Post, one of which we converted into a recording studio, pinning the map of Treblinka to the wall, choosing where William would sit—at some distance from Suchomel so that he wouldn't suspect anything.[33]

At the interview along with Lanzmann, Suchomel, and Lubtchansky were also the camera technician Jean-Yves Escoffier and an unnamed interpreter, the latter of whom does not appear on-screen but who is heard in the outtakes frequently speaking French with Lanzmann and German with Suchomel and who helps clarify difficult points of translation.[34] (Lanzmann can also be heard in the outtakes speaking French with Lubtchanksy and Escoffier, with whom he discusses the placement of the camera and the framing of shots.). At the end of the interview, Lanzmann paid Suchomel for his account, a financial agreement that was absolutely necessary for obtaining Suchomel's cooperation but that nevertheless, as Lanzmann admits in *The Patagonian Hare*, caused him some distress.[35] With this admission, Lanzmann reveals the idiosyncratic—or even arbitrary—ethical code he developed for the Suchomel interview, which inverted to some extent the ethical conventions documentarians tend to follow: first, he flagrantly and egregiously disregarded the prohibition on filming a subject without that person's knowledge; second, he objected to paying Suchomel not because that would violate his supposed objectivity vis-à-vis his subject, but because he believed it was deeply immoral to remunerate a former perpetrator for his testimony.[36]

The *paluche* transmitted the footage of the interview to an antenna attached to a van outside the hotel; the black and white transmission was recorded by a VCR, "copied onto 16mm film and magnetic soundtrack," and then edited for inclusion into the film.[37] At some point after the interview and in preparation for editing the footage, Lanzmann or one of his staff transcribed the interview, yielding 113 pages of typescript. When the outtakes of the interview arrived at the USHMM, they were thus recorded on separate audio and image tracks and had to be conformed during the restoration and digitization process.

Editing: Lanzmann's Construction of the Suchomel Interview for *Shoah*

At over four hours, the length of Lanzmann's full interview with Suchomel (the third reference set) exceeded many times over the excerpts of it included in the five discreet sequences in *Shoah* (the first set), which in total run to just under forty-five minutes and appear mostly in the middle of the nine-and-a-half hour film. (I include in this estimation of the total duration of the Suchomel scenes in *Shoah* lengthy interruptions within the sequences in which dialogue from the interview pauses and gives way to shots of trains and of the Treblinka memorial that are not accompanied by voice-over.) The parts of the interview included in the film sequences in *Shoah* originate chiefly in the first half of the full interview (and, in particular, the first third); the one exception to this is the notorious scene in which Suchomel sings the "Treblinkalied," which is placed in the finished film in the third sequence (and indeed opens the second part of *Shoah*) but that actually derives from the final half hour of the full interview. The content presented in the five sequences in *Shoah* (which I have chosen to designate according to their respective order in the finished film with the letters A, B, C, D, and E) thus hails almost exclusively from the first part of the full interview, in which Suchomel provides mostly a historical description of the camp and its operations, rather than from the second half, which focuses more prominently on Suchomel's relationship with the prisoners at Treblinka and his own complex feelings about his actions there. This is not at all surprising, given Lanzmann's obsession with documenting the machinery of genocide and his corresponding disdain for a psychologizing approach. However—and this is where Lanzmann and Postec's editing practices are critical—the portions of the full interview included in the sequences of the finished film are not simply whole sections lifted intact from the first part of the interview. Although each sequence in *Shoah* seems to be a discreet, continuous scene that unfolds logically and dialogically, this is an illusory effect of extensive postproduction editing.

In general, the sequences of Suchomel's interview in *Shoah* advance successively (but not exclusively) in the order of the original interview, meaning that segments from sequence A generally occur chronologically before segments from sequence B; segments from B tend to occur before segments from C, and so on. However, the product that results from the editing process is not always simply a boiled-down version of the original dialogue that preserves the existing skeletal structure of the interview and its progressive chronological movement. On the contrary, a large portion of the sequences is assembled outside the original chronological order of the interview, meaning that Lanzmann and Postec skipped back and forth proleptically and analeptically over the interview (i.e., forward or backward in the chronology of the men's discussion) to create seemingly seamless chains of dialogue that contain elements from diverse moments in Suchomel's testimony. Such heterogeneous assemblages of sections and even fragments are ubiquitous in the Suchomel sequences in *Shoah*, indicating the frequent anachronies created by edits, and they are often recognizable in the finished film by the fact that the audio track in these moments is not accompanied by corresponding images of Suchomel and Lanzmann in dialogue. Even scenes in which the audio and visual tracks are apparently synchronized may be heavily edited and thus asynchronous.[38]

As I have discovered by first identifying each discrepancy between the finished film and the unedited audio track of the interview and then by connecting each segment to the page number of the interview transcript to which it corresponds and to its original timestamp on the raw audio track, all of the sequences except B and E (the shortest of all of them) exhibit significant chronological movement back and forth throughout the interview. Sequence C in particular jumps on a macro level from the last part of the interview to the first and then to the middle parts; as my tracking of the sequence within the transcript indicates, there are many more instances of prolepsis and analepsis on the micro level (i.e., jumps back and forth between parts of the interview that are transcribed on a single page). As the extensive edits in sequences A, C, and D demonstrate in particular, far from reflecting an unmediated depiction of either Lanzmann's original dialogue with Suchomel or Suchomel's own characterization of his experience of Treblinka, the sequences featuring Suchomel in *Shoah* reveal Lanzmann and Postec's frequent, active and acute interventions as editors, an activity that is at least as formational for *Shoah* as Lanzmann's intradiegetic interpolation as interviewer. Whereas within the interview—or in narratological terms, within the fabula—Lanzmann constructs our perception of Suchomel through his performance and active manipulations as an interviewer (a phenomenon I explored in my article on the perpetrators in *Shoah*), on the level of auteurship or narrative discourse of *Shoah* he constructs this representation of Suchomel through his heavy hand as editor.[39]

As revealed by my painstaking work to track Lanzmann's construction of the film sequences in *Shoah* through examination of the raw audio track of the original interview, the conformed audio and video outtakes, and the transcript of the interview, large parts of the sequences (particularly sequences A and C) are a highly edited mishmash of small sections, discrete sentences, and even singular words that are edited together to create the semblance of a seamless, developing discussion. Each of the five sequences in *Shoah* contains multiple segments, by which I mean discrete, intact pieces of dialogue that were cut from the raw footage of the interview (the third reference set). Sequence A contains a minimum of sixty-two segments, sequence B contains at least fourteen; sequence C contains at least fifty-eight segments, sequence D twenty-seven segments, and sequence E two segments. (I say in all cases "at least" because I can only track the edits that are the result of the obvious insertion of segments containing dialogue, not those that potentially insert moments of silence). One example of the ways in which Lanzmann and his team edited Suchomel's dialogue on the sentence and word level is the section of the interview in which the two men discuss Suchomel's first days in Treblinka, a period in August 1942 in which the arriving Jewish deportees experienced particular chaos, fear, and brutality. This entire section of the original interview, as recorded in the raw, unedited audio track, proceeds in the following way (bolded text denotes dialogue that is also found in the scene of this exchange in *Shoah*, as cited below):

LANZMANN: Und diese Leute, die . . . zwei, drei Tage . . . gewartet haben, was haben diese Leute gedacht? Wußten sie schon? (And these people, who . . . waited . . . two, three days, what did they think? Did they know already?)

SUCHOMEL: **Die haben es geahnt. Die haben es geahnt. Sie waren vielleicht im Zweifel, aber manche werden es gewußt haben. Weil sie doch das Rattern der Motore gehört haben. (They sensed it. They sensed it. Perhaps they doubted it, but some of them will** have known it. Because they of course heard the rattling of the motor of the gas chamber.)

LANZMANN: Ah . . . Der Motore von der Gaskammer? (Ah. . . . The motor of the gas chamber?)

SUCHOMEL: Ja, **von der Gaskammer**. Das Rattern hat man gehört. (Yes, **of the gas chamber.** One could hear the rattling.)

LANZMANN: Was für ein Motor? (What kind of engine?)

SUCHOMEL: Diesel. (Diesel.)

LANZMANN: Diesel. Aber ein Tank . . . ein Panzermotor, oder was? (Diesel. But a tank. . . . a panzer engine, wasn't it?)

SUCHOMEL: **Ein Panzermotor war in dieser Gaskammer. (A tank engine was in this gas chamber.)**

LANZMANN: Aber **in Treblinka** es gab ein . . . eine [*sic*] Unterschied mit Auschwitz. Auschwitz . . . es war Zyklon. (But **in Treblinka** there was a difference from Auschwitz . . . it was Zyklon.)

SUCHOMEL: Na, na, na, na, na, na. In . . . in Polen **hat man nur Auspuff-gase genommen.** Nur Auspuffgase. (No, no, no, no, no, no. In . . . in Poland **only exhaust fumes were inhaled.** Only exhaust fumes.)

LANZMANN: Karbon-Monoxyd. (Carbon monoxide.)

SUCHOMEL: Ja. (Yes.)

LANZMANN: Nicht Zyklon. (Not Zyklon.)

SUCHOMEL: Nicht Zyklon. (Not Zyklon.)

LANZMANN: Zyklon war Auschwitz. (Zyklon was Auschwitz.)

SUCHOMEL: Na. **Zyklon war Auschwitz.** Also, das ist noch immer . . . ist die Periode Eberl. Ich hab Ihnen dann gesagt, daß Eberl von Wirth abgesetzt wurde. Binnen drei Tagen wurde das Lager . . . umorganis-iert. (Right. **Zykon was Auschwitz.** So, that was still . . . the period of Eberl. I told you that Eberl was ousted by Wirth. Within three days the camp was . . . reorganized.)

LANZMANN: Ja. (Yes.)

SUCHOMEL: Es kamen keine Transporte, **man hat die Leichen weg-geräumt.** (No transports arrived, **the corpses were cleared away.**)

LANZMANN: Alle die Leichen, die dort . . . (All the corpses that were there . . .)

SUCHOMEL: . . . die lagen, **die** da **herumlagen** . . . oder auch hier, in den Frauenbaracken, gel. (That were lying, **that were lying around** there . . . or here, in the women's barracks, right?)
LANZMANN: Ja. (Yes.)[40]

Lanzmann then edited this exchange for sequence A, creating out of what in the raw footage is a dialogue an uninterrupted monologue into which sections from earlier in the interview are inserted (bolded text denotes dialogue that derives from the excerpt of the outtakes cited above):

SUCHOMEL: In den Auffanglagern die Juden mußten warten, einen Tag, zwei Tage, drei Tage. Manche. **Die haben es geahnt. Die haben es geahnt. Sie waren vielleicht im Zweifel, aber manche werden es gewußt haben.** Zum Beispiel waren jüdische Frauen, die haben ihren Töchtern in der Nacht die Adern geöffnet, und sich selbst. Andere haben sich vergiftet. **Weil sie doch das Rattern der Motore von der Gaskammer gehört haben.** Da war **ein Panzermotor in dieser Gaskammer. In Treblinka hat man nur Auspuffgase genommen. Zyklon war Auschwitz.** Durch das, daß Menschen zwei bis drei Tage da waren, hat Eberl—Eberl war Lagerkommandant—endlich erreicht, hat in Lublin angerufen: "Es geht nicht mehr weiter, ich kann nicht mehr weiter, es muß ein Stop gemacht werden." Und eines Nachts kam Wirth. Der hat sich das angesehen und ist gleich wieder abgefahren. Und kam mit Leuten aus Bełżec. Also mit Praktikern. Und Wirth hat einen Transportstop erreicht. **Mat hat die Leichen weggeräumt, die herumlagen.**

(The Jews had to wait in the reception camp a day, two days, three days. **They sensed it. They sensed it. Perhaps they doubted it, but some of them will have known it.** For example [there] were Jewish women, at night they slit their daughters' wrists, and their own. Others poisoned themselves. **Because they of course heard the rattling of the motor of the gas chamber.** There was **a tank engine in this gas chamber. In Treblinka only exhaust fumes were inhaled. Zykon was Auschwitz.** Because the people had to wait two to three days, Eberl—Eberl was the camp commandant—finally achieved, he called Lublin, "It can't go on any longer, I can't do this any longer, there has to be a moratorium." And one night Wirth came. He inspected the situation and right away took off again. And returned with people from Bełżec—you know, with practitioners. And Wirth achieved a moratorium on transports. **The corpses that were lying around were cleared away.**)[41]

As is clear with the above example (which is one of a number of moments in the Suchomel interview in *Shoah* with a similar degree of editorial intervention), Lanzmann and his team made extensive and forceful edits to the original exchange, removing some bits of dialogue and adding others from elsewhere in the interview. Some of these cuts are the result of Lanzmann editing out his own questions, prompts, and responses to Suchomel's testimony; they thus served to make the sequences tighter, to allow Suchomel to provide elaboration on particular points when it is most needed, and to help Lanzmann and Postec to reduce their length (an important consideration, given that Lanzmann shot over 220 hours of footage). Moreover, the cuts also allowed Lanzmann to eliminate unnecessary repetitions and digressions in which linguistic and historical misunderstandings are clarified. Many of such edits are thus understandable, necessary, and even to be expected of the documentary filmmaker who wished to utilize his precious screen time wisely and effectively. At the same time, however, some of the cuts are evidence of precisely the type of editing practice to which Lanzmann so vehemently objected on ethical grounds, namely the "chopp[ing] up" and "transform[ation]" of the filmed "meeting between two people." As the above example demonstrates, in their amalgamation of different parts of the interview Lanzmann and Postec at times significantly altered the form of the men's original exchange, creating out of a dialogical interchange a monological, didactic lecture and thereby profoundly manipulating its content and meaning. In my 2013 article, I argued that, in his deliberate construction of the mise-en-scène of the interview (e.g., by supplying Suchomel with pedagogical props) and his feigned ignorance about the history about which Suchomel was educating him, Lanzmann cast Suchomel in the role of the "superior teacher who condescendingly explains to and then tests his student," a part that Suchomel appeared eagerly to assume.[42] However, it now also seems clear that Suchomel's didacticism and astonishing willingness to inform Lanzmann as represented in the theatrical release of *Shoah* are also the result of Lanzmann's calculated postproduction construction of his testimony in the editing room.

The fact that such highly edited scenes can appear to the viewer of *Shoah* as chains of uninterrupted, natural dialogue is attributable to a number of factors. On the one hand, there is the poor quality of the *paluche* footage, which is grainy and often contains visual distortions that result from weak radio reception and the foam that covered the camera lens, allowing the finished film to feature images of Suchomel and Lanzmann speaking that do not need to be synched with the corresponding audio track, since the viewer is unable to clearly see their mouths. On the other hand, Lanzmann and Postec utilized two different types of indexical crosscutting to maximize opportunities for disjoining the audio and visual tracks. First, Lubtchanksy's ability to manipulate the *paluche* through the pocket of the leather bag meant that he was able frequently to pan away from Lanzmann to Suchomel or from Suchomel to the large map of Treblinka that hung to Suchomel's left, a maneuver away from a focus on their mouths that thus allowed further cuts to the audio track. Second, as is the procedure throughout the film, in parts of the five *Shoah* sequences of the Suchomel interview, Lanzmann and Postec paired voice-over dialogue from the interview with two types of extended visual footage that serve different indexical and metonymical functions on the two narrative levels (Suchomel's narrative and *Shoah*'s narrative). On the one hand, they sutured in footage of trains and of present-day Treblinka that is metonymical to the content of Suchomel's testimony and that thus indexes the fabula of his narrative. On the other hand, they inserted establishing shots of a van parked ostensibly outside the building in which the interview took place that portray technicians purportedly watching the live feed from Lanzmann's hidden camera. These shots are designed to be metonymical to the clandestine interviewing situation itself; in this way, they index the fabula of *Shoah*'s narrative. In fact, however, the footage in *Shoah* that purports to show the radio reception of the interview from within the van is a further artefact of creative editing; when one looks at it closely, one realizes that this footage is not live feed from the interview with Suchomel, as the man shown on the small screen in the van is positioned at an entirely different angle than

Qu.: Ja, gut. Wenn Sie wollen jetzt über zweite Periode reden. Ich
glaube, das beste für mich - Sie werden beschreiben, ganz
genau, mit das: wie war es möglich, in Treblinka in Spitzen-
tagen, 18 000 Leute?

Rø.: 18 000 ist zu hoch.

Qu.: Ich habe das im Bericht gelesen. 18 000 Leute zu behandeln.
Zu liquidieren.

Rø.: Herr Lanzmann, das ist zu hoch gegriffen. Glauben Sie mir
das.

Qu.: Okay - wieviel?

Rø.: Zwölf- bis fünfzehntausend. Aber da wurde auch die halbe
Nacht dazu genommen. Nicht wahr. Die Transporte kamen oft
schon um sechs Uhr früh.

Qu.: Immer um 6 Uhr früh?

Rø.: Nicht immer. Manches Mal. Die Transporte kamen nicht pünkt-
lich. Die kamen manchmal um 6 Uhr früh, dann kam mittags
wieder einer, oder spät am Abend auch noch einer, nicht.

(C16) Qu.: Gut, gut. Ein Transport kommt (an.) Und ich möchte, daß Sie
schildern ganz genau den ganzen Prozeß. Von Anfang bis
zum Ende. Mit das, weil ich muß...

Rø.: Also, ohne Rücksicht auf Eberl, Stangl und Wirth.

(C17) Qu.: In der Hauptperiode.

Rø.: Aha, die Hauptperiode.

Qu.: Die Hauptperiode, Stanglperiode, wenn alles war...

(C18) *(C19)* Rø.: Also. Die Transporte (wir werden mal ganz von Anfang an
fangen) die kamen vom Bahnhof Malkinia zum Bahnhof Treblin-
ka. *départ* (Suc 7)

(C20) Qu.: Wieviel Kilometer zwischen Malkinia und Treblinka?

(C21) Rø.: Kann ich nicht sagen, gell. Zehn Kilometer oder mehr/viel-
(C22) leicht. Treblinka war ein Dorf. Ein kleines Dorf. Der Bahnhof gewann durch die Judentransporte an Bedeutung. Es kamen
dreißig bis fünfzig Wagons.

Qu.: Dreißig bis fünfzig?

(C23) *(C25)* Rø.: Ja. Da wurden immer zehn, zwölf, fünfzehn Wagen nach Treblinka hineingefahren. Der Rest blieb stehen. *(C30)*

(C27) *(C31)* Qu.: Mit Leute?

Rø.: Mit Leute. Am Bahnhof Treblinka.

Qu.: Also das heißt, ein Zug mit dreißig Wagen..

(C24) Rø.: Ja. Der wurde aufgeteilt je zu zehn. Zehn bis zwölf Wagons
(C26) Hat man ins Lager Treblinka...

Qu.: An die Rampe? *rb rajouté pour Traun (la nuit)*

Facsimile of a page from Lanzmann's original transcript of the Franz Suchomel
interview that has been altered to show the ways in which dialogue was edited into
sequence C of *Shoah*. Text within parentheses denotes dialogue included in the
film, while the corresponding letter and number identify the order of individual
segments when edited for the film. Created by Claude Lanzmann during the
filming of *Shoah*. (Used by permission of the United States Holocaust Memorial
Museum and Yad Vashem, the Holocaust Martyrs and Heroes' Remembrance
Authority, Jerusalem.)

REPRODUCED FROM THE HOLDINGS OF THE U.S. HOLOCAUST MEMORIAL MUSEUM ARCHIVES

Suchomel and, moreover, is illuminated from behind by a window that is altogether absent in the mise-en-scène of the Suchomel interview. It turns out that, with this first use of the *paluche*, Lanzmann's method did not yet include capturing interior footage of the radio reception of the Suchomel interview in the van; as I discovered by viewing the outtakes of Lanzmann's other clandestinely filmed perpetrator interviews, the image on the monitor we see in such establishing shots in *Shoah* is actually that of the former Auschwitz guard Pery Broad, whom Lanzmann interviewed in 1979 and who does not appear in the finished film. Thus, in the theatrical release of *Shoah*, the footage that purports to show the van receiving transmission of the Suchomel interview and that is meant to index the clandestine filming nature of that encounter is thus actually a scene that was staged much later in the film's production. Such editing strategies that disconnect the audio track from its visual correlate not only gave Lanzmann and Postec the freedom to construct at the sentence level Suchomel's dialogue for *Shoah*; they also visually bolster the truth effect of his testimony and the interviewing situation. At the same time, however, they violate Lanzmann's own ethics of editing, which insisted on "the rapport of image to sound" and emphatically eschewed the principle of contiguity.

Editing: Lanzmann's Construction of Suchomel in *Shoah*

In terms of content, the full interview as represented in the outtakes of course encompasses the topics and themes introduced in the *Shoah* sequences, which focus on Suchomel's impressions of the particularly brutal and chaotic period in the first weeks of Treblinka's existence and on his descriptions of how the people deported to Treblinka were compelled to undress and driven into the gas chamber. However, one cannot say that the sequences in *Shoah* are comphrehensively representative of the full interview, for the latter explores topics and contains compelling, expressive, and often highly ambivalent moments that are completely omitted from the finished film. For example, Suchomel describes the violent resistance of the transport of the survivors of the Białystok Ghetto Uprising and the extreme brutality of Christian Wirth, the supervising inspector for the Aktion Reinhard killing centers.[43] Suchomel further discusses his working relationship with the *Goldjuden*, which he characterizes as civil, if not friendly (according to

Shot from footage of the Suchomel interview included in *Shoah*. DVD capture from *Shoah* (1985). Directed by Claude Lanzmann. Released by Criterion.

Shot from footage of Lanzmann's interview with Pery Broad that has been edited into the Suchomel interview in *Shoah*. Broad's position in the framed shot on the van's monitor is easily distinguishable from Suchomel's position in the footage of his interview. DVD capture from *Shoah* (1985).

him, the Jewish prisoners who worked for him called him "Yom Kippur" because of his purported leniency), and what he alleges to have been his tacit support of the planned prisoner revolt (which took place on August 2, 1943).[44] Moreover, in addition to singing the Treblinka anthem (which we of course see in *Shoah*), he sings a Yiddish song and even tells Lanzmann a story he clearly intends to be humorous in a barely passable, heavily Germanized Yiddish, which he claims to have learned growing up among Jews in Bohemia and to have spoken with his *Goldjuden*.[45] Perhaps most astonishing, he reiterates throughout the interview his abiding feelings of guilt and shame regarding his role at Treblinka, and he even begins to cry at one point.[46] Such striking moments, revealing ambiguities, and astonishing revelations in the Suchomel outtakes stand in tension to the portrait that Lanzmann created in the finished film, which works to expose the stark discordance between Suchomel's volubility regarding his experience at Treblinka and his obtuseness with respect to its ethical implications but avoids opportunities to dwell on more nuanced instances of ethical ambivalence.

Nowhere is the tension between the ambivalence that occurs in outtakes of the interview and the more unequivocal framework erected in the finished film more pronounced than in the dynamics latent in sequence C of *Shoah*, which features Suchomel singing the "Treblinkalied." This not only is the film's central sequence featuring Suchomel and the one to which critics have most fervently responded in their characterization of him as the nefarious other who looks back gleefully on his past as a per- petrator, but it also occupies a pivotal role in the movement of *Shoah*, as it immediately precedes and, thus, as is customary between sequences of interviews of different witnesses in the film,[47] enters into dialogue with the powerful sequence in which Abraham Bomba testifies in an Israeli barber shop about his experience cutting women's hair within the gas chamber at Treblinka just moments before they were murdered.[48] As I mentioned previously, this sequence, which commences with Suchomel's singing, derives from the last part of the interview and then loops back to pick up threads from the beginning. In the film, Suchomel sings the "Treblinkalied" twice, exactly as he did in the interview. However, the order of the performances as they appear in the film is oddly reversed; in the film, Lanzmann places the second instance of singing first and the first instance second. (I am able to determine this because Suchomel sings one of the verses slightly differently in the two performances.) Moreover, the dialogue that in the film occurs after each rendition likewise deviates from its original order in the raw, unedited audio track. In my assessment, however, such remixing does not materially change the substance of the interview, although it does make it easier for Lanzmann to manipulate the ironies that emerge from the song and Suchomel's commentary on it. What intrigues me, however, about the original interview is Lanzmann's reaction to Suchomel's first rendition of the song, a response that is omitted in the theatrical release of *Shoah*. After finishing the song (which, as we learn from the outtakes, Suchomel sings at Lanzmann's specific request and not necessarily, as some critics have read his singing in the finished film, because he's "transported back" "in an uncanny enthusiastic reverie"), Suchomel delivers one of the most profoundly disturbing lines of dialogue to appear in the film: "Sind Sie zufrieden? Das ist ein Original. Das kann kein Jude heute mehr" ("Are you satisfied? That's an original. No Jew today can [sing] that any longer").[49] While this statement ends sequence C in the film, in the raw, unedited audio track, the exchange continues. Lanzmann responds to this first rendition of the song by encouraging him to sing it again: "Ja. Noch einmal" (Yes. One more time). And then, in French (either to Lubtchanksy, Escoffier or his interpreter), he says further, "Parce que c'est le début. Ce sera comme ça. Exactement comme ça" (Because that's the beginning. It will be like that. Exactly like that).[50] As I read it, this moment, which Lanzmann omitted in his reincorporation of the scene in the theatrical release of *Shoah* (as he did other moments during the Suchomel interview in which he makes comments in French), functions as a sort of epiphany for Lanzmann (although likely only one in a series of epiphanies that take place during the eleven years of the film's production), in which he suddenly realizes one of the organizing principles for the film—namely, what Lanzmann termed the "reincarnation" of past in the present, in this case through the acoustic and somatic dimension of song.[51] He recognizes at this moment the profundity of what he is witnessing, and, briefly but unmistakably donning his auteur's hat in place of that of the interviewer, envisions the way in which he will realize the scenario that is unfolding in front of his eyes at that very moment as a scene, as a constitutive or even originary moment of a film, the great bulk of which is yet to be shot. And, indeed, although Lanzmann decided to begin *Shoah* with another vocal performance—that of the Chełmno survivor Simon Srebnik—he did choose to open part two of the film with Suchomel's singing.[52] But in this moment, Lanzmann plays out his double role as both an undercover interviewer eliciting testimony and the film's director speaking with the crew. Lanzmann the interviewer transforms into Lanzmann the filmmaker, metaleptically collapsing the discourse of the film into the fabula of the raw footage of the interview.

A second notable interaction between the outtakes and the finished film occurs with the notorious exchange that ends sequence C and paves the way for the next scene, which features Bomba's wrenching testimony about cutting the hair of women he knew from his hometown. Suchomel, in one of the more protracted segments in the scene (in this section the audio track is synched with the visual track of the interview), describes the treatment of the arriving Jewish deportees as they were pushed through the "Schlauch," or the long, fenced-in corridor from the undressing area to the gas chambers. He mentions, almost offhandedly, that men, but not women, were driven by Ukrainian guards with whips. Lanzmann, astonished by this detail, queries further:

LANZMANN: Die Frauen sind nicht geschlagen worden? (The women weren't beaten?)

SUCHOMEL: Nein, nein, die sind nicht geschlagen worden. Also ich habe es . . . (No, no, they weren't beaten. That is, I didn't . . .)

LANZMANN: Warum diese Menschlichkeit? (Why this humanity?)

SUCHOMEL: Ich habe es nicht gesehen. Ich habe es nicht gesehen. Vielleicht sind sie auch geschlagen worden. (I didn't see it. I didn't see it. Maybe they were beaten too.)

LANZMANN: Warum nicht? Warum nicht? Sowieseo es war Tod, nicht? Warum nicht? (Why not? Why not? In any event it was death, wasn't it? Why not?)

SUCHOMEL: Vor den Gaskammern . . . sicher auch. (In front of the gas chambers . . . certainly as well.)[53]

Before answering Lanzmann's latter questions, Suchomel pauses in what appears to be his most profound and suggestive manner. He then responds slowly and dramatically, "Vor den Gaskammern . . . sicher auch." At this point, the theatrical release of *Shoah* cuts to Bomba's testimony; while the focal point of the scene remains with the women who travel from the "Schlauch" to the gas chamber, the focalization transfers from the former perpetrator to a former prisoner. In the outtakes, however, the focalization remains with Suchomel. Lanzmann, responding to Suchomel's weighty admission, converses further:

SUCHOMEL: Vor den Gaskammern . . . sicher auch. (In front of the gas chambers . . . certainly as well.)

LANZMANN: Vor den Gaskammern geschlagen. Frauen auch? Das glaube ich. (Beaten in front of the gas chambers. Women too? I believe so.)

SUCHOMEL: Ich meine, Herr Lanzmann, wenn's ich auch nicht sage, oft schäme ich mich. (I mean, Mr. Lanzmann, even if I don't say it, I'm often ashamed.)

LANZMANN [briefly touching Suchomel]: Bitte? (Excuse me?)

SUCHOMEL: Ich schäme mich, oft. Aber alles, was Sie sich vorstellen können, ist passiert. (I'm ashamed, often. But everything that you can imagine happened.)

LANZMANN: Ja, ja, ich bin sehr dankbar. Ich bin sehr dankbar. Und das ist wichtig für . . . Jetzt ist das Geschichte. (Yes, yes, I'm very grateful. I've very grateful. And that's important for. . . . Now it's history.)

SUCHOMEL: Das *ist* Geschichte. (It *is* history.)

ANOTHER VOICE (likely the interpreter): Non, il disait que même s'il ne dit pas tout . . . tout ce qu'on peut s'imaginer est quand-meme vrai . . . (No, he said that, although he does not say everything, everything we can imagine is true.)

SUCHOMEL: Verstehen Sie? Er hat Ihnen's jetzt gesagt. Ich schäme mich. (Do you understand? He's told you now. I'm ashamed.)

LANZMANN: Ja, aber Sie müssen nicht Schande haben, weil das ist Geschichte. Wir sind hier, Sie und ich, für Geschichte, und Sie müssen diese . . . Sie müssen bemühen. Sie müssen diese Bemühung machen. Das ist sehr wichtig. Ich kann nicht vorstellen, alles muß gesagt sein. Haben Sie keine Schande. (Yes, but you mustn't have disgrace, because that's history. We are here, you and I, for history, and you have . . . you have to exert yourself. You have to make an effort. It's very important. I can't imagine, everything has to be said. Don't have disgrace.)

SUCHOMEL: Herr Lanzmann, wir können sagen, wenn die Leute nicht wollten, wurden sie geschlagen. (Mr. Lanzmann, we can say that if people didn't want to [move forward], they were beaten.)

LANZMANN: Ja. (Yes.)[54]

There are a number of significant aspects to this exchange, not least of which is the repeated reference to "Geschichte," a word that is echoed later in the interview by Suchomel and appears, in sequence C of the film, just after Suchomel first sings the "Treblinkalied": "Sie wollen Geschichte haben, und ich sag Ihnen Geschichte" (You want to have history, and I'm telling you history). But I want to focus briefly on Suchomel's evocation of his shame, an element that appears throughout the outtakes but never makes it into the finished film. (Indeed, in *Shoah*, not one of the perpetrators expresses any sense of shame or remorse, a lack of contrition remarked upon frequently by scholarship on the film.[55]) Not surprisingly, when Suchomel first confides his sense of shame, Lanzmann is noticeably incredulous, perhaps outraged by what he is hearing or not quite in full comprehension of its import. After all, Lanzmann, who committed himself expressly to *not* understanding the perpetrators he interviewed, "refuses," as Jay Cantor writes, "to enter into the Nazis' psychology, to grant them inwardness"; he avoids entering Suchomel's mental space at all costs, as such an act would consequently grant Suchomel the ambivalent humanity Lanzmann wishes to deny him.[56] For this reason, perhaps hoping to stave off a confession or a more comprehensive statement of remorse, Lanzmann attempts to reroute the discussion away from Suchomel's admission of personal shame to the more public level of history, reminding him that the dictates of history require his testimony and even going so far as to weakly absolve Suchomel of the necessity to feel shame. Intriguingly, Lanzmann employs the word "Schande" (disgrace) in this context, not "Scham" (shame), the cognate of Suchomel's own assertion. This odd word choice could be the result of Lanzmann's less-than-perfect command of German, although, as I have argued, in his encounters with the perpetrators he interviewed, Lanzmann deliberately feigned a less fluent German than he in fact possessed in order to provoke attitudes of didacticism and superiority in his interlocutors.[57] At the same time, such a semantic shift may also indicate that Lanzmann wishes to deny Suchomel the opportunity to articulate feelings of opprobrium and contrition.

Suchomel's feeble but ultimately very human attempt here to express some sense of mortification, self-reproach, or even remorse provides constitutes one of the few public assertions of shame by perpetrators so intimately involved in the Judeocide. While I under no circumstances wish to accept uncritically his evocation of shame (indeed, it could be the case that he is lying!) or to imply that it is any way commensurate with his crimes, his statement does raise the question regarding whether any admission of anguish or remorse would be acceptable to us as viewers and what that admission might look like.[58] Moreover, the repeated assertions of shame and remorse by Suchomel, the perpetrator in whom critics of *Shoah* have been eager to see a monster, suggest not only that he may not be as horrific as Lanzmann has led us to believe. He himself may indeed also feel distress—if not what we might believe is the appropriate degree of remorse—as a result of the role he played in the genocidal violence at Treblinka. As Saira Mohamed writes in her astute investigation into the disquieting notion of perpetrator trauma,

The blind spot for perpetrator trauma is a symptom of [the] common assumption or expectation that perpetrators are monsters, incapable of the same humanity as the people they have attacked. For some people, surely, there is no trauma, no regret, no pain at the site of violence. But as researchers have shown, for many others, there is no innate evil; there are only terrible choices, an embrace of a world—or a slow sinking into it—in which ideology and hatred take over, at least for a time. To recognize trauma requires admitting that the sufferer of that trauma is human—no different in psychology or mental or emotional capacity from anyone else. The perpetrator is capable of being hurt just as he can inflict hurt; he is capable of suffering just as he can inflict suffering. He does not necessarily have a stronger stomach for violence than a person who does not inflict violence. . . . Dismissing perpetrators as monsters ignores the choices they made, and offers them an out. If they are mere monsters, then we cannot imagine that they might have behaved differently.[59]

Mohamed's point about the humanity of perpetrators of mass violence encourages us to avoid reflexively disregarding Suchomel's evocation of shame. Even though he dissembles about his own role in genocide and indeed imputes to himself more benign behavior at Treblinka than is credible, we should not so easily dismiss his expressions of anguish, for they may be evidence of the ways in which his experience of perpetrating violence continues to unsettle him. In an exchange that takes place shortly after he sings the "Treblinkalied" for the second time, Suchomel claims that he continues to be perturbed by his experience as a guard in Treblinka:

SUCHOMEL: Aber wir können's weiter singen, dass Treblinka unser Schicksal ist, nicht. Die Juden sind . . . die sind tot, aber wir leben noch. Mein Schicksal ist Treblinka weiter. (But we can still sing that Treblinka is our fate, right? The Jews are . . . they're dead, but we're still alive. My fate is still Treblinka.)

LANZMANN: Glauben Sie? (Do you believe that?)

SUCHOMEL: Ja, ich werde es nicht nicht so bald abschütteln. (Yes, I won't be able to shake it off so soon.)[60]

Assuming that Suchomel is exhibiting some modicum of honesty here (which of course may not be the case), his statements reveal a much more complex and indeed troubled relationship to his history as a perpetrator than does Lanzmann's portrait of him in *Shoah* as the gleefully remembering and morally stunted pedant who enthusiastically relives his past glory. However, for our purposes here, Suchomel's expression of shame is perhaps less interesting than Lanzmann's response to it, both as an interviewer, and—even more so—as a filmmaker. Suchomel, after providing Lanzmann with the compelling statement around which he will structure his film, takes the emotional logic of his remembrance of Treblinka one step further, in a direction Lanzmann is loath to follow. Having set the scene into motion, however, Lanzmann unexpectedly loses control of it and ends up confronted by the very aspect of Suchomel he most wishes to repress: his psychological response.[61] In this way, Lanzmann finds himself (as an interviewer in the fabula, at least) subject to the same dynamic that Felman locates in his interviewees, whereby "a complexity of truth" is brought forth that "is inadvertently no longer in the control or the possession of the speaker."[62] Lanzmann, who wished both to instrumentalize Suchomel as a pure conduit of history and to preserve him as maleficent other, encounters the very humanness in Suchomel he wishes to deny him. Moreover, by suppressing Suchomel's admittedly feeble feelings of distress, he denies space for Suchomel's expression of moral agency, however ambivalent and incomplete. In the end, however, both Lanzmann the interviewer and Lanzmann the filmmaker are able to reassert control. In the outtakes, Lanzmann steers the discussion back to the operations of Treblinka, while in the discourse of the film, Suchomel's expression of shame is intercepted just before its articulation.

Lanzmann's Editorial Interventions as Cultural Practice

The disclosure of the high degree of editorial manipulation of the Suchomel interview by Lanzmann and Postec made possible by close examination of the outtakes raises ethical questions about Lanzmann's method, especially for historians and other parties who look to the theatrical release of *Shoah* for a credible historical account of the Holocaust and an accurate and authentic depiction of the perpetrator's relationship to the past. As one of my colleagues, a scholar of the Holocaust in the Soviet Union, asked when I presented this material to her, How can we continue to teach *Shoah* to our students after knowing the scope of Lanzmann's manipulation of the interview? My answer to this is that I don't think we need to throw the baby out with the bathwater. In no way did Lanzmann distort or falsify history with his editing practices; on the contrary, particularly with regard to the portrait he created of the operations of Treblinka, he constructed from a digressive and at times chaotic dialogue an account that is coherent and comprehensible to the viewer, an effort that is not unlike the task of the historian, who creates a digestible narrative from the disorder of historical events. Lanzmann's redaction of the Suchomel interview in *Shoah* does not (or at least should not) prompt us to impugn the historical value and veracity of either the Suchomel sequences themselves or his larger *Shoah* project; the historiography on the Holocaust, Lanzmann's own meticulous research, and the credibility of the witnesses featured in *Shoah* are robust enough to withstand suspicions of falsification or significant deception.[63] What should give us pause is thus not the historical narrative of Treblinka that Lanzmann created in the Suchomel sequences, but rather his interpretation of Suchomel himself. This representation reflects—understandably and not without some ethical justification—Lanzmann's wish to suppress a more ambivalent image of the perpetrator that depicts him not only as shockingly insensible to the suffering and murder to which he personally contributed, boastful of his role at and knowledge of Treblinka, and avariciously interested in selling his story for money, but also as nuanced in his memory and characterization of the past, earnestly eager to impart what he knows about Treblinka for the purposes of history, and plagued by shame for his actions there: in short, as a fully human person, with all the ambivalent and contradictory baggage that such a designation brings with it. I do not argue here that we should condemn Lanzmann for his portrait of Suchomel, since not only was it (along with his entire *Shoah* project) a monumental achievement that recovered voices and narratives of the Holocaust that would have otherwise been consigned to oblivion, it was also the result of Lanzmann's justifiable antipathy toward and overt judgment of the men who perpetrated the Holocaust. Above all, his representation is a product of its cultural moment, which means that the particular cultural and ideological frameworks he employed in his construction are more easily recognizable to us now, over three decades since his film appeared, particularly given that public discourse on the Holocaust in general and perpetrators in particular has changed so much in the meantime.[64] (This is not to say that the field of Holocaust studies has exonerated perpetrators or that the current cultural imagination does not continue to demonstrate anxiety and ambivalence about them—just that our discourse has become more nuanced with the passing of time.) Finally, the revelation of Lanzmann's editorial intervention reminds us that we need to maintain the same sort of healthy skepticism with regard to the film and its filmmaker that we cultivate toward any document or cultural text, asking not only what it gives us but why it was made and especially how and through what means it was constructed. For, although *Shoah* is without question a masterwork, it is not a sacred text.

Notes

1. For in-depth analyses of Suchomel's performance of the "Treblinkalied," please see Zoltán Kékesi, "Die Falle der Erinnerung: das 'Treblinka-Lied' in Claude Lanzmann's *Shoah*," in *Ereignis Literatur: Institutionelle Dispositive der Performativität von Texten*, ed. Csongor Lörincz (Bielefeld: transcript, 2011), 331–57; "The Restoration of Difference: The Speech of the Perpetrator," in Zoltán Kékesi, *Agents of Liberation: Holocaust Memory in Contemporary Art and Documentary Film* (Budapest: Central European University Press, 2015), 37–57; and Erin McGlothlin, "The Voice of the Perpetrator, the Voices of the Survivors," in *Persistent Legacy: The Holocaust in German Studies*, ed. Erin McGlothlin and Jennifer Kapczynski (Rochester, NY: Camden House, 2016), 33–53.
2. *Shoah*, directed by Claude Lanzmann, New Yorker Films, 1985, DVD, disc 3, chapter 1. English translation mine.
3. Shoshana Felman, "The Return of the Voice: Claude Lanzmann's *Shoah*," in *Testimony: Crises of Witnessing in Literature, Psychoanalysis, and History*, ed. Shoshana Felman and Dori Laub (New York: Routledge, 1992), 204–83; Sue Vice, *Shoah* (London: Palgrave Macmillan, 2011).
4. Felman, "The Return of the Voice," 263.

5. Dominick LaCapra, "Lanzmann's *Shoah*: 'Here There Is No Why,'" *Critical Inquiry* 23, no. 2 (1997): 231–69; here, 245, 236.

6. Claude Lanzmann, *The Patagonian Hare*, trans. Frank Wynne (New York: Farrar, Straus & Giroux, 2012), 420.

7. In the original French, Lanzmann writes, "L'étonnement nu fut si grand que je me suis arc-bouté des toutes mes forces au refus de comprendre." *Le lièvre de Patagonie* (Paris: Éditions Gallimard, 2009), 605. Because the translation of this sentence in the published English version—"I braced myself with all my might against the refusal to understand" (*The Patagonian Hare*, 420)—implies with its ambiguous use of "against" the opposite of what the French sentence connotes, I have chosen to render my own translation.

8. In a 2015 interview, Lanzmann says with regard to his interviews with perpetrators (particularly "der SS-Mann," by which he means Suchomel), "Das Wichtigste war doch, diese Menschen zum Sprechen zu bringen. Zu erfahren, was sie getan haben. Wie man fünf Millionen vergast. Wie man das rein technisch schafft. Ich wollte keine Gefühle hören, ich wollte so genau wie möglich erfahren, wie alles ablief. Ich wollte Beschreibungen, akkurate, brutale, wertfreie Beschreibungen. Räumliche und zeitliche Präzision. Meine Gefühle habe mich dabei ganz und gar nicht interessiert. Und die Menschen haben geredet, weil sie, die heute bedeutungslos waren, über die Zeit reden durften, in der sie aktiv und wichtig waren, in der sie gebraucht wurden. Es waren gute Zeiten, wenn man so will, also habe ich sie reden lassen. Ich habe mich weder um ihre Psyche gekümmert noch um meine" (The most important thing was of course to make these people talk. To learn what they did. How 5 million were gassed. How that was accomplished at a purely technical level. I didn't want to hear any feelings, I wanted to learn as precisely as possible how everything was executed. I wanted descriptions, accurate, brutal, value-free descriptions. Spatial and temporal precision. My feelings in the matter didn't interest me in the least. And the people talked because they, who were today insignificant, were allowed to speak about the time in which they were active and important, in which they were needed. They were good times, if you will, so I let them speak. I was concerned about neither their minds nor my own). Gabriela Herpell and Thomas Bärnthaler, "Ich wollte erfahren, wie man fünf Millionen Menschen vergast." *Süddeutsche Zeitung Magazin* 48, November 26, 2015, https://sz-magazin.sueddeutsche.de/geschichte/ich-wollte-erfahren-wie -man-fuenf-millionen-menschen-vergast-81934 (accessed August 28, 2019); English translation mine.

9. Erin McGlothlin, "Listening to the Perpetrators in Claude Lanzmann's *Shoah*," *Colloquia Germanica* 43, no. 3 (2010; published 2013): 235–71; here, 239–40.

10. McGlothlin, "Listening to the Perpetrators," 260.

11. McGlothlin, 244.

12. Keith Moser, "The Poignant Combination of Beauty and Horror in The Aesthetic Representations of the Holocaust in Lanzmann's *Shoah* and Le Clézio's *Etoile Errante*," *Dalhousie French Studies* 92 (2010): 75–83; here, 76; Jacob Howland, "Reflections on Claude Lanzmann's *Shoah*," *Proteus: A Journal of Ideas* 12, no. 2 (1995): 42–46 [here, 44]; Timothy Garton Ash, "The Life of Death," *New York Review of Books*, December 19, 1985, 26–29.

13. Lanzmann reports that his meeting with Suchomel began at 9 a.m. and involved "long hours of complex and concentrated shooting." The men spent the morning in conversation, broke for lunch (for which Lanzmann paid) and resumed the interview in the afternoon. *The Patagonian Hare*, 453–54.

14. Of the early generation of critics of *Shoah*, few explicitly recognized the role that editing played in its representation of the Holocaust. LaCapra, an exception to this trend, observed the deliberate way in which interviews from disparate witnesses were combined in what he called "an editorially orchestrated sequence," a principle that Vice later described as "meaning . . . constructed through juxtaposition rather than chronology." But apart from Tzvetan Todorov, who wrote that "the depiction of the Germans in *Shoah* is just as schematic. . . . Not only has Lanzmann selected his characters according to an obvious bias, but he edits out whatever they say that might in any way complicate his simple picture," few acknowledged how the technical function of editing was employed to shape individual testimonies. LaCapra, "Lanzmann's *Shoah*," 251; Vice, *Shoah*, 30; Todorov, *Facing the Extreme: Moral Life in the Concentration Camps*, trans. Arthur Denner and Abigail Pollak (New York: Metropolitan, 1996), 275.

15. Jean-Michel Frodon, "The Work of the Filmmaker: An Interview with Claude Lanzmann," *Cinema and the Shoah: An Art Confronts the Tragedy of the Twentieth Century*, ed. Jean-Michel Frodon (Albany: State University of New York Press, 2010), 94. LaCapra asserts with regard to the function of the survivor-witnesses in the theatrical release of *Shoah*, "One difficulty in discussing *Shoah* as a 'fiction of the real' is that in it survivors both *play* and *are* themselves. Any boundary between art and life collapses at the point trauma is relived, for when a survivor breaks down, the frame distinguishing art from life also breaks down and reality erupts on stage or film." "Lanzmann's *Shoah*," 266. I argue that a

similar dynamic is at play with Lanzmann's double function as interviewer and filmmaker, although in this case the conflation of the two roles reifies rather than collapses the frame that unites reality with illusion.

16. LaCapra, "Lanzmann's *Shoah*," 233. The strength of LaCapra's argument that Lanzmann's "views are taken [by critics] to inform the film" is demonstrated by the fact LaCapra himself follows to some extent Lanzmann's framework for understanding *Shoah*. He writes that Lanzmann is both a "principal interlocutor or character in his film" and "an important viewer or interpreter of it." "Lanzmann's *Shoah*," 268

17. Lanzmann, *The Patagonian Hare*, 491.

18. Frodon, "The Work of the Filmmaker," 95.

19. See "Introduction: Claude Lanzmann's *Shoah* and its Outtakes: Inventing According to the Truth" in this volume.

20. See "Introduction" in this volume.

21. See contribution by Lindsay Zarwell and Leslie Swift in this volume.

22. H. Porter Abbott, *The Cambridge Introduction to Narrative*, 2nd ed. (Cambridge: Cambridge University Press, 2008), 22.

23. See Carl R. Plantinga, *Rhetoric and Representation in Nonfiction Film* (Cambridge: Cambridge University Press, 1997), 86.

24. Josef Oberhauser, with whom Lanzmann tried unsuccessfully to speak (and whose refusal to speak is a compelling moment in the theatrical release of *Shoah*), is considered to have been a much more central operator than was Suchomel in the Aktion Reinhard extermination program. At Bełżec, he was, in Yitzhak Arad's words, "third in the camp's chain of command" and the adjutant of Christian Wirth, the first commandant of Bełżec. When Wirth became Inspector of all three Aktion Reinhard camps in August 1942, Oberhauser accompanied him as his aide-de-camp. In this capacity he was promoted from SS–*Oberscharführer* to the officer rank of *Untersturmführer*. See Yitzhak Arad, *Belzec, Sobibor, Treblinka: The Operation Reinhard Death Camps* (Bloomington: Indiana University Press, 1987), 28, 89, 167.

25. Information regarding Suchomel's biography and his activities in the Aktion Reinhard program are taken from his 1965 verdict, which is included in *Justiz und Verbrechen: Sammlung deutscher Strafurteile wegen nationalsozialistischer Tötungsverbrechen, 1945-1966*, vol. 22, ed. Fritz Bauer, Irene Sagel-Grande, Adelheid L. Rüter-Ehlermann, H. H. Fuchs, and C. F. Rüter (Amsterdam: University Press Amsterdam, 1981).

26. According to his verdict, Suchomel was employed in Hadamar "nur als Foto-kopist" ("only as a photocopyist") und "keineswegs an den Gasöfen" ("in no way at the gas ovens"). *Justiz und Verbrechen*, 151; English translation mine.

27. From the testimony of Kalman Teigman in Chris Webb and Michal Chocho-laty, *The Treblinka Death Camp: History, Biographies, Remembrance* (Stuttgart: ibidem-Verlag, 2014), 156. According to Michael S. Briant, the survivor Rich-ard Glazar (who also appears in *Shoah*) testified at the first Treblinka trial that "'in view of the inhuman relationships in Treblinka, Suchomel was considered the mildest [guard]'"; at the same time, however, Briant notes that "subsequent witnesses stepped forward to paint a far less flattering portrait of Suchomel." Briant, *Eyewitness to Genocide: The Operation Reinhard Death Camp Trials, 1955–1966* (Knoxville: University of Tennessee Press, 2014), 106–7. The ver-dict from the Treblinka trial claims that Suchomel's behavior at Treblinka offers "ein zwiespaltiges Bild" ("an ambivalent picture"). On the one hand, he was reported to have behaved brutally during his time working at the ramp, where he whipped arriving deportees and shot with his pistol into the crowd. On the other hand, he was known to have treated his *Goldjuden* very well and addi-tionally to have attempted to save at least two people from gassing. *Justiz und Verbrechen*, 138–39; 150–51; English translation mine.

28. According to Kékesi, Suchomel "was convicted not as an accomplice (*Mittäter*) but rather only as an accessory (*Beihilfe*)" (*Agents of Liberation*, 38). As stated in the verdict at the Treblinka trial, "Suchomel ist nicht als Mittäter, sondern als Gehilfe anzusehen. Man kann nicht davon ausgehen, dass sein Wille über die Leistung eines Unterstützungsbeitrages hinausging und dass er die Mass-entötungen als eigene wollte" (Suchomel is to be seen not as a co-perpetrator but rather as a helper. It cannot be assumed that his volition exceeded the activity of a supporting contribution and that he harbored intent for the mass kill-ings). *Justiz und Verbrechen*, 192, 186. For this reason, the court was unable to characterize his mental attitude as "Täterwille" ("animus auctoris" or "will to perpetrate a crime"); English translation mine.

29. Lanzmann writes in *The Patagonian Hare* that the interview with Suchomel took place in March 1976, yet the USHMM catalog information states that "The date of April 27, 1976 is inscribed onto the cameraman's slates" (https://collections.ushmm.org/search/catalog/irn1004727, accessed August 27, 2019). Lanzmann further implies that the location of the interview was chosen so that Suchomel could conceal its existence from his son-in-law, who had violently

intervened to stop a previous meeting between Lanzmann and Suchomel. *The Patagonian Hare*, 447, 452.

30. Lanzmann writes that the he filmed the Suchomel interview "two years before the actual shooting of the film began." *The Patagonian Hare*, 452.

31. Lanzmann, 448–49.

32. At one point in the interview, Suchomel also requests that the audio recorder be turned off. Lanzmann responds, "Ja, ja, ja, ja," and then says to Lubtchansky, "Fais semblant d'arrêter" (Pretend to stop). Claude Lanzmann *Shoah* Collection, interview with Franz Suchomel (RG-60.5046, Film ID 3763, Camera Rolls 29–30), US Holocaust Memorial Museum and Yad Vashem and State of Israel; English translation mine.

33. Lanzmann, *The Patagonian Hare*, 453.

34. According to Jennifer Cazenave, the male interpreter in the Suchomel interview was anomalous for the entire *Shoah* project, as all the other interpreters were women. Jennifer Cazenave, *An Archive of the Catastrophe: The Unused Footage of Claude Lanzmann's* Shoah (Albany: State University of New York Press, 2019), 34.

35. Lanzmann, *The Patagonian Hare*, 446, 454.

36. Lanzmann writes in his autobiography that Suchomel specifically requested payment in German currency, and he describes paying him at the end of the interview: "When we had finished, I counted the 100 Deutschmark notes slowly in front of him and his wife." *The Patagonian Hare*, 452–54. However, at the end of the outtakes of the interview, Lanzmann can be heard explaining to Suchomel that he had no time to procure German currency and must thus give him 2,000 Swiss francs. Interview with Franz Suchomel (RG-60.5046, Film ID 3763, Camera Rolls 31–32). This small discrepancy serves as a reminder that, however much we must rely on Lanzmann's memory and his statements about the filming of *Shoah* for important contextual information about the film, they are not infallible.

37. See the contribution by Lindsay Zarwell and Leslie Swift in this volume.

38. For example, at one point in sequence C we see a long stretch of unedited visual track in which the camera pans from Suchomel's face to the map to which he is pointing. Lanzmann takes the opportunity to make some significant cuts to the audio track that are not at all perceptible because the camera no longer focuses on Suchomel's mouth. *Shoah*, disc 3, chapter 1.

39. For a discussion of the Lanzmann's performative self-production in *Shoah*, including his aggressive linguistic strategies, please see McGlothlin, "Listening to the Perpetrators," 245–48.

40. Interview with Franz Suchomel (RG-60.5046, Film ID 3754, Camera Rolls 3–4); English translation mine.
41. *Shoah*, disc 1, chapter 55; English translation mine.
42. McGlothlin, "Listening to the Perpetrators," 262.
43. Interview with Franz Suchomel (RG-60.5046, Film ID 3760, Camera Rolls 20–22; Film ID 3764, Camera Rolls, 31–32).
44. Interview with Franz Suchomel (RG-60.5046, Film ID 3762, Camera Rolls 26–28; Film ID 3760, Film ID 20–22).
45. Interview with Franz Suchomel (RG-60.5046, Film ID 3762, Camera Rolls 26–28). I possess basic facility in Yiddish and thus was able to analyze Suchomel's use of Yiddish only superficially; I therefore asked Maya Barzilai, a scholar of Hebrew and Yiddish literature, to confirm my appraisal of Suchomel's Yiddish. Barzilai confirmed that, although Suchomel "certainly had an ear for Yiddish," with the story he ostensibly narrates in Yiddish, he essentially "mix[es] a bit of Yiddish into his German" and speaks German with "Yiddish inflection." Private email to author, November 11, 2015.
46. Interview with Franz Suchomel (RG-60.5046, Film ID 3762, Camera Rolls 26–28; Film ID 3759, Camera Rolls 17–19).
47. According to Lanzmann, "The construction of this film follows a logic. Nobody meets anyone in *Shoah*. I already said this, but there is a corroboration in spite of this—I make them meet. They don't meet actually, but the film is a place of meeting." "Seminar with Claude Lanzmann 11 April 1990," *Yale French Studies* 79 (1991): 82–99; here, 84. By virtue of the ways in which he connects scenes of witnesses from often diametrically opposed experiences, Lanzmann creates these profound meetings with the process of editing.
48. Please see Brad Prager's contribution in this volume.
49. Leo Spitzer, "'You Wanted History, I Give You History': Claude Lanzmann's *Shoah*," in *Teaching the Representation of the Holocaust*, ed. Marianne Hirsch and Irene Kacandes (New York: Modern Language Association of America, 2004), 412–21; here, 416.
50. Interview with Franz Suchomel (RG-60.5046, Film ID 3763, Camera Rolls 29–30); English translation mine.
51. Vice, *Shoah*, 46–48.
52. In an interview, Lanzmann claimed that he consciously planned that the beginning of the second half of the film (which commences with Suchomel singing) would repeat the structure of the beginning of the first half of the film (in which Srebnik sings): "The film is organized according to a narrative structure

that plunges like a drill. In the beginning of the second period, it can seem as though it is all starting over from the beginning. But the witnesses are not the same." Frodon, "The Work of the Filmmaker," 100.

53. *Shoah*, disc 3, chapter 1; interview with Franz Suchomel [(RG-60.5046, Film ID 3755, Camera Rolls 5–10); English translation mine].

54. Interview with Franz Suchomel (RG-60.5046, Film ID 3755, Camera Rolls 5–10); English translation mine.

55. Director Marcel Ophüls writes, for example, "Most of the time, these criminals are asked very precise, technical questions about the details of their activities. Had Lanzmann asked any of these men about the state of their souls, they would have recoiled like rattlesnakes." "Closely Watched Trains," in *Claude Lanzmann's* Shoah: *Key Essays*, ed. Stuart Liebman (Oxford: Oxford University Press, 2007), 77–87; here, 84. In a similar vein, Moser writes, "Although Suchomel's disconcerting ecstatic demeanor as he is performing a song about Treblinka stupefies the viewer, his corporal language is perhaps a natural manifestation of his inability to confront sentiments of culpability. The former SS officer realizes that he played an important role in the genocidal horror perpetrated by the Nazi regime, but nostalgia functions as a coping mechanism that prevents him from opening old wounds and reflecting upon his own guilt." "The Poignant Combination of Beauty and Horror," 77. Among such critical assessments, Todorov's skepticism about the lack of remorse on the part of the perpetrators (quoted in note 14) is anomalous.

56. Jay Cantor, "Death and the Image," *Beyond Document: Essays on Nonfiction Film*, ed. Charles Warren (Hanover, NH: University Press of New England, 1996), 23–49; here, 34.

57. McGlothlin, "Listening to the Perpetrators," 245–47.

58. As Lawrence Douglas notes in his book about the trial of John Demjanjuk, the former guard at Sobibór, "In 1964, during the famous Frankfurt-Auschwitz trial, Fritz Bauer, the German-Jewish attorney general of Hessen, said in an interview that he often dreamed that 'sooner or later, one of the accused would step forward and say, '. . . what took place, it was horrific, I'm sorry' . . . Then the entire world would exhale, as would all the survivors of those who killed at Auschwitz, and the air would be cleared—if only at last one humane word were uttered.' And yet Bauer ruefully noted, 'it has not been uttered, nor will it be.'" *The Right Wrong Man: John Demjanjuk and the Last Great Nazi War Crimes Trial* (Princeton, NJ: Princeton University Press, 2016), 248. Bauer recognized here that his desire for statements of remorse on the part of the perpetrators

was inherently unfulfillable. Not only was it not to be expected that such statements would be issued; it also was pure fantasy to imagine that they could bear any meaning commensurate with the crimes.

59. Saira Mohamed, "Of Monsters and Men: Perpetrator Trauma and Mass Atrocity," *Columbia Law Review* 115 (2015): 1157–216; here, 1210–11.

60. Interview with Franz Suchomel (RG-60.5046, Film ID 3763, Camera Rolls 29–30); English translation mine.

61. In the interview cited in note 8, Lanzmann claims to have "let [the perpetrators speak]" and at the same time to have strenuously avoided eliciting their feelings. In the case of Suchomel's expression of shame, Lanzmann refused to "let [him] speak" precisely because Suchomel insisted on expressing the feelings Lanzmann was so loath to hear.

62. Felman, "The Return of the Voice," 263.

63. There is of course a real risk that the revelations presented here about Lanzmann's method of editing might give fodder to Holocaust denial. At the same time, however, Holocaust deniers have never required actual proof or logical arguments to make their specious claims. And, indeed, as I was conducting research for this article, I found a blog post by Peter Winter, author of *The Six Million: Fact or Fiction?* and a person who, according to the *Sunday Times*, "disputes the existence of the Auschwitz gas chambers and accuses Jews who survived the atrocity of 'outright lies and forgery.'" In this post, Winter argues that the "technical aspects" of the scenes with Suchomel in the theatrical release of *Shoah* (such as the blurred and flickering quality of the footage and the "differing focal lengths and perspectives") are evidence that Lanzmann "tamper[ed] with" or perhaps even falsified the Suchomel interview. Justin Stoneman and Robin Henry, "Holocaust Denial Books Sold on Amazon," *Sunday Times*, February 12, 2017, https://www.thetimes.co.uk/edition/news/holocaust-denial -books-sold-on-amazon-s5lrk9v5v (accessed August 27, 2019); Peter Winter, "The Suchomel Confession" in Claude Lanzmann's *Shoah* Movie, May 6, 2014, http://peterwinterwriting.blogspot.com/2014/05/the-suchomel-confession-in -claude.html (accessed August 27, 2019).

64. Since the catalyzation of what Rebecca Wennberg terms the "new perpetrator research" in the early 1990s with the publication of Christopher Browning's pioneering, nuanced study of lower-level perpetrators, *Ordinary Men: Police Reserve Police Battalion 101 and the Final Solution in Poland*, Holocaust studies has witnessed a wave of pathbreaking and illuminating work on perpetrators by historians, psychologists, sociologists, and, most recently, scholars of

literature, culture, and film that attempts to track the diversity of perpetrators with regard to temporal, geographical, and generational coordinates; class and social environment; ideological beliefs and degree of antisemitic and racist outlook; psychological disposition; self-understanding; and post-Holocaust cultural representation. Such scholarly approaches mirror a North American and European cultural climate that is less dependent on the trope of the "evil Nazi" for its image of Holocaust perpetrators and in which readers and viewers are willing to adopt in limited ways the perspective of the perpetrator. Rebecca Wennberg, "Between Sacred and the Profane: Holocaust Collaboration and 'Political Religion," *Religious Compass* 8, no. 1 (2013): 25–25. See also Erin McGlothlin, "Theorizing the Perpetrator in Bernhard Schlink's *The Reader* and Martin Amis's *Time's Arrow*," in *After Representation? The Holocaust, Literature, and Culture*, ed. R. Clifton Spargo and Robert Ehrenreich (New Brunswick, NJ: Rutgers University Press, 2009), 210–30; "Narrative Perspective and the Holocaust Perpetrator in Edgar Hilsenrath's *The Nazi and the Barber* and Jonathan Littell's *The Kindly Ones*," in *The Bloomsbury Companion to Holocaust Literature*, ed. Jenni Adams (London: Bloomsbury, 2014), 159–77; and "Empathic Identification and the Mind of the Holocaust Perpetrator in Fiction: A Proposed Taxonomy of Response," *Narrative* 24, no. 3 (2016): 251–76.

9 | The Real Abraham Bomba

Through Claude Lanzmann's Looking Glass

Brad Prager

In *The Era of the Witness*, Annette Wieviorka draws connections between the testimonies at Adolf Eichmann's trial in Jerusalem and Claude Lanzmann's *Shoah*, noting that three witnesses, "Simon Srebnik . . . and Mordechai Podklebnik, two of only three people to survive Chełmno; and Itzhak Zuckermann, a hero of the Warsaw ghetto uprising," were common to both.[1] Lanzmann interviewed at least three additional survivors who testified at the Eichmann trial (Hansi Brand, Abba Kovner, and Ada Lichtmann), and those interviews are now archived among the outtakes at the United States Holocaust Memorial Museum (USHMM). Lanzmann's roster of interviewees thus overlapped with Eichmann's prosecutors' witness list, and Lanzmann has since confirmed that when he made *Shoah*, he was indeed looking back to 1961. In *The Patagonian Hare*, he reflects: "It became clear to me that the [Eichmann] trial had been conducted by ignorant people: the historians at the time had done too little research, the president and the judges were poorly informed; Hausner, the chief prosecutor, thought that pompous moralizing flights of rhetoric compensated for what he lacked in knowledge—he made hundreds of mistakes."[2] Lanzmann adds: "Tearful witnesses gave a kind of show, making it impossible to re-create what they had truly experienced."[3] He describes the Eichmann trial as a "show," yet he concludes that it failed as a "re-creation" (*recréation*). During the many years he worked on *Shoah*, he continually explored the overlapping yet contradictory impulses that separate the testimonies in his documentary films—which include forms of re-creation and reenactment—from those that define public testimonies, such as one would encounter in a courtroom.

What, in Lanzmann's view, had Eichmann's prosecutors failed to accomplish? Because one could neither expect nor wish to "re-create" Nazi atrocities in a courtroom or as part of the production of a documentary film, re-creation is a misleading term, yet "dramatization," an alternative, implies histrionics. To describe witnesses as dramatists can be misleading insofar as we do not generally think of courtroom witnesses as participants in theatrical productions. However, where testimony is presented in front of a camera, witnesses' bodies may be situated and staged. Decisions concerning those matters affect the extent to which viewers empathize as they watch and listen to survivors in the process of recalling their suffering. Dominick LaCapra highlights some of the contradictory impulses that guide our interpretation of performative testimonies, relying on Lanzmann's own turn of phrase: "One difficulty in discussing *Shoah* as a 'fiction of the real' is that in it survivors both *play* and *are* themselves. Any boundary between art and life collapses at the point trauma is relived, for when a survivor-victim breaks down, the frame distinguishing art from life also breaks down and reality erupts on stage or film."[4] LaCapra begins from the position that a documentary such as *Shoah* is the work of an artist, but that the film's artifice can collapse when the uncontainable expression of traumatic experience erupts onto the screen. His interpretation thematizes the contradictions entailed in speaking of witness testimonies as though they were the end results of therapy sessions rather than sequences in highly controlled works that incorporate measured shot compositions and elements of mise-en-scène. Documentary films are the products of their directors' visions, just as much as features, and they pass through the many mediating layers that attend the filmmaking process; directors decide what to include, what to exclude, and in what order fragments of testimonies should be presented. They may actively seek and thus produce types of testimonies, bringing those testimonies into existence, soliciting them in accord with a preconceived design. Although Lanzmann's Jewish witnesses' emotions are surely genuine, the testimonies in *Shoah* become theatrical at the point the director implements organizational decisions. Lanzmann's witnesses play roles in his film, and their director takes on much of the responsibility for shaping, staging, and presenting their accounts.

In an interview at the time of *Shoah*'s release, Lanzmann acknowledged that his subjects "pass from the status of witnesses to History to that of actors."[5] He highlights in particular the Treblinka survivor Abraham Bomba, noting that Bomba, who was once a barber, became a "character" in *Shoah*, "because he was no longer a barber."[6] In *The Patagonian Hare*, in which Lanzmann writes about first meeting Bomba, subsequent to having been referred to him by Yad Vashem in 1975, he describes something remarkably akin to a performer's audition. Bomba, who had been born in Beuthen, Germany, raised in Częstochowa, Poland, and deported to Treblinka in 1942, had survived the Holocaust because he was assigned the task of cutting victims' hair shortly before they were executed in the gas chambers, and he had managed to escape from Treblinka in January 1943. When Lanzmann appeared at Bomba's door thirty years after the war's end, Bomba's daughter mistook Lanzmann for a Hollywood producer, and Lanzmann's description of his first prolonged interview with Bomba reads like the enthusiastic account of a director who had finally found his leading man.[7]

As Lanzmann had done in the cases of his other witnesses, he familiarized himself with his subject's testimony prior to filming. He explains in his memoir how he first "extricated" Bomba "from his terrible wife," who "hardly let the man get a word in edgeways," and how he subsequently interviewed him privately in upstate New York.[8] He writes that those two days of interviews "proved critical," not simply because of those aspects of Bomba's account that made him a unique witness, but because Lanzmann later followed a similar interview pattern with others. Lanzmann writes, "What [Bomba] told me then gave me the key to how I was to deal with the Jewish protagonists in my film."[9] He explains, "I encouraged him to rack his brain for every detail, forced him to plunge ever deeper into the unspeakable moments he had spent inside the gas chambers. I realized that in order to be able to film him, and people like him, I had to know everything about them in advance—or know as much as possible."[10] Contrary to Lanzmann's claim that he does not believe in retakes, the now-famous interview the two men conducted in a barbershop in Holon, near Tel Aviv, four years later, during the late summer of 1979—an interview that has since become one of the most famous interview scenes in documentary film history—was a *re*interview.[11] It was a version of the conversation the two men first conducted in New York, the one in which Lanzmann plunged "ever deeper into the unspeakable moments."

Lanzmann staged part of the 1979 interview—one of two settings for Lanzmann's three-and-a-half hours of interview footage with Bomba, all of which is now preserved among the USHMM's outtakes—in a barbershop because he felt the setting offered opportunities that an armchair interview would not have afforded him. He says, "If I had sat [Bomba] in a chair and said: 'Okay, now tell your story!' something completely different would have come out."[12] LaCapra's observation that the film's survivors "both *play* and *are* themselves" can be asserted with respect to nearly any documentary that involves testimonial performance, or the presentation of eyewitness accounts for theatrical or cinematic purposes.[13] Lanzmann has elsewhere asserted that this is no dissimulation, and that none of his choices, including placing a survivor in a position that somatically resembles elements of his traumatizing victimization, should be treated as opportunistic. He prefers to describe Bomba as truth "incarnate" (*incarné*), using that phrase to characterize the climax of his testimony.[14] Bomba's communication of trauma builds on a series of bodily expressions, particularly the strained and painful silence that has by now become his testimony's most famous aspect. Because it is not purely verbal but rather an "incarnation," and because the witness appears to come fleetingly into contact with his past, creating a feeling of immediacy, Bomba's testimony has been treated as though it possesses an exceptional measure of truth and authenticity. When Bomba experiences the memory of a traumatic moment, the barbershop is temporarily steeped in his palpable grief. Olaf Berg describes the sequence as an example of the "connotation mode" that is the defining signature of Lanzmann's work; ruptured, recollected pasts and testimonial presents overlap with one another without becoming identical.[15] Bomba survived his victimization, but, according to Shoshana Felman, Lanzmann, when he urges Bomba to speak, is facilitating his witness's emergence from death's grip. She ascribes tremendous significance to the silence and its interruption, asserting that it "is the silence of the witness's death, and of the witness's deadness which precisely must be broken, and transgressed."[16]

Most of the scholarship about this scene centers on this same haunting part of the interview: Bomba, while behaving as though he is giving an ordinary male customer a haircut, recalls for the camera how a barber alongside whom he worked at Treblinka encountered his own wife and his sister as they entered the gas chamber in the minutes before their execution. Bomba hesitates to recount the details of how his friend prepared his own family to die in the presence of SS men, but Lanzmann, who remains for the most part off-screen and present only as a voice, persuades him to say more. In the course of this sequence, Bomba grows overwhelmed and struggles to speak. He tries to maintain his composure, wiping his face with a handkerchief. Michael Renov seconds Lanzmann's own assessment of that moment, writing that in this difficult barbershop testimony, "the kernel of trauma, buried and of the Real, erupts less as language, more as signs of bodily distress—[the] grimacing, [the] tears, the cessation of activity."[17] Sven Kramer writes about this scene under the heading "Authenticity and Strategies of Authentication," noting, "Bomba omits the worst of the story, but Lanzmann lingers on the silence and registers his physical, bodily struggle to hold onto language as it slips away, to regain his composure, and to fight against the overwhelming memories and tears. Viewers become witnesses as Bomba is physically and psychologically overwhelmed by the past."[18] One of the long pauses is briefly broken by Bomba's interjection in Yiddish, which is not translated into English within the interview and typically remains untranslated in the subtitles. As much as these words can be distinguished, Bomba seems to be saying: "I feel like I am about to break. Just like back then in Germany." In the outtakes one finds other, prior instances when Bomba can be seen chatting, in a relaxed manner, with his barbershop client in Yiddish.[19] He is in communication with the man in the chair, but because other instances of that have been left out of the theatrical release of *Shoah*, critics have interpreted the Yiddish interjection as though it were an involuntary eruption from out of Bomba's past, an isolated reaction to his recollection of a traumatic episode.

Those other occurrences of Bomba speaking Yiddish, along with many other revealing details, were excluded from *Shoah*'s final cut, but, owing to the efforts of curators at the USHMM, it is now known precisely how much of Bomba's testimony found its way to the cutting-room floor. Examining the three hours and twenty minutes of additional material offers insight into Lanzmann's final product, particularly into the context and distinct perspective from which *Shoah* emerged.[20] The Bomba outtakes tell us a great deal about the film itself and about Lanzmann's vast number of formal decisions, and they also provide insight into how performance interacts with testimony. On the one hand, Bomba's physical responses seem to be involuntary expressions; his traumatic experience, which looks to be spontaneous rather than a preconceived articulation of ideas, attains a physical irrefutability akin to a tattoo on a survivor's arm. On the other hand, Bomba is, at that point, no longer a professional barber, and, at Lanzmann's behest, he is participating in a staged scene. Lanzmann was well acquainted with the details of his witness's testimony before the sequence was filmed. Like an attorney, he asks questions to which he, by and large, knows the answers, and the two men are attuned to the presence of the camera. If Bomba's testimony can be described as incontrovertible bodily evidence demonstrated at the moment of its undeniable eruption, can it also be treated as a reflection of a witness's unique ability to dramatize what he or she experienced—that is, the capacity to present a credible simulation? Can testimony be both an authentic eruption of incontrovertible truth *and* a dissimulating theatrical performance?

Abraham Bomba: Witness to Treblinka

Marianne Hirsch and Leo Spitzer assert that Lanzmann has a nearly singular purpose in *Shoah*, and they write that the "almost obsessive thrust" of the film, or "its primary goal, is to bring to memory and to record the workings of the Nazi machinery of destruction: to detail its operations and lethal course, from the ghettos, to the transports and trains, to the selections in the extermination camps, to mass murder in gas vans and gas chambers, to the burial and burning of the corpses."[21] Examining what Lanzmann chose to exclude from the final cut of Bomba's interview confirms Hirsch and Spitzer's impression: Lanzmann omits a substantial amount of interview footage that did not concern his or other survivors' direct confrontation with the machinery of death. As is obvious from *Shoah's* final cut, some of Lanzmann's 1979 interview with Bomba was filmed in another location, away from the barbershop. The outtakes include additional footage from the conversation the two of them conducted on a terrace in Jaffa, at an apartment belonging to the former French resistance fighter Théo Klein.[22] In the more than three hours of previously unreleased footage Bomba discusses the feelings he had while he was a prisoner in the Częstochowa Ghetto, as well as the circumstances under which Zelo Bloch, foreman of a labor detail at Treblinka and future leader of the August 1943 rebellion, helped him survive a kidney ailment, and, finally, the particulars of his escape from Treblinka in January 1943. The parts of his testimony that highlight redemptive and even heroic aspects of his experience were left out of the final cut of Lanzmann's film.

In the interviews on the terrace, Bomba touches on the thorny subject of whether Jewish deportees went to their deaths "like sheep," maintaining in the clearest possible terms that they did not. That contention, in both its affirmative and negative forms, has been often repeated, and historian Raul Hilberg writes in *The Destruction of the European Jews* that the rallying cry "Do not be led like sheep to the slaughter" was introduced by Jewish resistance organizations in Warsaw and Białystok in 1943.[23] The phrase was also invoked in Abba Kovner's testimony at the Eichmann trial, when Kovner described a manifesto he wrote in December 1941 (published on January 1, 1942), urging the prisoners of the Vilna Ghetto not to go like sheep to slaughter. At the trial, Kovner elaborated retrospectively on his attitude, explaining that he rejected any claim that Jewish prisoners did not revolt, if the claim was intended as an accusation. Kovner testified: "The surprising thing, in my opinion, is that a fighting force existed at all, that there was armed reaction, that there was a revolt. . . . It was like a struggle of any underground."[24] Lanzmann knew all this when he interviewed Kovner for *Shoah*—an interview entirely omitted from the theatrical release—and, in the outtakes from that interview, Lanzmann can be heard reading a French translation of Kovner's manifesto aloud to the camera, which indicates that he, at that point, likely expected to include discussion of it in his film.[25] In the course of that meeting, Lanzmann takes Kovner to task for having expected too much of the Jews in the Vilna Ghetto, asking him whether he would have written the document in precisely the same way, had he known what he later came to know about the challenges and complications of ghetto existence.[26] Although the topic of daily life and of resistance in the ghettos is discussed in Lanzmann's filmed interviews with Hilberg, surviving witnesses' judgments about the paucity of choices available to the demoralized residents of ghettos such as Vilna's were largely sidelined in *Shoah*'s theatrical release, and Lanzmann did not directly address them until he recut his interviews with Benjamin Murmelstein and Maurice Rossel decades after they took place, releasing them along with some additional, newly filmed footage under separate titles.

Although *Shoah* spends much time examining the choices faced by the *Sonderkommandos* at Auschwitz and the *Arbeitsjuden* in the Operation Reinhard camps, Lanzmann, throughout the film, avoids passing judgment on whether deported Jews went to their deaths courageously. The film's theatrical release, of course, does not exclude all redemptive narratives of resistance. Ferzina Banaji underscores the fact that the last words of the final cut of *Shoah* belong to Simcha Rotem, one of the fighters in the Warsaw Ghetto Uprising. In the film's penultimate sequence Rotem stands in the Ghetto Fighters' Kibbutz in Israel, and his placement underscores, according to Banaji, that Rotem "eventually found his way to Israel, a state that commemorates this tragedy in the memorial from which he speaks."[27] In this respect, *Shoah* thematizes Jewish resistance and heroism. However, very few of the witnesses in the film speak directly to the question of whether Jews went to their deaths "like sheep." That phrase, along with the entirety of the Kovner interview, does not appear in the final cut, and evaluative judgments about courage and resistance, whether they are made by Lanzmann or by his witnesses, are more implicit than explicit.

Insight into the formation of Lanzmann's perspective on this point, as well as into his framing of Bomba's testimony, can be drawn from the debate about Jean-François Steiner's 1966 novel *Treblinka* among French intellectuals at the time.[28] There were many objections to Steiner's book—a novelization based on witness testimony—because it allegedly emphasized the extent to which the Jewish workforce at Treblinka acted as the perpetrators' accessories. According to Samuel Moyn, who has written a history of Steiner's novel's reception, one of *Treblinka*'s major assumptions was that the Jews were their own worst enemies; many were complicit in their own peoples' destruction, and their responses to the machinery of death, whether one speaks of the "collaboration" of the commandos or the extent of the survivors' rebellions and escape attempts, were all characteristically

Jewish.[29] David Rousset, one of Steiner's critics, argued that Steiner's perspective was false: the camps were simply an effect of totalitarianism, and nothing about the victims' responses should be treated as having been specific to Jews.[30] Hannah Arendt also voices this idea in *The Origins of Totalitarianism*, where she similarly describes continuities among totalitarianisms.[31] According to Rousset and Arendt, the incapacity to resist in such circumstances, and the question of whether the Jews fought back heroically or went to their deaths like sheep, should not be treated as a singularly Jewish issue. All concentrationary regimes, German and Soviet ones alike, are manifestations of power, and their subjects all find themselves similarly subjugated.

Steiner had written a fictionalization based on witness accounts, and his novel, because it does not provide the verbatim texts of testimonies, served as a negative example for Lanzmann, who aimed to foreground survivors' voices. Rachel Auerbach, a survivor of the Warsaw Ghetto who became an early historian of Treblinka and collected important documentation on the camp, objected that Steiner reinterpreted survivors' stories, putting them to his own use and effectively effacing and distorting their words.[32] In a collection of documents entitled *The Death Camp Treblinka* (1979), editor Alexander Donat explains that some Jewish witnesses were suspicious when he approached them, and that they had to be convinced that he was "not 'another Steiner,' who was out to take advantage of the survivors in order to manufacture a distorted account of Treblinka."[33] Lanzmann aimed to present testimony in his film in a manner different from Steiner. His practice included reliance on firsthand accounts and a strategy for letting witnesses speak. Although Lanzmann enframes, coordinates, and edits his witnesses' testimonies, his intention was to let his audiences hear the survivors' accounts, a practice that comes into sharp relief when contrasted with Steiner's nearly wholesale repurposing.

Lanzmann, owing in part to his romantic involvement with Simone de Beauvoir, who authored a much-discussed preface to Steiner's book, became a participant in the *Treblinka* debate. In a roundtable in 1966, many years before he began production on *Shoah*, Lanzmann explains that unlike Steiner he harbored no doubts about the heroism of the Jews in the compulsory workforce, and he asks: "What is [Steiner] doing? He reflects on the case—I do not like the expression—of 'collaborating' Jews, that is to say those who, inside the camp, in the 'Sonderkommando,' helped the Germans do their work. . . . It is exactly like all these young people you talk to. [Steiner] asks: 'How did the Jews do that?' It never occurred to me to consider the men of the 'Sonderkommando' to be collaborators or traitors. I consider them martyrs, the same as all others, and I even hold up many of them as heroes."[34] Lanzmann then emphasizes the generational difference between himself and Steiner, noting that Steiner, born in 1938, is thirteen years younger. On that basis, Lanzmann explains: "[Steiner] seems to say that six million Jews, which is a huge mass (and thus a virtual power [*une puissance virtuelle*]), allowed themselves to be led like sheep to slaughter, as six million. In fact, [the Nazis] were not killing six million, but were instead killing one by one."[35] He acknowledges that Steiner had perhaps come around to the idea that the *Sonderkommandos* were heroic, but "he needs to do extensive work to get there, while I consider them from the start to be martyrs. . . . That's the big difference and it is a generational difference. He heard of it twenty years later, I heard about it at the time, so I do not have to justify the [behavior of the] men of the 'Sonderkommando.'"[36] Lanzmann is closer in age to his witnesses, and he therefore feels that he understands what those such as Bomba, who were brutally compelled into servitude in the camps, went through. His historical proximity, he believes, better acquaints him with the truth about the mimesis between executioners and their involuntary workforce, and it better prepares him to act as a survivor's co-witness.[37]

The stakes in the Steiner case turned on the distinction between concentration camps with their many survivors and the uniqueness of mass Jewish death in Treblinka and in the other Operation Reinhard camps. While Lanzmann can be said to have overemphasized the machinery of death in *Shoah*, the confrontation with that machinery, for him, defines Jewish experience during the war. Discussions of cowardice and resistance are red herrings based on misinformation about how expeditious and brutal the Operation Reinhard camps were. The level and extent of the mass killing that took place there was unique, and *Shoah* is, in this sense, neither about Jewish resistance nor weakness, but rather about the machine-like murder of Jews. Lanzmann fashions his film accordingly, and Bomba thus veers off topic when, in the outtakes, he addresses Jewish resistance and its singular nature, in particular the issue of courage and cowardice. He opines:

The Jewish people . . . is a strong nation. No nationality would [have] survived if that had happened to them. Take the Polish people, the French people or any other people, they would not. They would break down like flies. But the Jewish people have a will to live. I mean to live even in suffering. . . . No other people, it doesn't matter how they were, they started a revolution against the Germans, or the uprising against the Germans, but the Jewish people. It happened in the ghetto of Białystok, it happened in the ghetto of Częstochowa, and finally it happened in the ghetto of Warsaw, where the first uprising against the Germans started, only from the Jewish people and not from other ones. . . . Some people now today [say] that the Jewish people went to the slaughterhouse like sheep. That's not true. The Jewish people, they didn't go like sheep to the slaughterhouses. I would say that if that had happened to any other nationalities, they would be more frightened, they would be more afraid, they would be more behind the Germans.[38]

These statements were left out of *Shoah*. Lanzmann, of course, could not have been expected to include everything, and he justifies these particular exclusions in *The Patagonian Hare*, where he explains that he had been so absorbed in this interview that he chose not to interrupt Bomba, and he thus failed to account for the setting sun while the two of them were conversing, which rendered certain portions of the Jaffa terrace material unusable.[39] The sequence's audio is perfectly comprehensible, despite the low lighting, and it thus could have, in some form, been integrated in the film. But many of Bomba's reflections do not square with Lanzmann's narrative, the one correctly characterized by Hirsch and Spitzer as transfixed by the machinery of death. The footage containing Bomba's views on this point, like the entirety of Lanzmann's conversation with Kovner, did not make it to the editing table.

Rehearsal

Bomba is less commonly known for the Jaffa footage that made it into *Shoah* than he is for the story he tells in the barbershop, particularly for the moment he grows silent, and for Lanzmann's diegetic instruction: "Go on, Abe. You must go [on]. You have to." The interaction is remarkable because of the testimony's content, and also for the role played by the documentarian. It should be mandatory viewing for any student of the form. With the director's camera pointed at him, Bomba indicates that he is reluctant to speak further, asserting, "I won't be able to do it." Lanzmann replies: "You have to do it. I know it is very hard. I know and I apologize." A number of critics have written about the struggle in this scene. Joshua Hirsch, for example, highlights resonances with psychoanalysis, asserting: "It is clear that Lanzmann is interested not only in what happened at Treblinka but also in how the memory of Treblinka is experienced, or how it is re-experienced, or how its transmission is interrupted in a way that recalls the descriptions by psychiatrists of their traumatized survivor patients for whom language fails."[40] The sequence, however, can also be viewed as an allegory of the film's struggle for control: it is a clash between an interviewer, who wants to move things in one direction, and his interviewee, and it is also a clash between a documentarian and a subject who is attempting to contest his authority.

The French critic Jacques Mandelbaum similarly sees this exchange in terms of contestation, choosing to liken the sequence to the conclusion of Charlie Chaplin's *The Great Dictator* (1940). Mandelbaum writes: "And when, strangled by sobs, [Bomba] can no longer utter a word, how can we not hear the incredibly moving order given by Lanzmann . . . as an echo of the intense moment of truth that is the final speech in Chaplin's *The Great Dictator*?"[41] Mandelbaum emphasizes the "order" issued by Lanzmann, and although the parallel with Chaplin may at first seem objectionable, his implication is that Bomba, like the "real" Chaplin who steps out of his role and addresses the audience at the end of *The Great Dictator*, is in a position in which he finds himself ethically obligated to speak: in Lanzmann's eyes, Bomba, for similar reasons, "must" continue. Chaplin's film converges with nonfiction practice at the moment its lead actor steps out of character, suddenly pleading with viewers to fight in the name of democracy for a better world. At that moment, the real, authentic Chaplin appears; the film's artifice is sacrificed, its charade concluded. Chaplin's theme became, for him, too serious to withstand further simulation. Similarly, the moment where Bomba is urged to transition from silence to speech can be seen as a formal disruption. Whether it is treated as an exchange between analyst and patient, or between an autocratic director and his subject, Lanzmann takes it upon himself to force a rupture.

The outtakes reveal that Lanzmann and Bomba had previously engaged in an exchange similar to the one in the barbershop when they were on Théo Klein's terrace and Bomba was describing his transport to Treblinka. In that filmed interview, Bomba alludes to, without directly detailing, the painful loss of his first wife and child. Recalling the scene, he becomes emotional.[42] Lanzmann calls for a cut, and when filming is resumed, he begins by urging Bomba on. His words are recognizable to anyone familiar with the theatrical release of *Shoah*: "Yes, but you do have to do it. You have no choice."[43] When they subsequently reach a point comparable to the one in the barbershop, Bomba's emotions are undoubtedly genuine, yet their interaction is—contrary to Lanzmann's assertion that he does not do "re-takes"—a repetition of something that had happened earlier. When they filmed their barbershop interview in Holon, Lanzmann was already familiar with Bomba's story, and the path of the testimony had been paved.[44] It is possible he did not know every detail, yet the two men had spoken at length about Bomba's experiences, and they had already reached a similar breaking point.

This level of orchestration may give one pause where the use of mise-en-scène is concerned. It is often asserted that the barbershop is a contrivance: Bomba was no longer a barber, this was not his workplace, and he was, for the most part, making only superficial contact with the hair of the man seated in the chair. "There could be no question," Lanzmann writes, "of having him talk about [the cutting of Jewish women's hair inside the gas chamber] on that sunny terrace facing the blue sea."[45] On the terrace in Jaffa, the tone of voice Bomba adopts is intimate. The two men sit close to one another, and their interaction feels extraordinarily personal. In a profound performance of co-witnessing, they even clasp hands with one another. With the second filmed interview, Lanzmann was thus attempting to reach the same point in an alternate setting. In the barbershop, the two stand at a distance, which means that Bomba has to exert himself, using a theatrical or a stage voice, projecting his private story across a public space. Rarely does an interviewer sit so far from a subject when hearing testimony. Lanzmann's decision to assume a distant position opens up a theatrical space that is also reflective; his distance is a deliberately placed obstacle, one that affords the possibility that things will become difficult or volatile. Stuart Liebman takes note of additional elements of mise-en-scène, writing that in this barbershop, "so far removed from wartime Poland, the people reflected and refracted in the complicated, unstable spaces of the facing mirrors invoke invisible spectral presences that haunt Bomba's—and our—present. Indeed, the image of a woman with short-cropped hair in an advertisement just visible in the illusory depths of the frame makes the presence of the women who died uncannily palpable."[46] Lanzmann knew that these circumstances would provoke something profound in his subject, describing it as "a setting where something could happen."[47] Filming in a place of business, costuming Bomba as a barber, and standing at a distance secured for him a performance more profoundly affecting than the intimate and private conversation on the terrace.

As Liebman points out, the barbershop was also chosen because of its opposing mirrors. In *The Patagonian Hare* Lanzmann discusses the mirrors, writing that during the interview,

> I ask a question that is incongruous, absurd: "There were no mirrors [in the gas-chambers], no?"—knowing perfectly well, since I had seen the gas chambers at Auschwitz and Majdanek, that there was nothing but bare walls. However, the walls of the barbershop in which we are filming are lined with mirrors and [Bomba's] movements are infinitely reflected in them. These questions make it possible to recreate as precisely as possible the place, the situation.[48]

Lanzmann's remarks offer little insight: What was the allure of the mirrors, and what, especially in terms of "re-creation," was this deliberately naïve question meant to elicit? More insight is offered by Dorota Glowacka, who writes that "the theatrical effect of th[is] episode is enhanced by the presence of mirrors, which, reminiscent of the famous mirror episode in

Orson Wells's *Citizen Kane*, cast multiple reflections of the participants."[49] In her reading, the mirrors recall the presence of a subject as well as his persona—the witness and the performer, living both in the present and in the past. The nearly endless series of reflections highlights that "the viewer is forced to voyeuristically participate in the breakdown of Bomba's theatrical mask, reflected in the crumbling of his carefully composed and inexpressive facial features, and the shattering of his crafted, accented English."[50] As the mise-en-scène becomes a mise-en-abyme, documentary reality is forced into constellation with a series of simulations, and *Shoah*'s artifice presses up against its limits.

Lanzmann had employed a mirror as an element of mise-en-scène at another point during the production of *Shoah*. Among the outtakes is an interview with Karl Kretschmer, an SS-*Obersturmbannführer* who had executed Jews at Babi Yar and elsewhere, and who was notorious for having written a set of unusual letters from the front, in which he recounted the surprising pace at which he had grown accustomed to murder.[51] After the war Kretschmer was sentenced to eight years of forced labor but was released after only one year for reasons of bad health. Lanzmann, presenting himself pseudonymously as Dr. Claude-Marie Sorel, contacted Kretschmer, maintaining that he wanted to interview him about Marvin Chomsky's American television miniseries *Holocaust* (1978), which aired in Germany in January 1979 and was much discussed.[52] Before meeting with Kretschmer, Lanzmann films himself preparing for the encounter: Bernard Aubouy, the sound engineer, straps a hidden surveillance apparatus to Lanzmann's bare chest, and the very visible mirror is obviously a cherry-picked element of mise-en-scène, an inexorable part of the composition. The cinematographer films from one corner of the room, while Lanzmann readies himself for the confrontation. He prepares for his performance, doing some of his "lines" in German. Sue Vice likens Lanzmann's behavior in this sequence to that of Michael Moore or Sacha Baron Cohen, who have been known to adopt personae for the sake of confrontational interviews.[53] The apparatus, strapped to Lanzmann's chest, resembles a holster: the filmmaker is a secret agent. The camera shoots from slightly lower than eye level, and at some points the mirror is situated at the exact center of the frame. The prop is by no means incidental. It is intended to highlight Lanzmann's self-reflexivity vis-à-vis his film's

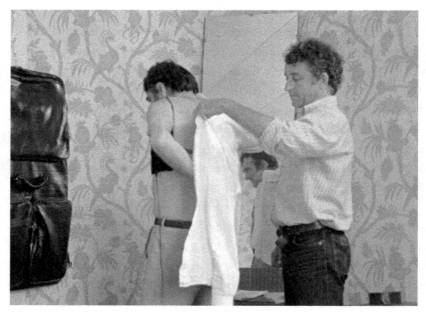

Claude Lanzmann prepares for his interview with Karl Kretschmer. Created by Claude Lanzmann during the filming of *Shoah*. (Used by permission of the United States Holocaust Memorial Museum and Yad Vashem, the Holocaust Martyrs and Heroes' Remembrance Authority, Jerusalem.)

artifice, and it calls to mind that he is about to engage in a simulation: he is on the verge of donning a mask.

Into the Mirror

The decision to film in front of mirrors in Holon was no less calculated, and one learns more about the mirrors' importance when watching the barbershop outtakes. Included among the first reels filmed in Holon, following clapperboard number fourteen, is what appears to be a practice reel. It contains no usable dialogue and could be described as "B-roll." The cameraman seems to search the space, finding his footing in a room filled with opposing mirrors. He pans back and forth, capturing the barber, the client in the chair, and the barber's image in the mirror, only to return again to the beginning. There is a practical reason for all of this: in order to work around the head of the customer—or, more specifically, the man who is pretending to be an ordinary customer—Bomba must periodically stand with his back to the camera. In the mirror, however, the cinematographer can capture Bomba's face. The set, with its numerous mirrors, thus affords the filmmaker a roomful of coverage without the burden of having to sweep in a circle, constantly compensating for the barber's movement around his client.

Now and again, the cameraman, while peering into the mirror, endeavors to conceal the seams between the mirrors, and in those moments, as the camera closes in, we lose sight of the fact that the mirror is a frame within a frame. We may feel that we have passed through the looking glass. Seams vanish, which leads to the fleeting apprehension that they are taking layers of mediation with them. Without these seams, we forget that we are still gazing into a mirror, and in zooming closer to the mirror Lanzmann is suggesting that his lens can venture deeper and reveal more.[54] But panning from Bomba's reflection back to the man, from image to image, is only a game. The filmed portrait of the survivor, whether reflected in a mirror or not, always has the same two-dimensionality, and not one of these images, each of which is enframed by Lanzmann's decisions, is more authentic than any other.

As the clapperboard falls before his protagonist for the sixteenth time, at the start of the reel that contained Bomba's now famous gas chamber testimony, the camera's first maneuver is to search for the barber's reflection. Indeed, in the final cut of the film, the sequence begins in the mirror. The lens first seeks out the false in order that Lanzmann can lead his viewers to the realm of the real. By the time we reach the most sensitive part of Bomba's testimony, the camera is pulling back from the mirror, revealing its seam. In response to a question about what he felt while working among the other forced laborers ("What was your impression the first time you saw these naked women arriving with children? What did you feel?"), Bomba explains, "Your feeling disappeared, you were dead. You had no feeling at all," and the camera, as though it were aware that Lanzmann was on the verge of reaching the very heart of Bomba's story, pulls away from the reflection and back into the seemingly more real space of the barbershop, bringing us with it, into the ostensibly authentic presence of the survivor. Rather than drawing our attention to the idea that the barbershop is a simulacrum, or to suggest that in *Shoah*, as in a hall of mirrors,

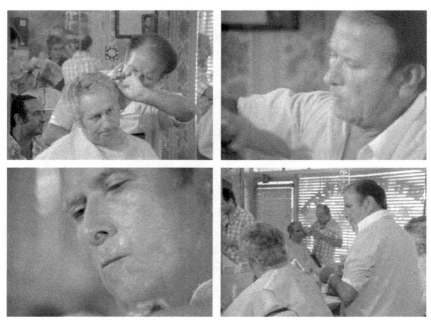

Lanzmann's cameraman finds his footing. Images are in order of appearance: the top two shots are in the mirror (with seams visible, left), and the bottom two are from the "real" (i.e., un-reflected) side. Images b and c show opposite sides of Bomba's profile. Created by Claude Lanzmann during the filming of *Shoah*. (Used by permission of the United States Holocaust Memorial Museum and Yad Vashem, the Holocaust Martyrs and Heroes' Remembrance Authority, Jerusalem.)

the truth is elusive and permanently obscured by apparitions, Lanzmann's camera movement, pulling away from the mirror and zooming in on Bomba, highlights his view that this interviewee is "truth incarnate." The very existence of the looking-glass Bomba, which acts as a foil for the real one, underscores the success of Lanzmann's quest; he has located a witness who embodies the truth. His decision to film in a hall of mirrors is not a sign that he has acquiesced to the restrictive limitations of mimesis, nor is he surrendering to the wholesale impossibility of Holocaust representation. Lanzmann is instead showing us that he can produce, before our eyes, the truth in its material or "incarnate" form.

The man who breaks down is thus meant to be perceived as the real thing, finally pinpointed by the camera. Having found the right witness, and having pushed him far enough, Lanzmann believes he can move the viewer from the one side of the mirror to the other, which is perhaps, contra Steiner, what he hoped to achieve in this interaction between interviewer and witness, analyst and patient, or documentarian and subject. With enough preparation, this real Bomba is neither a "character," nor is he *playing* himself. Lanzmann wants us to see Bomba *as* Bomba, as evinced by the fundamental truth of his bodily expression of trauma. All of this is, of course, misleading: although Bomba's experience is both genuine and genuinely moving, its presentation is the consequence of numerous stages of orchestration, including reperformance, mise-en-scène, and the choices made during the Jaffa interview, not to mention the decisions made during the editing process.

Owing to the eruption at the end of this scene, Mandelbaum is led to think of *The Great Dictator*. However, he is not the only one who recalls Chaplin in this context. The French film critic and historian Jean Narboni follows along similar lines to Mandelbaum, turning to *Shoah* in his study of *The Great Dictator*. He notes that the Jewish character played by Chaplin in that film is, like Bomba, a barber, and that Bomba and Chaplin each find themselves enjoined to speak the truth.[55] The philosopher and art historian Georges Didi-Huberman (in a book in which he takes a strong position against Lanzmann's resistance to archival images) also looks back to *The Great Dictator*, observing that: "The Jew and the dictator" in Chaplin's film,

> are more than fellows since they are the spitting image of one another; but at no moment do we find them indistinguishable. Everything sets them apart from one another at every moment. And when, in order to save his life, the Jew must dress in the robes of the dictator, the substitution itself only dissociates the elements of this structure, since it is Chaplin the artist who appears suddenly before the camera, beyond his two characters, as a citizen of the world assuming the responsibility of his ethical discourse.[56]

Didi-Huberman likely understands Chaplin's film as Mandelbaum does: the two parts, taken together—the two sides of Chaplin's performance—burst forth, uncontained, in the form of an ethical whole. Seen from this point of view, the pressure Lanzmann applies to Bomba is evidence not that he is a dictatorial filmmaker, but rather of the extent to which he is assuming an ethical responsibility. The documentarian and his subject dissimulate in order to produce the truth. The two of them were aware of what was going to emerge. They had made a pact early on; they agreed on the preconditions and had arrived at this point beforehand. Bomba knowingly puts himself in a position in which the past will overwhelm him, and producing a corporeal response is in the interest of their shared mission.

Return to New York

Abraham Bomba's videotaped USC Shoah Foundation testimony was recorded nearly seventeen years later, on August 14, 1996, in Monticello, New York. Coincidentally the duration of that interview is nearly identical in length to the unused portion of Lanzmann's interview with Bomba, and, in a practice reminiscent of Lanzmann's, the videographers have to call for several breaks in order to reload the camera. In the course of this three-hour-and-twenty-minute interview we learn a lot of significant personal history. Bomba recounts his conversation with a woman named Hanna Levinson, who urged him to live so that he could tell her story and that of other victims, and he also relates a distinctive account about a Jewish deportee who, as her last act, killed one of Treblinka's Jewish forced laborers with a razor, most likely under the mistaken impression that she was killing a German.[57] He recalls his escape from Treblinka and he mentions that he testified at the trials of former SS-*Scharführer* Josef Hirtreiter in 1951 and at the Düsseldorf Treblinka trial in 1964–65 in which Franz Suchomel, among others, was convicted. Finally, his wife Regina Bomba, to whom he had, at that time, been married for over fifty years, appears next to him at the interview's end, smiling, and she does not, in this brief appearance, remotely resemble the woman Lanzmann dismissively disparaged in his memoir.

Even in the course of this informative testimony, decisions must be made. The highly trained interviewer makes attempts to deemphasize affective response, and she has to consider where it is necessary to insist on further details. The choice to minimize the camera's movement, which is standard in such interviews, is also an enframing choice. Considering the form of interviews such as these, Oren Baruch Stier notes that videographers generally use a medium shot, focusing on the upper torso of the person who is testifying. The decision seems quite natural, yet "this frame is also somewhat deceptive—it gives the illusion (partially true) that the witness is speaking directly to us, the viewers. This illusion is beneficial, for it lends a sense of immediacy to the testimonial proceedings," but, Stier adds, it conceals the fact that "in actuality, the witness is speaking to us through intermediaries."[58] Numerous decisions have to be made about the testimony's pace, its setting, and the points at which the witness's story begins and ends. Video testimony aims for what might be described as a zero degree of narrative interference, or the pretense that no enframing is shaping the testimony.[59] That is, however, impossible. Here too, a story is being told, a narrative is shaped, and our relation to the narrating subject is determined by a wealth of formal decisions.

However genuinely emotive and affecting a witness's eruptions may be, there is always a dissimulating character to filmed testimony. The *Shoah* outtakes demonstrate how Lanzmann constructed his witness as "truth incarnate," staging Bomba's gestures as signs of his experience's undeniability. In Bomba, Lanzmann had found his leading man, and, owing to his cooperation, and to his success in the process of layering his response to the past atop Lanzmann's narrated and enframed present, it is unsurprising that Bomba is the one whom the director believed should set the tone for all other survivors in the film. To say as much is not to say that anything in Bomba's testimony is historically untrue; although individual facts within testimonies are sometimes inaccurate and can be disputed owing to the vagaries of memory, the fact of what happened at Treblinka, at the other extermination camps, and in the ghettos is not at all in question. This is only to say that where *Shoah* is concerned, conditions were created that facilitated a convincing testimonial performance, which included manufactured obstacles and even rehearsals. Some of what Bomba said did not fit the film's larger narrative, which meant excluding portions of the terrace testimony, but one expects no less from a documentarian. Filmmakers always decide to include what works and is most affecting, discarding what is not. Testimony, especially when captured on film, involves its construction and its performance, and these can hardly be regarded in isolation from one another.

Notes

1. Annette Wieviorka, *The Era of the Witness*, trans. Jared Stark (Ithaca: Cornell University Press, 2006), 81.

2. Claude Lanzmann, *The Patagonian Hare: A Memoir*, trans. Frank Wynne (New York: Farrar, Straus & Giroux, 2012), 425.

3. Lanzmann, *The Patagonian Hare*, 425.

4. Dominick LaCapra, "Lanzmann's *Shoah*: 'Here There Is No Why,'" *Claude Lanzmann's* Shoah: *Key Essays*, ed. Stuart Liebman (New York: Oxford University Press, 2007), 191–229; here, 220. The phrase "fiction of the real" is from Claude Lanzmann, "Site and Speech: An Interview with Claude Lanzmann about *Shoah*," trans. Stuart Liebman, in *Claude Lanzmann's* Shoah, 44. The phrase in French is "une fiction du réel." See "Le lieu et la parole: entretien avec Claude Lanzmann," *Cahiers du Cinema* no. 374 (1985): 18–23; here, 21.

5. Claude Lanzmann, "Site and Speech," 45. "History" is capitalized in Liebman's translation. Lanzmann's original words: "Le simple fait du tournage au présent fait passer ces gens du statut de témoins de l'Histoire à celui d'acteurs" ("Le lieu et la parole," 22).

6. Lanzmann, "Site and Speech," 45; "Le lieu et la parole," 22.

7. Lanzmann, *The Patagonian Hare*, 428.

8. Lanzmann, 428–29.

9. Lanzmann, 429.

10. Lanzmann, 429. On this point, Lanzmann differentiates between his preparation of Jewish witnesses and Polish ones. According to Lanzmann: "With the Poles I did not want to know anything in advance. With the Jews it was the other way around. With the Jewish witnesses I wanted to know everything in advance. These are two different levels of interrogation, of ethics, I would say." Claude Lanzmann, "Seminar with Claude Lanzmann. 11 April 1990," *Yale French Studies* 79 (1991): 82–99; here, 90–91.

11. Lanzmann says, "I didn't do a number of takes like people do when filming fiction. You stay in the moment; there are no retakes or second chances. How could I ask Abraham Bomba to repeat the emotion he feels, evoking what he lived through in the gas chamber in Treblinka? It is neither theatre nor the work of actors." See Jean-Michel Frodon, "The Work of the Filmmaker: An Interview with Claude Lanzmann," in *Cinema and the Shoah: An Art Confronts the Tragedy of the Twentieth Century*, ed. Jean-Michel Frodon (Albany: State University of New York Press, 2010), 97.

12. "Hätte ich ihn in einen Sessel gesetzt und gesagt: 'So, nun erzählen Sie mal!', wäre etwas völlig anderes dabei herausgekommen." See Heike Hurst, "Eine befreiende Wirkung. Gespräch mit Claude Lanzmann," *Shoah* (Claassen: Düsseldorf, 1986), 269–77; here, 275. Translation mine.

13. The phrase "testimonial performance" is used repeatedly by Oren Baruch Stier in *Committed to Memory: Cultural Mediations of the Holocaust* (Boston: University of Massachusetts Press, 2003). See chapter 3, on videotaped testimony, especially 84.

14. Lanzmann, "Site and Speech," 41. The original French: "Et c'est à partir de ce moment que la vérité s'incarne et qu'il revit la scène, que soudain le savoir devient incarné" ("Le lieu et la parole," 20). Translation slightly modified.

15. Olaf Berg, "The Challenge of Film Considered as Historical Research: Claude Lanzmann's Approach to the *Shoah*: Constructing History in Dialectical Time-Images," in *Cultural Studies Review: History Experiments* (ed. John Frow and Katrina Schlunke) 14, no. 1 (2008): 124–37; here, 130.

16. Shoshana Felman, "In an Era of Testimony: Claude Lanzmann's *Shoah*," *Yale French Studies* 79 (1991): 39–81; here, 53.

17. Michael Renov, *The Subject of Documentary* (Minneapolis: University of Minnesota Press, 2004), 127.

18. Sven Kramer, *Auschwitz im Widerstreit: zur Darstellung der Shoah in Film, Philosophie und Literatur* (Wiesbaden: Deutscher Universitäts-Verlag, 1999), 39; translation mine. Kramer draws here on Gertrud Koch, who places emphasis on Bomba's "somatic" response. See Koch, *Die Einstellung ist die Einstellung: Visuelle Konstruktionen des Judentums* (Frankfurt/M: Suhrkamp, 1992), 168.

19. See, especially, Claude Lanzmann Shoah Collection, interview with Abraham Bomba (RG-60.5011, Film ID 3202, Camera Rolls 13–15), US Holocaust Memorial Museum and Yad Vashem and State of Israel. Lanzmann's memory confirms this: "[Bomba's] customer, I think, spoke only Hebrew or Yiddish." See Lanzmann, "Seminar with Claude Lanzmann," 95.

20. Nearly thirty-two minutes of *Shoah*'s theatrical release are devoted to Bomba's face or voice, which is approximately 13 percent of the total footage of Bomba. Of those nearly thirty-two minutes, thirteen minutes and forty-five seconds of those were from footage filmed in Jaffa, and eighteen minutes and five seconds are from footage filmed in the barbershop.

21. Marianne Hirsch and Leo Spitzer, "Gendered Translations: Claude Lanzmann's *Shoah*," in Liebman, *Claude Lanzmann's* Shoah, 175–90; here, 176.

22. Lanzmann, *The Patagonian Hare*, 431.

23. Raul Hilberg, *The Destruction of the European Jews*, vol. 3 (New Haven, CT: Yale University Press, 2003), 1111n20.

24. Transcript of the Eichmann trial, May 4, 1961, session 27.

25. At the trial, Kovner read his manifesto in Hebrew. The document was published in Yiddish, but Kovner recalled writing it first in Hebrew. See Eichmann trial transcript, session 27. On the manifesto and its content, see Dina Porat, *The Fall of a Sparrow: The Life and Times of Abba Kovner*, trans. Elizabeth Yuval (Stanford, CA: Stanford University Press, 2010), especially 70–71.

26. See USHMM transcript of the *Shoah* interview with Abba Kovner, 42–43, https://collections.ushmm.org/film_findingaids/RG-60.5017_01_trs_fr.pdf (accessed August 27, 2019).

27. Ferzina Banaji, *France, Film and the Holocaust: From le génocide to la shoah* (New York: Palgrave Macmillan, 2012), 98–99. On the politics of Jewish resistance and Israel in Lanzmann's later films, see Manuel Köppen, "Searching for Evidence between Generations: Claude Lanzmann's *Sobibor* and Romuald Karmakar's *Land of Annihilation*," *New German Critique* 41, no. 3 (2014): 57–73.

28. Jean-François Steiner, *Treblinka*, trans. Helen Weaver (New York: Simon & Schuster, [1967] 1979). Abba Kovner was a significant reference point for Steiner, and Samuel Moyn's account of the Steiner controversy highlights the 1964 French language translation of Kovner's "Le miracle dans l'abdication," originally published in 1945, as a relevant influence. See Samuel Moyn, *A Holocaust Controversy: The Treblinka Affair in Postwar France* (Waltham, MA: Brandeis University Press, 2005), 22 and 174n31.

29. See Moyn, *A Holocaust Controversy*, 35.

30. Moyn, 55.

31. Hannah Arendt, *The Origins of Totalitarianism* (New York: Harvest/ Harcourt, [1951] 1968). See, especially, chapter 12, "Totalitarianism in Power," in which Arendt refers directly to Rousset's position.

32. Moyn, *A Holocaust Controversy*, 126.

33. Alexander Donat, in *Death Camp Treblinka*. See *The Death Camp Treblinka: A Documentary*, ed. Alexander Donat (New York: Holocaust Library, 1979), 284.

34. See "Ils n'étaient pas des lâches," *Le Nouvel Observateur* no. 75, April 27, 1966, http://tempsreel.nouvelobs.com/culture/20060428.OBS5784/ils-n-etaient-pas -des-laches.html# (accessed August 27, 2019). The word *Sonderkommando* appears in quotation marks in the original interview.

35. "Ils n'étaient pas des lâches," n.p.

36. "Ils n'étaient pas des lâches," n.p.

37. On "co-witnessing," see Irene Kacandes, "From 'Never Forgetting' to 'Post-Remembering' and 'Co-Witnessing': Memory Work for the Twenty-First Century," in *Being Contemporary: French Literature, Culture, and Politics Today*, ed. Lia Nicole Brozgal and Sara Kippur (Liverpool: Liverpool University Press, 2016), 193–210.

38. USHMM transcript of *Shoah* interview with Abraham Bomba, 45, 47, and 48–49, https://collections.ushmm.org/film_findingaids/RG-60.5011_01_trs _en.pdf (accessed August 27, 2019). Transcription slightly modified.

39. Lanzmann, *The Patagonian Hare*, 431.

40. Joshua Francis Hirsch, *Afterimage: Film, Trauma, and the Holocaust* (Philadelphia: Temple University Press, 2004), 75.

41. Jacques Mandelbaum, "Recovery," trans. Anna Harrison and Tom Mes, in *Cinema and the Shoah: An Art Confronts the Tragedy of the Twentieth Century*, ed. Jean-Michel Frodon (Albany: State University of New York Press, 2010), 33.

42. Hirsch and Spitzer note that such ruptures as this are occasioned by memories of women's fates, writing: "For Bomba, as for the others, encounters with women threaten whatever precarious emotional distance, whatever control and denial of feelings they had attempted to establish in order to survive. Indeed, the interruption within the powerful scene with Bomba demonstrates that the evocation of these encounters on screen endangers even the very continuity of the film's narrative flow" (180–81).

43. Claude Lanzmann *Shoah* Collection, interview with Abraham Bomba (RG-60.5011, Film ID 3198, Camera Rolls 4–6. Following Clapperboard no. 6, near time stamp 2:17:09:11).

44. Contrary to Lanzmann's claim that he had to know everything in advance, he says that he did not know the story of the friend whose wife and sister entered the gas chamber. In response to a question about whether he had heard that story, Lanzmann says: "No, not that precisely. There were new things too" ("Seminar with Claude Lanzmann," 95).

45. Lanzmann, *The Patagonian Hare*, 431.

46. Stuart Liebman, "Introduction," in *Claude Lanzmann's* Shoah, 3–24; here, 16.

47. Lanzmann, "Seminar with Claude Lanzmann," 95.

48. Lanzmann, *The Patagonian Hare*, 433.

49. Dorota Glowacka, *Disappearing Traces: Holocaust Testimonials, Ethics, and Aesthetics* (Seattle: University of Washington Press, 2012), 118.

50. Glowacka, *Disappearing Traces*, 118.

51. See Helmut Langerbein, *Hitler's Death Squads: The Logic of Mass Murder* (College Station: Texas A&M University Press, 2004), 121–27.

52. The name is likely an allusion to Julien Sorel, the romantic protagonist of Stendahl's *The Red and the Black* (1830). Of interest here is that in Jean-Paul Sartre's play *Les mains sales* (Dirty Hands, 1948), Hugo Barine, the communist protagonist, includes "Julien Sorel" among his potential pseudonyms. A film of *Les mains sales* was released in 1951, but the controversial play was first restaged in France, after a long hiatus, in 1976. Lanzmann, who was close to Sartre, might have had *Les mains sales* on his mind, when he conceived of this pseudonym. On his assumption of a false identity when in the presence of the perpetrators, see also Erin McGlothlin, "Listening to the Perpetrators in Claude Lanzmann's *Shoah*," *Colloquia Germanica* 43, no. 3 (2010): 245.

53. Sue Vice, "Representing the Einsatzgruppen: The Outtakes of Claude Lanzmann's *Shoah*," in *Representing Auschwitz: At the Margins of Testimony*, ed. Nicholas Chare and Dominic Williams (New York: Palgrave Macmillan, 2013), 144.

54. Aaron Kerner writes: "Analogous to the conventions of a typical narrative film, this highly emotionally charged moment is emphasized by the cinematic composition by zooming in on the character—in this case Bomba—during a moment of heightened emotion. In cinematic terms there is little or no difference between melodramatic fiction and documentary, a zoom in signifies an intensified emotional state and directs the audience in how they should respond." *Film and the Holocaust: New Perspectives on Dramas, Documentaries, and Experimental Films* (New York: Continuum, 2011), 209.

55. Jean Narboni writes, "La conjonction des trois motifs de la chevelure, de la mort programmée et de l'injonction voire du commandement fait à quelqu'un de prendre la parole au nom d'une valeur supérieure, comme c'est explicitement le cas à la fin du *Dictateur*, nous en connaissons une version difficilement supportable dans la scène de *Shoah* où figure l'ancien *sonderkommando* de Treblinka Abraham Bomba." Narboni, *Pourquoi les coiffeurs?: Notes actuelles sur* Le dictateur (Paris: Capricci, 2010), 48.

56. Georges Didi-Huberman, *Images in Spite of All: Four Photographs from Auschwitz*, trans. Shane B. Lillis (Chicago: University of Chicago Press, 2008), 154.

57. This remarkable story, including details about how the perpetrators made an exception and gave this Jewish man a proper burial, is recounted in Lanzmann's outtakes as well. See USHMM transcript of Bomba interview, 63–65.

58. Stier, *Committed to Memory*, 74.

59. Bill Nichols briefly outlines reservations about the concept of "zero degree" style in *Speaking Truths with Film: Evidence, Ethics, Politics in Documentary* (Berkeley: University of California Press, 2016), 240–41n8.

10

The Gender of Testimony

Ruth Elias and the Challenge to Lanzmann's Paradigm of Witnessing

Debarati Sanyal

A Czech survivor of Theresienstadt and Auschwitz, Ruth Elias is the subject of a two-and-a-half hour interview preserved in the outtakes of *Shoah*.[1] Her testimony discloses key aspects of the concentrationary system as it was experienced by women, such as sex, pregnancy, abortions, and infanticide. Elias became pregnant in the Theresienstadt Ghetto and gave birth in Auschwitz. A victim of Josef Mengele's experiments, she was forbidden to feed her newborn, and, faced with the prospect of the gas chamber, she put her infant to death. While Elias's testimony is transgressive in its contents, evoking as it does the taboo of maternal infanticide, its expression also challenges the forms of survival and testimony that we have come to associate not only with *Shoah*, but with Holocaust witnessing more generally. Given that Lanzmann selected his nine-and-a-half hours of film from over two hundred hours of additional footage, it is difficult to make any bold claims about the excision of this particular testimony from his cinematic monument. Nevertheless, I will suggest that the omission of Ruth Elias's interview speaks volumes about the gendering of testimony and the masculine paradigm of witnessing that emerges from *Shoah*.

The absence of women from Lanzmann's foundational representation of the Holocaust has not gone unnoticed. In the early 1990s, Marianne Hirsch and Leo Spitzer argued that Lanzmann's focus on the process of extermination necessarily eclipsed the subjective experience of victims and its gendered specificities, such as the liabilities of pregnancy and maternity. This had the unintended consequence of repeating the eradication of difference at work in the Final Solution itself in a gesture of historiographic transference. Hirsch and Spitzer speculate that women, due to their generative bodies, are doubly associated with death in Auschwitz and therefore expunged from *Shoah*, leaving the viewer with an orphic model of creation, where the Holocaust's memory is delivered by masculine subjects, and testimony is "an artificial 'birth' produced by men: by male couples that bypass the generativity of women."[2]

By contrast, Ferzina Banaji has argued that to criticize the paucity of women in *Shoah* is to forget the historical context of its production: "If *Shoah* is a largely male text, then the explanation lies not so much in an imagined chauvinism on the part of Lanzmann, but in the context of Holocaust historiography to which he belonged and that predated research on female histories."[3] Yet, while the belated emergence of feminist historiography may have had a role to play in the matter, Lanzmann's outtakes contain testimonies by no less than ten women, including Paula Biren, Inge Deutschkron, Ruth Elias, Gertrude Schneider, Hansi Brand, Ada Lichtman, and Hanna Marton, suggesting that he was well aware of the gendered specificities of survival in ghettos and camps. Furthermore, I find it hard to believe that any chauvinism imputed to Lanzmann is either imagined or explained by historical context. For instance, in his memoir, *The Patagonian Hare* (2012), Lanzmann evokes intimate details of his relationship with Simone de Beauvoir, the pioneer of feminism who diagnosed the myriad ways in which women are assigned to the pole of immanence, the body, reproduction, and finitude (*l'en-soi*) and thus opposed to the transcendence, consciousness, and agency attributed to masculine incarnation (*le pour-soi*). De Beauvoir's younger lover and protégé for several years, Lanzmann describes her bouts of existential anxiety thus: "So violent that it involved and altered her whole body and its function: her usually sweet breath, 'fragrant with long vegetal and rose-rich honeys', as Rimbaud says in 'Les Chercheuses de poux', suddenly became putrid and I had to force myself even to get close to her."[4]

De Beauvoir's body odor is either the perfume of Rimbaud's lyric or the stench of Baudelaire's decaying carcass (in his famous poem *Une charogne*). A minor detail, to be sure, but rife with irony insofar as Lanzmann has no qualms rehearsing the rhetoric of gender difference that de Beauvoir's *The Second Sex* had systematically dismantled, reducing his former companion and feminist intellectual to the reek of incarnation. More pertinent to the making of *Shoah*, however, is Lanzmann's dismissal of his translators, all of whom are women. Their failings are attributed specifically to their gender's irrepressible impulses: "It is a constant failing of female interpreters—even the best of them, especially the best—they give in to their fears, their emotions" (*Patagonian*, 482).[5] Once again, women engaged in the task of producing or transmitting knowledge are dismissed as hostages to their bodies and affects.

This essay will not pursue the path of Lanzmann's chauvinism, imagined or otherwise. Yet, as we turn to a woman survivor's testimony of unwanted pregnancy and unwilling infanticide in Auschwitz, what is worth retaining from *The Patagonian Hare* is the unease its author betrays toward the female body as the site of unpredictable effects and uncontrolled affects. By contrast, the male survivor's *face* is repeatedly celebrated in the memoir as a hieroglyph and resurrection of the Holocaust: "Abraham (Bomba)'s tears were as precious to me as blood, the seal of truth, its very incarnation," Lanzmann declares, while also recalling Podchlebnik's "splendid face of smiles and tears," a face that "*is* the site of the Shoah" (*Patagonian*, 435, 436). In these instances, the masculine face is the event made flesh, untouched by artifice and fiction. More generally, these men emerge as synecdoches and living traces of the Shoah, incarnations of its trauma.

What follows will suggest that the Ruth Elias outtakes resist such conversions of the survivor into the site of catastrophe. They offer alternate, less extreme, yet no less "true" forms of survival, memory, and testimony that we must reckon with in order to recover the range and nuance of concentrationary experience. For Jennifer Cazenave, women in *Shoah* are figures for the limits of visual representation; their frequent acoustic and *hors champ* presence, as voices or translators, are symptoms of their repressed centrality rather than their banishment. The omission of female testimonies such as that of Ruth Elias, Cazenave argues, is a sign that the knowledge these contain is "incompossible" within the logic of the film, that is to say, they are unfathomable and incommunicable.[6] In *The Patagonian Hare*, "incompossible" refers to the fact that there are categories that cannot coexist, for "to choose one is to preclude the existence of the other. Any choice is murder. . . . It is no accident that *Shoah* runs to nine and a half hours" (75). Lanzmann considers the issue of the outtakes in ethical terms, raising a number of questions: If for the director, to choose is to kill, both in an existential sense and—presumably at an entirely different, metaphorical level—in film editing, this axiom is of searing pertinence for the concentrationary realms of "choiceless choices," where actions were dictated by the imperative to survive against all odds.[7] Ruth Elias is an exemplary illustration of this axiom, for she was forced to administer morphine to her infant in order to save herself from certain death. The literal and horrible nature of Elias's incompossible choice in Auschwitz is far removed from Lanzmann's figural hyperboles about choices made in the cutting room. Yet is there a connection between the choiceless choice made by Elias when she euthanized her infant, Lanzmann's intransigent vision of Holocaust representation, and Elias's quasi-disappearance from the documentary's final cut? What does this particular register of "selection" mean in terms of the testimonial subject prized by Lanzmann? How does it invite us to read Ruth Elias's exclusion from the scene of representation in *Shoah* and to recover her testimony's significance from the outtakes?

In what follows, I argue that Ruth Elias's testimony, preserved in the outtakes, challenges Lanzmann's sacrificial vision of survival and testimony. We might rethink the concept of "incompossibles," not as what is unfathomable, unsayable, or what might lie beyond representation, but, more simply, as what is incompatible with the masculine modes of traumatic identification staged by *Shoah*. Ruth Elias's testimony functions as an incompossible in Lanzmann's documentary by virtue of its challenge to the exclusionary logics of incompossibles. The outtakes of her interview offer a way to recover modes of physical and psychic survival that have been eclipsed in Lanzmann's influential formulations of the survivor-witness.

The "true" witness that emerges from Lanzmann's classic work and continues to shape the legacy of Holocaust representation is a masculine subject of traumatic complicity. It is a male witness whose proximity to the site of extermination and implication in its machinery allows his testimony to emerge from "inside" the Final Solution. This survivor remains in the shadow of irreparable psychic damage and *personifies* the Holocaust in the form of a suffering face. A comparison between Ruth Elias and Filip Müller is instructive in this regard, for their respective functions in *Shoah* throw into relief Lanzmann's paradigmatic witness. Elias first appears in *Shoah* as a disembodied voice describing the arrival of her convoy from Theresienstadt to Auschwitz. Her face fleetingly appears in a close-up as she recounts her disbelief at the rumor that Auschwitz was an extermination center. The narrative of Auschwitz is then taken over by Rudolf Vrba, who reconstructs the attempt to form a resistance network with the Czech family camp's prisoners, and it culminates with Filip Müller's harrowing account of the camp's liquidation on the night of March 8, 1944. When the detainees entered the changing area and realized they were about to be gassed, they broke into the Czech national anthem and the Zionist hymn *Hatikvah*. Overcome by anguish, Müller, a *Sonderkommando* and Czech Jew, entered the gas chamber to die with his compatriots, but a group of women convinced him to stay alive and bear witness to their destruction.[8]

The contrast between Elias and Müller in this sequence of *Shoah* captures the key features of Lanzmann's exemplary witness: intimate knowledge of the extermination process, coerced implication as a participant, and hence a lasting sense of traumatic complicity as a survivor. If in *Shoah*, Elias's voice guides us to the gates of Auschwitz, Müller testifies from within its gas chamber.[9] Whereas in the film itself, Elias recalls her initial disbelief at detainees who told her that this was an extermination camp, we discover in the outtakes that she finally grasped this fact when she heard the Czech victims singing the *Hatikvah* from her locked barracks in the Czech family camp ("The moment we heard the *Hatikvah* being sung we knew these people were going to die").[10] In Müller's testimony, however, hearing the *Hatikvah* is what drives him *into* the gas chamber.

Lanzmann's intrusions in the two interviews underscore the difference between them. In the outtakes, Lanzmann expresses incredulity more than once at Elias's ignorance of the Final Solution during the months she spent in the Czech family camp: "Yes but you were four hundred meters from the crematorium"; "It is unbelievable, what you say, because when one sees Auschwitz today it's really four hundred meters from the place where you were and the crematoria."[11] Lanzmann appears to cast doubt on the reliability of Elias's testimony, on this eyewitness's capacity to *see* what was happening around her at the time, given what we know about Auschwitz today. His incredulity might also suggest that Elias *did* at some level know about the gas chambers but disavowed this knowledge until its evidence reached her ears, in the improbable form of a song. In any case, Elias's "unbelievable" incapacity to believe the fact of extermination, despite her physical proximity to the crematorium, could not be further from Müller's intimate view of its implementation, as a *Sonderkommando* who assisted the process and helped to erase its visible evidence. If Elias is initially positioned "outside" the site of extermination, Müller was embedded within it. When he narrates his attempt to join his doomed Czech compatriots "inside the gas chamber," Lanzmann presses him: "Already in the gas chamber? You were already inside?"

Lanzmann's focus on Müller's exact position in relation to the site of annihilation might remind us of Primo Levi's declaration that survivors of Auschwitz, the "saved," could not be the true or complete witness; only those who "drowned," "those who saw the Gorgon, have not returned to tell about it or have returned mute" are "the ones whose depositions would have a general significance."[12] As a *Sonderkommando*, Müller's multiple crossings into the site of killing bring him as close to the "Gorgon" as imaginable without turning to stone, or to ash. His position within the structure of the Final Solution resembles that of other male protagonists in *Shoah* who bear witness from within its implementation, such as Simon Srebnik, Michal Podchlebnik, and Abraham Bomba. These survivors were coerced into what Levi termed the "gray zone" of concentrationary realms, an "ill-defined sphere of ambiguity and compromise" that contaminated victims with "imposed complicity—."[13] As witnesses implicated in the process of extermination, their survival is steeped in traumatic complicity. Although Ruth Elias was also forced into the gray zone, albeit on a different scale, I will suggest that she does not fit this masculinized model of psychic destruction. This, too, is visually conveyed in her fleeting appearance in *Shoah*. Whereas the voice-over account of her disbelief regarding the extermination is followed by only a glimpse of her face, its composure highlighted by the close-up, the camera is fixed on Müller as he breaks down during his testimony of the family camp's annihilation ("Please, stop!" he begs Lanzmann). The contrast between Elias and Müller illustrates the joint protocols of proximity and trauma for testimonial authenticity in *Shoah*.

The paradigm of the witness that emerges from this monumental work is a masculine subject of traumatic complicity, one whose knowledge is at once unmediated, incommunicable, and "useless," as Charlotte Delbo understood the term.[14]

In *The Patagonian Hare*, Lanzmann consecrates the male protagonists of the gray zone—in particular, Auschwitz's *Sonderkommandos*—as "noble figures, gravediggers of their own people, at once heroes and martyrs" (15). Yet Primo Levi's ethical terrain of coerced complicity would also include the killing of newborn children to save a mother's life, even though the gray zone is not typically addressed in such gendered terms. Indeed, pregnancy in Auschwitz was a deadly liability: if a newborn was discovered, both mother and child were sent to the gas chambers.[15] Newborns were thus put to death, not only by female doctors and companions, but also by their mothers.[16] Akin to the men of the *Sonderkommando*, though on a different scale altogether, practitioners of these merciful infanticides could also be seen as "witnesses to the death of their people," as Lanzmann described the special squads.[17] A mother killing her own child in order to survive, as Ruth Elias was forced to do, embodies the gray zone of "choiceless choices." Yet, in stark contrast to the male survivors whose traumatized and traumatizing testimonies are privileged in *Shoah*, at no point does Ruth Elias show signs of having internalized the traumatic complicity imposed by Nazi gray zones. Instead, the outtakes of her interview with Lanzmann contain an astonishing account of persistence, survival, and resilience.

| Ruth Elias and the Arts of Survival

A Czech Jew from Ostrava deported with her family to Theresienstadt at the age of nineteen, Ruth Elias was reunited with a boyfriend she had met prior to their arrival. She married this boyfriend, who remains unnamed in the outtakes, on the eve of her family's deportation to the Łódź Ghetto in order to remain with him in Theresienstadt. She never saw her family again. Elias became pregnant and desperately sought to have an abortion, but to no avail. In December 1943, she was deported to the Czech family camp in Auschwitz, of which, as noted above, we hear her initial impressions in *Shoah*. In her eighth month of pregnancy, she managed to survive a selection by Mengele by concealing herself amid "beautiful young girls" and thus made it into a labor convoy sent to clear out a bombed oil refinery in Hamburg. Once her pregnancy was discovered, she, along with another pregnant woman, Berta, was deported back to Auschwitz by way of Ravensbrück. The two women were accompanied by an SS officer and a midwife (!), whose presence conveys the paradoxical logic of preserving life in order to better control its extermination.[18] As what Elias terms "the first living witnesses" to return to Auschwitz, and pregnant too, she and Berta were subjected to daily visits from the notorious SS doctor Josef Mengele in the *Frauenlager*.[19] When Elias gave birth to a healthy girl, Mengele ordered that her breasts be bound to see how long an infant could survive without food. After the sixth day, faced with the threat of the gas chamber for both mother and child, Elias administered a syringe of morphine to her baby. She was then transported to Taucha, a subcamp of Buchenwald, where she met her second husband, Kurt Elias, while organizing a variety program for the SS. Apart from an aunt, Ruth Elias lost her entire family in the Holocaust. A few years after the war, she moved to Israel and gave birth to two sons.[20]

Ruth Elias delivers her testimony with remarkable poise; the interview unfolds for the most part in a medium shot that frames the survivor as she sits outside on a terrace or in a courtyard at her home, with a German shepherd by her side. Elias's face is carefully made up and luminous, her manner is gracious, her limpid gaze seeks out the camera, as well as Lanzmann behind it, and it occasionally turns inward. As she speaks, in beautiful English with a light Czech accent, she is visibly in control of the story she passes on and attuned to the moments when her narrative deviates from Lanzmann's agenda of objective historical documentation. When he presses her for details about the mechanics of deportation to Theresienstadt, she takes a leisurely detour through her family's time in hiding near the town of Brno, where she learned to knit and fell in love with the young man she would later marry in the ghetto. Attuned to the director's impatience, she finally says with a twinkle in her eye and a brow raised in light mockery: "You want me to tell about Theresienstadt, now?"[21]

While Lanzmann seeks information about the mechanics of deportation, the ghetto conditions, and the physical and mental health of elderly Jews, Elias insists on the singularity of her own experience. To Lanzmann's query about whether Theresienstadt was "a shock," she responds, "I can only tell about my own feeling."[22] He asks again whether it was "a shock to live

Ruth Elias inquiring whether Lanzmann is ready to hear her story about Theresienstadt. Created by Claude Lanzmann during the filming of *Shoah*. (Used by permission of the United States Holocaust Memorial Museum and Yad Vashem, the Holocaust Martyrs and Heroes' Remembrance Authority, Jerusalem.)

suddenly, only among Jews," but instead of following his prompt to discuss the collective experience of Jews in the ghetto, she turns to the particular circumstances of her happy reunion with her boyfriend ("a big big luck"), the intensity of her perpetual hunger, which she equates throughout the interview with her thirst for life itself, the physical discomforts of living in cramped quarters, or her particular trials as a youthful nurse in the geriatric ward.[23] By stressing the continuities between before and after the ghetto and foregrounding her personal translation of historical experience, her narrative resists the joint protocols of rupture, trauma, and historical documentation that govern *Shoah*.

On occasion, Lanzmann steers her toward a more general account of the Jewish experience in Theresienstadt, addressing such topics as the survival rates of elderly German Jews and their dashed illusions about the Nazi promise that they could "rent a room in the sun." "Again I must disappoint you a little," apologizes Elias, who "ran away from it [the geriatric ward]" and had no further contact with its dying occupants.[24] As if in response to this, the camera recedes into a more distant shot.

After reminding her of the extraordinary death toll in the camp, Lanzmann inquires about how long elderly people "generally" survived. Perhaps feeling slightly defensive after disclosing that she fled the geriatric ward for more nourishing work in the kitchen, Elias remonstrates with a slightly skeptical expression that "you can't generalize" about such matters, her arms crossed in front of her chest, eyebrows elevated, shoulders rising in a subtle shrug.

Minutes later, Elias begins to muse in more general terms about Nazi dehumanization ("We were dancing to the Germans' music, they made the program and they broke us") and trails off, shaking her head, lost in thought. Lanzmann begins to offer his own generalization ("for me it was always one of the most horrible . . .") but Elias interrupts him with "a very hard story of what happened to *me*" (my emphasis).[25] We hear a sharp intake of breath by Lanzmann as Elias launches into the account of how she

"You can't generalize": Ruth Elias responding to Lanzmann's question as to how long elderly people survived in Auschwitz. Created by Claude Lanzmann during the filming of *Shoah*. (Used by permission of the United States Holocaust Memorial Museum and Yad Vashem, the Holocaust Martyrs and Heroes' Remembrance Authority, Jerusalem.)

received a letter from her father announcing that her mother (actually her stepmother, as we come to find out) was shot in Łódź.

Later, as Elias describes the terrifying selection at Auschwitz she survived despite her visible pregnancy, Lanzmann catches her off guard by asking her about Mengele, though it is unclear if he queries the perpetrator's frame of mind or his physical appearance:

LANZMANN: How was he? How was Mengele?
ELIAS: How?
LANZMANN: Yes. How did he look?
ELIAS: I will tell you a little later, ok?[26]

Lanzmann repeats the question of Mengele's appearance when Elias narrates her return to Auschwitz and the menace of his regular visits as her pregnancy came to term: "How was he? I heard he was a handsome man." He probes: "He was tall, or small?"; "Was he young?" It is once again unclear what Lanzmann seeks, since photos of Mengele were readily available at the time. Was he looking for signs of attraction or flirtation between the sadistic yet affable Nazi physician and his pregnant yet beautiful Jewish victim? Could he have been looking for the kind of erotic tension between perpetrators and victims that was suggested by Liliana Cavani's controversial *The Night Porter*, or Louis Malle's *Lacombe, Lucien*, films that around the same time that the Elias interview was conducted?[27] We might recall the cultural fascination for ambiguous, erotically charged rapports between Nazi perpetrators and their victims, designated in the mid-1970's as *la mode rétro*. This tendency was resisted in the following decade by *Shoah*'s unwavering ethical commitment to the victims. Yet it seems to me that, in this exchange, Lanzmann is inviting Elias to explore the ambiguities of Mengele's intentions and perhaps opening an inquiry into the erotic charge of their encounter. In any case, although Elias confirms that Mengele was attractive, charming, and self-assured, her response suggests that the physician's name and sinister reputation sufficed to instill terror and not much else: "And of course we heard Mengele and we were afraid, very afraid of him. My tongue was somehow stiff."[28]

I evoke these microinteractions to highlight the subtle tug-of-war between survivor and questioner in the interview's sequence, pacing, and aims, as well as to clarify their competing principles. Lanzmann seeks a collective account of the Jewish experience in the ghetto—specifically of the elderly—or an objective description of Mengele's appearance, or possibly an excursion into the erotic charge of their rapport, whereas Elias returns to her singular, embodied, and subjective experience as a young woman engrossed in her body's needs: its hunger, its terrors, but also its unpredictable pleasures, whether sexual pleasure with an unnamed husband in the ghetto ("I started to have some married life with my husband") or sharing food in the kitchen, where Elias and her companions would "cook with their mouth" (i.e., discuss recipes) and steal dough to make "a wonderful cake, which Elias stuffed into an apron," and "because of the yeast in the dough, I was growing and growing and all the kitchen was laughing!"[29] Elias's detours through personal anecdotes and the textures of embodied memory resist Lanzmann's combined aims of objective historical documentation and resurrected individual trauma. Along with the content of the testimony, such resistance also takes the form of nonverbal cues such as facial expression, bodily gesture, or vocal timbre. These embodied forms of testimony are as important as their contents; they summon us to develop what Noah Shenker calls "testimonial literacy"—that is to say, "an eye and ear for sensing the layers, ruptures, and tensions that mark the processes of giving and receiving accounts of the Shoah."[30] The Ruth Elias outtakes invite us to look beyond the verbal exchange that takes place between interviewer and interviewee, in order to decipher the gestural and vocal cues inflecting the testimony's content, but also to grasp the conditions of its transmission.

A strikingly similar—and similarly gendered—resistance to the pacing and orientation of Lanzmann's interview can be found in the Gertrude Schneider outtakes.[31] Like Elias, Schneider makes a fleeting appearance at the end of *Shoah*, when she sings a Yiddish song together with her mother.[32] Her recollections, like those of Elias, contain a wealth of information about how women experienced ghettos such as Theresienstadt and Riga, as well as pregnancies and abortions despite the Nazi prohibitions against sexual relations and programs of forced sterilization in the Riga Ghetto. Although in *Shoah* she is simply identified as a survivor of the ghetto, Dr. Schneider was also a historian who, by the time of the interview, had published a book on the Riga Ghetto in order to correct the historical misperception that

Latvian Jews were killed to make room for German and Austrian Jews such as her Viennese family. While narrating her family's journey by train to the Riga Ghetto, Schneider, like Elias, takes an anecdotal detour to convey a lesson learned at the ghetto's threshold. In her high-pitched voice and with precise diction, she recounts how her mother stashed several kilograms of marzipan pieces in their suitcase, hoping to set up some sort of commerce once they reached their destination. Fond of sweets, the young Schneider secretly devoured half of the suitcase's contents during the train journey. When they arrived in the ghetto, before her mother could discover her larceny, the SS confiscated their luggage. As Schneider wraps up her anecdote, Lanzmann interrupts her with an exasperated growl: "Don't go so fast! I want that you describe exactly the arrival, what time it was and so on . . . ," to which Schneider responds firmly, albeit with an amused grin and large placating gestures: "I will do that, this is just one particular story, this is a story just about the marzipan, and then I'll tell you everything."[33] Undeterred, she finishes up her tale, turns to Lanzmann and delivers the following adage, jabbing the air with her finger with gusto: "If you've got it, eat it, worry about later."[34] Despite this emphatic refutation of the Old Testament proverb, "The wise store up choice food and olive oil, but the fools gulp them down," her conclusion triggers what sounds like an annoyed huff from Lanzmann, after which Schneider concedes to "going back to how the arrival really was."[35]

The Gertrude Schneider outtakes disclose relations of force that remain implicit in Ruth Elias's interview. This is no subtle tug-of-war, but a stark exposition of the interview's competing aims: historical knowledge on the one hand, personal anecdote turned proverb on the other. Schneider, a self-assured survivor-witness who, like Lanzmann, is also a historian of the Final Solution, chooses to transmit "one particular story" and the life lesson she derived from it before submitting to the filmmaker's demand for objective and comprehensive historical description (or "how it really was").[36] The Schneider outtakes, like those of Elias, command attunement to what Shenker calls "the dialogic, mutual labor involved in testimony" as well as an attentiveness toward the fleeting moments when, from the margins, "witnesses assert agency in their testimony and at times even confront the interviewer on issues of the authoring of their interview." This means widening the frame of the outtakes even further to include off-camera moments that disclose not only the mutual labor of the interview, but also its competing aims and orientations.[37]

In the Ruth Elias outtakes, this reciprocal labor is thrown into relief in a brief but revealing off-camera moment. After the first roll runs out, the sound continues to record and we hear that the German shepherd has wandered off. Elias queries, "You need the dog the whole time here?" confirming that the German shepherd is part of Lanzmann's directorial mise-en-scène. "C'est bien, non?" Lanzmann asks a member of the crew, off-camera, though we don't know whether he is referring to Elias's performance or the dog's presence in the frame.[38] When Elias starts to sing two songs from Theresienstadt, the dog returns with a noisy rattle and Lanzmann asks her to take its chain off. Later still, as an unsmiling Elias recounts her arrival in Auschwitz, she holds the dog by the collar and gently strokes its scruff as she revisits the place in her memory.

The German shepherd is a docile, panting presence whose liquid eyes and cocked ears float in and out of the edge of the camera's frame during the first half of the interview. Why might Lanzmann have been attached to the dog's presence in the frame? The hound accompanying Ruth Elias's return to the memory of Auschwitz might have reminded viewers of the iconic relationship between German shepherds and the Third Reich: Hitler owned two German shepherds named Blondi and Bella, and the breed was deployed in camps not only as guard dogs, but also as killers. Charlotte Delbo gives the harrowing account of a detainee in Auschwitz who, consumed by thirst, runs to a ditch for a handful of clean snow and is killed by an SS man's dog.[39] Even in her own memoir, *Triumph of Hope*, Elias describes the acoustic assault of barking dogs, presumably German shepherds, upon her arrival in Auschwitz ("The horrible barking of dogs grew louder and louder").[40] Yet, decades afterward, in the outtakes, she sits by a German shepherd and holds on to its scruff as she revisits Auschwitz. If the barking dogs at the entrance of Auschwitz might evoke for us the mythic figure of Cerberus guarding the gates of Hades to stop the dead from leaving, by contrast, Elias's hound is a visible source of reassurance as she reenters the concentrationary inferno. Lanzmann's decision to place the German shepherd within the frame, not only as a companion and co-witness but also as a prop to the survivor's journey, introduces an ironic texture within the scene. I imagine he wished to stage the paradox of an animal breed that belongs to the brutal iconography of Nazi camps yet is domesticated and resignified as the gentle companion of a Holocaust survivor in an Israeli village.[41] The dog may initially have come to Elias of its own accord, but the director wishes it to remain in place, seen but not heard, in order to produce specific visual effects. The *hors scène* of the outtakes, in the form of a brief off-camera recording, illustrates the collaboration that takes place between interviewer and interviewee. It also signals a stylization or artistry that is essential to Lanzmann's documentary practice.

Despite their status as remnants of remnants, such off-camera moments within the outtakes can also reveal microtensions between interviewer and interviewee that help us better grasp the implicit gendered paradigm of the witness in *Shoah*. In the same sequence of sound recording, following the exchange about the wayward dog, Lanzmann compliments the survivor on her performance for the camera.

> LANZMANN: It's very good, you are extremely good. I like the . . . you're extremely good. Your voice is beautiful, and your face too.
> ELIAS: (*light laugh*) Thank you, I think it was natural, no?
> LANZMANN: You are a very beautiful woman.[42]

The bantering, even flirtatious, register comes as a surprise given that Elias's testimony has just paused on the abject conditions of the ghetto. Lanzmann's remarks beg the question of what it means to be "good" in the context of Holocaust testimony, and what role the beauty of the survivor's face or voice plays in her deposition. The recorded exchange offers us an unusual glimpse into forms of countertransference difficult to imagine with male survivors. Indeed, to my knowledge, none of Lanzmann's interviews with the protagonists of *Shoah* or the subjects of the outtakes carry such tones of seduction or aesthetic evaluation. As was perhaps the case with his queries to Elias about Mengele's looks, Lanzmann seems to find the possibility of heterosexual attraction irresistible in the most implausible of contexts. Furthermore, instead of hosting the transmission of a survivor's living memory, the director emerges in this recorded sequence as the producer of effects that can be assessed within normative codes for a successful performance.

Elias's response to Lanzmann's compliment is poignant in this regard ("It was natural, no?"). It betrays her intuition that for the director there exists a tension between the success of a performance and its authenticity. Such an intuition would not be incorrect given the privilege Lanzmann grants to the "truth" that is conveyed from the resurrection of the past, a truth transmitted more often than not by the breakdown of the witness: "C'est la transmission qui est le savoir même" (knowledge itself resides in its transmission), Lanzmann declares in his manifesto "Hier ist kein Warum" (Knowledge itself resides in its transmission).[43] If in *The Patagonian Hare* Lanzmann evokes Abraham Bomba's tears as the seal and incarnation of truth, he never alludes to their beauty, for such aestheticization of suffering would be markedly "obscene." In light of Elias's quasi-disappearance from the documentary, this inadvertent sound recording from the outtakes can be read as yet another trace of the opposition Lanzmann sustains between traumatic authenticity and artful performance, as if nature and artifice could be unraveled and opposed, as if the past's resurrection in *Shoah* was itself ever free of artfulness.

Elsewhere in the outtakes, and on more than one occasion, Lanzmann asks Elias to forget about the camera, look away, and act natural. But Elias is a performer whose musical gifts and "fröhliche" (happy) disposition—as one SS officer called it—earned her a coveted place in the Theresienstadt kitchen: the barracks' head cook overheard her singing with an accordion and offered her the job.[44] While in the Taucha camp, she was once again overheard singing a German operetta on New Year's Eve, 1944, this time by the camp commander, who promptly asked her to organize a variety show intended to distract the SS from Allied bombings. For Elias, performance was a key mode of physical and psychic survival.

While recalling the joie de vivre that persisted in the wretchedness of the Theresienstadt Ghetto, Elias exclaims, "How I was singing! And all the people with me were singing!"[45] Lanzmann invites her to share these songs of the ghetto, and she launches into a Czech call to resistance while accompanying herself on the accordion. The song mocks the conditions of ghetto life and concludes with a call to perseverance in the hope of liberation: "The day will come and we will laugh about the ruins of the ghetto," Elias translates.[46] Although she does not recall the song's origin, it is known as the Terezin March and was composed by Karel Svenk, who built a cabaret in the ghetto to sustain detainee morale. Svenk's march was featured at the end of each cabaret performance and became Theresienstadt's unofficial anthem.[47] Elias sings in a melodious voice, but soon interrupts herself to rehearse without the sound off ("Wait a second . . . I must once play it again").[48] She starts singing again, then stops and corrects herself once more. On her third attempt, she ends the song but looks up apologetically at the camera with a raised forefinger and says, "I made a little mistake there, I will sing it again . . ."

As she embarks on the fourth and final version of the same song, Lanzmann instructs, "But when you stop, don't look at the camera. Be natural, forget the camera."[49] With the evident desire to get it just right, she completes a fourth version of the Terezin March. In the next camera roll, Lanzmann requests once again that she "remain silent. When you want to go, you must go very naturally."[50] Elias complies and sings, with a joyful expression, first a song in Hebrew, and then a fifth rendition of the Terezin March; her eyes, however, continue to seek out the camera or the director, as if in search of a response to her musical testimony. It is evident that for Lanzmann, who urges her to ignore the camera, this awareness compromises the authenticity, spontaneity or "naturalness" of her performance. Yet

Ruth Elias playing the accordion and singing the Terezin March. Created by Claude Lanzmann during the filming of *Shoah*. (Used by permission of the United States Holocaust Memorial Museum and Yad Vashem, the Holocaust Martyrs and Heroes' Remembrance Authority, Jerusalem.)

Elias's desire to look at the recipients of her testimony, rather than losing herself in memory, may well be an authentic revisiting of her past. Her resurrection of these songs of resistance from the ghetto appears to insist on the reciprocity of gazes and relationships of solidarity that doubtlessly were elicited by the original performance.

Performance and theatricality are integral to an authentic restoration of the past in Elias's testimony, even if such intermingling does not fit the model of traumatic reimmersion privileged throughout *Shoah*. Elias's performances not only recall the experience of victims such as herself, but occasionally she conjures the perpetrators as well, by ventriloquizing the metallic tone of the SS announcing a selection ("AUFSTELLEN. ZU FÜNFT") or mimicking Mengele's languid hand selecting detainees for life or death.[51]

The register of theatricality imbues her entire experience. After all, when she and Bertha returned to Auschwitz in a state of advanced pregnancy, as the first witnesses to come back to the camp alive, they were "a very big sensation," she recounts wryly. Indeed, "such a sensation that Mengele heard about the sensation, and in he came to see us."[52] She recalls, with a dry smile of derision, Mengele's daily visits to her and Bertha, again mimicking his bantering tone when conveying his astonishment at having overlooked the two women's bellies during the selection. Lanzmann asks her to repeat Mengele's exact words in German, including his euphemism for selection, which she does once again in an assured and urbane voice: "Als ich die Leute für die Arbeit ausgesucht habe" (When I chose people for labor).[53]

The physical composure and narrative control that Elias maintains throughout the interview, her ironic mimicry of the perpetrators, as well as her sense of performance and her perfectionism while transmitting the songs of the ghetto, suggest that art and artfulness sustained her through the traumatic losses of her family and infant. These losses appear to be mastered, retrospectively, by the form of their delivery. Indeed, the narrative control she sustains throughout the interviews contrasts sharply with the loss of bodily control that she recounts: an unwanted pregnancy in the ghetto that she had no means of terminating, since by then abortions were forbidden: "I've known I'm pregnant, and can't do anything, can't help myself," she recalls, reliving the pain in the present tense.[54] Once in Auschwitz, her advancing pregnancy meant she had to wake up earlier than everyone else to wash in privacy: "Because I was pregnant, and my body started to grow, I was ashamed. . . . That was a terrible time for me. . . . My belly grew."[55] This exposure and vulnerability, as the body inside her grows toward a life destined for death while endangering its life-giver, culminates with the delivery of a big, beautiful girl in the infirmary and Mengele's order that Elias's breasts be bound to see "how long a baby can live without food."[56]

As Ruth Elias moves toward the crux of her testimony on her forced infanticide, tears quietly run down her face, but she does not break down into sobs. If her voice falters when narrating the lethal injection to her infant, she blots out her tears without pausing her account. In both the outtakes and her memoir, *Triumph of Hope*, Elias recounts how Maca Steinberg, a fellow detainee and doctor, procured morphine at great personal risk and convinced Elias to administer the injection to her baby in order to save herself from the gas chamber. Illustrating the twists in the gray zone's code of ethics, Steinberg believed that as a doctor who had sworn the Hippocratic oath, she could not administer the morphine herself. Of Steinberg, who facilitated her infant's death, Elias repeatedly says, "She is my mother today."[57] This is an astonishing reconfiguration of maternity, where the "midwife" of an infanticide becomes the mother's mother.

The Rescue of Possibles from Incompossibles

In order to fully grasp the significance of this maternal filiation born of a merciful infanticide in Auschwitz, we must return to Elias's memoir, published in 1998, which discloses her fraught relationship to motherhood. In *Triumph of Hope*, the survivor dwells on her parents' divorce in Ostrava, Czechoslovakia, when she was about five years old, after which her mother vanished, leaving her to be raised by relatives. Her mother reappeared briefly two years later bearing a book of waltz music for the piano and intercepted Ruth on the street. Distraught by her abandonment, however, Ruth turned away, screaming "Go away! You're not my mother anymore!" (*Triumph*, 9). She never saw or heard from her mother again.[58] While this brief encounter remained a secret (she does not disclose to Lanzmann that it was her stepmother, not her mother, who was shot in Łódź), throughout her childhood Ruth played waltzes from the piano book over and over again to remember her mother, crafting this loss into musical form.[59] It would not be far-fetched to imagine that such rehearsal of loss into form, whether through music, song, or theatricality, were integral to Ruth Elias's self-fashioning long before she arrived at the ghetto.

Elias's inability to continue working as a nurse in Theresienstadt's geriatric ward seems connected to this primary maternal loss. As we saw earlier, when Lanzmann presses her for details about the condition of elderly Jews in the ghetto, she merely responds that she "ran away from it," citing her youth, her hunger, and her desire to live. The memoir, however, lingers on her anguish as she held the dying in her arms at night: "I don't know how many patients crying out with longing for their children, died in my arms. I only know that most of them died deserted and alone, without children or relatives near them" (*Triumph*, 77). Yet if the elderly and the incurably sick were abandoned to their fate, they nevertheless died in the arms of Elias, a motherless and, at the time, childless girl of not quite twenty years. In those moments, whether intentionally or not, as she held the dying against her, Elias played the role of both mother and child to them.

Elias recalls that, as she went into labor in Auschwitz, she did not call out for her mother, as others in great pain might have done:

> But this one simple word that meant so much and brought so much relief was foreign to me. If only I could have called out "Mother!" and if only my mother could have stood by me in this difficult hour. What had I done that I should have to suffer like this? "Mother, Mother . . ." (*Triumph*, 145).

Although Elias was deprived of this solace at the time of her labor, she *does* call out to her mother at the time of the memoir's writing, when she relives the terror of giving birth in a site of death and transcribes this terror on the page. The temporalities of her experience in Auschwitz and the writing of the memoir become eerily entwined, for at this juncture of her account, the written cry to an absent mother—a symbolic reparation of her earlier inability to summon her mother—foreshadows the paradoxical mother to come. Indeed, several days after childbirth, as Elias's daughter wasted away, Mengele announced that he would return the next morning to take them both, presumably to the gas chamber.[60] In the memoir's haunting pages that describe their last night together, Elias addresses her unnamed daughter in the present tense, paradoxically resurrecting her as she anticipates their death the following day: "Come, my child, we'll spend our last hours close together. Your little body is already blue and covered with sores, but we have to make it through till tomorrow. Tomorrow we will go to the gas chambers together" (149). Yet, as the night progressed, Elias was overcome by anguish and began to scream. In the memoir, her screams are also relived and transcribed in the present tense: "I want to *live, to live!* Have I gone mad? Why am I screaming? I can't help it" (150). Elias's screams alerted Maca Steinberg, who reprimanded the young mother "harshly" with "that harsh voice of hers" for disturbing the other detainees, but whose voice turns into "the voice of an angel" when, risking her life to acquire some morphine, Steinberg handed Elias the syringe, persuading her to administer it to the infant (150). Steinberg thus materialized as the mother to whom Elias could not call out while delivering her child. Years later, then, as she writes the memoir, Elias implicitly links the call she was unable to make at childbirth ("Mother, Mother") to her screams of anguish on the eve of what she thought would be her condemnation to death. She thus retrospectively, in writing, summons Maca Steinberg to her side, as the mother to whom she was unable to call out in real life, and as the paradoxical mother she would become by virtue of assisting in the death of Elias's infant. The play of tenses and voices in the memoir thus offers evidence of how *writing* becomes an instrument for crafting traumatic loss into meaning, infanticide into maternity, rupture into filiation. *Triumph of Hope* ends with a 1977 photograph taken in Israel of Ruth Elias with Maca Steinberg, designated in the caption as "her camp 'mother,'" both of them smiling serenely. In the outtakes, Elias concludes, "She is my mother *today*."[61]

In Lanzmann's outtakes, the infanticide is conveyed with considerable visual intimacy, for, during this part of the testimony, the camera zooms into a close-up. Elias says through her tears, "She (Maca) started talking to me, talking *into* me, until I had no *Widerstand*," as Lanzmann proffers a translation, "resistance."[62] Elias refers to the erosion of her "resistance" to the imperative of killing her doomed child in order to save herself from the gas chamber. Yet, in this case, as in many others that have been documented, it was infanticide that functioned as a secret and concerted act of resistance to the Final Solution, since the practice sought to preserve the mother in the name of future children.[63] If the *Sonderkommandos* embody Nazism's diabolical contamination of its victims (for Primo Levi) and expose the machinery of annihilation (for Lanzmann), what the practitioners of infanticide reveal is a zone of necropolitics where childbirth continues during the mass production of death and is itself a death sentence, where doctors are humanitarian killers, yet where the Hippocratic oath trumps the taboo of maternal infanticide. In this paradoxical death-world, resistance to extermination mirrors the Darwinian principles of Nazi eugenics, their sterilization and euthanasia programs, and their selections. Terrence Des Pres characterizes such practices as a "strategic mimicry of the Nazi procedure" that strives to subvert the camp's ends, since the calculation was to preserve the mother's life so that she might bear future life.[64]

As the case of Ruth Elias reveals, the topography of concentrationary gray zones—so often associated with masculine figures of traumatic complicity whose extreme incarnation is the *Sonderkommando*—also requires us to consider the gender-specific phenomenon of secret abortions and infanticides. Elias virtually embodies the gray zone of circulation and reversal, where victims were coerced into perpetration: "Mengele had turned me into a child murderer," she reflects in her memoir.[65] Yet a gendered approach to the gray zone simultaneously opens up an alternate gendering of resistance to the Final Solution, the signs of which are nowhere to be found in *Shoah*, but remain to be decoded from outtakes such as these.

Sara Horowitz notes that scholarship on the phenomenon of pregnancy in the Nazi camps splits into two opposing narratives: the narrative of heroism, where pregnancy, childbirth and the community's protection of the baby is an arena for resistance over the genocide; or the narrative of atrocity, where the birth of a child signifies death and truncation.[66] However, like the testimonies that Horowitz examines, Ruth Elias's experience complicates this binarism considerably. Although a narrative of atrocity situated within the gray zone of the camps' coercive violence, it is also a tale of resistance and resilience. What is so striking in Elias's account, and what transgresses normative views of motherhood's sanctity, is that the "choiceless choice" of infanticide, in all of its horror, becomes generative of new bonds. For, by delivering Elias of her unnamed child, Steinberg delivered the survivor who would depart from Auschwitz the next day toward what she announces to be "the nice part of the story": an improbable romance in the Taucha camp on the eve of liberation, followed by emigration to Israel, where she would build another family and track down her symbolic mother.

What could be experienced as an intolerable breach is deliberately assumed as filiation; infanticide is transformed into midwifery. This reconfiguration of maternity is itself an act of resistance that transforms the gray zone's deadly complicities into chosen affiliations.

As we saw at the start of this essay, in Lanzmann's hyperbolic conflation of film editing and existential choices, all selection is deadly, or incompossible, for "to choose one is to preclude the existence of another." Ruth Elias's testimony unveils a gendered gray zone that is also a dreadfully literal site of "incompossible" choices, insofar as the infant's death, an act of mercy, is required for the mother's survival. Infanticide is perhaps the most transgressive materialization of the sacrificial axiom that "any choice is murder," that the existence of one is predicated on the extinction of the other. The scandal of Elias's testimony is its resignification of maternity as a bond formed in the shadow of infanticide, which she casts as the rescue of generative "possibles" from the eliminationist economy of "incompossibles."[67]

If Lanzmann interrogates Abraham Bomba about how he *felt* when he saw the doomed women from his home town in Treblinka, he asks no such question of Ruth Elias. During the last part of her testimony, when Elias narrates the "happy part of the story," the director withdraws into silence. The outtakes contain a fascinating sequence in which the camera is fixed on Lanzmann as he impassively looks on while an off-camera Elias animatedly recounts how she fell in love with Kurt Elias on stage and giggles about his bad singing voice. Lanzmann responds with a slight, constrained smile and then only intrudes to clarify a date.

Is this retreat into silence in the last portion of the outtakes due to *pudeur*, to modesty or reluctance about prying into the taboo of maternal infanticide and the psychological effects of its aftermath? Again, we can only speculate, but with its emphasis on hope, continuity, and resilience, Elias's testimony poses a challenge to Lanzmann's antiredemptive ethics and aesthetics.[68] What we can establish for certain is the marked contrast between Elias's story and the testimonies prized by Lanzmann. These are testimonies from male witnesses who become embodied hieroglyphs of the Shoah itself: Abraham Bomba's tears are, according to Lanzmann, the incarnation of truth, Michal Podchlebnik's face is "the site of the Shoah." As for Henryk Gawkowski, "his body wracked with remorse, his eyes wild, repeating a gesture of slitting his throat, his face gaunt, transfixed with

A silent Claude Lanzmann listening to Ruth Elias. Created by Claude Lanzmann during the filming of *Shoah*. (Used by permission of the United States Holocaust Memorial Museum and Yad Vashem, the Holocaust Martyrs and Heroes' Remembrance Authority, Jerusalem.)

pain," he "gives life and reality to the phantom train and makes it exist for all those who witness this stupefying scene" (*Patagonian*, 484). In these instances, the masculine face and body are signifying surfaces that legibly attest to irreversible and ongoing damage. We might imagine that the gendered bodily reality of childbirth and infanticide in Auschwitz, and the possibility that a survivor may psychologically survive and even thrive in its aftermath, would be far more difficult for Lanzmann to co-witness.

Lanzmann's investment in reenactment instead of representation, in the performative transmission of trauma instead of composed recollection and sequential delivery, permeates *Shoah*. At times, this positions him as a "midwife" of sorts, resurrecting and delivering the traumatic memory. In Abraham Bomba's barbershop scene, the re-creation of gestures and Lanzmann's persistent questioning seem to trigger a haptic and psychic resurrection of the past, producing the "seal of truth" that are Bomba's tears ("You have to do it," Lanzmann repeats). A similar act of midwifery is suggested in the interview with Podchlebnik, who smiles as he declares that everything died in him in Chełmno, where he found the body of his wife and children when unloading a gas van. As Lanzmann describes it, "I see him on the screen, *sensing my hand pressing on his shoulder to help him to find a voice* for his most grueling account. . . . I can do nothing but weep with him. Heroic and rigorous, Michael Podchlebnik" (436–37).[69] In each of these instances, Lanzmann functions as a midwife who facilitates the birth of testimony in male subjects.

It is difficult to imagine such gestures of compassion (or "feeling with") in the case of Ruth Elias, whose maternal immanence, beautiful face, and narrative self-possession preclude the performative transmission of trauma that Lanzmann seeks to deliver. Perhaps the identifications Lanzmann recalls in his memoir—"I can do nothing but weep with him"—are in the end predicated on homosocial bonds unavailable in the case of a woman, and even more so in the case of a mother who has literally given birth and symbolically reimagined motherhood from within the taboo of infanticide. After all, the Ruth Elias outtakes compel us to reimagine delivery in paradoxical terms, where helping a mother deliver herself of her child means delivering her as a survivor and witness, where the midwifing of death preserves the future possibility of life and testimony. The gender of testimonial *delivery* (in every sense of the word), however, remains resolutely masculine in *Shoah*. Its orphic mythology of masculine creation, as Hirsch and Spitzer term it, bypasses "the generativity of women."[70]

Elias's outtakes summon viewers to develop a "testimonial literacy" that moves beyond the paradigm of witnessing founded by *Shoah*, one that privileges an immersive relationship to past trauma and posits the emergence of "truth" in the (male) witness's breakdown. Abraham Bomba's testimony in the barbershop crystallizes a testimonial paradigm whose legacy continues to shape representations of the Holocaust. We need to unlock the opposition between bare life and triumphalist survival in order to recover the range and nuance of the experience in Nazi ghettos and camps. This would also require a full rethinking of influential polarities, not only in Lanzmann's thought—, but in Holocaust studies generally, between traumatic loss and reified redemption, between an immersive return to past violence and its questionable representation in stylized form.

Indeed, contemporary cultural representations of historical catastrophe continue to situate the truth of testimony as excessively "symptomatized" and authenticated in the masculine subject's body or face. We might evoke Oskar Schindler's sobs in Steven Spielberg's classic *Schindler's List* (1993), or the *Sonderkommando* protagonist's tormented, enigmatic face in László Nemes's *Son of Saul* (2015), or, in another genocidal context, the Indonesian perpetrator Anwar Congo's retching at the end of Joshua Oppenheimer's *The Act of Killing* (2012), a physical response widely read as the moment of the perpetrator's *prise de conscience*. Yet the privilege accorded to what I have called "traumatic complicity" in cinematic modes of witnessing disregards the extent to which performance and stylization are themselves integral to the "raw" experience of extremity. For Ruth Elias, performance, creativity, and generativity accompanied the greatest forms of destitution; "possibles" were fashioned out of "incompossibles," traumatic loss was shot through with the arts of survival.

At the end of her interview, after Elias has emphatically declared her commitment to Israel's survival, she looks toward Lanzmann, her head in an inquiring tilt, and tentatively offers: "It is a story. . . . I can tell you plenty of it, something more, I think. . . . Did you ask me something more, no?" Lanzmann gently but firmly tells her, "Don't talk now. Stay like this."[71] Elias maintains eye contact with him for a few seconds, then drops her eyes. This hesitant gesture to offer "something more," this unease with closure, is poignant in light of Elias's quasi-disappearance from *Shoah*. Within the outtakes of this interview are the ingredients of a cautionary tale concerning the limits of identification as the privileged mode for the reception of another's trauma. The issue at stake is not simply that such identification risks effacing gender difference from the question of testimony; it is also, as I've tried to suggest, that Ruth Elias points to performance itself as a mode of survival calling for attentive modes of reception that are open to "something more."

Notes

1. Claude Lanzmann *Shoah* Collection, interview with Ruth Elias (RG-60.50003, Film ID 3112, Camera Rolls 1–2; Film ID 3113, Camera Rolls 3–4; Film ID 3114, Camera Rolls 5–9A; Film ID 3115, Camera Roll 10; Film ID 3116, Camera Rolls 11–12; Film ID 3117, Camera Rolls 13–15; Film ID 3118, Camera Rolls 16–18), US Holocaust Memorial Museum and Yad Vashem and State

of Israel. In addition to the outtakes, this essay draws from the transcripts of Lanzmann's interview with Elias, as well as her memoir.

2. Marianne Hirsch and Leo Spitzer, "Gendered Translations: Claude Lanzmann's *Shoah*," in *Gendering War Talk*, ed. M. Cooke and A. Woollacott (Princeton, NJ: Princeton University Press, 1993), 3–19; here, 15.

3. Ferzina Banaji, "The Shoah after *Shoah*," in *L'Esprit Créateur* 50, no. 4 (2010): 122–36; here, 127.

4. Claude Lanzmann, *The Patagonian Hare: A Memoir* (New York: Farrar, Straus & Giroux), Kindle edition. Cited parenthetically hereafter.

5. Lanzmann recalls firing one interpreter because "her beautiful face was too Jewish for Poles to feel able to speak freely in front of her," replacing her with another interpreter of "good Catholic stock" who (therefore) distorted every aspect of the exchange between the priest, Srebnik and himself (*The Patagonian Hare*, 481).

6. Jennifer Cazenave, *Genèses des Figurations de la femme dans* Shoah: *Voix féminines et représentations cinématographiques de l'Holocauste (1946-1985)*; available from ProQuest Dissertations & Theses A&I; ProQuest Dissertations & Theses Global (893780498). See also *An Archive of the Catastrophe: The Unused Footage of Claude Lanzmann's* Shoah (Albany: State University of New York Press, 2019).

7. "Choiceless choices" is of course Lawrence Langer's term in *Versions of Survival: The Holocaust and the Human Spirit* (Albany: State University of New York Press, 1982).

8. Claude Lanzmann and Ziva Postec, *Shoah*, Les Films Aleph, 2003.

9. As Hirsch and Spitzer put it, "Elias's role—to set the scene, provide the atmosphere, the affect, and not the facts or the details—allows us to understand one way in which Shoah uses women." Hirsch and Spitzer, "Gendered Translations," 7.

10. Interview with Ruth Elias (RG-60.50003, Film ID 3116, Camera Rolls 11–12).

11. Interview with Ruth Elias (RG-60.50003, Film ID 3116, Camera Rolls 11–12).

12. Primo Levi, *The Drowned and the Saved*, trans. R. Rosenthal (New York: Vintage, 1989), 54.

13. Levi, *The Drowned and the Saved*, 67.

14. Charlotte Delbo, *Une Connaissance inutile: Auschwitz et Après*, vol. 2 (Paris: Minuit, 1970). That is not to say that there is only one kind of witness in *Shoah*, of course, but that these are *exemplary* or paradigmatic witnesses.

15. Mengele is reported to have said, "I don't know what to do with the child . . . it would not be humanitarian to send a child to the ovens without permitting

the mother to be there to witness the child's death. That is why I send the mother and the child to the gas oven together." Cited by Sara Nomberg-Prytyk in "Esther's First Born," in *Truth and Lamentations: Stories and Poems on the Holocaust,* ed. Milton Teichman and Sharon Leder (Champaign: University of Illinois Press, 1993), 86–89; here, 87.

16. For a discussion of pregnancy and motherhood in the camps, see Sara R. Horowitz, "Memory and Testimony of Women Survivors of Nazi Genocide," in *Women of the Word: Jewish Women and Jewish Writing,* ed. Judith R. Baskin (Detroit: Wayne State University Press, 1994), 258–82. Horowitz also evokes the gray zone in a discussion of sexuality and the gendering of moral categories in Holocaust memory: "The Gender of Good and Evil: Women and Holocaust Memory," in *Gray Zones: Ambiguity and Compromise in the Holocaust and its Aftermath* ed. Jonathan Petropoulos and John K. Roth (New York: Berghahn), 165–77. For a pertinent collection of essays on women's experience of the concentrationary system and the Final Solution, see Myrna Goldenberg and Amy Shapiro, *Different Horror/Same Hell: Gender and the Holocaust* (Seattle: University of Washington Press, 2013).

17. Lanzmann: "It was by now clear to me that the Jewish protagonists in my film had to be either the *Sonderkommandos* . . . the only witnesses to the death of their people . . . or those men . . . able to describe how the machinery of death functioned" (*The Patagonian Hare,* 421–22).

18. In Foucauldian terms, it illustrates the convergence of life-administering, or biopolitical, power with the sovereign right to kill.

19. Interview with Ruth Elias (RG-60.50003, Film ID 3117, Camera Rolls 13–15).

20. Interview with Ruth Elias (RG-60.50003, Film ID 3112, Camera Rolls 1–2).

21. Interview with Ruth Elias (RG-60.50003, Film ID 3112, Camera Rolls 1–2).

22. Claude Lanzmann *Shoah* Collection, interview with Ruth Elias (RG-60.50003, Film ID 3112, Camera Rolls 1–2).

23. Interview with Ruth Elias (RG-60.50003, Film ID 3112, Camera Rolls 1–2).

24. Interview with Ruth Elias (RG-60.50003, Film ID 3114, Camera Rolls 5–9a).

25. Interview with Ruth Elias (RG-60.50003, Film ID 3114, Camera Rolls 5–9a).

26. Interview with Ruth Elias (RG-60.50003, Film ID 3117, Camera Rolls 13–15).

27. Both films appeared in 1974, and the Elias interviews were conducted from 1978 to 1981.

28. Interview with Ruth Elias (RG-60.50003, Film ID 3117, Camera Rolls 13–15).

29. Interview with Ruth Elias (RG-60.50003, Film ID 3115, Camera Roll 10).

30. Noah Shenker, *The Modern Jewish Experience: Reframing Holocaust Testimony* (Bloomington: Indiana University Press), 2015.

31. Interview with Gertrude Schneider (RG-60.5015, Film ID 3221, Camera Rolls 3–5; Film ID 3222, Camera Rolls 6–9; Film ID 3223, Camera Rolls 92–93; Film ID 3224, Camera Rolls 94–95A; Film ID 3225, Camera Rolls 96–97).

32. For a reading of this interview and the song, see Doris L. Bergen, "What do Studies of Women, Gender, and Sexuality Contribute to Understanding the Holocaust?" in *Different Horrors, Same Hell*, 16–37. Also see Shoshana Felman on the song as a vector of the catastrophe's resurrection and as a mode of address in *Shoah*. Felman, "A l'age du témoignage: *Shoah* de Claude Lanzmann," in *Au Sujet de* Shoah, ed. Michel Deguy (Paris: Belin, 1989), especially 129–45.

33. Interview with Gertrude Schneider (RG-60.5015, Film ID 3222, Camera Rolls 6–9).

34. Interview with Gertrude Schneider (RG-60.5015, Film ID 3222, Camera Rolls 6–9).

35. Interview with Gertrude Schneider (RG-60.5015, Film ID 3222, Camera Rolls 6–9).

36. If in this instance Schneider resists the archival impetus of Lanzmann's questioning, elsewhere in the interview she provides ample information about well-known SS personnel such as Rudolf Lange and Gerhard Maywald.

37. Shenker, *The Modern Jewish Experience*, 14.

38. Interview with Ruth Elias (RG-60.50003, Film ID 3112, Camera Rolls 1–2).

39. Delbo, *Aucun de nous ne reviendra* (Paris: Minuit, 1970), 48. For more on the association between the German shepherd and Nazism, see Aaron Skabelung, "Breeding Racism: The Imperial Battlefields of the 'German' Shepherd Dog," *Society and Animals* 16 no. 4 (2008): 354–71.

40. Ruth Elias, *The Triumph of Hope: From Theresienstadt and Auschwitz to Israel*, trans. Margot Bettauer Dembo (New York: John Wiley, 1998), 107. Subsequent reference to the memoir will appear in the body of the essay as *Triumph* followed by page numbers.

41. Ruth Elias and her family settled in the village of Beit Yitzhak-Sha'ar Hefer, Israel, where she died in 2008.

42. Interview with Ruth Elias (RG-60.50003, Film ID 3112, Camera Rolls 1–2).

43. Claude Lanzmann in *Au Sujet de* Shoah, 279; translation mine.

44. Interview with Ruth Elias (RG-60.50003, Film ID 3114, Camera Rolls 5–9A).

45. Interview with Ruth Elias (RG-60.50003, Film ID 3114, Camera Rolls 5–9A).

46. Interview with Ruth Elias (RG-60.50003, Film ID 3114, Camera Rolls 5–9a). A more accurate translation of that final line would be: "The time is coming soon, we will pack up all our bundles then, and back home we'll return. If we wish. We'll succeed, hand in hand we'll be as one, on the ghetto ruins we shall laugh some day."

47. David Bloch, "'No One Can Rob Us Our Dreams': Solo Songs from Terezin," in *Israel Studies in Musicology* 5 (1990): 69–80; here, 79.

48. Interview with Ruth Elias (RG-60.50003, Film ID 3114, Camera Rolls 5–9a).

49. Interview with Ruth Elias (RG-60.50003, Film ID 3114, Camera Rolls 5–9a).

50. Interview with Ruth Elias (RG-60.50003, Film ID 3115, Camera Roll 10).

51. Interview with Ruth Elias (RG-60.50003, Film ID 3116, Camera Rolls 11–12).

52. Interview with Ruth Elias (RG-60.50003, Film ID 3117, Camera Rolls 13–15).

53. Interview with Ruth Elias (RG-60.50003, Film ID 3117, Camera Rolls 13–15); translation mine.

54. Interview with Ruth Elias (RG-60.50003, Film ID 3116, Camera Rolls 11–12).

55. Interview with Ruth Elias (RG-60.50003, Film ID 3116, Camera Rolls 11–12).

56. Interview with Ruth Elias (RG-60.50003, Film ID 3118, Camera Rolls 13–15).

57. Interview with Ruth Elias (RG-60.50003, Film ID 3118, Camera Rolls 16–18).

58. Rumor had it that Ruth Elias's mother emigrated to Palestine, married a Greek man, and moved to Salonika with him. Although Elias does not mention this, if the rumor is indeed true, it would be unlikely that she survived the war given that more than 95 percent of Salonika Jews perished during deportation or at the Nazi killing centers.

59. "In later years I often played the waltzes from that book as a reminder of my mother" (*The Triumph of Hope*, 9).

60. Ruth Elias's belief that she would be taken to the gas chamber with her child is supported by a number of testimonies, including Olga Lengyel. "When babies were delivered in infirmary, mother and child were sent to gas chamber. Only when the infant doesn't survive or is stillborn was the mother spared." Lengyel, *Five Chimneys: A Woman Survivor's Story of Auschwitz* (Chicago: Chicago Review, 2005), 113.

61. Interview with Ruth Elias (RG-60.50003, Film ID 3118, Camera Rolls 16–18); emphasis mine.

62. Interview with Ruth Elias (RG-60.50003, Film ID 3118, Camera Rolls 16–18).

63. For more on the mercy killings of newborns, see Rab Bennett, *Under the Shadow of the Swastika: The Moral Dilemmas of Resistance and Collaboration in Hitler's Europe* (New York: Macmillan, 1999), 88–90; and Myrna Goldenberg,

"Sex-Based Violence and the Politics and Ethics of Survival," in *Different Horror/Same Hell*, 99–127.

64. Terrence Des Pres, *The Survivor: An Anatomy of Life in the Death Camps* (New York: Oxford University Press, 1976), 129.

65. Elias, *Triumph of Hope, 151*.

66. Sara R. Horowitz, "Memory and Testimony of Women Survivors of Nazi Genocide," in *Women of the Word: Jewish Women and Jewish Writing* ed. Judith R. Baskin (Detroit: Wayne State University Press), 258–82.

67. Consider, for instance, the contemporaneous *Sophie's Choice*—William Styron's novel came out in 1979, and Alan J. Pakula's film in 1982—which presented suicide as a mother's immutable destiny in the aftermath of "selecting" one child over another, an incompossible choice par excellence. This gives us an inkling of the importance of Elias's testimony at the time.

68. Recall Lanzmann's response to Abraham Bomba's pleading recollection that as a barber in the gas chamber, "We did the best we could, the most human we could," which the director interrupts with "No no no no no."

69. Even Raul Hilberg functions in the film not simply as a historian of the Final Solution but as an incarnation of its resistance to understanding. Recall the knowing looks they share while deciphering the German railway timetable in *Shoah*. In a tribute to the historian, Lanzmann declared that "Hilberg literally embodied and accepted the essential dare that the Holocaust makes to all who seek to bring it to life." Claude Lanzmann, "Raul Hilberg, Actor in Shoah," in *Perspectives on the Holocaust: Essays in Honor of Raul Hilberg*, ed. James S. Pacy and Alan P. Wertheimer (Boulder, CO: Westview, 1995), 185–87; here, 187. See also Noah Shenker's chapter in this volume.

70. Hirsch and Spitzer, "Gendered Translations," 15.

71. Interview with Ruth Elias (RG-60.50003, Film ID 3118, Camera Rolls 16–18).

11

Challenging *Shoah*'s Paradigms of Witnessing and Survival

From Filip Müller to Ruth Elias

Markus Zisselsberger

... but my desire, it was dazzlingly clear, would prevail over everyone and everything.

—Claude Lanzmann, *The Patagonian Hare*

The testimony of Filip Müller, a Slovakian Jew and former member of the infamous *Sonderkommando* in Auschwitz, occupies a central role in Claude Lanzmann's *Shoah* and provides one of the most memorable scenes in the film. While providing an eyewitness account of the murder of the Czech family camp at Auschwitz in March 1944, Müller recalls a moment when he witnessed the victims enter the gas chambers. Prompted by their sudden singing of the Czech national anthem and the *Hatikvah*, he began to identify with his fellow countrymen. Realizing that his own people were being sent to their death, Müller suddenly considered his existence meaningless and, by his account, decided to end his life by entering the gas chambers with them. In the testimonial present, the memory of this identification triggers an emotional breakdown that causes Müller to momentarily fall silent and break into tears, providing one of the moments in the film when speech fails the witness, and silence and emotional distress communicate the persistent presence of unprocessed psychic trauma. Müller's breakdown ultimately embodies the aesthetics of testimony that permeate the film as a whole: the witnesses do not solely remember the past but, as Lanzmann insisted, ideally "act it out"; they relive it instead, and thereby invoke the experience of the Shoah in the only form Lanzmann deemed possible and appropriate—as an "incarnation" of the past in the present.[1]

However, Filip Müller was not the only one among Lanzmann's interviewees who bore witness to this scene. At the moment when Müller was ready to follow the members of the Czech family camp into the gas chamber, it seems that Ruth Elias, a Czech Jew and female inmate of a different part of the family camp, was very close by, in block six of Auschwitz-Birkenau, "just 400 meters away," as Lanzmann observes in his extended conversation with Elias included in the film's outtakes.[2] She, too, heard the group about to be gassed sing the Czech national anthem and the *Hatikvah*, even if for her the singing had a fundamentally different meaning.[3] For Müller it made for a moment of bonding and identification, making him aware of his national and cultural affiliation with the very victims whose bodies he would later be forced to cremate as part of a destruction process with which he had become intimately familiar. For Elias, on the other hand, it provided a moment of insight into the fate awaiting her fellow Czechs that had previously been unclear to her and that, unlike Müller, she never witnessed with her own eyes. In the absence of visual evidence, it was the aural experience that served as the basis for knowledge, as she notes in the outtakes: "The moment we heard the *Hatikvah* being sung we knew these people were going to die."[4] Despite the fact that both Müller and Elias bore witness to the fate of members of the Czech family camp, only one of them appears in *Shoah* with the authority to testify to their murder: it is Müller who tells their story, in testimony that totals over forty minutes, commensurate with a film whose narrative is carried mostly by the voices of male Jewish survivors. In contrast, Elias's voice is marginalized in the film's theatrical release, and the two-minute segment featuring her focuses exclusively on her deportation from Theresienstadt and her arrival in Auschwitz. Her individual experiences related in the outtakes—in particular as a woman, mother, and daughter in and outside the Czech family camp—remain excluded.[5]

This chapter investigates this disproportionality of voices in *Shoah* by turning to the film's extensive outtakes as a source for illuminating differences between and within the testimonies of two witnesses whose subjectivities are inevitably curtailed in a cinematic narrative focused on the death and destruction of an entire Jewish community. Although this narrative is carried by the individual voices of Jewish survivors, the film is not interested in their stories as individuals per se, or in the biographical details of their backgrounds and experiences, but rather in their ability to testify to the fate of the community as a whole. In fact, as critics have noted, despite its multiplicity of voices, the film works toward a homogenization of victimhood and, in the process, generally neglects, even disavows, differences among Jewish witnesses—including gender differences.[6] It might be too harsh, however, to charge Lanzmann, as Marianne Hirsch and Leo Spitzer do, with a "resolute unwillingness to contemplate and explore differences among the victims in *Shoah*."[7] Indeed, the extended interviews with Jewish survivors in the outtakes frequently show Lanzmann inquiring about the differences between the experiences of Jews, with respect, for instance, to origin, nationality, and treatment by the Nazis. Thus, it would be more accurate to say that any lack of attention to differences among the victims is primarily an effect of the film's final aesthetic form rather than a product of Lanzmann's "disinterest" as an interviewer. Precisely because it is the aesthetic form of the film through which differences are both disavowed and constructed, the outtakes offer themselves as a vital source through which to investigate the editorial choices that shaped Müller's and Elias's voices in *Shoah*.

Viewed solely within the film's thematic focus on the fate of a collective, the prominence of Filip Müller's testimony in *Shoah*—and, in turn, the marginalization of Ruth Elias's—seems at first glance congruent with the film, both in terms of its aesthetics and the auteurist vision that informs it. After all, Lanzmann always insisted that *Shoah* required a particular kind of witness: because the film was to focus on "death rather than survival," Lanzmann claims he was interested primarily in those survivors who were closest to the sites of mass murder, observed the death of others, or came close to death themselves. For Lanzmann, these witnesses, "those who had been in the very charnel houses of the extermination, direct witnesses of the death of their people," were the members of the *Sonderkommando*, the "special squads" charged with maintaining the crematoria that, incidentally, were comprised exclusively of men.[8] In his retrospective assessments of the film, Lanzmann in fact tends to elevate these "direct witnesses" (represented in the final version of the film by the likes of Filip Müller, Abraham Bomba, and Richard Glazar) to the "only" witnesses to the mass murder perpetrated by the Nazis because they were the last ones to come into contact with Jewish victims, "making them particularly able to describe in detail how the machinery of death functioned."[9]

Beyond his historical experiences as a member of the special squads, however, Müller also fulfilled the criteria for the metaphysical dimensions of Lanzmann's ideal witness. For Lanzmann did not merely want the interviewees to testify about death. Rather, he wanted them to do so as if they themselves *were* dead; they would, in other words, not speak so much as "survivors" but as "revenants," as ghosts who returned from the dead.[10] For that matter, they would not testify as individuals but instead "forget themselves" and be "self-effacing so that the dead might speak through them."[11] The conception of witnesses as ghostly "revenants" entails the expectation that survivors, in their testimony, would bear witness not so much to their own experiences as to "the fate of the people as a whole," as Lanzmann stresses.[12] This directorial expectation of "self-effacement" in turn implies a curious form of testimonial self-sacrifice, a disavowal of both individuality and subjectivity in which the witnesses would tell their own stories only for the sake of the film's narrative of collective death.[13]

It is Müller, rather than Elias, who embodies and exemplifies the qualities of Lanzmann's ideal witness. A storyteller with the distinct ability to invoke the individual voices of others, Müller employs a unique narrative and dramatic style that lends his testimony an epic quality and highlights the scope of murder and its impact on an entire community. Further, he is able to lead the viewer into the interior of the gas chamber not only because he was close to the victims and was an eyewitness to their murder, but also because he himself literally entered it: having committed himself to die with the Czech family camp, he had come close to death himself, indeed abandoned himself to it, and now he returns, as a "revenant," a kind of ghost, with a sense of obligation to testify to the fate of others, without regard for himself. Müller's own survival, as his testimony in the film suggests, is premised on the conviction that survival is necessary in order that he bear witness to the death of others—a paradigm of survival *as* and *by* witnessing that informs the film's aesthetics of testimony as a whole.

This chapter argues that the extended testimonies of both Müller and Elias in the outtakes complicate this paradigm and highlight how the film's representation of the relationship between survival and witnessing is the result of editorial choices. In turn, the complete interviews with Müller and the one with Elias suggest more complex relationships between survival and witnessing than the edited sequences included in *Shoah*. Müller's extended testimony in the outtakes offers a more detailed picture of the circumstances of his survival, puts into perspective the nature and scope of his decision-making, brings to light a more multifaceted subjectivity of the survivor as agent, and highlights a relationship between surviving and witnessing that is marked by the intervention of others. Ruth Elias, on the other hand, rejects, in the narrative and performative recollections of her experiences, the notion that survival was motivated by a desire to bear witness to the death of others. Considered in connection with one another, these testimonies suggest that Lanzmann—and, by extension, the film—is inattentive to the witnesses' complex subject positions as agents, both as agents in the past and, in the testimonial present, as testifying witnesses. Moreover, they demonstrate the film's neglect of the manifold ways in which the interviewees, in and through testimony, attempt to work through the memorial confrontation with their past in words and gestures that sometimes resist the kind of reenactments and emotional breakdowns envisioned by the film's cinematic auteur. Finally, both Müller's and Elias's extended interviews in the outtakes also offer new insights into the roles of gender and gender differences in witnesses' testimonies in the film.

Surviving and/as Witnessing: Filip Müller

Filip Müller seems to embody Lanzmann's ideal witness by virtue of his qualities as a storyteller alone, displaying seemingly little need for intervention by Lanzmann as interviewer or the elaborate staging of mise-en-scène; his testimony is carried primarily by a voice remarkable for its ability to invoke the voices of others and to render events in such vividness so as to make them present for the viewer. LaCapra describes him as a "bard of ultimate disaster," one who "seems to have recounted his tale many times before and is able to proceed with the virtuosity of a seasoned narrator," while Lanzmann, in turn, "does nothing to disturb Müller's narrative and is a patient, attentive, and responsive listener."[14] Indeed, Müller's style is distinctly theatrical in nature, marked by dramatic pauses, emphasis and intonation, the use of adverbial phrases and temporal markers that indicate sudden turns in events, an oscillation between direct and indirect speech, and by shifts in tone and pitch when dialogue between victims and Nazi perpetrators is rendered. He thus dramatizes the final moments before the former's murder. That Müller is able to offer this narrative in nonnative German makes the testimony all the more remarkable; however, as LaCapra intimates, it also raises questions about the extent to which his skills as a storyteller were natural, or might have developed over time, or were possibly influenced by repeated but formally and linguistically different acts of testifying to his experiences.[15]

Müller's ability to make the experiences of others vivid and tangible through his voice is ultimately also the source of his emotional breakdown in *Shoah*. Müller falls silent precisely at a moment when he "hears" the voices of the victims he has just so vividly conjured: their singing, in his native language, reminds him of their national and linguistic affiliation and prompts an emotional identification. In particular, the temporary silence of Müller—who sits on the couch in his living room for the entire duration of the interview—is not the result of a "performance" elicited through a complex mise-en-scène, as in the case of Abraham Bomba, whose breakdown occurs within the framework of a specular setting in which the bodily reality of persistent trauma is drawn out through an interplay of mirror reflections, which Brad Prager demonstrates in his chapter of this volume. Neither is the rupture in Müller's narrative the staged repetition of a prior interview: while Lanzmann had previously met with Bomba and heard his entire account before he interviewed him in front of the camera, he ostensibly had had no such prior conversations with Müller. Instead, the relationship with Müller was, from the very beginning, thoroughly "textual" in nature: Lanzmann had first read and learned about him through the latter's testimony at a local Slovakian court, the first account of his experiences he had given after the end of the war, which was subsequently included in the volume, *The Death Factory: Document on Auschwitz* (1966).[16] This book serves as the central means of engagement in the interview with Müller, as Lanzmann uses it frequently as a reference source, especially in the early takes, to ask Müller questions about the camp and have him identify the specific locations of the gas chambers and crematoria.[17] Beyond these functions, however, Lanzmann's use of the book also highlights the broader "textual" nature of his approach to interviewing Müller; in particular, it is evident in Lanzmann's attempts to elicit an emotional response from his witness through acts of reading—and the failure of this approach to elicit a testimonial "performance."

This textual approach and its failure are illustrated in Lanzmann's efforts to "test," so to speak, how Müller's voice could best be brought in touch with history so as to induce a return of and to the past in his witness. For that matter, Lanzmann explored how this return of the past might come from the substance of history itself, from a *Geschichte* whose horrific nature could not help but draw forth emotions. For that reason, Lanzmann asks Müller to engage in the reading of a story: the account of the murder of

Filip Müller reading the account of the murder of six hundred boys in Auschwitz in October 1944. Created by Claude Lanzmann during the filming of *Shoah*. (Used by permission of the United States Holocaust Memorial Museum and Yad Vashem, the Holocaust Martyrs and Heroes' Remembrance Authority, Jerusalem.)

six hundred boys at Auschwitz in October 1944, as recounted in the diary entries by Leib Langfus, a member of the *Sonderkommando* and the revolt movement.[18] Müller dutifully performs the reading and, in the process, offers the perhaps-hoped-for emotional response: on the verge of tears, he briefly stumbles in his reading and pauses.

This response, however, seems forced, particularly because his emotions are not drawn forth by an act of remembrance that has turned "incarnate," but by the reading of a story that is not his own. Indeed, at the end of the story, Müller acknowledges to Lanzmann that he did not witness the event directly.[19] This staged reading conveys that Lanzmann sensed Müller's qualities and skills as a storyteller but may have been unsure about how to best mobilize this voice so as to induce a "resurrection" of the past. As Lanzmann learned, for that to occur Müller would not have needed to "read" someone else's story but rather to tell his own.

Müller's testimony in *Shoah* is, like most other testimonies in the film, spliced together from different sections of the extended interview that are not in the order in which they were discursively presented. For instance, the first part of Müller's account in the film is assembled from twenty different excerpts that do not follow the order in which they were presented in the filmed interview. In contrast, Müller's last sequence in the film, in which he relates his encounter with the anonymous group of women in the gas chamber, consists of only three different parts, all of which remain in their original discursive order. In particular, the third of these segments is unedited and continuous, and it is at the end of this take that Müller breaks down. This emotional breakdown occurs when Müller recalls witnessing the fate of the members of the Czech family camp whom he observed—as he had previously with many other victims—entering the gas chambers. The encounter with the Czech Jews, however, brought about a breaking point: Müller describes both the extreme violence committed against the Jews when they were forced into the gas chambers and their simultaneous resistance, their refusal to take off their clothes, their proclamation of a desire to live, and their expression of solidarity and community through the singing of the Czech national anthem and the *Hatikvah*, even in the face of inevitable death. At this moment, driven undoubtedly by the identification with his Czech "countrymen" invoked by the songs, Müller ceases to speak and momentarily breaks into tears.[20]

In the film, Müller's subsequent emergence from this speechlessness is premised on the invocation of female voices, which makes for a moment that is significant in terms of gender, since it assigns to women the role of enabling male testimony while the women themselves appear deprived of the opportunity to speak about their own experiences. It suggests a paradigm of survival and, by extension, of witnessing that is central to *Shoah* and to its director more generally. Noting how emotionally "touched" he was by what he witnessed, Müller recalls thinking "dass mein Leben nicht mehr kein Wert hat" (that my life had no value anymore). For that reason, he decided at that very instant to enter the gas chambers, resolved to die with the other Czech Jews. If he nevertheless survived, that was because, as he notes in the film, a group of Jewish women compelled him to live, asking him to survive in order to bear witness to their experiences and the "injustice" of their death:

> Du willst ja sterben. Aber das hat doch keinen Sinn. Dein Sterben wird nicht unseres Leben bringen. Das ist keine Tat. Du must von hier raus, du musst ja noch berichten über den, was wir leiden, was für ein Ungerecht uns get[an], uns geschehen ist.[21]

> (So you want to die. But that's senseless. Your dying won't give us life. That's no deed. You must get out of here, you still have to report about our suffering, the injustice that was done, that happened to us.)[22]

Since these words conclude Müller's testimony in *Shoah*, the viewer never learns how Müller responded to the women, what actions he might have taken afterward, and under what circumstances he left the gas chamber and survived. However, because the interview with Müller ends here, with the women's demand to survive and bear witness, it is reasonable for the viewer to conclude that Müller's "report" to Lanzmann is indeed the result of a resolution and a decision to survive and return in order to testify to the murder of a collective. Indeed, the women's ethical demand that Müller survive to speak in their stead enables a double return, both in the past and in the present: Müller's physical return from the space of death, despite his firm resolution to die; and a linguistic return, from speechlessness to speech, in the present of the testimony, after Müller's emotional breakdown and silence in the recollection of his experience. Premised on this double return, Müller's testimony in *Shoah* enacts a particular paradigm of survival and witnessing in which the will to live is informed by a sense of responsibility to speak for the dead—an instance of what Dorota Glowacka calls "survival *by* witnessing."[23] It casts Müller in the (for *Shoah*) emblematic role of "heroic" storyteller who stays alive—indeed, returns from the dead, as the kind of privileged "revenant" who has literally seen and inhabited the "inside" of destruction and now bears witness for those who perished.

This paradigm of survival by witnessing, as embodied through Müller's testimony in the film, assigns and conveys different forms of agency to Jewish women and men, both in terms of their respective experiences and their corresponding testimonies. In Müller's account of his experience of survival, the women take on a double role that renders them both passive and active. As members of the family camp about to enter the gas chambers, they remind Müller of his national and cultural affiliations and cause him to succumb to hopelessness. Given Müller's resolution to die, the women in this scene do conform in part to the roles frequently assigned to female survivors in the film: they are associated with "danger and death," as Hirsch and Spitzer argue, and as such they appear to jeopardize the very possibility of male survival insofar as they "threaten whatever precarious emotional distance, whatever control and denial of feelings they [the men; MZ] had attempted to establish in order to survive."[24] However, the women also take on an active role in which they exercise agency precisely through their demand that Müller live in order to bear witness. Müller, as the film in turn suggests, decides to take on this responsibility and thus is assigned the agency of a survivor who willfully assumes the task of witnessing, ostensibly as a result of reflection and rational decision-making, a paradigm of survival that, as we will see, is complicated by his extended testimony in the outtakes.

On the level of testimony, however, *Shoah* assigns agency more unevenly along gender lines and attributes it primarily to Müller. For the film suggests that Müller's reemergence from speechlessness—and his very survival and presence as a living witness—depends on the "sacrificial" death of women who in turn depend on men to testify for them, illustrating the film's general treatment of women as testimonial subjects: they can be the objects of male testimony, but not necessarily agents with the capability of testifying to their own experiences. Within the economy of the film, then, the particular paradigm of surviving by witnessing as premised on a sense of obligation to bear witness for the dead also entails a general disavowal of women's testimonial agency. Offering a testimony that is both the embodiment and enactment of this paradigm, Filip Müller possesses the agency to speak; and only he, as one who has entered and returned from the gas chambers, can testify to the "inside" of death and destruction. To note these differences in agency is not to doubt or deny the historical reality and contingencies of survival expressed in Müller's testimony; women and children died in the gas chambers, while predominately men, such as the members of the *Sonderkommando*, survived due to having occupied "privileged" positions in the camps. Nevertheless, Müller's testimony is emblematic for the male-centered paradigm of witnessing that underlies the narrative of death and destruction in the film's "second era." In that phase of *Shoah*, female testimony tends to be used as a facilitating device to take the viewer "inside" the experience of extermination while women's experiences and voices mostly remain "outside."

Returning to Life: Agency and Testimony

This paradigm of survival as and through witnessing can be put into perspective, however, through Müller's extended testimony in the outtakes, where he offers a second, different account of his encounter with female members of the Czech family camp, as recorded in another take. This alternative version presents a relationship between survival and witnessing—in particular, with respect to Müller's motivations for living and taking action—that is more multifaceted than the edited testimony included in *Shoah* suggests. This difference is most strongly reflected at the level of agency: in the second take, Müller relates that the women who approached him once he had entered the gas chamber were, first of all, not entirely anonymous. Müller rather recounts that a particular woman, "ein schwarzes Mädchen" (a black [haired] girl) named Jana, stepped forth from the group of naked women and addressed him in similar yet more individualized, personal terms than suggested in the theatrical release of *Shoah*:

Ich bin Jana, und ich frage dich . . . : Was hat den dein Frei-
tod, was du machen willst, einen Sinn? Das hat doch keinen
Sinn. Du kannst uns nicht helfen. Im Gegenteil, du musst
leben und berichten, was für einen qualenvollen Tod wir da
erlitten haben.[25]

(I am Jana and ask you . . . : What purpose is there to the suicide you want to commit? That doesn't make any sense. You
cannot help us. On the contrary, you must live and report
what kind of agonizing death we suffered.)

While the testimony in *Shoah* indirectly suggests that Müller followed this
plea to bear witness and made a decision to go on living, his recollections
in the outtakes reveal that, while in the gas chambers, he had neither the
state of mind to process this plea nor to act upon it. As he notes, his immediate response to Jana's words was to consider them unrealistic, utopic:
"Mir scheint es als eine Utopie in dem Moment, was sie mir gesagt haben"
(What they told me seems to me a utopia at that moment).[26] In congruence
with his assessment of the situation, Müller decided not to act, and did not
leave the gas chamber; instead, it was the women who acted and forcefully
pulled him out of the space in which they themselves would die shortly
thereafter, as Müller recalls in dramatic terms: "Und plötzlich stürzten sich
diese Mädchen auf mich, nehmen mich, und ziehen mich bis zu der . . .
den . . . der Tür der Gaskammer, die ja geöffnet waren und schmeissten
mich heraus" (And suddenly these girls bore down on me, take me and
drag me to the door of the gas chamber, which were open, and threw me
out).[27] Thus, Müller's recollections in the outtakes convey a forced survival,
one that was not premised on Müller's agency and decision-making but
rather on that of others.[28] A consideration of the extended testimony in
the outtakes thus highlights the degree to which the paradigm of survival
as witnessing in *Shoah* is an effect of directorial and editorial choices.
While one can only speculate about the precise reasons for these choices,
it is likely that Lanzmann preferred the first version of Müller's account
because it led to Müller's emotional breakdown—a rupture in speech that,
moreover, seemed to occur naturally and was unforced. Moreover, in this
account, the women in the gas chambers remained anonymous and spoke

collectively, which may have appealed to Lanzmann's auteurist vision of a cinematic narrative about the death of an entire community in which there are no individual stories and in which survivors are passive victims who cannot escape the traumas of the past.

The fact that a desire to bear witness was not the primary motivation for survival is reinforced by Müller's account of his return to life after having been removed from the gas chamber. Müller relates that, immediately following his forced exit, he was seen and then beaten by an SS guard, who ordered him to go back to the crematoria. After his arrival there, Müller passed out and was taken to the coal storage room by fellow special squad members, where, upon his awakening, he was addressed by Kapo Kaminski:

> Filip, was hast du den so was gemacht?! Du wirst doch denen
> so einen Gefallen nicht machen? Und sich denn selbst er-
> legen? Wir brauchen dich noch! Du bist jung. Du kannst
> noch Vieles machen und vielleicht nochmal überleben.[29]

> (But Filip, why did you do such a thing?! You won't do them
> such a favor, after all, and kill yourself? We still need you!
> You are young, you can still do lots of things and perhaps
> survive again.)

Like Jana's words, those of Kaminski express a sort of reprimand for Müller's suicide attempt; however, unlike Jana, who compels Müller to stay alive to testify to the fate of the Czech family camp, Kaminski tries to remind Müller of his vital role within a (male) community, namely of both the special squad members and the resistance group. Müller credits this reminder, rather than Jana's words, with reinstilling in him a desire to live, as his subsequent commentary conveys:

> In dem Moment ist mir viele Kraft in mich gekommen. Ich
> hatte wieder Sehnsucht zum Leben, ich kann es nicht ver-
> stehen, wie es, wie es möglich war. Vorher wollte ich mir
> dem Leben nehmen, und jetzt eine grosse Sehnsucht. Der
> Kapo Kaminiski hat also so überzeugend auf mich gespro-
> chen dass also, dass das sehr eine grosse Wirkung auf mich

gemacht hat. Und so also hab ich diese, die schreckliche
Nacht dann überlebt.

(In this moment a lot of strength came into me. I had a longing to live again, I cannot understand how it was possible.
Before that I wanted to take my life, and now a great longing.
Kapo Kaminski spoke to me so convincingly that it had a
great effect on me. And that was the way, then, in which I
survived this terrible night.)[30]

In his testimony in the outtakes, Müller thus presents his survival as the
result of two distinctive factors: his forceful, physical removal from the gas
chambers at the hands of the women (a fact on which he does not explicitly
comment) and the return of a desire to live that was prompted by Kaminski's words. This sequence of events is significant insofar as it reverses the
relation between surviving and witnessing reflected and embodied through
Müller's testimony in the theatrical release of *Shoah*: survival, both as a
preservation of the physical self and a "longing" to live, precedes the desire
to bear witness and the possibility of doing so.

While this precedence of survival over witnessing might be considered
self-evident, it is nevertheless central to an understanding of how Müller
narratively relates his survival and how this survival ultimately led to a
material and immediate form of bearing witness that stands in contrast
to the more abstract and anonymous paradigm of testifying to the fate of
the people as a whole, as suggested by Müller's testimony in the film. For,
directly following the statement about having survived "diese schreckliche
Nacht" (this terrible night), Müller, without being prompted by Lanzmann,
immediately shifts the narrative back to the site of murder: "Aber, jetzt
will ich nochmal zurückgehen in die Gaskammer" (But, now I want to go
back once more into the gas chamber). This announcement marks another
double return: while Müller returns, in memory, to the site of murder (and
to his own suicide attempt), he actually relates a literal return to the inside
of the gas chamber that was motivated by a desire to keep a promise he had
made to Jana. Revisiting his encounter with the women, he recounts that
"bevor die Mädchen mich noch herausgeschmissen haben, sagte mir diese

schwarze Mädchen, Jana" (even before the girls threw me out, the black-haired girl Jana told me):

> Hier, in dieser Säule, wirst du mich finden, hier werde ich unter dieser Säule liegen. Ich habe hier eine goldene Kette. Ich habe einen guten Freund, Sascha, den sowjetischen Kriegsgefangenen. Der arbeitet in der Brotkammer. Gib ihm des [inaudible], und übergib ihm des, und einen letzten Gruss.[31]

> (Here, at this pillar, you are going to find me. Here I am going to be lying under this pillar. I have a golden necklace. I have a good friend, Sasha, a Soviet prisoner of war. He works in the bread storage room. Give him the [inaudible], hand it to him, and a final greeting.)

Müller recounts then that, after their murder, he did indeed go back to the gas chamber, retrieved the necklace and, the next morning, sought out Sasha, to whom he passed on Jana's final goodbye. According to Müller, Sasha, devastated by the news, explained that he had proposed to Jana and that they had intended to get married, and eventually broke into tears. This in turn, marked a breaking point for Müller, for the fates of Jana and Sasha for him evidently epitomized the tragedy of the family camp as a whole:

> Ich könnte schon nicht hören mehr weiter. Es war genug. Ich war voll, von Grausamkeiten, die ich erlebt hab. Mein Herz war entschüttert. Ich läufte weg auf der Strasse heraus. Und ging in meinen Block 13 zurück. So endete etwa, in ganz kurzen, das Schicksal des Familienslagers.[32]

> (I could not listen anymore. It was enough. I was filled, with cruelties I experienced. My heart was shattered. I walked away into the street and returned to my block 13. That's more or less, in brief, how the fate of the family camp came to its conclusion.)

Compared to the theatrical version of the film, Müller's extended testimony in the outtakes thus suggests another "double return," but one that implies a different relationship between witnessing and surviving: in *Shoah* Müller returns, by his own volition, both from the gas chambers to life, and from silence to speech, in order to testify to the fate of an anonymous collective; in the outtakes, he is brought back to life by others and only after that return to life—in the past as well as in the testimony—can he "return" to bear witness.

Outside the Frame: Ruth Elias

Ruth Elias was a Czech Jew and female survivor of the Theresienstadt Ghetto and Auschwitz. In an extended, two-hour conversation with Lanzmann in the outtakes (conducted in English), she describes her deportation to the ghetto in April 1942 at the age of eighteen and her subsequent imprisonment in the Czech family camp at Auschwitz. In particular, Elias relates her experiences as a daughter, pregnant woman, and mother, and thereby offers insights into the "family" aspect of the camp and the experiences of women that tend to be neglected in the theatrical version of the film: she arrived at Auschwitz as a pregnant woman but was able, in part due to her own resourcefulness, to conceal her pregnancy and escape selection for an extended period of time, even managing to temporarily leave the camp as part of a work detail sent to Hamburg. There, however, her pregnancy was discovered and she was sent back to Auschwitz, leading to a fateful encounter with the infamous "doctor" Mengele, who, astonished that he could have overlooked a pregnant woman during the selection process, took a special interest in her. As part of a "medical" experiment, Mengele allowed Elias to give birth to a daughter but then prohibited her from feeding the child in order to see how long it would take for the baby to die without her mother's nourishment. Forced to witness the newborn's health steadily deteriorate, Elias, at the urging and with the assistance of a Jewish doctor, decided to end the child's suffering by lethally injecting her with morphine.

However, none of these experiences are related in the final version of the film, where Elias's voice can be heard only for a little over two minutes. The testimony included in the film is used to facilitate entry into Auschwitz as a historical site and a geographical space of experiences to which exclusively male survivors like Müller bear witness but from which she herself is excluded. Elias's voice opens the fourth part of the film, in which she recalls her deportation from Theresienstadt to Auschwitz and the internment of the Czech Jews in the family camp. Her testimony is presented as voice-over that is accompanied by present-day footage of a train traveling through a deserted landscape, seen from a passenger's perspective. The detailed description of her deportation and the arrival and unloading at Auschwitz then opens the gates to the camp, as it were, visualized through a present-day tracking shot of the rail tracks leading into the extermination site. Lanzmann's interest, as the unfolding cinematic narrative suggests, is to follow the traces of the Czech Jews to their eventual murder in the gas chambers. Elias's testimony, it appears, is not useful for the further construction of this narrative, because her perspective was too limited to bear witness to the extermination process—at least that is what the sequences in this part of the film suggest. Indeed, in contrast to the extended interview in the outtakes, where Elias describes moments in which she had developed awareness of the murder taking place in Auschwitz, the testimony included in the film emphasizes her narrow perspective as a deportee and her lack of knowledge of the destination: "I didn't know anything about Auschwitz."[33] And she recalls that, once she was inside the camp—after the tracking shot of the railroad has taken the viewer inside the camp, the film at this point cuts back to a shot of Elias—when men told her that Auschwitz was an extermination camp, "we didn't believe it."

Considered as part of the broader narrative constructed in the second era of *Shoah*, Elias's testimony highlights how the film consistently forecloses the possibility of creating cinematic spaces in which female experiences could be articulated, other than within male testimonies. In fact, the narrative framing of the segment tracing the murder of the Czech Jews from the family camp denies women the space in which, as in the cases of Müller and, later, Bomba, a traumatized inner life emerges both through speech and speechlessness; instead, there is only an "outside" (Elias entering the camp) and an absolute "inside" (the gas chambers), in which "life" is already death; there is no space *as experientia*, in which women could narrate and articulate what they went through, even though the film simultaneously constructs gendered dichotomies of knowledge and insight. Rather than simply omitting testimonial materials that would offer insights into the specific experiences of women, the film in this sense forecloses the construction of a cinematic space in which women's voices could even emerge. While *Shoah*'s narrative in this segment leads the viewer—both visually and linguistically—from the outside to the "inside" of murder, in the case of Elias, the direction is reversed: as the film approaches the center of destruction in the gas chambers, Elias's experiences are moved "outside" the camp. They are subsumed in the "family" of the family camp, in that anonymous group of women who compel Müller to live, highlighting the premise on which the film's narrative rests more generally: the construction of a paradigm of witnessing that assigns agency predominately to male Jewish witnesses.

In her extended interview with Lanzmann in the outtakes, Ruth Elias challenges this disavowal of testimonial agency and complicates the paradigm of survival by witnessing embodied by Müller and central to *Shoah* both through the content of her testimony and her choices of narrative self-representation. While Elias's testimony in *Shoah* is used instrumentally for a cinematic narrative that tends to assign women primarily to a realm of death and speechlessness, her extended testimony in the outtakes is marked by the dominance of life over death and hope over hopelessness and narratively permeated by a will to live, which she repeatedly calls "instinct." This instinct not only motivated her choices and helped her survive; it also informs the structure and form of her testimony and indicates particular narrative choices in the representation of her experiences. In its emphasis on the preeminence of life itself, this testimony offers an alternative conception of the relationship between survival and witnessing: a form of witnessing *by* surviving that proves at odds with *Shoah*'s aesthetics of testimony and the filmmaker's obsessive focus on death that drives it.

Witnessing by Surviving: Testimonial Agency and the Instinct to Survive

The kind of agency that characterizes Elias's testimony is aptly brought into focus in the outtakes in a contentious moment between the witness and Lanzmann. When Elias is in the process of recounting her deportation to Auschwitz and her first encounter with Mengele, Lanzmann suddenly interrupts her, posing a seemingly innocent question. While Elias tells of

Mengele's presence at Auschwitz, Lanzmann interjects rather unexpectedly: "How was he?" Elias, clearly surprised by the question and unclear about its meaning, seems somewhat incredulous and asks Lanzmann for clarification ("How?"). Lanzmann in turn rephrases the question to suggest that he is interested in Mengele's appearance: "Yes. How did he look?"[34] An interruption of this kind is generally not uncommon in Lanzmann's role and performance as an interviewer whose gestures are often designed to interrupt the flow of the narrative in order to return his interviewees to particular moments in memory and, at times, to induce a literal return of the past suitable to elicit an emotional breakdown.

In this case, however, the question seems abrupt and somewhat intrusive, not only because it shifts the focus of the testimony from victim to perpetrator, but also because Lanzmann seems to casually inquire about the condition and "well-being" of one of the most notorious and cruel Nazi murderers who was responsible for the death of Elias's child. Despite the casualness of Lanzmann's interjection, one might see this question as another reflection of Lanzmann's self-proclaimed obsession with death and perhaps as an attempt to gauge Elias's reaction while she recalls the man responsible for the death of her child. However, if Lanzmann's question is indeed designed to reconfront the witness, in memory, with the face of the "angel of death," Elias refuses to respond to the director's cue and instead insists on deferring a possible answer by responding calmly, with a smile on her face: "I will tell you later."[35] Although this deferral constitutes a seemingly minor moment in the interview, it suggests a sense of testimonial agency on behalf of a witness who wishes to control the direction and structure of the narrative and thereby, at least at this particular moment, to resist Lanzmann's attempts to bring her back to the experiences of destruction and her literal face-to-face encounter with death. Indeed, while Elias eventually relates her encounter with Mengele and the loss of her child, her account is embedded within a broader narrative that emphasizes life, hope, survival, and community even in the face of such atrocity. The structure and form of this narrative, in turn, is informed by a discourse on "instinct," which Elias credits with her survival but that also influences the discursive order of her story.

In her testimony, Elias frequently invokes "instinct" as a trope to explain actions that clearly involved rational consideration and quick thinking but that she believes cannot be explained through recourse to "thought": "It was all instinct to be able to live. . . . I was only acting instinctively."[36] Thus, Elias recalls that, when she was first facing selection at Auschwitz, she asked a group of beautiful young women to stand in front of her in the hope that this might help make "the man which is in Mengele" overlook her despite the fact that she was eight months pregnant.[37] Having followed her instinct, Elias, veiled by the young women, was waived to the right and put on a work transport to Hamburg. Later, when arriving at the women's camp in Ravensbrück, where she was taken after her pregnancy was discovered in Hamburg, she proposes to Berta, a fellow pregnant prisoner, that they identify themselves as sisters and claim that Berta was feeling sick, so that Elias could justify staying with her and prevent their immediate return to Auschwitz. When asking herself "When I think today, where did I get these thoughts? Where did I get the courage to think of things like that?" she notes only that "it was again this instinct."[38] That same instinct, she relates, later made them remove the yellow star from their clothing and provide false names in order to hide their identities as Jews. For Elias, this instinct ultimately amounted to a will to live, a relentless desire to stay alive, and hope in the face of murder: "Every time there was hope, and the will to live was so very strong. We were only thinking of how to live, how to come over all this."[39]

As a force equated with life itself, however, "instinct" does not serve merely as an explanatory function in Elias's recollections. Rather, the structure and chronological order of Elias's narrative as well as recurring temporal markers within it indicate that the memories of "life" and the instinct to survive are not simply the object of her testimony but are rather also narratively reenacted in the present in complex ways. While her story testifies to her experience of survival, it is life itself, the very instinct she credits with her survival, which guides—indeed seems to dictate—the form of her story and the narrative reconstruction of her memories. This symbiotic relationship between the content of experience and its narrative representation is reflected in her testimony on various levels. For one, as illustrated by the deferral of the story recounting the confrontation with Mengele, Elias frequently includes temporal markers in her narrative, indicating which part she is going to tell: "You will afterwards hear how I was eating and how I was stealing."[40] These markers suggest that she knows how she wants to or must tell her story, predetermining, as it were, the narrative presentation of events and possibly making it resistant to the kind of digressions and redirections introduced by Lanzmann's interruptions and questions. Whether these markers in turn are indicative of conscious decisions with regard to the order and form of the narrative, however, is subject to debate. In particular, the seemingly predetermined structure of Elias's testimony raises the question as to what extent her choices in narrative self-representation may be influenced by the fact that Elias, like Filip Müller, seems to have told her story many times before.[41] Whatever the influence of previous experiences of relating her story on her interview with Lanzmann, it is noteworthy that while the testimony itself suggests that its witness possesses testimonial agency, in the sense of her control over any decision-making concerning the presentation of events, Elias herself seems to disavow any agency she may have exercised in her quest to survive even though many of her previously described choices involved rational thought and decision-making. However, Elias vehemently denies that her actions involved "thought," because she considers the "instinct" she followed "animal" rather than human in nature; such an instinct, as she notes in her memoir, "dictated" her behavior and did not allow for rational thinking.[42]

From this notion of instinct emerges an understanding of survival that posits individual self-preservation as its main driving force rather than a need and desire to bear witness to the lives and deaths of others, as Elias repeatedly emphasizes in her statements to Lanzmann:

> ELIAS: I'll tell you something: *people in misery act like animals. That is instinct,* and when today I listen to people, they were doing this and this in concentration camps—*to be able to tell it afterwards, I don't believe it.* I'm sorry to say I don't believe it, because I saw the animal instinct in people.
>
> . . .
>
> ELIAS: All these thoughts are thoughts of today, as I told you. Instinct is not the thought of today. I said I was only acting instinctively.
>
> . . .
>
> ELIAS: Again, *I can't fetch it that people are telling that they wanted to live to be able to tell afterwards.* I didn't know what would be afterwards; you know what "carpe diem" means?

LANZMANN: Yes.

ELIAS: That's what we had to do. "Carpe diem." I didn't know what would be the next hour, I couldn't say what would be the next day. *I didn't want to live to be able to tell people, I wanted to live because I was young, and I wanted to live. That's it: I wanted to live, nothing else.* You will see afterwards—I have got a very long story—but you will see how *the will to live is so very strong, without any thoughts behind it. I don't believe in thoughts in misery like this.*[43]

In her conception of survival as premised on an "animal instinct," Elias rejects the idea of futurity inherent in the notion of survival by witnessing, finding it inconceivable that the "misery" of the camp could have allowed even the possibility of thinking of an "afterwards" ("to be able to tell if afterwards, I don't believe it"; "I can't fetch it that people wanted to live to be able to tell afterwards"). In fact, being driven by instinct for Elias precludes the very possibility of "thought," as there is only a "will to live . . . , without any thoughts behind it."[44] In a paradoxical sense, survival here has no object other than life itself, as Elias's circular statement intimates: "I didn't want to live to be able to tell people, I wanted to live because . . . I wanted to live."[45] In this conception of survival, then, it is life itself that serves as testimony: witnessing *by* surviving rather than surviving by witnessing. The latter's difference from a survival premised on the need to speak for others is reinforced by Elias's repeated insistence that she can only "talk for herself," not for others.[46] This also suggests a resistance, if not refusal, of the kind of self-effacement Lanzmann expects from the ideal witness. This resistance to self-effacement is inseparable from the affirmation of life that permeates the testimony—indeed, is constitutive of it, and as such offers a counterpoint to the presence and proximity of death Lanzmann often seeks to solicit in his interviewees' testimonies.

At the same time, however, the oral dimension of Elias's testimony, elicited in part through Lanzmann's presence and interventions, seems to draw forth the preeminence of life in a distinct way. This distinctness is best illustrated through a consideration of the differences between Elias's recollection of an experience while working in the kitchen in the Theresienstadt Ghetto in her memoir and her subsequent testimony to this experience in the interview with Lanzmann. In the *Shoah* outtakes, this episode occurs within the framework of an extensive discourse on food that Elias describes as one particular manifestation of her "instinct" and as an essential component in the drive for "self-preservation." In this context, she recalls a day in the kitchen when she placed bread dough under her apron, an act she describes in her memoir in a chapter devoted to life in the Theresienstadt Ghetto:

> One day I decided to take a little of the yeast dough for my roommate and her child. I took a handful and put it under the big oilcloth apron I wore over my work clothes. I was about to leave the kitchen when two police officers (*Kripo*) walked in. One of them started a routine inspection while the other guarded the door. Because of the heat the dough under my apron began to rise, and the dimensions of my bosom became larger and larger. Terrified that the dough would expand beyond my apron, I gave my chest a hard thump. The dough collapsed, but only for a moment. It immediately started to rise again. The *Kripos* didn't notice. My coworkers, though, were highly amused by these antics. Finally, after what seemed an eternity, the detectives left. Instead of a handful of dough for my roommate, I returned with dough smeared all over my clothes. We were able to scrape it off, and she and her daughter received a little additional nourishment.[47]

In her memoir, Elias explains the act of putting dough under her apron as being motivated by a desire to help others, to pass on food to her roommate and the latter's child—an act, one should note, that once more highlights her agency as a survivor who undertakes actions directed at the survival (here, of others) on the basis of rational decision-making, even if she disavows such rational thinking in retrospect. The unexpected rising of the dough, in turn, is recollected as leading to a moment of danger insofar as it threatens to expose her transgression during a routine inspection. If there is a potential humor in this situation, it is only intimated by a reference to coworkers who, as Elias notes, "were highly amused by these antics."

In contrast to the description of this episode in the memoir, Elias's recollection in the interview with Lanzmann in the outtakes places this experience in a fundamentally different context. Here, the episode is remembered—notably, by an animated and smiling Elias, who has just performed a musical piece for Lanzmann—purely as a lighthearted moment in which the placement and rising of the dough is a result of horseplay among kitchen workers, without any altruistic motivation and devoid of any danger. Thus, Elias merely notes that after she had hidden the dough beneath her apron in order to smuggle it to her living quarters, her friends, as a joke, held her back, to "see what the yeast dough does when it starts to grow." As Elias recalls, "It started to grow, here, behind my apron. . . . All the time I had to clasp here, and I was growing and growing, and all the kitchen was laughing. You see, there was humor in our heart."[48] Within the context of her oral testimony, this recollection functions as—and is emblematic of—a particular affirmation of life that is characteristic of her testimonial performance in the outtakes more generally: despite experiences of suffering and death, there was life inside here, driving her, beyond her control, expanding, like the dough, as it were. This affirmation of life is accentuated by the formal differences between the memoir and the oral interview: within the chapter-structure of the memoir, this episode is far removed, in the discursive order of presentation, from Elias's later incarceration in the family camp; in the narratively condensed version of her story in the conversation with Lanzmann, on the other hand, the shorter time of narration puts the event at Theresienstadt much closer to her experiences at Auschwitz.

This experiential and memorial proximity lends the dough story a different testimonial weight and suggests the possibility of a gendered reading of its unexpected expansion. It was late 1943 and Elias was, ostensibly, not yet aware of her pregnancy, although she was undoubtedly, like the dough, already "growing and growing."[49] It is difficult not to read this memory of the expanding dough and a growing belly as a narrative figuration of the life within her—the life of the child that would be in her, the life of the child she lost, but also the "life" and "instinct" to survive in the face of utmost destruction that she carried with her through the Shoah and that remains in her even in the present of the testimony. One might then see the permeation of Elias's testimony with life as another instance of a gendered form of recall designed to "break the frame of Auschwitz" in the testimonial present.[50] If Elias, in the decision to end her child's life, faced an impossible moral choice, the latter is countered by the choices of narrative self-representation

"I was growing and growing": Ruth Elias sharing the story of how dough expanded under her apron. Created by Claude Lanzmann during the filming of *Shoah*. (Used by permission of the United States Holocaust Memorial Museum and Yad Vashem, the Holocaust Martyrs and Heroes' Remembrance Authority, Jerusalem.)

through which Elias asserts the dominance of life over death in her memory. This "breakage" of the frame of death also extends, however, into the aesthetic frame that underlies *Shoah*: in framing her death experiences with "life," Elias also interrupts Lanzmann's auteurist obsession with death. And insofar as at the heart of this obsession is the "inside" of the gas chambers, Elias, in testifying to the horrifying experience of a mother ending the life of her child, also offers glimpses into a different, gendered "inside" of the Shoah that remains, perhaps by aesthetic necessity, excluded from *Shoah*.

Coda: The Afterlife of Victims as Survivors

The complex subjectivities of Filip Müller and Ruth Elias as survivors and witnesses that emerge from an examination of the *Shoah* outtakes highlight the limited attention of Lanzmann's film to its interviewees as agents, both in the past and in the testimonial present. As Dominick LaCapra observes in his seminal article on *Shoah*, the film not only offers "a limited construction of the role of Jewish agency and resistance in the Holocaust," but in the end also pays very little attention to the interviewees' multifarious attempts and diverse forms of "working-through" the past, rather than simply reliving it, as Lanzmann would have it.[51] The filmmaker instead seems to be interested in the witnesses solely as victims of an event from which they "return" but cannot redeem themselves.[52] Perhaps driven partly by his own melancholy repetition-compulsion, Lanzmann—and ultimately the final version of the film itself—remains "blind," as it were, or at least inattentive to the complexities of how survivors, as filmed witnesses and as subjects of the director's questions, narratively represent and negotiate their relationship to a traumatic past in the testimonial present—what LaCapra calls "the afterlife of the victims as survivors."[53] The "force" of the filmmaker's desire, as LaCapra puts it, may then ultimately "desensitize one to the problem and process of attempting to move, however incompletely, from victim to survivor and agent in survivors themselves."[54]

In critically examining the testimonies of Filip Müller and Ruth Elias—both in the *Shoah* outtakes and in the film itself—this chapter ultimately also sought to make a contribution to the "extensive study" of the "afterlife of victims as survivors" that LaCapra calls for.[55] In particular, the cases of Müller and Elias suggest that a focus on the agencies of witnesses as survivors might also open up possibilities to further investigate the role of gender in the testimonies of the *Shoah* interviewees without falling into the trap of reaffirming the gender dichotomies that permeate the theatrical version of the film. As Hirsch and Spitzer note, *Shoah* inscribes gender differences that associate femininity largely with "hiding, passivity, lament, and invisibility" and, furthermore, present women as an embodiment of "danger and death" that threatens the emotional stability and survival of male witnesses. The presence of females in the film, Hirsch and Spitzer conclude, ultimately serves the function of enabling male testimony while women themselves are largely rendered speechless.[56] In her insistence on witnessing *by* survival, the preeminence of instinct, and the existence of hope, Ruth Elias undoubtedly challenges gender dichotomies that resign women to death and speechlessness; it would be problematic, however, to take her testimony as a basis for making broader claims about the experiences of women in the film and its outtakes. Attending to the voices of female Jewish survivors like Ruth Elias in the film and its outtakes would instead require finding a gender-conscious position that is empathetic toward the witnesses' voices but, at the same time, offers a critical and analytical perspective that highlights the complexities of their subjectivities as witnesses, without succumbing to the risk of identification and gender essentialism. Such an approach would, as its starting point, require a careful analysis of the many other female voices in the film's outtakes.[57]

A continued reassessment of the film's legacy would also necessitate a sustained comparative reconsideration of the extended testimonies by male Jewish survivors such as Filip Müller, Richard Glazar, and Abraham Bomba, whose voices are the central, indispensable "fixtures" around which the film's narrative is constructed, but whose singular and diverse experiences *as men* remain in need of critical attention, especially as they may emerge from the juxtaposition of their extended testimonies to both those by women and to the edited interviews in the film itself. As the discussion of Filip Müller's testimony in this chapter intimated, such a reconsideration would require particular attention to the role women play in the men's representation of their experiences, both in the film and in the outtakes. As Hirsch and Spitzer note, some of the most powerful and memorable scenes in the film involve the breakdown of speech in the testimonies of male Jewish survivors precisely at moments when their discourse focuses and revolves around their encounters with women, most conspicuously in the interviews with Filip Müller and Abraham Bomba.[58] While these scenes contribute substantially to the film's construction of gender differences and the casting of women as the embodiment of "death and danger," the extended interviews with male Jewish witnesses in the outtakes suggest a more complex representation of their relationship to the past and their experiences, in which references to women take on the precarious function of both a threat and an encouragement to survival; in this way, their testimonies both complicate the binary gender distinctions that Hirsch and Spitzer have discerned in the film and further highlight how the "gendered" nature of testimonies in *Shoah* emerges from, but is also obscured by, the aesthetic and interrogative choices of the film's director and interviewer. Like this analysis of the testimonies by Filip Müller and Ruth Elias, such an examination would not counter but rather further complement Lanzmann's "vision" as an auteur, who, after all, hoped that the film would not become "an icon of the past" but remain a living testimony to the presence of the Holocaust in our time.[59]

Notes

This article was made possible (in part) by funds granted to the author through a Sosland Family Fellowship at the Center for Advanced Holocaust Studies.

Epigraph: Claude Lanzmann, *The Patagonian Hare: A Memoir*, trans. Frank Wynne (New York: Farrar, Straus & Giroux, 2012), 438.

1. As Lanzmann notes: "In a certain way these people had to be transformed into actors. They recount their own history. But just retelling is not enough. They had to act it out, that is, they had to give themselves over to it. . . . They have to be put into a certain state of mind but also into a certain physical disposition. Not in order to make them speak, but so that their speech can suddenly communicate, become charged with an extra dimension." Marc Chevrie and Hervé Le Roux, "Site and Speech: An Interview with Claude Lanzmann about *Shoah*," in *Claude Lanzmann's* Shoah: *Key Essays*, ed. Stuart Liebman (London: Oxford University Press, 2007), 3750; here, 41, 44–45.

2. Claude Lanzmann *Shoah* Collection, interview with Ruth Elias (RG-60.50003, Film ID 3112, Camera Rolls 1–2; Film ID 3113, Camera Rolls 3–4; Film ID 3114, Camera Rolls 5–9A; Film ID 3115, Camera Roll 10; Film ID 3116, Camera Rolls 11–12; Film ID 3117, Camera Rolls 13–15; Film ID 3118, Camera Rolls 16–18), US Holocaust Memorial Museum and Yad Vashem and State of Israel. All transcriptions from the interview, which was conducted in English, are my own. The transcriptions give Elias's original statements; errors in grammar or diction are reproduced without any corrections.

3. Though Müller and Elias give different dates, it is clear that they are both referring to the same events. Müller "think(s) it was March 8th or 9th," while Elias identifies the date as March 7, 1944, noting that the people from the camp who were murdered that day belonged to the "September transport—the transport that came in three months before us in the family camp."

4. Interview with Ruth Elias (RG-60.50003, Film ID 3116, Camera Rolls 11–12).

5. Whereas Ruth Elias's extended testimony in the outtakes totals 3.4 hours in length, she appears in *Shoah* for 4:34 minutes; the extended interview with Filip Müller is 4.8 hours, while his testimony in the film comprises 65:01 minutes.

6. On the film's simultaneous neglect and inscription of gender differences, see Marianne Hirsch and Leo Spitzer, "Gendered Translations: Claude Lanzmann's

Shoah," in Liebman, *Claude Lanzmann's* Shoah, 175–90; here, 177. First published in *Gendering War Talk*, ed. Miriam Cooke and Angela Woolacott (Princeton, NJ: Princeton University Press, 1993), 3–19.

7. Hirsch and Spitzer, "Gendered Translations," 182, 178.

8. Marc Chevrie and Hervé Le Roux, "Site and Speech: An Interview with Claude Lanzmann about *Shoah*," in Liebman, *Claude Lanzmann's* Shoah, 37–50; here, 38.

9. Lanzmann, *The Patagonian Hare*, 421–22. See also the interview with Jean-Michel Frodon, in which Lanzmann notes: "I wanted only men of the special commandos. This choice had tremendous consequences and still does: *they were the only witnesses to the extermination of their people.*" Frodon, "The Work of the Filmmaker: An Interview with Claude Lanzmann," in *Cinema and the Shoah*, ed. Jean-Michael Frodon, trans. Anna Harrison and Tom Mes (Albany: State University of New York Press, 2010), 93–106; here, 96; emphasis mine.

10. Lanzmann, *The Patagonian Hare*, 423.

11. Lanzmann, 423.

12. Lanzmann, 423–24: "I became convinced that there would be no archive footage, no individual stories, that the living would be self-effacing so that the dead might speak through them, that there would be no 'I,' however fantastical or fascinating or atypical an individual fate might be; that, on the contrary, the film would take a strict form—in German a *Gestalt*—recounting the fate of the people as a whole, and that those who spoke for them, forgetting themselves and supremely conscious of their duty to pass on their memories, would naturally express themselves in the name of all, considering the question of their own survival almost as anecdotal, of little interest, since they too were fated to die—which is why I consider them as 'revenants' rather than as survivors." For the notion of "Gestalt" in the context of Hilberg's influence on Lanzmann and *Shoah*, see Noah Shenker's chapter in this volume.

13. "*Shoah*, as I've said a thousand times, is not a film about survival; it is, not, in particular, a film about their survival, their personal survival. And it is not of themselves that they speak in in the film. They never say 'I,' they are never telling us their their personal story or how they escaped. . . . The survivors do not use the 'I,' they say 'we,' they are literally the spokepersons of the dead." Frodon, "The Work of the Filmmaker," 96.

14. Dominick LaCapra, "Claude Lanzmann's *Shoah*: 'Here There Is No Why,'" in *History and Memory After Auschwitz* (Ithaca, NY: Cornell University Press, 1998), 95–138; here, 106.

15. Müller had given testimony in 1945 at a Slovakian court before later testifying, on his own initiative, at the Auschwitz trials in Frankfurt. By the time he met Lanzmann in 1975, he ostensibly was living in Germany and in the middle of writing his memoir in collaboration with a German editor. Many accounts in the outtakes, down to specific phrases, echo Müller's recollections in the memoir, thus raising the question as to what extent his work on the memoir—and collaboration with the editor—may have shaped his testimony and language in the interview with Lanzmann. In general, a further investigation of the complex subjectivities of Jewish witnesses in the outtakes would also require a consideration of how these subjectivities are articulated and performed differently across diverse media, including memoirs.

16. *The Death Factory: Document on Auschwitz*, ed. Ota Kraus and Erich Kulka, trans. from the Czech by Stephen Jolly (Oxford: Pergamon, 1966). The volume was first published in Czech in 1946. For Müller's testimony, see 156–60.

17. Interview with Filip Müller (RG-60.5012, Film ID 3206, Camera Rolls 1–4; Film 3207, Camera Rolls 5–7; Film ID 3208, Camera Rolls 8–11; Film ID 3209, Camera Rolls 12–14; Film ID 3210, Camera Rolls 15–17; 3211, Camera Rolls 18–21). When quoting from the Müller outtakes, I first provide the original German and then English translations. All transcriptions and translations are my own. As with the outtakes of Ruth Elias's interview, I have retained grammatical and syntactical errors as well as errors in diction in Müller's original statements in German.

18. In the conversation with Müller Lanzmann attributes the story to Zalman Levental, who also kept a diary (found in 1962). However, in *The Scrolls of Auschwitz*, which includes the diaries of both men, the story is attributed to Leib Langfus. See *The Scrolls of Auschwitz*, ed. and trans. from the Hebrew by Bernard Mark (Tel Aviv: Am 'Oved, 1985), 211.

19. Interview with Filip Müller (RG-60.5012, Film ID 3211, Camera Roll 18).

20. Müller confirms this identification and its mediation through the singing in his memoir: "To me the bearing of my countrymen seemed an exemplary gesture of national honour [sic] and national pride which stirred my soul. I proudly identified with them." Filip Müller, *Eyewitness Auschwitz: Three Years in the Gas Chambers*, literary collaboration with Helmut Freitag, ed. and trans. Susanne Flatauer (Chicago: Ivan R. Dee, 1979), 111. Originally published in German under the title *Sonderbehandlung: Drei Jahre in den Krematorien und Gaskammern von Auschwitz*, Deutsche Bearbeitung von Helmut Freitag (München: Steinhausen, 1979).

21. *Shoah*, directed by Claude Lanzmann, New Yorker Films, 1985. Unless otherwise indicated, all transcriptions and translations from the film are my own.

22. The English translation in the film's subtitles of "berichten" as "to bear witness" (rather than "to report") and of "Du must hier raus" as "You must get out *alive*" (my emphasis) further reinforces the paradigm of survival as motivated by a desire to witness. The full translation of the passage in the film's subtitles reads as follows: "So you want to die. But that's senseless. Your death won't give us back our lives. That's no way. You must get out alive. You must bear witness to our suffering, and to the injustice done to us."

23. Dorota Glowacka, *Disappearing Traces* (Seattle: University of Washington Press, 2012), 28; my emphasis.

24. Hirsch and Spitzer, "Gendered Translations," 180–81.

25. Interview with Filip Müller (RG-60.5012, Film ID 3210, Camera Rolls 15–17).

26. Interview with Filip Müller (RG-60.5012, Film ID 3210, Camera Rolls 15–17).

27. Interview with Filip Müller (RG-60.5012, Film ID 3210, Camera Rolls 15–17). Müller also recounts his forceful removal from the gas chambers by the women in his memoir in the chapter devoted to "The tragedy of the Family Camp," where he adds that he actually resisted the women's actions: "Before I could give an answer to her spirited speech [*Bevor ich noch weiter darüber nachdenken konnte*], the girls took hold of me and dragged me protesting [*trotz meiner Gegenwehr*] to the door of the gas chamber" (*Eyewitness Auschwitz/ Sonderbehandlung* 114/180). While both the German and English versions of Müller's recollections emphasize his reluctance to leave the gas chambers, thus further mitigating his agency as a survivor-witness at this moment, the German original also conveys a lack of reflection (*nachdenken*).

28. Nevertheless, Müller also notes elsewhere in the interview that bearing witness, combined with the prospect of an uprising, was a motivation for survival. Ironically, given the film's affirmation of this desire as a basis for survival, it is Lanzmann who questions it in the outtakes, asking Müller whether such a motivation is not "constructed" after the fact.

29. Interview with Filip Müller (RG-60.5012, Film ID 3210, Camera Rolls 15–17).

30. Interview with Filip Müller (RG-60.5012, Film ID 3210, Camera Rolls 15–17).

31. Interview with Filip Müller (RG-60.5012, Film ID 3210, Camera Rolls 15–17).

32. Interview with Filip Müller (RG-60.5012, Film ID 3210, Camera Rolls 15–17).

33. Interview with Ruth Elias (RG-60.50003, Film ID 3116, Camera Rolls 11–12).

34. Interview with Ruth Elias (RG-60.50003, Film ID 3117, Camera Rolls 13–15).

35. Interview with Ruth Elias (RG-60.50003, Film ID 3117, Camera Rolls 13–15).

36. Interview with Ruth Elias (RG-60.50003, Film ID 3114, Camera Rolls 5–9A).

37. Interview with Ruth Elias (RG-60.50003, Film ID 3117, Camera Rolls 13–15).

38. Interview with Ruth Elias (RG-60.50003, Film ID 3117, Camera Rolls 13–15).

39. Interview with Ruth Elias (RG-60.50003, Film ID 3117, Camera Rolls 13–15).

40. Interview with Ruth Elias (RG-60.50003, Film ID 3114, Camera Rolls 5–9A).

41. In addition to her oral testimonies, Elias also wrote a memoir that, as its title suggests, emphasizes hope and survival instead of death: *Triumph of Hope: From Theresienstadt and Auschwitz to Israel*, trans. from the German by Margot Bettauer Dembo (New York: John Wiley, 1998). Originally published in German under the title, *Die Hoffnung erhielt mich am Leben* (München: Piper, 1988).

42. Describing her arrival and first experiences at Auschwitz, Elias notes: "In the morning a disgusting brew they called tea was served, and we pounced on it like a wild mob. . . . I can't explain our unbridled behavior in any other way except to say that animal instincts had taken over. All of us had come from the same social milieu; we were quite civilized and peaceful people. From now on, our instinct for survival would dictate our behavior" (Elias, *Triumph of Hope*, 109).

43. Interview with Ruth Elias (RG-60.50003, Film ID 3114, Camera Rolls 5–9A); my italics.

44. Interview with Ruth Elias (RG-60.50003, Film ID 3114, Camera Rolls 5–9A).

45. Interview with Ruth Elias (RG-60.50003, Film ID 3114, Camera Rolls 5–9A).

46. Interview with Ruth Elias (RG-60.50003, Film ID 3116, Camera Rolls 11–12).

47. Elias, *Triumph of Hope*, 82; italics in original.

48. Interview with Ruth Elias (RG-60.50003, Film ID 3115, Camera Roll 10).

49. Interview with Ruth Elias (RG-60.50003, Film ID 3115, Camera Roll 10).

50. I refer here to Dori Laub's call to assess the content of survivor testimonies not purely by historiographical standards of truth, but also by its narrative form, and by what this form in turn may suggest about the witness's relationship to the past. Laub cites the case of a survivor who, in recalling a revolt at Auschwitz, remembered the destruction of four chimneys, a number contested by historians, who questioned the reliability of the testimony. Laub, however, argues that the number, judged to be inaccurate by historical standards, reflects how the witness relates and tries to work-through a traumatic past. Thus, the recollection of destroyed crematoria was not a false memory of the past, but rather an indication of a "breaking of the frame of death" and "assertion of survival" in the testimonial present—according to Laub, the witness's "way of being, of

surviving, of resisting." Dori Laub, "Bearing Witness, or the Vicissitudes of Listening," in *Testimony. Crisis of Witnessing in Literature, Psychoanalysis, and History,* ed. Shoshana Felman and Dori Laub (New York: Routledge, 1992), 57–74; here, 59–60, 62.

51. LaCapra suggests that "working-through" traumatic experiences might take place when "language functions to provide some measure of conscious control, critical distance, and perspective." While such a "working-through" one's relation to the past "may never bring full transcendence of acting out (or being haunted by revenants and reliving the past in its shattered intensity)," it may nevertheless "enable processes of judgment and at least limited liability and ethically responsible agency." See "Holocaust Testimonies. Attending to the Victim's Voice," in LaCapra, *Writing History, Writing Trauma* (Baltimore: Johns Hopkins University Press, 2001), 86–113; here, 90.

52. On this point, see also LaCapra, who observes that "Lanzmann seems to have been more interested in victims, especially dead or shattered victims, than in survivors—except for survivors who remained close to their experience as victims" ("Claude Lanzmann's *Shoah*," 133).

53. Lanzmann, in the context of his epistemological insistence on the "obscenity of understanding," describes "blindness" as the "vital condition of creation" for the film, stressing, however, that it amounts to a form of "seeing": "Blindness should be understood here as seeing in its purest form, the only way not to avert the gaze from a reality that is literally blinding: blindness as clear-sightedness itself." Lanzmann, "Hier ist kein Warum," in Liebman, *Claude Lanzmann's Shoah*, 51–52; here, 51. I would like to thank Erin McGlothlin for reminding me of this passage.

54. LaCapra, "Holocaust Testimonies," 98.

55. LaCapra borrows and mobilizes the Freudian term "working-through" not solely as a psychoanalytical tool to describe a survivor's way of relating to and processing a past (or that of a traumatized subject more broadly), but rather also as a critical trope to conceptualize the relationship of historical studies to trauma, and theory to practice—that is, the way the researcher, as reader and viewer, relates to objects (and subjects) of study. In particular, LaCapra's reflections on *Shoah* call for the viewer of the film to be conscious of his or her own subject position vis-à-vis the film's interviewees (and any potentially "unchecked" transferential investments)—in other words, to "work-through" the potential identifications the film provokes (with particular witnesses, but also with Lanzmann himself, as both actor and auteur).

56. Hirsch and Spitzer, "Gendered Translations," 179, 180, 186.

57. The film includes testimonies by twelve male and five female Jewish survivors, the latter including Paula Biren, Inge Deutschkron, Ruth Elias, and Gertrude Schneider, as well as the latter's mother, Charlotte Hirschhorn, who is not identified by name in the film. The outtakes include interviews with two women that were not included in the film: Ada Lichtman and Rita Wassermann, Gertrude Schneider's sister, who participated in the extended interview, together with her mother. As I have argued elsewhere, the subjectivities of these female Jewish witnesses are in themselves testimonies to alternate oral histories with implications for gender that cannot be subsumed into a single, homogenous narrative: Rita Wasserman, in a gendered form of recall, reveals an imagination of resistance that also translates into the frame of the testimony, in its refusal to acknowledge the hopelessness of death in place of an affirmation of life; Paula Biren engages in a sustained reflection on survivor guilt that suggests efforts at working-through the past that escape Lanzmann's attentiveness and are not visible in the film, where her testimony is integrated into a broader narrative of collective amnesia; Ada Lichtman distances herself, in memory, from her experiences of death and thus disappoints the filmmaker's desire both for a proximity to the gas chambers and a literal repetition of the past. See my "The Afterlives of Victims as Survivors: Female Voices and Gendered Testimony in the Outtakes of Claude Lanzmann's *Shoah*" (unpublished manuscript).

58. Hirsch and Spitzer, 180 and elsewhere.

59. Graham Fuller, "Searching for the Stamp of Truth. Claude Lanzmann reflects on the making of *Shoah*," *Cineaste* (Spring 2011): 16–19; here, 16.

12 | The Role of Song in Claude Lanzmann's *Shoah* Outtakes

"They were killing us and we were singing"

Leah Wolfson

In the opening credits to his epic 1985 documentary *Shoah*, Claude Lanzmann introduces the haunting voice that will begin the film. Simon Srebnik, member of the infamous *Sonderkommando* at Chełmno, one of the first Nazi death camps, outlives his fellow slave laborers by virtue of his singing voice. Indeed, the first sound we hear in the film is Srebnik's haunting song, sung from a rowboat along the Narew River. The highly evocative, visually stunning scene evokes Charon rowing along the River Styx: a silent, peaceful sylvan scene that erases the bodies buried beneath the deep green trees. With these opening moments, Lanzmann establishes role of music in *Shoah*: to function as a voice from the dead. Lanzmann reinforces this with the two other instances of song that feature prominently in the film: the guard Franz Suchomel's chilling "work song" from the Treblinka death camp that, the latter notes, "no Jew knows today"; and a Yiddish song from Gertrude Schneider and her mother that goes untranslated and unsubtitled and that functions as a depiction of the trauma of survival. With the notable exception of Schneider's song, these performances are framed as singular, individual acts of memory. The communal aspects of the songs and singing are almost completely absent in *Shoah*. This choice too reflects Lanzmann's vision of the singular voice, and of the singular story that "speaks" for the whole, and, in many cases here, on behalf of the dead. As Marianne Hirsch and Leo Spitzer explicate in their article "Gendered Translations": "In this sense they are like Orpheus, the witness: the one who has come out of Hades alive, and whose song is made hauntingly beautiful by an encounter no other living human being has been able to experience and to speak about."[1] These songs—and their singers—serve and shape the overall narrative of *Shoah* as a tome of witnesses whose voices emanate from inside the machinery of death.

Left on the cutting-room floor, however, were hours of footage that depict a very different story.[2] Rather than featuring voices from those who serve merely as living corpses, the songs from the outtakes of *Shoah* (at least those sung by survivors) instead portray the complex reality of life and living inside the most extreme of circumstances. While Lanzmann's film takes his audience into the heart of the Gorgon, his unused footage—in particular, his unused musical "performances"—depict a far more nuanced portrait of life inside the graveyard itself: a complexity that has no place in the final film. Indeed, amid these musical moments that could serve as mere additional carefully planned acts of pathos, an aspect of each survivor's story—and by extension, his or her ownership over it—escapes and overtakes the narrative that Lanzmann seeks to control. It is in this way that the film's musical outtakes of survivors become markedly different from those that Lanzmann frames in the final cut of the film. The performances in the outtakes thus reveal the complex interplay between life and death that the final film belies or ignores altogether.

This essay will read the instances of song performed in the outtakes alongside those included in the final cut of the film in order to illuminate the ways in which a universal language of death is countered by complex individual realities. While the songs that Lanzmann features in the final film exist as powerful remnants of genocide and mass murder, I argue that they simultaneously evacuate the particular and at times very contradictory meanings that music assumes in these and other testimonies more broadly. By examining the outtakes of songs and singing, we learn something new about the blind spots within the final film, and the ways in which, in service of giving voice to the dead, the many voices of the living are all too often made mute. As Shirli Gilbert notes in her article about Yiddish songs, "Buried Monuments: Yiddish Songs and Holocaust Memory": "We may no longer believe that songs will enable us to 'fathom the soul of a people,' but they can perhaps help us to memorialize the victims more honestly by acknowledging their diverse human-ness."[3] This "diverse human-ness" is what Lanzmann and others elide when the machinery of death—and not the individuals who were themselves caught up within it—becomes the primary signifier for the Holocaust experience. Ultimately, then, by examining the songs in both the outtakes and the final film, we begin to see a complication of a normative narrative, an interruption, and a challenge to any simplified meaning of "survivor" or "victim."[4]

"You hear a song, you cry": Gertrude Schneider and Songs of Youth

Lanzmann's interview with Gertrude Schneider and her mother demonstrates the ways in which the outtakes and the final film depict contrasting meanings using the same musical source. While the finished film relies upon gendered and flattened imagery of pathos—most often depicted as women crying or unable to speak at all—the outtakes instead reveal the Schneiders' nuanced relationship to music during the war and its multiple meanings and significations. The two minutes devoted to Gertrude Schneider and her mother occur in the film's final segment, just before the section that outlines the Warsaw Ghetto Uprising. The outtakes of Dr. Gertrude Schneider's interview last a little over two hours. Schneider received her PhD from the City University of New York and wrote two books about Austrian Jewry during the Holocaust: *Journey into Terror: The Story of the Riga Ghetto* (1979) and *Exile and Destruction: The Fate of Austrian Jews, 1938–1945* (1995).[5] Schneider was already a recognized scholar during the time that Lanzmann was interviewing; a Jewish Telegraph Agency article from February 17, 1977, entitled "War Criminal Faces Deportation," cites Schneider as an authority on the Holocaust in Latvia and further identifies her as "a City University of New York professor, Latvian history scholar, survivor of the Riga Ghetto and a naturalized citizen."[6] Unlike with Raoul Hilberg and Leib Garfunkel, fellow historians who are addressed as such, the film's final segment refers only to "Gertrude Schneider and her mother."

In *Shoah*'s theatrical release, the scene opens with a shot of an unidentified open field in winter. A woman's voice slowly, softly invades the landscape, at first barely audible, then growing louder. We are reminded of Simon Srebnik's haunting melody from the beginning of the film, floating over a very different, lush green landscape. Here, we see only a barren winter landscape, indistinguishable and unspecific. As the voice grows louder, Lanzmann cuts to the face of an old woman, who is barely singing along with the dominant, younger voice. The camera is in extreme close-up at this moment; the woman's face fills the whole screen as she buries her head in her hands (her nails painted in bright red polish), crying silently. Only then does the camera pull back, showing Gertrude Schneider and her mother seated on a couch, thus revealing the singer's face. The subtitle identifies both women merely as: "Gertrude Schneider and her mother (New York)." The scene also invokes traditional domesticity; Schneider is pictured knitting on the couch next to her mother. The published English-language transcript of the film, *Shoah: An Oral History of the Holocaust: The Complete Text of the Film*—but not the film—identifies these women as survivors of the ghetto.[7] Even here, however, what little context is provided is not specific. This scene commences the final segment of the film devoted to the Warsaw Ghetto. The viewer, then, would not be blamed for assuming that these two women were also from this locality. In this way, the most well-known ghetto swallows what is really the very specific experience of Viennese Jews being deported to the Riga Ghetto, whose Latvian Jews had already been killed by the time Schneider and those like her arrived.

The song itself (in Yiddish) goes completely untranslated and unexplained; it is the only portion of the film in Yiddish, Hebrew, or Polish that remains untranslated into French, English, or German for Lanzmann's comprehension. The scene becomes one of pure affect and emotional performance. Once again, as Hirsch and Spitzer note about this moment in the final film, "Gertrude Schneider sings but does not speak, and her nameless mother, overcome with the emotional weight of memory and the event captured by the camera, gestures but neither sings nor speaks." They are both, as Hirsch and Spitzer point out, heard only as the "emotional background" of the film.[8]

The interview with Schneider and her mother (as well as with her sister, whose voice, but not face, appear in the final film) takes place in Gertrude's

New York City apartment, in English, with smatterings of German taking place between her and her mother. It focuses on the German Jewish population who arrived in the Riga Ghetto just after the extermination of Latvian Jewry. Thus, the context in which this interview is placed within the final film is misleading at best. Lanzmann begins by asking Schneider about her book *Journey into Terror* and then transitions into the topics of arrival at the ghetto, ghetto life, transports, and extermination. Lanzmann seeks specific detail: "I want that you describe exactly the arrival"; "How did [the gas vans] look?" "During the trip, you were escorted by what kind of people?"[9] This type of detail-oriented question is typical of Lanzmann, who consistently asks for precision from his interview subjects. Schneider generally leads the interview, with her sister at times contributing additional information. Their mother is largely silent throughout the interview, and when she does speak, she uses German and often veers off topic.

Lanzmann does not ask about music until roughly halfway through the interview, during their discussion of ghetto life. Schneider and her sister have just finished describing pregnancy and abortion in the ghetto. Lanzmann asks: "But tell me about the songs, you used to sing them in the ghetto in which circumstances?" Schneider answers: "Well, at first . . . you know, when young people come together and there is no television and no movies and very few books and everything . . . you sing."[10] Songs are therefore described as a logical extension of youth, and the story that follows confirms this impression. Schneider recalls a song based on a song composed in the Börgermoor camp for "political prisoners" (a category that quickly included Jews) in Lower Saxony, Germany, circa 1933. The German song, entitled "Die Moorsoldaten," was composed by a young man in this camp whom Schneider does not name but refers to as "the Casanova of the ghetto."[11] "Die Moorsoldaten" (known also as "Börgermoorlied"), a communist song reminiscent of a march, is sung by Schneider and her sister as her mother looks on.[12] Schneider later relates how this young man was killed: "In Stützpunkt, where . . . you know, Stützpunkt was the place where they exhumed the bodies and burned them. And . . . and that is where he was killed eventually."[13] A song and a story of youth become a story of mass graves.

The second song introduces the melody that was ultimately incorporated into the final cut of the film: a Yiddish song entitled "Azoy muz seyn"

("That's how it must be"). Schneider explains that this was a song from the Latvian Jews, most of whom had been murdered prior to the arrival of the German Jews. In a grisly description of the state of the house Schneider and her family were assigned to occupy in the ghetto, she recalls a scene frozen in time, complete with food still on the table, blood on the walls, and a dead baby in the toilet.[14] The murders had, it seemed, just taken place, and the evidence was left frozen (literally and figuratively) in this particular ghetto house. Schneider thus describes the song (which is in Yiddish and originated in the Latvian Jewish population killed prior to Schneider's arrival at the ghetto) as "very, very poignant, it meant a lot to all of us. There were lots of songs, but these two . . . mean more than others."[15]

The final cut includes none of this context. Indeed, Schneider and her mother appear just prior to the film's extended final segment on the Warsaw Ghetto Uprising, which implies that they were Yiddish-speaking Polish survivors. Their status as German Jews in Latvia is elided. The mise-en-scène of this moment provides its own form of historical erasure. Schneider and her mother's voice are heard initially only as a voice-over to an unnamed, unidentified snowy empty field—an unusual departure for a film so intent on the specificity of place. When Schneider and her mother do appear, we first see only a tight shot of her mother, crying, her head in her hands, with red fingernail polish punctuating the visual. Only when the camera backs away do we see two people: Gertrude is shown knitting while turned toward her mother, now completely bereft and silent. The subtitle reads only: "NEW YORK—GERTRUDE SCHNEIDER and her mother."[16] Schneider's doctorate—and the expertise that goes with it—are not acknowledged, and the specificity of their story is completely erased. They instead embody affect and feminized emotional archetype. This is particularly striking in that it occurs just before the film's extended sequence on the Warsaw Ghetto Uprising: an event that centers almost completely on the agency and narratives of men.

Schneider's most vivid recollections of music—excluded from the final film but striking in the outtakes—is from the Kaiserwald concentration camp: she recalls the so-called Vilna girls, a transport from the Lithuanian ghetto.[17] In this segment of the interview Schneider's songs shift from commemoration of the dead to a far more complicated memory of life in an untenable situation. Whereas "Azoy muz seyn" recalled the near-complete extermination of Latvian Jewry, the songs of the "Vilna girls" conjure a somewhat joyous—if conflicted—affect between Schneider, her sister, and her mother.[18] Schneider frames these songs as both hopeful and bittersweet:

> When the . . . the Vilna transport came to Kaiserwald, to Riga, on September 25, 1943, and, uh, it was a young transport, most of the people were very young, and among them were some . . . extremely talented girls, and they sang those songs. They sang others as well, and they awoke a lot of . . . heartache in us, because Kaiserwald was totally different from the ghetto, and it was so harsh, and so bad that their songs made us long not only for our original homes but even to some extent for the ghetto as well.[19]

Schneider goes on to recall their songs, including a German song about the world outside, which went on unabated, in spite of their plight; and a Russian prewar melody about a soldier departing for war.[20] During both of these performances, Schneider's mother becomes animated for the first time in the nearly two-hour interview. Whereas the clip included in the final cut of the film depicts her as only a passive, tragic figure, here she has agency and voice. The Schneiders' songs enable them to speak as individuals in a way that exceeds the expectations of Lanzmann's interview. Ultimately, it is because Lanzmann does not control their testimony in these moments that he must excise them from his final film.

With one of the final songs of this outtake we begin to understand the full force of Lanzmann's exclusion. Schneider recalls a Polish song sung in Stutthof, another forced labor camp near the Chełmno death camp. Schneider sings only one line and hums the rest. She begins: "Mały biały domek . . . you know it?"[21] This very song begins Lanzmann's nine-and-a-half hour epic: Chełmno death camp survivor Simon Srebnik, being rowed down the Narew River, singing the song about little white houses in the countryside. As Srebnik performs it in the film, it is slow and mournful. As performed popularly, the melody can be upbeat and up-tempo. Lanzmann explains in his prologue that this and other songs prolonged Srebnik's life. A young boy recognized for his singing voice, the SS guards taught him folk melodies from their home and commanded him to entertain them. Srebnik survived longer than most on the *Sonderkommando* detail because of this talent. At the close of the war, Srebnik was shot and left for dead. However, he survived in the ditch in which he was shot. Lanzmann "discovered" Srebnik after viewing footage from the trial of Adolf Eichmann, where Srebnik testified in 1961. Lanzmann frames Srebnik as a ghostly visitor from another planet whose very presence haunts the film. He is frequently used as a speaker from and of the dead. We know only his brief wartime story; indeed, as with all the survivors in the film, we have no sense of him outside of this specific context.

By contrast, Schneider's rendering of the song encompasses many different associations simultaneously. While we do not see Lanzmann's reaction in the Schneider interview, her own response implies a look of surprise on Lanzmann's face. Schneider explains the meaning of the melody for her:

> Stutthof, when you walked in, there were little white houses
> with flowers and green roofs, and . . . and then there were

Gertrude Schneider sings a line from the Polish song "Mały biały domek," which she learned at the Stutthof forced labor camp. Created by Claude Lanzmann during the filming of *Shoah*. (Used by permission of the United States Holocaust Memorial Museum and Yad Vashem, the Holocaust Martyrs and Heroes' Remembrance Authority, Jerusalem.)

the girls from Łódź. . . . And all of a sudden, in the evening when it was quiet, they would sing. And, you know, little white houses: "Mały biały domek . . ." [Schneider hums the tune.] And it was also . . . it helped, it just helped. You know, don't forget my age at the time, a teenager, you hear a song, you cry.[22]

Schneider's performance of Mały biały domek (incomplete, and hummed in parts) assumes a sing-song quality that aligns with her largely positive memories of the moment in which she heard it. For Schneider, the song brought comfort; for Srebnik, it was part of the horror of his role as a slave to the German guards. The meaning of the song is, of course, both, as even Schneider points out when she explains that, "they [Polish girls] were thinking of their little white houses in Poland, but to us it was Stutthof. And it was horrible, it was . . . very, very, very upsetting, very upsetting."[23] The song is at once comfort and at the same time "upsetting" as a reminder of the slave labor camp in which they resided. Indeed, this song, which is not included in Schneider's rendering, is the reason she and her mother appear in the final film at all. This story is revealed in an oral history taken by United States Holocaust Memorial Museum musicologist Dr. Brett Werb in November 2006, twenty-one years after the release of *Shoah*. In this interview, Schneider recalls her time with Lanzmann. As Schneider remembers, Lanzmann began crying when she recalled this Polish melody in recognition of this connection.[24]

Ultimately, then, the full force of the complexity of meaning of this song, as Schneider explains it, is lost in the final film. Doris Bergen similarly reflects on the inherent contradictions of the song and narrative in this out-take: "Muted in Lanzmann's film but not silenced, Gertrude Schneider, her mother, and her sister embody and express a view of history that integrates past and present and encompasses victims, witnesses, and scholars of the Holocaust. Together, these women convey the reality of bottomless trauma at the same time that they offer a glimpse at the astonishing human capacity to survive, live, and connect."[25] Trauma and survival live side by side, as indeed, they must. Overall, Schneider's songs present a multifaceted portrayal of life within a place of death rather than a voice as emissary *from* the dead. Lanzmann's final film aimed for the former and wrote out the latter.

"We were so young": Ruth Elias and the Murder of Motherhood

Like Schneider, Ruth Elias's interview also depicts a complicated story of youth, survival, and death. Elias, a Czech Jew, was deported from her home in Ostrava (now in the Czech Republic) to Theresienstadt and later to Auschwitz. Of her two hour and forty minute interview, Lanzmann includes in the final film only a few minutes in which Elias describes the transport from Theresienstadt to Auschwitz. Ruth Elias's full interview teases out a far more complex and disturbing story of infanticide: a story in which music does not figure per se, but instead foreshadows. Like Schneider, Elias understands music—even within the Holocaust context—as an expression of youthful exuberance. This narrative of youth and survival amid death and murder will become the linchpin of the devastating story that Elias tells.

Elias emphasizes her youthful naïveté throughout the interview. The first example of this comes with her decision to marry her then "boyfriend," as she calls him, just before her father's transport from Theresienstadt to Auschwitz. Elias's memory of innocence becomes one of death—a theme throughout her testimony that the musical interludes will highlight. She describes her quick marriage and her father's reaction:

> I'll never in my life forget the expression of my father's face. He started to cry. And . . . I didn't know—instead that my father shall be glad and it is a joy for him that his daughter is married, he started to cry, and I didn't understand why. Today I understand it very well. . . . My father somehow gave me his blessings, and I told him goodbye and that was the last time I ever saw my father. I never saw him again in my life.[26]

Because of her marriage, Elias was spared a spot on the transport that sent her father to his death—a reality that she could not (or would not) see at the time. Her love for her boyfriend prevented her from understanding the implications of her decision, and, by extension, from truly saying goodbye to her father. Elias clings to this narrative of youthful naïveté even as she describes wrenching experiences in Theresienstadt and Auschwitz: "Youth, you know, it's all connected to youth."[27]

Elias's songs are all related to her time in Theresienstadt and reflect the mentality of a young woman who wants to live at all costs. She sings two songs: one composed in the ghetto in Czech, and a Hebrew liturgical standard, "Hine Ma Tov" ("Behold, how good"), based on the first verse of Psalm 133. Elias accompanies herself on the accordion for both songs and presents an upbeat, expressive style that completely belies the tragic story she will relay just a few minutes later. She translates the Czech song:

> Everything goes when it is possible. Even if the, if the time is so very hard, some kind of humor is still in our hearts. Every day we have to move there and forth, and only in thirty words we can write home, but tomorrow the time is beginning again. And the time is coming nearer and nearer when we will again pick up our *Päckele* and go home again, and everything goes when you want that it shall go. And the day will come and we will laugh about the ruins of the ghetto. . . . It is full of hope when you think about the words. That is what we sang there, and everyone who went through Terezin and will hear this song, will sing the words with you.[28]

Elias performed the Hebrew melody, "Hine Ma Tov," in a similarly upbeat manner, although it can be and has been played in slow and mournful fashions as well. Elias uses the song to portray the community of young, optimistic people of which she was a part. Elias ends her description and performance of song with an anecdote: she recalls stealing bread dough in the Theresienstadt kitchen where she worked. Elias received this privileged position, she explains, due to her "cheerful," or "fröhlich," attitude and voice.[29] She hides the dough under her apron, and her friends refuse to let her out of the kitchen. Elias remembers: "And it started to grow, the yeast dough, here, behind my apron, and I started to grow, and I wanted to leave to put the dough into my living quarters. And all the time I had to clap here [she pats her chest] and I was growing and growing and all the kitchen was laughing. You see, there was humor in our heart, as just the hymn, which I sang, said."[30] Song, music, and performance are all intimately intertwined with memories of life and survival embodied by Elias's time at Theresienstadt.

The story that follows this depiction, however, casts a pall on the innocence of youth and the songs that represent it. The remainder of Elias's interview concerns the discovery of her pregnancy and its implications as she is deported "to the East," to Auschwitz. When Elias's attempt to procure an abortion in Theresienstadt fails, she is forced to conceal her condition as long as possible. She survives a selection at Auschwitz, a transport to Ravensbrück, and a further transport to Auschwitz under an assumed name. Finally, however, Elias finds herself in one of Mengele's experiments: to see how long a child can live without food. Elias describes the agony of watching her malnourished daughter slowly die of hunger, until "a woman doctor" (as Elias describes her)[31] gives her the opportunity to kill her baby

Ruth Elias sings the Hebrew melody "Hine Ma Tov" to portray the community of young, optimistic people in Theresienstadt of which she was a part. Created by Claude Lanzmann during the filming of *Shoah*. (Used by permission of the United States Holocaust Memorial Museum and Yad Vashem, the Holocaust Martyrs and Heroes' Remembrance Authority, Jerusalem.)

with an overdose of morphine. Elias recalls the doctor's words: "I've made an oath, of Hippocrates, and I must save lives. You're young, and I must save your life. The child can't live; look at the child, how it's looking. But you are young and I must save you. And you will give this to your child because I can't."[32] Youth becomes an integral part of this searing narrative of infanticide.[33] The songs, then, while not an explicit part of this story, play an implicit role in what they represent. Indeed, for Elias, the song becomes part of a larger landscape of her experience of the Holocaust as a young woman. In that experience, youth and death cannot be separated; one becomes intertwined with the other.[34] Elias thus relates youth to life and survival. Indeed, it is this narrative that Elias will deploy to explain the infanticide at the heart of her testimony.

This incongruous image of youth, survival, and sacrifice stands in stark contrast to the ways in which a moment of song is remembered by Filip Müller, who appears in the final cut of the film. A Czech survivor from the *Sonderkommando* at Auschwitz, Müller (whose interview is conducted in German) recalls the liquidation of the Czech family camp on the nights of July 10 and 11, 1944. He describes a chaotic, desperate scene in which the surviving Jews (including approximately one hundred children) begin to grasp their fate. Müller recalls: "Suddenly, as though in a chorus, like a chorus, they all began to sing. The whole 'undressing room' rang with the Czech national anthem, and then the *Hatikvah*. That moved me terribly that . . ."[35] Müller paints a portrait of a single voice, in its final death throes. "I realized that my life had become meaningless," he says. "Why go on living? For what? So I went into the gas chamber with them, resolved to die." He reports that he is stopped by a young woman who tells him, "'So you want to die. But that's senseless. Your death won't give us back our lives. That's no way. You must get out of here alive, you must bear witness to our suffering, to the injustice done to us."[36] Here, then, song (and women's songs at that) are both of and from the dead, literally and metaphorically. This example—one of the more striking and memorable testimonies in the film—typifies Lanzmann's use of song as a relatively straightforward signifier for death. Indeed, this is the role that the majority of the survivors in his film plays: voices of and from the dead. The last lines of the film highlight this portrayal. Simha Rottem, survivor of and participant in the Warsaw Ghetto Uprising, wanders the now-destroyed streets of the ghetto after its final liquidation: "Yes, I was alone all the time. Except for that woman's voice, and a man I met as I came out of the sewers, I was along throughout my tour of the ghetto. I didn't meet a living soul. At one point, I recall feeling a kind of peace, of serenity. I said to myself, I'm the last Jew. I'll wait for the morning, and for the Germans."[37] The voice of the last survivor in the film is a voice consigned to its own eventual silencing. While Rottem survives to tell the tale, his own anticipated, even hoped-for, death gets the last word.

Given this narrative, the larger question posed by the Schneider and Elias outtakes concerns the potential reasons for their exclusion from the final cut of the film. Lanzmann's focus of his film remains quite explicit: only the extermination process, and only those people who served as witnesses, perpetrators, and bystanders to that particular chapter of Holocaust history. In an interview with *Cahiers*, Lanzmann describes the "types" of survivors he sought to find for his film: "I wanted very specific types—those who had been in the very charnel houses of the extermination, direct witnesses of the death of their people."[38] For this reason, he includes short clips of the testimony (musical and otherwise) of both of these women. However, the full force of their song, and, by extension, the full force of their testimony, is lost. I suggest that their exclusion speaks to the role of music in both Gertrude Schneider's and Ruth Elias's accounts, and the ways in which that music escapes the careful control of the interview process that Lanzmann wants to contain. Songs break both the language and the medium of Lanzmann's interviews. Moreover, they serve as an active memory that defies the "script" that Lanzmann seeks to impose upon them.

For both women, music speaks to the "performance" of youth, and, even more profoundly, the performance of a youth closely intertwined with the experience of death. For Schneider, this came in experiencing the remnants of death: hearing songs from an exterminated Latvian Jewish community, young Jewish women from Łódź singing about the white houses of Stutthof, Russian songs about leaving for war that became anthems for the coming and goings of the ghetto that could end in death. "They were killing us and we were singing, isn't this, isn't this a scream?" she sarcastically remarks.[39] For Elias, songs represent youth, but a youth that remains linked to the death of her baby girl. In both instances, life, death, and survival all exist simultaneously. Lanzmann's film does not seek to stage such dynamics; it asks instead for emissaries *from* the dead. The songs Lanzmann features in the film highlight the machinery of death over the individual stories of complicated survival. Srebnik's haunting song stands in for those killed at Chełmno. Müller's recollection of the Hatikva in the gas chamber is literally of screams from the dead. The songs of the living—and the conflicting narratives that they represent—have no place in the final film.

Ultimately, then, Lanzmann's specific framing of these complex musical performances and narratives in the final film excises the complexity of what are multilayered identities of victimhood and survival. In the context of *Shoah*, the film's time and attention are devoted not only to the death camp process, but also to the "survivor" as himself (or, as we have seen all too rarely, *herself*) as a signifier *for* that death. If we consider the full interviews, however, a very different portrait emerges. In these cases, the binaries of death and life, celebration and defeat, murder and survival, are blurred; at times, the borders between them are elided completely. The question then becomes: what—and whose—story is remembered through these performances. They do not simply (as perhaps Lanzmann might have hoped) memorialize or inhabit the dead. Instead, they inhabit a far more complex space between history and memory; life and death; artifact and changing, living entities. Shirli Gilbert reminds us of the many ways in which music and song both transform and are transformed by memory:

> When considering song in a memorial context, then, the object is slippery: how do we define 'the song itself,' when it exists in various transcriptions and recordings, across an extended time-span? [Different versions] further complicate the question of song's potential role as a bearer of memory. In short, in order to function as agents of memory, songs unavoidably have to be recreated.[40]

Gilbert points to the ways in which songs are living embodiments of the present as much as relics of the past. In a similar fashion, both Elias's and Schneider's songs become enmeshed in the larger narratives of the ways in which they conceive of themselves and their wartime identities. For Schneider, songs were part of a tenuous camaraderie that quickly unraveled with every passing day. For Elias, music symbolizes a remembrance of youth—youth that is complicated by its simultaneous connection to both survival and infanticide. In both cases, the song and its performance are haunted by past and present at the same time.

In Lanzmann's final film, song and music are powerful representations of a process of death that would otherwise be rendered silent. Neither purely redemptive nor clear acts of resistance, songs and singing in *Shoah* become haunting reminders of the murdered. To that end, they reach beyond any individual story. In fact, they rely upon a single voice to represent an entire category of death: Srebnik's haunting voice accompanies his narrative of mechanized killing; Müller's narrative of the *Hatikvah* in the gas chambers becomes the last words of the soon-to-be-annihilated Czech family camp; Schneider's song in the film is the precursor to the destruction of the Warsaw Ghetto. Lanzmann's film—focused as it is on the enormity of the crime—elevates these voices from their individual stories to the status of voices and representatives of what the writer and survivor Ka-Tzetnik (Yehiel Dinur) called "Planet Auschwitz." In the process of this elevation, Lanzmann evacuates the complex individual meaning from within each of these stories. Indeed, he erases what Thomas Trezise calls the "'how' of memory":

> At stake in the stories told by survivors is not only what happened but *how* it is remembered; and the "how" of memory in turn not only has, itself, a history but suggests accordingly that, as an event, a traumatic historical event whose repercussions have far from diminished with time, the Holocaust must be understood to include its own aftermath.[41]

With a focus on the "what" over and above the "how" of memory, *Shoah*, in its finished form, skews toward the collective truth as opposed to the individual voice. The final film aims to show the horror of the Holocaust in all of its painstaking and devastating detail. In so doing, it (perhaps necessarily) evacuates the individual voice. While songs are a critical element in the final film, they are parts of a larger argument about the enormity of genocide. Indeed, Lanzmann reminds his audience of the power of these voices as evidence over the course of what is nothing short of a monumental film. By creating this powerful collective, however, Lanzmann's final film removes the individual complexity—and contradictions—inherent in the very witnesses his documentary takes such pains to elevate.

In the outtakes, the songs that are captured on film become something very different; they serve as pointed reminders of the complexities of and contradictions within survivor narratives and experiences. It would be easy to merely excoriate Lanzmann for the film that might have been, and for the ways in which Schneider's or Elias's voices might have made for a different work, perhaps even a more inclusive one. Yet the presence of these songs on film, both Lanzmann's solicitation and his recording of them, speak to a larger set of questions. By viewing the two products side-by-side—an exercise that we are only now able to do thanks to the availability of the outtakes themselves—we begin to understand the profound ways in which, as Trezise points out, survivor stories and narratives are always already a part of their own aftermath. The testimony that occurs through music highlights this point; indeed, both Elias's and Schneider's songs introduce a new form of memory and a new form of remembering that the viewer witnesses evolving on many planes (and in many languages) at once. The songs instead become multivalent signifiers that destabilize as much as they illustrate the narrative presented. In this way, their very presence, and the very audacity of Lanzmann to record them at all, disrupts the carefully crafted story that *Shoah* seeks to tell. And so, perhaps in the end, these voices are not silenced at all, but instead have been left to languish on the cutting-room floor for nearly thirty years. Their emergence now, sharpened rather than mollified by the passage of time, affords us the opportunity not simply to hear, but also to listen to the ways in which their melodies alter our own assumptions about survivors and survival.

Notes

1. Marianne Hirsch and Leo Spitzer, "Gendered Translations: Claude Lanzmann's *Shoah*," in Stuart Liebman, *Claude Lanzmann's* Shoah: *Key Essays* (New York: Oxford University Press, 2007), 175–90; here, 185.
2. This article focuses on the victims who sing as opposed to perpetrator testimonies, which encompass much different concerns. To that end, please note that one of the more famous—and infamous—instances of song (Franz Suchomel's "Treblinkalied" and the outtakes related to it) will not be addressed. For further

reading about Suchomel's vocal performance, please see Erin McGlothlin, "The Voice of the Perpetrator, the Voices of the Survivors," in *Persistent Legacy: The Holocaust in German Studies*, ed. Erin McGlothlin and Jennifer Kapczynski (Rochester, NY: Camden House, 2016), 33–53, as well as McGlothlin's chapter in this collection.

3. Shirli Gilbert, "Buried Monuments: Yiddish Songs and Holocaust Memory," *History Workshop Journal* 66 (2008): 107–28; here, 124.

4. Indeed, Hirsch and Spitzer argue that the voice of the women within *Shoah* often disrupt this narrative of death. They write: "And yet Inge Deutschkron, Ruth Elias, Gertrud Schneider, and her mother do offer their own examples of survival, curtailed as they are by Lanzmann's mythic vision. Together with the translators, they disrupt the film's relentless pursuit with traces of alternative stories. Their presence, minimal as it is, serves as a reminder of the *price* this film pays for its remarkable ability to make possible the testimony from the *inside*." Hirsch and Spitzer, "Gendered Translations," 187.

5. Gertrude Schneider, *Journey into Terror: The Story of the Riga Ghetto* (New York: Ark House, 1979); *Exile and Destruction: The Fate of Austrian Jews, 1938–1945* (Westport, CT: Praeger, 1995).

6. See "War Criminal Faces Deportation," *Jewish Telegraph Agency*, February 16, 1977, http://www.jta.org/1977/02/16/archive/war-criminal-faces-deportation (accessed June 20, 2017).

7. Claude Lanzmann, *Shoah: An Oral History of the Holocaust* (New York: Pantheon, 1985), 194.

8. Hirsch and Spitzer, "Gendered Translations," 180.

9. Claude Lanzmann *Shoah* Collection, interview with Gertrude Schneider (RG-60.5015, Film ID 3222, Camera Rolls 6–9), US Holocaust Memorial Museum and Yad Vashem and State of Israel.

10. Interview with Gertrude Schneider (RG-60.5015, Film ID 3224, Camera Rolls 94, 94A, 95, 95A).

11. Interview with Gertrude Schneider (RG-60.5015, Film ID 3224, Camera Rolls 94, 94A, 95, 95A).

12. Interview with Gertrude Schneider (RG-60.5015, Film ID 3224, Camera Rolls 94, 94A, 95, 95A). For more about the Börgermoor camp and this song, see Geoffrey Megargee, ed., *Encyclopedia of Camps and Ghettos, 1933–1945, Volume I: Early Camps, Youth Camps, and Concentration Camps and Subcamps under the SS-Business Administration Main Office (WVHA), Part A* (Bloomington: Indiana University Press, 2009), 1–10.

13. Interview with Gertrude Schneider (RG-60.5015, Film ID 3224, Camera Rolls 94, 94A, 95, 95A).

14. Interview with Gertrude Schneider (RG-60.5015, Film ID 3222, Camera Rolls 6–9).

15. Interview with Gertrude Schneider (RG-60.5015, Film ID 3224, Camera Rolls 94, 94A, 95, 95A).

16. *Shoah*, directed by Claude Lanzmann, New Yorker Films, 1985, DVD, disc 4, chapter 17.

17. Kaiserwald, located in the Mežaparks Forest resort near Riga, Latvia, was established on March 14, 1943, with Albert Sauer as its commandant. It housed Jews from Latvia and Estonia as well as Viennese Jews, like Schneider and her family, who had already been deported to the Riga Ghetto. It also held a significant population from Vilna, Lithuania. For more information about the camp, its inhabitants, and its administration, see Megargee, *Encyclopedia of Camps and Ghettos, 1933–1945*, vol. 1, 1230–32.

18. Schneider is not the only survivor to recall this transport of young women and the songs that they brought with them. In USC Shoah Foundation testimony, Esra J. (36824) speaks of vivid memories of this transport and the songs that they brought with them. For a full analysis of this interview, see Leah Wolfson, "'Is there anything else you would like to add?' Visual Testimony Encounters the Lyric," *South Atlantic Review* 73, no. 3 (2008): 86–109.

19. Interview with Gertrude Schneider (RG-60.5015, Film ID 3225, Camera Rolls 96, 96B, 97).

20. This type of song (although not the identical lyrics or melody) is reflected in another USC Shoah Foundation interview, that of Robert N. (5388). For a full analysis of this and other songs that Robert N. recalls, see Wolfson, "'Is there anything else you would like to add?,'" 86–109.

21. Interview with Gertrude Schneider (RG-60.5015, Film ID 3225, Camera Rolls 96, 96B, 97).

22. Interview with Gertrude Schneider (RG-60.5015, Film ID 3225, Camera Rolls 96, 96B 97).

23. Interview with Gertrude Schneider (RG-60.5015, Film ID 3225, Camera Rolls 96, 96B 97).

24. Oral history interview with Gertrude Schneider, USHMM Archives RG 50.613.000, tape 3, 4:25–6:05.

25. Doris Bergen, "What Do Studies of Women, Gender, and Sexuality Contribute to Understanding the Holocaust?" in *Different Horrors, Same Hell: Gender and*

the Holocaust, ed. Myrna Goldenberg and Amy H. Shapiro (Seattle: University of Washington Press, 2013), 16–37; here, 29.

26. Interview with Ruth Elias (RG-60.5003, Film ID 3113, Camera Rolls 3–4).

27. Interview with Ruth Elias (RG-60.5003, Film ID 3113, Camera Rolls 3–4).

28. Interview with Ruth Elias (RG-60.5003, Film ID 3114, Camera Rolls 5–9A).

29. Interview with Ruth Elias (RG-60.5003, Film ID 3114, Camera Rolls 5–9A).

30. Interview with Ruth Elias (RG-60.5003, Film ID 3115, Camera Roll 10).

31. Interview with Ruth Elias (RG-60.5003, Film ID 3117, Camera Rolls 13–15).

32. Interview with Ruth Elias (RG-60.5003, Film ID 3118, Camera Rolls 16–18).

33. This type of narrative could be viewed as the kind of "choiceless choice" that Lawrence Langer discusses at length in his book *Holocaust Testimonies: The Ruins of Memory* (New Haven, CT: Yale University Press, 1991). See in particular chapter 1, "Deep Memory: The Buried Self," and chapter 3, "Humiliated Memory: The Besieged Self."

34. Like Elias, Ruth Klüger also describes a certain sense of community—alongside a simultaneous feeling of ostracization. For Klüger, too, Theresienstadt was both the place where she became a Jew and "a mudhole, a cesspool, a sty." *Still Alive: A Holocaust Girlhood Remembered* (New York: Feminist Press at the City University of New York, 2001), 84–88.

35. *Shoah*, disc 4, chapter 5. Müller's original German: "Und plötzlich hörte ich, wie ein Chor fängt . . . fängt an, wie ein Chor fangen an sich singen. Ein Gesang verbreite sich in dem Auskleideraum, und da fing an zu klingen, sich singen die tschechische Nationalhymne und die Hatikwa. Es hat mich sehr berührt, dieser . . . dieser."

36. *Shoah*, disc 4, chapter 5. Müller's original German: "Also, dieser Vorfall machten meine Landsleuten, und ich habe mich erfaßt, dass mein Leben nicht mehr kein Wert hat. Was sollte man leben, für was? Und da ging ich in die Gaskammer, mit denen, und entschieden zu sterben. Mit ihnen. . . . Und plötzlich kam eine kleine Gruppe von Frauen zu mir, guckte mich an und sagte. . . . In den . . . schon in den Gaskammern. . . . Da sagte eine: 'Du willst ja sterben. Aber das hat doch keinen Sinn. Dein Sterben wird nicht unseres Leben bringen. Das ist keine Tat. Du mußt von hier raus, du mußt ja noch berichten über dem, was wir leiden, was für ein Ungerecht uns getan . . . geschehen ist.'"

37. *Shoah*, disc 4, chapter 20. Rottem delivers his testimony in Hebrew, which is translated on screen into French by Lanzmann's interpreter, Francine Kaufmann, and then subtitled for the English-language version of the film.

38. See Marc Chevrie and Hervé Le Roux, "Site and Speech: An Interview with Claude Lanzmann about *Shoah*," in Liebman, *Claude Lanzmann's* Shoah, 37–49; here, 37.

39. Interview with Gertrude Schneider (RG-60.5015, Film ID 3225, Camera Rolls 96, 96B, 97).

40. Gilbert, "Buried Monuments," 122.

41. Thomas Tresize, "Between History and Psychoanalysis: A Case Study in the Reception of Holocaust Survivor Testimony," *History and Memory* 20, no. 1 (2008): 7–47; here, 32–33.

Coda

Ownership, Authorship, and Access: The Claude Lanzmann *Shoah* Collection

Regina Longo

I spent six years of my life as the film and video archivist at the United States Holocaust Memorial Museum (USHMM) in Washington, DC. This archive houses unique collections of actuality footage—recordings of real or actual events, shot by professional or amateur camera operators, usually unedited and lacking a formal narrative structure—from the time period of the Holocaust, as well as significant collections of documentary footage shot after the fact. One of the most important collections in the USHMM's care is the Claude Lanzmann *Shoah* Collection, which was officially acquired by the museum in 1996. It arrived slowly, in boxes, crates, and bins, between 1997 and 1999, after protracted negotiations between Lanzmann, the USHMM, and Yad Vashem, who partially funded Lanzmann's film in the early stages of research and filming in the 1970s.

I did not join the USHMM staff until 1999. Fresh out of the archival program of the L. Jeffrey Selznick School of Film Preservation at the George Eastman Museum (GEM) in Rochester, New York, I was eager when I began my first official archival job, which included restoring, reconstructing, and reconforming what, at the time of the original purchase in 1996 and subsequent acquisition in 1997, was estimated at over three hundred hours of original camera negative, positive workprint, and original quarter-inch magnetic audio tape that were produced by Lanzmann and his crew for the film that would eventually become *Shoah*.[1] I worked diligently on this project for six years.

I was the only professionally trained film archivist that the USHMM had ever had on staff, and I managed to persuade Raye Farr, then director of the Film and Video Archive—who had the foresight to acquire this collection and did so against great odds—to spend a great deal of money to get this preservation project moving to the next level. Raye Farr was instrumental in bringing the outtakes collection to the USHMM, and she knew the collection better than anyone else there.

Only two other individuals knew the outtakes collection better than she did: Claude Lanzmann and Sabine Mamou. Mamou was the editor with whom Lanzmann worked on the first two films he would make from the *Shoah* outtakes (*A Visitor from the Living* [*Un vivant qui passe*, 1997] and *Sobibór, October 14, 1943, 4 p.m.* [*Sobibór, 14 octobre 1943, 16 heures*, 2001]).[2] The status and extent of the outtakes were virtually unknown to anyone beyond a small circle of individuals until the release of *A Visitor from the Living* in the United States in 1999, the same year I joined the USHMM archives staff. This was also the year in which the museum seized the opportunity to promote their acquisition of this collection on the heels of the US and international release of *A Visitor from the Living*, which had originally premiered in France in 1997. While the legal sale of Lanzmann's outtakes to the USHMM was completed in 1996, it would take another two years for all of the outtakes to arrive there.

The international success of *A Visitor from the Living*, which focused solely on Lanzmann's damning interview with Maurice Rossel, the Swiss Red Cross representative who visited Theresienstadt in 1944 and gave the camp a seal of approval, propelled the museum to begin work in earnest on a systemized preservation plan for the outtakes and propelled Lanzmann to begin work on a second film from the outtakes. By the time this film premiered in the United States, Lanzmann was already at work on that second film, which became *Sobibór*. And during this time it was revealed that Lanzmann had sold the outtakes to the USHMM in order to fund the production of *A Visitor from the Living*.

With *Sobibór*, Raye Farr became instrumental in ensuring that Lanzmann and Mamou had access to the materials from the *Shoah* outtakes that were necessary to produce the film. Many of the outtakes had arrived at the museum in a state of disarray. The elements had been stored in three locations in France in the years prior to their consolidation and arrival at the USHMM, and the task of sorting through these materials was a multi-year process. While the majority of the labels on the elements' containers corresponded to their contents, this was not always the case. Thus, while the paper records could lead to most of the materials, there were some out-takes that had to be hunted for by going through more than just the boxes labeled "Sobibór." Several subjects interviewed by Lanzmann were inter-viewed on the subject of Sobibór, including Jan Piwonski, Yehuda Lerner, Ada Lichtman, Hans Prause, Jacob Arnon, Henryk Gawkowski, Franz Suchomel, Perry Broad, Richard Glazar, Filip Müller, Alfred Spiess, Benja-min Murmelstein, and Jan Karski. It was no easy task to gather together all the necessary materials and deliver elements to France in a timely manner. Film production schedules are usually quite intensive, and this meant that the USHMM Film and Video Archive was functioning as part of a film production team while also fulfilling all its daily duties and responsibilities for the archives and the institution.

A good portion of the original quarter-inch audio open reels required triage at an outside laboratory (Specs Bros. LLC, in Lodi, New Jersey). This project was my responsibility, and, at times, work on the audio outtakes became all-consuming for me. While Raye Farr and I had organized a pres-ervation priority schedule for the outtakes based on both their material condition and their historical importance, this schedule took a back seat to the exigencies of Lanzmann's project. In fact, the museum prioritized and paid for the preservation and transfer of the outtakes that Lanzmann used in this film. Therefore, even after selling the outtakes in order to continue funding his projects, a good portion of the cost for making *Sobibór* also fell on the shoulders of the USHMM.

As the team of two managing these materials at the USHMM, Raye Farr and I had developed a close working relationship with Mamou, who func-tioned as the *porte-parole* for the collection. She alone knew where every reel of original audio or film materials had been stored; she alone understood the edit logs, and she helped us to decode their lexicon. Most important,

Lanzmann relied on Mamou to provide information to him and to the USHMM staff for locating the selects he needed to complete *Sobibór*. Thus, in the early years of managing the outtakes collection at the USHMM, the exigencies of Lanzmann's post-*Shoah* films created with the *Shoah* outtakes formed—by default—the preservation priority schedule.[3]

There was, however, one event that occurred that was not determined by Lanzmann's new productions and individual ambitions: the death of Jan Karski on July 13, 2000. Karski had lived in the Washington, DC, metro area, worked closely with some members of the USHMM curatorial staff over the years, and been a pillar of the Georgetown University community. Karski's death at age eighty-six pushed to the fore the completion of the reconstruction and restoration of his testimony for *Shoah* and the creation of a special tribute video comprised of the *Shoah* outtakes for a memorial held at the USHMM on January 16, 2001.[4] By 2001, it was clear that Farr, in her capacity as the archives' director, could not devote all of her time to the hands-on work of preserving this collection, and the day–to-day management of the project became my responsibility.

Working on this collection was never a chore: it was both an honor and an obligation to history. It was also never a solo venture. It required collaboration among several staff members at the USHMM who became part of the project in the early 2000s when they joined the staff of the Film and Video Archive. These individuals, Lindsay Zarwell and Leslie Swift, continue to manage these materials today. The restoration of the collection also necessitated collaboration between two different film preservation laboratories: first, Commonwealth Film Labs of Richmond, Virginia, which went out of business in 2002, and then Colorlab Corporation of Rockville, Maryland, which began the work in earnest in 2003 and went on to do the remainder of the film-to-film and film-to-digital preservation work.

When I left the USHMM in August 2005, my position was frozen. As is often the case in large US government museums, a portion of the staff positions are funded directly by the federal government, and others are supported with donated or endowed funds from private entities. While I worked at a federal agency, my position was not federally funded, and the designated line could not be transferred. I was therefore classified as a "donated" employee rather than a federal employee. When a donated position is vacated at the USHMM, the directors of the museum assess the status of that position and have the full purview of the institution to reallocate the donated funds to another line. I knew that this meant that the work I had advanced with Colorlab could potentially come to a halt—not because the staff of the Film and Video Archive was incapable of managing the work, but because the archive was already understaffed.

The *Shoah* outtakes were only one collection among many that demanded their attention and expertise. I understood that it was time for me to move on, but this work had been so close to me for so many years that the thought of losing the momentum on this preservation project was something I did not want to imagine. I had reached perhaps an unhealthy level of obsession with the *Shoah* outtakes and with the larger-than-life character of Lanzmann. Before leaving, I had taken care to work closely with Lindsay Zarwell to train her in the hands-on work of film inspection and handling. She was a quick study, and I was certain that, if given the time to focus on this project, she would deftly manage this work. However, she was also the department's principal cataloger. So, in addition to the possibility of taking over this physical aspect of the work, she would have to continue to split the task of cataloging and documentation with Leslie Swift, who held the position of film researcher for the department at that time. One of the last things I wrote in my capacity at the museum was a letter to Lanzmann, dated August 15, 2005. However, I never sent that letter.

In fact, until 2007, I did not even recall writing it. In my haste to clean up my office, organize my files, and move to California to embark on a new phase of my career, I had neglected to send the letter. Instead, I filed it in a manila folder marked "*Shoah* most recent" that I took with me to California. The folder contained copies of some of my files and USHMM work that I intended to incorporate into my professional archival portfolio. I pulled this letter from the file box in the bottom of my closet for the first time the night I came home from a graduate seminar screening of *Shoah* on the University of California, Santa Barbara campus. When I came across the letter mixed with all the other bits and pieces of communication with Lanzmann, film labs, and colleagues, I was genuinely surprised. I was also taken aback by the sheer hubris of my own words. How could I forget writing such a passionate plea?

As part of a newer generation of audiovisual archivists, both in my own archival practices and in the theoretical scholarly work I was engaged in, I believed I was actively challenging the entrenched power dynamics of the gatekeeping practiced by archival professionals and institutions. While my letter to Lanzmann does indeed stress the need for continued work and access, it did seem that I myself had fallen prey to the notion that I had the power to stop or start a large-scale preservation project that was set in motion before I arrived at the USHMM, and that would undoubtedly continue once I had gone. A brief funding hiccup would be just that: a short-term stoppage. In hindsight, I realize that my not remembering to send the letter in 2005 was subconsciously intentional. My subsequent scholarly work on the subject of *Shoah* in particular, and on archival labor in general, has shed light on the motivations for my strongly emotional response to my archival work with the Claude Lanzmann *Shoah* Collection. I had to first forget in order to remember.

In 2007, when I began my first critical assessment of my professional work preserving and restoring the *Shoah* outtakes, I decided to sit down and write another letter to Lanzmann, which I sent off to Paris in March 2007. This time, I wanted to directly challenge my own biases, and I desperately wanted to reconcile the mixed emotions I continued to harbor regarding Lanzmann's approach to the initial production of *Shoah* and his ongoing exploitation of the experiences and labors of others under the guise of righteousness, human rights, and the insistence that the story of the Holocaust as he understood it could only be told from first-person accounts, rather than from archival images or documents. As other authors in this volume demonstrate in their chapters, and as I have noted here in relation to the hidden archival labors of managing these vast outtakes, Lanzmann first exploited his subjects and then exploited the custodians of the outtakes. Each time the director of *Shoah* returned to his materials—now an archive of images and documents—he would continue to repurpose these archives to craft new narratives and histories. With each repurposing, the status of Lanzmann as a singular force for the retelling of the Shoah seemed to grow. Likewise, my fascination with Lanzmann's outsized persona continued to grow, and it troubled me. If the theories I was struggling to develop regarding archival work were to withstand my own critique and that of established scholars, I believed I had to somehow persuade Lanzmann that he too was a custodian and not the architect of these histories. But in order to do so, I entered into a game of cat and mouse that would inevitably be beyond my control. From my letter to Claude Lanzmann, dated March 13, 2007:

Dear Mr. Lanzmann,

This will be my second attempt at writing to you. You will find a copy of that first attempt included in this envelope. The first letter was written over a year ago. Much has changed since that time, and much remains the same. I would like to suggest that you begin by reading the letter I originally intended to send to you in August of 2005, and then that you read this follow-up. So, please read on to the following page for that original letter, and then come back to the text that follows below.

Perhaps I should now enumerate what has changed and what has remained the same. Much has happened as I predicted that it would. No more work has been completed with the outtakes of your film. However, the ten interviews that we did preserve at USHMM have now been cataloged, so that is some degree of progress. While it is not the type of progress I would have liked, and would have pushed for if I were still at the museum, I still do not regret my departure. I am still in close contact with many of my former colleagues, and for this reason I am able to provide you with this information despite the fact that I have been absent from the museum for over a year and a half.

Leaving the museum, and the daily, hands-on work of restoration and reconstruction of films has enabled me to think about the work I was doing, and the work that you were doing, in new and interesting ways. I was just in touch with Stuart Liebman, as his new anthology of articles on *Shoah* was recently released here in the US. I recall many conversations with Stuart while he was in residence with us at the center, about this book, and the many times that I told him there was so much more to study and to write about in relation to your film. I find myself echoing this sentiment often, and it was not until a few months ago that I decided perhaps I would be the person to do this writing—or at least a part of it.

In one of my graduate film seminars titled "History, Memory and Media," one of the first films we screened was *Shoah*. I must admit I was filled with a sense of dread; I had not looked at much related to the Holocaust since leaving the museum. I felt I needed the break from the daily confrontation with the unspeakable and the constant barrage of images. However, I spoke of my work often, I even lectured about the archival process, and I presented public programs with select outtakes from *Shoah*, but I could not really bring myself to engage with the subject of the Holocaust. Suddenly, there I was, three thousand miles away from Washington, DC, and looking at your film again.

In a darkened room, miles away from the gray walls of the museum where I had watched your film so many times, viewed the outtakes, cleaned off film cans, wound through reel upon reel of the outtakes, separated each moldy quarter-inch audio reel into its own plastic bag and box for shipment to the lab for cleaning and remastering, stacked and restacked the cans, labeled and relabeled the elements, I suddenly could not bear to watch what I had seen and heard and touched so many times before. For the first time in my life, I looked away from a movie screen. If you knew me, you would understand that this is something that I never do. I will watch anything, at least once.

Each time I forced myself to return my gaze to the screen, what flashed before me in your film was only a fraction of what was projected in my mind's eye. Flashing in my head were the corridors of the museum, the warehouse where we store your film materials, my hands winding through the reels, that one odd reel of archival photos that is mixed in with the collection, my discussions with my colleagues about your work, bits and pieces of the faces and people I worked with daily for six years, fragments of stories they told about you—the myth that is Lanzmann. Needless to say, it was much too much to process in addition to the content of your film. I left the room, I drove home, and I began to cry. Then, I began to write.

I have been writing since that day. I am currently working on an article about reconstructing Jan Karski's interview. I am looking at parallel forms of reconstruction: the term I am using instead of restoration, because it allows for the idea of reestablishing a text rather than trying to restore some sort of wholeness or integrity. The levels of this reconstruction would be your reconstruction of the extermination of the Jews in your original film, Karski's own reconstruction of his testimony in his book, in the article that is in Liebman's anthology and in his experience that you captured in roughly five hours of interview time with the man in 1978, and finally USHMM's reconstruction of your work through a case study of the Karski interview. As I am sure you know, much of the theory surrounding art and film restoration is borrowed from Gestalt psychology. At present I am engaging some of these ideas of perception and positioning them against the type of psychoanalytic approach that Felman uses to discuss your work, which embraces the fracturing, rather than "the whole" that LaCapra would prefer and that he finds troubling in your film.

I felt compelled to write to you again, and this time to send you the letter. I am not certain how this article will end up, or whether or not it will ever be published, but I would like to send you a copy of this article when it is complete. I have come to realize that we are drawn to our work for a reason, and that it becomes sutured to our life in ways that we could not have imagined, but that we need to confront and to embrace.

I never did receive a response from Lanzmann to this letter: at least not in 2007. And, as luck would have it, Raye Farr was finally able to convince the head of the Collections Division and the director of the USHMM that the work should continue in earnest; more funds were allocated for this project; and, by 2008, Lindsay Zarwell was working full steam ahead with Colorlab to continue systematically preserving, cataloging, and making available the materials in the outtakes collection. I breathed a huge sigh of relief and moved along with my scholarly work on archives, content in knowing that the outtakes were becoming more and more accessible to a larger group of researchers and historians. But I had not entirely let go of my own curious obsession with the man behind the myth. His persona had taken hold of me in a way that compelled me to eventually find a way to confront him face to face and to demand some answers. That moment had not yet arrived in 2008, but it was drawing nearer. It would take time before other filmmakers were granted access and permission to use these materials in new film productions, but that day was drawing nearer too.

As an archivist, I find it reassuring to know that the work I do resonates. It is not enough to save materials, preserve them, and document their content and creation. Their afterlife is of equal importance. Access to the materials for ongoing study, for reuse and reinterpretation by successive generations of scholars, artists, educators, and the general public are important aspects of this afterlife. In the digital age, digital preservation for access is also an integral component of this process. When one works with an archive of Holocaust histories, anticipation of the myriad uses of such archival records is a constant concern, but, as a general principle at the USHMM, access to view materials is usually granted to all who request it. When it comes to the opportunity to license and reuse such materials in new visual or textual productions, the institutions or individuals who own or manage archives are able to exercise a certain degree of control over this part of the process. Unfortunately, for several years after the *Shoah* outtakes arrived at the USHMM, the museum remained beholden to the whims of Lanzmann and his insistent proclamations that his authorship superseded the legalities of the contract he signed with the USHMM. Despite the fact that the legal technicalities of Lanzmann's selling of the outtakes to the museum gave it and Yad Vashem this jurisdiction over the filmmaker, Lanzmann still made a great fuss about the potential use of the outtakes in any new creative works. This was indeed the case throughout my tenure at the museum. Any reuse of the materials by anyone other than Lanzmann, even by the USHMM, was always fraught with struggles between the museum and the filmmaker.

In the case of the public interest and requests for materials from the Claude Lanzmann *Shoah* Collection, since the USHMM first preserved and reconstructed the interview with Jan Karski between 1998 and 2000 (which Lanzmann recorded at Karski's home in Washington, DC, in the winter of 1978–79), these outtakes and the full interview transcript have been the most requested, accessed, studied, and copied of all the interviews associated with the *Shoah* project. By all accounts, including Karski's own, Lanzmann had made him a star.[5] It is because of his forty minutes of screen time, and the intensity of his on-screen testimony, alongside those of Simon Srebnik and Abraham Bomba—which stand out as some of the most emotionally and historically compelling recorded testimonies—that others also contacted Karski. In the late 1980s the *Shoah* outtakes were not a known or available entity, and therefore historians and filmmakers seeking to further elaborate Jan Karski's story went directly to the living witness.

The first to follow on the heels of *Shoah* and to feature newly recorded testimonies with Jan Karksi was the 1986 release *Messenger from Poland*, directed by Martin Smith for British, German, and American public television. Also in 1986, Karski appeared in an extensive interview on Polish language television in Canada on the CBC weekly show *Teleponica Montreal* (Channel 24). In 1991 came *They Risked Their Lives: Rescuers of the Holocaust,* directed by Gay Block, and in 1995 Renee Firestone interviewed Jan Karski for the USC Survivors of the Shoah Visual History Foundation. In 1996, historian E. Thomas Wood, who published the book *Karski: How One Man Tried to Stop the Holocaust* in 1994, conducted a series of video interviews with Karski that he deposited with the Hoover Institution archives. Then, two Polish productions, *Silent Witness* (1999) and *They Fought Back* (2000), both of which were directed by Francisco Roel, also featured newly recorded testimonies of Jan Karski. None of these interviews carry the same gravitas as his testimony in *Shoah*. With each successive interview and recorded appearance, Karski's telling of his own story changes. The facts do not change, but his delivery varies.

The Karski recorded by Lanzmann in 1978–79 did not laugh or boast; he barely even looked directly at the camera. In *Messenger from Poland*, Karski still exhibits a degree of reserve, but his composure is markedly different than what it is in *Shoah*. I viewed each of these productions during my time working on the outtakes at the USHMM. As Karski becomes more practiced at sharing a story that he had ostensibly kept to himself from the late 1940s or early 1950s until his appearance in *Shoah* in the mid-1980s, the accounts become more wooden, which is not meant as a slight against Karski; this can be an unfortunate consequence of repetition and performativity in recorded testimony.

By the time *They Fought Back* was in production, news of the USHMM's acquisition of the *Shoah* outtakes was common knowledge among Holocaust historians, but the outtakes were not yet available to other filmmakers.

Thus, the first use of the outtakes in a new video production was for the January 2001 memorial tribute event referenced earlier in this chapter. Even this use of the Karski outtakes was met by blustering consternation from Lanzmann. This memorial video was never broadcast beyond the public event on January 16, 2001, but it remains available in the USHMM archives. Between 2001 to 2010, the Karski materials were requested and viewed with consistency and frequency, but until the Karski centenary in 2014 again brought Jan Karski back into the larger public consciousness, the Karski video outtakes had only been reused for one publicly distributed new film work made in 2010 by Lanzmann himself: *The Karski Report* (*Le Rapport Karski*).

In 2015, Sławomir Grünberg's documentary *Karski and the Lords of Humanity*, a Polish-Russian coproduction, would make use of passages of Karski's testimony from both the completed film *Shoah* and from the *Shoah* outtakes. While it is encouraging to see these outtakes made available for new productions, Grünberg's film—like all the other films that have attempted to harness the essence of Karski's energy and testimony that burst onto and out of the screen in *Shoah*—doesn't quite achieve this aim. Andy Webster's review of the film in *The New York Times* sums it up quite well: "*Karski & the Lords of Humanity* focuses exclusively on Karski's courageous adventures in intrigue and espionage. . . . In 2010, Mr. Lanzmann (whose footage Mr. Grünberg often borrows from) devoted a documentary, *The Karski Report*, to the man, who ultimately taught for years at Georgetown University. *Karski & the Lords of Humanity* is fascinating, but Mr. Lanzmann's efforts tower over it."[6]

| Mimetic Obsessions and Reflections

In March 2010, Lanzmann made news again, this time in relation to *The Karski Report*, another film he made from the *Shoah* outtakes, produced by the Franco-German television channel Arte. The choice of subject did not come organically from Lanzmann, but rather was prompted by the French author Yannick Haenel's novel *Jan Karski*, published by Gallimard in December 2009 and subsequently published in English in 2011 as *The Messenger*. The book was on the French bestseller list for weeks. It won the Goncourt Prize and the Interallié Prize. I read, intrigued, the review of the film and an analysis of the dispute between Lanzmann and Haenel written by Rémy Besson, one of very few scholars to have delved as deeply into the *Shoah* outtakes as the USHMM archivists. Besson had spent a great deal of time working with many of the testimonies and had interviewed Lanzmann during the course of his doctoral research. Besson's substantiated argument summed up my instincts quite well:

> For Lanzmann the subject of the book was less problematic than its three-part structure and overall point of view. In the first part, the novelist appropriates Karski's account in *Shoah* of his role as a courier for the Polish resistance. In the second part, he uses Karski's autobiography, published during World War II, as the thread of his narrative. And in the third part he attributes his own ideas to Karski. The crux of the controversy was Haenel's fictionalized version of Karski's verbal report to Roosevelt: Lanzmann found the author's style flippant and challenged his attribution to Roosevelt of responsibility in the destruction of the Jews of Europe. The book as a whole and this section in particular seemed to him anachronistic and insufficiently respectful of historical fact and the persons involved. The issue, then, was two conflicting visions of Karski's testimony. For Lanzmann only the account given by the witness in 1978 could be taken as trustworthy; Haenel, on the other hand, stressed the freedom of interpretation inherent in writing a work of fiction.[7]

The film was not yet available in the United States, but after reading Remy's review and speaking to my former USHMM colleagues, who also did not have access to the new film, I was compelled to find a copy. I took the opportunity to write to Lanzmann's assistant, and I requested a copy of *The Karski Report*. The disc arrived with no note, just the requested contents. I had followed all the French reports on the novel, on the film, and on the public debates in the French press between Haenel and Lanzmann. Lanzmann's position amounted to more or less what I expected: an assertion that only Claude Lanzmann understood Jan Karski; that only he could dare to interpret the transcripts and the outtakes of *Shoah*; and, without a doubt, that only he could make a claim regarding the footage of Karski that appears in *Shoah*. He insisted, both implicitly and explicitly, on his exclusive authorship of that material. According to Lanzmann, the only story of Karski's work with the Polish underground that needed to be told was the story that Lanzmann told. The timing of this very public intellectual debate just seemed too perfect for everything to simply be about historical integrity or philosophical arguments over Holocaust history and the veracity of testimony. Lanzmann had also published his memoir *The Patagonian Hare* (*Le lièvre de Patagonie*) with Gallimard in 2009. The final chapters of his memoir end with the production and release of *Shoah* in 1985. His public and provocative intervention in the debate around the release of Haenel's book was undoubtedly a well-timed act. This was clearly a man taking stock of his life and his work, and someone who wanted to maintain control over his public image and his legacy.

This dismayed and unsettled me. Lanzmann's insistence on his version of history and his version of Karski's story—as told first in *Shoah* and now reinforced in *The Karski Report*—being the only acceptable truths were banal. I didn't agree with his basic argument about the nature of testimony, documentary, and "truth," but I couldn't help recognizing that no other interviewer or filmmaker had ever come close to eliciting the types of testimonies from his subjects that Lanzmann did. Was it because of Lanzmann's persistence? Was it because he was a bully? Was it his own passion and determination? Once again, I found myself back in the intellectual and emotional throes of my work with the *Shoah* outtakes. While I had presented a few academic papers on the subject of archival labor and the role of the archivist as witness with the Jan Karski interview as my case study, I had decided that I would stake my scholarly reputation on something other than *Shoah*. Yet, somehow, I couldn't stay away from it. In May 2010, I was in Paris as a representative of the US State Department to present my work on the Italian productions of the Marshall Plan Film Unit. I took an afternoon away from these activities and showed up unannounced at Lanzmann's door. I brought with me copies of my 2005 and 2007 letters to him.

His assistant let me in, after I claimed in awkward French that I had made an appointment with her a couple of months earlier, when I had requested the DVD copy of *The Karski Report*. I had done no such thing; I did not know in March that I would be in Paris that May. Instead, I emulated Lanzmann's "guerilla" interview style and gained entry to his office without an appointment. I showed Lanzmann's assistant my letters and asked her to see if she could find the 2007 letter in his files. She found it, filed neatly in a binder marked "mars 2007." She placed the binder, open to the letter, on the blotter on Lanzmann's rather crowded desk. She then informed me that Lanzmann was around the corner finishing lunch, and that she did not know when he would be back. I pleaded with her to call him to let him know that I was waiting. She acquiesced, and Lanzmann appeared within less than a half hour. At once curious and angry, he entered, looked me up and down, went to his desk, and demanded to know who I was and what I wanted from him. I pointed to the letter and asked him to read it. He pointed to the seat opposite him and said brusquely in English, "Sit down."

He read the letter then, in front of me, for the first time. Once he had read the entire letter, he looked at me across the desk and said, "What do you want from me? I have no money for this work." I assured him that much had changed since I had written that letter. I had not come to implore him to give more money to the USHMM for the work, for, as he well knew—since he himself had since used elements of the restored outtakes—the work was indeed continuing, and, in fact, accelerating. I had come to see him because, even after five years away from the daily work of preserving *Shoah*, I was haunted by it.

Lanzmann went on to complain about everyone at the USHMM who had worked on these materials and were not carrying out his wishes. I suddenly felt guilty for my own selfish impulses in visiting him, and for the possibility that my letter, and my emotional connection to the film, could make trouble for my former colleagues. I did my best to reassure him once again that everything had changed, and that I was now visiting him for more personal reasons. I was only partially successful. Lanzmann seemed visibly upset that he had not been kept in the loop on each and every step. He bore a grudge that originated with events leading up to an important public presentation in 2007 at the Austrian Film Museum in Vienna, during which restored footage from one of the earliest interviews conducted for *Shoah*, footage never used in the completed film (the lengthy interview shot in Rome in in the winter of 1975–76 with Benjamin Murmelstein, the last head of the Jewish Council in Theresienstadt), was first screened publicly.

Lanzmann was present at that event, as was Raye Farr.[8] But something happened at that event that angered Lanzmann. It is still unclear to all who were present what it could have been. The event was a huge success, as the interview with Murmelstein is a magnum opus in and of itself, and it helped to confirm his reputation and to demonstrate the important role of preserving outtakes along with completed films. Because of the meticulous restoration work done with matching the original audio with the original image tracks by Colorlab technicians, Lanzmann was once again able to resurrect from the ashes of *Shoah* a new film, *The Last of the Unjust* (*Le dernier des injustes*), which premiered to great acclaim in 2013.

I pushed Lanzmann, but got no definite answer as to why he was so angry with my former colleagues. I defended them, as I firmly believed, and still believe, that there is no better repository for these materials than the USHMM, and no better-equipped group of experts than the staff there for continuing to ensure the conservation, preservation, and access to these materials. This last issue—the question of access—was where the trouble lay. Lanzmann continued to insist, in 2010, that only he should be making new films from these outtakes. Regardless of the millions of dollars that have gone into preserving and restoring these films since 1996, with funding from the US government and the Max Foundation, and regardless of the sum Lanzmann was paid when he first transferred possession of the materials to the USHMM in the late 1990s, he continued to consider himself the sole intellectual creator, author, and owner of these outtakes.

I assert here an opinion that is held by most media scholars: in the collaborative medium of filmmaking, there is really no such thing as a sole creator or sole author. Lanzmann has attempted to retain control and authorship where the authorship of testimony is in question. Lanzmann's very struggle to control the material—and, in fact, the truths about Karski's testimony—reveal how filmed testimony often exceeds any one author's control.

A simple look at the full cast and crew credits for *Shoah* make this abundantly clear. The producers, cameramen, translators, and editors who worked side by side with Lanzmann on this project for years are part of the picture, part of the production history. The traces of their handiwork can be seen in *Shoah*, as well as in the outtakes. These marks take nothing away from the director, but the status of the auteur should be consistently questioned in the writing and rewriting of histories. And now there is another set of authors to consider. In light of the twenty years of work that have been put in to reconstruct these outtakes, it is also evident that the hands of all the staff members at the USHMM who have served as custodians of these elements over the years have an equally weighty and authorial charge as the keepers of this material history. And yet, because in the case of the USHMM this group of authors is made up of interns, survivor volunteers, permanent staff, part-time researchers and scholars, and outside contractors such as film laboratories, much of this archival labor remains invisible to anyone who accesses these collections at the USHMM. Sometimes, the marks of the cultural custodians are evident in the paper files and digital records, and sometimes an actual name is present, but a list of credits acknowledging the labor of these individuals does not exist in the same way as it did for the original production team.

I met two more times with Lanzmann during my stay in Paris. Our second meeting was a lunch date in the neighborhood along the Canal Saint Martin in the 11th arrondissement. He came to pick me up at my hotel in his car, and we barreled through the streets of Paris while he hollered out his car window at pedestrians who crossed his path. Despite this show of bravado, a more charming Lanzmann had replaced the gruff one I had met that first day. As I took my place in the passenger seat, I looked in the back seat of his car and saw a bulletin and death announcement for William Lubchantsky, the cameraman for *Shoah* who had also worked with Jean-Luc Godard, Agnès Varda, Jacques Rivette, François Truffaut, Philippe Garrel, and others. Lubchantsky had recently died on May 4, 2010.[9] He was buried a few days later in a small ceremony at Père Lachaise cemetery. Lanzmann was of course in attendance, and he recounted his experience of the funeral to me. He was genuinely, deeply saddened by Lubchantsky's death and could not help but reflect on his own mortality, a subject that had figured heavily in his writing, films, and public appearances since the publication of his memoir in 2009. In *The Last of the Unjust*, made with the restored outtakes of the Murmelstein interview, it has been observed that Lanzmann deliberately presents himself as an aged man, having trouble managing steep stairs. Reflecting on this film passage after Lanzmann's death in 2018, and after viewing the videos and still images of his state memorial and subsequent burial at Père Lachaise, which streamed live on French TV and online, I cannot help but wonder if there will be yet another coda to write. On the day of his state funeral in Paris, Raye Farr, Lindsay Zarwell, Leslie Swift, and I exchanged a flurry of emails sharing our feelings and also our observations of the actuality footage of Lanzmann's public memorials. We felt compelled to reach out to each other on that day and on subsequent days. We were compelled to process this event, and our experiences of the legend that is Lanzmann, together.[10]

During our 2010 luncheon I learned from Lanzmann that he had in fact known about the publication of Yannick Haenel's book well before its release. *Jan Karski* was published by the same editor at Gallimard who was working with Lanzmann on *Le lièvre de Patagonie*. For a moment, I wondered to myself if the entire public debate and Lanzmann's outcries against Haenel were simply carefully orchestrated marketing ploys to further the success of Lanzmann's own memoir and subsequent books and films. Lanzmann told me at that time that he was already at work on a second volume of his memoir, *The Tomb of the Divine Diver* (*La Tombe du divin plongeur*, 2012), as well as on the Murmelstein film. The subject of the conversation eventually returned to my original purpose for arriving

The author, Regina Longo, with Claude Lanzmann in 2012 at Stanford University. From the author's personal collection.

unannounced on Lanzmann's doorstep: the recontextualization of *Shoah* vis-à-vis the reconstruction of the *Shoah* outtakes. I brought him a copy of the 2008 working draft of my unpublished paper, which used the Jan Karski outtakes as a case study. To my surprise, he read and responded to it rather thoroughly over the course of our four-hour lunch.

Ownership or Authorship: Between Jan Karski and *Shoah*

Jan Karski's words and image recorded for *Shoah* have been interpreted, reinterpreted, appropriated, and reappropriated in documentary films, public lectures, museum exhibitions, and novels. Yet Jan Karski's story did not begin with *Shoah*, and the use and reuse of the outtakes did not end with *The Karski Report*. Sławomir Grünberg's 2015 documentary film *Jan Karski and the Lords of Humanity*, for example, made a splash on the festival and university circuits. This is in fact the first mainstream documentary film account of Karski's role as a member of the Polish underground that claims that Karski did not actually visit the Bełżec extermination camp during World War II, but rather the Izbica transit camp-ghetto, which was the stopover for the victims en route to Bełżec and other camps. This is the now commonly acknowledged and corroborated historical account of Karski's experiences. The 2010 edition of Karski's own *Story of a Secret State* contains the following footnote: "The camp to which Karski was taken was Izbica Lubelska and not Bełżec. . . . After a de-lousing operation in Izbica Lubelska, the Jews were either executed in the camp or (the majority) transported to Bełżec, amidst the violence and horrors described by Karski."[11]

Jan Karski and the Lords of Humanity is not a remarkable film for professional historians or those most knowledgeable about Holocaust history. Yet it is remarkable for the way in which the long-disputed fact of precisely where Karski found himself in 1942 is simply and matter-of-factly presented. This film has chosen to present what Holocaust historians call the "Izbica thesis," which allows for much of Karski's earlier written testimony of his experiences during the war as a messenger for the Polish resistance to be validated, without giving credence to certain particulars of Karski's accounts that many historians have questioned for some time. Details and facts are always critical, but for Holocaust historians they hold a double weight. There have been, and will always be, revisionists who seek to deny the extent of Hitler's Holocaust. In pointing out the importance of facts and chronologies, historians are seeking not to discredit Karski so much as to contextualize his role.

For this reason, the archives can potentially perform another function of bearing witness, removing some of the burden of testimony from eye-witnesses, who, recounting their stories weeks, months, or—in the case of Karski in *Shoah*—years after the fact, are bound to reinterpret even their own accounts. Yet this "fact" of the archives is not without controversy. Lanzmann includes a long excerpt from the Karski interview in the final cut of *Shoah*, and *The Karski Report* is comprised of a forty-eight-minute-long selection from the outtakes, but in neither film does Lanzmann use any of the footage in which Karski recounts his experiences of Bełżec, though nearly thirteen pages of the transcript of Karski's testimony recorded in 1978 and 1979 are devoted to his emotional, physical, and very visceral responses to his experience in what Karski believed to be Bełżec.[12] Instead, in both films, Lanzmann's interpretation of Karski's role is identical. For his account of his role as a representative of the Polish Underground to the Warsaw Ghetto in 1942, Karski proved credible, and, as a result, forty minutes of Karski's nearly five hours of testimony are included in *Shoah*.

And yet, when he insists in the introductory scroll of *The Karski Report* that Karski must be taken at his word as recorded by *Shoah's* cameras, Lanzmann takes liberties with his own interpretation of this history. Were filmmaking a court of law, the remaining four hours, thirteen minutes, and twelve seconds that comprise the outtakes of his interview with Karski would be entered into the official record, and a judge or a jury would be required to make some sense of them. Without the outtakes, we only have part of the story, and in continuing to put forth *Shoah's* version of Karski's role, Lanzmann does not allow for a full examination of the facts of Karski's original recorded testimony.

Lanzmann went to Karski seeking answers about Warsaw, Bełżec, Sobibór, and his missions to London and the United States. He got many: some satisfied him, others did not. What is remarkably revealed in the Karski outtakes is just how patient, persistent and seemingly nonjudgmental Lanzmann remained—at least on camera—in the face of Karski's account of Bełżec, which was full of emotion and bluster, and perhaps sowed the seeds of doubt about precisely which camp Karski had visited. This could have made the entirety of his testimony unusable for Lanzmann's film. But perhaps Lanzmann had already made up his mind, along with Hilberg and other historians, that Karski had not experienced Bełżec, yet in his quest for finding any and all eyewitnesses to the heinous acts of killing and in his efforts to thoroughly document the architecture of this killing machine, he pressed on with his interrogation of Karski.

The research Lanzmann conducted for *Shoah* began with a reexamination of Jan Karski's own written words. Karski's "forgotten" missives—official government reports from the mid-1940s and the *Collier's* magazine article "Polish Death Camp" from 1944, written by Jan Karski and illustrated by William Pachner, which was an advance excerpt from his memoir *Story of a Secret State* (1944)—formed the basis of a number of questions that Lanzmann asked of him during what was one of the first interviews he conducted for *Shoah* in 1978. Lanzmann did not find Karski on his own. He admittedly relied heavily on Raul Hilberg's research, particularly *The Destruction of the European Jews*, originally published in 1961. Lanzmann had corresponded with the historian prior to his arrival in the United States to film interviews for what would become *Shoah*, and yet when he interviewed Hilberg for the film he based his questions on the 1944 material, instead of on the written correspondence that had transpired between the two men.

Hilberg is the only professional academic historian on whom Lanzmann relies, and the only such academic who appears in *Shoah*. His interview was conducted in the winter of 1978–79, during the same period in which Lanzmann interviewed Karski. In the 1970s, Karski's *Story of a Secret State* experienced a second round of popularity. While *The Destruction of the European Jews* does not mention Karski by name, it does have several references to the Bełżec camp. Undoubtedly, Hilberg had read Karski's personal accounts of his wartime experiences, but according to my conversations with Lanzmann, Hilberg had begun to question the veracity of Karski's personal accounts by the time of Hilberg's encounter with Lanzmann at his home in Vermont, where he was interviewed for *Shoah*. By the 1990s, Hilberg critically questioned Karski's accounts of his visit to Bełżec, and in *Perpetrators, Victims, Bystanders* (1993) Hilberg notes that

Above all, trains did not leave Bełżec or Treblinka so that the passengers could die in the cars. Bełżec and Treblinka were death camps with gas chambers, and these facilities were not mentioned in Karski's account.[13]

Lanzmann, the author/filmmaker/interrogator, has chosen to hold to the "Hilberg thesis," (the Izbica thesis) since Karski's own written accounts and his subsequent interview by Lanzmann cannot confirm with certainty Karski's visit to Bełżec. Lanzmann insistently grapples with history, both personal and general, and related issues of nostalgia, retrospection, and temporality. More specifically, his work often refutes the image of history as a neat trajectory moving smoothly forward in time. He acknowledges instead the possibility of working against time—of creating work that deliberately counters received ideas of what the present should look like, what the past was, or what the future will be—and thus directs attention to the seams in the construction and presentation of history. As an archivist who worked to reconstruct Lanzmann's work, I often found myself on a parallel path to the filmmaker himself.

How does an archivist, traditionally labeled a custodian of history who is not typically expected to make the same interventions into the historical record as historians are expected to make, redress enduring inequities and retrieve lost histories? In diverse ways, archival work is not so much or certainly not only about histories or historical events as it is a reflection on and questioning of the temporalities implicit in history's unfolding—past, present, and future. It is also a reflection on the act of witnessing as discussed by Shoshana Felman in her work *Testimony*, a view shared by both Lanzmann and myself.

Archival reconstruction is a form of testimony. Film archiving is both a critical act and material work. Throughout my years in the profession, I have noticed some troubling consistencies. Scholars often take for granted that, because an institution such as the USHMM is well funded, the entire outtakes collection will be in ideal order. To me, this demonstrates a naïveté not only about the importance of archival labor, but also about the filmmaking process in general, and the labors inherent therein. Thus, in addition to the role of the archivist in redressing larger historical inequities, such as those related to the veracity of whether or not Karski visited Bełżec in 1942, there remains the pressing task to redress, among a learned group whose professional reputations are often staked on their archival "discoveries," the implications of archival labor and the hidden variables of which many researchers remain blissfully naïve in relation to the accessibility of archival collections: collections management in the digital "dark age," funding struggles, institutional mandates and priorities, and donor rights and restrictions, to name just a few.

Felman can actually be quite useful for both of these forms of redress, where she carefully examines the role of testimony and how Lanzmann approaches it. Most astutely, she points out that *Shoah* is a film about the complexity of the relationship between history and testimony, and, further, about the relationship between art and testimony. She suggests that *Shoah* constantly poses questions regarding what testimony means and what significance there may be in testimony concerning the Holocaust. She asserts that testimony, in this area, is simultaneously necessary and impossible. According to Felman, the impossibility of witness testimony is actually the most profound and most critical subject of the film. She speaks of *Shoah* as a film about silence, the loss of voice, and a paradoxical attempt to recover the memory of amnesia. She further describes the survivor's desire *not* to speak as born of the fear of hearing oneself, of being witness to one's self.

These ideas resonate strongly with me. It was not until I was forced to confront myself and an important part of my professional identity through a reintroduction to *Shoah* in a very different setting that I was able to relocate my own displacement and fracturing in my role as archivist. The voice of the archivist is often subsumed by the work itself. Here, I reclaim my voice, not as the voice of authority, but as the critical, individual, and informed voice that it is.

In 1986 Karski published a brief essay about his interview in *Shoah*, describing his encounter with Lanzmann as follows:

> The movie includes an interview with me. The circumstances
> surrounding the interview speak to the methods employed
> by Lanzmann and the planned parameters of *Shoah*. He vis-
> ited me in 1977, providing me with materials attesting to his
> qualifications, previous movies, etc. . . . The interview took
> place at my house in 1978. He filmed for two days, in total

about eight hours. Lanzmann is a difficult person. Passionate. Completely devoted to his work. Uncompromising in
his questioning and establishing of facts. A few times I broke
down emotionally. Once he broke down. My wife, unable to
bear it, left the house.[14]

Karski goes on to say that, out of the hours of filming that Lanzmann did
with him, he had only ever seen the roughly forty minutes that appear in
Shoah that discuss his visit to the Warsaw Ghetto in 1942 as a representative
of the Polish Underground. Karski himself believes that this is not the most
critical element of his testimony—or, rather, it is not the way in which he
wants to represent himself for history. Karski believes his most important
contributions to his testimony, and, by proxy, to his history, were his visits
out of Poland to the United States and the United Kingdom to deliver the
message and therefore to testify to what he saw in the Warsaw Ghetto as
well as in the extermination camp of Bełżec. After viewing all of Karski's
testimony, I find that the most compelling and emotionally raw material
in this interview occurs when Karski discusses his visit to Bełżec. As he
testifies, it is clear that he has more trouble talking about the Bełżec experiences than he does recounting his own torture at the hands of the Gestapo,
his suicide attempt while in captivity, and Szmul Zygielbojm's own suicide
attempt. The wounds of what he saw at Bełżec, which was actually Izbica,
have never closed. One has to draw the conclusion, however fraught it may
be, that the most moving part of his testimony is actually the "incorrect"
part. Here, we see another fracturing of Karski's self; again the path bifur-
cates en route to understanding Karski's public and private histories, and
the way others have chosen to further give voice to, or to further silence,
Karski's testimony.

Lanzmann has made a number of comments about the role of Karski's
testimony in *Shoah* in relation to authorship and intentionality. Particularly
with regard to Haenel's novel *Jan Karski*, which does not contain a table of
contents. Instead it includes an un-numbered page simply titled "NOTE,"
from which the reader learns that the book is divided into three parts. Part 1
contains the words spoken by Karski in the film *Shoah*, part 2 is a summary
by Haenel of Karski's book *The Story of a Secret State*, and part 3 is a fiction-
alized account of Karski's life based partially on the 1994 biography *Karski:*

How One Man Tried to Stop the Holocaust, written by E. Thomas Wood and Stanislaw M. Jankowski. From this page, the reader can launch into part 1; indeed, in some ways she is forced to begin there, because there is no table of contents to indicate where one might find the beginning of part 2. Of course, most readers could easily skip to another section if they wished, but this explicit lack of a guide tends to mimic the work of Lanzmann in *Shoah*: the viewer is brought into the story in a particular way, which insists on a form of searching and interrogation.

What struck me when I first read Haenel's *Jan Karski* was just how much the portions of Karski's testimony in *Shoah* echo, at least in terms of Karski's behaviors, the Karski outtakes. Moments in which Karski breaks down on camera, which occur several times in *Shoah*, are in fact fairly frequent in the outtakes as well, as are times when Karski recounts and interprets the emotions of others. Haenel attempts to reckon with Karski's stiffness as an interview subject and all this talk of motion and breakdowns. I frequently found myself in the same position viewing the outtakes: I was forced to stop and start again; I counted the times Karski breaks down on camera; I wondered whether Lanzmann asking for an immediate retake was the best tactic. I still tense up physically when I think of Karski leaving the room during one particularly tense moment of the interview, when he could no longer hold himself together. In one instance, he returns to the room with his large scrapbook of recollections from the war years, including the drawings by William Pachner that accompany the *Collier's* article.[15] He and Lanzmann pore over these pages together, Karski seated on his sofa, Lanzmann standing and leaning over him from behind, witnessing with him.

This rite of return of Karski to Lanzmann, and Karski to a revisionist history not written by Lanzmann, was made possible by the physical and material work of reconstructing Karski's interview. But even this reconstruction leaves gaps. Because the USHMM does not own the materials that were included in the film *Shoah*, if one wishes to view the Karski outtakes in their entirety, there will be moments of black leader, and moments of extradiegetic silence. Of course, by consulting the detailed catalog records and the full transcripts of the complete interview with Karski, one could reconstitute Lanzmann's interview with Karski as it was shot, over a few meetings in Karski's Washington, DC, living room between 1978 and 1979.

From Claude Lanzmann's interview with Jan Karski in Washington, DC, in 1978. Created by Claude Lanzmann during the filming of *Shoah*. (Used by permission of the United States Holocaust Memorial Museum and Yad Vashem, the Holocaust Martyrs and Heroes' Remembrance Authority, Jerusalem.)

Yet, if one did perform this editing work, Lanzmann would never allow the fully reconstructed interview to be shown or shared publicly. As long as Lanzmann retains the rights to *Shoah*, this will not come to pass. This is unfortunate.

Karski describes the film as "full of bewitching poetry." Perhaps in his call for more films to follow, he wants to find a way to come to terms with this bewitching quality. This is where the archivist, as a secondary witness to these testimonies, makes his or her mark. The archivist leaves a critical trace by bringing out the "bewitching poetry" of Karski's retelling of his journey through Bełżec. It is because of the detailed and meticulous work by every archivist on the USHMM staff who had a hand in this work that Karski's story can continue to be retold and reimagined. Yet Karski's testimony of his brief visit to Bełżec is also a retelling, because, as he claims in his interview with Lanzmann and in his own written words, he first told this story to American and British diplomats who refused to listen, or—more important—refused to hear.

Karski portrays himself as a machine and a camera. He claims he could only experience Bełżec as if he were a camera—as if he were "not human."[16] As he goes on to describe what he saw while in the camp, the viewer understands why Karski had to consider himself anything but human at that point. Karski fractured himself in order to make it out of the camp and away from this teeming sea of human faces that were facing certain death at Bełżec. This declaration occurs about halfway through Lanzmann's two-day interview with Karski in 1978. The camera roll begins with Karski seated on his velvet divan in his living room, looking directly at the camera and then breaking down, unable to look at the camera, getting up and leaving the room as Lanzmann physically reaches out an arm and begs him to stay.

We understand from this scene that this is not the first time Karski has lost his composure on camera. There is another scene in the film *Shoah* that recalls precisely this moment, yet the two scenes are not part of the same interview segment, as evidenced by the fact that Karski is wearing a different shirt and tie in this particular scene of his breakdown. The fact that Karski breaks down more than once during the filming does not change the reading or the placement of the scene in *Shoah*, but rather reinforces it.

Karski's notion of himself as a camera is a theme to which he returns throughout his testimony. At times he interchanges the word "camera" with the word "machine"; at one point he refers to himself as a tape recorder and then as a human form of microfilm. Karski had to think of himself as a mechanized object, displacing his own humanity, turning his eyes into something other than the proverbial "windows to the soul." I vividly recall the first time I watched a portion of the Karski outtakes, and how I was struck by the way his eyes seem to stare through the camera lens, through Lanzmann and through me, the captive viewer. They are an icy blue-gray, they pierce through the focal length, they shift, they seem cold, and then, at moments, when he must look away from the camera or when he leaves the room to cry, they flash to a lighter shade of gray. During these moments, when he is at the breaking point, Karski also begins to lose his voice. His voice, much like his eyes, has a rigid, mechanical quality to it. When the words no longer come, Lanzmann's camera often lingers on Karski, moving in closer and capturing his mouth, his tongue, his teeth, and his lips as they move without speech, grasping for words as he gasps for air. It is painful to watch these scenes, yet it is impossible to look away.

In these outtakes, as in *Shoah*, the camera technique is commonplace in its simplicity. In the location footage that appears in *Shoah*, the camera looks for us, points, walks, and pans; it functions as the arm of a guide sweeping across the land. There seems to be no trickery; it simply leads the viewer and shows locations. The viewer is invited to scour the landscape for meaning, to contemplate the places, and to enter the present while attempting to decipher its relationship to the past. This same camera invites us to search the faces of those Lanzmann asks to speak, as we search the landscape. It invites the viewer to weigh the witnesses' words and watch their eyes. The eyes of Karski, the witness, are not so clear about the matter of reliving the past. Lanzmann has described how he sought to reanimate, to reincarnate, the process of extermination. Karski's relationship to Lanzmann's endeavor shifts and changes; his words, his silences, and his face reflect. Can one uncover what lies beneath the stones at Bełżec? Should we? Must we? Karski seems to ask this as he resists in varying degrees the prodding of Lanzmann, who says, "Professor Karski, I understand that . . . I know how difficult it is . . . I am asking you to describe the indescribable."[17]

Thus, as I watch Lanzmann in his armchair, watching Karski on his divan describing his experience on the train platform at Bełżec in November 1942, I begin to understand what Lanzmann means when he says that his technique and his film reject memory and simultaneously restore a sense of immediacy. Karski's testimony is immediate to the point of being overwhelming. For Lanzmann, "a film on the Holocaust has to set out from the principle of the rejection of memory. The refusal to commemorate. The worst moral and artistic crime that can be committed in producing a work dedicated to the Holocaust is to consider the Holocaust as past. Either the Holocaust is a legend or it is present; in no case is it a memory."[18] Karski's words and emotions are immediate, at times almost pleading. Yet I am often aware that he does not plead with the viewer or with Lanzmann, but with himself. In the immediate present Karski pleads with his past. In this way, what appears on-screen is the historical continuum and the rupture of which both Felman and Lanzmann speak. This is the moment of the impossibility of witnessing. For the moment during which Karski gave his testimony, during which that testimony was captured, and during which I, the archivist, view the testimony, the rupture is present, no longer absent.

Not only as a custodian of Lanzmann's film elements, but also as a custodian and witness of history, I see and hear in Karski's testimony about Bełżec another part of the story that many must hear. Karski had not spoken about his Holocaust experiences from 1946 until 1978, when Lanzmann's determination enabled him to lift his veil of silence. Karski had been teaching the history of World War Two and of Eastern Europe at Georgetown University for twenty-six years, yet he claimed he never once mentioned his own story. This conscious decision and desire *not* to speak is born of the fear of hearing himself, of being witness to himself. Karski felt like a failure. He had done everything in his power to deliver the message, yet no one would listen. He had failed to save the Jews, he had failed to complete his mission, and he had failed as a human being. Lanzmann listened, yet he then silenced this voice in *Shoah*. I listened, and I found his testimony so moving that I cannot let it go.

| Notes

1. See the chapter in this volume by Lindsay Zarwell and Leslie Swift of the USHMM as well as Appendix 1 for complete and accurate inventory information.
2. Lanzmann went on to direct and produce *The Karski Report* (2010), *The Last of the Unjust* (2013), and *The Four Sisters* (2018), all of which were made from the outtakes.
3. This would change after the completion of *Sobibór*, when USHMM began a more systemized preservation plan, which remains in place today and has enabled a more rigorous and thorough approach to the preservation, restoration, and study of these materials.
4. See *USHMM Memorial Tribute to Jan Karski*, Film ID: HMM156, https://collections.ushmm.org/search/catalog/irn1003656 (accessed August 27, 2019).
5. Jan Karski, "Shoah," trans. Marek Nowak, in *Claude Lanzmann's* Shoah: *Key Essays*, ed. Stuart Liebman (New York: Oxford University Press, 2006), 171–74. This essay was originally published not long after *Shoah's* initial release in *Together*, July 2, 1986, 14–16.
6. Andy Webster, "Review: In *Karski and the Lords of Humanity*, a Holocaust Spy," *New York Times*, November 27, 2015.
7. Rémy Besson, "*The Karski Report*: A Voice with a Ring of Truth," trans. John Tittensor, *Etudes Photographiques* 27 (May 2011): https://etudesphotographiques.revues.org/3467 (accessed August 27, 2019).
8. For more information on the event, see "*The Last of the Unrighteous*: Benjamin Murmelstein, filmed by Claude Lanzmann," Austrian Film Museum, Vienna, Austria, October 14, 2007, http://www.filmmuseum.at/jart/prj3/filmmuseum/main.jart?rel=en&reserve-mode=active&content-id=1219068743272&schienen_id=1215680368518 (accessed August 27, 2019).
9. For a thorough account of Lubchanstky's career and influence on cinema, see Richard Brody, "In Memoriam William Lubchantsky," *New Yorker*, May 5, 2010,

http://www.newyorker.com/culture/richard-brody/in-memoriam-william
-lubtchansky (accessed August 27, 2019).

10. The last time we were together was in October 2017, at the Film Society of Lincoln Center. We met to attend the New York City premiere of Lanzmann's last films made from the outtakes, *The Four Sisters*. Lanzmann was in attendance and refused to acknowledge the USHMM or any of us in his onstage remarks, or in the conversations he had with other audience members after the screenings. I was not personally offended by his rebuff, but I was dismayed that he emphatically refused to speak with Raye Farr when she approached him in the theater after the end of *The Hippocratic Oath*, the first of the four films. It was a moment I will not soon forget, for it was such a harsh and violent dismissal of the woman, the archivist, the researcher, the custodian of history who made his legacy and his last period of success as a filmmaker possible. I cried for Raye and with her that afternoon.

11. Jan Karksi, *Story of a Secret State: My Report to the World* (Washington, DC: Georgetown University Press, 2013), 382n4. Karski's memoir was first published in 1944.

12. Transcripts from USHMM, 28–41, https://collections.ushmm.org/film_finding aids/RG-60.5006_01_trs_en.pdf (accessed August 27, 2019).

13. See Raul Hilberg, *Perpetrators, Victims, Bystanders: The Jewish Catastrophe, 1933–1945* (New York: Harper Collins, 1992), 223.

14. Karski, "Shoah," 173–74.

15. Jan Karski, "Polish Death Camp," illus. William Pachner, *Collier's*, October 14, 1944, 18–19, 60–61.

16. Interview with Jan Karski (RG-60.5006, Film ID 3137, Camera Rolls 16–18).

17. Interview with Jan Karski (RG-60.5006, Film ID 3136, Camera Rolls 13–15).

18. Claude Lanzmann, "From the Holocaust to Holocaust," in *Claude Lanzmann's Shoah: Key Essays*, ed. Stuart Liebman (New York: Oxford University Press, 2006), 35.

Appendix 1

The Claude Lanzmann *Shoah* Collection: A Guide to the Outtakes

Compiled by
Lindsay Zarwell
and Jennifer Cazenave

The Claude Lanzmann SHOAH Collection of outtakes is publicly available for research with streaming video in the United States Holocaust Memorial Museum's online catalog, Collections Search: https://collections.ushmm.org/search/. Refer to this catalog for the most up-to-date information about the collection.

USHMM RG #	Name	Summary	Length	Language
RG-60.5022	Arnon, Jacob	Jacob Arnon was a Dutch Jew and leader of a Zionist student organization. Arnon's uncle was one of the chairmen of the Jewish Council in Amsterdam, and though he admired his uncle greatly, he condemns the council's actions, especially their choice of whom to deport. Arnon's uncle survived the war but the two never spoke again.	2 hrs	English
RG-60.5000	Avriel, Ehud	Ehud Avriel was born in Vienna and became active in escape and rescue operations after the Anschluss. He continued this work once he reached Palestine in 1940. Avriel later held several positions in the Israeli government.	2.4 hrs	French
RG-60.5084	Bass, Bedrich	Bedrich Bass discusses the present-day Jewish community in Czechoslovakia and the cost of maintaining the old Jewish cemetery in Prague.	47 mins	French
RG-60.5049	Bauer, Yehuda	Scholar Yehuda Bauer talks about how he first became involved in the study of the Holocaust and how he tries to strike a balance in his work between emotional involvement and objectivity. He talks about the Jewish Councils and Israeli attitudes to them after the war. Lanzmann and Bauer debate Rudolf Kasztner's actions and motivations and the Nazi fantasy of "world Jewry."	2.3 hrs	English
RG-60.5052	Becher	An Orthodox Jew affiliated with Rabbi Weissmandel's Yeshiva in New York, Mr. Becher talks about Weissmandel, the "Blood for Goods" and other rescue efforts, and the Orthodox prohibition on violent resistance. He also discusses the German boycott in the United States and Rabbi Stephen Wise's actions.	39 mins	English

Date	Location	Crew	Included in 1985 Film?	Lab preservation work	Transfer Complete?	# of Reels
September or October 1979	Israel	Corinna Coulmas (assistant); William Lubtchansky (cinematographer)	No	Aug 2007	Yes	5
1979	Israel	Corinna Coulmas (assistant); William Lubtchansky (cinematographer)	No	Nov 2004	Yes	5
Spring 1979	Prague, Czechoslovakia		No	Dec 2017; Dec 2016	Yes	2
1979	Israel	Corinna Coulmas (assistant); William Lubtchansky (cinematographer)	No	Aug 2016	Yes	7
November 1978	Mount Kisco, New York, USA	William Lubtchansky (cinematographer); Bernard Aubouy (sound engineer); Dominique Chapuis (cinematographer); Irena Steinfeldt (assistant)	No	Aug 2016	Yes	3

USHMM RG #	Name	Summary	Length	Language
RG-60.5020	Bergson, Peter and Merlin, Samuel	Peter Bergson and Samuel Merlin were activists in the United States during the war. They talk about conflicts with other Jewish groups and Rabbi Stephen Wise. Bergson and his group organized the We Will Never Die pageant and other bold publicity moves aimed at influencing US policy in favor of helping the Jews of Europe.	1.8 hrs	English
RG-60.5001	Biren, Paula	Paula Biren survived the Łódź Ghetto and Auschwitz. She describes ghettoization, the children's Aktion of September 1942, and her deportation to Auschwitz.	2.2 hrs	English
RG-60.5037	Bolkowiak, Gustaw Alef	Gustaw Alef Bolkowiak addresses the tension between Polish and Jewish resistance movements and the question of Polish antisemitism. He talks about arms in the Warsaw Ghetto, the Bund, the Zegota Council to aid the Jews of Poland, Poles who hid Jews, and Communist partisans.	1 hr	French
RG-60.5011	Bomba, Abraham	Abraham Bomba, a barber from Czestochowa, Poland, is featured prominently in the film *Shoah*. In the outtakes, he talks about the treatment the Jews received when the Germans first arrived in his town, deportation to Treblinka, and his work cutting the hair of people before they entered the gas chambers. Bomba escaped from Treblinka and tried to warn the remaining ghetto residents of Czestochowa but they did not believe him.	3.5 hrs	English
RG-60.5032	Borowi, Czeslaw	Czeslaw Borowi is a Polish peasant who lived his entire life in Treblinka. He describes the transports and the experience of living in the shadow of the camp. When the Germans were shooting at Jews, his family slept on the floor to avoid stray bullets. He repeats some common refrains about how rich Jews arrived in fancy trains and the Jews offered no resistance.	1.5 hrs	Polish

Date	Location	Crew	Included in 1985 Film?	Lab preservation work	Transfer Complete?	# of Reels
November 15, 1978	New York, New York, USA	William Lubtchansky (cinematographer); Bernard Aubouy (sound engineer); Dominique Chapuis (cinematographer); Irena Steinfeldt (assistant)	No	Aug 2007	Yes	5
Winter 1978–1979	Panama City, Florida, USA	William Lubtchansky (cinematographer); Bernard Aubouy (sound engineer); Dominique Chapuis (cinematographer); Irena Steinfeldt (assistant)	Yes	Sep 2002; Feb 2001	Yes	4
March–April 1979 (Pologne II Hiver)	Poland	William Lubtchansky (cinematographer)	No	Sep 2009	Yes	3
September 1979	Israel	Dominique Chapuis (cinematographer)	Yes	May 2016; Feb 2009; Jul 2005; Dec 2000	Yes	10
July 1978	Poland	Barbara Janica (interpreter); Jimmy Glasberg (cinematographer)	Yes	Jan 2009	Yes	4

USHMM RG #	Name	Summary	Length	Language
RG-60.5002	Brand, Hansi	Hansi Brand and her husband Joel were members of the Relief and Rescue Committee of Budapest, Hungary, as was Rudolf Kasztner. Brand details her husband's experiences with Adolf Eichmann and the "Blood for Goods" rescue scheme. She also addresses the controversy over whether Kasztner neglected to warn the Jews of their fates. She states emphatically that by 1944 everyone knew what it meant to be deported to the east.	1.7 hrs	English; German
RG-60.5053	Broad, Pery	Pery Broad spent two years as a guard in Auschwitz-Birkenau. Broad voluntarily wrote a report of his activities while working for the British as a interpreter in a POW camp after the war. Broad's report corroborates details of killing installations and the burning of corpses. This interview was filmed in 1979 with a hidden camera, known as a *paluche*.	5.8 hrs	English; German
RG-60.5044	Deutschkron, Inge	Inge Deutschkron, a German Jew, witnessed the increasing persecution and violence against Jews in Berlin, including the promulgation of the Nuremberg Laws and *Kristallnacht*. Her father escaped to England but she and her mother remained behind and went into hiding in 1943. Lanzmann interviews her in a coffeehouse in Berlin in which she remembers seeing a "Jews Not Wanted" sign during the Nazi years.	3.8 hrs	English
RG-60.5003	Elias, Ruth	Ruth Elias was a Czech Jew who was sent with her family to Theresienstadt, where she became pregnant. She managed to hide her pregnancy in Auschwitz but was eventually discovered and she and her baby were experimented upon by Mengele. She speaks of these experiences and of her solidarity with other women prisoners.	3.4 hrs	English
RG-60.5059	Falborski, Bronislaw	Bronislaw Falborski witnessed the deportation of Jews from Koło, Poland to Chełmno. From 1941 to 1942, Falborski was a private driver for the supervisor of the German forest wardens in the area. He talks about the slow speed of the gas vans and the mass graves in the forest. This interview takes place in Falborski's home and was recorded during Lanzmann's second trip to Poland.	40 mins	Polish

Date	Location	Crew	Included in 1985 Film?	Lab preservation work	Transfer Complete?	# of Reels
September or October 1979	Israel	Corinna Coulmas (assistant); William Lubtchansky (cinematographer)	No	Nov 2004	Yes	3
Summer 1979	Germany	Dominique Chapuis (cinematographer); Corinna Coulmas (assistant/interpreter); Bernard Aubouy (sound engineer)	No	Mar 2015; Nov 2014	Yes	23
Late Spring or Early Summer 1979	Berlin, Germany; Wannsee, Germany	Dominique Chapuis (cinematographer); Corinna Coulmas (assistant/interpreter); Bernard Aubouy (sound engineer); William Lubtchansky (cinematographer)	Yes	May 2012	Yes	12
1979	Tel Aviv, Israel	Corinna Coulmas (assistant)	Yes	Aug 2004	Yes	7
March–April 1979 (Pologne II Hiver)	Poland	Barbara Janica (interpreter); William Lubtchansky (cinematographer)	No	Aug 2016	Yes	2

USHMM RG #	Name	Summary	Length	Language
RG-60.5060	Feingold, Henry	Henry Feingold, a distinguished scholar on the subject of America and the Holocaust, discusses American Jewry, the German-American Bund, refugee visas, Jewish leaders in the United States, and the War Refugee Board.	1.7 hrs	English
RG-60.5004	Forst, Siegmunt	Siegmunt Forst escaped Vienna and moved to New York after the war broke out. He talks about his dealings with Rabbi Weissmandel, a Slovakian Jew who begged American Jewish leaders and others for money to bribe the Nazis and save Jews.	2.8 hrs	English
RG-60.5067	Ganzenmüller, Albert	As chief of the German Reichsbahn, Albert Ganzenmüller was responsible for the deployment of deportation trains. In July 1942, he wrote a letter to Karl Wolff, Himmler's chief of staff, describing the deportation trains from Warsaw to Malkinia to Treblinka. Lanzmann speaks about Ganzenmüller's letter in a short recording in French.	14 mins	French
RG-60.5005	Garfunkel, Leib	Leib Garfunkel describes the Kovno ghetto in Lithuania, where he was vice-chairman of the Jewish Council, and the Aktion of October 1941, during which 9,200 Jews were murdered at the Ninth Fort. This was most likely the first interview Lanzmann conducted in the making of *Shoah*.	2.2 hrs	English
RG-60.5036	Gawkowski, Henryk	Henryk Gawkowski was a locomotive conductor at the Treblinka station and estimates that he transported approximately 18,000 Jews to the camp. He drank vodka all the time because it was the only way to make his job and the smell of burning corpses bearable. He describes the black market and the prostitution that developed around the camp. This interview also includes conversations with several Polish witnesses who were railway workers.	3.9 hrs	Polish

Date	Location	Crew	Included in 1985 Film?	Lab preservation work	Transfer Complete?	# of Reels
February 1979	New York, New York, USA		No	Mar 2019; Oct 2014	Yes	3
November 1978	New York, New York, USA	William Lubtchansky (cinematographer); Bernard Aubouy (sound engineer); Dominique Chapuis (cinematographer); Irena Steinfeldt (assistant)	No	Mar 2019; Aug 2016; Jun 2002; Dec 2000	Yes	7
1978–1979	Poland		No	Mar 2019; Oct 2014	Yes	1
February 1976	Israel	Irena Steinfeldt (interpreter); William Lubtchansky (cinematographer); Bernard Aubouy (sound engineer)	No	Aug 2004	Yes	8
July 1978	Treblinka, Poland; Malkinia, Poland	Barbara Janica (interpreter); Jimmy Glasberg (cinematographer)	Yes	Aug 2016; Apr 2009	Yes	13

RG #	Name	Summary	Length	Language
RG-60.5027	Gewecke, Hans	Hans Gewecke was the Territorial Commissioner of Siauliai, Lithuania. He is evasive about when he arrived in the town stating that the killing actions there took place "before my time." He claims he was not a crass antisemite and provides as proof the fact that he didn't pursue a legal case when the dog of a Jewish woman bit his wife. He talks about his postwar trial and stresses that the court did not find him to be a perpetrator but an administrator. Lanzmann used a false name and filmed Gewecke with a hidden camera.	5.3 hrs	German
RG-60.5028	Glazar, Richard	Richard Glazar, a survivor of Treblinka, is featured prominently in *Shoah*. He talks about his Czech heritage, Theresienstadt, his experiences at Treblinka, and witnessing the transports as they arrived from Grodno, Bialystok, Saloniki, and other places. He also describes the prisoner revolt and his escape from the camp.	7.4 hrs	German
RG-60.5068	Goldberg, Malka	Malka Goldberg talks about being in the Warsaw Ghetto, Majdanek, Auschwitz, Ravensbrück, and Malhof before immigrating first to Sweden and then returning to Warsaw. At Lanzmann's prompting, Goldberg explains that she was part of the resistance and sings part of the Yiddish resistance song "Undzer shtetl brent!" ("Our Town is Burning!").	10 mins	German; Hebrew; French; Yiddish
RG-60.5082	Goldmann, Nahum	Nahum Goldmann was president of the World Jewish Congress, which he founded with Rabbi Stephen Wise, from 1948 to 1977. He was a Zionist activist but was often critical of Israeli public policy. Lanzmann and Goldmann discuss when the Jews realized the reality of the Final Solution, the Jewish Councils, and the Hannah Arendt controversy.	1.2 hrs	English
RG-60.5042	Grassler, Franz	Franz Grassler was the assistant to Heinz Auerswald, the Nazi commissioner of the Warsaw Ghetto. Lanzmann tries to get him to talk about the ghetto, but he pretends not to remember. Lanzmann asks about Jewish Council chairman Adam Czerniakow and his suicide, typhus, the black market, the ghetto wall, and filming in the ghetto. Grassler seems to remember things only when he thinks they might be documented in Czerniakow's diaries.	1.6 hrs	German

Date	Location	Crew	Included in 1985 Film?	Lab preservation work	Transfer Complete?	# of Reels
Late Spring or Early Summer 1979	Moelln, Germany	Corinna Coulmas (interpreter); Dominique Chapuis (cinematographer); Bernard Aubouy (sound engineer)	No	Nov 2008	Yes	14
Late Spring 1979	Basel, Switzerland	Corinna Coulmas (assistant)	Yes	Nov 2008; Feb 2001	Yes	17
May or September 1979	Tel Aviv, Israel	Corinna Coulmas (interpreter); Bernard Aubouy (sound engineer)	No	Aug 2017; Oct 2014	Yes	2
February 3–10, 1975	Jerusalem, Israel		No	Jun 2016	Yes	3
1978–1981	Germany		Yes	Sep 2009	Yes	4

USHMM RG #	Name	Summary	Length	Language
RG-60.5045	Hilberg, Raul	Historian Raul Hilberg was one of the main protagonists of *Shoah*, laying out for Lanzmann in great detail the primary elements of the Nazis' killing process. The interview contains details about the bureaucracy that supported the Holocaust, as well as the involvement of the German Army, among many other topics.	6.2 hrs	English
RG-60.5075	Hilse, Willy	Willy Hilse was a German railroad worker at the Auschwitz train station. He discusses the technical details of the train platforms, the arrival and separation of men and women at Auschwitz, and the shipment of Jewish property back to Germany.	47 mins	German
RG-60.5006	Karski, Jan	Jan Karski tells of his capture and torture by the Gestapo when he was a courier for the Polish underground. He also describes his clandestine visit to the Warsaw Ghetto and meeting with Szmul Zygielbojm, six months before Zygelbojm's suicide. Karski attempted to expose conditions in the Warsaw Ghetto and the existence of Bełżec when he met with President Franklin D. Roosevelt and Supreme Court Justice Felix Frankfurter. In 2010, Lanzmann made *The Karski Report*, based almost entirely on this interview.	4.2 hrs	English
RG-60.5017	Kovner, Abba	Abba Kovner was a central figure in the Zionist youth resistance movement in Vilna, Lithuania. He commanded an underground partisan resistance group throughout the war. Kovner provides oblique and poetic answers to Lanzmann's questions throughout the interview.	4.7 hrs	Hebrew; French
RG-60.5018	Kretschmer, Karl	Karl Kretschmer was *Obersturmführer* with *Einsatzgruppe* 4a and wrote an infamous letter to his wife and children about witnessing mass killings. In this hidden-camera interview, Kretschmer is reluctant to talk. Lanzmann asks about Babi Yar and Kretschmer says he wasn't there. He says he doesn't remember what his letter said since he doesn't have it any more.	44 mins	German; French
RG-60.5035	Kryshak, Eduard	Eduard Kryshak accompanied two or three train transports of Jews to Treblinka and was a witness at postwar trials in Düsseldorf and Bielefeld. In this hidden-camera interview obtained with a *paluche*, Kryshak claims he did not know that people were killed at Treblinka until after the war.	1.8 hrs	German; French

Date	Location	Crew	Included in 1985 Film?	Lab preservation work	Transfer Complete?	# of Reels
January 1979	Burlington, Vermont, USA	William Lubtchansky (cinematographer)	Yes	Aug 2016	Yes	17
1978–1981	Germany		No	Mar 2015	Yes	3
October 1978	Washington, DC, USA	William Lubtchansky (cinematographer); Dominique Chapuis (cinematographer); Irena Steinfeldt (assistant)	Yes	Oct 2000	Yes	11
September 27–28, 1979	Israel	Francine Kaufmann (interpreter); William Lubtchansky (cinematographer)	No	Aug 2007	Yes	10
Summer 1979	Germany	Bernard Aubouy (sound engineer); Corinna Coulmas (interpreter); Dominique Chapuis (cinematographer)	No	Aug 2007	Yes	2
Summer 1979	Germany	Corinna Coulmas (interpreter); Dominique Chapuis (cinematographer)	No	Apr 2009	Yes	5

USHMM RG #	Name	Summary	Length	Language
RG-60.5025	Laabs, Gustav and Lettre Becker	Lanzmann attempted to interview Gustav Laabs, who drove a gas van at Chełmno. Lanzmann is challenged by two neighbors after Laabs refuses to open the door to his apartment. Additional reels show industrial scenes, a Saurer truck in transit (Saurer manufactured gas vans during the war), and Lanzmann reading a letter written by engineer Dr. Becker, who details the operation of a gas van.	1.3 hrs	German; French
RG-60.5007	Landau, Hermann	Hermann Landau talks about the rescue work of Rabbi Weissmandel as well as rescue efforts in Switzerland and the United States. He describes Weissmandel as an increasingly desperate man who would not hesitate to bribe the Nazis or commit violence if it would help save Jews.	1.7 hrs	English
RG-60.5030	Lerner, Yehuda	One of the leaders of the revolt in Sobibór, Yehuda Lerner talks about his arrival, escape from eight camps, and pivotal role in the Sobibór uprising. Lanzmann found this interview so compelling that he used it to make the film *Sobibór, October 14, 1943, 4 P.M.*	2.5 hrs	Hebrew; French
RG-60.5023	Lichtman, Ada	Ada Lichtman talks about her experiences in the Kraków ghetto, her father's murder, and her transport to Sobibór. She was chosen to do the SS laundry in Sobibór and remembers cleaning dolls and toys seized from a transport of children and given to SS families. At Lanzmann's urging, Lichtman sews doll clothes during the interview; this is a duty she used to perform in Sobibór.	2.7 hrs	German; Yiddish
RG-60.5008	Marton, Hanna	Hanna Marton is from Romania, where both she and her husband were lawyers and Zionists. She was aboard the controversial rescue train organized by Rudolf Kasztner. She talks about Kasztner, the libel trial in Israel after the war, and his assassination.	3.5 hrs	French; Hebrew
RG-60.5047	McClelland, Roswell	Roswell McClelland was the US representative to the War Refugee Board (WRB) in Switzerland before serving as a US ambassador to the Republic of Niger. McClelland recounts his personal experiences, motivations, and work with the WRB.	1.9 hrs	English

Date	Location	Crew	Included in 1985 Film?	Lab preservation work	Transfer Complete?	# of Reels
Summer 1979	Germany; Switzerland	Corinna Coulmas (assistant); Dominique Chapuis (cinematographer)	No	Aug 2016; Sep 2009; Nov 2008; Aug 2007	Yes	5
1979	New York, New York, USA	William Lubtchansky (cinematographer); Irena Steinfeldt (assistant)	No	Jun 2002; Feb 2001	Yes	4
October 11, 1979	Jerusalem, Israel	Francine Kaufmann (interpreter)	No	Jan 2009	Yes	5
September or October 1979	Israel	Corinna Coulmas (assistant); William Lubtchansky (cinematographer)	No	Aug 2007	Yes	8
October 10–11, 1979	Jerusalem, Israel	Francine Kaufmann (interpreter)	No	Sep 2016; Aug 2004	Yes	10
November 1978	Chevy Chase, Maryland, USA	William Lubtchansky (cinematographer); Irena Steinfeldt (assistant)	No	Dec 2013	Yes	5

RG #	Name	Summary	Length	Language
RG-60.5033	Michelsohn, Martha	Martha Michelson was the wife of a Nazi schoolteacher in Chełmno. She talks about the *Sonderkommando*, Jews killed in a church, the terrible smell that pervaded the town when bodies were burned, the Poles' attitude toward the Jews, and the operation of gas vans. She says that she told people in Germany about the killing of Jews in 1942 or 1943 but they accused her of spreading atrocity propaganda.	1.5 hrs	German
RG-60.5012	Müller, Filip	Filip Müller worked in a *Sonderkommando* detail at Auschwitz, one of the prisoners chosen to help the SS dispose of corpses after gassing. Müller undressed the dead and stirred the fires of the crematoria. He describes how the SS lied to the victims to the very end in order to keep them calm, telling the doomed that they were at the camp in order to work but that first they must be disinfected. He was a member of the camp resistance and tells of the October 1944 uprising as well as his liberation from Gunskirchen by US forces.	4.8 hrs	German
RG-60.5009	Murmelstein, Benjammin	Benjamin Murmelstein, a rabbi and intellectual, worked closely with Adolf Eichmann in Vienna and became the last head of the Jewish Council in Theresienstadt. He defends his behavior against the many who have criticized him since the war and provides important details about the functioning of Eichmann's Central Office for Jewish Emigration. This is the longest interview in the outtakes and the basis for Lanzmann's 2013 film *The Last of the Unjust*.	11.4 hrs	German
RG-60.5065	Oberhauser, Josef	Josef Oberhauser was an SS officer in Bełżec. Lanzmann attempts to interview him in a Munich beer hall and he refuses to answer many questions. Oberhauser discusses his work selling beer, but remains silent in response to questions about his days as an SS officer.	12 mins	German
RG-60.5051	Oppenheimer, Lore and Ziering, Hermann	Lore Oppenheimer and Herman Ziering, copresidents of the Society of the Survivors of the Riga Ghetto, share their experiences during the war. They address the conflicts between German Jews and Eastern Jews, deportation to the Polish border in 1938, propaganda, arrival in Riga and witnessing the evidence of murdered Latvian Jews, and life in the Riga Ghetto. The interview takes place during a 1978 conference of Riga survivors.	1.6 hrs	English; German

Date	Location	Crew	Included in 1985 Film?	Lab preservation work	Transfer Complete?	# of Reels
Summer 1979	Laage, Germany	Corinna Coulmas (assistant); William Lubtchansky (cinematographer); Bernard Aubouy (sound engineer)	Yes	Jan 2009	Yes	3
Spring 1979	Germany	Corinna Coulmas (assistant); William Lubtchansky (cinematographer); Bernard Aubouy (sound engineer)	Yes	Jul 2005	Yes	10
February 1976	Rome, Italy	Angelika Schrobsdorff (interpreter); William Lubtchansky (cinematographer)	No	Jul 2005	Yes	34
Spring or Summer 1979	Munich, Germany		Yes	Mar 2019; Oct 2014	Yes	2
November 1978	New York, New York, USA	William Lubtchansky (cinematographer); Irena Steinfeldt (assistant)	No	Aug 2016	Yes	5

USHMM RG #	Name	Summary	Length	Language
RG-60.5014	Pankiewicz, Tadeusz	Tadeusz Pankiewicz was a Pole who ran a pharmacy within the confines of the Kraków Ghetto, refusing the Germans' offer to let him relocate to another part of the city. He aided Jews by providing free medication and allowing the pharmacy to be used as a meeting place for resisters.	1 hr	German
RG-60.5021	Pehle, John	John Pehle, the first director of the War Refugee Board, discusses US policy and inaction, the Riegner cable of March 1943, Rabbi Wise and the rally at Madison Square Garden, antisemitism, the bombing of Auschwitz, the International Red Cross, and the Vatican.	2.4 hrs	English
RG-60.5054	Pictet, Jean	A leading member of the International Council of the Red Cross, Jean Pictet was responsible for the preparatory work which led to the conclusion of the four Geneva Conventions in 1949.	1.4 hrs	French
RG-60.5055	Pietyra, Helena	Helena Pietyra describes her experience as a Pole living near the city of Auschwitz, Poland.	25 mins	Polish
RG-60.5031	Piwonski, Jan	Jan Piwonski gives a detailed description of the killing process at Sobibór. He provides a harrowing account of the brutal treatment the Jews received in the process of building the camp. He could hear the screams of the victims from his home 3 kilometers from the camp.	3.3 hrs	Polish; French
RG-60.5026	Podchlebnik, Mordechai	Mordechai Podchlebnik discovered the corpses of his wife and children while working on a work detail unloading bodies from a gas van in Chełmno. He escaped the camp and attempted to warn the Jews of a nearby town but the residents did not believe him. Podchelbnik says that his whole family died in Chełmno and that it is not good to talk about it but he feels obligated. He testified at the Eichmann trial and other postwar trials.	2 hrs	French; German; Hebrew; Yiddish

Date	Location	Crew	Included in 1985 Film?	Lab preservation work	Transfer Complete?	# of Reels
March–April 1979 (Pologne II Hiver)	Kraków, Poland	William Lubtchansky (cinematographer)	No	Apr 2007	Yes	3
November 1978	Washington, DC, USA	William Lubtchansky (cinematographer); Irena Steinfeldt (assistant)	No	Aug 2007	Yes	6
April 19, 1979	Geneva, Switzerland	Corinna Coulmas (assistant); William Lubtchansky (cinematographer)	No	Nov 2014	Yes	4
March–April 1979 (Pologne II Hiver)	Oswiecim, Poland	Barbara Janica (interpreter); William Lubtchansky (cinematographer)	Yes	Nov 2014	Yes	1
1978–1981	Poland	Barbara Janica (interpreter); Jimmy Glasberg (cinematographer)	Yes	Jan 2009	Yes	9
May 1979	Israel	Fanny Apfelbaum (interpreter); Corinna Coulmas (assistant); William Lubtchansky (cinematographer)	Yes	Nov 2008	Yes	4

USHMM RG #	Name	Summary	Length	Language
RG-60.5029	Prause, Hans	Hans Prause was an engineer with the German *Reichsbahn* stationed in Warsaw, Radom, Lvov, and Malkinia, Poland. He talks about relations between the German and Polish railroads, preparing trains for the invasion of the USSR, hostile relations between Poles and Jews, and visiting the Warsaw Ghetto. He defends the fact that he signed orders by saying that the trains would have gone regardless of anyone's signature. He also defends Reichsbahn Chief Ganzenmüller, another *Shoah* interviewee, regarding transports to Treblinka.	1.5 hrs	German
RG-60.5061	Reams, Robert	Ambassador Robert Borden Reams was interviewed about American diplomats during a fishing and golfing trip in Panama City, Florida. He was the secretary of the Intergovernmental Committee during World War II and a guest of the German government in 1942. He represented the United States at the Bermuda Conference and was a deputy of Breckinridge Long.	1.7 hrs	English
RG-60.5019	Rossel, Maurice	As a representative of the Swiss Red Cross in 1944, Maurice Rossel was asked to inspect the Theresienstadt camp in Czechoslovakia. He admits that he gave Theresienstadt a clean bill of health and would probably do so again today. He was also given a tour of Auschwitz, which he did not realize was a death camp. Lanzmann's questioning points to the degree to which Rossel and others were manipulated by the Nazis and to what extent they were willing to be fooled because of their own politics and prejudices. This interview is the basis of Lanzmann's 1999 film *A Visitor from the Living*.	2.3 hrs	French
RG-60.5048	Rotem, Simha and Zuckerman, Itzhak	Simha Rotem and Itzhak Zuckerman talk about their involvement in the Jewish Combat Organization (ŻOB) in the Warsaw Ghetto and the Warsaw Ghetto Uprising. Some of the interview takes place at the Ghetto Fighters House in Israel.	3.7 hrs	Hebrew; French

Date	Location	Crew	Included in 1985 Film?	Lab preservation work	Transfer Complete?	# of Reels
1978–1981	Germany		No	Jan 2009	Yes	3
Winter 1978/1979	Panama City, Florida, USA	William Lubtchansky (cinematographer); Dominique Chapuis (cinematographer)	No	Aug 2017; Oct 2014	Yes	5
April–May 1979	Switzerland	Dominique Chapuis (cinematographer)	No	Aug 2007	Yes	6
October 4–6, 1979	Jerusalem, Israel	Francine Kaufmann (interpreter); Corinna Coulmas (assistant); William Lubtchansky (cinematographer)	Yes	Incomplete; Oct 2019; Oct 2015	No	11

USHMM RG #	Name	Summary	Length	Language
RG-60.5062	Rubenstein, Richard	Richard Rubenstein, an American scholar, discusses stateless people, bureaucracy, and the role of churches during the Holocaust. He argues that, at the Evian Conference, Western democracies were not genuinely concerned for Jewish refugees. Rubenstein also details the fundamental differences between the Jewish and Christian religions, and how that led to European Christians viewing the Jews as dangerous to their beliefs.	1 hr	English
RG-60.5034	Schalling, Franz	In a hidden-camera interview, Franz Schalling, *Ordnungspolizei*, describes the process of execution by gas vans at Chełmno.	50 mins	German
RG-60.5071	Schilanski, Dov	Dov Schilanski was born in Siauliai, Lithuania. He survived the Holocaust and moved to Israel in 1948, where he later served as Speaker of the Knesset from 1988 to 1992. This interview was conducted in the Knesset.	45 mins	Hebrew; French
RG-60.5015	Schneider, Gertrude	Gertrude Schneider was a Viennese Jew deported with her family to the Riga Ghetto. The interview, which also includes Schneider's mother and sister, covers topics such as the perception of Viennese Jews by Latvian Jews, sex and pregnancy in the ghetto, and the deportation of March 26, 1942. At Lanzmann's urging, the women sing several Yiddish songs they learned in the ghetto.	2.3 hrs	English; German; Yiddish
RG-60.5013	Schubert, Heinz	Lanzmann used a false name and filmed this interview clandestinely. Heinz Schubert was a member of *Einsatzgruppe* D and was convicted and sentenced to death (later commuted) for his role in the massacre of Jews in the Crimean town of Simferopol. Schubert never admits to much criminal or moral guilt. The interview ends when Schubert discovers that Lanzmann has been filming it.	1.7 hrs	German
RG-60.5038	Smolar, Hersh	Hersh Smolar was the editor of a Yiddish daily newspaper. After the war began, he became a leading member of the resistance in the Minsk Ghetto and the commissar of a partisan group operating in the Belarusian forests. He discusses conditions in the ghetto and resistance activities.	1.9 hrs	Yiddish; French; German

Date	Location	Crew	Included in 1985 Film?	Lab preservation work	Transfer Complete?	# of Reels
Winter 1978/1979	Tallahassee, Florida, USA	William Lubtchansky (camera operator)	No	Aug 2017; Oct 2014	Yes	5
1978–1981	Germany	Corinna Coulmas (interpreter)	No	Jan 2009	Yes	2
September or October 1979	Jerusalem, Israel		No	Mar 2015	Yes	5
November 1978	New York, New York, USA	William Lubtchansky (cinematographer); Dominique Chapuis (cinematographer); Irena Steinfeldt (assistant)	Yes	May 2007	Yes	5
Summer 1979	Ahrensburg, Germany	Corinna Coulmas (interpreter, off-camera); Bernard Aubouy (sound engineer); Dominique Chapuis (cinematographer)	Yes	May 2006	Yes	4
September or October 1979	Tel Aviv, Israel	Corinna Coulmas (interpreter, off-camera); Bernard Aubouy (sound engineer); William Lubtchansky (cinematographer)	No	Sep 2009	Yes	7

USHMM RG #	Name	Summary	Length	Language
RG-60.5063	Spiess, Alfred	Alfred Spiess was a prosecutor at the Treblinka trial. He talks about the reorganization of the camp and gas chambers. Speiss discusses the challenges of conducting the Treblinka investigation, since the camp was almost razed to the ground. He describes the arrival process for Jews in the camp, the gas chambers, and the cremation process as well as the destruction of the camp by the Germans.	2.2 hrs	German
RG-60.5024	Srebnik, Simon	Simon Srebnik was thirteen years old when he was deported to Chełmno from the Łódź ghetto. He worked on a *Sonderkommando* burying those who had been murdered by gas. Srebnik was seriously wounded by gunfire during the liquidation of the camp, but managed to escape and find refuge with a Polish farmer. Srebnik's story is a focal point in *Shoah*.	5.1 hrs	German; Polish; French; Hebrew; English
RG-60.5010	Steiner, Andre	Andre Steiner, an architect, discusses Jewish Councils and resistance activities in Slovakia. He recounts his interactions with Rabbi Weissmandel and Gisi Fleischmann in their attempts to rescue Slovak Jews from deportation.	2.7 hrs	English
RG-60.5064	Stier, Walter	As a *Reichsbahn* official, Walter Stier scheduled the journeys of special trains to different death camps. He claims he knew nothing of their destinations in this hidden-camera interview. He says he never saw the trains that he scheduled. Stier was a witness in many of the postwar trials for high-ranking Nazis, and he voices his disapproval of the statute of limitations on further convictions of Nazis.	1.7 hrs	German
RG-60.5046	Suchomel, Franz	Lanzmann filmed Franz Suchomel, who was with the SS at Treblinka, in secret in March 1976. This was the first interview Lanzmann filmed with the newly developed hidden camera known as the *paluche*. Lanzmann also used an alias and paid Suchomel 500 German marks. Suchomel provides further details about the treatment of Jews at the camp as well as a more ambivalent memory of his experiences than is apparent in the released film.	4.6 hrs	German

Date	Location	Crew	Included in 1985 Film?	Lab preservation work	Transfer Complete?	# of Reels
Spring or Summer 1979	Wuppertal, Germany		Yes	Dec 2017; Oct 2014	Yes	5
September 1978 (Poland) and Fall 1979 (Israel)	Israel; Chełmno, Poland	Corinna Coulmas (interpreter); Barbara Janica (interpreter); Jimmy Glasberg (cinematographer); William Lubtchansky (cinematographer)	Yes	Aug 2007	Yes	15
Winter 1978/1979	Atlanta, Georgia, USA	William Lubtchansky (cinematographer)	No	Nov 2012; Aug 1998	Yes	6
Spring or Summer 1979	Frankfurt, Germany	Dominique Chapuis (cinematographer)	No	Nov 2017; Aug 2016; Oct 2014	Yes	7
March 1976	Austria	William Lubtchansky (cinematographer); Jean-Yves Escoffier (camera assistant)	Yes	Feb 2015	Yes	12

USHMM RG #	Name	Summary	Length	Language
RG-60.5040	Tamir, Shmuel	Shmuel Tamir represented the defendant Malchiel Grünwald in the Kasztner libel trial in Israel. He speaks passionately about the virtues of Rabbi Weissmandel and the perfidy of Rudolf Kasztner.	1.6 hrs	English
RG-60.5016	Vrba, Rudolf	Rudolf Vrba was a Slovakian Jew who escaped from Auschwitz in April 1944 in hopes of warning the world about the imminent destruction of the Hungarian Jews and inciting the Jews to revolt. He describes working on the arrival ramp for ten months and witnessing as Jews from various countries went to the gas chambers. He and Lanzmann debate the culpability of the Jewish Council members and other Jewish leaders, whom Vrba describes as traitors who collaborated with the Nazis.	4 hrs	English
RG-60.5078	Wiener	Dr. Wiener leads Lanzmann around the Jewish quarter of Kraków, Poland, and describes various buildings, sites, and his personal connection to the Holocaust. Wiener points out the street where many Orthodox Jews lived before the war, the old synagogue, and the old wall to the Jewish quarter. Wiener and Lanzmann talk with Israël Hertzl, a Polish Jew who was a driver and German interpreter in the Soviet Army during the war.	1 hr	Polish; German
RG-60.5050	Zaidel, Motke and Dugin, Itzak	Motke Zaidel and Itzak Dugin are survivors of Vilna, Lithuania. They tell the story of their extraordinary escape from the Ponari camp, digging a tunnel for months, and how the dogs that caught them backed away whimpering because the men smelled of death. The interview took place over two days in the forest of Ben Shemen (an Israeli forest resembling Ponari) and in Mr. Zaidel's apartment in Peta'h Tikva.	3.8 hrs	Hebrew; French
RG-60.5072	Ziegelbaum, Faivel	The story of Szmuel (Artur) Ziegelbaum through his brother, Faivel. Faivel reads his brother's letters and occasionally offers his own reflections. Szmuel wrote letters describing his feelings of powerlessness and guilt about family members and thousands of others living in Europe. Faivel reads his brother's suicide letter, which accuses the Allied countries of not doing enough to help the Jews. This interview takes place in Tel Aviv.	1.2 hrs	English

Date	Location	Crew	Included in 1985 Film?	Lab preservation work	Transfer Complete?	# of Reels
September or October 1979	Israel	Corinna Coulmas (interpreter, off-camera); Bernard Aubouy (sound engineer); William Lubtchansky (cinematographer)	No	Apr 2010	Yes	4
November 1978	New York, New York, USA	William Lubtchansky (cinematographer); Dominique Chapuis (cinematographer); Irena Steinfeldt (assistant)	Yes	Jul 2007	Yes	10
March–April 1979 (Pologne II Hiver)	Kraków, Poland	William Lubtchansky (cinematographer)	No	Nov 2017; Aug 2017; Mar 2015	Yes	3
September 18–19, 1979	Israel	Francine Kaufmann (interpreter); Corinna Coulmas (interpreter, off-camera); Bernard Aubouy (sound engineer); William Lubtchansky (cinematographer)	Yes	Aug 2016	Yes	11
September or October 1979	Tel Aviv, Israel	Corinna Coulmas (interpreter, off-camera); Bernard Aubouy (sound engineer); William Lubtchansky (cinematographer)	No	Nov 2017; Aug 2017; Mar 2015	Yes	2

USHMM RG #	Name	Summary	Length	Language
RG-60.5080	Assembled Shots (Poland and Israel)	Assembled color reels containing location filming in Poland and Israel. Some of the cans were marked "Retirages de *Shoah*," which roughly translates to "Miscellaneous Reprints of *Shoah*."	1 hr	Silent
RG-60.5070	AJC offices	Claude Lanzmann interviews an American Jewish Committee (AJC) employee at the New York City office. The employee guides Lanzmann on a tour of the building housing the AJC, which is comprised of several departments.	37 mins	English
RG-60.5057	Auschwitz	Location filming of Auschwitz and Birkenau in winter. Shots of the remains of various buildings on the grounds, including the barracks, the railway to the main entrance, the guard-tower, and the remains of the crematorium.	1.5 hrs	Silent
RG-60.5088	Bełżec	Location filming in Bełżec, Poland.	22 mins	Silent
RG-60.5058	Camionnette	Minibus with equipment for hidden-camera interviews, staged in the suburbs of Paris at Saint Cloud, near the LTC Studio where the final film's editing was done, in May 1983. This could have been staged in France rather late in the film's production to illustrate a sequence about the hidden-camera interviews for the final film.	24 mins	Silent
RG-60.5066	Chełmno	Lanzmann interviews local Polish people in and around Chelmno, Poland and reads a letter from Mr. May regarding operations at Chelmno. Reels also include the landscape of the camp and church services.	4 hrs	French; Polish; Silent
RG-60.5043	Corfu	Lanzmann filmed the few surviving Jews of Corfu, Greece. Many are craftsmen who experienced deportation to Auschwitz and Birkenau. Some interviews take place in the synagogue.	4.5 hrs	French; Hebrew; Italian; Silent
RG-60.5083	Cracow	Scenes of Kraków, Poland, including Nisko, Piotrkow Trybunalski, Wieliczka, and Mielec.	20 mins	Silent

Date	Location	Crew	Included in 1985 Film?	Lab preservation work	Transfer Complete?	# of Reels
Spring 1979	Łódź, Poland; Kraków, Poland; Chełmno, Poland; Warsaw, Poland; Israel	William Lubtchansky (cinematographer)	No	Incomplete; Mar 2019; Aug 2004	No	7
December 1978	New York, New York, USA		No	Jan 2018; Mar 2015	Yes	2
March–April 1979 (Pologne II Hiver)	Oswiecim, Poland	William Lubtchansky (cinematographer)	No	Incomplete; Oct 2019; Sep 2018; Nov 2014	No	9
	Bełžec, Poland		No	Oct 2019; Aug 2019; Jun 2016	Yes	2
May 19, 1983	Saint Cloud, France		No	Mar 2019; Feb 2018; Nov 2014	Yes	2
March–April 1979 (Pologne II Hiver)	Chełmno, Poland		Yes	Oct 2019; Mar 2019; Dec 2017; Dec 2016	Yes	15
September 1978	Corfu, Greece	Jimmy Glasberg (cinematographer); Bernard Aubouy (sound engineer)	Yes	Sep 2019; Aug 2019; Jun 2016; Sep 2009	Yes	13
	Kraków, Poland	Corinna Coulmas (assistant)	No	Nov 2017; Jun 2016	Yes	4

USHMM RG #	Name	Summary	Length	Language
RG-60.5085	Germany; Switzerland	Location filming of scenes in Germany and Switzerland.	3 hrs	Silent
RG-60.5039	Grabów (Maisons)	Interviews with Polish people who live in the village of Grabów. During the war, the synagogue of Grabów was transformed into a furniture warehouse and Jews were deported to Chełmno, less than 20 kilometers away. Lanzmann reads a letter from January 19, 1942, about the killing of Jews at Chełmno that the Grabów rabbi, Jacob Schulmann, wrote to friends in Łódź. The outtakes also include shots of the town and daily life.	2.2 hrs	Polish; French
RG-60.5069	Israel	Location filming of life at the seashore in Tel Aviv, Israel. Men fish at the water's edge, and families gather to enjoy the ocean views. Additional reels show the desert landscape, cemeteries, and the city of Jerusalem.	6 hrs	Silent
RG-60.5076	Lettre Just	Lanzmann reads two versions of the June 5, 1942 letter (Lettre Just) from Willy Just to Walter Rauff concerning gas vans in Chelmno.	42 mins	German
RG-60.5090	Łódź	Location filming in Łódź, Poland of the ghetto, train station, and landscape.	1 hr	Silent
RG-60.5087	Lublin; Majdanek	Location filming of scenes in Lublin and Majdanek camp for *Shoah*.	30 mins	Silent
RG-60.5074	Mengele Factory	Lanzmann talks to German workers and peasants in the present-day Mengele family factory in Günzburg, Germany. The workers are unresponsive, saying things like, "Auschwitz was part good and part bad" or "it's all in the past." Most of them only admit to a vague idea of who Josef Mengele was.	1 hr	German

Date	Location	Crew	Included in 1985 Film?	Lab preservation work	Transfer Complete?	# of Reels
Spring or Summer 1979	Essen, Germany; Wannsee, Germany; Berlin, Germany; Munich, Germany; Geneva, Switzerland; Basel, Switzerland	Corinna Coulmas (assistant)	Yes	Mar 2019; Feb 2018	Yes	13
August 1978; Winter 1978/1979	Grabów, Poland	Barbara Janica (interpreter)	Yes	Jan 2009	Yes	10
September or October 1979	Tel Aviv, Israel		No	Incomplete; Feb 2015	No	15
May 1983	Germany		No	Jan 2018; Mar 2015	Yes	3
	Łódź, Poland		No	Incomplete; Sep 2019; Jun 2016	No	3
	Lublin, Poland; Majdanek, Poland		No	Mar 2019; Jun 2016	Yes	2
July 5, 1979	Günzburg, Germany		No	Incomplete; Dec 2017; Mar 2015	No	4

USHMM RG #	Name	Summary	Length	Language
RG-60.5056	New York	Location filming in New York City including shots of various buildings and bridges in both Manhattan and Brooklyn: the Empire State Building, the World Trade Center, the Brooklyn Bridge, and the Statue of Liberty.	2.5 hrs	Silent
RG-60.5079	Sobibór and Wlodowa	Interviews with local Polish people around Sobibór, Poland, including long sequences of a Catholic mass in Wlodowa. Lanzmann asks about the Jews in Wlodawa before the war and inquires how non-Jewish residents got along with the Jews. Also includes shots of the Sobibór camp and environs.	4 hrs	Polish; French
RG-60.5041	Society of the Survivors of the Riga Ghetto (New York)	Lanzmann films at a New York conference for survivors of the Riga ghetto. He interviews several former Jewish policemen from Riga, Latvia who describe the division of the ghetto into sections for Latvian Jews and German Jews, dealing with the Nazi discovery of a secret weapons cache, and responsibilities as Jewish police. He also interviews veteran frontline soldier, Friedrich Baer.	35 mins	German
RG-60.5081	Theresienstadt; Prague	Location filming in and around Terezin and Prague in Czechoslovakia.	40 mins	Silent
RG-60.5077	Treblinka	Location filming of Treblinka and the train station. Includes short interviews with individuals in Iladou, Poniatowo, and Wolka Okraglik, Poland. Lanzmann talks with Polish men and women who describe having lived and worked in the fields in the shadow of Treblinka during its operation. Some discuss finding corpses of Jews and being able to smell the burning bodies, while others describe their fears of being killed by the Ukrainians who served as camp guards simply for looking at the camp.	7 hrs	Polish; French; Silent
RG-60.5089	Warsaw	Location filming in Warsaw, Poland including the ghetto, Mila 18, the Rappoport memorial, the cemetery, the railway station, and archival documents and photographs.	2 hrs	Polish; French; Silent

Date	Location	Crew	Included in 1985 Film?	Lab preservation work	Transfer Complete?	# of Reels
November 1978	New York, New York, USA		Yes	Incomplete; Aug 2019; Nov 2014	Yes	5
1978–1981	Wlodowa, Poland; Sobibór, Poland; Poland	Barbara Janica (interpreter)	Yes	Jul 2019; Jun 2016; Mar 2015	Yes	19
November 1978	New York, New York, USA	William Lubtchansky (cinematographer); Irena Steinfeldt (assistant)	No	Incomplete; Mar 2019; Feb 2018; Aug 2016; Mar 2010	No	5
March–April 1979	Terezin, Czechoslovakia; Prague, Czechoslovakia	William Lubtchansky (camera operator)	No	Mar 2019; Feb 2018; Oct 2015	Yes	2
July 1978 and 1981	Iladou, Poland; Wolka Okraglik, Poland; Poniatowo, Poland	Jimmy Glasberg (cinematographer)	Yes	Oct 2019; Jul 2019; Aug 2016; Apr 2009	Yes	36
	Warsaw, Poland		Yes	Incomplete; Oct 2019; Sep 2018	Yes	8

USHMM RG #	Name	Summary	Length	Language
RG-60.5086	US cities: Atlanta, Washington, DC, and Panama City	Location filming in Atlanta, Georgia, Washington, DC, and Panama City, Florida. Several interviews were conducted in these regions, including Steiner, Reams, Karski, McClelland, and Biren.	42 mins	Silent
RG-60.5073	Yad Vashem	A university course debate by a professor in front of an assembly of military school students after a film showing at Yad Vashem. They debate the resistance actions of the Jews during the Holocaust and the world's reluctance to help the Jews. The students voice their concerns about the Holocaust happening again.	1.2 hrs	Hebrew

Date	Location	Crew	Included in 1985 Film?	Lab preservation work	Transfer Complete?	# of Reels
July 1978 and 1981	Washington, DC, USA; Atlanta, Georgia, USA; Panama City, Florida, USA	William Lubtchansky (cinematographer); Dominique Chapuis (cinematographer)	Yes	Mar 2019; Feb 2018	Yes	3
October 12, 1979	Jerusalem, Israel	Francine Kaufmann (interpreter); Corinna Coulmas (interpreter, off-camera); Bernard Aubouy (sound engineer); William Lubtchansky (cinematographer)	No	Nov 2017; Mar 2015	Yes	3

Appendix 2 | Works by and about Claude Lanzmann

Films Directed by Claude Lanzmann

The Four Sisters (*Les quatre soeurs*). 2018; Synecdoche, 273 min.

Israel, Why (*Porquoi Israël*). 1973; Stéphan Films, Compagnie d'Entreprise et de Gestion (CEG) and Parafrance Films, 185 min.

The Karski Report (*La rapport Karski*). 2010; Arte, 48 min.

The Last of the Unjust (*Le dernier des injustes*). 2013; Synecdoche, Le Pacte, Dor Film Produktionsgesellschaft, 220 min.

Lights and Shadows. 2008; Why Not Productions, 40 min.

Napalm. 2017; Margo Cinema, Orange Studio, Centre National de la Cinématographie, Région Ile-de-France, 100 min.

Shoah. 1985; BBC, Historia, Les Films Aleph, Ministère de la Culture de la Republique Française, 566 min.

Sobibór, October 14, 1943, 4 p.m. (*Sobibór, 14 octobre 1943, 16 heures*). 2001; France 2 Cinéma, Les Films Aleph, Why Not Productions, 95 min.

Tsahal. 1994; Bavaria Film, France 2 Cinéma, Les Films Aleph, Les Productions Dussart. 316 min.

A *Visitor from the Living (Un vivant qui passe)*. 1999; La Sept-Arte, Les Films Aleph, MTM Cineteve, 65 min.

Writings by Claude Lanzmann

"À propos de *Shoah*." In *Shoah le film: des psychanalystes écrivent*, 199–214. France: James Grancher, 1990.

Commentary (with Angelika Schrobsdorff). *Der Vogel hat keine Flügel mehr: Briefe meines Bruders Peter Schwiefert an unsere Mutter*, edited by Angelika Schrobsdorff. München: Deutscher Taschenbuch Verlag, 2012.

"Concerning the Accounts given by the Residents of Hiroshima." In *Trauma: Explorations in Memory*, edited by Cathy Caruth. Baltimore, MD: Johns Hopkins University Press, 1995, 221–35.

Das Grab des göttlichen Tauchers: Ausgewählte Texte. Translated by E. W. Skwara. Reinbek: Rowohlt, 2015.

"De l'Holocauste à Holocauste ou comment s'en débarrasser." *In Au sujet de* Shoah: *Le film de Claude Lanzmann*, edited by M. Deguy, 306-16. Paris: Éditions Belin, 1990.

"Filip Müller, fossoyeur et martyr." *Le Nouvel Observateur* (1980): 135–55.

Foreword. *I Shall Live: Surviving Against All Odds*. By Henry Orenstein, ix–xii. New York: Beaufort, 1987.

"From the Holocaust to 'Holocaust.'" In *Claude Lanzmann's Shoah: Key Essays*, edited by Stuart Liebman, 27–36. Oxford: Oxford University Press, 2007.

"Hier ist kein Warum." In Liebman, *Claude Lanzmann's Shoah*, 51–52.

"Holocauste, la représentation impossible." *Le Monde*, March 3, 1994.

"Ihr sollt nicht weinen. Einspruch gegen *Schindlers Liste*." *Frankfurter Allgemeine Zeitung*, March 5, 1994.

"J'ai enquêté en Pologne." In Deguy, *Au sujet de* Shoah, 211–17.

"La question n'est pas celle du document, mais celle de la vérité." *Le Monde*, January 19, 2001.

"Le lieu et la parole." In Deguy, *Au sujet de* Shoah, 407–25.

Le lièvre de Patagonie. Paris: Éditions Gallimard, 2009.

"Le monument contre l'archive?" *Cahiers de médiologie* 11 (2001): 271–79.

"Les non-lieux de la mémoire." In Deguy, *Au sujet de* Shoah, 280–92.

"Parler pour les morts." *Le Monde des Débats* (2000): 14–16.

The Patagonian Hare: A Memoir. Translated by Frank Wynne. New York: Farrar, Straus & Giroux, 2012.

"Réponse à Marcel Ophüls." *Les Cahiers du Cinéma* (2002): 54–55.

"*Shoah.*" *Jewish Quarterly* 198 (Summer 2005): 43–48.

Shoah: The Complete Text of the Acclaimed Holocaust Film. Cambridge, MA: Da Capo, 1995.

Shoah. Translated by Nina Börnsen and Anna Kamp. Hamburg: Rowohlt Taschenbuch Verlag, 2011.

"Un cineaste au-dessous de tout soupçon?" *Le Nouvel Observateur* (1991): 70–73.

"Why Spielberg has Distorted the Truth." *Guardian Weekly*, April 3, 1994.

Interviews with Claude Lanzmann

Blouin, Patrice, Franck Nouchi, and Charles Tesson. "Claude Lanzmann: Sur le courage." *Cahiers du cinema* 561 (October 2001): 47–57.

Chevrie, Marc, and Hervé Le Roux. "Site and Speech: An Interview with Claude Lanzmann about *Shoah.*" Translated by Stuart Liebman. In Liebman, *Claude Lanzmann's Shoah,* 37–49.

Dax, Max. "Claude Lanzmann im Gespräch mit Max Dax." In *Shoah,* 279–303. Hamburg: Rowohlt Taschenbuch Verlag, 2011.

Gantheret, F. "Das Aussetzen der Erinnerung. Ein Gespräch mit Claude Lanzmann." *Psyche* 42, no. 3 (1988): 245–57.

Frodon, Jean-Michel. "The Work of the Filmmaker: An Interview with Claude Lanzmann." In *Cinema and the Shoah: An Art Confronts the Tragedy of the Twentieth Century,* edited by Jean-Michel Frodon, translated by Anna Harrison, 93–106. Albany: State University of New York Press, 2010.

Herpell, Gabriela, and Thomas Bärnthaler. "Ich wolle erfahren, wie man fünf Millionen Menschen vergast," *Süddeutsche Zeitung Magazin* 48 (2015): https://sz-magazin.sueddeutsche.de/geschichte/ich-wollte-erfahren-wie-man-fuenf-millionen-menschen-vergast-81934.

Hoberman, J. "The Being of Nothingness: An Interview with Claude Lanzmann." In *The Faber Book of Documentary,* edited by Kevin Macdonald and Mark Cousins, 322–25. London: Faber, 1997.

Jeffries, Stuart. "Claude Lanzmann on why Holocaust Documentary *Shoah* Still Matters." *Guardian,* June 9, 2011.

Khalfa, Jean. "Claude Lanzmann in Conversation." *Wasafiri* 44 (2005): 19–23.

Laub, Dori, and Laurel Vloch. "An Evening with Claude Lanzmann." Video Archive for Holocaust Testimonies at Yale University, May 4, 1986.

"The Obscenity of Understanding: An Evening with Claude Lanzmann." *American Imago* 48 (1991): 473–95.

"Sartre's 'J'accuse': Ein Gespräch mit Claude Lanzmann." *Babylon* 2 (1987): 72–79.

"Seminar with Claude Lanzmann 11 April 1990." *Yale French Studies* 79 (1991): 82–99.

Stone, Judy. *Eye on the World: Conversations with International Filmmakers.* Los Angeles: Silman-James, 1997, 180–82.

| Reviews of Claude Lanzmann's Films

Ascherson, Neal. "The *Shoah* Controversy." *Soviet Jewish Affairs* 16, no. 1 (1986): 53–61.

Ash, Timothy Garton. "The Life of Death." *New York Review of Books,* December 19, 1985, 26–29.

Asséo, Henriette. "La premiere fois." *Les Temps Modernes* 471 (1985): 530–38.

Audé, François. "Tsahal: L'agressivité est l'onde de choc du passé." *Postif—Revue mensuelle de cinema* (1994): 43–44.

Bernstein, Richard. "An Epic Film About the Greatest Evil of Modern Times: An Epic Film about the Holocaust." *New York Times,* October 20, 1985.

Brody, Richard. "Witness." *New Yorker,* March 19, 2012, https://www.newyorker.com/magazine/2012/03/19/witness-5.

———. "Claude Lanzmann's *The Last of the Unjust.*" *New Yorker,* September 27, 2013, https://www.newyorker.com/culture/richard-brody/claude-lanzmanns-the-last-of-the-unjust.

Brumberg, Abraham. "What Poland Forgot." *New Republic,* December 16, 1985, 46–48.

Brumlik, Micha. "Der zähe Schaum der Verdrängung." *Spiegel,* February 17, 1986, 192–97.

Buchka, Peter. "Was ein Leben vom Menschen ist. *Shoah* von Claude Lanzmann: eine Dokumentation der Judenvernichtung im Dritten Reich." *Süddeutsche Zeitung,* March 1–2, 1986, 151.

Canby, Vincent. "*Shoah*: Memories of the Death Camps." *New York Times,* October 23, 1985.

Cohn, Bernard. "Lettre de lecteur: À propos du *Dernier des injustes* de Claude Lanzmann." *Positif—Revue mensuelle de cinema* (2014): 82.

Corliss, Richard. Review of *Shoah. Time,* November 4, 1985, 96.

Cremonini, Giorgio. "La Memoria Della Shoah: Nel Vento. In DVD Il Film-Documento di Claude Lanzmann sui Lager Nazisti." *Cineforum* 48, no. 4 (2008): 48–50.

Demeure, Jasques. "Les insuffisances de l'honnêteté (pourquoi israël?)." *Postif—Revue mensuelle de cinema* (1974): 71–72.

Denby, David. Review of *Shoah. New York Magazine,* October 28, 1985, 130.

———. "Look Again: The Current Cinema." *New Yorker,* January 10, 2011, 80–81.

Dickstein, Morris. "*Shoah* and the Machinery of Death." *Partisan Review* 53, no. 1 (1986): 36–42.

Dupont, Joan. "An Auteur's Postscript to *Shoah*; With *Last of the Unjust,* Director Finds New Voice in Interviews with Rabbi." *International Herald Tribune,* May 18, 2013.

Ebert, Roger. Review of *Shoah. Chicago Sun-Times,* November 24, 1985.

Edholm, Felicity. "*Shoah*: A Film by Claude Lanzmann." *History Workshop* 25 (1988): 204–6.

Erens, Patricia. Review of *Shoah. Film Quarterly* 39, no. 4 (1986): 28–31.

Giavarini, Laurence. "Sur les héros de Sobibór: Le Dernier Film de Claude Lanzmann et la représentation de la Shoah." *Cahiers du Cinéma* 565 (2002): 46–48.

Hoberman, J. "*Shoah*: Witness to Annihilation." *Village Voice,* October 29, 1985, 46.

———. "Shoah Business." *Village Voice,* January 28, 1986, 24.

———. "*The Last of the Unjust,* the New Film by the Director of *Shoah,* Is a Moral and Aesthetic Blunder." *Tablet,* February 5, 2014, https://www.tabletmag.com/ jewish-arts-and-culture/161448/last-of-the-unjust-lanzmann-hoberman.

Hynes, Eric. "Film: What Is *Shoah*?" *Village Voice,* December 8, 2010, 46.

Jacobowitz, Florence. "Claude Lanzmann's *The Last of the Unjust.*" *Cineaction* 92 (2014): 68–70.

Jones, Kent. "Present Tense." *Film Comment* 47, no. 1 (2011): 62–67.

———. "Truth Be Told." *Film Comment* 48, no. 2 (2012): 78.

Joyard, Olivier. "Vous n'avez encore rien vu." *Cahiers du cinéma* 557 (May 2001): 97.

Kael, Pauline. Review of *Shoah. New Yorker,* December 30, 1985, 70–72.

Kauffmann, Stanley. Review of *Shoah. New Republic,* October 28, 1985, 39–40.

Kermode, Mark, and Peter Dean. Review of *Shoah. Sight and Sound* 4, no. 12 (1994): 59.

Kissel, Howard. Review of *Shoah. Women's Wear Daily,* October 21, 1985.

Kreimeier, Klaus. "Unsagbares sagen. Claude Lanzmann's Film *Shoah.*" *Epd Film* 3, no. 2. (1986): 24–27.

Kuryluk, Ewa. "Memory and Responsibility: Claude Lanzmann's *Shoah.*" *New Criterion* 4 (1985): 14–20.

Lewis, Anthony. "'Remember, Remember': *Shoah* Means Annihilation." *New York Times,* December 2, 1985.

Liebman, Stuart. "*The Last of the Unjust.*" *Cineaste* 39, no. 2 (2014): 42–44.

Lilla, Mark. "The Defense of a Jewish Collaborator." *New York Review of Books,* December 5, 2013.

Luft, Hebert. Review of *Shoah*. *Films in Review*, May 1986, 306.

Macnab, Geoffrey. "Return to *Shoah*: Claude Lanzmann's New Film *The Last of the Unjust* Revisits Holocaust Epic." *Independent*, March 14, 2014.

McGill, Hannah. "*The Last of the Unjust*." *Sight and Sound* 25, no. 2 (2015): 66–67.

Mertens, Jacob. "Criterion Core: Time Distorts All Things." *Film International* 12, no. 3 (2014): 143–46.

Nichols, Peter M. "Spoken Memories of the Unspeakable." *New York Times*, December 19, 1999.

Rabinbach, Anson. Review of *Shoah*. *Nation*, March 15, 1986, 313–17.

Romano, Carlin. "Portrait of the Artist as a Glamorous Existentialist." *Chronicle of Higher Education* 58, no. 28 (2012): B4–B5.

Rosenbaum, Jonathan. "Beyond Good and Evil." *Artforum International* 52, no. 6 (2014): 65–66.

Rubenstein, Lenny. Review of *Shoah*. *Cineaste* 14, no. 3 (1986): 39.

Sanaker, John Kristian. "Claude Lanzmanns *Shoah*: TV-dokumentar utenom det vanlige." *Z: Filmtidsskrift* 6, no. 2 (1988): 8–9.

Seitz, Michael H. Review of *Shoah*. *Progressive* 49 (1985): 49.

Seligsohn, Leo. Review of *Shoah*. *Newsday*, October 23, 1985.

Sklar, Robert. "Lanzmann's Latest: After *Shoah*, Jewish Power." *Forward* 10 (1994): 10.

Solle, Dorothee. "Von Gott verlassen: Augenzeugen des Holocaust: Claude Lanzmanns Film *Shoah*." *Die Zeit*, February 21, 1986.

Sterritt, David. Review of *Shoah*. *Christian Science Monitor*, November 22, 1985.

Thomas, Kevin. Review of *Shoah*. *Los Angeles Times*, December 27, 1985.

Toumarkine, Doris. "*A Visitor from the Living*." *Film Journal International* 103, no. 2 (2000): 75–76.

———. "Buying and Booking Guide: *The Last of the Unjust*, Directed by Claude Lanzmann." *Film Journal International* 117, no. 3 (2014): 58.

———. "*The Last of the Unjust*." *Film Journal International* 117, no. 3 (2014): 58.

Turowicz, Jerzy. "*Shoah* w polskich oczach." *Tygodnik Powszechny*, November 10, 1985.

Ward, Geoffrey C. Review of *Shoah*. *American Heritage* 37 (1986): 15.

Webster, Robert M. Review of *Shoah*. *French Review* 61, no. 6 (1988): 976–77.

Wiesel, Elie. Review of *Shoah*. *New York Times*, November 3, 1985.

Wieseltier, Leon. Review of *Shoah*. *Dissent* 33, no. 1 (1986): 27–32.

Winsten, Archer. Review of *Shoah*. *New York Post*, October 23, 1985.

Articles on Claude Lanzmann's Films

Angress, Ruth K. "Lanzmann's *Shoah* and its Audience." *Simon Wiesenthal Center Annual* 3 (1986): 249–60.

Avni, Ora. "Narrative Subject, Historic Subject: *Shoah* and *La Place de l'Etoile*." *Poetics Today* 12, no. 3 (1991): 495–516.

Banaji, Ferzina. "The Shoah after *Shoah*: Memory, the Body, and the Future of the Holocaust in French Cinema." *Esprit Createur* 50, no. 4 (2010): 122–36.

Bellour, Raymond. "Le tremblement." *Trafic* 47 (2003): 67–70.

Biró, Yvette. "The Unbearable Weight of Non-Being." *Cross-Currents* 6 (1987): 75–82.

Blouin, Patrice, Franck Nouchi, and Charles Tesson. "Claude Lanzmann: Sur le courage." *Cahiers du Cinéma* 561 (2001): 46–57.

Braganca, Manuel. "Faire parler les morts: sur Jan Karski et la controverse Lanzmann-Haenel." *Modern and Contemporary France* 23, no. 1 (2015): 35–46.

Brinkley, Robert, and Steven Youra. "Tracing *Shoah*." *PMLA* 111, no. 1 (1996): 108–27.

Carter-White, Richard. "Towards a Spatial Historiography of the Holocaust: Resistance, Film, and the Prisoner Uprising at Sobibór Death Camp." *Political Geography* 33 (2013): 21–30.

Cesarani, David. "Memory and Forgetting: Twenty-Five Years after Its Release, *Shoah*, Claude Lanzmann's Documentary about the Extermination of the Jews, Has Lost None of Its Power." *New Statesman* 139, no. 5029 (November 29, 2010): 42–43.

Champetier, Caroline. "C'est quoi une camera." *Cahiers du cinéma* (2005): 10–11.

Chare, Nicholas. "Gesture in *Shoah*." *Journal for Cultural Research* 19, no. 1 (2015): 30–42.

Charny, Israel W. "A Study of Attitudes of Viewers of the Film *Shoah* towards an Incident of Mass Murder by Israeli Soldiers." *Journal of Traumatic Stress* 5, no. 2 (1992): 303–18.

Clendinnen, Inga. "Representing the Holocaust: The Case for the History." *Michigan Quarterly Review* 37, no. 1 (1998): 80–100.

Cuau, Bernard. "Dans le cinema une langue étrangère." In Deguy, *Au sujet du Shoah*, 13–19.

De Urabain, Ainara Miguel Sáez. "Can the Photography Show the Unimaginable? The Debate on the Representation of the Shoah?" *Revisita Fotocinema* 10 (2015): 1–36.

Desplechin, Arnaud. "Les Films de Claude Lanzmann." *Infini* (2002): 54–64.

Doherty, Thomas. "Representing the Holocaust: Claude Lanzmann's *Shoah*." *Film & History* 17, no. 1 (1987): 2–8.

Erlewine, Robert A. "When the Blind Speak of Colour: Narrative, Ethics, and Stories of the Shoah." *Journal of Visual Art Practice* 1, no. 1 (2001): 25–37.

Esquenazi, Jean-Pierre. "Qu'est-ce que tu as vu à Chelmno? *Shoah*, un monumentaire." *Cinemas* 12, no. 1 (2001): 147–65.

Felman, Shoshana. "In an Era of Testimony: Claude Lanzmann's *Shoah*." *Yale French Studies* 79, Literature and the Ethical Question (1991): 39–81.

———. "Theaters of Justice: Arendt in Jerusalem, the Eichmann Trial, and the Redefinition of Legal Meaning in the Wake of the Holocaust." *Critical Inquiry* 27, no. 2 (2001): 201–38.

Fornara, Bruno. "Recontre avec Claude Lanzmann à propos de *Pourquoi Israël*." *Jeune Cinéma* (2007): 77–81.

Franklin, Ruth. "On Film: *Shoah*, by Claude Lanzmann." *Salmagundi* (2011): 26–34.

Frappat, Hélène. "Les chemins de la liberté." *Cahiers du cinéma* (2001): 77–78.

Friedman, Elisabeth R. "The Anti-Archive? Claude Lanzmann's *Shoah* and the Dilemmas of Holocaust Representation." *English Language Notes* 45, no. 1 (2007): 111–21.

Friedman, Régine Mihal. "'Du wirst nicht mehr töten'—Der erste von Claude Lanzmann für TSAHAL vorgesehene Titel." *Frauen und Film* 61 (2000): 65–83.

Frodon, Jean-Michel. "Le fameux débat' Lanzmann-Godard: Le parti des mots contre le parti des images." *Le Monde*, June 18, 1999.

———. "Juste des images." *Cahiers du Cinéma* 587 (2004): 19–22.

———. "Repliques: L'horizon ethique." *Cahiers du Cinéma* (2004): 60–63.

Fuller, Graham. "Searching for the Stamp of Truth: Claude Lanzmann Reflects on the Making of *Shoah*." *Cineaste* 36, no. 2 (2011): 16–19.

———. "The Unimaginable Imagined." *Sight & Sound* 23, no. 8 (2013): 94–95.

Gantheret, François. "Das Aussetzen der Erinnerung. Ein Gespräch mit Claude Lanzmann." *Psyche* 42, no. 3 (1988): 245–57.

Garbus, Lisa. "The Unspeakable Stories of *Shoah* and *Beloved*." *College Literature* 52, no. 1 (1999): 52–68.

Geller, Jay. "The Rites of Responsibility: The Cinematic Rhetoric of Claude Lanzmann's *Shoah* (1985)." *Film & History* 32, no. 1 (2002): 30–37.

Gelley, Ora. "A Response to Dominick LaCapra's 'Lanzmann's *Shoah*.'" *Critical Inquiry* 24 (1998): 830–32.

Goutte, Martin. "Rendez-vous avec l'Histoire: les trains et la Shoah: motif de l'Histoire, histoire d'un motif." *CinémAction* (2012): 138–42.

Habib, André. "Delay, Estrangement, Loss: The Meanings of Translation in Claude Lanzmann's *Shoah* (1985)." *SubStance* 44, no. 2 (2015): 108–28.

Halkin, Hillel. "Claude Lanzmann and the IDF." *Commentary* 99, no. 6 (1995): 45–51.

Hansen, Miriam Bratu. "*Schindler's List* Is Not *Shoah*: The Second Commandment, Popular Modernism, and Public Memory." *Critical Inquiry* 22, no. 2 (1996): 292–312.

Hoberman, J. "The Being of Nothingness: An Interview with Claude Lanzmann." In *The Faber Book of Documentary*, edited by Kevin Macdonald and Mark Cousins, 322–25. London: Faber, 1997.

Howland, Jacob. "Reflections on Claude Lanzmann's *Shoah*." *Proteus* 12, no. 2 (1995): 42–46.

Jeffries, Stuart. "Claude Lanzmann on Why Holocaust Documentary *Shoah* Still Matters." *Guardian*, June 9, 2011.

Kaufmann, Francine. "Interview et interprétation consécutive dans le film *Shoah*, de Claude Lanzmann." *Translators' Journal* 38, no. 4 (1993): 664–73.

Kellmann, Steven. "Cinema of/as Atrocity: *Shoah*'s Guilty Conscience." *Gettysburg Review* 1, no. 1 (1988): 22–30.

Kippen, Lorelee. "Performing the Gendered Holocaust Body: Traumatic Style, Memory, and the Search for Proper Identities." *South Atlantic Review* 68, no. 1 (2003): 34–63.

Koch, Gertrud. "The Aesthetic Transformation of the Image of the Unimaginable: Notes on Claude Lanzmann's *Shoah*." *October* 48 (1989): 15–24.

———. "The Angel of Forgetfulness and the Black Box of Facticity: Trauma and Memory in Claude Lanzmann's Film *Shoah*." *History & Memory* 3, no. 1 (1991): 119–34.

Köppen, Manuel. "Searching for Evidence between Generations: Claude Lanzmann's *Sobibór* and Romuald Karmakar's *Land of Annihilation*." *New German Critique* 123 (2014): 57–73.

LaCapra, Dominick. "Lanzmann's *Shoah*: 'Here There Is No Why.'" *Critical Inquiry* 23, no. 2 (1997): 231–69.

———. "Equivocations of Autonomous Art." *Critical Inquiry* 24 (1998): 833–36.

Lawless, Kate. "Memory, Trauma, and the Matter of Historical Violence: The Controversial Case of Four Photographs from Auschwitz." *American Imago* 71, no. 4 (2014): 391–412.

Le Fanu, Mark, and Paul Coates. "Letters: Criticizing *Shoah*." *Encounter* 69 (1987): 79–80.

Leone, Massimo. "*Shoah* and Humour: A Semiotic Approach." *Jewish Studies Quarterly* 9, no. 2 (2002): 173–92.

Leszczyńska, Dorota, and Reinhold Vetter, eds. "In letzter Konsequenz antipolnisch . . . Warschauer Kommentare zu dem französischen Film *Shoah* über das jüdisch-polnische Verhältnis." *Osteuropa* 36 (1986): 568–78.

Linke, Uli. "Murderous Fantasies: Violence, Memory, and Selfhood in Germany." *New German Critique* 64, Germany: East, West, and Other (1995): 37–59.

Listoe, Daniel. "Seeing Nothing: Allegory and the Holocaust's Absent Dead." *SubStance* 35, no. 2 (2006): 51–70.

McGlothlin, Erin. "Listening to the Perpetrators in Claude Lanzmann's *Shoah*." *Colloquia Germanica* 43, no. 3 ([2010] 2013): 235–71.

Mongin, Olivier. "Se souvenir de la *Shoah*: histoire et fiction." *Esprit* 1 (1988): 85–98.

Moser, Keith. "The Poignant Combination of Beauty and Horror in the Aesthetic Representations of the Holocaust in Lanzmann's *Shoah* and Le Clézio's *Etoile Errante*." *Dalhousie French Studies* 92 (2010): 75–83.

Naveh, Gila Safran. "A Speck of Dust Blown by the Wind across Land and Desert: Images of the Holocaust in Lanzmann, Singer, and Appelfeld." In *Jewish American and Holocaust Literature: Representation in the Postmodern World*, edited by Alan L. Berger and Gloria L. Cronin, 103–14. Albany: State University of New York Press, 2004.

Ochman, Ewa. "The Search for Legitimacy in Post-Martial Law Poland: The Case of Claude Lanzmann's *Shoah*." *Cold War History* 6, no. 4 (2006): 501–26.

Olin, Margaret. "Lanzmann's *Shoah* and the Topography of the Holocaust Film." *Representations* 57 (1997): 1–23.

———. "Graven Images on Video? The Second Commandment and Jewish Identity." *Discourse: Journal for Theoretical Studies in Media and Culture* 22, no. 1 (2000): 7–30.

Paisova, Elena. "Opyt: Klod Lantsman: 'Ne vernut' k zhizni, a umertvit' snova.'" *Iskusstvo Kino* 1 (2010): http://kefisrael.com/2011/01/26/le-montage-du-film -shoah-ziva-postec/.

Pătrăşconiu, Cristian. "La Auschwitz/ Citeşte şi taci . . ." *Orizont* 12 (2002): 18–19.

Plank, Karl A. "The Survivor's Return: Reflections on Memory and Place." *Judaism* 38, no. 3 (1989): 263–77.

Postec, Ziva. "Le montage du film *Shoah*." *Kef Israël*, January 26, 2011.

Rabinowitz, Paula. "Wreckage upon Wreckage: History, Documentary, and the Ruins of Memory." *History and Theory* 32, no. 2 (1993): 119–37.

Renga, Dana. "Staging Memory and Trauma in French and Italian Holocaust Film." *Romanic Review* 97, nos. 3–4 (2006): 461–82.

Richards, Jeffrey. "*Shoah* and Four Films after *Shoah.*" *History Today* 65, no. 3 (2015): 63.

Richmond, Thomas. "The Perpetrator's Testimonies in *Shoah.*" *Journal of Holocaust Education* 5, no. 1 (1996): 61–83.

Robbins, Jill. "The Writing of the Holocaust: Claude Lanzmann's *Shoah.*" *Prooftexts* 7, no. 3 (1987): 249–58.

Rogerson, Edward. "Movies and Metaphysics: Steiner, Coates, *Shoah.*" *Encounter* 70 (1988): 63–65.

Roth, Michael S. "*Shoah* as Shivah." *Etnofoor* 6, no. 1 (1993): 83–94.

Saxton, Libby. "Fragile Faces: Levinas and Lanzmann." *Film-Philosophy* 11, no. 2 (2007): 1–14.

———. "Influential: Filming the 'Unfilmable.'" *Vertigo* 3, no. 6 (2007): 14.

Scheel, Kurt. "Grosses Unheil, Katastrophe. Zu Claude Lanzmanns Film Shoah." *Merkur: Deutsche Zeitschrift für europäisches Denken* 40, no. 6 (1986): 529–32.

Singleton, Daniel. "Exhausting Documentary: The Affects of Adapting Histories within and between Three Holocaust Documentaries." *South Atlantic Review* 79, nos. 1–2 (2015): 177–95.

Skloot, Robert. "Lanzmann's *Shoah* after Twenty-Five Years: An Overview and a Further View." *Holocaust and Genocide Studies* 26, no. 2 (2012): 261–75.

Stoekl, Allan. "Lanzmann and Deleuze: On the Question of Memory." *Symplokē* 6, nos. 1–2 (1998): 72–82.

Stoicea, Gabriela. "The Difficulties of Verbalizing Trauma: Translation and the Economy of Loss in Claude Lanzmann's *Shoah.*" *Journal of the Midwest Modern Language Association* 9, no. 2 (2006): 43–53.

Tsuchimoto, Noriaki. "'*Shoah* m'aide à repenser les possibilities du cinêma': Un Lettre à Claude Lanzmann." *Cahiers du Cinéma* 596 (2004): 63–64.

Vice, Sue. "Claude Lanzmann's Einsatzgruppen Interviews." *Holocaust Studies: A Journal of Culture and History* 17, nos. 2–3 (2011): 51–74.

———. "Generic Hybridity in Holocaust Cinema." *Short Film Studies* 4, no. 2 (2014): 199–202.

Vulliet, Armand. "Letters to Claude Lanzmann and to the Grand Larousse." *Yale French Studies* 85 (1994): 152–59.

Wajcman, Gérard. "'Saint Paul' Godard contre 'Moïse' Lanzmann, le match." *L'Infini* 65 (1999): 26–30.

Williams, Linda. "Mirrors without Memories: Truth, History, and the New Documentary." *Film Quarterly* 46, no. 3 (1993): 9–21.

Wilson, Emma. "Material Remains: Night and Fog." *MIT Press Journals* 112 (2005): 89–110.

Zeitlin, Froma I. "The Vicarious Witness: Belated Memory and Authorial Presence in Recent Holocaust Literature." *History & Memory* 10, no. 2 (1998): 5–42.

Books and Book Chapters on Claude Lanzmann's Films

Alterman, Aline, *Visages de Shoah: Le film de Claude Lanzmann*. Paris: Cerf, 2006.

Ash, Timothy Garton. "The Life of Death: *Shoah*—A Film by Claude Lanzmann." In Liebman, *Claude Lanzmann's* Shoah, 135–47.

Avisar, Ilan. *Screening the Holocaust: Cinema's Images of the Unimaginable*. Bloomington: Indiana University Press, 1988.

Bernauer, James S. J. "The Flawed Vision in Claude Lanzmann's *Shoah* (1985) and the Corrective Lens of Pierre Sauvage." In *Through a Lens Darkly: Films of Genocide, Ethnic Cleansing, and Atrocities*, edited by Raymond G. Helmick and John J. Michalczyk, 107–14. New York: Peter Lang, 2013.

Boswell, Matthew. *Holocaust Impiety in Literature, Popular Music, and Film*. London: Palgrave Macmillan, 2012.

Brodsky, Claudia. "'Auf das Wo komme es eigentlich an': Memory, Catastrophe, and Society in Lanzmann, Rousseau, and Goethe." In *Katastrophe und Gedächtnis*, edited by Thomas Klinkert and Güter Oesterle, 320–32. Berlin: de Gruyter, 2013.

Brown, Adam. "Bridging History and Cinema: Privileged Jews in Claude Lanzmann's *Shoah* and Other Holocaust Documentaries." In *Judging "Privileged" Jews: Holocaust Ethics, Representation, and the "Gray Zone."* Studies on War and Genocide. Vol 18. New York: Berghahn, 2013.

Bruzzi, Stella. *New Documentary*. New York: Routledge, 2006.

Burns, Bryan. "Fiction of the Real: *Shoah* and Documentary." In *Representing the Holocaust: Essays in Honour of Bryan Burns*, edited by Sue Vice, 81–88. London: Vallentine Mitchell, 2003.

Camper, Fred. "*Shoah*'s Absence." In Liebman, *Claude Lanzmann's* Shoah, 103–11.

Cantor, Jay. "Death and the Image." In *Beyond Document: Essays on Nonfiction Film*, edited by Charles Warren, 23–49. Hanover, NH: University Press of New England, 1996.

Cazenave, Jennifer. *An Archive of the Catastrophe: The Unused Footage of Claude Lanzmann's* Shoah. Albany: State University of New York Press, 2019.

Colombat, André. *The Holocaust in French Film*. Metuchen, NJ: Scarecrow, 1993.

Cuau, Bernard. "Dans le cinema une langue étrangère." In Deguy, *Au sujet du Shoah*, 13–19.

D'Arcy, Michael. "Claude Lanzmann's *Shoah* and the Intentionality of the Image." In *Visualizing the Holocaust: Documents, Aesthetics, Memory*, edited by David Bathrick, Brad Prager, and Michael D. Richardson, 138–61. Rochester, NY: Camden House, 2008.

Dayan-Rosenman, Anny. "*Shoah*: L'écho du silence." In Deguy, *Au sujet du* Shoah, 188–97.

De Beauvoir, Simone. "*Shoah*." In Liebman, *Claude Lanzmann's* Shoah, 63–65.

Deguy, Michel, ed. *Au sujet de* Shoah. Paris: Belin, 1990.

Delacampagne, Christian. "Claude Lanzmann (1925–)." In *The Columbia History of Twentieth-Century French Thought*, edited by Lawrence D. Kritzman, 571–72. New York: Columbia University Press, 2006.

Denby, David. "Out of Darkness." In Liebman, *Claude Lanzmann's* Shoah, 73–76.

Didi-Huberman, Georges. "The Site, Despite Everything." In Liebman, *Claude Lanzmann's* Shoah, 113–24.

Didier, E., A. M. Houdebine, and J. J. Moscovitz, eds. Shoah *le film. Des psychanalystes écrivent*. Paris: Jacques Grancher, 1990.

Elsaesser, Thomas. "Subject Positions, Speaking Positions; From *Holocaust, Our Hitler,* and *Heimat* to *Shoah* and *Schindler's List*." In *The Persistence of History: Cinema, Television, and the Modern Event*, edited by Vivian Sobchack, 145–83. New York: Routledge, 1996.

Elsner, Anna Magdalena. "'L'obscénité absolue du projet de comprendre': The Communicability of Traumatic Knowledge in Claude Lanzmann's *Shoah*." In *Anamnesia: Private and Public Memory in Modern French Culture*, edited by Peter Collier, Anna Magdalena Elsner, and Olga Smith, 41–55. Bern: Peter Lang, 2009.

Farr, Raye. "Some Reflections on Claude Lanzmann's Approach to the Examination of the Holocaust." In *Holocaust and the Moving Image: Representations in Film and Television since 1933*, 161–67. London: Wallflower, 2005.

Felman, Shoshana. "The Return of the Voice: Claude Lanzmann's *Shoah*." In *Testimony: Crises of Witnessing in Literature, Psychoanalysis, and History*, edited by Shoshana Felman and Dori Laub, 204–87. New York: Routledge, 1992.

———. "Film as Witness: Claude Lanzmann's *Shoah*." In *Holocaust Remembrance: The Shapes of Memory*, edited by Geoffrey H. Hartman, 90–103. Oxford: Blackwell, 1994.

———. "Education and Crisis, or the Vicissitudes of Teaching." In *Trauma: Explorations in Memory*, edited by Cathy Caruth, 13–60. Baltimore, MD: Johns Hopkins University Press, 1995.

———. "Introduction to Claude Lanzmann's Speech." In *Trauma: Explorations in Memory*, edited by Cathy Caruth, 201–4. Baltimore: Johns Hopkins University Press, 1995.

Forecki, Piotr. *Reconstructing Memory: The Holocaust in Polish Public Debates*. New York: Peter Lang, 2013.

Forges, Jean-François. *Shoah de Claude Lanzmann*. Paris: L'Eden Cinéma, 2002.

Fridman, Lea Wernick. *Words and Witness: Narrative and Aesthetic Strategies in the Representation of the Holocaust*. Albany: State University of New York Press, 2000.

Frodon, Jean-Michel. "Le travail du cinéaste: Entretien avec Claude Lanzmann." *Le Cinéma et la Shoah: Un art à lépreuve de la tragédie du 20e siècle*. Paris: Cahíers du Cinéma, 2007.

Furman, Nelly. "The Languages of Pain in *Shoah*." In *Auschwitz and After: Race, Culture, and "the Jewish Question" in France*, edited by Lawrence D. Kritzman, 299–312. New York: Routledge, 1995.

———. "Called to Witness: Viewing Lanzmann's *Shoah*." In *Shaping Losses: Cultural Memory and the Holocaust*, edited by Julia Epstein and Lori Hope Lefkovitz., 55–74. Urbana: University of Illinois Press, 2001.

Hartman, Geoffrey H. *The Longest Shadow: In the Aftermath of the Holocaust*. Bloomington: Indiana University Press, 1996.

Hellig, Jocelyn Louise. "Recalling the Holocaust: Lanzmann's *Shoah* and Spielberg's *Schindler's List*." In *Literary Responses to the Holocaust, 1945–1995*, edited by Yehoshua Gitay, 55–68. San Francisco: International Scholars, 1998.

Hilberg, Raul. *The Destruction of the European Jews*. New Haven, CT: Yale University Press, 1961.

Hirsch, Joshua. *Afterimage: Film, Trauma, and the Holocaust*. Philadelphia: Temple University Press, 2004.

Hirsch, Marianne, and Leo Spitzer. "Gendered Translations: Claude Lanzmann's *Shoah*." In *Gendering War Talk*, edited by Angela Woollacott, 3–19. Princeton, NJ: Princeton University Press, 1993.

Hofmann, Gert. "Claude Lanzmann's *Shoah* and the Aesthetics of Ohnmacht." In *German and European Poetics after the Holocaust: Crisis and Creativity*, 267–72. Rochester, NY: Camden House, 2011.

Houdebine-Gravaud, Anne-Marie. *L'écriture de Shoah: Une lecture analytique du film et du livre de Claude Lanzmann*. Limoges: Lambert-Lucas, 2008.

Huppert, Elisabeth. "Voir (*Shoah*)." In Deguy, *Au sujet de* Shoah, 150–56.

Jacobowitz, Florence. "*Shoah* as Cinema." In *Image and Remembrance: Representation and the Holocaust*, edited by Shelley Hornstein and Florence Jacobowitz, 7–21. Bloomington: Indiana University Press, 2003.

Jochimsen, Jess. "'Nur was nicht aufhört, weh zu thun, bleibt im Gedächtnis': Die Shoah im Dokumentarfilm." In *Shoah: Formen der Erinnerung: Geschichte, Philosophie, Literatur, Kunst*, edited by Nicolas Berg, Jess Jochimsen, and Bernd Stiegler, 215–31. Munich: Wilhelm Fink Verlag, 1996.

Kaplan, E. Ann, and Ban Wang. *Trauma and Cinema: Cross-Cultural Explorations*. Hong Kong: Hong Kong University Press, 2004.

Karski, Jan. "*Shoah*." In Liebman, *Claude Lanzmann's* Shoah, 171–74.

Kékesi, Zoltán. "Die Falle der Erinnerung: Das 'Treblinka-Lied' in Claude Lanzmann's *Shoah*." In *Ereignis Literatur institutionelle Dispositive der Performativität von Texten*, edited by Csongor Lörincz, 1331–50. Bielefeld: Transcript Verlag, 2011.

———. *Agents of Liberation: Holocaust Memory in Contemporary Art and Documentary Film*. Budapest: Central European University Press, 2015.

Kerner, Aaron. *Film and the Holocaust: New Perspectives on Dramas, Documentaries, and Experimental Films*. New York: Continuum, 2011.

Koch, Gertrud. *Die Einstellung ist die Einstellung: Visuelle Konstruktionen des Judentums*. Frankfurt/M: Suhrkamp Verlag, 1992.

Kramer, Naomi. "The Transformation of the Shoah in Film." In *Building History: The Shoah in Art, Memory, and Myth*, edited by Peter M. Daley, Karl Filser, Alain Goldschläger, and Naomi Kramer, 143–48. New York: Peter Lang, 2001.

Kramer, Sven. *Auschwitz im Widerstreit: Zur Darstellung der Shoah in Film, Philosophie und Literatur*. Wiesbaden: Deutscher Universitäts-Verlag, 1999.

LaCapra, Dominick. *History and Memory after Auschwitz*. Ithaca, NY: Cornell University Press, 1998.

———. "Holocaust Testimonies: Attending to the Victim's Voice." In *Catastrophe and Meaning: The Holocaust and the Twentieth Century*, edited by Moishe Postone and Eric Santner, 209–31. Chicago: University of Chicago Press, 2003.

Lange, Sigrid. *Authentisches Medium: Faschismus und Holocaust in ästhetischen Darstellungen der Gegenwart*. Bielefeld, Germany: Aisthesis Verlag, 1999.

Lichtner, Giacomo. *Film and the Shoah in France and Italy*. London: Vallentine Mitchell, 2008.

Liebman, Stuart, ed. *Claude Lanzmann's* Shoah: *Key Essays*. Oxford: Oxford University Press, 2007.

Loewy, Ronny, and Katharina Rauschenberger, eds. *"Der Letzte der Ungerechten": der Judenälteste Benjamin Murmelstein in Filmen 1942–1975*. Frankfurt: Campus Verlag, 2011.

Loshitzky, Yosefa. "Holocaust Others: Spielberg's *Schindler's List* versus Lanzmann's *Shoah*." In *Spielberg's Holocaust: Critical Perspectives on* Schindler's

List, edited by Yosefa Loshitzky, 104–18. Bloomington: Indiana University Press, 1997.

Lowy, Vincent. *L'histoire infilmable: Les camps d'extermination Nazis à l'ecran*. Paris: L'Harmattan, 2001.

McGlothlin, Erin. "The Voice of the Perpetrator, the Voices of the Survivors." In *Persistent Legacy: The Holocaust and German Studies*, 33–53. Rochester, NY: Camden House, 2016.

Millet, Kate. *The Politics of Cruelty: An Essay on the Literature of Political Imprisonment*. New York: Norton, 1994.

Naveh, Gila Safran. "A Speck of Dust Blown by the Wind across Land and Desert: Images of the Holocaust in Lanzmann, Singer, and Appelfeld." In *Jewish American and Holocaust Literature: Representation in the Postmodern World*, edited by Alan L. Berger and Gloria L. Cronin, 103–14. Albany: State University of New York Press, 2004.

Neufeld, Amos. "Claude Lanzmann's *Shoah*: Annihilation." In *Celluloid Power: Social Film Criticism from* The Birth of a Nation *to* Judgment at Nuremberg, edited by David Platt, 457–66. Metuchen, NJ: Scarecrow, 1992.

Ophüls, Marcel. "Closely Watched Trains." In Liebman, *Claude Lanzmann's* Shoah, 77–87.

Pacy, James S., and Alan Wertheimer. *Perspectives on the Holocaust: Essays in Honor of Raul Hilberg*. Boulder: Westview, 1995.

Pickford, Henry W. *The Sense of Semblance: Philosophical Analyses of Holocaust Art*. New York: Fordham University Press, 2013.

Reichel, Peter. *Erfundene Erinnerung: Weltkrieg und Judenmord in Film und Theater*. Munich: Carl Hanser Verlag, 2004.

Renov, Michael. *The Subject of Documentary*. Minneapolis: University of Minnesota Press, 2004.

Richardson, Michael, and Meera Atkinson, eds. *Traumatic Affect*. Newcastle upon Tyne: Cambridge Scholars, 2015.

Robson, Kathryn. "*Shoah*." In *The Cinema of France*, edited by Phil Powrie, 165–73. London: Wallflower, 2006.

Rosenbaum, Ron. "Claude Lanzmann and the War against the Question Why." In *Explaining Hitler*, 251–66. New York: Random House, 1998.

Rothberg, Michael. *Traumatic Realism: The Demands of Holocaust Representation*. Minneapolis: University of Minnesota Press, 2000.

Saxton, Libby. "Anamnesis and Bearing Witness: Godard/Lanzmann." In *Forever Godard*, edited by Michael Temple, James S. Williams, and Michael Witt, 364–79. London: Black Dog, 2004.

————. *Haunted Images: Film, Ethics, Testimony, and the Holocaust*. London: Wallflower, 2008.

Schlüter, Bettina. "'Raum und Zeitpassagen' im Film: Claude Lanzmann's *Shoah*." In *Passagen: Theorien des Übergangs in Musik und anderen Kunstformen*, edited by Christian Utz and Martin Zenck, 219–32. Saarbrücken: Pfau, 2009.

Segler-Meßner, Silke. "Topographien der Auslöschung: Cayrol, Resnais, Lanzmann." In *Katastrophe und Gedächtnis*, edited by Thomas Klinkert and Günter Oesterle, 445. Berlin: de Gruyter. 2013.

Spitzer, Leo. "'You Wanted History, I Give You History': Claude Lanzmann's *Shoah*." In *Teaching the Representation of the Holocaust*, edited by Marianne Hirsch and Irene Kacandes, 412–21. New York: Modern Language Association of America, 2004.

Stern, Anne-Lise. "Ei Warum, Ei Darum: O Why." In Liebman, *Claude Lanzmann's Shoah*, 95–102.

Szurek, Jean-Charles. "*Shoah*: From the Jewish Question to the Polish Question." In Liebman, *Claude Lanzmann's Shoah*, 149–69.

Talbot, Daniel. "Distributing *Shoah*." In Liebman, *Claude Lanzmann's Shoah*, 53–65.

Theweleit, Klaus. *Das Land, das Ausland heißt*. Munich: Deutscher Taschenbuch Verlag, 1995.

Thiele, Martina. *Publizistische Kontroversen über den Holocaust im Film*. Munster: LIT Verlag, 2001.

Todorov, Tzevtan. "*Shoah*." In *Facing the Extreme: Moral Life in the Concentration Camps*, translated by Arthur Denner and Abigail Pollak, 271–78. New York: Metropolitan Books, 1996.

Vice, Sue. Shoah. London: Palgrave Macmillan, 2011.

————. "Representing the Einsatzgruppen: The Outtakes of Claude Lanzmann's *Shoah*." In *Representing Auschwitz: At the Margins of Testimony*, 130–50. New York: Palgrave Macmillan, 2013.

————. "Supplementing *Shoah*: Claude Lanzmann's *The Karski Report* and *The Last of the Unjust*." In *Holocaust Cinema in the Twenty-First Century: Memory, Images, and the Ethics of Representation*, edited by Gerd Bayer and Oleksandr Kobrynskyy, 38–55. New York: Wallflower, 2015.

Vidal-Naquet, Pierre. "The Shoah's Challenge to History." In *The Jews*, translated by David Ames Curtis, 142–50. New York: Columbia University Press, 1996.

Wajcman, Gérard. *L'objet du siècle*. Lagrasse: Verdier, 1998.

Walker, Janet. *Trauma Cinema: Documenting Incest and the Holocaust*. Berkeley: University of California Press, 2005.

Wiesel, Ellie. "A Survivor Remembers Other Survivors of *Shoah*." In Liebman, *Claude Lanzmann's* Shoah, 67–72.

Wieseltier, Leon. "*Shoah*." In Liebman, *Claude Lanzmann's* Shoah, 89–94.

Wiessberg, Liliane. "Claude Lanzmann's *Shoah*—eine Bootsfahrt auf dem Styx." In *Wer zeugt für den Zeugen?: Positionen jüdischen Erinnerns im 20. Jahrhundert*, edited by Dorothee Gelhard and Irmela von der Lühe, 139–55. Frankfurt: Peter Lang, 2012.

Weissman, Gary. *Fantasies of Witnessing: Postwar Efforts to Experience the Holocaust*. Ithaca, NY: Cornell University Press, 2004.

Wildmann, Daniel. "Emotionen, Körper, Mythen: Lanzmann interviewt Murmelstein." In '*Der Letzte der Ungerechten': Der 'Judenälteste' Benjamin Murmelstein in Filme 1945–1975*, 101–24. Frankfurt: Campus Verlag, 2011.

Zepp, Susanne. *Le Regard du Siècle: Claude Lanzmann zum 90. Geburtstag*. Marburg: Tectum Verlag, 2017.

Zolkos, Magdalena. "'Un Petit Geste': Affect and Silence in Claude Lanzmann's *Shoah*." In *Traumatic Affect*, edited by Meera Atkinson and Michael Richardson, 59–79. Newcastle upon Tyne: Cambridge Scholars, 2013.

Contributors

Jennifer Cazenave is Assistant Professor of French and Film at Boston University. Her research focuses on documentary cinema, Holocaust and genocide studies, feminist theory, and the Anthropocene. She is the author of *An Archive of the Catastrophe: The Unused Footage of Claude Lanzmann's Shoah* (2019). She has also published articles in *Cinema Journal, Memory Studies,* and several edited volumes.

Tobias Ebbrecht-Hartmann is Lecturer in Film and German Studies at the Hebrew University of Jerusalem, Israel. His research focuses on cinematic and digital Holocaust memory and the use and reuse of archival footage. Currently he participates in the collaborative EU-funded project "Visual History of the Holocaust—Rethinking Curation in the Digital Age" (2019–2022). He is the author of *Geschichtsbilder im medialen Gedächtnis: Filmische Narrationen des Holocaust* (2011).

Dorota Glowacka is Professor of Humanities at the University of King's College in Halifax, Canada. Her research and teaching interests include Holocaust and genocide studies, theories of gender and race, and critical theory. She is the author of *Po tamtej stronie: świadectwo, afekt, wyobraźnia* (From the other side: testimony, affect, imagination, 2017) and *Disappearing Traces: Holocaust Testimonials, Ethics, and Aesthetics* (2012) and coeditor of *Imaginary Neighbors: Mediating Polish-Jewish Relations after the Holocaust* (2007, with Joanna Żylinska) and *Between Ethics and Aesthetics: Crossing the Boundaries* (2002, with Steven Boos).

Regina Longo is an audiovisual archivist, historian, researcher, and producer. She manages the MCM archives and teaches in the department of Modern Culture and Media at Brown University. She has led digitization and preservation efforts at the Albanian National Film Archives, the US Holocaust Memorial Museum, and the Smithsonian's Human Studies Film Archives. She authored the Page Views column in *Film Quarterly* from 2014 to 2018. Her work has appeared in *Velvet Light Trap*, *California Italian Studies*, and *Screening the Past*. She continues to volunteer her skills to aid moving image archives at risk in various parts of the world.

Erin McGlothlin is Associate Professor of German and Jewish Studies at Washington University in St. Louis. Her research focuses on Holocaust literature and film and German-Jewish literature. She is the author of *Second-Generation Holocaust Literature: Legacies of Survival and Perpetration* (2006) and coeditor of two additional volumes, *After the Digital Divide? German Aesthetic Theory in the Age of New Digital Media* (2009, with Lutz Koepnick) and *Persistent Legacy: The Holocaust and German Studies* (2016, with Jennifer Kapczynski).

Brad Prager is Professor of Film Studies and German Studies at the University of Missouri. He is the author of *After the Fact: The Holocaust in Twenty-First Century Documentary Film* (2015) and *The Cinema of Werner Herzog: Aesthetic Ecstasy and Truth* (2007). He is the coeditor of *Berlin School Glossary: An ABC of the New Wave in German Cinema* (2013), *The Collapse of the Conventional: German Cinema and its Politics at the Turn of the Twenty-First Century* (2010), and *Visualizing the Holocaust: Documents—Aesthetics—Memory*. He serves on the editorial boards of *German Studies Review* and *New German Critique*.

Debarati Sanyal is Professor of French at the University of California, Berkeley. She is the author of *Memory and Complicity: Migrations of Holocaust Remembrance* (2015) and *The Violence of Modernity: Baudelaire, Irony, and the Politics of Form* (2007). Her book-in-progress examines the poetics of flight, containment, and detention in representations of the current refugee "crisis." She serves on the editorial boards of *Representations* and *Critical Times*.

Noah Shenker is the 6a Foundation and N. Milgrom Senior Lecturer in Holocaust and Genocide Studies at Monash University in Melbourne, Australia. His research focuses on representations of the Holocaust and other genocides through film, testimony, and new media. He is the author of the monograph *Reframing Holocaust Testimony* (2015) and of articles and chapters including "Post Memory: Digital Testimony and the Future of Witnessing" (2019), "Through the Lens of the Shoah: The Holocaust as a Paradigm for Documenting Genocide Testimonies" (2016), and "Embodied Memory: The Institutional Mediation of Survivor Testimony in the United States Holocaust Memorial Museum" (2010).

Leslie Swift has worked at the United States Holocaust Memorial Museum for more than twenty years, first in the Photo Archives and then in the Film and Video Archive, which houses the museum's extensive collection of archival film from the Holocaust period. Since October 2014 she has been the Chief of the Film, Oral History, and Recorded Sound branch. Leslie has an undergraduate degree in history from Elmira College and a master's degree in American Studies from George Washington University.

Sue Vice is Professor of English Literature at the University of Sheffield, where she teaches and researches contemporary literature, film, television, and Holocaust studies. Her most recent publications include the coedited volume *Representing Perpetrators in Holocaust Literature and Film* (2013) with Jenni Adams, the monograph *Textual Deceptions: False Memoirs and Literary Hoaxes in the Contemporary Era* (2014) and the coauthored study *Barry Hines: "Kes," "Threads," and Beyond* (2017, with David Forrest). She is currently working on a study of rescue and resistance in Claude Lanzmann's *Shoah* outtakes.

Gary Weissman is Associate Professor of English at the University of Cincinnati. He is the author of *The Writer in the Well: On Misreading and Rewriting Literature* (2016) and *Fantasies of Witnessing: Postwar Efforts to Experience the Holocaust* (2004). His work in the fields of literary studies and Holocaust studies has appeared in journals including *College English, Post Script, Reader, Shofar,* and *Style,* and in volumes including *The New Jewish American Literary Studies* (2019), *Third-Generation Holocaust*

Narratives: Memory in Memoir and Fiction (2016), and *Elie Wiesel's* Night (2010).

Leah Wolfson is the Rosalyn Unger Director of Campus Outreach Programs at the Jack, Joseph and Morton Mandel Center for Advanced Holocaust Studies at the United States Holocaust Memorial Museum. She received her PhD in Comparative Literature with an emphasis in Jewish Studies from Emory University. She is the author of the book *Jewish Responses to Persecution, 1933–1946* (2015). She also serves as one of two project leads for the Mandel Center's first digital humanities effort. Her article examining the USC Shoah Visual History Foundation Archive, "Is there anything else you would like to add: Visual Testimony Encounters the Lyric," appeared in *South Atlantic Review* in 2008. She is the Product Owner of the digital project *Experiencing History: Holocaust Sources in Context*.

Lindsay Zarwell has worked since 2000 as a film archivist at the United States Holocaust Memorial Museum, where she acquires, conserves, manages, and promotes audiovisual media. She is particularly focused on collecting and interpreting amateur film collections and preserving the Claude Lanzmann *Shoah* collection. She was instrumental in launching the first web-based catalog with streaming video for public access to Holocaust film footage in 2006. Ms. Zarwell has contributed to several collaborative projects promoting digital access to historic film.

Markus Zisselsberger was Assistant Professor of German at the University of Miami, Florida, from 2008 to 2017 and currently teaches English at St. Frances Academy in Baltimore. His research focuses on twentieth-century and contemporary German language and Austrian literature and culture as well as Holocaust and memory studies. He is the editor of *The Undiscover'd Country: W. G. Sebald and the Poetics of Travel* (2010) and *"If we had the word": Ingeborg Bachmann. Views and Reviews* (with Gisela Brinker-Gabler, 2004).

Index

Page numbers in *italics* refer to figures.

delay, 27, 182, 210, 223–24, 225, 226–27; in translation, 178, 179, 197, 198

Delbo, Charlotte, 94–95, 309, 316

Deleuze, Gilles, 90

Denby, David, 21

Derrida, Jacques, 65–66, 74

Desbois, Patrick, 14

Desplechin, Arnaud, 20

Des Pres, Terrence, 324

Destruction of Kovno's Jewry, The (Garfunkel), 93–95, 98

Destruction of the European Jews, The (Hilberg), 116, 117, 118–22, 130–31, 135n4, 137n21, 281, 411; editions of, 130–31, 137n21

Deutschkron, Inge, 386n4, 426

diaries, 92–94, 106–7, 127–31, 342, 364n18

Didi-Huberman, Georges, 29n10, 293

diegesis, 239, 248, 286

digitization, 45–46, 78–79, 213, 242, 400

Dinur, Yehiel, 384

discourse, 242–43, 249, 258, 263

documentary, 11, 60; as archive, 61; as construction, 25, 276–77; Lanzmann's rejection of term, 6–7; participatory, 19, 31n27; *Shoah* not as, 13, 209

dogs, 88, 310, 316–17, 446

Donat, Alexander, *The Death Camp Treblinka*, 283

double return, 343–44, 348, 350

Douglas, Lawrence, 272–73n58

Dowody na istnienie (Krall), 168n27

Dugin, Itzak, 446

durational time, 210, 211, 221, 223, 227

Dylewska, Joanna, *Po-lin*, 146, 168n27

Eberl, Irmfried, 250, 251–52

Ebert, Roger, 12

Edelman, Marek, 145

edge codes, 36–37, 40

editing, 8, 25, 42, 43, 59, 210–11, 276–77; intercutting, 271n47; in *The Last of the Unjust*, 226; long takes, 79, 210, 223; montage, 79, 224, 226; processes of, 79; in *Sobibór*, 183, 185. *See also* ethics: of editing

editing, *Shoah*, 24–27, 75, 79, 88, 117, 127, 156, 220, 223, 267n14, 277, 337; Abraham Bomba interview, 59, 210–11, 280; Filip Müller interview, 342, 346; Franz Suchomel interview, 238–41, 247–55

Ehrlich, Edith, 100

Ehrlich, Leonard H., 100

Eichmann, Adolf, 49, 99, 217, 218, 426, 436; Kasztner negotiations and, 92, 104, 107; trial of, 53, 91, 99, 100, 101, 275–76, 438

Eichmann in Jerusalem (Arendt), 9, 99, 103, 105, 214

Einsatzgruppen, 49, 55n6, 95, 126, 135–36n5, 432, 442

Elias, Kurt, 310, 325

Elias, Ruth, 49, 88, 307–10, *311*, *312*, 316–25, 336, 350–59, *359*, 378–81, 386n4, 426; attitude of, 310–14, 339; "choiceless choices" and, 110n11; in *The Four Sisters*, 64; "gray zone" and, 308–9; incompossible and, 306; marginalization of, 16, 43, 303, 307–8, 337, 382; song and, *319*, 379–81, *380*, 383–84, 385; *The Triumph of Hope*, 316, 321–23

embodied memory, 211, 314

Engelking, Barbara, 146

English language, 48, 77, 156, 183, 195, 198

Eppstein, Paul, 66

Era of the Witness, The (Wieviorka), 275

erasure, 163, 374

Estonia, 387n17

ethics: of editing, 90, 108–9, 239–40, 255, 306, 325; of filmmaking, 12, 98, 109,

Hirschhorn, Charlotte, 368n57, 369, 371–75, 377, 386n4

Hirtreiter, Josef, 294

historians, 22, 92, 100, 120, 214, 432; ancient, 101, 219; contrasts between, 126, 132; role of, 129, 132–33, 212, 333n69, 411; women as, 124–25, 283, 314–15, 371

historiography, 216, 218–19, 366–67n50. *See also under* Holocaust

Holocaust: historiography of, 22, 45, 92, 93, 264, 304; as incomprehensible, 92, 111–12n21, 201; narratives of, 16–17, 148, 165; study of, 422; temporal distance from, 209–10; terminology of, 201; as unrepresentable, 196–97

Holocaust (Chomsky), 200, 289

Holocaust denial, 273n63, 409–10

Holocaust memory, 27, 35, 88, 102, 147, 330n16

Holon, Israel, 278

Horowitz, Sara, 324

Horsey, Charlotte, 58n38

Hungary, 47, 92, 102–6, 107

"In an Era of Testimony: Claude Lanzmann's *Shoah*" (Felman), 12–13

incompossible, 8, 89–90, 91, 96, 102, 106, 109, 305–6, 325

incomprehensibility, 14, 92, 111–12n21, 152, 201

infanticide, 49, 64, 110n11, 303, 310, 321, 323–26, 327; as merciful, 16, 309, 380–81

instinct, 352, 353–57, 358, 366n42

Intergovernmental Committee, 440

International Red Cross, 438

"International Scholars Conference on the Holocaust—A Generation After," 92–93, 99, 121

interpreters, 19, 94, 98, 106, 146, 178–79, 183, 270n34, 386n4; difficulties for,

142, 150, 156, 169n45; effacement of, 184, 185, 187–88; function of, 205n46; Lanzmann's frustration with, 184–85; in *Shoah* book, 176–77; women as, 37, 150, 305, 329n5. *See also* translation

intertitles, 24

interviewees: agency of, 359–60; choice of, 142, 155; as contributors, 19, 22; excluded from *Shoah*, 68, 103, 166n3, 179, 214; Lanzmann's attitude toward, 148, 149; selection of, for preservation, 46–50; translation attributed to, 184–85; treatment of, 12–13, 148. *See also* witnesses

interview techniques, 76, 198, 235, 236, 293–94, 362n1, 373, 404; as aggressive, 21–22, 149; interruption, 352–53, 355; pressuring, 279, 286, 287; repetition, 156, 277–78; resistance to, 310–11, 314–16, 331n36, 353, 355, 356

Into That Darkness: An Examination of Conscience (Sereny), 235

irony, 68, 71, 78

Izbica, 409, 412, 414

Jaffa, Israel, 281, 285, 287

Jakubowska, Wanda, *The Last Stage*, 88

Jana (Auschwitz victim), 345–46, 347, 348–49

Janicka, Barbara, 146, 149, 150, 156

Jan Karski (Haenel), 78, 402–4, 408, 414–15

Jaruzelski, Wojciech, 143

Jedwabne, Poland, 145

Jewish Aid and Rescue Committee (Vaada; Hungary), 92, 102, 104

Jewish cemetery, Prague, Czech Republic, 422

Jewish Combat Organization (ŻOB; Poland), 440

Jewish Council, Amsterdam, 65, 422

necropolitics, 324
negatives, film, 36, 38, 40, *42*
Nemes, László, *Son of Saul*, 7, 328
New York City, New York, 452
Nichols, Bill, 19, 31n27
Night and Fog (Resnais), 20–21, 88, 89, 209
Nisko, Poland, 217
Niziołek, Grzegorz, 143
"Noah's Ark." *See* Kasztner train
Nowicka, Magdalena, 149
Nowicki, Maciej, 149
Nuremberg Laws, 426

Oberhauser, Josef, 21, 268n24, 436
Ochab, Maryna, 146
Ochman, Ewa, 143
On Listening to Holocaust Survivors (Greenspan), 198
Operation Barbarossa, 126
Operation Reinhard camps. *See* Aktion Reinhard camps
Ophüls, Marcel, 20–21, 272n55; *The Sorrow and the Pity*, 20
Oppenheimer, Joshua, *The Act of Killing*, 328
Oppenheimer, Lore, 1–2, 436
Origins of Totalitarianism, The (Arendt), 283
Orpheus and Eurydice myth, 216, 218, 225, 370
Oświęcim, Poland, 63, 154, 438
Other: Jews as, in Poland, 151, 157; perpetrators as, 13, 236, 263; Poles as, to Lanzmann, 155
outtakes: accessibility of, 64, 78, 213, 233–34, 400, 406; as "anti-archive," 60; as archive, 7, 10, 11, 35–37, 41, 44–45, 60, 78, 165, 213; cataloging of, 44–45, 79; contradictions in, 118; deterioration of, 43–44; Lanzmann's desire to destroy, 6, 117; Lanzmann's reworking of, 27,

58n46, 60, 64, 65, 108–9, 282, 392–4, 400; online availability of, 36, 42, 45, 50, 79, 213; ownership of, 23, 78, 406; preservation of, 5–6, 36, 41–46; prioritization of, 47; reasons for excluding, 3–4, 46, 66–78, 91, 109, 166n3, 179, 214, 280–81, 285, 375, 382; scope of material, 36–41; synchronicity of, 61; use of, by other filmmakers, 23–24, 58n46, 78, 220, 402, 405–6; use of, by scholars, 50, 51, 403. *See also* location footage
overidentification, 126, 149

paluche cameras, 48, 56n13, 63, 69–70, 245–46, 253, 426, 432, 444
Panama City, Florida, 454
Pankiewicz, Tadeusz, 68, *69*, 438
Paris, France, 88–89
Paris Match, 149
partisans, 424, 432, 442
Patagonian Hare, The (Lanzmann), 8, 15, 53, 235, 404; on Lanzmann's research, 93; on making of *Shoah*, 87–89, 237, 239, 277–78, 285, 288; on Poland, 145, 148, 157; translation of, 146; women in, 146, 304–5
payment, for interviews, 15, 30n23, 246, 264, 270n36; declined, 100
Pehle, John, 438
perpetrators: clandestine recording of, 245, 253, 255; documents of, 117, 120, 122–23; Lanzmann's disinterest in mentality of, 235–36, 260–63, 266n8; mentality of, 234–36, 259–63, 267n14, 272–73n58, 272n55, 273n6, 289–90; motivations of, 126–27; scholarship on, 236, 260, 273–74n64; self-exculpation of, 69, 70–71; written accounts of, 75
perpetrator trauma, 261–62
Pictet, Jean, 438
Pietyra, Helena, 63, 438

Piwoński, Jan, 49, 148, 152, 155–56, 157, 438

Podchlebnik, Mordechai (Michael), 73, 150, 275, 305, 325, 326–27, 438

Polacy/Żydzi: Zderzenie stereotypów (Szlajfer), 165

Poland: as concentration camp location, 148; history of, 151, 164; Lanzmann's attitude toward, 155–56; reception of *Shoah* in, 18, 141–45, 146–47, 151; showing of *Shoah* in, full, 23, 145, 148; showing of *Shoah* in, truncated, 142, 144–45; underground publications in, 144. *See also* resistance: Polish

Poles: as aiding Jews, 152–53, 161, 424, 438, 444; attitude toward Jews, 151–53, 436, 440; depiction of, 18, 118, 142, 144, 148, 155–56, 159, 163; Lanzmann's attitude toward, 163–64; self-perception of, 151–52; suppression of testimony, 18, 150–51, 163; as witnesses, 12–13, 50, 142, 145, 150, 155–56, 158–59, 164–65, 296n10, 438, 448, 452

Poliakov, Léon, *Bréviaire de la haine*, 173n89

POLIN. *See* Museum of the History of Polish Jews

Po-lin (Dylewska), 146, 168n27

Polish language: embedded prejudice in, 157; errors in, 154–55, 159, 172n75; fluency in, 153–54, 156; Lanzmann's attitude toward, 154–57, 158, 163; misspelling and, 154; subtleties of, 152; translation of, 155–56; as unsubtitled, 178; as untranslated, 154, 159; uses of, 142; Yiddish traces in, 162, 173n87

Polish Righteous among the Nations, 142, 166n3

Polityka, 144

Pomsel, Brunhilde, 59

Ponari, 446

Ponary Forest, Lithuania, 68–69

Postec, Ziva, 43, 73, 240, 241, 247, 248, 252, 253, 255, 263

Pourquoi Israël (Lanzmann), 21

Pracovná Skupina. *See* Working Group

Prague, Czech Republic, 452

Prause, Hans, 440

pregnancy, 303, 309–10, 314, 320–21, 324, 373, 442; in Auschwitz, 309, 350, 380, 426

presentness, 207, 208, 210, 227n1

prolepsis, 248

propaganda, 226, 436; Nazi, 61, 208, 220, 225–26, 227; *Shoah* seen as, in Poland, 142–43

prosthetic identification, 90

prosthetic memory, 88–90, 109

pseudonyms, 77, 289, 300n52, 430, 442, 444

Rabinbach, Anson, 18

Rabinovici, Doron, 215, 218

railroads, 119, 440

railroad workers, 50, 428, 432

Rauff, Walter, 73, 450

Ravensbrück, 310, 354, 430

Reams, Robert, 440

recomposition, 27

re-creation, 68, 123, 127–28, 129, 155, 160, 181, 210, 276, 288, 326

Red Army, Jewish officers in, 184, 194

Red Cross. *See* International Red Cross; Swiss Red Cross

reenactment, 163, 173n79, 209, 235, 276, 336, 354; vs. representation, 326

reference sets, 8–9, 241–43

Reichsbahn, 428, 440, 444

reincarnation, 26, 31n26, 68, 72, 124, 235, 258, 336

Relief and Rescue Committee of Budapest, Hungary, 426

Religious Association of Mosaic Faith (Poland), 143

CPSIA information can be obtained
at www.ICGtesting.com
Printed in the USA
BVHW060020020320
573705BV00007B/22